Oxford University Press

London   Edinburgh   Glasgow   Copenhagen
New York   Toronto   Melbourne   Cape Town
Bombay   Calcutta   Madras   Shanghai
Humphrey Milford Publisher to the UNIVERSITY

William Wilberforce

From the portrait by John Rising in the possession of Sir H. G. Conway

WILBERFORCE

A NARRATIVE

BY

R. COUPLAND

FELLOW OF ALL SOULS COLLEGE
BEIT PROFESSOR OF COLONIAL HISTORY IN THE
UNIVERSITY OF OXFORD

OXFORD
AT THE CLARENDON PRESS
1923

Printed in England

PREFACE

THIS book makes no pretence of extending the bounds of historical knowledge. There is very little that is new in its materials or ideas Its only excuse lies in the fact that, except for Leslie Stephen's admirable summary in the *Dictionary of National Biography*, there is nothing in modern literature to recall the memory of Wilberforce and his work to the present generation. Harford's *Recollections* (1865), Colquhoun's *Wilberforce and his Friends* (1866), and Stoughton's short *Life* (1880), are all out of print. The ' official ' biography, by two of Wilberforce's sons, Robert and Samuel (2nd edition, 1839), is also out of print and rather difficult to read. It is not a three decker merely ; it is a quinquereme, each volume stretching on the average to 400 pages ; and much of it is more like a manual of devotion than a biography of one who was certainly a saint but also a statesman. Croker, indeed, described it in a letter to Lord Wellesley as ' the shreds and patches of morbid *pictastery* in which the injudicious biographers have disfigured their father, or, to speak more justly, allowed him to disfigure himself '. But it has one great merit. It quotes profusely from Wilberforce's Diary. The present writer was enabled to compare it with the original manuscript of the Diary over a period of some years ; and he found that virtually nothing of interest or importance was left unquoted. Hence nearly all the numerous references to the *Life* in the following pages are references to extracts from the Diary.

2759

My warm thanks are due to Mr. H. W. W. Wilberforce for allowing me to read the portion of the Diary in his possession and to quote from it ; and to Mrs. A. M. Wilberforce for permitting the full reproduction of a letter of Pitt's from her *Private Papers of William Wilberforce* (1897). I am also very specially indebted to my friend, Professor H. W. C. Davis, for his kindness in reading the book in proof and for his many valuable suggestions and emendations.

R. C.

Wootton Hill,
October, 1923.

Note. The term 'Hansard' is used, for convenience, in the footnotes to cover both the *Parliamentary History* and the successive series of *Parliamentary Debates*.

CONTENTS

PORTRAITS

I
YOUTH

On March 25, 1784, a great public meeting was held in the Castle Yard at York. More than most English counties, Yorkshire was interested in politics, and politics at that moment were more than usually interesting The crisis was approaching in the strange parliamentary battle between the Fox-North Coalition which George III, by the least unwise of his constitutional adventures, had thrown out of office in the previous December and the young, untried Prime Minister whom he had appointed in its place. Public opinion had long been hardened to the cynicism of eighteenth-century political life. Every one knew that the making and unmaking of Governments were dictated by personal interests, by the concert or conflict of individual ambitions, by the intrigues of the great families, by the King's masterfulness or caprice, by anything rather than the welfare of the nation. But there was something novel and refreshing, something almost suggestive of a new political era, in Pitt's appointment. He was, of course, absurdly young—he was only twenty-four—but he was Chatham's son , and like Chatham, he was not closely tied to the old oligarchy of great families, and like Chatham, he had not gone into politics to make money for himself or for his friends. Three years of political apprenticeship, moreover, had proved him the possessor of great parliamentary gifts—a cool head and, for his age, an astonishing self-assurance ; a skill and weight in argument that made him already a match for any veteran in the House of Commons ; and an eloquence, not indeed as inspired, as overwhelming as his father's—colder, stiffer, prosier—but fluent and logical and convincing. He was obviously an interesting, an attractive figure, this new young man, so capable and with such hereditary claims. At the start the electors were willing enough to support him, within the limits of good electoral business ; and in a few weeks' time he had made himself positively popular. It was not only that his bold and lonely stand against almost all the experience, prestige, and debating power in the House had appealed to English instincts. Fox had made one of the worst blunders of his career. He had denounced Pitt's maintenance of office against the will of the Commons and at the same time done all he could to prevent him taking the verdict of those of whom the Commons were but the representatives To all his enemies' assaults, therefore, to their repeated votes of censure, to their address to the King for the removal of Ministers, to the rejection of his first big Government measure, Pitt could make a confident reply. His constitutional position might indeed be irregular . Fox might even threaten him with impeachment ; but, with increasing certainty as those stormy weeks went by, he could assert that, if the House were against him, the people were on his side. At last the time was ripe, and the machine was ready, for this assertion to be tested. On March 24 Parliament was dissolved. The subsequent election was not conducted, as has often been supposed, on a new and purer system. The ' influence ' of the King and of the Whig nobles flowed along its well-known channels ; and the great commercial houses made a special effort at corruption. But corruption, as a Tory chronicler admitted, ' for once became almost unnecessary '. The electors returned Pitt to power with a great majority ; and save for one brief interval, they kept him there for the rest of his life.

It was on the day after the dissolution and before the news of it had reached the North that some thousands of the electors of Yorkshire—yeomen, clothiers, squires, county magnates—had poured into York to hear the issue of the hour publicly debated, according to custom, by the rival spokesmen of the Coalition and of the King's young Minister. It was a bleak wintry day. A gale of wind, with occasional storms of hail, swept through the Yard. Yet from ten in the morning till late in the afternoon the huge crowd stood patiently listening to the oratorical contest. At last, however, even those sturdy Yorkshiremen had begun to weary of the verbiage and the weather when suddenly their attention was recaptured The young Member for Hull had climbed on to the speakers' table—

a figure so youthful and slightly built that it seemed, said
an observer, as if it would be unable to make head against
the violence of the storm.   But Wilberforce kept his feet ;
and, whereas several previous speakers had been hardly
audible in the uproar, his exceptionally beautiful and well-
pitched voice penetrated to the farthest fringes of the
crowd. ' He spoke like an angel ', said one of its members :
and, though the speech lasted over an hour, from the first
sentence to the last the young orator held the whole
meeting in chains.   It chanced that Boswell was there,
and Dr. Johnson's biographer was a well-schooled critic.
' I saw ', he reported to Dundas, ' what seemed a mere
shrimp mount upon the table ; but, as I listened, he grew,
and grew, until the shrimp became a whale.'

In the course of the speech a note was handed to the
speaker.   It had just arrived by a special messenger who
had started on horseback from London two days before.
' Dear Wilberforce,' it ran, ' Parliament will be prorogued
to-day and dissolved to-morrow. . . . I send you a copy of
the speech which will be made in a few hours from the
Throne. . . . You must take care to keep all our friends
together, and *to tear the enemy to pieces.* . . . Ever faithfully
yours, W. Pitt.'   A less skilful speaker might have been
disconcerted by this interruption, but not Wilberforce.   In
half a minute he had mastered the contents of the note, and
in the next he was telling his audience the great news that
Pitt had appealed to the people.   It was a dramatic stroke,
and the speech ended in a clamour of applause.   It had not
been merely the best speech of the day : it had won the
hearts of the Yorkshire freeholders.   ' We'll have this little
man for our county member ', they shouted : and, true
enough, despite the seeming futility of a young man quite
unconnected with the great local families disputing one of
the seats for the county with the nominees of the Cavendishes
and Fitzwilliams and Carlisles, Wilberforce and his colleague,
Duncombe, obtained such a ' vast majority ' at the show of
hands at the election that the magnates accepted their
defeat without asking for a poll.   And the price of the
victory was the small one—for those days—of less than

£5,000. 'I can never enough congratulate you on such glorious success,' wrote Pitt.*

II

Born in the same year, 1759, Pitt and Wilberforce had become acquainted as undergraduates at Cambridge, but no more than acquainted. In University standing Pitt, who had come into residence at the precocious age of fourteen, was three years Wilberforce's senior. They were at different colleges—Pitt at Pembroke, Wilberforce at St. John's—and they were not thrown together by similar pursuits. Pitt was a not unworthy member of a college which he described as ' a sober staid college, and nothing but solid study there '. He solidly studied Thucydides and Polybius and the ancient orators commended to him by his father, and ranged beyond them over the whole field of Greek and Roman literature ; he translated obscure classics and wrote classical verses with equal facility ; and he studied mathematics and astronomy and Shakespeare and civil law. But Wilberforce, at any rate in his first years when he overlapped with Pitt, was making a different use of Cambridge. He had no Chatham to supervise his training : he had lost his father when he was eight years old. He had more money to spend than Pitt ; for his father, a successful merchant in the Baltic trade at Hull, had left his family well provided for, and his father's elder brother, who had a house in London and a villa at Wimbledon, had promised to make nephew William his heir. And he was unfortunate in the atmosphere he found awaiting him at St. John's. Years afterwards, when his views of life were far more serious, he spoke rather bitterly of his first companions. ' On the very first night of my arrival I was introduced to as licentious a set of men as can well be conceived. They were in the habit of drinking hard, and their conversation was in perfect accordance with their principles. Though

* *Life of William Wilberforce*, by Robert and Samuel Wilberforce (2nd ed., London, 1839), i. 53–63.

often mingling in their parties, I never relished their society
—indeed I was often horror-struck at their conduct, and
felt miserable.' At the end of the year he drifted away
from this set, and thenceforward he was taken up by the
fellows of his college   But his afterthoughts of those dons
were scarcely kindlier   ' Their object seemed to be to make
and keep me idle. If I occasionally appeared studious, they
would say to me, " Why in the world should a man of
great fortune trouble himself with fagging ? " I was a good
classic, and acquitted myself well in some of our examina-
tions ; but I greatly neglected mathematical lectures and
was often told that, being so quick of apprehension, it was
needless for me to toil.' In the Universities, as in the
Church, there were plenty of men in those days who did no
justice to their vocation , and, though something perhaps
should be discounted from the stern judgements of the older
Wilberforce, it is to be feared that some of the dons at
St. John's did their best to spoil the wealthy and attractive
young man   They frequently invited him to play cards
with them . they petted him and praised his gifts : they
even declared, in his hearing, that men who ' were fagging
hard and constantly attended lectures ' were ' mere saps,
but that he did everything by real talent '. So he had little
inducement and no natural desire to shut himself up in his
rooms and work.   Indeed he hated being alone.   If he
could not play cards, at least he must talk   And there were
usually plenty of undergraduates ready to come and talk,
and eat ' the great Yorkshire pie ' which was always to be
found in his rooms.   As a last resort he could rout out the
man who lived next door, a studious man, a ' mere sap '
indeed, called Gisborne.   Often after a hard day's work,
when he was raking out his fire at ten o'clock, bent on early
sleep and a good start next day, Gisborne would hear
Wilberforce's ' melodious voice calling aloud to me to come
and sit with him before I went to bed '   ' It was a dangerous
thing to do ', he adds, ' for his amusing conversation was
sure to keep me up so late that I was behindhand the next
morning '

It was not Cambridge, then, but London and politics that

brought Wilberforce and Pitt together. Wilberforce had
soon determined not to bury himself in the family business
at Hull The obvious career, he thought, for an English
gentleman of parts and leisure lay in the House of Commons ;
and it was easy enough for him, with his wealth and his
local position, to get there. His family had been originally
settled in the township of Wilberfoss, eight miles east of
York. In the seventeenth century it had moved to Beverley,
where a William Wilberfoss was mayor at the time of the
Civil War, and later to Hull. The great-grandson of the
mayor of Beverley, another William and the first to spell
his surname, Wilberforce, was twice mayor of Hull ; and
in his old age he would tell his little grandson, the William
of this narrative, great stories of his past—how the Duke of
Marlborough, no less, had invited him to come out to
Flanders and witness an approaching battle from a neighbouring hill, an offer which the prudent merchant had
declined , and how in 1745 the news had come to Hull
that the young Pretender was in England and the north
country up in arms, and how the mayor had set his townsfolk
to strengthen the defences of the arsenal. Our William's
father, too, had been a highly respected citizen of Hull ;
and with such a local tradition—and with a little expenditure
of money—the present representative of the family, young
as he was, might make a confident bid for the votes of the
Hull electors. So, early in 1780, before indeed he had come
of age, Wilberforce made his preliminary canvass, shook
hands with Johnny Bell, the butcher, and all the rest, and
then drove off to London to lay siege to the affections of
the three hundred freemen of Hull who lived on Thames-
side. Great suppers were held at sundry public-houses in
Wapping , and amid the candles and the beer, Wilberforce
would get on his feet and beguile his simple, seafaring
guests with his Yorkshire patriotism and a voice so beautiful
that it was soon to win him the title of ' the nightingale of
the House of Commons '

A useful training this for politics , still better the long
nights spent in the gallery at Westminster, listening to the
historic debates on the American War, to North's cool and

capable defence of the King's disastrous policy, to Burke's
eloquence and Fox's passion. It was all intensely interesting,
intensely attractive. Night after night he haunted the
gallery, and night after night he found Pitt there. For
Pitt, too, was serving his apprenticeship in politics. On
taking his degree in 1776 he had gone into chambers at
Lincoln's Inn and was now about to be called to the Bar.
But this was nothing but a step to Parliament; and like
Wilberforce, but without his local or financial advantages,
he was already thinking of a seat. It was in the gallery of
the House of Commons, then, that the Cambridge acquaintance began to ripen into intimacy. They were not senior
or junior now, in different colleges and cliques, but fellow
apprentices, almost exactly of an age, bent on the same
career. And, almost inevitably, their politics were the same.
If Wilberforce had sat up there alone, it is probable enough
that his very youth and his vivacious, adventurous spirits
would have enlisted him on the Opposition side against
North's placid majority and a policy already darkened with
the shadows of humiliation and defeat by Saratoga and
the French alliance. But with Chatham's son beside him,
burning with detestation of the whole American war and
of his father's enemies who made it, never forgetting the
dreadful day when he had listened to his father's last
faltering protest in the Lords, run to his side when he fell
back fainting in his seat, and helped to carry him away—
with the younger Pitt beside him, it was impossible for
Wilberforce to be anything but an opponent of the Government and the war. He was included, therefore, with other
young politicians who were already looking to Pitt as their
leader, with Eliot and Bankes and Pepper Arden and
Grenville and some twenty others, in the new and small
and exceedingly select political club which established itself,
in the course of 1780, in the premises of a certain Goosetree
in Pall Mall—' a society of young Ministers ', George Selwyn
sarcastically called it, ' who are to fight under Pitt's
banner '.

Suppers and long talks at Goosetree's, when the House
was up, brought Pitt and Wilberforce still closer to each

other. They were sufficiently alike and sufficiently unlike to make the best of friends. Both had been so delicate from early childhood as to cause continual anxiety to their parents. Even the American colonists had scarcely worried Chatham more than the fear lest his precocious William, fortified though he was with poisonous quantities of port, should overstrain himself. And Wilberforce had been so tiny, so feeble, with weak eyesight inherited from his mother and a quite inadequate digestion, that he seriously thanked God, in after days, that he had not come into the world ' in less civilised times, when it would have been thought impossible to rear so delicate a child '. Pitt was taller than Wilberforce : but he was not so very much bigger or broader ; and if nobody could call him a ' shrimp ', it was chiefly because he held himself stiffly erect while Wilberforce had early acquired the rounded shoulders and the bent, peering posture of the short-sighted man. And they were alike in other things than physique—in their intellectual eagerness and subtlety, their love of literature as well as politics, their passion for talk and the ready wit that irradiated it, and in a natural refinement which kept them from the uglier pastimes of young London. Yet they were very different. Pitt's was the cooler temper. He was earnest rather than ardent, resolute rather than enthusiastic. No sparks—and no smoke either—rose from that clear, steady fire. But Wilberforce was impulsive and emotional, easily exalted, easily depressed. He could show at need, indeed, a courage and a patience no less stubborn than Pitt's ; he was never a weak man ; but there was something of gentleness and sweetness in his character, something of almost womanly grace and sensibility, which gave him a charm denied to Pitt. Both of them could still be frivolous ; but Pitt was shy and reserved with strangers—almost super-ciliously aloof, he seemed to some ; he kept his laughter for children and his intimates, and no stranger saw his tears but once ; while Wilberforce, who could laugh—and cry—more easily, was almost as voluble and sportive in the coldest company as with his friends. All in all, they were a wonderful pair of young men, so attractive, so gifted, with such historic lives ahead of them ; and for two or three years, at any rate, they were more closely drawn to one another than to any one else. If it was never quite the same afterwards as in those first years in the gallery of the House and at Goosetree's, still, for Wilberforce at any rate, if not in the same degree for Pitt, their friendship remained to the end one of the things that most mattered in their lives *

III

In the early autumn of 1780 Wilberforce returned to Hull to celebrate his coming of age on August 24. It was a great day in the town and for the local candidate for its seat. All and sundry were invited to attend the feast, and an ox was roasted whole in one of Wilberforce's fields. As his biographers put it, ' the election opportunely followed '. Despite the opposition of the Rockingham ' interest ', of Sir George Savile, and of the King's Government, the result was almost a foregone conclusion. Wilberforce belonged to Hull like his fathers before him, he was personally very popular indeed .   and he spent between eight and nine thousand pounds   He received 1,126 votes   his two opponents exactly the same number between them

At the same election Pitt stood for Cambridge University, a seat he hankered after, partly because it was honourable and independent and partly because it was cheap   He was defeated ; but, before the year was up, Sir James Lowther, monarch of Cumberland, made him a present of the borough of Appleby. And so, in January 1781, the alliance which had been struck up in the gallery was transferred to the floor of the House   Of the two, Pitt quickly took the lead. Within a few weeks he had proved his heredity with a maiden speech on financial reform, which Burke declared to be not a chip merely, but the old block itself ; which Lord North described as the best speech he had ever heard ; and which prompted Fox to

* *Life*, 1 1-17   Holland Rose, *Life of Pitt*, 1, chaps iii-iv

' put up ' the orator forthwith for Brooks's. In the following
May he made an even abler speech on the audit of public
accounts. This ' famous speech ', wrote Wilberforce to a
friend at Hull, ' did not convince me, and I staid in with
the old fat fellow ' (Lord North to wit). But in the same
letter he described Pitt as ' a ready-made orator '. ' I doubt
not but that I shall, one day or other, see him the first man
in the country.' The day soon came. In June Pitt delivered
a violent attack on the American War, and in December he
drove home the fatal news of Yorktown and demanded
immediate peace. Six months later, at the age of twenty-
three, he was appointed Chancellor of the Exchequer in
Shelburne's Government. A year and a half more, and he
was Prime Minister. With so swift a rocket Wilberforce,
for all his talents, could scarcely keep pace. But at every
stage of the advance he was at Pitt's back; his vote and his
voice almost, if not (as has been seen) quite, always at Pitt's
service. His maiden speech, on May 17, was a brief attack
on the revenue laws, introducing a petition of protest from
Hull ; his second speech a light essay in criticism of the
Government's failure to increase the navy, with a note on
Hull's capacity for building ships. Thus for a year, it seems,
he watched and waited ; but in 1782 he let himself go.
Speaking on General Conway's motion for putting an end
to the war, he told Ministers that they were more like
furious lunatics than prudent statesmen and had conducted
the war in ' a cruel, bloody and impracticable manner '. It
is probable that at this period he spoke more often, it is
certain that he spoke better, than the few and brief reports
in Hansard suggest. At any rate he had made his mark by
the time the North Ministry collapsed ; and when Rockingham was in office, so strong was the rumour about town that
Wilberforce was shortly to be included in the Government,
with a seat in the Upper House, that several tradesmen
requested his custom for the supply of peer's robes. If
such a plan was really in Rockingham's mind—and certainly
he made himself very agreeable to the eloquent upstart
who had beaten his own nominee at Hull—he did not live
long enough to execute it ; and Shelburne, his successor,

was satisfied with securing the abler of the two young
allies. But Pitt could still count on Wilberforce's support ;
and it was at Pitt's request that he seconded the Address
on the Preliminaries of Peace. Already there was talk of
the impending Coalition ; and, the rumour having been
confirmed by Bankes whom he met on his way to the
House, Wilberforce took occasion in his speech to denounce
what he regarded as an infamous intrigue. And when it
materialized, when the Coalition was in power and Pitt left
in the cold, he made a series of fiery and not ineffective
attacks on Fox and North. The report of his speech on
Fox's ill-fated India Bill may be quoted in full. ' Mr. Wilberforce answered Mr. Burke, and with humour and ability
compared the seven Commissioners [and eight Directors [1]]
to seven physicians and eight apothecaries come to put the
patient to death *secundum artem*. After laughing with this
idea he became more serious and said he wished that in
the end, if the present Bill passed, we might not see the
Government of Great Britain set up in India instead of that
of India in Great Britain.' A few days later he made a more
personal assault on Fox. Once the country had believed in
him, he said, but now that he had joined hands with North,
he had lost its trust ; and then, with that musical resonant
voice, he declaimed Satan's famous greeting to Beelzebub in
Hell : ' But O how fall'n, how chang'd, from him who in
the happy Realms of Light. . . .'

Wilberforce, in fact, was thoroughly enjoying himself.
He had found his feet in the House. He had proved himself
too clever and too eloquent to be snubbed or ridiculed. He
could be as offensive as he liked, in the best parliamentary
manner, to any one on the Government bench. And soon
it was still more pleasantly exciting. For, presently, he
was on the Government bench himself, not indeed a Minister,
but almost the only ready and attractive speaker—for
Dundas was neither—whom the young Prime Minister
could call to his aid in his unequal battle with the ousted
Coalition. He had naturally been one of the inner circle
about Pitt throughout the crisis that brought him into

[1] There were nine directors in Fox's Bill, not eight.

power. 'Lord Temple resigned', notes his diary for
November 22 : ' No dissolution declared. Drove about for
Pitt ' ; and for the 23rd, ' Morning Pitt's . . . Pitt nobly
firm '. ' We had a great meeting that night ', he afterwards
recalled, ' of all Pitt's friends in Downing St. . . . I remember
well the great penetration showed by Lord Mahon. " What
am I to do ", said Pitt, " if they stop the supplies ? "
" They will not stop them ", said Mahon, " it is the very
thing they will not venture to do." ' Anxiously the little
clique awaited the meeting of Parliament in January : and
on the very first day Wilberforce's gloves were off and his
heart on his sleeve. ' My right honourable friend ', he said,
' did not look up to ease and emolument solely, as the right
honourable gentleman opposite to him did, when he came
into office. He is another sort of patriot. He considered
the good of his country and the salvation of the constitution
as matters of infinitely greater moment than his own
personal interests.' ' Mr. Wilberforce ', adds Hansard,
drily, ' pursued his panegyric for some minutes in terms of
great eloquence.' A fortnight later he roundly asserted
that there was nothing unconstitutional in the circumstances
of the Coalition's dismissal and Pitt's appointment. Were
all those noble lords who voted against the India Bill to be
charged with servile obedience to the royal wishes ? And
what had it to do, in any case, with the appointment of the
present Government ? ' If the India Bill had passed the
Lords with as great a majority as it did the Commons,
I should still have thanked the Crown for dismissing the
late Ministers.' But Wilberforce could do better than that.
His speech in the debate on March 1 on the Address for the
removal of Ministers was in a quieter and more rational
vein—a capable exposition of the only valid constitutional
defence that could be made for George III and Pitt. Wisely
treating the dismissal of Fox and North as past history,
he concentrated on the present facts. It was clear, he
argued, from the stream of addresses daily flowing in from
all parts of the country, that the Government and not the
majority of the House of Commons possessed the confidence
of the people ; and the policy of the Coalition was to make

the Government's position impossible, to force the King to
change it, without considering the people's will. He confessed that, not long ago, he had voted with Fox, ' whose
abilities every one with discernment must admire ', when he
was trying to reduce the undue influence of the Crown by
abolishing certain places and pensions. But the Constitution
might just as easily be undone by the undue influence of
a corrupt majority of the House of Commons. A despotic
faction in the Commons, unsupported by the people, could
not only destroy the just prerogative of the Crown but
subvert the very pillars of our freedom : and were not many
tyrants worse than one ?

A few weeks later came the General Election of 1784 ;
and when Wilberforce took his seat for the new session, he
had become, as one of the members for Yorkshire, a very
important person in the House, second only in importance
to Ministers and the Opposition chiefs. But it was no longer
quite such an exciting game. He attended very regularly :
he was immensely interested in the daily ebb and flow of
party conflict : but to fight for Pitt in a minority had been
far more thrilling than it was to stand at ease among his
safe majority. Nor was there much to rouse his youthful
ardour in the quiet measures, mainly financial, by which
Pitt began his great work of nursing England back to
strength after the crushing losses of the American War.
His vote, of course, was still always at Pitt's command ;
but for the next two years he seems to have taken an active
part only in two questions—Reform and Ireland. With
Reform the member for Yorkshire was necessarily concerned.
For Yorkshire was the cradle of the movement. Christopher
Wyvill was as deep-rooted a Yorkshireman as Wilberforce
himself ; and the meeting and petition he organized in
1779 and his foundation of the Yorkshire Association in
1780 had been the first steps in the mobilization of public
opinion for its fifty-years' campaign. Naturally, therefore,
Wilberforce, as he reminded Fox, had supported Burke's
measures of ' economical reform ' ; and he had voted with
the minority for Pitt's first proposal for ' parliamentary
reform ' in 1782. And now that Pitt was in office and faced

with the hazardous duty of pressing his Reform ideas on
a following by no means unitedly or eagerly in favour of
them, Wilberforce was one of the few on whose assistance he
could safely count. Thus, when Wyvill and his colleagues
grew impatient and when Alderman Sawbridge, in the
summer of 1784, tried to draw Pitt on with a motion of
his own, Wilberforce, speaking ' as a hearty and zealous
well-wisher to a parliamentary reform ', seconded Pitt's
plea for a few months more delay. By mid-winter Pitt
was ready to move, and he wrote off to Wilberforce, who was
spending Christmas with his family at Nice, to warn him
that his presence would be needed. ' I have some remorse ',
he says, ' in the immediate occasion of my writing to you
just now, which, however, all things considered, I am bound
to overcome. Be it known to you, then, that, as much as
I wish you to bask on under an Italian sun, I am perhaps
likely to be the instrument of snatching you from your
present paradise and hurrying you back to " the rank
vapours of this sin-worn mould ".' He intends, he goes on,
to fix a day early in February for the introduction of his
Bill. ' I would not for a thousand reasons have you absent,
though I hate that you should come before your time ; and
if any particular circumstances make a week or ten days
a matter of real importance to you, I think I could postpone
it as long as that. Only let me hear from you positively
before the meeting of Parliament.' Although other things
than politics, as will be seen, were now already beginning
to occupy Wilberforce's mind, he at once responded to this
summons ; but he was obstructed by snow-drifts and
dangerous roads in the hills of Burgundy, and he only
arrived in London on February 22. He was in plenty of
time. Parliament had been sitting since January 25, but
it was not till April 18 that Pitt moved for leave to introduce
his Bill. His plan, though it completely satisfied Wyvill,
was by no means revolutionary. It merely provided for
the establishment of a public fund for the gradual purchase
of thirty-six ' rotten boroughs ' from their present proprietors and for the distribution of the seventy-two seats
thus obtained to increase the representation of London,

Westminster, the counties, and the new and wholly unre-presented big towns. Wilberforce duly spoke in its support. It was not a great speech : he thought it bad himself : but its main point is interesting in view of the line he was presently to take in politics. The chief merit of the plan, he argued, was the effect it would have on the party system which was largely maintained by the corrupt use of the ' rotten boroughs '. ' By destroying them, the freedom of opinion would be restored, and party connexions in a great measure vanish . . . and for his part, he wished to see the time when he could come into the House and give his vote divested of any sentiments of attachment which should induce him to approve of measures from his connexion with men.' But there were too many enemies of Reform in any shape on both sides of the House for even this mild measure to pass. Leave to introduce the Bill was refused by a majority of 74. ' Terribly disappointed and beat,' comments Wilberforce in his diary ; ' extremely fatigued— spoke extremely ill, but commended.' And next day : ' Called at Pitt's—met poor Wyvill.'

On the Irish Question the member for Yorkshire was in a far more difficult position. In the West Riding lay the centre of the English woollen industry as well as important ironworks and many allied businesses : and the British manufacturing interest as a whole was up in arms against Pitt's proposal to establish equal trade between Britain and Ireland. But Wilberforce's allegiance to Yorkshire came second to his allegiance to Pitt. He was ' extremely anxious ' as to the political risk Pitt was running. He suggested to him that the matter might well be postponed. He dreaded, he told him, a conflict between the Irish Parliament and the Irish nation or a conflict between the Irish and British Parliaments, especially in view of the ' unprincipled and mischievous ' Opposition. ' God bless you, my dear Pitt, and carry you thro' all your difficulties ! ' But, finding Pitt firm, he supported him with a long and closely argued defence of his ' propositions '. He could not, of course, make light of the manufacturers' apprehensions of Irish competition ; he confesses, indeed, in his diary

how much it pained him to differ from his constituents ; but
he suggested that experience would not bear those apprehensions out. The cheapness of Irish labour would be more
than compensated by the greater skill, ingenuity, and, above
all, the greater capital of British manufacturers And he
warned the Opposition to remember the other side of the
case, the safety of the market for British goods in Ireland.
' For I know ', he said, ' that, if anything were to interrupt
the harmony between the two nations, this would be the first
point at which Ireland would suffer her jealousy to operate.'
Protective duties, he continued, had already been talked of
in Ireland ; and perhaps their actual imposition had only
been delayed by the introduction of these new proposals.
And then he took higher ground. ' I trust ', he said, ' that
these propositions will manifest to Ireland that we consider
her not with the jealousy of a rival but with the affection of
a sister-kingdom, and that mutual confidence and good-will
will produce a unity of effort for the promotion of the common
welfare of both countries. And that would infinitely repay
us for any sacrifices we are now asked to make.' It was true
enough. If Pitt's scheme had succeeded, something at
least would have been done to appease the tormented spirit
of Irish nationalism But it was not yet appeased ; and
Fox could easily evoke its quick instinctive jealousy in
order to thwart the Government plan. So on the Irish
Question, as on Reform, the first shoots of Pitt's young
liberalism were promptly nipped and withered. He won
his case, after fierce debates, by great majorities at Westminster, only to lose it at Dublin.

When Parliament rose that summer, the first phase of
Wilberforce's political career had ended. A new force was
beginning to work on him—a force that was to change his
views of politics and of everything else. But those five
years had given to his politics a colour that they could never
lose They had been years of the closest intimacy with
Pitt. It had been something more than friendship, it had
been a brotherhood-in-arms, especially in those unforgettable
first months of 1784. And inevitably the more adult mind,
the mind that had been trained so long and anxiously for

C

politics and politics alone, had captured the younger mind, the mind that had so far never troubled about politics at all. Wilberforce, in fact, had become the first of the Pittites, and in the root-principles of his politics he remained a Pittite to the end. But there was an important distinction between Wilberforce and the Pittites of a later generation. Their hero was the Pitt who fought Napoleon, his the Pitt of 1781 to 1785.*

IV

Indeed, to fight for Pitt and his new party, with the comfortable assurance that Pitt's supremacy was quite essential to the welfare of the country, was all that politics yet meant to Wilberforce. It was not a highly serious business, not very much more than a fine intellectual game ; and as a regular occupation it accorded admirably with the rest of his London life. It was a crowded, varied, exciting, fatiguing life. To be lonely or dull or at a loss for amusement, mental or physical, were impossibilities for a young man in his ' twenties ' whose means and manners and county standing had won him easy entrance into ' Society ' in the reign of George III—that brilliant, cultured, extravagant, restless, tireless Society, with its magnificent homes in town and country, its august oligarchic chiefs, its political dames, its *beaux* and reigning beauties ; riding, hunting, shooting, dining, dancing, gambling, flirting ; out-of-doors all day and up all night, starting with the opera or the play, and on to a midnight masquerade at Ranelagh or Soho Square ; modish, but quick to change, arrogant but open-minded, many-sided but not unbalanced, not ' enthusiastic ', not running to extremes ; laughing at the new sobriety and thrift at Court, but almost as disdainful of the vulgar excesses of York House ; bent on wresting from every hurrying hour all the pleasure it could give to mind and body.

* MS. Diary, 1783–5. *Life*, i. 13–79. *Private Papers of William Wilberforce* (ed. A. M. Wilberforce, London, 1897), 8–9. *Hansard*, xxii (1781), 800, 1042 ; xxiii (1782), 439–41, 1247 ; xxiv (1783), 50, 312, 485–7, 702–5, 977, 1004 ; xxv (1785), 462–3, 651–6. G. S. Veitch, *The Genesis of Parliamentary Reform* (London, 1913), chap. iv.

Into this aloof, compact little world Wilberforce had plunged
with gusto. He had enjoyed his popularity in Yorkshire
where, especially after his election for the county, he was
a leading social figure, a faithful patron of race-meetings and
horse-shows, a marked man at the county ball. But London
left Yorkshire in the shade ; and in London he was scarcely
less popular. Society opened its arms to this attractive,
responsive little man from the North. If he was shy, he
did not show it ; and he was never *gauche* or dumb. He was
ready, indeed, to talk and laugh with any one in the world.
He was a godsend to anxious hostesses. His boyish spirits,
his unextinguishable merriment, could melt the iciest
company. And he had some valuable drawing-room accom-
plishments. He was an admirable mimic. His caricature
of a speech by Lord North, of its substance as well as its
delivery, never failed to bring down the house till his old
godfatherly friend, Lord Camden, warned him that mimicry
was a dangerous habit for a young politician. And his
wonderful voice, untrained though it was, made him a
moving singer of parlour-ballads. ' We must have you
again,' they told him at Devonshire House after a *soirée*
at which he had first met the Prince of Wales ; ' the Prince
says he will come at any time to hear you sing.' He often
sang in public in Yorkshire ' to please his constituents '.
So he was very soon right inside the magic circle and very
much at home there—equally at ease with statesmen and
duchesses and actresses, and they with him. He dined with
Fox two or three times and found him ' very pleasant and
unaffected '. Like the other young bloods, he sat at the feet
of Mrs. Crewe and burned his incense to Mrs. Siddons. The
beautiful Duchess of Gordon, who raised the regiment of
Gordon Highlanders, it was said, by giving each recruit
a shilling from her mouth, was a frequent guest in his house.
He was a member of five fashionable clubs and was very
soon an habitual and ardent participator in the gambling
which was then the rage in them. ' I remember the first
day I went to Brooks's,' he recalled, many years afterwards,
' when I was just twenty, knowing scarcely anybody.
Through mere shyness I played a little at the ' faro ' table

where George Selwyn, of fashionable notoriety, presided,
keeping the bank. An acquaintance of mine, who saw me
at play and was aware of my inexperience, exclaimed, in
a tone akin to pity as though he viewed me as a victim
dressed out for sacrifice, " What, Wilberforce, is that you ? "
George Selwyn seemed quite disconcerted by this interference, and, patting me on the back, said, " Don't interrupt
him. He couldn't be better employed ".' But the novice
was not necessarily a victim. ' The first day I went to
Boodle's ', he used to say, ' I won twenty-five guineas from
the Duke of Norfolk.' He often won larger sums than that ;
and, after a time, he was shrewd enough to set a limit of
£100 to his losses on a single night. His diary records an
occasion when he reached this limit and left the club and
then returned and won a guinea, just to keep on the right
side of the line. But gambling never gripped him quite as
fast as it gripped Fox ; and about 1785 he swore off at least
the more devastating games like ' faro '—for a reason that
reveals the gentleness that underlay his gaiety. One night
he was challenged by Bankes, who never played himself, to
take the bank : he did so, and at the end of the game he
had won £600 ; but among those who had lost most heavily
he found young men who had not yet inherited their fortunes
and could not easily afford to pay.

Wilberforce had not been long in London before the
death of his uncle made him still wealthier and the owner
of a spacious house at Wimbledon, with enough bedrooms
to entertain eight or nine guests. Always, if he could, he
slept there, finding in the quiet and ' country-air ' a much-
needed antidote to the racket and fogs and stuffiness of the
town ; and he would often persuade friends, who came out
to dine or sup, to stay the night. Every day while Parliament was sitting, he rode or drove or walked to town. How
he spent his time there before a late, sometimes a very late,
return to Wimbledon (unless he slept at Bankes's house in
town) may best be seen from the brief diary of the period,
written up regularly from day to day, with scarcely one
omission, in his small, rather illegible, shortsighted hand-
writing.

Jan. 24, 1783.	At the House—indifferent day—dined Goosetree's Bankes got drunk and some others—called Eliot's [1]—Home and bed before 12.
Feb. 3	Very bad morning—feverish—went in carriage to House—obliged to pair off by the heat : dined Pitt's. Home evening.
Feb. 5.	Exceeding rainy bad day. No fever or very little. Missed House Dined Goosetree's and played billiards afterwards. Home and bed before 12.
Feb 7 (Sunday).	Morning, Philip Green called at 10 and detained me from church—walked—dined Woodly's . . afterwards Goosetree's where supped. Bed at 2 o'clock.
Feb. 11.	Morning delightful—carriage to City Custom House. Too late and walked home. House over soon. Dined Advocate's [2] and staid till 11. Goosetree's. At Pharoah, [?] and Pitt—supped late—lost money £100 which had been owed me. Bed about 4.
March 12.	Fine but cold. . . . House. Lord Abingdon's concert. Supped Goosetree's and bed about 2
March 27.	Walked to House. Dined Lord George's and went with them to Mrs. Siddon's Grecian Daughter.
March 29.	Morning fine, frosty . . . Walked for 5 hours—called in Union Club, dined Goosetree's—drank much wine—Pitt, Bankes and Pratt—played Pharoah.
May 20.	Morning, walked—made calls. Dined Woodly's, then Goosetree's and Almack's where danced till 4 o'clock in the morning.
May 26.	Up early. Chaise to East Grinstead where breakfast—then Godstone, 2 old men basking—rode to Croydon and chaise to town—House—spoke—dined Advocate's. Mr. and Mrs Johnstone, Thurlow, Pepper, Pitt. After the rest went, we sat till 6 in the morning.
Oct. 28.	Morning walked John Villiers—sat at

---

[1] Afterwards Pitt's brother-in-law.
[2] Dundas, Lord Advocate for Scotland.

	home—then Kemble Hamlet—Goosetree's, no fire there, tried Cocoa Tree, returned Goosetree's. Bed ½ past 1. Began vegetable diet.
Nov. 27.	Great day in the House Sat till past 4 in morning. Bed without supper at 5.
Nov. 28.	No House Dined Tom Pitt's.[1] Mrs. Crewe, charming woman.
Nov. 29.	Evening went to Mrs Siddons—Mrs. Crewe at play.
Nov. 30.	Morning walked. Dined Lord Chatham's. Meeting. Wrote for ladies to get to the Gallery, but disappointed
Dec 2.	Up late. Dined Steele, Catch Club. Sandwich.—Then opera—Mis. Crewe there—supped Lord George's—Lord John there, Mrs Crewe, Duchess of Portland, converts. Mrs Crewe made the party (promise ?) to adjourn to Downing St.[2] next night. Bed 3 o'clock.
Dec. 3.	Dined Goosetree's—played cards and supped Duchess of Portland's, Downing St. Chas Fox came in—whispering over chair. Heavy evening. Bed about 3.
Dec. 6.	Walked Dined Hamilton's Opera—supped Burlington House—Mrs Crewe—Duchess of Portland—Mrs Sheridan sang old English songs angelically—promised her our votes Bed about 3.
Jan. 29, 1784.	Windy. House—dined White's by way of forming a Club—then Play and supped Goosetree's.
Feb. 21.	Continued thaw—dined Lord Camden's—Prince of Wales' Levée—opera—supped Goosetree's—took off [3] people—Bed 3.
Feb. 22 (Sunday).	Very much fatigued—church—dined G. Hardinge's. Mrs. Siddons sang charmingly.
Feb. 24.	Very tired—walked—dined Mr Smith's—then Lady Howe's Ball, danced till ½ past 4.
March 7 (Sunday)	Morning, church—dined Lord Salisbury's.

[1] William Pitt's cousin, afterwards Lord Camelford

[2] The Duke of Portland was Prime Minister of the Coalition Government (March to December, 1783).

[3] i.e. mimicked.

Then with Dundas to Mr. Seaton's to sup
with Mrs. Siddons—Sir C. and Lady
Dorothy. Bed ½ past 2.

June 21.   Rode in goggles 6 miles, then to town—
House—dined Pitt.

August 5   Dined Pitt's—jolly large party—at night
returned to Wimbledon. Bed ½ past 4.

An exacting life. One wonders, indeed, how a man of
Wilberforce's poor physique could live it. As it was, the
body rebelled. It was not only his eyes, which were frequently indifferent and sometimes ' very bad ' in cold or
dusty weather or after playing cards, so bad now and then
that the lines of the diary run into one another. He suffered
also from occasional fever and sickness and the *mal du pays*.
One suspects that he enjoyed those two meals every night
too much, and that the ' vegetable diet ' was a reluctant
and not very long sustained experiment. Brief as it is,
there is room in the diary for a mention of duck and asparagus
and turtle and venison : and once, it confesses—' eat
enormously '. He slept badly too. One night, indeed,
at Hampstead, there was some excuse ; he was ' kept awake
by fleas ' but often at clean, comfortable Wimbledon,
when he came home late from the House, he would lie
tossing and dreaming about the debate. No doubt it was
only his love of out-of-door exercise, his walks and rides,
that kept him fit at all for this London life ; and happily
those late sittings and those ' heavy evenings ' did not run
on all through the year. When Parliament rose, Wilberforce
was off into the country—preferably to the Lakes, where he
had taken a house at Rayrigg on the edge of Windermere—
with a great box of books to read, ' classics, statutes at large,
and history ', and, better still, congenial folk to talk to
St. John, who often supped and gamed with him in London,
spent several months at Rayrigg in the summer of 1782 :
other friends, Cambridge contemporaries some of them,
came to stay from time to time , and his mother and sister
paid visits from Hull. So the books, it seems, often remained
in their box. ' Boating, riding, and continual parties at
my own house and Sir Michael le Fleming's fully occupied

my time,' says Wilberforce in one of the many stray notes
he kept of his doings. Another year he tried the West
Country and found Teignmouth greatly to his liking—
' a delightful place in delightful country, mild air, good and
cheap provisions, many things in the neighbourhood to see,
but lodgings very indifferent and a smell arising from the
stagnant sea-water in some of them ' One June he drove
to Southampton to meet Pitt, visiting Salisbury and Stone-
henge on the way and returning by Romsey and Winchester
And sometimes he went to Brighton to take the warm sea-
water baths, now coming into vogue, or to Cambridge where
he dined in Hall at St. John's and drank with his old
admirers in the Combination Room, and played cards with
them once more. There was plenty of change, therefore,
and plenty of fresh air and exercise—enough, apparently,
to keep that slight, delicate frame going, and that lively
brain working, at full speed through all the noise and dazzle,
the drinking and gambling and singing, the debates and
levées, the balls and routs of those hectic London nights.*

V

In all this social side of Wilberforce's early life, just as
in his politics, Pitt is the dominant, ever-present figure
There are not many pages of the diary without a mention
of his name. They had the same tastes, followed the same
pursuits, haunted the same places. Wilberforce was always
calling at Goosetree's, and Goosetree's at this time was
almost Pitt's home · he dined there every night one winter.
They became addicted to gambling about the same time
and with the same fervour. ' I well remember ', said
Wilberforce once, ' the intense earnestness he displayed.'
And they gave it up about the same time, though Pitt's
reason was characteristically different from Wilberforce's.
Cooler headed than Fox, Pitt realized that it was getting
so strong a hold on him, taking so much of his time, as to

* MS Diary, 1783–5 *Life*, 1, chaps 11 and 111. J. S Harford,
Recollections of Wilberforce (London, 1865), 205, 210.

endanger his political career And there were plenty of other amusements. Wilberforce, for his part, was never happier than when they sat in a circle of intimates, jesting and 'ragging' and exchanging witty repartees—*foyning* or *foining* as they called it. It was Pitt's quick and merry wit that Wilberforce admired perhaps more than anything else in him. ' He was the wittiest man I ever knew,' he declared, long after Pitt was dead ; and he recalled one hilarious evening when they joined a party gathered at the Boar's Head tavern in East Cheap to celebrate the memory of Shakespeare. ' Many professed wits were present, but Pitt was the most amusing of the party and the readiest and most apt in the required allusions.' If Pitt's youth was very short, at least it was—to those who really knew him—very youthful. ' When I left the House,' noted the old *roué*, George Selwyn, in his diary one day in 1782, ' I left in one room a party of young men, who made me, from their life and spirits, wish for one night to be twenty. There was a tableful of them drinking—young Pitt, Lord Euston, Berkley, North, &c., singing and laughing *à gorge déployée*. some of them sang very good catches ; one Wilberforce, a M. of P., sang the best.'

Moreover, unable himself to afford a suburban villa, Pitt often made use of Wilberforce's. He too felt the better for a night in the ' country air ', and Wilberforce would often get a note like the following, hastily scribbled from Pitt's seat in the House of Commons : ' Eliot, Arden and I will be with you before curfew, and expect an early meal of peas and strawberries.' ' Wimbledon,' notes the diary for April 3, 1783, ' where Pitt etc. dined and slept— Pratt and Bankes foyned Mrs. Hayes etc etc. Evening walk. Bed a little past 2.' And next day : ' Lounged morning at Wimbledon with friends Night foyned and ran about the garden for an hour or two.' Sunday, July 6 ' Morning fine. Persuaded Pitt and Pepper to church . . . Pitt and Pepper and Lawrence and Johnson at night— walked ladies on Common.' And the following Friday . ' Fine hot day—went on water with Pitt and Eliot fishing— came back, dined, walked evening. Eliot went home, Pitt

staid.' Wilberforce would often bring Pitt home with him
when the House sat late , one spring Pitt lived there for
three or four months together , and again continuously
from April 1783, when he left the Chancellor of the Exchequer's official residence, till the following December
when he entered the Prime Minister's. With some reason,
therefore, Wilberforce could claim in after days to have been
' the depositary of his most confidential thoughts '. ' Hundreds of times ', he says, ' I have roused him out of bed
in the morning and conversed with him while he was
dressing.' And it was by no means a one-sided friendship.
Pitt wanted Wilberforce in those days to talk to, to confide
in, just as much as he wanted Dundas later on. ' Pray
come to Wimbledon as soon as possible,' he writes in the
early days of his premiership to hasten him back from the
Midlands : ' I want to talk with you about your navy
bills . . . and about ten thousand other things.' And
he adds in a postscript . ' For the sake of this letter I am
leaving a thousand others unanswered and a thousand
projects unread. You will probably think it was hardly
worth while.'

Once more, the dominant note of this close personal
intercourse is the gaiety, the rollicking spirits, of both young
men. The note is worth stressing ; for it might well seem
incredible that Wilberforce and Pitt as history knows them—
the revered humanitarian and saint, and the silent, cold,
haughty statesman—could ever have behaved like that.
Happily the incredible is true. They did engage in interminable bouts of ' foyning ' : they did run about the garden in
the dusk : and Pitt did get up early one morning and carefully
sow the flower-beds with fragments of an opera-hat which
Ryder had worn down from London the night before. And
Pitt's letters to Wilberforce, in those years, exhale the same
light-heartedness. ' I am as well as it is possible ', he writes
from London in July 1782, ' in the midst of all this *sin and
sea-coal* , and for a Chancellor of the Exchequer who has
exchanged his *happier hour*, pass my time very tolerably.
Even Goosetree's is not absolutely extinct, but has a chance
of living through the dog days. I shall be happy to hear

from you, whether in the shape of an official dispatch or
a familiar epistle ' ' *Anderson's Dictionary* I have received,'
he writes next summer from Brighton, ' and am much obliged
to you for it. I will return it safe, I hope not dirtied, and
possibly not read. I am sorry you give so bad an account
of your eyes, especially as this very letter looks as if it would
put them to a severe trial . . . The lounge here is excellent,
principally owing to our keeping very much to ourselves—
that is Pulchritudo, Steele, Pretyman, and myself. The
Woodlys have been here in high foining, and have talked
me to death   .   Mrs Johnstone and Mrs. Walpole are
left to dispute the prize here. The first is clearly the
handsomer woman, but the husband of the latter looks
the quieter man, and the better part of love as of valour
is discretion. I conclude as you did by desiring you to write
immediately.'

Sometimes they spent their holidays together. One
Easter, for instance, they went to Brighton, and then
immediately and impulsively, so disgusting was the weather,
drove off to Bath. ' As Pitt was then upon the western
circuit,' notes Wilberforce of this holiday, ' he entertained
the barristers . . . We had, too, abundance of corporation
dinners and jollity.' And sometimes they met on visits to
the same country-houses and walked and rode together.
On one such occasion, which Wilberforce was not easily
allowed to forget, his bad sight and clumsy handling of
a gun nearly cost Pitt his life—or so at least his friends
averred. But the best, the longest remembered, of these
joint holidays was the great tour in France in the autumn
of 1783, just before the Coalition fell and Pitt came in. It
was carefully and keenly planned. ' The party to Rheims
holds, of course,' wrote Pitt some weeks beforehand, ' at
least as far as depends on me , which is at least one good
effect certain. I wrote yesterday to Eliot, apprising him
that I should be ready to meet him at Bankes's before the
last day of August ; that I conceived we must proceed from
thence to London, and that we ought to start within the
three or four first days of September. I hope you will bear
all these things in mind, and recollect that you have to do

with punctual men who could not risk their character by
being late for any appointment.' ' Do not verify my prophecy
of detaining us a fortnight,' he writes on the 22nd, ' and
jilting us at the end of it : ' and on the 30th, ' Your letter
has relieved me from two fears I have for some time entertained ; the one of losing the pleasure of your company,
the other of being made to wait for it. I am very sorry
for the state of your eyes, but I am quite of opinion that the
air of Rheims is exactly the thing for you. I hope to find
it equally sovereign for toothaches and swollen faces, which
have persecuted me ever since I have been here [at Burton
Pynsent] as if it was the middle of a session. We shall
agree excellently as invalids, and particularly in making
the robust Eliot fag for us, and ride bodkin, and letting him
enjoy all the other privileges of health.' But it was not,
after all, till September 11 that the three of them met at
Canterbury and set out for France via Dover and Calais.
The stay at Rheims was a great success, largely owing to
the benevolence of the Abbé de Lageard, a high official of
the town. The good Abbé was told by the superintendent
of police that three strange Englishmen had arrived. They
had no servants, he said, and had taken wretched lodgings :
and yet they pretended to be *grands seigneurs* and one of
them, forsooth, ' a son of the great Chatham.' ' It is
impossible,' declared the agitated policeman ; ' they must
be *des intrigants*.' ' Let us be in no hurry,' replied the Abbé :
' I will inquire about them myself.' So he visited the
travellers, and was ' at once satisfied by their appearance '—
so much so that he invited them forthwith to dinner, gave
them ' the best vintage of the country ' (since Pitt had complained that even in the middle of Champagne they could get
no ' tolerable wine '), and kept them talking for several
hours. Nor was this all. ' The Abbé ', wrote Wilberforce,
' was a fellow of such extraordinary humanity that to prevent
our time hanging heavy on our hands he would sometimes
make us visits of five or six hours at a stretch.' Similarly
overwhelming was the compliment paid to the Englishmen
by a rich wine-merchant of the town at whose house, after

supper had been started with a series of light dishes in the
French mode, ' a vast joint of ill-roasted beef . . . was placed
upon the table amongst the winks and smiles of the company.'
' A sad party,' records Wilberforce, ' a drunken prior—
sang—[*aet.*] seventy-three.' And Paris was no less diverting.
A week of social activities in the city itself—dinners, recep-
tions, cards, the opera, hunting—and then four days with
the Court at Fontainebleau, Marie Antoinette bewitching
Wilberforce with her ' engaging manner and appearance ',
Louis, on the other hand, striking him as ' a clumsy, strange
figure in immense boots . . . worth going a hundred miles
for a sight of him, a-boar-hunting '. As for Pitt, the men
and women crowded round him ' in shoals '. ' He behaved
with great spirit, though he was sometimes a little bored
when they talked to him about the parliamentary reform.'
But their stay in Paris was cut short A special messenger
arrived summoning Pitt to London , and before the end of
October they were back in town.

They found London agog with ' secret plottings—the
King groaning under the Ministry which had been imposed
upon him ' ; and in two months the Coalition had fallen
and Pitt was in power. Never again could he and Wilberforce have quite so gay and care-free a holiday. ' The
foinsters ', as Eliot called their little group, were now on
the Government bench ; and a short letter from Pitt to
Wilberforce in the next year, discussing co-operation with
Wyvill for Reform, significantly ends, ' Adieu . I must
conclude, having no time for *foining* '. The same serious
note is sounded in a letter from Wilberforce to Pitt in 1785.
' You may reckon yourself most fortunate in that cheerfulness of mind which enables you every now and then to throw
off your load for a few hours and rest yourself. I fancy it
must have been this which, when I am with you, prevents
my considering you as an object of compassion, tho' Prime
Minister of England ; for now, when I am at a distance,
out of hearing of your *foyning* . . I cannot help representing
you to myself as oppressed with cares and troubles ; and
what I feel for you is more, I believe, than even Pepper feels

in the moments of his greatest anxiety ; and what can I say more ? . . . ' For both of them, indeed, young as they still were, their youth was nearly over. It had been all too short, but it was very glorious while it lasted.*

* MS. Diary. *Life*, i, chap. ii. *Private Papers*, 3–6, 10–11. *The Correspondence of William Wilberforce* (ed. R. and S. Wilberforce, London, 1840), i. 1–2, 4–5. Harford, 202. Holland Rose, *Pitt*, i. 95, 282.

II
THE CALL

MIDDLE-AGE came quickly to Pitt. A Prime Minister of twenty-four must needs soon double his years : and beneath the cares of office, and presently of war, his short youth was smothered. But the change was not sudden, nor complete. The method and purpose of his life were unaltered. He still enjoyed such social relaxations as his duties permitted. He could still be merry, now and then, with children and his intimates. And, if, as the strain increased and the weak body, which was to fail him altogether before those twenty-four years had become forty-eight, began to revolt against its exacting master, if his stern self-sufficiency became more marked, if there was a touch of hauteur in his aloofness, if his cold, stiff bearing in the House seemed at times a little stilted, these were but the old manners growing on the man : it was the same Pitt to the end. With Wilberforce it was otherwise. In 1785 he underwent an abrupt and profound psychological change It was not merely the passing of his youth He would himself have been the first to admit that he became a different man.

The Evangelical movement was perhaps the most striking event in the domestic life of England in the second half of the eighteenth century : but it was mainly among the poorer classes that Whitefield and Wesley made their conquests , and to the average, comfortable, well-to-do Englishman this new conception of religion, so revolutionary in its simplicity, so extortionate in its demands on a man's whole manner of life, seemed not merely inconvenient but dangerous. No wonder, therefore, that Wilberforce's mother should have promptly summoned her ten-year-old son home to Hull from his school at Putney, when she heard that his aunt, with whom he lodged at Wimbledon, was trying to 'convert' him. After anxious consideration the boy was entrusted to the charge of the correct clerical head master of Pocklington Grammar School. There he would assuredly be safe : for it was a more expensive and exclusive institution than its name suggests. There, at the cost of some £300 or £400 a year, he would be certain to learn nothing dangerous. And in the holidays he should be left no time for mischief ' Hull ', said the victim himself in after days, ' was then one of the gayest places out of London. The theatre, balls, large supper and card parties were the delight of the principal merchants and their families.' As the son of a principal merchant, young Wilberforce was deluged with invitations, and his mother saw to it that none of them was needlessly declined. ' No pious parent ever laboured more to impress a beloved child with sentiments of religion than my friends did to give me a taste for the world and its diversions.' Their labours were not in vain. In the seductive gaieties of Hull, as in the costly seclusion of Pocklington, the temptations of Wimbledon, his aunt's insidious discourses, the hearty chapel services, the long sermons—it was soon all forgotten : and Mrs. Wilberforce could rest content in the belief that she had plucked her brand from the burning.

Yet, had she known it, the train of circumstance which was to lead to her son's conversion—' perversion ', she would have called it—had already been laid. Before he went to Putney the boy had attended the Grammar School at Hull, and shortly before he left it, a certain Isaac Milner had become an usher there. Left in poverty on his father's death, this able young man had found in this ushership the first rung of the ladder which was to lead him far from the weaver's loom where he had begun to earn his living. A sizarship at Cambridge presently gave him the requisite scope for his genius in mathematics. In the tripos of 1774 so brilliant were his papers that the examiners placed him first and ' wrote the word *incomparabilis* after his name '. Two years later he was elected a Fellow of Queens' College and of the Royal Society as well. At one time he held the chair of Natural Philosophy and later that of Mathematics ; and in 1792 he became Vice-Chancellor of the University. In 1778 he was appointed rector of St. Botolph's, Cambridge ; in 1791 Dean of Carlisle ; and till his death in 1820 he was better known as a preacher and religious writer than as

a scientist. Rarely then, since the days when Andrew
Marvell's father was its head master, can the Grammar
School at Hull have possessed so remarkable an usher : and
if the youthful 'shrimp' was naturally attracted by
Milner's energetic personality, by his great size and strength,
and by the jovial and sometimes uproarious humour in
which, despite the seriousness of his religious views, he
indulged to the end of his life, the remarkable usher was as
quick to recognize the gifts of his remarkable pupil. He
noted especially the wonderful voice : and he used to set
the lad on a table and make him read aloud to the assembled
school as a model of elocution. The friendship thus struck
up between the two outlasted Wilberforce's excursion to
Putney, and his subsequent removal to Pocklington and
later to Cambridge ; and it was not forgotten when he found
himself a favourite among people so different from his
Yorkshire schoolmaster as the Duchess of Portland or
George Selwyn or Mrs. Siddons. So it happened that when
in the summer of 1784, a year after his trip to Paris, having
celebrated his twenty-fifth birthday in style at the York
races, he met Milner, now a Cambridge don, at Scarborough,
he told him he was contemplating a second visit to the
Continent and asked him to join the party.

The invitation was accepted , and in the autumn they
set out for the Riviera by way of Lyons and Avignon,
Wilberforce with Milner in one carriage, his mother and
sister and two female cousins in the other. Talking is easier
in a carriage than in a railway train and there is more time
for it, but it was not during this journey, nor at Nice,
where the ladies of the family settled down in a villa for the
winter, but on the return journey to London, whither Pitt
had summoned him to support his Reform scheme, that the
subject of religion was first seriously discussed. Wilberforce
had casually picked up a copy of Doddridge's *Rise and
Progress of Religion* ; and since Milner thought it ' one of
the best books ever written ', they read it together as they
drove slowly along those snow-clogged roads. When they
reached Dartford late on a February night, they heard that
a critical division in the House of Commons on the unfor-

tunate business of the Westminster Election was expected
in the early hours of the morning; but though Pitt's
position might have been, and indeed was, in danger,
Wilberforce did not push on to London. Was it fatigue?
Or had politics and Pitt begun already to lose something of
their hold? At any rate the first symptoms of a change
are soon discernible in the pages of Wilberforce's diary.
The life recorded is outwardly the same—constant social
engagements, dinners with Pitt twice or thrice a week:
'Sitting up all night,' 'Shirked Duchess of Gordon at
Almack's,' 'Danced till five in the morning'. . . . But a
new note has begun to sound. Of a christening ceremony,
for instance, he writes, 'Very indecent—all laughing round';
and of the opera, 'Shocking dance of Festin de Pierre, and
unmoved audience.' Still more significant is this comment:
'Strange that the most generous men and religious do not
see that their duties increase with their fortune, and that
they will be punished for spending it in eating, etc.' With
such new thoughts in his mind—disquieting thoughts for
a man of his wealth and his tastes—Wilberforce set out,
when the session was over, to rejoin his family. And Milner
was again his companion. They met the ladies in July at
Genoa and travelled thence to Geneva and the Bernese
Oberland. This time, on Milner's suggestion, they read the
New Testament in the Greek; and on the way home by
the Rhine and Spa, their discussions became so absorbing
that Wilberforce was taken to task for the infrequency of
his visits to the other carriage. 'By degrees', he wrote
long afterwards, 'I imbibed his (Milner's) sentiments,
though I must confess with shame that they long remained
merely as opinions assented to by my understanding but
not influencing my heart.' And now the change could be
detected by his fashionable friends, some of whom he
encountered among the 'curious assemblage from all parts
of Europe' at Spa. 'Mrs. Crewe', he notes, 'cannot believe
that I can think it wrong to go to the play. . . . Surprised
at hearing that halting on the Sunday was my wish and not
my mother's.' Clearly the days of Sunday suppers with
Mrs. Siddons are now over. Wilberforce's leisure, indeed,

is now more and more occupied with introspection and
reflection. 'Began three or four days ago to get up very
early ', says the diary for October 25. ' In the solitude and
self-conversation of the morning had thoughts which I trust
will come to something.' In the following month, besides
the diary, he began to keep a private journal of his inner
life It might help him, he thought, to be ' humble and
watchful '. And certainly some outlet was needed for the
emotionalism of a nature now wrung to its depths by a
bitter spiritual conflict ' Often while in the full enjoyment
of all that this world could bestow, my conscience told me
that, in the true sense of the word, I was not a Christian.
I laughed, I sang, I was apparently gay and happy, but
the thought would steal across me, "What madness is
all this , to continue easy in a state in which a sudden call
out of the world would consign me to everlasting misery,
and that when eternal happiness is within my grasp ! " '
The process of conversion soon reached its climax. ' For
months I was in the deepest depression from strong conviction of my guilt.' The London life became wellnigh
unbearable ; and the diary at this period is a tragically
different document from that of 1783-4. ' I feel quite
giddy and distracted by the tumult, except when in situations of which I am rather ashamed, as in the stagecoach :
the shame, pride : but a useful lesson.' ' All religious
thoughts go off in London.' ' I must awake to my dangerous
state, and never be at rest till I have made my peace with
God.' ' My heart is so hard, my blindness so great, that
I cannot get a due hatred of sin.' ' True, Lord, I am
wretched, and miserable, and blind, and naked.' ' At the
levée, and then dined at Pitt's—sort of cabinet dinner—
was often thinking that pompous Thurlow and elegant
Carmarthen would soon appear in the same row with the
poor fellow who waited behind their chairs ' ' In vain
endeavoured in the evening to rouse myself. God grant it
may not all prove vain. Oh, if it does, how will my punishment be deservedly increased ! ' ' As I promised, I went
to Pitt's—sad work—I went there in fear, and for some time
kept an awe on my mind.' ' I am too intent on shining in

company, and must curb myself here ' ' Sunday . . . I felt
sometimes moved in church, but am still callous.'

This new seriousness, this constant watching for little
faults and bitter self-condemnation when he marks them,
were to grow into a permanent habit of Wilberforce's life :
but happily he was soon rescued from the initial phase of
excessive self-distrust and misery. After ' a good deal of
debate ' with himself he decided, early in December, to
ask for spiritual advice from the Rev. John Newton, the
rector of St. Mary Woolnoth in Lombard Street and one of
Whitefield's most celebrated successors in the Evangelical
line. Whitefield spent his youth as a tapster at the Bell
Inn, Gloucester ; but the contrast between the young
Newton and the old was even more remarkable. Son of a
master-mariner, he had gone to sea at the age of twelve ;
and after some years of service, partly on his father's ship,
partly as a ' pressed man ' on a man-of-war, he had drifted
into the position of an overseer at one of the dépôts on the
Gold Coast where slaves were collected for shipment to
America. Himself a slave to dissolute habits and to the
brutal caprices of his master and his master's negro concu-
bine, he was fast sinking into that irrecoverable degradation
which is so often the doom of an outcast white man among
blacks when he was rescued, more or less against his will,
by a friend of his father's, brought back to England, and
finally given the command of a slave-ship. It was during
his career as a ' slaver ' that ' conversion ' came upon him ,
and, oddly enough, the transformation of his beliefs and his
morals brought with them no sense of repugnance to his
occupation. On one side of a partition in his ship the slaves
lay packed in chains, many of them dying, all of them in
appalling filth and discomfort, while, on the other side,
from time to time, the lord and master of the infernal vessel
conducted the prayers of his European crew. He desired,
however, to bear witness to a wider circle ; and presently
he was admitted to deacon's orders and obtained a curacy
at Olney in Buckinghamshire where he became an intimate
friend of the poet, Cowper. Thence, after sixteen years,
he was transferred to London, and, till his death in 1807

at the age of 83, ' the old African blasphemer ', as he called
himself, continued to depict with ruthless candour and in
lurid hues the foulness of the pit from which he had been
so miraculously lifted. Such was the scarred and seasoned
warrior to whom the young novice turned for aid, and not
in vain. Doubtless the mere outpouring of his trouble to
another was itself a great relief : doubtless, too, the old
pastor, though he would rack and harrow his penitents, knew
also how to console them. At any rate, now that he is
definitely within the Evangelical fold, Wilberforce's spirits
begin to mend. The accusations continue : ' I go off sadly '
... ' I tremble ' ... ' I am in a most doubtful state ' ... ' Very
wretched—all sense gone.' But the sufferer is no longer
alone : ' Very unhappy—called at Newton's, and bitterly
moved : comforted me.' And presently, through Newton,
he finds other sympathizers in that dangerous aunt of bygone
days and in her brother, John Thornton. So gradually the
pages of the diary are less profusely strewn with ' coldness ',
' darkness ', ' weakness ', and in place of them there is more
of ' peace ' and ' hope ' ; till, as time goes on, Wilberforce
renews his old cheerfulness, almost his old gaiety. If
' gravity ' indeed, he tells his sister, should be the business
of life, ' gaiety ' should be its relaxation ; but, he adds,
' I will give it a more worthy epithet than gay. Let me call
it serenity, tranquillity, composure which is not to be
destroyed.' *

II

To all his friends the passing of Wilberforce's soul-
sickness was a great relief, and to no one greater, we may
be sure, than to Mrs. Wilberforce. The rumour had run
through Yorkshire that the young member for the county
had ' gone mad ', and it was with anxious feelings that the
mother awaited her son's first visit after this strange new

* MS. Diary, 1784–5. *Life*, i, chaps. i–iv ; v. 53. Harford,
chap. iv. *D. N. B.* ' Isaac Milner ', ' John Newton '. Sir James
Stephen, *Essays in Ecclesiastical Biography* (London, 1860), 400–13

fanaticism, which she had tried to fence off years before,
had come upon him. Was it melancholy that possessed
him, or, in the language of the day, ' enthusiasm ' ? Was
it some silent, dreamy anchorite that she would have to
welcome home, or, more likely, some wild hot-gospeller,
ranting of hell-fire and Eternity ? Happily it was neither.
It was just her son—older, certainly, and quieter, but as
alert and affectionate and companionable as ever, and more
constantly considerate now than he had once been and less
quick-tempered. ' If this is madness ', said a friend to
whom Mrs. Wilberforce had opened her heart, ' I hope that
he will bite us all.'

In the judgement of serious-minded people, indeed, the
charm of his personality had been deepened by the change,
and the new Wilberforce made many new friends. It was
about this time that at Bath, whither he was frequently
driven by ill health, he made the acquaintance of Hannah
More, whose experience of life had been so like his own.
Born fourteen years before him, she too had been a delicate
and a precocious child. During her girlhood at Bristol she
mastered French, Italian, Spanish, and Latin At the age
of seventeen she published an ' edifying ' drama called *The
Search for Happiness*. When she came to London she soon
found herself a favourite in the world of art and letters.
Burke, Reynolds, Garrick were her constant friends . and
Dr. Johnson, who treated her with playful affection, declared
her to be ' the most powerful versificatrix in the English
language '. Others, it seems, were of a like opinion : for no
less than four thousand copies of her tragedy, *Percy*, were
sold in a fortnight. And then suddenly, in the midst of
these social and literary triumphs, under the influence (it
is said) of Garrick's death in 1779, she began to break away
from her London circle and its manner of life The theatre,
above all, seemed now so evil that she even refused to be
present when her own *Percy* was revived with Mrs. Siddons
as the heroine And it was divines like Dr. Kennicott and
Bishop Porteus she now made her friends Finally, withdrawing from London to live with her sisters at Bath or at
a cottage she had built at Cowslip Green in Somerset, she

began with *Thoughts on the Importance of the Manners of the Great to General Society* that series of moral writings which were so widely, and so appropriately, read by her contemporaries. It was a little before the publication of the *Thoughts* that she first became fully acquainted with Wilberforce at Bath : and, soon afterwards, he paid a visit to her and her sisters at Cowslip Green. It was the beginning of a close and lifelong friendship. Like two exiles drawn together by a common patriotism, their spirits had recognized and acclaimed their kinship. ' That young gentleman's character ', said Hannah More at the outset of the acquaintance, ' is one of the most extraordinary I ever knew for talents, virtue and piety.' ' This is truly magnificent,' wrote Wilberforce of her devotion to the ignorant rustics of Somerset instead of to London rank and fashion, ' the really sublime in character.'

What was attractive in the new Wilberforce to Hannah More may well have been repugnant to some of his earlier friends. Writing to one of them many years later—he was then over sixty—he recalls the circumstances with characteristic, if somewhat laborious, sincerity. ' I grant ', he says, ' that, though the interest I took in the well being of my old friends was even greater than it had been before the change I have been speaking of, yet, from natural and obvious causes, we were not likely to be such agreeable intimates to each other as heretofore. There was no longer the " eadem velle " and " eadem nolle " in the same degree ; and therefore we were likely to retain, full as strong a desire to SERVE such friends as formerly, but not to have the same pleasure in each other's society.' It was probably true. While Wilberforce, as will presently be seen, never lost contact with the closest and greatest of his old intimates, he could never again be quite at ease in his earlier circle. His tastes, his manner of life, were too completely changed for that. He no longer sat up into the small hours if he could help it. He took his name off all his five clubs. Gossip and aimless wit no longer amused him. ' Foyning ' and dancing and singing over the wine had gone the way of cards and mimicry. And the play, whether *Hamlet* or *The*

Grecian Daughter, had gone too ' I think the tendency of the theatre most pernicious ', he writes to his sister in 1787, begging her to set a good example to the people of Hull by abstaining from it. He did not, however, after those first weeks of misery, seclude himself from the world : he was careful, indeed, to keep in touch with it and if he resolved to devote his mornings to study and reflection, the evenings were to go to society. But society was now a duty rather than a pleasure Though he was no longer haunted by morbid visions of his fellow guests standing stripped beside the waiters before the Judgement Seat, he was worried by the apparent lack in others of the high seriousness he felt in himself. The diary of the period is all too full of this impatience. ' How vain and foolish all the conversation of great dinners : nothing worth remembering ' . . ' Dined Lord Chatham's—Duchess of Gordon, Lady Charlotte, Duke of Rutland, Graham, Pitt, Dundas, etc. How ill-suited is all this to me ! How unnatural for one who professes himself a stranger and a pilgrim ! ' . . . ' Obliged to dine at the Speaker's ' . . . ' Forced out to breakfast at the Bishop of London's.' Sociability, it is clear, is no longer the easy virtue it once was ; and he is happier when he writes · ' Dined at home—Milner and I had some serious talk.' His continued interest in society is mainly due, in fact, to the hope that a surreptitious opportunity may be given him at those gay gatherings for a little ' serious talk ' with others than Milner Some quiet words of his, in the corner of the drawing-room, may carry through the music and the laughter to a friend's heart, and—who knows— may set the inner forces moving that may lead him, from just such an accidental start as in his own case, to share in the end his own felicity. When, moreover, the Abolition of the Slave Trade became the main purpose of his life, social intercourse provided another field of good work He could use it to propagate the cause. There is a quaint item in the diary in 1793 which reveals both these motives in combination ' Doubtful whether or not I ought to go to Windsor to-morrow to take the chance of getting into conversation [on the Slave Trade] with some of the royal family. Lady E. may afford me the opportunity. Also I may do good to N and H '

Yet, at times, the old Wilberforce breaks through. ' Dined at E 's—rout afterwards—what extreme folly is all this ! Yet much entertained ' And again, after a luxurious country-house party, he writes to Hannah More . ' How difficult it is to be merry and wise.' Yes ; with all his seriousness he can still be merry. And therein lies the clue to what would otherwise be a puzzling mystery. How was it that Wilberforce was still so popular with so many diverse types of men and women ? How was it that hostesses still invited him to entertainments which he thought so vain and foolish ? Nay, indeed, why was he not regarded as an insufferable prig ? Because always, whatever the company, however frivolous to his inner mind its chatter, he was still the same kindly, courteous, engaging little man ; not, perhaps, as of old, the source and centre of all the fun, but ready to be ' merry '—within the limits of decorum—with the rest. It is only in the diary that he seems a kill-joy at the feast ; and many men might be misjudged by later generations if they ventured to keep and to leave unburnt behind them so candid a record of their innermost thoughts. Thus, if cynics smiled at the ' convert ', if friends ' take him to task ' over some of his ' peculiarities ', such as always saying ' grace ' at meals, or dislike some of his habits, such as that which grew on him in later life, of humming hymn-tunes about the house, nobody seems ever to have spoken of him, or thought of him, as a prig.

It was impossible, too, no doubt, to regard as a prig one whose virtues were so genuine and yet so unostentatious. Those, for instance, who knew of Wilberforce's wealth and how he spent it must perforce have respected him. He soon abandoned his pleasant house at Wimbledon because it entailed unnecessary expense as well as being inconvenient for his servants ; and thenceforward his purse was always open to private and public charity—to Hannah More's schools, to which for a time he subscribed £400 a year ; to a Yorkshire society ' for catching the colts running wild on Halifax Moor . . and sending them to college ', to the unemployed and destitute at Pudsey ; to some hundreds of Lascars stranded in the East End ; to sufferers in Germany from the devastations of the Napoleonic War ; and so forth without stint. One year he finds that on such objects and in helping friends he has spent nearly £3,000 of his capital. So he takes stock of his finances and plans domestic economies which will enable him in future ' by management to give away at least one fourth ' of his income to the poor. Was this a prig ? It was certainly a saint.*

III

And what of politics and of Pitt ?

In the first days of his spiritual conflict, as soon as Wilberforce began to realize what was happening to him, he must at once have wondered what effect it would have on his relations with his most intimate friend. Pitt had never, he knew, given much thought to religion ; and to his quieter, cooler temperament anything so precipitate, so tumultuous, as an evangelical conversion might well seem strange, if not positively distasteful. Might he not find it hard to understand and to sympathize ? Only a few months back Wilberforce had entered in his diary : ' Sat up late chatting with Pitt—his good hopes of the country, and noble patriotic heart.' Could he realize that even patriotism might seem a secondary thing ? Would he see that one who had felt a higher call must needs give less of time and mind to politics, and in so far as he remained a politician could no longer render strict allegiance to a person or a party, but, whatever might be at stake, must speak and vote only as conscience should prescribe ? And must not such independence mean, if not indeed a ' loss of friends ', at least a loss of intimacy ? Deeply anxious as to the answer to these questions, Wilberforce hesitated for

* *Life*, i, chaps. v–vii ; iii. 4 ; iv. 154 ; v. 149–50. *Correspondence*, i. 50–1. Harford, 216. J. J. Gurney, *Familiar Sketch of the late William Wilberforce* (1838), 10. *D. N. B.* ' Hannah More '.

several weeks to grasp the nettle It was not till the beginning of December 1785, when his inner struggle had reached its final stage, that he wrote to Pitt, telling him what had happened and of his intention to withdraw for a time from public life and declaring that, though he would 'ever feel a strong affection for him' and though he saw no likelihood of their differing in politics, he could no longer be 'so much of a party man' as he had been before. But even now, and even with one who had hitherto shared so freely in his thoughts, he dreaded argument over matters which he felt could not be argued ; he shrank from discussing face to face the cause and meaning of his transformation. He suggested that, when next they met, it would be better not to talk about the subject of his letter.

Pitt's prompt reply, disclosing as it does not only the strength of his feeling for Wilberforce but, better perhaps than any other published document, what manner of man Pitt was, must be quoted in full :

Downing St
December 2, 1785.

'My dear Wilberforce, Bob Smith mentioned to me on Wednesday the letters he had received from you, which prepared me for that I received from you yesterday I am indeed too deeply interested in whatever concerns you not to be very sensibly affected by what has the appearance of a new æra in your life, and so important in its consequences for yourself and your friends. As to any public conduct which your opinions may ever lead you to, I will not disguise to you that few things could go nearer my heart than to find myself differing from you essentially on any great principle.

' I trust and believe that it is a circumstance which can hardly occur. But if it ever should, and even if I should experience as much pain in such an event, as I have found hitherto encouragement and pleasure in the reverse, believe me it is impossible that it should shake the sentiments of affection and friendship which I bear towards you, and which I must be forgetful and insensible indeed if I ever could part with. They are sentiments engraved in my heart, and will never be effaced or weakened. If I knew how to state all I feel, and could hope that you are open to consider it, I should say a great deal more on the subject of the resolution you seem to have formed. You will not suspect me of thinking lightly of any moral or religious motives which guide you.

As little will you believe that I think your understanding or judgment easily misled. But forgive me if I cannot help expressing my fear that you are nevertheless deluding yourself into principles which have but too much tendency to counteract your own object, and to render your virtues and your talents useless both to yourself and mankind. I am not, however, without hopes that my anxiety paints this too strongly. For you confess that the character of religion is not a gloomy one, and that it is not that of an enthusiast. But why then this preparation of solitude, which can hardly avoid tincturing the mind either with melancholy or superstition? If a Christian may act in the several relations of life, must he seclude himself from them all to become so? Surely the principles as well as the practice of Christianity are simple, and lead not to meditation only but to action.

'I will not, however, enlarge upon these subjects now. What I would ask of you, as a mark both of your friendship and of the candour which belongs to your mind, is to open yourself fully and without reserve to one, who, believe me, does not know how to separate your happiness from his own. You do not explain either the degree or the duration of the retirement which you have prescribed to yourself. you do not tell me how the future course of your life is to be directed, when you think the same privacy no longer necessary. nor, in short, what idea you have formed of the duties which you are from this time to practise. I am sure you will not wonder if I am inquisitive on such a subject The only way in which you can satisfy me is by conversation. There ought to be no awkwardness or embarrassment to either of us, tho' there may be some anxiety and if you will open to me fairly the whole state of your mind on these subjects, tho' I shall venture to state to you fairly the points where I fear we may differ, and to desire you to re-examine your own ideas where I think you are mistaken, I will not importune you with fruitless discussion on any opinion which you have deliberately formed.

'You will, I am sure, do justice to the motives and feelings which induce me to urge this so strongly to you. I think you will not refuse it if you do not, name any hour at which I can call upon you to-morrow. I am going into Kent, and can take Wimbledon in my way. Reflect, I beg of you, that no principles are the worse for being discussed, and believe me that at all events the full knowledge of the nature and extent of your opinions and intentions will be to me a lasting satisfaction.

'Believe me, affectionately and unalterably yours,

W. PITT.'

With such an appeal in his hands Wilberforce could not
evade discussion : and next morning ' the young saint and
the young minister ' were closeted at Wimbledon for nearly
two hours. It was a conversation which neither of them
was likely to forget. ' He tried to reason me out of my
convictions ', recalled Wilberforce long afterwards, ' but
soon found himself unable to combat their correctness if
Christianity were true. The fact is, he was so absorbed in
politics that he had never given himself time for due
reflection on religion. But amongst other things he
declared to me that Bishop Butler's work raised in his
mind more doubts than it had answered.' Clearly Pitt
discussed their differences with all the candour he had
promised · clearly, too, those differences could not be
compounded. So the two parted, one fearing that his
country had lost a statesman, the other knowing that he
had not lost a friend. And as soon as events put it to the
test, Wilberforce discovered that, for the time at any rate,
his anxiety lest politics should create a breach was quite
unfounded. Whole-hearted converts to any doctrine are
apt to expect—almost, sometimes, to welcome—disagreement with the unconverted on other issues : and when a
few months later Wilberforce resumed his duties in the
House of Commons—his emergence from seclusion hastened,
maybe, by Pitt's arguments—he expressed a naive surprise at
finding how generally he agreed with Pitt. Something like
the old intimacy could, therefore, be recaptured. Once
more the diary records their constant intercourse   ' Pitt's
before House—dined.' ' After House to Pitt's—supped.'
' Dined Pitt's and sat with him.' ' Went to Holwood with
Pitt.' ' Hurried to House, no business, Pitt having got the
gout—saw him ' To all appearance the relationship was
all it had ever been. ' They were exactly like brothers,'
said one who often saw them together at this time. And
yet there was, inevitably, a change   Not only the increasing
pressure of business on the Prime Minister's time but
Wilberforce's new dread of spending leisure in mere talk or
of keeping late hours (and those were Pitt's freest hours)
so as to impair his strength for good next day reduced the

opportunities of meeting. Again the diary tells its tale :
' Called in at Pitt's . . . and stayed supper—Apsley, Pitt
and I. Too late, particularly for Saturday—will not again.'
' Called on Pitt and lounged too long.' ' A note from Pitt,
desiring me to dine and go to Holwood with him, and stay
two or three days. Would not do the latter that I might
get out of town, and while in it might be quiet and reform.'
There must have been occasions, moreover, when Pitt
could no longer give all his confidence to Wilberforce. Not
that Pitt's politics were dirty. He was above a fraud and
far above a bribe   The notorious example of his personal
incorruptibility in that cynical age was one of his greatest
services to England. But the maintenance of a majority,
if not so directly mercenary an affair in Pitt's time as in
Walpole's, was still an unsuitable subject of discussion with
Wilberforce's conscience. On a point of party tactics, too,
or in the heat of party combat, Pitt could no longer turn
first to Wilberforce for counsel and aid. Would there not
be something incongruous now in bidding him ' tear the
enemy to pieces ' ? So, in the daily round of party duties,
it was the man of the world, not the saint, that Pitt naturally
chose for his comrade—Dundas, not Wilberforce. And
Wilberforce on his side was, for a time at least, content
He saw all he wanted of Pitt , and the more he saw, just
as in the old days, the greater his affection and respect.
' In the midst of all these disquieting circumstances ', he
wrote during the Regency crisis of 1788 (a crisis, by the way,
in which party fortunes were deeply involved), ' my friend
is every day matter of fresh and growing admiration   I wish
you were, as constantly as I am, witness to that simple and
earnest regard for the public welfare   . you would love him
more and more ' *

* *Life*, 1 94–5, 113, 158–9, 191, 204, 210, &c   *Private Papers*,
12–15. Cf. Lord Rosebery's Preface to the privately printed edition
of Pitt's letters

III
NOVITIATE

I

In the course of that interesting interlude between the
Wars of the American and the French Revolutions it was
not so very difficult for a politician with a conscience to
support the Government   Only the crudest partisans can
withhold their tribute of admiration for the manner in which
the ' schoolboy ', as the Whigs dubbed the young Prime
Minister, nursed his country back to health and strength
in that critical decade.   When the Treaty of Versailles was
signed in 1783, British fortunes were at a lower ebb than they
had been for centuries.   A wretchedly conducted war had
ended in a decisive defeat and a humiliating peace.   Our
kinsmen beyond the Atlantic, weak and divided at the
moment, despite their triumph, but bearing in their young
untainted vigour and in the unfathomed wealth of their
vast country the seeds of a splendid future, had determined
not to share that future, for good or ill, with the mother-
country.   The English-speaking commonwealth, in fact,
had split asunder ;   and to the rival states of Europe it
seemed that the blow they had helped to deal had
struck Britain down for ever to the second rank.   And
if they were soon proved wrong, if with the advent of the
next war only ten years later—a stubborn long-protracted
war, enmeshing, bleeding, exhausting all the Powers—Britain
proved herself inferior to none in strength and endurance, it
was principally Pitt she had to thank for it.   By a steady
pursuit of peace abroad he secured just that little breathing-
space which his countrymen needed to throw off the despondent mood engendered by defeat and to recover all their
old resilient self-confidence.   By resolute financial retrenchment and reorganization at home, he enabled them to lift
themselves swiftly and surely from the economic morass
in which the American war had left them sunk to the neck.
More than that, it was a decade in which, in politics as in
religion, a new spirit was abroad ;   and if Pitt was never
a disciple of Wesley or Whitefield, he was an early and zealous
disciple of Adam Smith.   He failed, as has been seen, in

1785, to establish commercial equality between Britain and Ireland ; but in 1787 he secured a measure of free trade in the famous commercial treaty with France. He never renewed, it is true, his attempt to introduce the new spirit into the heart of the whole political system, but it must not be forgotten that Reform was stubbornly opposed by a majority of his colleagues in the Cabinet and a majority, in which there were Whigs as well as Tories, of the House. It must be remembered, too, that Pitt's insistence on the sovereignty of Parliament and the authority of the First Minister of the Crown did as much as the fiasco of George III's American policy to defeat the last attempt of an English king to reverse the judgement of 1688.

In all this Wilberforce could support his friend with a single mind. Peace, public frugality, freer trade—it was an honest and not un-Christian programme. And the resolve to live up to his faith in politics as in everything else had not carried Wilberforce quite into the clouds. He was no fanatic, and the fanatic's temptation to embrace the rigours of the logical extreme made no appeal to him. He remained a good man of the world, seeking peace but not a quietist, a champion of the weak but not an enemy to all government, considerate to the poor but dreaming no dreams of primitive Christian communism. Save only in the matter of Slavery and the Slave Trade he had no radical propensities. But on Reform, with Yorkshire behind him, he could venture a little farther than Pitt, or, rather, he could do what Pitt would have done in his place. Thus his first achievement on his return to politics in 1786 was the successful conduct through the Commons of a Bill which ' aimed directly at purifying county elections by providing a general registration of the freeholders and holding the poll in various places at the same time '. It was not Wilberforce's fault that this useful little measure never became law: the country magnates in the Lords, Tory and Whig, combined to kill it. In 1793, again, more free as a private member than Pitt to prove himself unshaken in his principles by the tremors of the cataclysm across the Channel, he kept in close touch with his fellow Yorkshireman, Wyvill, and declared his sympathy with ' all moderate Reformers '. It was right, he said, ' to pay great regard to them and to the object of bringing them to act cordially for the constitution and against the republicans '. He intended to express these sentiments openly during the Reform debate of that year, but he failed repeatedly to catch the Speaker's eye. Some notes have been preserved, however, which may have been jotted down in preparation for the speech he meant to make. They reveal, at any rate, the trend of his thought and especially the dominance of moral ideas. To argue from the actual results of the existing machinery of election, he notes, and not to consider how corruptly it works is ' the expediency gentleman's system ' and it ' has this grand vice inherent in it—that national morals [are] of no account whatever in it '. Again, ' many boroughs now, where interest (often family interest) must either be at once abandoned or maintained by the most unjustifiable means. How wrong to reverse the Divine procedure and make duty and interest incompatible.'

High notions, likewise, inspired Wilberforce's support of the Commercial Treaty with France. He did not neglect the material arguments—that the British business world was in favour of it, that the free exchange of British manufactured goods for French raw materials would tend to prevent France from setting herself to develop new industries in competition with Britain, and so forth. But ' the most pleasing view he had of the Treaty ', he told the Commons, ' was in the tendency which he hoped it would have to check destructive contentions between the two countries by making the preservation of a harmonious intercourse the mutual interest of both '. And in the course of this speech, not for the first time, he crossed swords, on Pitt's behalf, with Fox. It was a curious encounter ; for by opposing a measure which, except for the fact that the government of France was still the most famous, if no longer the most powerful, embodiment in Europe of the principle of absolutism, was in accordance with all his liberal sympathies, the great Whig had enabled his opponent to use language which might more naturally have fallen from his own lips Is it necessary, asked Wilberforce, to remain perpetually at feud with France, simply in order to maintain the tradition of the Balance of Power and the policy of allying ourselves always with the weaker states against the stronger in order to maintain the liberty of Europe ? ' This principle ', he said, ' has made us splendid in the page of history ; but I wish the country could at length learn that important lesson—that the greatness and happiness of a people are not the same. . . . If the right honourable gentleman's system has made us often reap the laurels of victory, yet has it not loaded us with 250 millions of debt ? Has it not laid us under the necessity of abridging every cottager in the kingdom of his comforts ? And what are the feelings of the poor creature who, with his windows stopped up, with scarce food to eat or a house to live in, by the miserable light of a candle he can scarce afford to burn, is to be compensated for all his distress by reading over a speech of the right honourable gentleman in which he is dignified by the honourable appellation of the Adjuster of the Balance of Power and Guardian of the Liberties of Europe!' Yes! Fox was forced to answer, such is the poor cottager's compensation ' That it is that enables him to bear his poverty with cheerfulness, and to feel the satisfaction, amidst all his distress, of reflecting on the thought of his being one of the subjects of a free country, whose characteristic it is to balance the power of Europe.' And he belaboured Wilberforce for belittling the power and prestige of England. ' Is not his country, then, in a situation to take a part in preserving the liberties of Europe ? Does the honourable gentleman mean to hold that language to the world ? ' Effective debating stuff, no doubt, but it sounds more like Pitt's voice than Fox's. And indeed from time to time hereafter Pitt, as well as Fox, was to find himself somewhat embarrassed by the conscientious Wilberforce's habit of transcending the authoritative party arguments. It can never be very comfortable for Ministers to have their policy earnestly vindicated in the language of the Opposition.

Two other causes taken up by Wilberforce in this first phase of his new political life were not so much exposed to party contention. He had made friends with Samuel Romilly and had been much impressed by the pamphlet which heralded his great crusade against the barbarities of the English penal law. In 1786, therefore, he himself introduced an amending Bill, and carried it through the Commons. It was a mild measure, considering how wide was the scope for humane improvement. Its most striking provision was the substitution of hanging for burning as the capital punishment for women convicted of murdering their husbands. But Lord Loughborough denounced it on points of law, although, or rather because, it had been drafted by Pitt's Law Officers; and on Lord Loughborough's high authority his fellow peers rejected it. The subject, however, had set Wilberforce thinking along another line. He had been brought up against the old problem of the effectiveness of punishment as a preventive. ' The barbarous custom of hanging ', he wrote to Wyvill in the following year, ' has been tried too long, and with the success which might have been expected of it. The most effectual way of preventing the greater crimes is by punishing the smaller and by endeavouring to suppress that general spirit of licentiousness which is the parent of every species of vice.' But by what special means, beyond the customary agencies of school and church and penal code, was this end to be sought? A perusal of Dr. Woodward's *History of the Society for the Reformation of Manners in the year 1692* gave Wilberforce his cue. He proposed to found a similar society. It was to assume the rôle of ' the ancient censorship ', to be ' the guardian of the religion and morals of the people '. The project was well received in high quarters. The Archbishop of Canterbury blessed it. The Duke of Montagu undertook to be the society's first president. And we are informed by his filial biographers that Wilberforce ' spared no labour to attain his object, visiting in succession the episcopal residences of the prelates of Worcester, Hereford, Norwich, Lincoln, York, and Lichfield, and gaining many of the bishops as the first promoters of his scheme '. Influential lay support was also forthcoming on both sides of politics. Pitt was ready to help. Fox, seemingly, was not approached;

but Lord North gave his name. Finally the royal sympathies were engaged. The conduct of the Prince of Wales had been more than usually embarrassing of late, rumours of his secret marriage with Mrs. Fitzherbert were abroad; and it was only when the Prince had authorized Fox to give the House a direct, quite untrue, but convincing denial of the marriage—' that miserable calumny, that low malicious falsehood . . . which had not the smallest degree of foundation '—that the Commons had consented to pay his debts from the nation's purse to the tune of £161,000. The King, however, was still sane, it was a year later that his mind gave way, and since Wilberforce's plan appealed strongly to his genuine domestic piety, a Royal Proclamation against Vice and Immorality was issued on June 1, 1787, to provide the new society, which was consequently known as the Proclamation Society, with a pretext and a programme. Its activities, in which Wilberforce took a vigorous part for many years, were mostly directed against blasphemous and indecent publications, but it busied itself also with attempts to enforce a stricter observance of Sunday among the poor, to suppress such indecorous rustic festivities as ' wakes ', and so forth. In 1802 its place was taken by the better-known Society for the Suppression of Vice—better known if only as the butt of Sydney Smith's mordant humour ' A corporation of informers,' he called it, ' supported by large contributions ' and bent on suppressing not the vices of the rich but the pleasures of the poor, on reducing their life ' to its regular standard of decorous gloom ', while ' the gambling houses of St. James's remain untouched '. These were well-aimed shafts, and they hit the Proclamation Society as truly as its successor. It was fortunate, surely, that Wilberforce's fine enthusiasm was soon to find a wider and worthier field.*

---

* *Life*, i 78, 114, 130–8 , ii. 9, 24, 446–7. *Hansard*, xxvi (1786–8), 440–4 *Memoirs of Romilly* (London, 1840), i 90, 334 S Smith, *Works* (London, 1840), iv 84–100

II

There was one vastly wider field of human relations in which any one who believed, like Wilberforce, in the application of Christian principles to politics was bound sooner or later to find himself profoundly interested From the Age of Discovery onwards the peoples of Europe had been brought into contact with the peoples of Asia and Africa—a multitude of races, infinitely dissimilar in their capacities and in their standards of civilization, but all alike in this , they were the weaker and the white men the stronger. To any candid Christian mind there could be no clearer case of the eternal issue between might and right   Asia and Africa lay at Europe's mercy—ever more helplessly as her material power grew. Her treatment of them was a palpable test of the validity of her moral and religious professions And of all the European peoples the test was especially applicable to the British   Masters of the sea-ways of the world, they had already assumed in Wilberforce's day the leading rôle in the relations between Europe and Asia and, in one respect at least, the leading rôle also in the relations between Europe and Africa.

It so happened that, when Wilberforce first entered Parliament, the British connexion with Asia had reached a critical stage. Since the middle of the eighteenth century the East India Company had slipped with rapid and dangerous momentum into a new phase of its career. It had started, at the beginning of the seventeenth century, as a purely commercial concern. For more than a hundred years it had confined itself, almost without a break, to the peaceful routine of trade. Its foothold on Indian soil had been limited to the two or three settlements it had established with the permission of Indian rulers, for the purpose of carrying on its business. But all this had suddenly been changed. The Mogul Empire, by which the unity and peace of India had been more or less effectively maintained, had collapsed. Released from its binding rim, the kaleidoscopic pattern of Indian races, dynasties, and creeds had broken into a tangle of discordant fragments. That huge country, those millions of men and women, had drifted helplessly towards anarchy and chronic warfare. And to make confusion worse confounded, the French had sought to direct the turbid, masterless forces of rapine and racial passion to the assault and overthrow of their British rivals. The subsequent struggle, with Clive as its protagonist, is a familiar chapter of British history. At its close the members of the East India Company had found themselves no longer merchants merely but the virtual rulers of Bengal and possessors of a great—it might soon be the greatest—political power throughout India. It was a drastic transformation, and it had come about much too swiftly. The Company was unable to face its new obligations. Political power, in Bengal at any rate, it could not now evade, but it would have nothing to do with political responsibility. Its sole object in India was still to be the Indian trade ; the maintenance of law and order, the welfare of the Indian people, these were not its affair, these were to remain the business of Indian princes and officials. True, the Bengal Government was entirely the Company's creature. The Company controlled the revenue ; paid its puppet rulers ; called their tune. And on the Company's military strength they depended, in the last resort, for defence against their enemies. Yet, all the time, the Company declined to hold itself responsible for the manner in which they ruled. The results were inevitable. Power divorced from responsibility offers a temptation which human nature cannot easily resist. There were men of honour and humanity in the Company's service in India—and there were others. The opportunities not only for legitimate or illegitimate private trading but for corruption and extortion were almost infinite ; and presently a stream of men, with the bronzed faces and luxurious habits of the East, began to trickle back to England, still in the prime of life but already owners of enormous fortunes. They were not altogether welcome. The old landed families looked askance at the invasion of Mayfair and the countryside by these *nouveaux riches*. The man in the street shook his head at their extravagance

and ostentation   And politicians, observing how keenly
and with what inexhaustible purses the ' nabobs ' pushed
into the borough market, recalled the precedent of the
Proconsuls and the fate of the Roman Republic.

The British Commonwealth, in fact, was standing at the
cross-ways   If the true principles that should control
British relations with India had not now been quickly
recognized and applied, imperfectly and haltingly at first,
but with increasing conviction and consistency as time went
on, to the concrete problems of Indian government, the
consequences would have been disastrous both for India
and for Great Britain and in the long run for all the world.
The relations between Europe and Asia would have hardened
into soulless exploitation on the one side and on the other
into servile fear and hate   Visions of bridging the gulf
between East and West, Christian ideals of human unity
and fellowship, would have faded into idle dreams.
That the worst did not happen, that Britain presently
took the right path, gave the right lead, was mainly
due to one Irishman.   Burke's vivid pictures (not always
accurately drawn) of the sufferings of the Indian people and
his flaming denunciations (not always scrupulously just) of
British misrule in India awakened the public conscience and
created the atmosphere of reform.   More than that, he was
the first to state in unequivocal terms the new doctrine
on which the reconstruction of British rule in India was to
rest   In his great speech on Fox's India Bill he declared
that ' all political power which is set over men . . . ought
to be some way or other exercised ultimately for their
benefit ', and that the rights and privileges derived there-
from ' are all in the strictest sense a trust '.   Truisms, no
doubt, of political thought in England, but startlingly novel
in their application to India.   In fact, it is not too much
to say that Burke's publication of that idea marks a decisive
moment in history   The principle of trusteeship as the
governing rule in the relations between strong and weak,
advanced and backward, peoples had been set before the
world.

Even in his unregenerate days, Wilberforce must have

been shocked, like most Englishmen, at the revelation of the
Indian scandal. He had been in the House when the famous
Reports of the two Committees of 1781, on one of which
Burke had been the outstanding figure, were laid on the
table, with their overwhelming mass of black and authoritative evidence. He had probably voted for the damnatory
resolutions, moved by Dundas in 1782, one of which had
demanded the recall of Warren Hastings, whom Burke
was not alone in regarding as the villain of the piece. And he
had probably supported Dundas's challenge to the Coalition
in its early days of office, when he introduced a Bill to transfer
the power of recall from the Company to the Crown and
urged that Hastings should be the first to suffer under it.
And yet he had joined quite happily in the denunciation
of Fox's India Bill by Pitt and his party. It was only
natural. The Bill might be, as impartial critics have long
recognized, a not unworthy embodiment of Burke's ideals.
It might at least attempt to do the essential thing—to force
responsibility for British rule in India on the British Parliament and people by entrusting the supreme authority over
the personnel and conduct of the Company to a Commission
appointed in the first instance by Parliament and after
four years by the Crown. It might be supported by Fox
at his best and by Burke in a speech which ranks among
his masterpieces. But quite naturally—for those were his
unregenerate days—Wilberforce would have none of it. It
was the product of the Coalition, a child of that unseemly
marriage. It was Fox's Bill, not Pitt's. So, as we have seen,
he was content to match his cheap witticisms and his party
clap-trap against Burke's burning sincerity and the purple
and the thunder of his eloquence—content, too, to go all
lengths with Pitt in exaggerating the weak point of the Bill,
the appointment of the first Commissioners by Parliament,
into an incredible intrigue to give to Fox and his friends
a really effective and lasting stranglehold on the whole of
British public life. As every one knows, these tactics were
gloriously successful. No need to tell the King that to let
the Bill go through was to surrender his crown to Fox. He
jumped at his chance, secured the Bill's defeat in the Lords,

and promptly dismissed the Coalition. And so, when, next summer, another India Bill was introduced, which was grounded on the same cardinal principle as Fox's Bill and which, if it was on the whole a better Bill, differed from it in form rather than in substance, Wilberforce was free to support it. It was Pitt's Bill, not Fox's.

But the Act of 1785 had by no means shelved the Indian Question. It had initiated a new era It had placed the exercise of the British ' trust ' in India under the unquestionable control of British Ministers and the British Parliament With modifications in detail, it was to remain the governing Act till the great re-settlement in 1858. But Burke and those who felt as he did were not satisfied. The future of India might be brighter now, but what of the black past ? Could a new era be built up on unredressed injustice ? It was impossible, doubtless, to mark what had been done amiss by every Englishman in India—impossible to wrest from every guilty ' nabob ' his ill-gotten gains. But there was one of them whose punishment could atone for the immunity of the rest—the man who had been primarily responsible for British policy in India since 1772, the man whose recall Parliament had demanded in 1782 and who, a year after the passing of Pitt's Act, was still the Governor-General of Bengal. In 1785-6, therefore, the Indian Question was right to the front again in the guise of the Hastings Question ; and the Wilberforce of 1786 was not the Wilberforce of 1784 What was the man who had severed all party ties going to think and say about it ?

Few *causes célèbres* have occasioned such cross-swearing as the Hastings case. Quite reputable students have held opinions of him not merely differing in emphasis, but as discordant as vinegar and oil, and contemporary judgements were at least as violently contradictory. But the reason is not far to seek. In the first place the case became, all too quickly, a party question ; and, secondly, the presentation of it was lamentably one-sided For years past, Francis had been pouring his stream of jealousy and spite into the ears of the Whigs till they had come to conceive Hastings as a monster of iniquity ; and, while his enemies were ransacking the archives for evidence that could be twisted into proof of his guilt, Hastings was too much occupied with his overwhelming task in India, and perhaps too proud, to busy himself with propaganda in his own defence. There is something ironical, indeed, in the alliance of Burke's untainted moral passion with so much that was mean and malignant. For in two main respects Hastings had been trying to do in India what Burke wanted done. He had striven from the beginning to awaken and enforce a sense of responsibility among the Company's officials He could not abolish the bad custom of private trading ; but he had cleansed it of its worst impurities. He had reorganized the collection of the revenue under the more direct supervision of his Council. He had established law-courts in Calcutta and in the outlying districts of Bengal to make justice easily accessible to the Indian population. Hastings, in fact, more than any other man, was the initiator of the tradition of efficient and just administration for the common people of India which was one day to become the unquestionable hall-mark of the British Raj. Moreover, it was due to Hastings that the British Raj continued to exist, and whatever Burke might think of the Company's government, he never desired that Britain should abandon altogether the trust with which Providence, so he held, had charged her. In the dark days of the American War, when France was once more striving for mastery in the East and Britain was no longer in undisputed command of the sea, that far-off British outpost in India would have been overwhelmed but for Hastings's vigour and tenacity. But if Burke could scarcely disapprove the end, the means appalled him Hastings could not fight without money for his troops. When his official treasury was exhausted, he could get none from England, where, indeed, his own Directors were clamouring for dividends. Yet he had to find it, not for himself, as so many lesser men had done in India, but for his country. And he found it, in one case at least, by methods which, like the power behind them, were those of an Oriental despot, except that the rich man, not the poor, the prince, not the peasant, was the victim of his extortion.

When Raja Cheyt Singh, the wealthy *zemindar* of Benares,
refused the payment of £50,000 which, in addition to his
regular annual tribute, Hastings had demanded of him in
accordance with the Indian custom that vassals might be
called on to assist their paramount chief in time of emergency, Hastings treated the refusal as proof of disaffection
and determined ' to exact (as he said himself) a severe
vengeance for his delinquency and to draw from his guilt
the means of relief to the Company's distress '. So, after
giving him more than one warning, he fined him £500,000.
On his continued recalcitrance, Hastings ordered his arrest,
and when this was met by rebellion, he deposed Cheyt Singh
and installed a new *zemindar* Equally notorious was
Hastings's treatment of the Begums of Oudh.   Those
exalted ladies were unfortunate in being nearly related—one
of them as grandmother, the other as mother—to the Nawab
Wazir of Oudh whose tribute to the Company had fallen
heavily in arrears.   To enable him to pay this debt the
Nawab demanded that the Begums should surrender to
him a share of the family treasure which they had unjustly
been allowed to appropriate , and at the instigation of the
British Resident the sum of £300,000 was grudgingly paid
out, a pledge being given by the Governor-General-in-
Council that no further claim should be made.   Six years
later, the Nawab was again in arrears , and Hastings, in
serious financial straits, acceded to his request that the
family wealth should be tapped once more.   Since the Begums
had undoubtedly favoured Cheyt Singh's rebellion, Hastings
was able to maintain that the pledge had been invalidated ;
and when they resisted, British troops were dispatched to
assist the Nawab's forces, and the treasure was seized.
These things happened in 1780 and 1781, but another of
the leading charges against Hastings belongs to an earlier
date. In 1774 he had allowed the Nawab of Oudh the use
of British troops wherewith to conduct an attack on a border
hill-tribe, the Rohillas They had been sternly suppressed
and the survivors driven from the country.
    The assault came to a head in 1786. From the moment

when Hastings landed in England in the previous summer
the great body of public opinion had ranged itself in opposing
camps. The Court at once took Hastings's part, so did
influential peers like Lord Mansfield and Lord Thurlow.
Burke and Fox and the Whig party as a whole stood already
committed on the other side. Every one was wondering
what Pitt would do, for on Pitt's attitude, every one knew,
the fate of Hastings depended. But never was Pitt's reserve
more baffling It was thought that the influence of Dundas,
his intimate adviser, who, man of the world as he was,
could scarcely change the colours he had worn so openly
four years before, must go far with Pitt ; but, if this were
so, he gave no sign of it. And when Burke presently forced
the question on the House of Commons, his official declaration
was studiously impartial. ' I am neither a determined
friend nor foe of Mr. Hastings,' he said, ' but I will support
the principles of justice and equity. I recommend a calm
dispassionate investigation, leaving every man to follow the
impulse of his own mind '

The curtain was now rung up and the drama rapidly
developed In the early months of 1786 Burke brought
forward a series of motions for papers. To all of them, save
two which involved the publication of confidential matter,
Pitt promptly assented, and the motions were carried
without a division The prosecution then demanded that
certain witnesses should be called before the House To
this Pitt demurred on the ground that the accused should
in justice be heard before his accusers. At this point
Wilberforce first intervened. He applauded Pitt's steady
course and he begged him not to be driven from it by
intemperate attacks. Then came Hastings's appearance at
the Bar of the House. It would have been a notable
opportunity for an orator. But Hastings was a man of
action, and all he could do was to try to set the facts, as he
saw them, before his judges So throughout, not one sitting
only, but two, he prosed away from a long written narrative
of his thirteen-years administration. But the House could
not be bothered with all those details. It yawned and

emptied. Then, after a month's respite, during which both
sides were busy with the papers, the climax came. On June 2
Burke propounded the first of his definite charges against
Hastings—his conduct with regard to the Rohilla War.
Whatever its merits, the charge was weakened by its stale-
ness, and to those members of the House who had not resolved
a priori to vote for Hastings or against him on every point it
seemed unreasonable to press it. Wilberforce spoke before
the Government had given a lead. He agreed with the censure passed on the Rohilla War, but he was not prepared to
make it the ground of an impeachment. It was Lord North's
duty, he argued, to have recalled Hastings at the time.
Twelve years had since gone by, and during those years
Hastings had spent his life and health in the public service,
and had left our affairs in India in a more prosperous state
than they had been for long before. To punish him now for
his earlier mistakes was ' like eating the mutton of a sheep
which we had previously shorn of its fleece '. The argument
was obviously equitable, and Dundas, seizing the chance of
a little trimming, strengthened it by pointing out that
Hastings had received in the interval ' what might be
considered as a parliamentary pardon ' ; he had been
reappointed Governor-General of Bengal by statute. Pitt
spoke only on a technical point arising from the wording of
the motion, and the House, assuming from his silence that
the Government was on the whole opposed to the charge,
rejected it by 119 votes to 67.

So far Hastings was safe, and his friends were hopeful.
If Pitt holds to this moderate line, they thought, there can
be no impeachment. And Pitt, for his part, was well aware
of his peculiar responsibility. Only eleven days supervened
before the second charge—as to Hastings's treatment of
Cheyt Singh—was raised, and every moment of those days
which he could spare from other pressing business at
Downing Street he gave to the study of the case. ' I have
had hardly hours enough ', he wrote to a friend, ' to read all
the papers on that voluminous article.' And when, all too
soon, the day arrived, he was still not perfectly certain of
his judgement. On this charge he knew he must break

silence, and if the Prime Minister spoke, it would be proper
that he should not wait till the end of the debate. It opened
with a long and vehement speech by Fox, followed by a
shorter and more bitter one from Francis   Pitt sat stiffly
in his seat, attentive to every word, and as he winnowed the
justice from the rhetoric, the wavering balance of his mind
began to settle. But before he spoke the irrevocable words,
on which, more than on any others uttered in the House,
the fate of a great public servant must depend, he determined to take one man's advice—the only man, perhaps,
in that assembly whose conscience he could absolutely trust
Catching Wilberforce's eye, he beckoned him to his place,
and they retired together behind the Speaker's chair.
' Does not this look very ill to you ? ' asked Pitt. ' Very ill
indeed,' said Wilberforce. It was enough. The scales had
settled.   And when Francis had been followed by an
unflinching advocate of Hastings who declared downright
that he had acted very properly, Pitt rose to deliver one of
the most candid and unequivocal speeches ever made by
a front-bench politician on a burning issue. He frankly
told the House that, if he had followed his inclinations
rather than his duty, he would not have been there, such
was the difficulty and uneasiness he felt at having to form
a judgement on the question. But by a most laborious
investigation he had satisfied himself as to the vote which
in his conscience he was bound to give. . . . At last, then,
the decisive word, for which both sides had so long been
waiting, was to be spoken. And soon the friends of Hastings
were rubbing their hands. For Pitt, with the quiet logic
of which he was a master, was busy tearing up Fox's plea
that in all his transactions with Cheyt Singh, from first to
last, Hastings had been wrong. He had been right, he
declared, to demand the *zemindar's* feudal aid, over and above
the tribute, in an emergency   Such was the old-established
custom. And the sum required had not been too high.
Cheyt Singh was admittedly capable of paying it. Hastings
had been right, too, in inflicting punishment when the
payment was contumaciously refused. . . . But presently
it was the turn of Hastings's enemies to rejoice. For Pitt

went on to say that the actions of Englishmen in India
must conform to other standards besides those of Oriental
custom. ' Though the constitution of our Eastern possessions is arbitrary and despotic, still it is the duty of every
administration in that country to conduct itself by the
rules of justice and of liberty as far as it is possible to
reconcile them to the established government.' And in
fixing the fine which he had levied on Cheyt Singh Hastings
had not been ' guided by any principle of reason or justice '.
It was ' beyond all proportion exorbitant, unjust, and
tyrannical '. Since, then, in this respect he had committed
' a high crime and misdemeanour ', if an impeachment
should be preferred against him upon the whole of the
charges—and as to that he did not now commit himself—
this must be one of its articles. A few words more—on
the subsequent deposition of the *zemindar*, which was, he
held, the inevitable result of his rebellion—and, without any
peroration to break the cool judicial tenor of the speech,
Pitt resumed his seat

From that moment the impeachment of Hastings was
a certainty. A few Tories spoke, several voted, against their
chief, but there could be no question of a general revolt,
and the motion was carried by 119 votes to 79. The raising
of the charge relating to the Begums of Oudh a few weeks
later was scarcely necessary, for after what had happened
Pitt's vote and the consequent result were a foregone conclusion. The decisive moment had come and gone on
June 13 behind the Speaker's chair.

There was uproar, of course, among the Hastings faction,
and bitter recriminations were heaped on the young Prime
Minister's head. Never, it was said, had British statesman
committed so gross, so coldly calculated, an act of treachery.
He had waited to see which way the current of opinion was
going to flow, and at the chosen moment he had sacrificed
a far greater man than himself to his petty love of popularity
and power. Nay, it was worse than that. He had thrown
Hastings to the wolves merely to appease a mean Scot's
jealousy. Had he not been closeted with Dundas for hours
on the morning of the debate ? And was it not a well-

known fact that Dundas regarded Hastings as a dangerous
rival ; that Lord Chancellor Thurlow had a ' scheme for
making him a peer, perhaps a minister ' , that the King
was bent on obtaining his admission to the Cabinet ? . . .
What matter that the evidence for these calumnies was of
the slightest ? It was enough for the passions of the time ;
it was enough for the magisterial eloquence of Macaulay ,
it has even been enough for partisans of our own day. But
Wilberforce knew better. One evening, many years afterwards, the old man was recalling, as he loved to do, the
memories of his long, eventful life. ' Oh, how little justice ',
he exclaimed, ' was done to Pitt on Warren Hastings's
business ! People were asking what could make Pitt support
him on this point and that, as if he was acting from political
motives, whereas he was always weighing in every particular
whether Hastings had exceeded the discretionary powers
lodged in him   . . He paid as much impartial attention
to it as if he were a juryman.'

More reasonable are those critics who regret Pitt's decision
because the impeachment, when at last it came, was so
wretched a business—dragging on with such intolerable
languor through its seven years' course, tainted by such self-
conscious stagy pleading and by the exaggerated invective
that betrayed Burke's failing mind, and so unfair, when
all is said, despite the ultimate acquittal, to the culprit at
the bar. Yet Pitt's decision—and Wilberforce's—had been
right in principle. Impeachment, as we can see to-day
better than they could then, was the wrong process : but
it was essential that Parliament, by some such other means
as a committee of inquiry, should minutely investigate and
decide upon the charges against Hastings. The inclusion
of Indian territories within the British Commonwealth had
introduced a strange anomaly into its political system.
Britain was the traditional foe of autocracy in the Western
world. Yet in the East she herself played the autocrat.
In those days any other kind of rule in India was inconceivable ; already, indeed, experience had proved that the
powers committed to the Governor-General, so far from
being over-despotic, were not despotic enough , and Pitt's

Act of 1784 had strengthened them. But only on one condition could those two discordant principles of government be maintained side by side in a single political community—only if the one controlled the other, only if Parliament controlled the Governor-General. Nor, secondly, could the British ' trust ' in India be anything but a pretentious catchword to salve the conscience of the public and gratify its moral pride, unless the public saw to it that its servants were true to the ' trust '. And, lastly, what of the Indian people ? It was not autocracy they minded, they were used to that ; but the autocrat of Bengal was now a white man and a Christian, more alien to all its life than any conqueror of an earlier age. How long would they endure the British Raj unless indeed, in solid fact, it gave them what it promised—justice and security such as the East had never known ? And what hope was there of that if the actual practice of the British Raj, however high its theories, meant the unmodified dictatorship of a series of irresponsible Englishmen ; if the man who governed British India, however fine his object and however good his other deeds, could do such things as Hastings had done, and never be required to justify them ? *

III

If the European record in Asia in Wilberforce's day had its dark spots, in Africa it was wellnigh wholly black. It might almost seem as if Nature had decreed that the destiny of Africa should be sacrificed to that of other continents Cut off from Europe by the vast Sahara, the great mass of it lay for centuries outside the stream of history. Its unindented, harbourless, inhospitable coast, the bars and rapids of its few great rivers, the deadly climate of its tropical belt made exploration difficult and unattractive. And if, as old rumour ran, somewhere in its

* *Life*, v. 340-1. *Hansard*, xxv (1785-6), 1408-9 ; xxvi (1786), 59-60, 101-13 *Warren Hastings' Papers* (ed Forrest), vol 1 Gleig, *Life of Hastings*, vol 1 Rose, *Pitt*, 1, chap x

dark interior immeasurable wealth was to be found, the
difficulty of finding it, of getting it away, of developing any
systematic commerce in such an uncivilized country and
with so primitive a population, repelled the pioneers of
European trade Africa was little more to them than a
gigantic obstacle to a straight sea-voyage to Asia. Diaz
and da Gama attempted and achieved its circumnavigation
merely as a means of reaching India. The Dutch settlement
at its southern extremity, from which a great European
nation was one day to grow, was only established, and for
some centuries of its existence was only valued, as a
strategic outpost on the sea-road to the East and a port-
of-call for Indian merchantmen. Only in one part of
Africa (save where it fronted Europe across the Mediterranean) had Europeans begun to settle and trade in those
early days. In the fifteenth century the Portuguese crossed
from Madeira to the West coast, planted trading stations
along it towards the Equator, and trafficked with the
natives for gold and ivory and pepper But the African
trade would never have been very lucrative, it would never
have been worth a fraction of the Indian trade, if other
products than those had not been found there—products
for which there presently developed an almost inexhaustible
demand among the leading European nations, and the
exploitation of which brought Africa at last into the main
current of the world's business.

While Africa was yet barely known, Europe, still groping
for the East, had found America . and soon from Carolina
through the West Indies to Brazil a chain of European
colonies had been created which promised their creators an
infinite supply of sugar and tobacco and other desirable
commodities, provided only they could find the labour
wherewith to till the soil. Unhappily, it could not be found
in America The redskins of the North were not of the type
to be persuaded or compelled to give up hunting buffalo
and take to digging on the pale-faces' plantations. The
feebler Indians of the South had been decimated or driven
deep into the forests by their Spanish conquerors, and in
any case they were not physically fit for the work Yet

somehow or other civilized Europe must have its sweets and
solaces · if Nature had imposed obstacles thereto, civilized
Europe must use its strength and ingenuity to break them
down   And not much ingenuity or strength was needed
The idea came straight from those Portuguese traders who
had found something else in Africa than gold   The first
cargo brought to Lisbon by the first European company
for the exploitation of West Africa had consisted of two
hundred negro slaves · and if negroes could work in
Portugal, they could work in Brazil. Simple, childlike folk,
hot-blooded but docile under the whip, inured to tropical
heat, very strong and tough, they might almost seem to
have been created for the special needs of colonial planters
Nor was it difficult or dangerous to get them   They could
be got, in fact, more easily and in more paying quantity
than gold or ivory. So the dilemma was quickly overcome ;
and in due course the men, women, and children of West
Africa were being bundled across the ocean, not in hundreds
merely, but in thousands and tens of thousands. The life
of America had been saved, so to speak, by a transfusion of
blood from Africa

The merchants of other countries were soon sharing the
trade with Portugal and Spain · but it was not till the
middle of the sixteenth century that an Englishman first
took a hand in it.   In 1562 that notable buccaneer,
Sir John Hawkins, shipped 300 negroes from Sierra Leone
and sold them to Spanish planters in St. Domingo—an
exploit to which his Queen's attitude was seemingly somewhat equivocal. ' If any Africans should be carried away
without their free consent ', Elizabeth is reported to have
said to Hawkins on his return, ' it would be detestable and
call down the vengeance of Heaven on the undertaking '
but it appears that she lent him one of her own ships
for his next voyage in quest of slaves, and the coat of
arms with which she honoured him was supported by
' a demi-moor in his proper colour, bound captive '. Thenceforward, however, for many years the English took little, if
any, part in the Slave Trade. The agent of the African
Chartered Company, established in 1618, told a negro who

offered him slaves that Englishmen did not buy or sell
' any that had our own shapes '. But when the demand
occasioned by the establishment and growth of English
colonies in North America and the West Indies increased,
these high sentiments were soon forgotten In 1662 a
third African Company, which undertook to supply 3,000
slaves a year to the West Indian colonies, was given its
charter by Charles II, and one of its members was the
King's brother, the future James II. From that time
onwards the expansion of the Slave Trade was steadily
encouraged by English statesmen as an integral factor in
the commercial and naval strength of England Forts
were built on the Gold Coast, and in 1713 a treaty was
concluded with Spain, the notorious *Assiento*, which transferred from French to English merchants the monopoly of the
supply of slaves to the Spanish colonies. By the beginning
of the eighteenth century the rivalry of the Dutch and the
French was overcome, the largest share of the Trade was in
English hands, and English traders were dumping about
25,000 negroes on the other side of the Atlantic every year.
About 1770, out of a rough total of 100,000 slaves exported
annually from West Africa by traders of all nations, British
ships were carrying from 40,000 to 60,000 : and though
the British figure dropped as the result of the American
War, it was still the highest on the list in 1787, standing at
38,000, with France a good second at 31,000 Of the
English ports engaged in the Trade Liverpool easily held
the lead. In 1771, for example, 107 ships cleared from
Liverpool to carry 29,250 slaves, 58 from London to carry
8,136, 23 from Bristol to carry 8,810, 4 from Lancaster to
carry 950. At the beginning of the nineteenth century,
Liverpool had captured six-sevenths of the whole English
trade with West Africa.

The slaves were obtained in three ways—by direct
seizure, by purchase from professional traders, or by barter
from a chief. If it was an unfrequented part of the coast,
or if the inhabitants could be taken by surprise, a sudden
armed landing might be made and the natives kidnapped
by force or guile The grossest treachery was regarded by

some slave-captains as legitimate. On one occasion the British military Governor of Goree was entertaining a merry party of over a hundred natives—men, women, and children —when three slave-captains, who chanced to be present, suggested to him that the whole party should be seized and carried off to their ships, alleging that a former Governor, on a similar occasion, had consented. The professional traders, mostly Arabs of old-established ' firms ', which had carried on the traffic in the heart of Africa for ages past, obtained their slaves in the interior and brought them down to the coast for sale. But a deal with a native chief was the easiest and most productive method of getting the goods. British agents would be sent up-country with orders ' to encourage the chieftains by brandy and gunpowder to go to war and make slaves ', and a chief was rarely to be found who could long hold out against such encouragement, particularly against the lure of the raw, fiery spirit. The usual result was an order to his soldiers to round up a neighbouring village in the night and bring back all the captives they could make ; but sometimes, if his greed were desperate, a chief might sell his own subjects into slavery. And there was yet another way of doing business. Enslavement, it was observed, became an increasingly favourite penalty for crime—not only for witchcraft and adultery, but for petty offences. Or again, a fine would be levied in slaves, and if the offender had none to pay it with, he would be himself enslaved. Even *agents provocateurs* of a sort were not unknown: if an unwary fellow tribesman could be tempted astray, there would be brandy and gunpowder for somebody. Inevitably, therefore, the season of the coming of the slave-ships was a season of terror and violence all along the coast. When a slaver was seen in the offing, the inhabitants left their work in the fields and gathered together for safety in armed groups. Raids meant reprisals. Chief went to war with chief and tribe with tribe—each victory rewarded by a sale of slaves—until at last, their holds filled by one means or another with living cargo, the ships set sail for the West and peace, for a season, settled down again on Africa—on villages lying wrecked and empty among the neglected corn, on childless parents and orphaned children, on a people decimated as by some demoniac visitation.

Meantime the sufferings of the slaves themselves had only begun. The direct voyage to the West Indies might take three or four weeks or more in unfavourable weather, and if the complement was not yet complete the ships might hang about along the coast. The 'hunting-ground' from Cape Verde to the Gulf of Guinea lay close to the Equator and the route thence to the West Indies was entirely within the tropical belt. On a luxurious modern steamship it would be a trying voyage. For the slaves in their small sailing-ships this 'Middle Passage' was an inferno The bigger the cargo, the bigger the profit—it averaged between £2 and £3 per slave in the eighteenth century—and a boat of 100 to 150 tons was made to carry from 300 to 600 slaves The space between decks was usually about five feet, and this was divided into two by a broad shelf on each side with a passage-way in the middle. On the floor and on the shelves the male slaves were laid, manacled together in pairs and so closely packed that often they had not room to lie flat on their backs Suddenly torn from their homes, wholly unused to the sea, terrified by their present fate and the prospect of unknown sufferings to come, squeezed together, like sardines, in sultry heat and rank air, fed on the coarsest food—it is not surprising that numbers of them fell ill. Dysentery of a kind was always rife among them ; and there was no sanitary equipment. In fine weather they would be taken on deck for a time, and forced to dance in their chains for exercise, while their quarters below were being cleaned. In rough weather they had to stay where they were. What the conditions must have been like in a severe Atlantic gale of some days' duration it is impossible to imagine. No wonder that sometimes as many as a quarter of the slaves died on the voyage. No wonder that sometimes a slave took advantage of a chance release from his fetters and his captors' surveillance to leap into the sea. The women and children were not chained together or so closely imprisoned, but the women were habitually exposed to the lust, and the children to the cruelty—sometimes the fatal cruelty—of the captain and crew. Nor were the slaves the only sufferers. The captains of the slave-ships were a peculiar class : and their crews were exposed in a special degree to the hardships and the brutal treatment which in those days were more or less a regular part of the sailor's life at sea. And the contagion of disease was unescapable. The death-rate among the white men engaged in the Slave Trade was far higher than in any other field of the merchant service.

As the end of the voyage approached, the slaves were examined and prepared for sale. Wounds, caused by storm or ill usage, were doctored up and, as far as possible, concealed. But all traces of the Middle Passage could not always be removed ; and the reports of the agents at the ports in the early records are full of complaints : ' The parcel of negroes were very mean.' ' Very bad, being much abused.' ' These . . included some little boys and dying negroes.' Strong men were singly and quickly disposed of at good prices—as much as £40 apiece—but the sick and injured would be lumped with women and children in a batch and sold off cheap. ' Refuse ' such were called. And so, at last, those wretched Africans found in far-away plantations oversea their second ' homes ', where some of them might in time be happy—happier, perhaps, than they had ever been in Africa, if the master were kind-hearted and the meaning of freedom forgotten—and some of them might not . . .*

* For the Slave-Trade, see *Report of the Lords of the Committee of Council . concerning the present state of the Trade to Africa and particularly the Trade in Slaves*, 1789 (see p 116 below) ; Wilberforce's speeches and writings (cited below) , T. Clarkson, *History of the Abolition of the Slave-Trade* (London, 1808) , Bryan Edwards, *History of the British West Indies* (London, 1819) ; F W Pitman, *The Development of the British West Indies, 1700–1763* (Newhaven, U S A., 1917) , C. C. S Higham, *The Leeward Islands, 1660–1668* (Cambridge, 1921), &c

IV

How was it—we may well ask—that eighteenth-century Englishmen, who, whatever their faults, were not devilishly cruel, could tolerate the continuance of this hideous scandal ? Doubtless the facts were not very widely known. Doubtless the public as a whole knew as little and cared as little about Africans as Indians. And it required, no doubt, an unusual effort of imagination to realize the sufferings of those remote black men. But why was there no organized attempt to enlighten the public, to awaken its imagination and its conscience ? Why did the leaders of State and Church do nothing ? Partly, no doubt, for economic reasons—because the Slave Trade was a profitable element in British business and because the productivity of the West Indies and hence of the West Indian trade seemed indissolubly linked up with it ' The impossibility of doing without slaves in the West Indies ', wrote a London publicist in 1764, ' will always prevent this traffic being dropped. The necessity, the absolute necessity, then, of carrying it on, must, since there is no other, be its excuse ' Partly, again, for political reasons—because the withdrawal of Britain alone from so large a field of the carrying-trade might greatly injure her maritime strength in comparison with that of less scrupulous European rivals ; partly because any interference with the Trade by the mother-country would arouse the bitterest resentment in the colonies ; even because—so it was actually argued—the filling-up of the islands with a slave population would tend to keep them more loyal to the imperial connexion than if, like those tiresome New England colonies, they developed into little democracies of white men, with English notions of political freedom Doubtless all these reasons helped in different degrees to keep the humaner feelings in their proper place But there was one other check, and that not the least effective. The agents and connexions of the Slave Trade on the one hand and the colonial planters on the other constituted in course of time a powerful vested

interest in England. The ' West Indians' became as well
known and almost as formidable a body in politics and in
society as the ' nabobs ' ; and it must be a bold man who
would face their anger and their influence.

   This was a powerful array of arguments and interests,
powerful enough to keep the leaders of English opinion and
the makers of English policy from interfering with the
Slave Trade for a very long time. But the silence of consent
was not unbroken No sooner had the Trade firmly established itself than individual protests began to make themselves heard. The first of them, it is safe to assume, were
made not in England itself but in the American colonies.
In America imagination was not needed. The thing was
there. It was to maintain Slavery in the southern continental colonies as well as the West Indies that the Trade
existed ; and if the plantations which required slave-labour
lay only in the South, they were very close to the Puritan
consciences of the middle and northern colonies. In 1688
both the two allied questions—the Slave Trade and Slavery
itself—were raised at a meeting of German Quakers in
Germantown, Pennsylvania. ' Tho' they are black ', it
was said, ' we cannot conceive there is more liberty to have
them slaves as it is to have other white ones . . . Those
who steal or robb men and those who buy or purchase
them, are they not all alike ? ' In 1696 the Yearly Meeting
of the Quakers of Pennsylvania advised ' that Friends be
careful not to encourage the bringing in of any more
Negroes ' This warning was constantly repeated, but
without complete effect, until in 1774 a decree of expulsion
from the Society was passed on any Friend who should
persist in concerning himself with the Trade. At the same
time, manumission of existing slaves was recommended to
all Friends and in 1776 it was made compulsory. But in
America as in England the claims of justice and humanity
were no match for economic interests. To the planters of
the South and the merchants of the North the Trade was
a ' necessity ' ; and such restrictions on it as were imposed
by the colonial legislatures, usually in the form of import
duties, were mainly inspired by fear, by the alarming

results of the great influx of black men into their small white communities, by occasional negro-risings in Carolina and even by a 'negro plot' in New York. And those restrictions were mostly disallowed by the British Government in the interests of the British element in the Trade.

Meantime Englishmen at home had not been silent. As early as 1680 an Anglican clergyman, named Godwyn, who had been a student of Christ Church, Oxford, and had gone out to Barbados, published a tract entitled *The Negro's and Indian's Advocate, suing for their admission into the Church*, in which he asserted that the planters excused their brutal treatment of their slaves by the plea that they were brutes, proved by sundry arguments that as a matter of fact they were not apes or drills but men, and incidentally described the traffic in them as ' a Cruelty capable of no Palliation, and for which *Vengeance* cannot be long expected ere it fall upon the *inhuman Authors* '. About the same time, Richard Baxter, the great Nonconformist, roundly declared in his *Christian Directory* that slave-pirates ought to be regarded as the common enemies of mankind. Similar protests were made at intervals by individual preachers and publicists of lesser note ; and in 1766 Bishop Warburton, an outstanding figure in more than one crucial question of his time, proclaimed from the pulpit that ' the infamous traffic for slaves directly infringes both divine and human law '. But there was no organized movement, religious or secular, against the Trade till in 1724 the Quakers, the first Christian community in England as in America to make a stand collectively and consistently against this negation of Christianity, passed a resolution condemning Slave Trade and Slavery together In 1758, in step with their brothers in Pennsylvania, they proceeded to warn, and in 1761 to disown, all Friends who continued to participate in the Trade. The Wesleyans, meantime, had followed the Quakers' lead In 1739, Whitefield, who was then in America, had plainly hinted, though he had not declared outright, that the Slave Trade was anti-Christian ; and in 1774 John Wesley himself entered the lists with his widely read *Thoughts upon Slavery*.

Nor was it only in religious circles that attention was being drawn to the African scandal. Already before the end of the seventeenth century the tragedy of enslavement had begun to figure in fashionable literature. *Oroonoko*, by Mrs. Aphra Behn, the first novel with a negro for its hero, was posthumously published in 1698 and afterwards dramatized by Southerne. Early in the eighteenth century Defoe took up the cudgels. He condemned the Slave Trade in his poem on *The Reformation of Manners*; he pleaded for kindlier treatment of the negroes in his *Life of Colonel Jacque*; and in *Robinson Crusoe* (1719) he drew a picture, to be adored by every English child for centuries to come, of a black man who could rise above the normal level of his race and prove himself a shrewd, devoted, lovable comrade to a white man. Pope's *Essay on Man*, published in 1733, contained the famous lines on the ' poor Indian ', dreaming of

> Some happier island in the watery waste,
> Where slaves once more their native land behold,
> No fiends torment, no Christians thirst for gold.

And Thomson broke the homely quietude of the *Seasons* (1726–30) with a grim picture of a shark as it follows a slave-ship,

> And from the partners of that cruel trade,
> Which spoils unhappy Guinea of her sons,
> Demands his share of prey.

' Why must I Afric's sable children see, Vended for slaves ? ' wrote Richard Savage a few years later ; and ' See the poor native quit the Libyan shores, Ah ! not in love's delightful fetters bound ', sang Shenstone, not without bathos.

Meantime something more practical than the poets could do was being done for the slaves by the cold machinery of English law. It may seem strange to the present generation of Englishmen that less than two hundred years ago a negro slave was a commonplace sight in England. Till past the middle of the eighteenth century, planters and merchants resident in the colonies were accustomed to bring some of their domestic slaves with them in their visits to the home-

country It was more comfortable, no doubt, and cheaper
than hiring English servants ; but it had its drawbacks.
Many masters were kind to their slaves ; many slaves were
devoted to their masters : but slaves in less happy house-
holds, observing the freedom of white servants and the
opportunities of escape afforded by a crowded town, frequently absconded ; and their masters were put to the
trouble of hunting after them and bringing them back, if
necessary by force. And this, though they can never have
suspected it, did more than anything else to set in motion a
train of events that was ultimately to bring not only the
Slave Trade but Slavery itself to an end. For it thrust
realities, hitherto far off, under the very eyes of the English
people. In the streets of London now, just as if it was in
Georgia or Jamaica, Englishmen and Englishwomen could
see miserable negroes dragged along to captivity and
punishment For the most part they did not like the
spectacle. It startled their imagination. It stirred their
sympathies. It was unseemly, un-English. It hurt their
pride in the tradition of personal liberty which was rooted so
deep in English soil. It was repugnant to their general
notions of English law Surely, they muttered behind their
windows, every one in England was free, provided, of
course, he had been baptized.

Whether this was indeed the law or not, it was an idea
that intelligent slaves were quick to appreciate and to act
upon And they had no difficulty, if once they could slip
away, in finding Christian ministers to baptize them and
warm-hearted citizens to be their godfathers By this means
they obtained at least some measure of protection, ineffective
as it often might be, against the arbitrary power of their
masters. Godfathers could not always prevent the recapture
of fugitive slaves, but, if they were stout, contentious
Englishmen, they could, and often did, threaten their
masters with a suit at law if they attempted to remove the
slaves from England Interference of this kind became in
fact so frequent, so tiresome, and, in the uncertainty of the
law, so menacing that in 1729 the West Indian community
appealed for an opinion to the Law Officers of the Crown

It got all it could want. Attorney-General Yorke and
Solicitor-General Talbot pronounced that neither residence
in England nor baptism affected the master's ' right and
property ' in the slave and that ' the master may legally
compel him to return again to the plantations '. Naturally
the masters gave all the publicity they could to this reassuring doctrine ; and now that the law was unequivocally
behind them, they abandoned such reticence and discretion
as they had hitherto observed out of deference to English
taste They saw no reason now why the whole slave-
business should not be treated with the same frankness in
England as in the colonies. They advertised the sale of
slaves by auction in the newspapers. They advertised, too,
for runaways, and offered rewards for their apprehension.
To capture slaves and put them safe on board ship at a
price became almost a regular trade in the East end of
London. But again the West Indians had not reckoned
with the instincts of stay-at-home Englishmen. Slave-
hunts, slave-auctions ! Such things might happen every
day in Africa or America ; but they could not go on in
England Before very long, they had jolted the nascent
movement against Slavery and all its concomitants one
stage farther : they had created the first of the Abolitionists.

Granville Sharp was born in 1735 of an eminent ecclesiastical family. Though his grandfather was Archbishop of
York and his father Archdeacon of Northumberland, he
started life himself in the humble station of apprentice to
a linen merchant. In 1758, however, he obtained a clerk-
ship in the Ordnance Department, where he employed his
leisure in writing treatises on the text of the Old Testament
and the use of the English tongue. It happened one day in
1765 that he was in the house of his brother, William Sharp,
a surgeon, noted for his readiness to help the London poor,
when a slave, called Jonathan Strong, appealed for medical
aid He belonged, he told them, to a certain David Lisle
who had brought him from Barbados and had so maltreated
him in his lodgings at Wapping, especially by beating him
over the head with a pistol, that his eyesight had become
affected ; then he had been attacked by an ague which had

left him lame in both legs ; and finally, being useless for
work, he had been deserted by his master. William Sharp
soon cured him ; and Granville, whose sympathies had
been keenly excited, provided him temporarily with money
and presently found him a situation with an apothecary.
Unfortunately, some two years later, Jonathan was observed
by his old master, while he was taking medicine to a
customer's house Too obviously, he was quite fit again for
work or for sale. So David Lisle procured two men to
kidnap him and promptly sold him to John Kerr, a
Jamaican, for £30. Jonathan Strong at once appealed to
his godfathers, and they to Granville Sharp, who hastened
to the Lord Mayor, Sir Robert Kite, and persuaded him to
intervene Kite sent for Strong and, after some legal
debate, discharged him on the ground that he had been
deprived of his liberty without a warrant. As the parties
were leaving the court, the captain of the ship that was to
carry Strong to Jamaica attempted to drag him away, but
on being charged by Sharp in formal terms with an assault,
he released his hold. So Strong went off in safety with his
protector, and apparently Kerr made no further effort to
recover his property

This case, though it had ended happily, had made a deep
and permanent impression on Sharp's mind. The wretched
Jonathan, despite the desertion and the two years' interval,
had still been legally Lisle's to sell and Kerr's to buy—and
this in England ! The ruling of the Crown lawyers had been
quoted in the court and the Lord Mayor had not ventured
to contest it. But was that ruling inexpugnable ? Sharp
applied to no less an authority than Blackstone and was
told it was. Still he would not accept it. He would study
the law himself. And after two or three years of hard work
he produced a book on *The Injustice and dangerous Tendency
of tolerating Slavery in England* in which he resuscitated
the earlier opinion of Chief Justice Holt that every slave
entering England became free and supported it with a
learned exposition of the principles of villenage and of the
Common Law Soon after the publication of this book, he
rescued another slave from a ship on the point of sailing for

the West Indies by means of a writ of *Habeas Corpus*
Neither in this case nor in Strong's had the broader legal
issue been faced ; and the continual evasion of it—for there
were other cases besides those in which Sharp was concerned—began seriously to disquiet the legal authorities,
until, in 1772, Chief Justice Mansfield, the greatest lawyer
of his day, arranged with Sharp that the case of James
Somerset, a captured runaway, should be made a test case
for definitely resolving the conflict between Holt's ruling
and that of Yorke and Talbot. Naturally the West Indian
community was alarmed Planters and merchants rallied
to the side of Somerset's owner, Stewart, and put up the
money for engaging the professional services, if not the
personal sympathies, of the brilliant Whig barrister,
Dunning. The case was heard at three sittings, and at
each the court was crowded. For it was far more than a
West Indian concern. The general interest of the public
had been roused. English history, it was felt, was in the
making ; and certainly when Mansfield delivered judgement
on June 22, a conspicuous piece of English history was
made. ' Tracing the subject to natural principles ', he said,
' the claim of slavery never can be supported The power
claimed never was in use here or acknowledged by the law.'
Slavery was still to exist, for more than sixty years, on
English soil overseas , but from that moment it ceased to
exist on the soil of England.

Religion, literature, individual philanthropy, and finally
the law had thus played their part in the gradual awakening
of English opinion to the anachronism of Slavery and the
Slave Trade. But the only positive result of it all was the
Somerset judgement ; and that in itself had done no more
than prevent slaves being brought to England The whole
inhuman business on the Guinea Coast, on the Middle Passage,
in the island slave-markets, could go on exactly as before.
Neither churchmen nor poets nor lawyers could stop it for
an hour. Only Parliament could do that. No one questioned
its legality outside England . it could only be stopped by
an Act of Abolition. And Parliament, through all those

years, had done virtually nothing. It had, indeed, in 1750,
passed an Act to regulate the Trade, which, after reciting
its advantages to Britain and its necessity to the colonies
in the preamble, had solemnly pronounced any deed of
' fraud, force, or violence ' committed against a native in
the process of carrying him off from Africa to be an offence
punishable by a fine of £100. Palpably the preamble was
more important than the clause   Parliament continued to
regard the advantages and necessity of the Trade as unquestionable ; but Parliament did nothing to enforce the
punishment of a single trader for any of the countless acts
of fraud and violence without which the Trade—as everybody knew—could not be carried on. It was not that the
sympathies of the average Englishman, in Parliament or
out of it, had been quite untouched. When he read about
the wrongs of Slavery or the Trade or saw some faint
reflection of them on the stage, he was moved to pity and
sometimes perhaps to indignation. And at close quarters, of
course, he could not endure them. But as long as they were
out of his sight, he could. He came, in fact, to regard them
as part of the inevitable evil in the order of creation. Men
were but men ; everybody was involved in it ; every other
maritime nation was as eager as England to profit by the
Trade and envied her the lion's share of it. The American
colonists, it was true, protested at having it forced on them
by the disallowance of their restrictions ; but there was
more politics than morals in their indignation. When
Congress banned the Trade in 1774, it was mainly as a part
of the general policy of severing all commercial connexion
with the mother-country, a move in the preliminaries to
rebellion. And when the war itself had come, when the
Declaration of Independence was being framed, it was not
only morals that inspired the charge levied against the King
in the first draft of the document, of waging ' cruel war
against human nature itself, violating its most sacred rights
of life and liberty in the persons of a distant people who never
offended him, captivating and carrying them into slavery
in another hemisphere or to incur miserable death in their
transportation thither '. Jefferson, the draughtsman, him-

self confessed later on that this clause ' was struck out in complaisance to South Carolina and Georgia who had never attempted to restrain the importation of slaves and who, on the contrary, still wished to continue it. Our northern brethren also, I believe, felt a little tender under those censures ; for though their people had very few slaves themselves, yet they had been pretty considerable carriers of them to others.' In any case, as soon as the war was over, the Trade was complacently and profitably resumed in Georgia and the Carolinas and New England just as it was resumed in England as soon as the seas and the markets were reopened. It made no difference that some of the most notable men of the day had joined, during the war period, in the attack upon the Trade—that Adam Smith had demonstrated in the *Wealth of Nations* that slave-labour was uneconomic ; that Robertson's widely read *History of America* had denounced the Trade as equally repugnant to humanity and religion ; that Paley in his *Moral Philosophy* had expressed the fond hope that ' the great revolution which had taken place in the western world may conduce (and who knows but that it was designed ?) to accelerate the fall of this abominable tyranny ' ; that Bishop Porteus had preached a sermon on the wrongs of the negroes before the Society for the Propagation of the Gospel. Nor did it matter much that the thorny question had been revived in Parliament. It had been quickly shelved again by the appointment of a Commission in 1775 to take evidence on the conditions of the Trade. And in 1776 the House of Commons had promptly rejected the first of the long series of ineffective resolutions against the Trade moved by Hartley, a predecessor of Wilberforce's in the seat for Hull, and seconded by that generous Yorkshireman, Sir George Savile. All this was of small account. The sacrifice of Africa was still a ' necessity ' for Europeans across the Atlantic. The Trade, indeed, could never satisfy the planters' needs. Conditions of slave-life on the plantations were not conducive to any large natural increase in the stock. Always more imported slaves were wanted, and some day more islands might be British, more land available for cultivation. There seemed no reason why the Trade should ever come to an end.*

V

Thus resigned, thus fatalistic was the attitude of the House of Commons when Wilberforce became a member of it. And he was soon enabled to judge its temper for himself. The Quakers were not minded to let the matter drop ; and, when in 1783 a Bill was introduced to prevent servants of the Crown from engaging in the business of the African Company, they took advantage of this incidental reference to the Slave Trade to present a petition against it. The Coalition had just come into office, and Lord North responded with urbanity. ' The object and tendency of the petition ', he said, ' ought to recommend it to every humane breast ; and it did credit to the feelings of the most mild and humane set of Christians in the world But still he was afraid that it would be found impossible to abolish the Slave Trade . . . for it was a trade which had, in some measure, become necessary to almost every nation in Europe ; and as it would be next to an impossibility to induce them all to give it up and renounce it for ever, so he was apprehensive that the wishes of the humane petitioners could not be accomplished ' Two years later, another appeal was made to Parliament. The inhabitants of Bridgwater petitioned for ' the extinction of that sanguinary traffic ' The petition was presented by Poulet and Hood, the members for the borough ; and in due course they reported to their constituents that it had been ordered to ' lie on the table ' ' There did not appear ', they said, ' the least disposition

---

* Godwyn, *The Negro's and Indian's Advocate*, &c (London, 1680) Clarkson, *op. cit.*, i, chaps ii–v. Prince Hoare, *Memoirs of Granville Sharp* (London, 1820), chaps i–iv. W. E B. Du Bois, *The Suppression of the African Slave-Trade to the United States of America* (Cambridge, U S A , 1896), chaps ii–v. S. H Swinny, ' The Humanitarianism of the 18th Century ' in *The Western Races and the World* (ed Marvin, Oxford, 1922) Lecky, *History of England in the 18th Century* (Cabinet edition), vii. 357 ff.

to pay any further attention to it.' What Wilberforce thought is not recorded.

The Quakers, meantime, had not by any means resigned themselves to Parliament's cool *non possumus*. In 1784 the Meeting for Sufferings, a sort of standing committee to which the matter was entrusted, prepared a written statement entitled *The Case of our Fellow-creatures, the oppressed Africans, respectfully recommended to the serious Consideration of the Legislature of Great Britain, by the people called Quakers.* Copies were sent to the King and Queen and the Prince of Wales, to Pitt, who was now Prime Minister, to Lord Chancellor Thurlow and Chief Justice Mansfield, to Lord Howe, First Lord of the Admiralty, to the Speaker, and to the members of both Houses of Parliament. Twelve thousand copies in all were printed and circulated. In 1785 they likewise promoted the circulation of a book by Anthony Bezenet, an American Quaker, on ' the calamitous state of the enslaved negroes in the British Dominions ', and deputations waited on the head masters of Winchester, Eton, Harrow, Westminster, Charterhouse, and other schools to ask them to allow their scholars to be given copies of it. Since 1783, moreover, a small committee of six—William Dillwyn, George Harrison, Samuel Hoare, Thomas Knowles, John Lloyd, and Joseph Woods—had been acting as a sort of permanent executive ' for the relief and liberation of the negro slaves in the West Indies and for the discouragement of the Slave Trade on the coast of Africa ' by means of personal influence, publication of books, and propaganda in the newspapers. This little body soon found itself drawn into collaboration with other pioneers outside the circle of Friends—chief among them Granville Sharp, who had continued ever since the Somerset case to write for the cause on his own account, corresponding with Bezenet and other Abolitionists in the United States and with the leaders of the established Church in England. Another useful ally was the Rev. James Ramsay, who had spent nineteen years in St. Christopher and had returned to take up a living at Teston in Kent burning to redress the negroes' wrongs. His *Essay on the Treatment and Conversion of the African*

Slaves in the Sugar Colonies, published in 1784, was the
first of a series of outspoken pamphlets from his pen. And
presently a recruit was found who was ready to devote the
whole of his life to the cause. Thomas Clarkson, son of the
head master of Wisbeach Grammar School, had come into
residence at St. John's College, Cambridge, about the time
that Wilberforce went down. He was evidently a ' sap ' ;
he had come up with an exhibition from St. Paul's , he
worked hard for his degree ; and in 1784 he won the first
prize for the Latin Essay for B A 's of ' middle ' standing.
It so happened that in 1785 the Vice-Chancellor, whose duty
it was to choose the subjects for the Latin Essays, was
Dr. Peckard, Master of Magdalen College and a determined
foe of the Slave Trade , and the subject he set for ' senior '
B A.'s was *Anne liceat invitos in servitutem dare* ? or *Is it
right to make men slaves against their will ?* Clarkson again
competed ' In studying the thesis ', he afterwards said,
' I conceived it to point directly to the African Slave Trade,
and more particularly as I knew that Dr. Peckard (in a
sermon in the previous year) had pronounced so warmly
against it.' It was a safe assumption , and Clarkson, having
devoured all the books about West Africa he could find and
discussed the question with military friends who had served
in the West Indies, won the first prize. In due course he
read his essay in the Senate-house ; and as he rode back
to London he found himself unable to think of anything
but the Slave Trade. ' I became at times very seriously
affected,' he records, with the zest for personal detail which
protracts but enlivens his *History of the Abolition of the
Slave Trade.* ' I stopped my horse occasionally, and dis-
mounted and walked I frequently tried to persuade myself
in these intervals that the contents of my essay could not
be true . . . Coming in sight of Wades Mill in Hertfordshire,
I sat down disconsolate on the turf by the roadside and held
my horse. Here a thought came into my mind—that, if
the contents of the essay were true, it was time some person
should see these calamities to their end. Agitated in this
manner, I reached home.' The agitation continued. When
he set himself to translate his essay into English for publica-

tion, the truth of the evils it described once more stared
him in the face, stared him out of countenance. Presently
he made Dillwyn's acquaintance and learned from him—
what he had not hitherto suspected—that other Englishmen
were troubled by those facts and had banded together to
deal with them Then he met Granville Sharp and Ramsay
Finally, in 1787, he came to his decision. He would abandon
the clerical career he had begun—he was already in deacon's
orders—and devote the whole of his life to the destruction
of the Slave Trade.

In the summer of 1787 this band of fellow workers formally
consolidated itself, with the original group of Quakers for
its kernel, into a Committee for the Abolition of the Slave
Trade, with Granville Sharp as its first chairman It was
well manned for its initial task—to elicit, to master, and to
spread broadcast the widest possible amount of evidence
as to the realities of the Trade. But that was not enough.
If the country must first be schooled and roused, the second
step must be to break through the apathy of Parliament,
to defy such fatalistic doctrine as Lord North's, to introduce
and—tremendous task !—to carry a Bill for the abolition
of the Trade. And for this a politician was needed, and
a politician endowed with very rare gifts indeed He must
possess, in the first place, the virtues of a fanatic without
his vices He must be palpably single-minded and unself-
seeking He must be strong enough to face opposition
and ridicule, staunch enough to endure obstruction and delay.
In season and out of season, he must thrust his cause on
Parliament's attention. Yet, somehow or other, Parliament
must not be bored He must not be regarded—and the
planters, no doubt, would do their best to cultivate this
idea—as the tiresome victim of an *idée fixe*, well-meaning
possibly, but an intolerable nuisance. Somehow or other
he must be persistent, yet not unpopular. Secondly, he
must possess the intellectual power to grasp an intricate
subject, the clarity of mind to deal with a great mass of
detailed evidence, the eloquence to expound it lucidly and
effectively. He must be able to speak from the same brief
a score of times without surfeiting his audience with a hash

of stale meat And, since the Slave Trade is his theme, he must have a certain natural delicacy of feeling He will have terrible things to say , they will foim an essential part of his case , but in the choice of them and in the manner in which he says them he must avoid the besetting sin of the professional humanitarian. He must never be morbid. He must not seem to take a pleasure in dwelling on the unsavoury vices of his fellow men. He must not pile up the horrors and revel in atrocious details. He must shock, but not nauseate, the imagination of his hearers. Finally, he must be a man of recognized position in society and politics. It must be impossible for wealthy West Indians to deride him in London drawing-rooms as an obscure crank, a wild man from beyond the pale And he must have, or by some means must obtain, a footing in Downing Street. For without at least some shadow of support from Government his task may well prove desperate.

Such were the requisite qualifications for the politician needed to lead the movement for the abolition of the Slave Trade in Parliament ; and, as we know, a politician so qualified was available. Like many other Englishmen of good feeling, Wilberforce had early been impressed with the abuses, actual and potential, of Slavery and the Trade Indeed the precocious boy had written, at the age of fourteen, a letter to a York newspaper ' in condemnation of the odious traffic in human flesh '. But the subject had not haunted or depressed him, and it was not till he was twenty-one that his active interest was reawakened. A friend of his chanced to be going to Antigua, and Wilberforce wrote to ask him to collect some first-hand information as to the treatment of slaves in the West Indies ' I expressed ', he said afterwards, ' my determination, or at least my hope, that some time or other I should redress the wrongs of those wretched and degraded beings.' Three years later, in 1783, he first met Ramsay, but it was not till 1786 that the acquaintance bore fruit. In the interval Ramsay had published his first pamphlet, and among its many readers were his old friend and patron, Sir Charles Middleton, afterwards Lord Barham, First Lord of the Admiralty in the days of Trafalgar, and his

public-spirited wife. So shocked was the latter at Ramsay's
revelations that she entreated her husband to take the
matter up in Parliament and cast about in her mind as to
which of the front-rank politicians might be prevailed upon
to undertake the championship of the cause. Her choice
fell on the young member for Yorkshire whose ability and
eloquence were already well known and who was, moreover,
so usefully intimate with Pitt. So Wilberforce was invited
to Teston ; Ramsay was reintroduced to him ; and to the
rector's torrent of appalling facts Lady Middleton added her
own earnest prayers.

It has sometimes been asserted that Lady Middleton's
initiative decided the issue. ' The abolition of the Slave
Trade ', wrote the venerable Ignatius Latrobe in 1815, ' was,
under God and when the time was come, the work of a
woman.' But Wilberforce himself put the case in truer
perspective when he said in after life that ' it was just one
of those many impulses which were all giving to my mind
the same direction ' One such impulse was certainly the
intercourse he had with Clarkson in 1787.

' On my first interview with him ', the latter's faithful prose
records, ' he stated frankly that the subject had often
employed his thoughts and that it was near his heart. He
seemed earnest about it and also very desirous of taking the
trouble of enquiring further into it. Having read my book,
which I had delivered to him in person, he sent for me.
He expressed a wish that I would make him acquainted
with some of my authorities for the assertions in it, which
I did afterwards to his satisfaction. He asked me if I could
support it by any other evidence. I told him I could. I
mentioned Mr. Newton, Mr. Nisbett, and several others to
him. He took the trouble of sending for all these. He made
memorandums of their conversation, and, sending for me
afterwards, showed them to me. On learning my intention
to devote myself to the cause, he paid me many handsome
compliments. He then desired me to call upon him often
and to acquaint him with my progress from time to time.
He expressed also his willingness to afford me any assistance
in his power in the prosecution of my pursuits '

John Newton's name suggests another ' impulse '. No one
at this period was more intimate with Wilberforce , none

had greater influence over him ; none knew better what
torments the young penitent had lately passed through,
what vows he had made to prove himself worthier of grace.
Is it not likely that the old pastor seized the opportunity
and spoke long and earnestly to Wilberforce of the field
in which, as he knew too well, a great redeeming work was
crying to be done ?   At any rate it was Wilberforce's
' conversion ', whatever the personal suggestions which
followed it, that primarily accounts for his fateful decision.
He returned to his place in the House of Commons, as has
been seen, with quite a new conception of his political
career. He felt that in previous sessions he had been merely
wasting his time. ' The first years that I was in Parliament ',
he once said, ' I did nothing.   . My own distinction was my
darling object.' Now he was determined—partly, maybe,
owing to Pitt's kindly and practical sympathy—at any rate
to do *something*. But what was it to be ? What cause could
pass the test of his new conscience ? It must be something
outside or above the party programmes, untainted and
unwarped by the pretences and compromises of party strife
It must be something big ; for otherwise the talents which
he knew had been given him to use had better be used elsewhere than in politics. Up to a point the notion of a great
campaign against vice might seem to satisfy these conditions.
But was this enough ? It did not readily lend itself to
parliamentary treatment , and surely some more tangible,
more exacting, more drastic task was needed than the
constricted and rather humdrum activities of the Proclamation Society.   To Wilberforce, in some such questioning
mood, the thought of taking up the cause of the slaves
must at once have made a strong appeal. Here was a cause
which no party had cared or dared to touch   Here, if you
like, was a big cause—a cause on which depended the moral
and physical welfare of hundreds of thousands of human
beings. Here, above all, was a challenge which no Christian
could evade. Coming when it did, in fact, the idea seemed
to Wilberforce to be charged with higher than human
inspiration ; and his mind was soon made up.   ' God
Almighty ', he wrote in his journal, ' has set before me two

great objects, the suppression of the Slave Trade and the reformation of manners.' The order is significant. The Proclamation Society may still claim part of his thoughts and his time, but most of them will henceforward be occupied elsewhere.

Wilberforce promptly set himself to master the facts. He sought out and closely questioned the London merchants in the African and West Indian trade. 'I found them', he says, 'at this time ready to give me information freely, the Trade not having yet become the subject of alarming discussion.' Any one, indeed, who knew or cared anything about the matter became the prey of his tact and charm and curiosity. There were constant interviews at the house he had now taken in town in Palace Yard   Clarkson called to report progress at least once a week. And there were breakfast-parties at Sir Charles Middleton's and long talks over the fire, and finally regular meetings at Palace Yard between Granville Sharp, Ramsay, and Clarkson on the one side and one or two friendly members of Parliament on the other   Thus, in the course of 1787, Wilberforce began to feel that, though he had a great deal more to learn, he was sufficiently equipped to open the case in the House of Commons. But one thing remained to be done before he finally committed himself to political action.   Just as Pitt had consulted him before making his decisive speech on the Hastings case, so now he consulted Pitt. The opportunity came when he was staying at Pitt's country-house at Holwood ; but he hesitated, it seems, from modesty or shyness, to raise the question himself   And Pitt, who was doubtless aware of what had been occupying so much of Wilberforce's mind for many months past, may well have hesitated too   The political championship of Abolition was not a task to be lightly urged upon a friend, especially upon one so sensitive and seemingly so fragile. It might leave him broken in health, and isolated and crippled in politics. Had not Burke himself, before he became engrossed in India, contemplated the task, but refrained from undertaking it for fear of rousing a storm that might rend and shatter the Whig party ?   And was not Pitt himself, *mutatis*

mutandis, in the same position as Burke? But he knew
that the plea of party loyalty and unity did not apply to
Wilberforce. He knew, too, how closely the cause must
harmonize with his new religious zeal; and to his practical
mind this was probably the determining argument. The task
might be painful and exhausting; but, once absorbed in
it, Wilberforce would be safe at least from the temptation,
which not so long ago he had confessed to him, of secluding
himself altogether from the world of affairs; safe from
drifting into extravagant or ineffective pietism; safe from
spending all his days on nothing more fruitful than the
Proclamation Society In a sense, indeed, the idea must
have seemed as providential to Pitt as it had to Wilberforce.
And so, as they sat one day, with Grenville for a third, ' at
the root of an old tree just above the steep descent into
the vale of Keston ', Pitt asked the question which his friend
wanted most to hear ' Why don't you, Wilberforce,' he
said, ' give notice of a motion on the subject of the Slave
Trade?' Had he not ' taken great pains to collect evidence '?
Was not the credit therefore his due? And was not the
subject admirably ' suited to his character and talents '?
' Do not lose time,' he added, with a touch of worldly
wisdom, ' or the ground may be occupied by another.'

There was now no reason why Wilberforce's decision
should not be made known to the world of politics and
business; and Clarkson, so he tells us, was conspiring to
bring this very thing about, anxious doubtless to get the
brilliant young politician committed beyond recall. Accordingly he arranged with his old friend, Langton, a well-known
London host whose table had been honoured by Johnson
and Burke and most of the great men of the day, that
Wilberforce should be invited to a dinner-party and tactfully
drawn into a positive declaration. The party duly assembled.
Joshua Reynolds, Boswell, Windham, and Middleton were
among the seven guests. And the subject of the Slave Trade
was duly broached. It was a rich subject for the dinner-
table; and Boswell expatiated on the planters' plea that
the negroes were happier on their plantations than they
had ever been in Africa. ' Be it so,' he sagely remarked,

' but we have no right to make people happy against their will.' ' But what about the welfare of the West Indies and the prosperity of Liverpool?' suggested some one. That fired Windham. ' Rather let Liverpool and the Islands be swallowed up in the sea ', he said, ' than this monstrous system of iniquity be carried on.' And then Langton delivered his attack on Wilberforce ' in the shape of a delicate compliment '. There had been, of course, no need whatever for all this finesse. Wilberforce had committed himself at Holwood ; and he at once replied to Langton's question that he was quite prepared to take up the cause in Parliament ' provided no more proper person could be found '. Nor, of course, had he any objection to Clarkson's mentioning this avowal to his ' friends in the City '. So the news was quickly spread. With very different feelings Abolitionists and West Indians heard that the Prime Minister's intimate friend had taken the field against the Slave Trade.*

* *Life*, i, chap. vi. Clarkson, i, chaps. vii–x. *Memoirs of G. Sharp*, 229–39. Harford, 138–9. *D. N. B.* ' T. Clarkson '.

IV
CRUSADE

I

WHEN Pitt recommended Wilberforce to take up the Slave Trade question, he had not washed his hands of it himself. He must already have felt that the Trade was an outrage on Africa and a disgrace to Europe and that it ought to be, and could be, stopped . for he would scarcely have encouraged Wilberforce to divert his talents and enthusiasm into a blind alley. At the same time, with his cooler judgement and his closer knowledge of the political world, he probably realized better than his sanguine friend what a long and laborious task it well might be. If he did not know already, he very soon discovered that his own colleagues and followers were by no means prepared to risk the fortunes of the Government and the party on such an idealistic and controversial issue that Sydney, his Secretary of State who dealt with colonial questions, was stubbornly opposed to it : that Thurlow, his cynical and disloyal Chancellor, whose influence with the King was almost as strong as his own, was dead against it : that the King himself would do all he could to prevent his admirable young Minister from disturbing the present comfortable adjustment of political forces. And Dundas, who had now become Pitt's most intimate and influential political adviser, though, like most people, he had a warm liking for Wilberforce, was the last person to encourage Pitt to go crusading with him. One thing, therefore, was very soon plain Pitt could not commit his Government to an official assault on the Trade for the simple reason that his Government was not agreed on it. Presently, perhaps, he might prove himself so indispensable to the King and to the country as to be able to do as he chose. Some day, perhaps, he might contemplate resignations in the Cabinet with indifference : he might break outright with Thurlow he might impose Abolition on the King. But not yet. To force the issue now would probably mean his own dismissal or, at the best, another General Election , and with his party divided, with Thurlow and his pack and possibly the King against him, with the

currents of corruption working quite incalcutably, an
Election might mean downfall and the breaking-off of his
patient, systematic work for the restoration of his country.
Those critics who maintain that Pitt betrayed his littleness
by refusing in so great a cause to stake all and face the
consequences, should reflect that Wilberforce, to whom also,
as it happens, the cause seemed a great one, had no suspicions of Pitt's littleness Whatever he may have thought
later on, he never supposed at the outset that Pitt should
have done anything more than he did. He quite understood, he fully concurred, he had never expected anything
else, when Pitt told him that the opening move of his
campaign—a motion in the House of Commons calling for
consideration of the Trade—must be a non-party move ;
that Ministers and their following must be left free to speak
and vote on the motion as they pleased.

Of course this did not mean that Pitt himself was going to
be neutral He would be as free as anybody else ; and he
can have had little doubt from the first which way he
would speak and vote. Having settled that the motion
should come on early in the following year, he gave a good
deal of his time during the autumn and winter of 1787 to
studying and discussing the case. He saw almost as much
of Wilberforce as in the Wimbledon days ; witness the diary.
' Called at Pitt's and staid supper—Apsley, Pitt and I.'
' Pitt, Bearcroft, Graham, &c. dined with me.' ' Pitt's
before House—dined ' ' After House to Pitt's—supped '
And one entry shows that Pitt was going to first-hand
sources for his information ' Unwell and so did not dine
at Pitt's, but met Ramsay there in the evening and discussed ' ' It would delight you to hear Pitt talk on this
question,' Wilberforce told Wyvill in January ; and in the
same month Pitt wrote from Holwood begging Wilberforce
to give him yet more talk. ' If you could contrive to come
here to-night or to-morrow, I would stay another day
quietly in the country, and should like extremely to have
a full prose on all this business Remember you owe me at
least a week.' And there was more than talk Pitt's
political insight had instantly seized on the argument which

the defenders of the Trade would make the most of—the
economic folly and the national danger of giving up the
Trade as long as other countries continued to pursue it
and in the course of the autumn he began, in concert with
Wilberforce, to make soundings abroad Obviously, it would
cut a big slice of ground from under the West Indians' feet
if some sort of provisional agreement could be made with
foreign Governments ; and in this hope, this rather desperate hope, Pitt was ready to thrust the thorny question
into the delicate field of international diplomacy. ' You
have had a letter from my friend Wilberforce ', he wrote
to Sir William Eden, British Ambassador at Paris, on
November 2, ' on a scheme which may appear to some people
chimerical, but which I really believe may, with proper
management, be made practicable. If it can, I am sure it
is an object well worth attending to, and perhaps you may
be able to learn the private sentiments of the French
Government upon it, in a general way , so as to enable us
to judge whether it can be carried further. I mean the idea
of the two nations agreeing to discontinue the villainous
traffic now carried on in Africa.' A few days later Pitt
wrote again : ' The more I reflect upon it, the more anxious
and impatient I am that the business should be brought as
speedily as possible to a point ' ; and since Eden was
shortly to be transferred to Madrid, he added · ' If you
see any chance of success in France, I hope you will lay
your ground as soon as possible with a view to Spain also.
I am considering what to do in Holland.' Eden cannot
have relished his task   His relations with the French
Government were not of the smoothest. M. de Montmorin,
indeed, had just been telling him that France had recently
been ' much nearer going to war than from a view of the
circumstances I might suppose ' and was now complaining
bitterly of the effect on French industries of the new
Commercial Treaty which, it had been hoped, would
initiate a real *entente*. ' He says ', Eden informed Pitt,
' that the representations from the different parts of
Normandy, and even from Bordeaux also, against our
pottery and against the cottons are again urgent to a degree

of clamour and violence. . . . In Normandy above 4,000 manufacturers are begging in the streets.' Eden cannot, therefore, have welcomed his rather imperious Prime Minister's move ; and he would have been still more uneasy if he had known that Wilberforce was impulsively bent on a visit to Paris, and was only dissuaded by Grenville's tactful suggestion that ' the appearance of our being over-solicitous upon the subject would not forward the attainment of our point '. But Eden's diplomacy, however free from amateur intrusion, however correct and cautious, could get little out of Montmorin. ' It is in a more hopeful way than I expected,' he reported to Wilberforce on December 19 ; ' but I am not sanguine as to the success of any proposition, however just and right, which must militate against a large host of private interests.' And he went on to suggest half-measures—an agreement with France and Spain to denounce the Trade and to prepare measures for its abolition or to suspend it temporarily with a view to its final cessation later on. But these half-measures were firmly combated by Wilberforce in his reply, and he was as firmly backed by Pitt. ' On the subject of the Slave Trade ', the latter wrote to Eden on January 7, ' you will hear from Wilberforce more at large than I have time to write, and it is the less necessary for me to do it as I concur entirely in his ideas. I am persuaded a temporary interruption of the Trade would be as full of difficulty and inconvenience as to abandon it entirely. . . . Besides this, if the principle of humanity and justice, on which the whole rests, is in any degree compromised, the cause is in a manner given up. I therefore trust you will find the French Government in a disposition to concur with the measure in its full extent.' But Eden's further efforts were quite unavailing. M. de Montmorin was vague. ' It is one of those subjects ', he said, ' upon which the interests of men and their sentiments are so much at variance that it is difficult to learn what is practicable.' And he repeated grave opinions he had heard as to the ruinous effect of Abolition on the French West Indies. He said in fact precisely what Sydney would have said, *mutatis mutandis*, to the French

Ambassador if he had raised the question in London. And, apart from other arguments, the French Government was naturally unwilling to commit France to Abolition until it was quite certain that England was committed. That was, in fact, the cardinal crux in all these negotiations, not to be overcome by the most confident assertions on Wilberforce's part. He told Eden about the activity of the Quakers, about the Abolition Committee and its increasing influence, about the enthusiasm for the cause at Manchester, about the foundation of an Abolitionist Society at Birmingham with ' a liberal subscription '. He even declared that, so far as he could judge during the recess, ' there appears an universal disposition in our favour in the House of Commons '. ' On the whole, therefore,' he concludes, ' *assure yourself that there is no doubt of the success.*' It may be questioned if even those italics convinced Eden ; and certainly, in the light of after events, M. de Montmorin cannot be blamed for requiring some rather more positive proof of the British Government's and Parliament's intentions. So Pitt's assault on France proved ineffective ; and, if France held out, it was useless to press the matter on Spain or Holland.

Meantime Wilberforce was better engaged in London than he would have been in Paris. Since the impending motion was to be ' unofficial ', it was decided that he should move it rather than Pitt . and throughout those winter months he was busy arming himself with more facts. The diary is full of it. ' Mr. Hartley, African, &c. breakfasted with me.' ' Dined Sir C. Middleton's—Ramsay and Collins.' ' Collins, Ramsay, Edwards, Gordons supped—Slave Trade discussed.' And he was corresponding with friends of the cause in the provinces. ' At this place ', writes one from Manchester, ' large subscriptions have been raised for the slave business, and *te duce Teucro* we are warm and strenuous.' But it was from the Abolition Committee, which Wilberforce was not yet invited to join on the ground that his influence would be greater if he acted independently, that he obtained the best and fullest information, and particularly from Clarkson   That autumn Clarkson set

out on the first of those laborious missions of inquiry which
were to do so much—more, indeed, than anything else—to
give the Abolition movement its essential basis of hard
fact.   Bristol, Liverpool, and Lancaster, the three ports
outside London concerned in the Trade, were naturally his
first quarry.   At Bristol he found the subject ' in everybody's
mouth '.   ' Everybody seemed to execrate it, though no one
thought of its abolition '   Of the evidence he was hunting
there was enough and to spare.   He discovered, by checking
the muster-rolls, that the proportion of deaths among
British seamen on slave-ships was exceptionally high.   He
was told some gruesome stories, one at least at first hand,
of the cruelty of captains to their crew.   He took the
measurements of the slaves' quarters in two small ships then
in port and worked out the allowance of space for each
slave as two square feet in one and four in the other.   At
Liverpool, and at Lancaster too, the muster-rolls told him
the same tale of high mortality.   He saw in the window of
a Liverpool shop the leg-shackles, hand-cuffs, thumbscrews,
and mouth-openers used on slave-ships, and wisely purchased
a specimen of each.   And everywhere and all the time he
was asking questions, disagreeable questions, questions that
presently gave rise to the idea that this mad busybody was
actually proposing to destroy the traffic which made Liverpool the great and wealthy place it was !   The atmosphere
grew warm.   Traders and captains and their friends began
to frequent the ' King's Arms ' where Clarkson habitually
dined , they talked loudly at him , they drank provocative
toasts to the Trade ; they tried to engage him in argument.
Fortunately Clarkson had always with him a companion of
the martial name of Falconbridge, who could explain, if
counter-attack were needed, his own experience of the
Trade on the African coast.   Better still, he was, says
Clarkson, ' an athletic and resolute-looking man '.   And he
had a pistol in his pocket   But before he left Liverpool
Clarkson had a narrow escape   He had got on the track of
the murder of a seaman by his captain ; and one day a
gang of eight or nine men, the suspected murderer among
them, tried to hustle Clarkson into the sea as he was watching

a big gale from the pier-head   ' I escaped, not without
blows '   And so back to London by way of Manchester,
where he preached one of his few sermons, and Birmingham,
where he stimulated the local zeal of which Eden had been
told.   A letter from George Rose to Wilberforce reveals
him still at work on his return   ' It is quite unprecedented ',
he writes, ' to allow any one to rummage the Custom House
papers for information, who has no employment in the
revenue   I will, however, without delay obtain for
Mr. Clarkson all the information which he wants—though
I am a West Indian planter, would I were not ! '   It was at
this time, too, that Wilberforce arranged for Clarkson to
lay his evidence before Pitt   He went twice to Downing
Street and his minute account of the interviews shows that
Pitt was well acquainted with the statesman's art of eliciting
information.   He was rather cold, thought Clarkson, and
uncertain in his sympathies.   He confessed to doubts about
the validity of the case for Abolition and was not easily to
be satisfied.   It was not till Clarkson had fetched his copies
of the muster-rolls and Pitt had himself ' looked over about
a hundred pages accurately ', that he admitted conviction.
Not unnaturally, perhaps, Clarkson was deceived by these
tactics.   He knew nothing of Pitt's earlier talk with Ramsay,
nothing of the negotiations with France ; and he came away
with the conviction that the interviews ' had given birth to
an interest in favour of our cause '.   He found Grenville
better informed and troubled by fewer doubts: so it is
probable that Grenville got much less out of him than Pitt.

But the activity that winter was not all on one side.
The representatives of the Trade had awakened to the
gravity of the danger implied in Wilberforce taking the
field as a champion of Abolition—Wilberforce the popular,
the eloquent, the unimpeachable, the member for Yorkshire,
the friend of Pitt.   Anxiously they began to set the
machinery of the African and West Indian vested interest in
motion.   Wherever they had influence, they tested and
strengthened it—in Society, in Parliament, at the Court.
In all quarters conversation began to turn upon the Trade.
Its value to England, it seemed, had never been adequately

estimated. Did critics realize, it was asked, what the cessation of the Trade would mean to the West Indies ? Nay, were they aware of the unsuspected blessings it bestowed on the people of Africa ? As the case for the defence took shape, it became clear to Pitt, clear to Wilberforce, too, that the obstacles to Abolition were greater than they had at first foreseen. ' Called at Pitt's at night ', says the diary early in 1788 ; ' he firm about African trade, though we begin to perceive more difficulties in the way than we had hoped there would be ' It was soon obvious that the attack could not be opened as early as February 2, the date originally fixed for the motion. More time was needed, and, despite Clarkson's energy, more evidence. Nothing could so damage the cause at the beginning as unsubstantiated accusations : and Wilberforce agreed with Pitt that, in face of the concerted opposition of the Trade, some more authoritative evidence was required, whatever delay it might entail, than could be obtained by the private efforts of Clarkson or himself or anybody else. And here the Prime Minister could help officially without violating his Government's neutrality. Pitt directed the Trade Committee of the Privy Council to make an inquiry into the conditions of British commercial intercourse with Africa. It was a straight challenge to the Trade, and the Trade met it squarely. They could prove, said the African merchants, that the traffic in slaves was at once necessary and humane. On the other side the Abolition Committee, with which Wilberforce kept in constant touch, prepared its evidence and marshalled its witnesses.*

* *Life,* 1 151–66 Clarkson, i, chaps xiv–xxii *Journal and Correspondence of Lord Auckland* (London, 1861), 1. 266–7, 269, 277, 304–8. Holland Rose, *Pitt,* 1. 459–60

II

At this exciting moment, when the opposing forces were already lining up for the first battle, the Abolitionists were suddenly deprived of their parliamentary leader. Wilberforce's frail physique had mutinied. In the course of February and March his recurrent indigestion developed into serious intestinal trouble. He could eat little and assimilate nothing Intermittent fever and tormenting thirst robbed him of sleep He rapidly lost weight. ' There 's Wilberforce,' said one Cambridge acquaintance to another, pointing out the enfeebled invalid : ' he can't last three weeks.' And when his friends compelled him to summon the fashionable Dr. Warren to consult with Dr. Pitcairne, the great man came to much the same conclusion. Whether or not they diagnosed the case in the drastic language of Wilberforce's biographers as ' an entire decay of all the vital functions ', the doctors shook their heads and gave it up ' He has no stamina to last a fort-night ', they told the family, and advised the prompt removal of the dying man to Bath on the desperate chance that its mysterious waters might work a miracle beyond the reach of human skill. It was practically a death-sentence, and Wilberforce was not deceived. He was ready to go and die at Bath if such was God's will. But there was one thing he must do before he went He sent for Pitt and, fighting down the physical languor and mental exhaustion which had begun to assail him, he entreated him to under-take, if he should die, the cause to which he had meant to give his life Would he, in any case, he asked him, move the resolution in Parliament which, whatever happened, he would not now be able to move himself ? Pitt's answer came straight from his heart. His innate political caution, his party difficulties, the problems of his own career were forgotten. ' With a warmth of principle and friendship ', as Wilberforce said afterwards, ' that has made me love him better than I ever did before ', he promised not only to introduce the motion but to do anything, if his friend so

wished, which it 'would be proper for him to do himself'.
The sick man was deeply moved. This was more than he
had dared to hope. If the greatest statesman of the day
should succeed him in the conduct of it, the cause would
lose nothing—might it not even gain ?—by his own dismissal. And so, the one thing done and so well done,
Wilberforce prepared for his journey with a quiet and
thankful mind.

He reached Bath on April 5 in a state of collapse ; and a
week later, since he was now unable to attend to business,
his mother and two other friends wrote jointly on his behalf
to Pitt, saying the time had come for the formal commitment of the Abolition cause into his hands. And then the
miracle began to happen. Not indeed by drinking the
Bath waters but by taking minute doses of opium—a drug
which Dr. Pitcairne had had the greatest difficulty in
forcing on his scrupulous patient—Wilberforce began to
mend. And his progress, once the corner had been turned,
was astonishingly rapid. On May 5, exactly a month after
his arrival *in extremis*, he was strong enough to leave Bath
for a visit to Cambridge, travelling mostly in a carriage, but
at times—a miracle indeed !—on horseback. There followed
a peaceful month in comfortable quarters in the Warden's
Lodgings at St. John's. ' Lived more regularly and quietly ',
he wrote in the Journal, ' than I had done for a long time.
Chiefly with Milner [1] in the evenings Dined commonly in
Hall. . . . In health mended.' But he was not yet fit for
London and politics, and in June he left Cambridge for the
Lakes, where he settled down for the summer in his house
at Rayrigg He was able now to continue his correspondence with the Abolition Committee in London, and he had
hoped to find in his retirement an opportunity for unbroken
study and contemplation , but his days were soon encroached
on by a stream of visitors. ' The tour to the Lakes has
become so fashionable ', he wrote to John Newton, ' that the
banks of the Thames are scarcely more public than those of
Windermere . . At this moment my cottage overflows with
guests.' And there was one day in the week on which this

[1] Now Fellow of Queens'

constant irruption was especially irksome. ' Sadly taken
up on Sundays ', he complains, ' with company in the
house.' But there were precious hours he could still make
his own. Early in the morning, before any of his guests
were stirring, he would take a boat and row out by himself
and ' find an oratory under one of the woody islands in the
middle of the lake '.*

III

While Wilberforce was thus gathering strength to return
to the stage he had nearly left for ever, Pitt was faithfully
playing his part as understudy. From the moment of
Wilberforce's departure from London he began to devote
yet more time and thought to the question than he had
hitherto assigned to it. He at once arranged to superintend
the Privy Council inquiry henceforth in person ; and on
receiving Mrs. Wilberforce's letter from Bath, he promptly
invited Granville Sharp to come to Downing Street and
discuss with him the policy of the Abolition Committee.
The invitation was eagerly accepted, and the conference
was held on April 21. Sharp had decided to state the
Committee's case without reserve, and he told Pitt that its
object was nothing less than the complete abolition of the
Trade. Pitt replied ' that his heart was with them and that
he considered himself pledged to Mr Wilberforce that the
cause should not sustain any injury from his indisposition '.
But he pointed out that success could not be won in an
instant. No Bill could be introduced before the Privy
Council inquiry was completed , in other words, till next
session. To Sharp this delay was doubtless irksome ; for
already the Committee's propaganda in the country was
bearing fruit and impatient supporters were demanding
that, since Wilberforce was out of action, another parliamentary leader should at once be chosen to press the
business on. Pitt's attitude, on the other hand, was manifestly as sincere as it was practical ; and Sharp could use

* *Life*, 1 167–84

the knowledge of his pledge to Wilberforce to propitiate the hotheads.

A few days later, on May 9, Pitt fulfilled the first and smallest of the promises he had made. In a short speech he moved a resolution binding the House to consider the circumstances of the Slave Trade early in the next session. It was a short speech because Pitt 'studiously avoided', as he frankly told the House, giving his own opinions on the Trade at this stage. A full discussion of the question, he declared, was now neither useful nor desirable. Some held that the Trade should be abolished outright; others that it only needed regulation. The matter must be considered deliberately and in detail, and this was impossible until the result of the inquiry instituted by his Majesty's Ministers elsewhere was known. He alluded to Wilberforce's illness, and expressed the hope that his honourable friend would be able to 'resume his charge' and introduce the question himself next session: for in no one's hands could 'any measure of humanity and national interest' be better placed. But if he were still too unwell, he (Pitt) would undertake the task again himself. In this tribute to Wilberforce Fox promptly concurred. He had meant himself, he said, to raise the question of the Slave Trade, but 'when he heard that the member for Yorkshire had resolved to take it up, he was unaffectedly rejoiced, not only knowing that gentleman's purity of principles and sincere love for the rights of humanity, but because, from a variety of considerations as to the characters and situations in which different men stood in that House, there was something that made him honestly think that it was better that the business should be in the hands of the honourable gentleman than in his, and that it would come from him with more weight, more authority, and more probability of success than from himself'. But his faith in the cause was as strong as Wilberforce's own; and in contrast to Pitt's official caution—a contrast he was careful to bring out—he openly asserted it. 'I have no scruple to declare, at the onset', he said, 'that my opinion of this momentous business is that the Slave Trade ought not to be regulated

but destroyed.' Burke also spoke. He, too, had previously
thought of taking up the question of the Slave Trade, and
he, too, at once committed himself to the full, clean course of
Abolition. Of the other speeches Sir James Johnstone's
was the most interesting. He was the first to raise the
question of the effect of these discussions at Westminster on
the minds of the slaves themselves. Others were presently
to point to restlessness among the negroes on the plantations
as a reason for doing nothing and even saying nothing ;
but to Johnstone, who declared himself an Abolitionist, it
was a reason for doing something and doing it without
delay, lest ' the poor creatures' hopes might be raised too
high and bad consequences follow '. The slaves, he told the
House, were already aware of the Abolitionist movement in
England. He had recently heard from Grenada that they
were going about invoking the champions of their cause in
a crescendo of excited hope and faith—' Mr. Wilberforce
for negro. Mr. Fox for negro. The Parliament for negro.
God Almighty for negro.' The rest of the debate was only
remarkable for the silence of the West Indian group. They
had decided, it appeared, to reserve their defence. Only one
member had the impatience to assert that Abolition was
' unnecessary, visionary, and impracticable ' ; and not one
voted against the resolution. It was carried *nem. con*

The general question of Abolition was thus temporarily
shelved , but the session was not to close without one at
least of the particular scandals of the Trade being forced on
Parliament's attention Old Sir William Dolben, member
for Oxford University, had been moved to go on board a
slave-ship that was lying in the Thames and had been so
horrified at the arrangements for packing the slaves between
decks—' like books on shelves ', as Lord Stanhope put it—
that he had promptly given notice of a Bill for limiting the
number of slaves in proportion to the tonnage which a
ship should be allowed to carry The Bill was read a first
time on May 26, and in the debate on the second reading,
since the House was not now discussing the theoretical
rights and wrongs of slave-trading but a single, definite
abuse connected with it, the champions of the Trade were

forced into the open. Lord Penrhyn flatly denied the cruelty and unhealthiness alleged. ' It was absurd to suppose ', he said, ' that men, whose profit depended on the health and vigour of the African natives, would purposely torment and distress them during their passage so as to endanger their lives ' But when, in support of the petition Lord Penrhyn presented, the Liverpool merchants were heard by counsel at the bar, their representatives were compelled to admit that the average death-rate on the Middle Passage was at least 10 or 5 per cent. according to its length and that in one case no less than a third of the slaves had died It was useless, after that, to plead that ' the voyage from Africa is the happiest period of the slave's life ! ' These disclosures made a marked impression on the House ; and Pitt showed that he had made up his mind on this particular aspect of the Trade at any rate by moving and carrying the unusual proposal that the Bill, if passed, should operate retrospectively from June 10. The partisans of the Trade would have been wise if they had taken the hint, made as graceful a retreat as possible, and dug their trenches farther back against the next attack. But they were not wise They declared that they would have none of these regulations. To regulate the Trade would ruin it. Every negro lost by regulation to a British ship would be a negro won by a French ship. To argue thus, at this stage, was a tactical mistake. It raised the general question and raised it in a provocative manner. It amounted to a claim that, so far from contemplating the abolition of the Trade, Parliament must put no limits on it at all. And this was more than Pitt could stomach. At the outset of the debate he had asked the House to judge the particular regulations proposed in the Bill on their own merits, and not to go back on its previous decision to reserve the broader discussion on the fate of the Trade as a whole till next session. But now he himself was provoked into taking the wider ground. ' I have no hesitation to declare ', he said in the closing speech of the debate, ' that, if the Trade cannot be carried on in a manner different to that stated by the honourable members opposite me, I will retract what I said on a former day against going into the general question, and, waiving every other discussion than what has this day taken place, I will give my vote for the utter abolition of a trade which is shocking to humanity, is abominable to be carried on by any country, and reflects the greatest dishonour on the British senate and the British nation. The Trade, as the petitioners propose to carry it on, without any regulation, is contrary to every humane, to every Christian principle, to every sentiment that ought to inspire the breast of man.'

This discharge of high explosive seems to have blown the opponents of the Bill right out of Westminster Hall. Only five members in a thin House voted against the third reading, while fifty-six voted for it. But the Trade had still a chance, and a good chance, in the House of Lords. It mattered not at all to Lord Chancellor Thurlow that the Prime Minister had given the Bill such wholehearted support in the Commons as almost to make it his own measure. He derided it as the product of a ' five days' fit of philanthropy '. It might well teach the slaves ' to proceed of their own accord to an abolition of this Trade '. Unhappy merchants who had embarked their all in ships already sailed would be ruined by it. The Duke of Richmond and Lords Carlisle, Stanhope, Hopetown, and Townshend supported the Bill : but the rest followed Thurlow's lead. Lord Heathfield had ascertained by careful calculations that a negro in a slave-ship had nearly twice as many cubic feet of air to breathe as a British soldier in a tent. The Duke of Chandos was convinced by a letter he had just received from Jamaica that the passage of the Bill might very well lead to a negro rising in the West Indies and a universal massacre of the whites. More reasonable and more respectable was Lord Rodney's blunt anxiety at the prospect of losing commerce to the French. Obsessed by the idea that to tamper with the Slave Trade might somehow mean a weakening of our strategic hold on the West Indies, the great sailor not only minimized the hardships of the Middle Passage, but went beyond his brief to repudiate current notions of the sufferings of the slaves on the plantations.

He had never heard of a negro being cruelly treated, he
avowed, in all the time he had been at the West Indies ; and
he had often expressed the wish that the English labourer
might be but half as happy. Finally, Lord Sydney, the
Secretary of State primarily concerned, declared his
preference for leaving the matter over for the general discussion in the next session   It seemed, indeed, as if the Bill
was lost   and it would have been lost if the Lords had been
left to themselves. But Pitt's back was up. When he
heard how the debate was going, he told Grenville that, if
the Bill were defeated, he would not remain in the same
Cabinet with its opposers ; and he used all his personal
influence with individual peers to save it. By a narrow
margin he won and Thurlow lost   On June 30 the Bill was
carried, with certain useful amendments of its hasty drafting,
by 14 votes to 12.*

<h2 style="text-align:center">IV</h2>

Events at Westminster during the summer of 1788 were
thus calculated to hasten Wilberforce's convalescence. He
could assure himself that the cause had lost little, if anything,
through his illness. The Government and the House of
Commons stood committed to a full discussion of the Trade
next year. The amelioration of the negro's lot had already
been begun with Dolben's Act. Pitt had not only confessed
to the world his detestation of the cruelties of the Trade
as it was then carried on, but had proved his earnestness
by staking the existence of his Government on the necessity
for its instant regulation

In October Wilberforce returned to town and dined with
Pitt ; but he was soon off again to Yorkshire and to Bath ;
and it was not till the beginning of December that he finally
settled down again in London and resumed his parliamentary
duties   It was a critical moment in politics. The King
had gone out of his mind. The Whigs were demanding the

* *Life*, i. 171–3. Clarkson, i. 504–60. *Hansard*, xxvii (1788–9),
495–506, 576–99, 638–52

automatic assumption of the Regency by the Prince of
Wales, whose first act, they assumed, would be to dismiss
Pitt and send for Fox And Thurlow, scurrying betimes
from the ship, all gratitude for his sick master's past favours
forgotten, had sold his support to the Prince, and continued
to sell him the secrets of the Cabinet to which he still belonged,
at the price of retaining the woolsack in the new Ministry.
But Pitt had still to be reckoned with. He was determined
that if and when the medical evidence should leave no doubt
as to the need for the appointment of a Regent, it should
be made by the will of Parliament and under such conditions
as Parliament might desire. And Wilberforce, now quite
himself again, joined eagerly in the struggle on Pitt's side,
admiringly convinced that his friend was standing, not only
for constitutional right, but for plain honesty and patriotism
in a world of selfish intrigue. Before Christmas the crisis
was practically over. The Prince had acknowledged the
sovereignty of Parliament—' the sacred principles which
seated the House of Brunswick on the throne '—and
Thurlow in the House of Lords had prayed God to forget
him if ever he should forget the loyalty he owed the King.
In the following February Pitt introduced a Bill to confer
the powers of Regent with certain restrictions on the Prince,
but it never became law. Before the end of the month
George III recovered his reason as quickly as he had lost it.

The Regency crisis over, Wilberforce could concentrate
once more upon the Slave Trade ; and from the beginning
of the new year he was occupied all day and every day
in preparation for the imminent parliamentary struggle.
Somehow or other his health, though he refused to play
the invalid and spare it, kept up to the old indifferent level
of the days before his breakdown. ' House till near six,'
says the diary for January 26 · ' slave business all the
evening, with only biscuit and wine and water—nervous at
night, and dreamed about slavery ' Again, a month later :
' Slave business till near bed, and slept ill, as I commonly
do when my mind is occupied before bedtime—nervous and
tossing, haunted by thoughts about trifles.' But there was
one thing he could do, and do willingly enough, to ease the

pressure. After dining one night in February at Lord Salisbury's he sets down this characteristic resolution : ' On full conviction from experience that it is impossible for me to make myself master of the slave subject and to go through my various occupations except I live more undistractedly, I determine scarce ever to dine out in parties, and in all respects to live with a view to those great matters till the slave business is brought to some conclusion. May God bless the work and my endeavour.'

But abstention from parties meant no rest. The insatiable ' slave business ' streamed into the vacuum. Almost every day the diary bears witness to it. ' Evening. Eliot staid and we looked at slave business.' ' Very unwell—kept the house all day—slave business, Eliot.' ' Frewen and Clarkson at dinner—Jonas Brown, Muncaster, and Eliot at night—slave business, but interrupted often and much by people on other matters which sadly obstruct my progress.' ' Morning to Pitt's on business. Then Slave Trade. Dined Bayham's. Slave business evening.' ' Obliged to dine at Speaker's. Found Ramsay and Clarkson at home, so kept up.' And all the time those ' other matters ' were pressing and obstructing. There were the various duties he had to perform as member for Yorkshire and the calls on his time of his numerous private charities. Not many public men can have spent busier days. Already while he sat at breakfast—to which some Abolitionist colleague was often invited to discuss the latest evidence—his ante-room began to fill with callers, the earliest of whom was generally summoned to the breakfast-room before the meal was ended. It was a queerly mixed company that gathered in that ante-room. ' On one chair sat a Yorkshire constituent, manufacturing or agricultural ; on another a petitioner for charity or a House of Commons client ; on another a Wesleyan preacher ; while side by side with an African, a foreign missionary, or a Haytian professor, sat perhaps some man of rank who sought a private interview and whose name had accidentally escaped announcement.' That is the description of Wilberforce's biographer-sons—a little pompous, a little early-Victorian. Hannah More's was more succinct : ' Noah's

Ark, full of beasts, clean and unclean.' And certainly not all the callers were immaculate ; for it appears the small books which had originally been kept in the room had to be exchanged for heavy folios ' which could not be carried off by accident in the pocket of a coat '. The morning calls disposed of, Wilberforce was off to a meeting of the Abolition Committee or to the House of Commons ; or if nothing took him from home, he was closeted with his collaborators in his library, examining, winnowing, tabulating the gigantic mass of detailed evidence that was to smash the Trade. It was at this period that he first became acquainted with James Stephen, who had lived for the past eleven years as a barrister at St Kitts, and had been so deeply stirred by the evils of slavery as he saw it at close quarters that he had refused, in the teeth of universal custom, to own a single slave himself Such experience, such burning convictions were the best credentials ; and Wilberforce promptly took Stephen to his heart—and to his library. As likely as not, he would find Clarkson there, or Ramsay who was often up from Teston, staying in the house As the date of the debate drew near, this little band of zealots were labouring at their papers for eight or nine hours every day. ' Wilberforce's white negroes ' Pitt once dubbed them , but, if Wilberforce was in a sense their master, he toiled no less than they. Their presence and their example, indeed, made it almost impossible for him, even if he had wished it, to slacken the strain To return home from some tiring business was not to find an easy-chair and restful solitude. Once, towards the end of March, he thoroughly exhausted himself travelling to Cambridgeshire and back between nine at night and noon next day. ' Reached London about twelve very faint,' he says. The rest of the day's record in the diary is brief but significant. ' Ramsay and Clarkson '—that is all, and quite enough.

Meantime the other side was also hard at work. The debates on Dolben's Bill, and especially Pitt's uncompromising attitude, had convinced the Trade of the reality of the danger threatening it. At public meetings all over the country, in the newspapers, in a host of pamphlets, the

British people were assured that their interests were inextricably interwoven with the interests of the Trade. Abolition meant the end of our colonial empire—more, it meant the commercial downfall of the mother-country. Not only from Liverpool, but from Bristol and from London also, though neither of these latter ports enjoyed a quarter of Liverpool's share in the Trade, came the same lurid warnings. Even Alderman Sawbridge, that old, robust exponent of the City's traditional devotion to liberal causes, was induced to confess his belief that any further tampering with the Trade would spell ruin for his constituents. And, while Abolition would cripple England, it would do no good to the negroes. Those morbid tales of cruelty and suffering, those fantastic statistics of mortality were only the hysterical inventions of pietistic old women who knew nothing about the West Indies and less than nothing about Africa.

'It is well known', wrote the author of a pamphlet entitled *Slavery no Oppression*, 'that the eastern and western coasts of Africa are inhabited by stupid and unenlightened hordes ; immersed in the most gross and impenetrable gloom of barbarism, dark in mind as in body, prodigiously populous, impatient of all control, unteachably lazy, ferocious as their own congenial tigers, nor in any respect superior to these rapacious beasts in intellectual advancement but distinguished only by a rude and imperfect organ of speech, which is abusively employed in the utterance of dissonant and inarticulate jargon. Such a people must be often involved in predatory battles, to obtain a cruel and precarious subsistence by the robbery and destruction of one another. The traffic has proved a fortunate event for their miserable captives '

Not all the apologists of the Trade were quite so dishonest or so imbecile as that. There were candid merchants who did not deny the hardships of the negroes, but held that business is business and that the weak must suffer for their weakness in this hard world. Some, indeed, were willing, if not anxious, that everything should be done to improve the conditions under which the Trade was carried on— anything, that is, which would not diminish its profits. Others, like Rodney, thought first and foremost of British sea-power and set their faces stubbornly against endangering it for a sentiment. Others, again, like Admiral Barrington, had seen only the happier side of the slave's life in the West Indies and were as unconvinced of its evils as were many of the better slave-holders in the Southern States of America in the nineteenth century. And behind all these was the English legal mind. When negroes were suffering in London, the legal mind had concentrated—after some hesitation—on the slave's right to freedom ; but when negroes were suffering on the Guinea Coast or in mid-Atlantic, the legal mind was more concerned with the owner's right of property. Were numbers of Englishmen to be suddenly deprived of what the law allowed them to possess, of a livelihood, which, unpleasant though it might be, they had so long been permitted to pursue by public opinion and with at least the tacit authority of Parliament ?

Amid all this discussion, public and private, passionate and sober, the Privy Council Committee was quietly finishing its inquiry. Before the end of April its Report was presented to Parliament in a stout sub-folio volume. It did not state any conclusions on the Committee's part for or against the Trade ; it was simply a collection of the evidence given before it and of information otherwise obtained—declarations submitted to it, tables of statistics, and so forth. These materials were marshalled in five sections : (1) on the civilization of West Africa and the manner in which slaves are made ; (2) on ' the manner of carrying slaves to the West Indies ' ; (3) on the treatment of slaves on the plantations ; (4) on the extent of the trade and population, slave and free, of the West Indies ; (5) on the Slave Trade and Slavery as practised by other nations. Of these sections the first three, and of their contents the statements of the witnesses, were the most interesting and important. A variety of persons gave evidence—ex-governors, naval officers, captains of slave-ships, surgeons, traders, travellers. One of these last, Dr. Andrew Spaarman, Professor of Physic at Stockholm, the record of whose travels in South Africa has long been known and valued by geographers and historians, is worth quoting because of his palpable disinterestedness. On the question as to how slaves were obtained, he gave evidence as follows :

'When the kings of the country want slaves for the purchase of goods, they send their horsemen in the night to the villages to make as many slaves as they can. In the neighbourhood of Goree he saw one of these expeditions. The King of Barbessia came to him in the night to tell him that he was going to send out a party to make slaves as he wanted brandy to encourage his officers. In the course of the conversation, the King became so intoxicated with madeira by Dr. Spaarman's bedside that he was carried away speechless. Dr. Spaarman saw the party set out and saw them return with some slaves they had made. They conceal part of those they make on these occasions in order to enhance their price.'

A good deal of evidence was given on both sides, but rather more against the Trade than for it. Clarkson's first journey had not been taken in vain. He gave evidence himself on what he had discovered at Liverpool and Bristol, and he is named as presenting several of the other witnesses. The most whole-hearted defender of the Trade was Robert Norris, a slave-captain, whose rose-coloured caricature of the Middle Passage was to be dealt with presently by Wilberforce in Parliament. Its most outspoken assailant was James Arnold, one of Clarkson's witnesses, a Bristol surgeon who had served on slave-ships and told a ghastly story of a captain's fiendish cruelty not only towards the slaves, male and female, in his power, but towards his white crew too. But, apart from the more extreme statements, if half what the moderate men said was true—as they took oath it was—it was more than enough. On the issue of bare humanity, uncrossed by political or material considerations, any ordinary kindly human being who read the Report must instantly, by simple, instinctive standards, have condemned the Trade.

The Report presented, there was no reason for further delay ; and already on April 10 Pitt had written to Wilberforce to fix the day for the debate. ' Grenville and I ', he said, ' have formed a project of reducing the case, as it appears from the Report, into a string of resolutions, which

we will send you as soon as they are complete. . . . The more
we consider the case, the more irresistible it is in all its
parts.' Wilberforce was now at Teston, making his final
preparations away from the interruptions of town ; but he
went to Holwood twice in the next few weeks to discuss the
campaign with his chief. ' Pitt very earnest about the Slave
Trade,' he notes. And now at last the day came—May 12.
Its events are thus typically recorded in the diary. ' Tuesday
very indifferent. Came to town sadly unfit for work, but
by Divine grace was enabled to make my motion so as to
give satisfaction—three hours and a half—I had not prepared
my language, or even gone over all my matter, but being
well acquainted with the whole subject I got on. My breast
sore, but *de ceteris* pretty well. How ought I to labour,
if it pleases God to make me able to impress people with
a persuasion that I am serious, and to incline them to agree
with me ! '

Who would suppose from this entry that its author had
made that day one of the finest speeches in all that golden
age of Parliamentary oratory ? The greatest of the orators
had been quick to acclaim it. ' The House, the nation, and
Europe ', said Burke, ' are under great and serious obligations to the hon. gentleman for having brought forward
the subject in a manner the most masterly, impressive, and
eloquent. The principles were so well laid down, and
supported with so much force and order, that it equalled
anything I have ever heard in modern times, and is not
perhaps to be surpassed in the remains of Grecian eloquence.'

Only an incomplete and, as Wilberforce himself complained,
an inaccurate record has survived ; but it is worth while to
try to catch some echoes, faint and broken though they be,
of a speech so praised by such a master.*

---

* *Life*, i, chaps. vii and viii. Clarkson, ii. 12–20. *Report of the
Lords of the Committee of Council, &c.* (1789).

V

Imagine, then, the crowded House that afternoon of May 12, 1789—Grenville in the Speaker's chair, Pitt and Fox facing each other across the table, and behind them, close-ranked, the country gentlemen of eighteenth-century Britain with a sprinkling of new-comers from the commercial middle-class among them. Imagine the small, bent, slender figure, rising to propose the motion Imagine a speech far better phrased than these clipped and mutilated fragments ; and imagine, as it is delivered, the speaker's eager, mobile face, the natural gestures, the earnest, persuasive, beautiful voice.

' When I consider, Sir, the magnitude of the subject which I am to bring before the House—a subject in which the interests not of this country nor of Europe alone, but of the whole world and of posterity are involved—and when I think, at the same time, on the weakness of the advocate who has undertaken this great cause, I cannot but feel terrified at my inadequacy to such a task. But when I reflect on the encouragement which I have had, through the whole course of a long and laborious examination of this question, on how much candour I have experienced and on how conviction has increased within my own mind in proportion as I have advanced in my labours—when I reflect, especially, that, however averse any hon gentlemen may now be, yet we shall all be of one opinion in the end—when I turn myself to these thoughts, I take courage, I determine to forget all my fears, and I go forward with a firmer step in the full assurance that my cause will bear me out and that I shall be able to justify, upon the clearest principles, every resolution in my hand, the avowed end of which is the total abolition of the Slave Trade

' I wish exceedingly, at the outset, to guard both myself and the House from entering into the subject with any sort of passion. It is not your passions I shall appeal to I ask only for your cool and impartial reason . . . I mean not to accuse any one, but to take the shame upon myself in common with the whole Parliament of Great Britain for having suffered this horrid trade to be carried on under our authority. We are all guilty. We ought all to plead guilty, and not to exculpate ourselves by throwing the blame on others. And I therefore deprecate every kind of reflection against the various descriptions of people who are more immediately involved in this wretched business.

' In opening up the nature of the Slave Trade, I need only observe that it is found by experience to be just such as every man who uses his reason would infallibly conclude it to be. For my own part, so clearly am I convinced of the mischiefs inseparable from it that I should hardly want any further evidence than my own mind would furnish by the most simple deductions. Facts, however, are now laid before the House. A report has been made by His Majesty's Privy Council, which I trust every hon gentleman has read and which ascertains the Slave Trade to be just such in practice as we know from theory it must be. What should we suppose must naturally be the consequence of our carrying on a slave trade with Africa—with a country vast in its extent, not utterly barbarous but civilized in a small degree ? .. Is it not plain that she must suffer from it—that civilization must be checked, that her barbarous manners must be made more barbarous, that the happiness of her millions of inhabitants must be prejudiced by her intercourse with Britain ? Does not every one see that a slave trade carried on round her coasts must carry violence and desolation to her very centre—that in a continent just emerging from barbarism, if a trade in men is established, if the men are converted into goods and become commodities that can be bartered, it follows that they must be subject to ravage just as goods are ? We see, then, in the nature of things how easily the practices of Africa are to be accounted for. Her kings are never compelled to war, that we can hear of, by public principles, by national glory, still less by the love of their people. In Europe it is the extension of commerce, the maintenance of national honour, or some great public object, that is ever the motive for war with every monarch. In Africa it is the personal avarice and sensuality of her kings. These two vices of avarice and sensuality—the most powerful and predominant in natures thus corrupt—we tempt, we stimulate, in all these African princes. We depend upon these vices for the very maintenance of the Slave Trade. Does the King of Barbessia want brandy ? He has only to send his troops in the night time to burn and desolate a village The captives will serve as commodities that may be bartered with the British trader. What a striking view, again, of the wretched state of Africa is furnished by the tragedy of Calabar ! Two towns, formerly hostile,

had settled their differences and by an intermarriage among
their chiefs had pledged themselves to peace. But the trade
in slaves was prejudiced by such pacifications, and it became,
therefore, the policy of our traders to renew the hostilities.
This policy was soon put into practice, and the scene of
carnage was such that it is better perhaps to refer gentlemen
to the Privy Council's report than to agitate their minds by
dwelling on it.

'The Slave Trade, in its very nature, is the source of such
kind of tragedies. . . . It is a trade in its principle inevitably
calculated to spread disunion among the African princes,
to sow the seeds of every mischief, to inspire enmity, to
destroy humanity ; and it is found in practice, by the most
abundant testimony, to have had the effect in Africa of
carrying misery, devastation, and ruin wherever its baneful
influence has extended.

'I must speak now of the transit of the slaves to the West
Indies. This, I confess, is in my opinion the most wretched
part of the whole subject. So much misery condensed in
so little room is more than the human imagination had
ever before conceived. I will not accuse the Liverpool
merchants. I will allow them—nay, I will believe them—to
be men of humanity. And I will therefore believe that, if
it were not for the multitude of these wretched objects,
if it were not for the enormous magnitude and extent of
the evil which distracts their attention from individual
cases and makes them think generally and therefore less
feelingly on the subject, they never would have persisted
in the trade. I verily believe that, if the wretchedness of
any one of the many hundred negroes stowed in each ship
could be brought before their view, there is no one among
them whose heart would bear it. Let any one imagine to
himself six or seven hundred of these wretches, chained two
and two, surrounded with every object that is nauseous and
disgusting, diseased and struggling under every kind of
misery ! How can we bear to think of such a scene as this !
One would think that it had been determined to heap upon
them all the varieties of bodily pain for the purpose of blunt-
ing the feelings of the mind , and yet in this very point—to
show the power of human prejudice—the situation of the
slaves has been described by Mr. Norris, one of the Liverpool
delegates, in a manner which, I am sure, will convince the
House that interest can draw a film over the eyes so thick
that blindness itself could do no more. . . . " Their apartments ", says Mr Norris, " are fitted up as much for their

advantage as circumstances will admit. The right ankle of
one, indeed, is connected with the left ankle of another
by a small iron fetter, and, if they are turbulent, by another
on their wrists They have several meals a day—some of
their own country provisions with the best sauces of African
cookery—and, by way of variety, another meal of pulse etc.
according to European taste After breakfast they have
water to wash themselves, while their apartments are
perfumed with frankincense and lime-juice Before dinner
they are amused in the manner of their country The song
and the dance are promoted "—and, as if the whole were
really a scene of pleasure and dissipation, it is added that
games of chance are furnished   " The men play and sing,
while the women and girls make fanciful ornaments with
beads with which they are plentifully supplied."

' Such is the sort of strain in which the Liverpool delegates,
and particularly Mr Norris, gave evidence before the Privy
Council. What will the House think when by the concurring
testimony of other witnesses the true history is laid open.
The slaves, who are sometimes described as rejoicing in
their captivity, are so wrung with misery at leaving their
country that it is the constant practice to set sail at night,
lest they should be sensible of their departure. The pulse,
which Mr. Norris talks of, is horse-beans , and the scantiness
both of water and provisions was suggested by the very
Legislature of Jamaica in the report of their committee
to be a subject that called for the interference of Parliament.
Mr. Norris talks of frankincense and lime-juice, when the
surgeons tell you the slaves are stowed so close that there is
not room to tread among them and when you have it in
evidence from Sir George Yonge that even in a ship which
wanted 200 of her complement the stench was intolerable.
The song and the dance, says Mr Norris, are promoted.
It would have been more fair, perhaps, if he had explained
that word " promoted ". The truth is that, for the sake of
exercise, these miserable creatures, loaded with chains,
oppressed with disease and wretchedness, are forced to
dance by the terror of the lash and sometimes by the actual
use of it. " I was employed ", says one of the other evidences,
" to dance the men, while another person danced the women."
Such, then, is the meaning of the word " promoted " ! And
it may be observed, too, with respect to food, that an instrument is sometimes carried aboard in order to force the
slaves to eat—which is the same sort of proof of how much
they enjoy themselves in that instance also. As to their
singing, what shall we say when we are told that their songs

are songs of lamentation on their departure and that, while they sing them, they are always in tears, insomuch that one captain—more humane, as I should conceive him than the rest—threatened one of the women with a flogging because the mournfulness of her song was too painful for his feelings !

' In order, however, not to trust too much to any sort of description, I will call the attention of the House to one species of evidence which is absolutely infallible. Death, at least, is a sure ground of proof · and the proportion of deaths will not only confirm—it will, if possible, even aggravate—our suspicions of their misery in the transit. It will be found, on an average of all the ships of which evidence has been given at the Privy Council, that, exclusive of those who perish before they sail, not less than $12\frac{1}{2}$ per cent. perish in the passage. Besides these, the Jamaica report tells you, not less than $4\frac{1}{2}$ per cent. die on shore before the day of sale which is only a week or two from the time of landing. One-third more die in the " seasoning ", and this in a country exactly like their own—where they are healthy and happy as some of the evidence would pretend ! The diseases which they contract on board, the astringent washes which are used to hide their wounds, and the mischievous tricks employed to make them up for sale, are one principal cause of this mortality Upon the whole there is a mortality of about 50 per cent., and this among negroes who are not bought unless quite healthy at first, unless—as the phrase is with cattle—they are " sound in wind and limb " How, then, can the House refuse its belief to the multiplied testimonies before the Privy Council of the savage treatment of the negroes in the Middle Passage ? Nay, indeed, what need is there of any testimony ? The number of deaths speaks for itself and makes all such inquiry superfluous.

' As soon as I had arrived thus far in my investigation of the Slave Trade, I confess to you, Sir, so enormous, so dreadful, so irremediable did its wickedness appear that my own mind was completely made up for the abolition. A trade founded in iniquity and carried on as this was must be abolished, let the policy be what it might. Let the consequences be what they would, I from this time determined that I would never rest until I had effected its abolition. Such enormities as these having once come within my knowledge, I should not have been faithful to the sight of my eyes, to the use of my senses and my reason, if I had shrunk from attempting the abolition. It is true, indeed, my mind was harassed beyond measure. For when West

India planters and merchants retorted it on me that it was
the British Parliament had authorized this trade—when
they said to me, " It is your Acts of Parliament, it is your
encouragement, it is faith in your laws, in your protection,
that has tempted us into this trade and has now made it
necessary to us "—it was difficult to find an answer. If the
ruin of the West Indies threatened us on the one hand,
while this load of wickedness pressed upon us on the other,
then indeed the choice of alternatives was awful ! But it
naturally suggested itself to me how strange it was that
Providence, however mysterious in its ways, should so have
constituted the world as to make one part of it depend for
its existence on the depopulation and devastation of another.
I could not help, therefore, distrusting the arguments of
those who insisted that the plundering of Africa was
necessary for the cultivation of the West Indies. I could
not believe that the same Being, who forbids rapine and
bloodshed, had made rapine and bloodshed necessary to the
well-being of any part of His universe. I felt a confidence in
this principle. I took the resolution to act upon it. And
soon the light broke in upon me. The suspicion of my mind
was every day confirmed by increasing information. The
truth became clear. The evidence I have to offer on this
point is now decisive and complete. And I wish to observe—
with submission, but with perfect conviction of heart—what
an instance is this of how safely we may trust the rules of
justice, the dictates of conscience, and the laws of God in
opposition to the seeming impolicy of these eternal principles.
 ' I hope now to prove by authentic evidence that in truth
the West Indies have nothing to fear from the total and
immediate abolition of the Slave Trade. . . . What are the
causes of the slave-mortality in the West Indies ? In the
first place the disproportion of the sexes—an evil which, when
the Slave Trade is abolished, must in the course of nature
cure itself. In the second place, the disorders contracted
in the Middle Passage. . . . A third cause of deaths in the
West Indies is excessive labour joined with improper food.
I mean not to blame the West Indians ; for this evil springs
from the very nature of things. In this country the work
is fairly paid for and distributed among our labourers
according to the reasonableness of things. If a trader or
manufacturer finds his profits decrease, he retrenches his
own expenses, he lessens the number of his hands, and every
branch of trade finds its proper level. In the West Indies
the whole number of slaves remains with the same master.
Is the master pinched in his profits ? The slave allowance

is pinched in consequence. For, as charity begins at home, the usual gratifications of the master will never be given up so long as there is the possibility of making the requisite retrenchment from the allowance of the slaves There is therefore a constant tendency to the very minimum with regard to slaves' allowances : and if in any one hard year the slaves get through upon a reduced allowance, from the very nature of man it must happen that this becomes a precedent on other occasions. Nor is the gradual destruction of the slave a consideration sufficient to counteract the immediate profit that is got by hard usage. . . . Another cause of the mortality of slaves is the dreadful dissoluteness of their manners. Here it might be said that self-interest must induce the planters to wish for some order and decency around their families : but in this case also it is slavery itself that is the mischief. Slaves, considered as cattle, left without instruction, without any institution of marriage, so depressed as to have no means almost of civilization, will undoubtedly be dissolute . and until attempts are made to raise them a little above their present situation, this source of mortality will remain . . .

' It is now to be remarked that all these causes of mortality among the slaves do undoubtedly admit of a remedy. And that remedy is the abolition of the Slave Trade. When the manager shall know that a fresh importation of slaves is not to be had from Africa and that he cannot retrieve the deaths he occasions by any new purchases, humanity must be introduced An improvement in the system of treating the slaves will thus infallibly be effected An assiduous care of their health and of their morals, marriage institutions, and many other things as yet little thought of, will take place, because they will be absolutely necessary. Births will then increase naturally. And instead of fresh accessions of the same uncivilized negroes from Africa, each generation will improve upon the former, and thus will the West Indies themselves eventually profit by the abolition of the Slave Trade. . . .

' I have in my hand an extract from a pamphlet which states, in very dreadful colours, that thousands and tens of thousands will be ruined—how our wealth will be impaired and one-third of our commerce cut off for ever—how our manufactures will droop in consequence, how our land-tax will be raised, our marine destroyed, while France, our natural enemy and rival, will strengthen herself by our weakness. (Cries of assent from several parts of the House)

I beg, Sir, that gentlemen will not mistake me. The pamphlet
from which this prophecy is taken was written by Mr. Glover
in 1774 on a very different occasion : and I would ask
gentlemen whether it has been fulfilled. Is our wealth
decayed ? Our commerce cut off ? Our manufactures and
our marine destroyed ? Is France raised up upon our
ruins ? On the contrary, do we not see from the instance
of this pamphlet how men in a desponding moment will
picture to themselves the gloomiest consequences from causes
by no means to be apprehended ? We are all apt sometimes
to be carried away by a frightened imagination. Like the
poor negroes, we are all in our turn subject to Obiha. And
when we have an interest to bias us, we are carried away
ten thousand times more. The African merchants told us last
year that, if less than two men to a ton were to be allowed,
the Trade could not continue. Mr. Tarleton, instructed by
the whole trade of Liverpool, told us that commerce would
be ruined and that our manufactures would migrate to
France. We have petitions on the table from our manufacturers, but I believe they are not dated at Havre or any
port in France. And yet it is certain that out of twenty
ships last year from Liverpool, not less than thirteen carried
this very ruinous proportion of less than two to a ton. It
is said that Liverpool will be undone. The Trade, says
Mr. Dalziel, now hangs upon a thread, and the smallest
matter will overthrow it. I believe indeed that the Trade
hangs upon a thread : for it is a losing trade for Liverpool.
It is a lottery, in which some men have made large fortunes,
chiefly by being their own insurers, while others follow the
example of a few lucky adventurers and lose money by it.
It is absurd to say, then, that Liverpool will be ruined by
the abolition. Liverpool will not even feel it very sensibly,
since the whole outward-bound tonnage of the Slave Trade
amounts only to one-fifteenth of the outward-bound tonnage
of its port.

‘ The next subject I shall touch upon is the influence of the
Slave Trade on our marine. Instead of its being a benefit
to our sailors, as some have ignorantly argued, I assert it
is their grave. The evidence upon the point is clear : for,
by the indefatigable industry and public spirit of Mr. Clarkson, the muster-rolls of all the slave ships have been collected
and compared with those of other trades ; and it appears
in the result that more sailors die in one year in the Slave
Trade than die in two years in all our other trades put
together. It appears by the muster-roll to 88 slave ships
which sailed from Liverpool in 1787 that the original crews

consisted of 3,170 sailors. Of these only 1,428 returned.
642 died or were lost , and 1,100 were discharged on the
voyage or deserted either in Africa or the West Indies

' There is one other argument—in my opinion a very weak
and absurd one—which many persons have dwelt upon ·
I mean, that, if we relinquish Slave Trade, France will take
it up   If the Slave Trade be such as I have described it,
if it be in truth both wicked and impolitic, we cannot wish
a greater mischief to France than that she should adopt
it.   For the sake of France, however, and for the sake of
humanity, I trust—nay, I am sure—she will not.   France
is too enlightened a nation to begin pushing a scandalous
as well as a ruinous traffic at the very time when England
sees her folly and resolves to give it up   And, in any case,
it is clearly no argument whatever against the wickedness
of the Trade that France will adopt it   Those who argue
thus may argue equally that we may rob, murder, and commit any crime which any one else would have committed
if we did not.   But the truth is that by our example we shall
produce the contrary effect   . . Let us therefore lead the
way   Let this enlightened country take precedence in this
noble cause and we shall soon find that France is not backward to follow, nay, perhaps to accompany, our steps. . .

' I believe, Sir, I have now touched on all the objections
of any consequence which are made to the abolition of the
Slave Trade.   When we consider the vastness of the continent
of Africa—when we reflect how all other countries have for
some centuries past been advancing in happiness and
civilization—when we think how in this same period all
improvement in Africa has been defeated by her intercourse
with Britain—when we remember that it is we ourselves
that have degraded them to that wretched brutishness and
barbarity which we now plead as the justification of our
guilt ; how the Slave Trade has enslaved their minds,
blackened their character, and sunk them so low in the scale
of animal beings that some think the very apes are of
a higher class and fancy the orang-outang has given them
the go-by—what mortification must we feel at having so
long neglected to think of our guilt or to attempt any
reparation ! It seems, indeed, as if we had determined to
forbear from all interference until the measure of our folly
and wickedness was so full and complete, until the impolicy
which eventually belongs to vice had become so plain and
glaring, that not an individual in the country should refuse

to join in the abolition—it seems as if we had waited until the persons most interested should be tired out with the folly and nefariousness of the Trade and should unite in petitioning against it

'Let us then make such amends as we can for the mischiefs we have done to that unhappy continent Let us recollect what Europe itself was no longer ago than three or four centuries. What if I should be able to show this House that in a civilized part of Europe, in the time of our Henry II, there were people who actually sold their own children ? What if I should tell them that England itself was that country ? What if I should point out to them that the very place, where this inhuman traffic was carried on, was the city of Bristol ? Ireland at that time used to drive a considerable trade in slaves with these neighbouring barbarians : but, a great plague having infested the country, the Irish were struck with panic, suspected (I am sure very properly) that the plague was a punishment sent from Heaven for the sin of the slave trade, and therefore abolished it All I ask, therefore, of the people of Bristol is that they would become as civilized now as Irishmen were four hundred years ago. Let us put an end at once to this infamous traffic ! Let us stop this effusion of human blood ! The true way to virtue is by withdrawing from temptation Let us then withdraw from these wretched Africans those temptations to fraud, violence, cruelty, and injustice, which the Slave Trade furnishes ! Wherever the sun shines, let us go round the world with him, diffusing our beneficence. But let us not traffic only that we may set kings against their subjects and subjects against their kings, sowing discord in every village, fear and terror in every family, setting millions of our fellow-creatures a-hunting each other for slaves, creating fairs and markets for human flesh, through one whole continent of the world, and under the name of policy concealing from ourselves all the baseness and iniquity of such a traffic. . . .

'I have one more word to add, upon a most material point ; but it is a point so self-evident that I shall be extremely short It will appear from everything I have said that it is not regulation, it is not mere palliatives, that can cure this enormous evil Total abolition is the only possible cure for it The Jamaica Report admits, indeed, much of the evil, but recommends it to us so to regulate the Trade that no persons should be kidnapped or made slaves contrary to the custom of Africa But may they not be made slaves unjustly, and yet by no means " contrary

to the custom of Africa " ? I have shown they may . for
all the customs of Africa are rendered savage and unjust
through the influence of the Trade. Besides, how can we
discriminate between the slaves justly and unjustly made ?
Can we know them apart by physiognomy ? And, if we
could discriminate, does any man believe that the British
captains can be prevailed on by any regulation in this
country to refuse all such slaves as have not been fairly,
honestly, and uprightly enslaved ? .   . Again, as to the
Middle Passage, the evil is radical there also. The merchant's
profit depends upon the number that can be crowded together
and upon the shortness of their allowance. Astringents,
escatories, and all the other arts of making them up for sale,
are of the very essence of the Trade. These arts will be
concealed both from the purchaser and the legislature. They
are necessary to the trader's profit and they will be practised
Chains, again, and arbitrary treatment must be used in
transporting the slaves   Our seamen must be taught to
play the tyrant, and that depravation of morals among them,
which some judicious persons have thought the very worst
part of this business, cannot be hindered while the Trade
itself continues. As to the slave merchants, they have
already told you that, if two slaves to a ton are not permitted,
the Trade cannot continue , so that the arguments for regulation are done away by themselves on this quarter. And as
to the West Indies, I have shown that the abolition is the
only possible stimulus whereby a regard for population and
consequently for the happiness of the negroes can be effectually excited in those islands.
    ' I trust, then, I have proved that, upon every ground,
the total abolition ought to take place. I have urged many
things which are not my own leading motives for proposing
it, since I have wished to show every description of gentlemen and particularly the West India planters, who deserve
every attention, that the abolition is politic upon their own
principles. Policy, however, Sir, is not my principle, and
I am not ashamed to say it. There is a principle above
everything that is politic   and when I reflect on the command which says, " Thou shalt do no murder ", believing
its authority to be divine, how can I dare to set up any
reasonings of my own against it ? And, Sir, when we think
of Eternity and of the future consequences of all human
conduct, what is there in this life that should make any man
contradict the dictates of his conscience, the principles of
justice, and the laws of God ?
    ' Sir, the nature and all the circumstances of this Trade

are now laid open to us. We can no longer plead ignorance.
We cannot evade it   We may spurn it   We may kick it
out of the way   But we cannot turn aside so as to avoid
seeing it. For it is brought now so directly before our eyes
that this House must decide, and must justify to all the world
and to its own conscience, the rectitude of the grounds
of its decision. A society has been established for the
abolition of this Trade, in which Dissenters, Quakers,
Churchmen—in which the most conscientious men of all
persuasions—have united and made common cause. Let
not Parliament be the only body that is insensible to the
principles of national justice   Let us make reparation to
Africa, so far as we can, by establishing a trade upon true
commercial principles, and we shall soon find the rectitude of
our conduct rewarded by the benefits of a regular and
growing commerce.'

Wilberforce then moved twelve resolutions, summarizing
the main facts he had expounded in his speech as to the operation of the Slave Trade on the African coast and the effects
of its methods on the civilization of the natives, as to the
hardships of the Middle Passage and the loss of life entailed
among both slaves and seamen, and as to the lack of natural
increase among the slaves in the West Indies and the causes
of it ; and declaring that the interests of the planters would
suffer no considerable or permanent damage from the discontinuance of the Trade and that for the merchants engaged
in it a substitute might be found in the export of those
special products of the African soil which were required for
the manufactures of this country *

* From the report in *Hansard*, xxviii (1789–91), 41–67   Short-
hand reporting not yet having come into vogue, it must be, at the
best, a very imperfect reproduction of the actual speech , and for
present purposes it has seemed justifiable to make some alterations
in punctuation and a few slight verbal changes for the sake of
clearness

VI

So forcible, yet so moderate, an appeal, the fruit of so many months' unresting labour, deserved a better fate. But almost from the moment of its delivery the long, intolerable sequence of Wilberforce's disappointments began. It made no difference that the few great men in the House of Commons of that day were on his side Burke devoted not only his incomparable eloquence but all his powers of lucid reasoning to show that the threatened loss of commerce would not be great enough to justify, on the plea of necessity, the terrible inhumanity of the Trade : and if some loss there must be, ' were they not prepared ', he asked, ' to pay the price of virtue ? ' Pitt followed Burke with the frank avowal which everybody had expected since his outburst on Dolben's Bill. Though he was willing, he said, to listen to arguments for the continuance of the Trade, he did not believe that any of them could be reconciled with the principles of justice and humanity. One particular plea —that Abolition would simply lead to the smuggling of slaves into the British West Indies by traders of other nations—he dealt with in advance ' Should that be the case ', he said, and it was the Prime Minister speaking, ' our language must be that Great Britain has resources to enable her to protect her islands and to prevent others carrying on a traffic which she has thought it for her own honour and character to abandon.' And Fox followed Pitt, applauding Wilberforce's clear demand for Abolition, applauding, too, Pitt's firm attitude on the question of smuggling by foreign slavers, but avowing the hope that other countries might follow our example and the belief that France, at any rate, might be expected ' to catch a spark from the light of our fire and to run a race with us in promoting the ends of humanity '. But it made no difference that Fox and Pitt and Burke were all with Wilberforce, nor that the case against him was feebly put by lesser men—by Alderman Newnham, who predicted in

K 2

all seriousness that Abolition ' would render the City of
London one scene of bankruptcy and ruin '—by Mr. Demp-
ster, who asked whether Wilberforce or Pitt or Fox possessed
plantations of their own, and declared that, though sugar
could indeed be cultivated more profitably by free labour
than by slaves, Parliament had no pretence of right ' to
prescribe to the gentlemen of the West Indies by what hands
their plantations should be cultivated '—by Mr Drake,
who insisted that Abolition would be in the highest degree
unjust unless everybody who might lose by it were fully
compensated from the public purse—by Mr. Henniker,
who read a very long letter, which purported to have been
sent by the King of Dahomey to George I, in order to prove
that the cruelties practised in Africa could not be ascribed
to the operation of the Slave Trade—by Mr Molyneux,
who asked whether they meant ' to swallow all the property
of the planters in order to gratify a humane disposition
towards the Africans ' and produced what he described as
a proof that slaves were not cruelly treated, to wit, a letter
from his agent in the West Indies, complaining that a
certain Rev. Mr. Frazer, who was paid £50 a year by
Mr. Molyneux for looking after his slaves, had neglected to
give proper attention to ' a negro that was ill in the hot-
house with a sore throat '—by Viscount Maitland who,
cleverer than the rest, appealed to the jealousy of the
Commons on a point of privilege and urged that they would
be surrendering their historic rights if they accepted the
evidence given before the Privy Council and did not insist
on its being given all over again at their own bar.

All these arguments, good and bad, except the last,
mattered little   What mattered was the disinclination of
the average silent member of the House to screw himself
up to a definite decision on such a controversial subject.
The brief report in Hansard of one speech from a back
bench may be taken to illustrate the mood of the great
majority.

' Sir Guy Cooper confessed himself a friend to the inquiry.
He thought, however, that the representatives of a generous
and brave people might be carried by too rapid steps to the

adoption of a measure which introduced such novelty in the commercial concerns of the West Indies. Men distinguished for philanthropy might be hurried to the adoption of a measure which tended to the injury of our West India islands. He confessed he entertained much doubt and perplexity on the subject.'

A jejune, perfunctory report of what was probably a poor enough speech : but it may serve as a not unfair reflection of the frame of mind that defeated Wilberforce. They were not insensible nor inhumane, these country gentlemen They were not unmoved by Wilberforce's unimpeachable sincerity Indeed, he had sharply pricked their consciences. But between conscience and the interests of the State and of the planters and of the innumerable individuals whose livelihood, one way or another, depended on the Trade, they were most uncomfortably perplexed. And, for once, the traditional way of escape from such a dilemma was barred. Compromise, for once, was impossible . for had not the Trade declared that further regulation would be as fatal as Abolition itself ? Puzzled and uneasy, therefore, they leaped at the chance, obligingly suggested by Lord Maitland, of at least postponing a decision. Yes ; let the evidence be recited all over again. Then, surely, they would be able to make up their minds

It was useless for Pitt and Fox to expose the flimsy pretext of privilege. The great majority on both sides, if they could decide nothing else, had decided to procrastinate. So it was agreed, without a division, to go into committee on nine specified days. And when those days had passed with the long task of hearing evidence still far from finished the end of the session was close at hand, and further discussion of the subject was squeezed out by other business. This did not mean, of course, that the twice-told evidence had convinced the House that the Trade was right and Wilberforce wrong It meant nothing so definite as that. And indeed, when Wilberforce displayed anxiety at the possibility of the whole question being shelved, a motion was promptly brought forward ' that this House will, early in the next session of Parliament, proceed to consider

further of the circumstances of the Slave Trade '. Alderman
Newnham himself proposed it, and the House carried it
nem con. And there was time for one more good deed.
A Bill for amending and continuing Sir William Dolben's
temporary Act of the previous year was quickly and
smoothly passed before the session closed Then members,
their duty done, carried off their consciences for a holiday.

Time was to prove abundantly that Wilberforce possessed
a wonderful patience. Throughout these disappointing
debates he maintained the same temperate, conciliatory
attitude he had shown in his opening speech. Bitter things
were said by some. One champion of the Trade, in particular, was so violent in his personal abuse of Wilberforce
that the Prime Minister himself rebuked him But however
violent the invective, its object remained unruffled. And
when the session from which he had hoped so much ended
with so little done, Wilberforce quietly resumed his labours.
At any rate he had learned something from those otherwise
futile debates The opposition had declared its hand.
There were new arguments to be met, new evidence to be
sought for, weak points in the Abolitionist case to be
strengthened Above all, some further attempt might be
made to win the co-operation of France, and thus to nullify
the most weighty, genuine, and respectable argument
against Abolition To its weight even young Charles Grey,
the most promising of the Whig cadets and more liberal-
minded than most of the older members of the party, had
yielded. ' If France alone ', he had written in answer to
a letter from Wilberforce appealing for his support, ' would
consent to abolish this detestable and inhuman traffic, the
proposed plan would not have a more zealous supporter
than myself ' But, without that condition, he confessed
that he would probably cast a silent vote against his feelings
and for the Trade. Wilberforce, accordingly, again proposed
that he should go himself to Paris, and this time no official
objection was raised For the moment relations with
France were friendlier , and M. Necker, who was now Chief
Minister, was known to favour Abolition. Unofficial
conversations might, therefore, be more effective than

formal diplomacy. But befoie Wilberforce was ready to start there was a sudden change in the whole political situation. The first rumbles of the great earthquake became audible across the Channel. ' The news came of Necker's being out ', he records in his diary for July 14, ' and of insurrections, firing, &c.' For one so eminent in British political circles as himself to visit Paris just at this crisis seemed obviously unwise . and it was decided that Clarkson should go in his place. So, on August 7, Clarkson set out, accompanied by a French secretary and interpreter, and furnished by Wilberforce with written instructions and a consideiable sum of money from his private purse. Of the results of this mission, more anon.

Meanwhile there had occurred in England an event which must have strained even Wilberforce's patience. The vicar of Teston, whose knowledge and zeal had been such important factors in determining Wilberforce to take up the cause, and who had worked so unsparingly and in such close intimacy with him ever since, had been singled out by the more violent of the West Indian planters as the special victim of the bitter and revengeful feelings which the attack on them and on their fortunes had excited. Hard things had been said about their indifference to the horrors of the Trade and their treatment of the slaves on their plantations —not without occasional distortion and exaggeration of the facts. And they meant to repay the debt with interest. If Wilberforce himself was beyond their reach, too popular and influential, too famous, and too notoriously good, at any rate the obscure Kentish clergyman could be assailed with impunity. So the sewers were opened, and a stream of calumny poured out on Ramsay. His life in the West Indies, it would seem, had been one black story of depravity. By such a merciless assault the sturdiest spirit might well have been shaken, and Ramsay, a sensitive man, never robust, and now suffering from his excessive labours, bent to the storm His character, indeed, could easily be cleaied. James Stephen, on his return to the West Indies, carefully inquired into the accusations and reported the results to Wilberforce ' I have not heard ', he wrote, ' a crime or

a blemish imputed to Mr. Ramsay which has not been
refuted afterwards in my presence by some of his most
inveterate enemies, better acquainted with the facts.' But
the damage could not be undone. Ramsay's health was
completely broken, and Wilberforce's diary for July 21 thus
records the end. ' Heard that poor Ramsay died yesterday at ten o'clock   A smile on his face now '   Not such
the victor's comment.   ' Mr Molyneux ', wrote Stephen,
' announced the decease of the public enemy to his natural
son in this island in these terms " Ramsay is dead—I have
killed him ".' *

VII

When Parliament reassembled in the New Year, Wilberforce made an attempt to speed up the procedure of taking
evidence. On January 27 he proposed that the witnesses
should henceforth be heard before a Select Committee
instead of before a Committee of the whole House as in the
preceding session   The spokesmen of the Trade opposed it,
for the wiser heads in their party had realized that the case
against them was too strong to be met by simple contradiction and that their best policy at the moment was delay—
delay on the plea of fair-play, delay in the interests of
national security, delay on any grounds and at any price
And delay, as has been seen, was by no means unpalatable
to the average member of Parliament   But to insist on
devoting the meagre space of time of the whole House to
witnesses whose statements would have just as much or as
little weight in committee ' above stairs ' was palpably to
shelve the business almost indefinitely and was dangerously
suggestive of a definite decision in favour of the Trade
So on this occasion, at any rate, Wilberforce and Pitt and
Fox and Burke had their way. A Select Committee was
appointed, and during the next three months steady progress
was made.

The evidence in defence of the Trade was taken first

* *Life*, 1, chap \11   *Hansard*, xxviii (1789–91), 68–101. Clarkson,
11 40–118.

it was completed during April, and then came an unexpected interruption. The Trade party had decided on a daring change of tactics. Having only heard one side of the case, the House was presumably at that moment in a more favourable mood towards the Trade than it was ever likely to be again. Might it not be worth while, then, to drop the policy of procrastination and press for an immediate decision? A vote snatched now for the maintenance of the Trade as it stood might smash the Abolitionist movement for years to come! The news of this audacious plan took the Abolitionists by surprise and filled them with alarm. As soon as it reached Wilberforce's ears he hastened straightway to Downing Street. 'Saw Pitt in bed,' he notes on April 20, ' and talked with him on the enemy's impudent attempt to resist our calling evidence ' Pitt suggested that he should go at once to Fox, since the proposal for the vote was to come from Lord Penrhyn and his friends on the Whig side of the House So Wilberforce hurried off to the Leader of the Opposition, who, no less determined than the Prime Minister to keep the Slave Trade question above the party conflict, undertook to make inquiries and to do what he could to prevent the threatened move. He was apparently successful; for he told Pitt, two days later, that the forthcoming motion—so he was informed—was not intended to force a decision at once but merely to fix a day, in about three weeks' time, for closing the evidence, on the supposition that by then all the witnesses against the Trade would have been heard.

But Fox had been deceived When the House got to business next day, Alderman Newnham at once rose to protest against the calling of any further evidence The House, he argued, must already be convinced that Abolition was quite impracticable. Further evidence, therefore, was unnecessary and would merely cause delay from which—he coolly confessed—the question had already suffered too much Let the House give forthwith a manly and decisive vote and so put an end to these protracted and dangerous discussions This plea was underlined by Lord Penrhyn with a frank appeal to fear ; he begged for an immediate

decision on the ground that the vast negro majority in the
West Indies might be so excited by the continuance of these
debates as to rise and massacre the whites. This was not
the first time that this argument had been used nor was
it by any means the last At every stage of its slow progress the cause of the negroes was to be damaged and
obstructed by the cry that Englishmen and Englishwomen were in danger. And at times, as will be seen,
they were in danger.

With the whitewashing evidence fresh in their minds,
members were doubtless more susceptible to such arguments
than they had been in the previous year But, their in-
grained sense of fair play combining with their inveterate
irresolution, they declined to be hustled into conceding to
Lord Penrhyn the swift decision they had refused to Wilberforce So the indecent manœuvre failed The House
decided, without a division, that the evidence should be
continued ' Our opponents, blessed be God, fairly beat,'
says the diary

All through May and on into June the Committee was
meeting almost daily, and Wilberforce was invariably
present, watching and assisting his witnesses ' I am almost
worn out,' he writes, ' and I pant for a little country air
and quiet.' But even the close of the session on June 10
did not bring him rest A General Election was imminent,
and the member for Yorkshire hurried off on the 9th to
conduct a three-weeks' canvass. In the last few years he
had become almost a stranger to his constituents He had
no country house on his scattered Yorkshire property and
he rarely visited the county In the biographical notes he
left behind him, he confesses and excuses his neglect
' I must mention ', he says, ' the uncommon kindness and
liberality which I experienced from my constituents In
former times the county members displayed their equipages
annually at the races and constituted a part of the grand
jury at the summer assizes ; the latter, indeed, I should
have been glad to attend but for the unseemly festivities
which annually take place at that period. I was not,
however, wanted , the number of gentlemen of larger

fortune in the county were far more than sufficient to
constitute a most respectable grand jury, both at the spring
and summer assizes. I could not consistently with my
principles frequent the theatre and the ball-room, and I
knew I should give offence by staying away, were I actually
at York, but no discontent was ever expressed at my not
presenting myself to the county on those occasions. My
friends appeared tacitly to admit my claim to the command
of my own time during the recess.' And Wilberforce was
no more subservient to his constituents' political opinions
than to their social conventions ; more than once, he was
to set himself against the popular tide It is to the credit
of the Yorkshire electors that, under these circumstances,
his seat was always safe

The election over—a dull election, increasing, as every
one expected, Pitt's hold on the House of Commons—
Wilberforce was able to spend the rest of the summer in
the country, taking the waters at Buxton and touring in
Wales with Mr. Babington, a zealous Abolitionist and now
one of his closest friends. In October they both settled
down at Yoxall in Staffordshire, where, on the fringe of
Needwood Forest, the Rev. Thomas Gisborne had his home—
Gisborne the 'mere sap', the receptacle of Wilberforce's
midnight eloquence at Cambridge, but now and for the
rest of his life a far more intimate friend of his than he
ever could have been in those old gay days at St. John's.
For a whole month the two labourers stayed at Gisborne's,
wrestling with the Privy Council Report and with the
evidence—nearly 1,400 folio pages of it—given before the
House of Commons. ' Mr Wilberforce and Mr Babington ',
writes a visitor in the house, ' have never appeared downstairs since we came, except to take a hasty dinner and for
half an hour after we have supped, the Slave Trade now
occupies them nine hours daily. . . They talk of sitting up
one night in each week. . . . The two friends begin to look
very ill, but they are in excellent spirits, and at this moment
I hear them laughing at some absurd questions in the
examination.' That one of them, at any rate, was once more
taxing his strength to the limit is clear enough from the

diary, Oct. 8. ' Unwell Hard work—slave evidence.'
Oct 9 : ' Eyes bad. Hard at work.' Oct. 11 ' Slave
evidence, and very hard at it with Babington all this
week. wherein by God's blessing enabled to preserve a
better sense of heavenly things than for some time before '
Nov. 1 : ' Continued to work very hard at the evidence all
this week. Slept ill, not being well, partly through working
too much.'

On November 19 he is back in London, ' plunging at once
into a dinner-circle of Cabinet Ministers ' , and the diary
resumes its old complaint of wasted hours Many men
might have envied Wilberforce an evening spent with Pitt,
Chatham, Grenville, Dundas, and Ryder, discussing Burke's
newly published onslaught on the French Revolution—
Pitt, Chatham, and himself on one side, Grenville and Ryder
on the other, Dundas apparently on neither—but his characteristic comment is merely, ' kept up late, and unfit for
prayer '. ' Oh ! how I regret Yoxall Lodge,' he cries a little
later And, when the new session began and the hearing of
evidence in committee was resumed, not without renewed
opposition, the hours available for work were still further
curtailed Yet work was more imperative than ever ,
for the evidence was drawing to an end, and then, surely,
Parliament must give its verdict. At last, in the early
spring of 1791, Wilberforce was forced to retreat from
Palace Yard to Clapham where he prepared, as at Teston
two years before, for the imminent debate. The prospects
of success were certainly no more favourable than in 1789.
Abolitionist enthusiasm in the country had begun to lose
its edge as the novelty of the crusade wore off. Pitt was
still warm in his support, like Fox and Burke, and his
dominion over the House of Commons was now stronger
than it had ever been , but he was still unable to commit
the Government to Abolition, still unable, therefore, to
compel his followers to vote with him In the House of
Lords there was one change for the better. Sydney had
resigned because he felt that, differing, as he did, from the
Prime Minister on the Slave Trade, he could not remain
in charge of the department in which colonial matters were

then dealt with. And Pitt had made the most of this opportunity. He had appointed Grenville, a staunch Abolitionist, Home Secretary in Sydney's place and had raised him moreover to the peerage in order that he might act, on the Slave Trade question amongst others, as a check to Thurlow in the Upper House But what was one friend among so many enemies ? And if Wilberforce was hopeful, it was not to human allies that he looked. He had received, late in February, a letter from the aged Wesley—written a week before his death, perhaps the last he ever wrote— which echoed his own inmost convictions ' Unless the Divine power has raised you up ', it ran, ' to be as *Athanasius contra mundum*, I see not how you can go through your glorious enterprise. . . Unless God has raised you up for this very thing, you will be worn out by the opposition of men and devils , but if God be for you, who can be against you ? . . Go on, in the name of God and in the power of His might, till even American slavery, the vilest that ever saw the sun, shall vanish away before it.' In the same spirit in which the old crusader put off his armour, the young crusader girded his on ' May I look to Him ', he writes in his spiritual journal a few days before the debate, ' for wisdom and strength and the power of persuasion . . . and ascribe to Him all the praise if I succeed, and if I fail, say from the heart " Thy will be done ".'

He had need to pray for resignation ; for the debate of 1791 followed much the same course as the debate of 1789 to a worse end. Wilberforce opened it—moving for ' leave to bring in a Bill to prevent the further importation of slaves into the British islands in the West Indies '. His speech was as eloquent as its predecessor, as moderate in tone, as careful not to underestimate the strength of the opposition's case, but now more closely packed with detailed evidence. The fruit of those long laborious hours with Babington, it stands as the clearest, most circumstantial, and yet most succinct account, given then or since, of the case against the Slave Trade. And again the great trio supported Wilberforce. Burke's speech was short and sharp, but both Pitt and Fox made longer and bigger efforts than in 1789.

Others might be squeamish but certainly not Fox ; and whether he won votes by it or lost them, he forced the House to listen to the grim realities which Wilberforce had mostly left to the imagination. He told them of the planter who had ordered his surgeon to cut off a fugitive negro's leg and, on his humane refusal, had broken the leg himself, and of the young female slave, tied naked to a beam by the wrists and burnt about the body as she writhed and swung. Was there not, he asked, in the cruelty of the little despots of the slave-ship and the plantation a streak of insanity as in the cruelty of the great Roman despots, of Caligula and his like ? And he bade each doubtful member of the House to ' make the case his own '. ' What would any of us say, and how would we feel, if conquered and carried away by a tribe so savage as our countrymen on the coast of Africa show themselves to be ? How would we bear the same treatment ourselves which we do not scruple to inflict on the Africans ? ' Pitt's speech, as usual, was the antithesis of Fox's. It was not primarily a question of humane feeling, he insisted at the outset, but a question of moral justice ' It is impossible ', he said, ' for me to support the Slave Trade unless gentlemen will, in the first place, prove to me that there are no laws of morality binding upon nations and that it is not the duty of a country's legislature to restrain its subjects from invading the happiness of other countries and from violating the fundamental principles of justice ' Intent on gaining votes, he devoted most of his speech to removing the objections of those members who desired the Trade to cease but feared that the labour-supply in the West Indies could not be maintained without it. Coolly setting forth the facts and figures, and reviewing separately the different circumstances in each of the islands, he argued that better conditions in the life of the plantations —the new thought and care for the slaves which the planters would be forced to take in their own interests if the Trade were abolished—would lead to a natural increase of the slave population and nullify the need of further importation. And in this connexion he touched on what he called ' a rather delicate point ', the possibility of emancipating the slaves—

not rashly, not at once—it was madness to talk like that—
but when they had been raised from their present degradation and made capable of freedom. But perhaps the most
important feature of the speech was the unequivocal lead
it gave. He said nothing now of his willingness to listen to
the arguments on the other side. He had listened to them—
to all the elaborate defences the West Indian party had put
up in the committee—and they had not shaken his previous
opinions in the least. At the beginning of his speech, he
declared that never, since he entered the House, had there
been a question in which his heart was so deeply interested.
' How can we hesitate a moment ', he asked at the end of it,
' to abolish this commerce in human flesh which has too
long disgraced our country and which our example will
contribute to abolish in every corner of the globe ? ' But,
as in 1789, the great men pleaded in vain This time the
opposition was better managed. The Trade had realized
that something more was needed than bluster and *gaucherie*
from the back benches. Quiet, not unreasonable, effective
speeches were made by Sir William Yonge, Colonel Jackson,
and Lord John Russell. Mr. Molyneux was wisely silent.
One fool, only, was irrepressible—a colonel who had spent
ten months in the West Indies and solemnly contended that
the slaves must be happy because they were fond of ornaments. But folly, no more than wisdom, could now affect
the issue. At last the country gentlemen had made up their
minds. There were some on both sides of the House who
were ready to take the leap of Abolition—all honour to
them. But there were more, on both sides, who had come
to the conclusion that the Trade must go on. Property,
precedent, prescription—these were stronger forces than
Pitt's justice or Fox's humanity ; and the strongest of them
was property. A little speech towards the close of the debate put the whole case with admirable brevity and candour
' The leaders, it is true,' said Mr. Drake, ' are for Abolition.
But the minor orators, the dwarfs, the pygmies, will, I trust,
this day carry the question against them. The property
of the West Indians is at stake ; and though men may be
generous with their own property, they should not be so

with the property of others.' Mr. Drake's trust was justified. After two days' debate, prolonged till half-past three in the morning of April 20, the House of Commons rejected Wilberforce's motion by 163 votes to 88.*

* *Life*, 1 265–308. *Hansard*, xxviii (1789–91), 311–15, 711–14; xxix (1791–2), 250–359. Clarkson, 11. 212–338.

V
CHECK

WITH his defeat in the session of 1791 Wilberforce had lost his last chance of carrying Abolition for a long time to come. Why this was so will be clear if we return to Clarkson and follow him on his visit to Paris in 1789. For it so happened that this zealous Abolitionist was present in person at the beginnings of two interlinked series of events, which in their consummation were to have the effect of stopping dead the progress of his cause for fifteen years

Clarkson, of course, was unaware of this. The fact that the Bastille had fallen only a few weeks before his arrival in Paris was for him the best of good omens, signifying the advent of a new era in which Slavery and the Trade could have no place. While the foundations of the society in which he moved began to quiver and crack around him, he devoted himself to his mission with single-minded and confident industry. He was greatly encouraged at the start by the sympathetic reception accorded him In France as in England, it need scarcely be said, there were sensitive philanthropists as well as cynical business-men and timid politicians. 'Men are born free and with equal rights,' proclaimed the first article of the Declaration of the Rights of Man in 1789 'free and equal they remain.' And there were Frenchmen prepared to apply the doctrines of Rousseau beyond France, to black men no less than white. The Abbé Raynal had denounced Slavery at the same time as Dr. Paley was denouncing the Slave Trade Within a decade of the *Wealth of Nations* had appeared Necker's *De l'Administration des Finances de la France* in which he suggested the possibility of abolishing the Trade within a generation by a general European compact And the foundation of the Abolition Committee in 1787 had at once attracted attention in Paris. Brissot, whom the new dispensation was bringing to the forefront of French politics, had written to congratulate the Committee and to ask that he and his friend Clavière might be regarded as

associates in its work ; and, when passing through England
on his way to visit the United States in 1789, he had attended
a meeting of the Committee in London. Lafayette had also
communicated with the Committee and announced that he
proposed to found a similar society in France. Accordingly,
in 1788, *Les Amis des Noirs* had come into being. It was
a more distinguished body than its prototype of quiet
Quakers and the like. Condorcet was its president, and
Rochefoucauld and Lafayette were enrolled as its first
members.

Clarkson, therefore, was not coming to preach in a wholly
heathen land ; and he was promptly and warmly welcomed
by the *Amis des Noirs* as the representative of the sister
society in England and as a useful ally in France. A joint
deputation was arranged to lay the case for Abolition before
Necker, and Clarkson, at any rate, was pleased with the
result. The Minister was kindness itself. He flattered
Clarkson with the suggestion that better progress would
be made if they discussed the matter privately, without the
distinguished Frenchmen of the deputation, and he begged
him to dine with him from time to time for the purpose. If
it should happen by ill luck that he were called away on
business of state, Madame Necker—she promised it herself—
would take her husband's place and would receive and
converse with Clarkson ' on all occasions in which this great
cause of humanity and religion might be concerned '. And
Madame Necker, if not so useful, was at least as ardent as
the Minister ; like the Marquise de Lafayette, she was one
of the *Amis des Noirs*. The Archbishop of Aix, the Bishop
of Chartres, the Abbé Grégoire were as keenly interested as
the churchmen of England. The Abbé Sieyès presented
Clarkson with a set of his works and expressed his pleasure
at making the acquaintance of ' the friend of man ' Rochefoucauld, ' the most virtuous man in France ', held a meeting
of sympathizers at his house. Mirabeau welcomed Clarkson
with open arms. He had just drafted the outlines of a speech
on the Slave Trade for the Assembly ; the only thing lacking
to complete it was the ' circumstantial knowledge ' which
Clarkson was just the man to supply. Clarkson supplied it,

Every other day for a month he wrote him a letter of sixteen to twenty pages ; and Mirabeau, he tells us, ' usually acknowledged the receipt of each '. But there was one piece of information available in more graphic and compendious form ; for Clarkson had with him some copies of a plan printed for distribution in England, showing a section of a slave-ship's interior with its shelves of human cargo Mirabeau was delighted. He summoned a carpenter, gave him the plan, and told him to make forthwith a wooden model of a slave-ship as an ornament for his dining-room. It was about a yard long, we are told, and it contained the authoritative number of little men and women, painted black, and stowed tightly in their proper places . . . Mirabeau, Rochefoucauld, Lafayette, Condorcet, Brissot, Sieyès, Necker, Madame Necker—these were great French names, and Clarkson proudly capped the list with Louis XVI himself. His Majesty, Necker informed him, was desirous of making himself master of the question and had expressed a wish for two copies of his *Essay on the Impolicy of the Slave Trade* (published in 1788), one in French and the other in English. The volumes were duly presented together with specimens of native African handicrafts. The plan of the slave-ship was not submitted, since Necker ' thought it would affect His Majesty too much, as he was then indisposed ' The outcome was highly gratifying, at any rate to Clarkson. Louis admired the specimens, ' particularly those in gold ', and he devoted himself, it was said, to an ' unwearied ' perusal of the book

Clarkson's temperament was at least as sanguine as Wilberforce's ; and perhaps it is not to be wondered at that so kindly an interest, in quarters so varied and so high, should have excited fond delusions in his mind. Quite early in his mission he wrote that the question of Abolition would be raised in the National Assembly in eight or ten days' time. And once they were at it, these quick Frenchmen would put slow, deliberate England to shame. ' Evidence will not be necessary,' he declared, ' and I should not be surprised if the French were to do themselves the honour of voting away the diabolical traffic in a single night.' Some

weeks later he is less confident as to speed but not as to
the ultimate result. ' I am convinced in my own mind ',
he writes, ' that the Slave Trade will, in a couple of months,
fall in France ' When in the autumn, after nearly six
months stay, he at last left Paris, the sympathy of his French
allies had been as cordial as when he came ; Lafayette had
condoled with him in his disappointment ; Mirabeau had
told him that he had won over at least a quarter of the
members of the Assembly and had given him a letter for
Pitt , Brissot had accompanied him to his carriage—but the
Slave Trade had not fallen. In France, as in England,
though supported by some of the best and ablest men of
the day, the cause had failed, and largely for the same
reasons. Bordeaux and Havre had defended the Trade as
stoutly as Liverpool and Bristol. The planters had fought
as hard in Paris as in London, and their weapons were as
sharp. The press had been virulent. Clavière had been
anonymously threatened with assassination. Clarkson himself had been personally denounced as, among other things,
an English spy. And the average Frenchman had been
confronted with the converse of the argument which had
weighed so much with the average Englishman. If France
relinquished the Trade before England, would not England
sit still and reap the profit ? Nay, how was it that England,
peaceful and prosperous, unshaken by the throes of Revolution, having considered the question coolly and at length,
had not given the lead herself ?

Revolution ! There, though nobody, perhaps, and certainly not the busy English visitor could then have guessed
it, lay the insuperable obstacle to the success of Clarkson's
cause, not only for the moment in France but for years
ahead in England. It was actually while he was in Paris
that Versailles was invaded by the starving mob and the
King and Queen escorted, prisoners of the people, to the
Tuileries. And from that instant the tragedy proceeded to
its climax with the seeming certainty of Fate—first, a year
of illusory calm , then the flight to Varennes and the
conference of the despots of Central Europe at Pilnitz ;
next, the gathering of the *émigrés* and their allies on the

frontier ; and then, in quick succession, the outbreak of
war, the September Massacres, and the execution of the
King

Already in 1791, still more darkly in 1792, the shadow
of this tragedy was falling over England, dimming the light
and distorting the perspective along the whole range of
British politics. No great stir had been created at the first
appearance of Revolutionary France on the European stage.
Observers on this side of the Channel had looked the new
actor up and down and concluded that he was not unlike
themselves—almost an Englishman, a very old-fashioned
Englishman, about a century behind the times. It was
Burke's shrill cry of ' wolf ' that first roused alarm, not very
deep or widespread to begin with, till presently those seemly
garments of the orthodox cut fell off and a new and utterly
un-English figure was disclosed, gaunt, ferocious, in rags
and a red cap, with bared teeth and dripping knife. And
then, indeed, throughout the political classes of England,
excepting only a tiny minority of unrepentant Whigs and
a negligible handful of Republicans, alarm stiffened into
a complex of anger, fear, and hate. Thenceforward it was
impossible for the British people to determine British
questions on their merits. Cases were still elaborately argued
at Westminster Fox answered Pitt. Whig voted against
Tory. But appeals to logic, to justice, to humanity, even
to party principles were now of secondary importance. The
grim figure of the Jacobin brooded over every debate. It
was he, not really Pitt or Fox, that dominated the discussion ,
inspired, chiefly by reaction, the arguments ; decided,
mostly by repulsion, the votes. Inevitably, under these
conditions, that little burst of liberalism, which had broken
out so hopefully since 1783 and might, if peace had lasted,
have gained strength to do the work of the Reform Act
forty years before its time, was promptly and utterly suppressed.

The cause of Abolition was among the first of good causes
to suffer from this process of reaction. It was not only
affected, in general, like all other questions, by the results
of the Revolution in France ; it was affected, also, in parti-

cular, by the results of the Revolution in the West Indies.
And in the approaches to this second tragedy we meet again
the busy, rather self-important, very English Clarkson,
not this time merely a silent spectator as when the doomed
King and Queen drove by, but in close and constant intercourse with one of the principal actors. Dining one day with
Lafayette, he met the six representatives of the mulatto or
' coloured ' population of the French half of St. Domingo,
who had been sent to Paris with a gift of six million *livres*
to the National Assembly, a request to Lafayette to accept
the post of Commander-in-Chief of the People of Colour in
the island, and a mission to obtain from the Assembly a
pledge that, when, as was shortly expected, it framed a new
constitution for the colony in accordance with the new
ideas, the mulatto population should be put on the same
political footing as the Europeans. Clarkson was naturally
interested in these indirect products of the Slave Trade.
As he sat among them at the dinner-table, he noted that their
behaviour was ' modest ' and their appearance ' genteel '—
they had donned the uniform of the French National Guards,
and one of them wore the Cross of St Louis—and that their
complexion, though ' sallow and swarthy ' was ' not darker
than that of some of the natives of the south of France '.
On several subsequent occasions Clarkson met and talked
with these ' Deputies of Colour ' ; and their mutual acquaintance ripened into something like a transient friendship.
When Clarkson left Paris one of them, he says, ' gave me
a trinket, by which I might remember him '. And indeed
there was much common ground between them. The six
men were ardent Abolitionists and Clarkson was in genuine
sympathy with their claim to political equality. But he
was somewhat disturbed at the growing impatience they
displayed as week after week went by and their mission
remained unfulfilled. Soon after their arrival, they had
been called before the National Assembly, in which the
European delegates from St. Domingo had already taken
their seats, and the President had bidden them take courage
since the Assembly ' knew no distinction between Blacks
and Whites, but considered all men as having equal rights '.

But when they had pressed for admission as regular members, they had met with nothing but evasion and delay. The whole colonial interest in Paris was up in arms against them ; and, even in that new sanguine atmosphere, interest was still a match for principle. Six times a day was fixed for the discussion of their claim , six times it was postponed ; and the disappointed deputies grew more and more restive. At last their leader, Ogé, confided to Clarkson that he no longer cared what the Assembly did. ' But let it beware of the consequences,' he added. ' Dispatches shall go directly to St Domingo and we will soon follow them. We can produce as good soldiers on our estates as those in France. Our own arms shall make us independent and respectable.' Clarkson—so he tells us in his book—begged them to be patient, to make allowance for the domestic difficulties of France, to reflect on the miseries which hasty action might bring to their own island. ' At my last conference with them I recommended moderation and forbearance as the best gifts I could leave them.'

But before Clarkson's departure Ogé, heedless of this pacific counsel, had angrily shaken off the dust of Paris and returned to St. Domingo. Some months later, he put his threat into execution ; he armed his slaves and called on his fellow mulattoes to rise and fight for their rights. The rebellion was quickly suppressed. Oge himself escaped to a Spanish port, but was surrendered to the French authorities and broken on the wheel.

The second act of the tragedy was a conflict among the Europeans themselves. Since the first days of the Revolution in the mother-country the partisans of the Assembly and of the King in the island had been on the brink of civil war , and early in 1791, encouraged by some mutinous French regulars, recently sent from France, the soldiers of the garrison of Port au Prince tore off their white cockades, murdered their Royalist colonel, and set the Government at defiance. The situation was clearly very delicate and very dangerous. At the back of the 40,000 divided whites were 40,000 embittered and revengeful mulattoes ; and at the back of the mulattoes were 450,000 negro slaves. And this complex of inflammable human nature was perilously isolated from the civilized world, shut in upon itself by the encircling sea. Yet the left wing of the National Assembly took a recklessly precipitate course. It began at precisely the wrong end. It made no attempt to restore order in the island or to establish a single effective government. Brushing aside the opposition of the colonial party, it straightway applied the principle of equality for which Ogé had pleaded in vain, and applied it in a manner which was bound to be regarded as invidious and provocative. On May 15, on the motion of the Abbé Grégoire, a decree was carried bestowing on mulattoes born of free parents an equal political status with the whites. At once the great majority of the mulattoes, whose mothers had been slaves, were up in arms. Treated like slaves themselves, they summoned the slaves to make common cause with them against the whites. And this time the revolt was far more formidable. The call was answered by 100,000 slaves; within two months, in the early autumn of 1791, 2,000 whites, of both sexes and all ages, had been massacred, more than 1,000 plantations destroyed, and 1,200 planters' families reduced to beggary. Bestial cruelties were perpetrated by the blacks; and the whites, sinking to their level, gave like for like. The beautiful, fertile colony had become—and was long to remain—a little hell on earth.

Thus a second and more direct argument was established against the cause of Abolition. To the White Terror in Paris was added the Black Terror in St. Domingo; the one an awful warning of the perils of idealism in general, the other of its perils as applied particularly to the negroes. And when the contagion of rebellion spread to Martinique and the smaller French islands, and finally to the British island of Dominica—where a small and soon-suppressed slave-rising occurred in 1791—the case, to the cautious conservative temper of the British Parliament, at any rate, seemed proved. The reasoning might be weak. It might, indeed, have been argued that, if the slaves in the West Indies were in a rebellious mood, it was better not to let the Trade bring more of them from Africa. But into the minds of British legislators, stiffened and hardened by the impact of horrible events, logic could now scarcely penetrate.*

II

The petrifying effects of the French Revolution were slower to reach the rank and file of the British people than their so-called representatives at Westminster, and it is a significant commentary on the character of the unreformed Parliament that, at the very time when its attitude to Abolition was at freezing-point, the country at large had never been so hot for it. This recovery of all and more than all the initial enthusiasm for the cause was mainly due to the indefatigable propaganda of Wilberforce and Clarkson and the Committee. The torments of the slave-ships were not only popularized by the Committee's literature and by the publication of the debates in Parliament ; other means of the most diverse kind were employed. The poet Cowper, who had already attacked the Slave Trade, somewhat heavy-handedly, in *The Task*, was inspired to write three shorter pieces on the theme   Of these *The Negro's Complaint* was perhaps the best calculated to appeal to the popular taste   The following are three of its seven stanzas :

> Still in thought as free as ever
>   What are England's rights, I ask,
> Me from my delights to sever,
>   Me to torture, me to task ?
> Fleecy locks and black complexion
>   Cannot forfeit Nature's claim ;
> Skins may differ, but affection
>   Dwells in black and white the same.
> Why did all-creating Nature
>   Make the plant, for which we toil ?
> Sighs must fan it, tears must water,
>   Sweat of ours must dress the soil.

* *Life*, i 229-32   Clarkson, i 446, 466, 492-3, 500 , ii 118-66 Bryan Edwards, *History of the British West Indies* (London, 1819), vol. iii   T Southey, *Chronological History of the West Indies* (London, 1827), iii 33-7, 40-7   M Rainsford, *The Black Empire of Hayti* (London, 1805), chap iii   De Poyen, *Histoire Militaire de St. Domingue* (Paris, 1899), 1-15

Think, ye masters, iron-hearted,
  Lolling at your jovial boards,
Think how many backs have smarted
  For the sweets your cane affords

Is there, as you sometimes tell us,
  Is there one, who rules on high ;
Has he bid you buy and sell us,
  Speaking from his throne, the sky ?
Ask him if your knotted scourges,
  Fetters, blood-extorting screws,
Are the means which duty urges
  Agents of his will to use ?

The Abolitionists made prompt use of a poem which, as Clarkson puts it, ' gave a plain account of the subject with an appropriate feeling '. It was printed on the finest paper, and thousands of copies, neatly folded and aptly superscribed *A Subject for Conversation at the Tea-table*, were circulated throughout the country. It was also set to music, and presently the unhappy negro could be heard complaining in the streets of London and many provincial towns Another propagandist device was due to the ingenious generosity of Wedgwood, the famous Quaker master-potter and an ardent Abolitionist He had a cameo made depicting a negro in a posture of piteous entreaty on a white ground and distributed hundreds of them among the supporters of the cause. The cameo soon became as popular as the poem. It was to be seen everywhere—inlaid in gold on the lids of gentlemen's snuff-boxes, inserted in ladies' bracelets or worked up into heads of ornamental hair-pins. The wearing of it, it is said—and it is not incredible—became quite the fashion. Even more significant was the success of a campaign against the use of West Indian sugar. All the more zealous Abolitionists had resolved to abstain from it on the morrow of the parliamentary failure of 1791. ' We use East Indian sugar entirely ', wrote Babington to Wilberforce, ' and so do full two-thirds of the friends of Abolition in Leicester.' The venerable John Newton, on the other hand, regarded this move as premature and likely to alienate moderate men ; and Wilberforce decided not to make it an essential part of the official programme. But when Clarkson travelled through the country in 1792 he found that numbers of individual Abolitionists in all parts had adopted the ban. He estimated—probably somewhat over-estimated in his sanguine way—an average of 200 to 500 abstainers in the larger towns ' who had made this sacrifice to virtue '. He came upon grocers who had ceased to sell West Indian sugar, and children old enough to be persuaded to abstain, on principle, from sweets

These symptoms of popular zeal were not to be disregarded ; and after the signal defeat in the House of Commons in 1791 and when in the subsequent months the damaging effects of the French Revolution and the St Domingo affair became increasingly manifest in political circles, Wilberforce and his colleagues decided that the time had come to appeal from Parliament directly to the people on a comprehensive scale   Then, with an emphatic popular mandate behind him, Wilberforce was to return to the charge in the Commons   ' The best course will be ', he wrote at the beginning of 1792, ' to endeavour to excite the flame as much as possible in a secret way, but not to allow it more than to smoulder until after I have given notice of my intention of bringing the subject forward. This must be the signal for the fire's bursting forth.' So a new abstract of the evidence against the Trade was prepared by Clarkson and this, together with the report of the last debate, was circulated broadcast.   On its heels Clarkson set out on another of his exhaustive and exhausting tours through England, while Dr. Dickson was dispatched to Scotland.   The results of this mission were immediate. Corresponding Committees, linked to the parent body in London, sprang up at Newcastle, Nottingham, Glasgow, and then all over Britain   The second step was the organization of public meetings , the third and last the presentation of petitions to Parliament.   For three months the flame was thus excited according to plan.   And there was no doubt whatever as to its heat   Throughout the Midlands and the North enthusiasm for Abolition ran riot.   It was reported from Scotland that ' the clergy to a man were favourable to the cause ', and in Scotland the opinions of the clergy were the opinions of the people. Even the City of London returned at last to its old liberal traditions The proposal of a petition in the Common Council was stifled by the Lord Mayor and a majority of the Aldermen, but they could not override a meeting of the Livery. The Liverymen attended in full strength, drowned their protests in groans and hisses, and triumphantly carried the motion

The campaign was controlled by the London Committee, with which Wilberforce was closely associated, though not actually a member till 1794. His own duties were heavy, for his lieutenants in the country were always asking how they should proceed even in details. Should they raise the question of the sugar ban ? What were they to say about St. Domingo ? When was the precise moment for launching a petition ? How was a public meeting to be organized ? ' Give us precise instructions ', wrote one agent on this last point . and precise instructions were forthcoming day after day. Never was Wilberforce's intimate knowledge of society more useful. He could warn one man of Lord Harrowby's dislike of public meetings, advise another how best to approach Lord Fitzwilliam, suggest to a third that the father of a Staffordshire M.P. might persuade his son to propose the motion for a petition if he were informed that by so doing his son would secure the votes of the Wedgwood interest at the next election And, in the intervals, there was his own speech to be prepared—the culminating effort of the whole campaign. Once more the physical strain was severe. ' I thank God I keep well ', he wrote.

Meantime the enemy were not idle Paris and St. Domingo had given them two new cards to play, and they played them for all they were worth And there was a weakness in their opponents' hand of which they were quick to take advantage It may be a salutary dispensation that human progress is always retarded not only by the people who want to go too slow, but also by the people who want to go too fast. The history of all great causes is full of set-backs from the ' Left ' , and the cause of Abolition was no exception to the rule. The Abolitionists in the mass were not fanatics, but every fanatic was an Abolitionist and a great deal more. It was an easy game, then, for the Trade to spy out the Jacobins among the British *Amis des Noirs*, to suggest that the good, simple-minded Wilberforce was unaware of the sinister forces that had enlisted under his banner; to give out that, however moderate and respectable their leaders might be, the mob behind them was bent on securing Abolition only as. a lever wherewith to thrust the British Empire down the primrose path of Equality into the flames of St Domingo. The danger of these insinuations was clear to Wilberforce; and when, in this year, the Convention made him a citizen of France, he quickly parried the unwelcome compliment by joining, on Burke's suggestion, a committee in aid of the French emigrant clergy. But Clarkson was not so wise. He failed to realize that a public expression of his eager sympathy with the Revolution might damage the cause of Abolition, the triumph of which was, after all, the supreme, the single motive of his life. His friends realized it well enough. After a long talk with him Milner wrote to Wilberforce, ' I wish him better health, and better notions in politics'. ' You will see Clarkson', wrote Wilberforce to Lord Muncaster: ' caution him against talking of the French Revolution ; it will be the ruin of our cause.' But cautions were thrown away on so sanguine an apostle, and there was rejoicing in the enemies' camp when it was known that Clarkson had ventilated Jacobinical opinions at a meeting at a pothouse in the Strand And it was not only the Trade that marked his indiscretion. Government circles, already sniffing the scent of a Republican bogey in England, were annoyed ; and Dundas wrote a sharp note to Wilberforce. ' What business had your friend, Clarkson, to attend the " Crown and Anchor " last Thursday ? He could not have done a more mischievous thing to the cause you have taken in hand ' And if Dundas was angry, Pitt must have been more so, and for a better reason. He was a confessed Abolitionist—and Prime Minister ; and since, at this time, he was maintaining the strictest official neutrality towards the French Revolution, it was not pleasant for him to find a cause, which he had so notoriously supported, tainted ever so little with Jacobinism.

The incident, indeed, may well have been one reason for Pitt's betraying, at this time, the first faint touch of embarrassment at the conflict between his personal sentiments and his official position. St. Domingo had made it difficult enough, without any gossip about Jacobins, for the Prime Minister to reassert, just at this moment, his uncompromising condemnation of the Trade. 'People here are all panic-struck with the transactions in St Domingo', wrote Wilberforce 'I am pressed on all hands . . . to defer my motion till next year.' And, to his dismay, one of those who pressed for delay was Pitt. There is a painful note in the diary of a committee-meeting on the question 'Pitt threw out against Slave motion on St. Domingo account . . . I could hardly bring myself to resolve to do my duty and please God, at the expense (as I suspect it will turn out) of my cordiality with Pitt, or rather his with me.' The little storm was over in a moment · Pitt was willing still to yield to Wilberforce and his own instincts . but the entry was sadly prophetic. If Pitt should retire from the conflict, the friends would part ; for Wilberforce assuredly would stay behind. 'Do not be afraid', he said to Babington at this time, 'lest I should give ground this is a matter wherein all personal, much more all ministerial, attachments must be as dust in the balance.'

And now the campaign had reached its climax. Wilberforce had given notice of his motion, and on this, the appointed signal, the well-prepared machinery for the launching of petitions for Abolition all over the country was instantly set in motion It went like clock-work. Petitions poured into Westminster—312 from England and Wales, 187 from Scotland On the other side only five petitions were presented—two of them from individuals and a third in favour at least of regulation. 'You will perhaps be surprised', wrote one of Wilberforce's correspondents, 'that Liverpool does not petition for the Trade. Liverpool will never again, I think, petition on this subject , conviction of the truth has spread amongst us widely.' And he hinted that the vehement support of the Trade by Tarleton, the local member, might cost him his seat at the next election—as indeed it did   Never before had the politically passive, quiescent, oligarchic Britain of the eighteenth century witnessed such a lively and widespread movement. It had shown how much could be done to mobilize public opinion outside the walls of Parliament, yet strictly within the liberties of the constitution. It was a new and a great fact in British politics. ' Its methods ', writes an eminent authority on nineteenth-century British history, ' became the model for the conduct of hundreds and even thousands of other movements—political, humanitarian, social, educational—which have been and still are the chief arteries of the life-blood of modern Britain ' And not the least effective part of its organization was the admirable timing, so as to bring the maximum of pressure on the House of Commons at the latest possible moment. The last of the petitions, that from the Livery of the City, was presented on April 2 at the very hour at which Wilberforce rose to make his motion.

Meantime, only a fortnight earlier, something had happened outside England that was bound to affect the question   On March 16, Christian VII of Denmark had signed an edict declaring that ' with the beginning of the year 1803, all traffic in the Slave Trade by our subjects shall cease '. The Danish possessions in the West Indies were few and small. On a yearly average, only some fifty or sixty ships of from 80 to 120 tons were engaged in trading with them. Denmark's share in the Slave Trade was thus incomparably less than Britain's. But, none the less, that enlightened country had achieved the honour of giving the lead to Europe And from the point of view of British Abolitionists the edict might at first sight have seemed peculiarly timely. The preamble to it bristled with their arguments—the conditions of the Trade were undesirable : the plantations could be cultivated by labourers born and trained in the islands instead of by imported slaves : and this would eventually prove a benefit to the masters themselves. But there was a dangerous flaw in the plan—the date. Wilberforce and Sharp and Clarkson, Pitt and Fox and Grenville, the Abolition Committee and all that host of petitioners desired immediate Abolition. Not so the King of Denmark. He had indeed condemned the Trade· but he had postponed the execution of the sentence ten whole years *

III

The invasion of the eighteenth-century House of Commons by such an undesirable stranger as Public Opinion was somewhat disconcerting to the representatives of the people In the last session they had achieved, not without throes and twinges, a decision ; and now it appeared that this decision was repudiated by a very large number of their countrymen, less properly impressed than themselves by those plain warnings from oversea. For those members, at any rate, whose seats were not positively secured by influence or bribery, it meant at least a reconsideration of the thorny question. And another full-dress debate meant for all, or most of them, a reopening of their minds to the Abolitionist logic and a re-exposure of their consciences, still a little raw, to the painful facts of the Trade case To the spokesmen of the Trade the spectacle of the heaped petitions on the table might have been even more unpleasant if they had not known what was coming But they had known, and they were ready. The possibility that this volume of public protest might just succeed in turning the scale against them had compelled them to reconsider their strategy. Their old policy of direct and complete opposition to Abolition had been discarded and a new and skilful plan concocted. And, to make victory certain, they had secured for the chief part in its execution the services of a very big man indeed A few weeks earlier Wilberforce had jotted down this characteristic note in his diary, quite unsuspicious

* *Life*, 1 333–69 Clarkson, 11 188–92, 346–55 G M Trevelyan, *British History in the 19th Century* (London, 1922), 51.. T. Southey, *op. cit*, 111. 50, 71.

of its irony : ' January 21. Went with Pitt to Wimbledon.
. . . A long discussion with Dundas after dinner *tête-à-tête*—
most excellent man of business. Oh, what a pity he is not
alive to what is best ! ' It was indeed a pity. This excellent
man of business, the most indispensable of Pitt's colleagues,
the most powerful and *rusé* of his party managers, the
master-broker of Scottish seats, was to be the mainspring
of the Trade's device. They could scarcely have done
better   Not only was the House of Commons to be impressed
by this professional exponent of plain horse-sense, this
personified antithesis and antidote to Wilberforce's sensibility and Fox's passion ; but his performance would also
rub in the important point that, if Pitt still spoke for
Abolition, he would not be speaking for his Government.
So the enemies of Abolition could face the debate, despite
those piled petitions, with a fairly easy mind   Let Wilberforce make the most of Pitt : they had a Roland for his
Oliver.

Wilberforce's opening speech was a masterly example of
the art of variation on a familiar theme. He was bound, as
in his previous speeches, to make the two same cardinal
points—that the Slave Trade was an abomination and that
its continuance was not essential to the welfare of the
planters. But there was no hackneyed clap-trap in his
arguing of them, no sentimental clichés, no stale illustra-
tions. It was to the first of the two points that he paid
most attention, bent on convincing the House that the
inevitable concomitants of the Trade were so hideous that
no civilized community could know of them and let it be ,
and for this, of course, the evidence was so voluminous that
there was never need for him to tell the same story twice.
One striking phrase deserves quotation. ' Europeans ', he
said, ' are hovering round the coast like vultures : and like
vultures they feed on blood.' And of the two or three
telling incidents he chose to recount, one made a peculiarly
sharp impression   Six British slave-ships, he told the House,
had anchored off the little African coast-town of Calabar :
and their captains, on learning that the native traders were
obstinately demanding more than the usual payment for

those of their countrymen whom they were willing to sell as slaves, took counsel together and decided to open fire on the town in order to compel a lowering of the price Some time was wasted in discussion with a French slave-captain who happened to be present and who, being ready to pay the higher price, declined to take part in the operation ; but in the course of the morning fire was opened with sixty-six guns. Not a shot was fired in reply, but the inhabitants could be seen running in all directions like ants in a broken nest. The bombardment was continued for three hours and resumed again in the evening, until at last, some twenty people having been killed and many injured, the natives consented to sell their slaves at any price the captains fixed The Abolition debates had accustomed the House to horrors ; but this particular story created a sensation. There was—says sober Hansard in one of his rare interpolations—' a sudden burst of indignation '. The House rang with cries of ' Name ! Name ! ' ' Mr. Wilberforce ', the chronicler continues, ' resisted for a long time , at last the cry overpowered him and we heard the names.' Those of the captains may well be left in obscurity. The ships were *Thomas, Recovery, Anatree* (?) of Bristol, *Betsy* and *Thomas* of Liverpool, and, more appropriate than these humanities, *Wasp*, her port not stated.

Wilberforce was followed by orthodox champions of the Trade—Baillie, agent for Grenada, and Tarleton, member for Liverpool Their part was to state the case against Abolition as clearly as before and to make all possible capital out of St. Domingo Baillie indeed, detecting in the irresponsible propaganda of Wilberforce and his friends a more sovereign source of evil for the world than the French Revolution itself, declared that ' the causes of all these calamities have originated in Great Britain ' But it was not according to plan that the opposition should be quite inexorable These first speakers were to show themselves not impervious to reason, not altogether unmoved by the weight of evidence against them, not quite irresponsive to the popular clamour Accordingly they were readier to make admissions than in earlier debates. Baillie was

' far from denying that many acts of inhumanity have been committed '. Tarleton even confessed that, if the Trade were not an old-established interest but about to start *de novo*, he would himself be its most strenuous opponent And then, when one or two minor Abolitionists had had their say, Dundas got up. Those of his honourable friends, he said, with whom he was most closely associated, knew very well that he had long shared their opinion as to the desirability of abolishing the Slave Trade. In fact, he fully agreed with all the material parts of the honourable mover's argument. But he differed as to method His friends' plan was precipitate abolition, a plan which showed their zeal for a great object. But was it prudent ? Was it practical ? Might it not run counter to an equally great object, ' the sacred attention which Parliament had ever shown to the interests of individuals ' ? And the speakers on the other side had been no less rigorous, no less unequivocal : they had asserted that the Slave Trade must continue for ever or the West Indies be ruined. Let no one suppose that he admitted that. He was for abolition, total abolition, but by a method no less speedy, nay, even speedier, than that of his friends. The most direct method. Indeed, the only method. He would proceed by regulations. ' What regulations ? ' interjected Fox. Regulations, replied Dundas, to promote the breeding of negroes in the West Indies; to put an end by a gradual process to hereditary slavery , to improve the conditions of the existing slaves ; and to provide for the education of their children. Two results would accrue : not only would the practicability of abolishing the Trade without injury to the planters' interests be proved by experience, but in course of time a transition would be effected from slave labour to free. Having thus outbidden the Abolitionists both in immediate respect for the rights of property and in prospective philanthropy, Dundas turned to the defenders of the Trade and begged them in their own interest to accept his proposal. Let them only try his regulations, and in a few years' time they would be of one mind with him. The speech concluded with a plain appeal to all ' gentlemen of the moderate or middle way of thinking ' to form a coherent group in favour of this policy and so ' reduce the question to its proper bounds '.

Two gentlemen of the moderate or middle way of thinking, both destined, possibly on that account, to become Prime Ministers, responded to this shrewd proposal. Addington at once left the Speaker's chair to thank Dundas for relieving him from ' the utmost anxiety ', torn as he had been between his hatred of the Trade and his respect for individual rights. The new method, he declared, could hardly be improved on Certainly the Trade ' ought to exist a few years longer, perhaps for a period of eight   or ten . . . or twelve years ', but under regulations. And he suggested a few more of these—a heavier duty on male slaves than on female, to increase the importation of the latter , a bonus to slaves for large families , a premium on the introduction of agricultural machines The second ' moderate ', Jenkinson, who was one day to bear a title taken from the greatest Slave Trade port, showed himself decidedly more averse to Abolition than Addington ; but he, too, welcomed Dundas's method and added his quota to the stock of regulations—premiums to such planters and overseers as promoted an increased birth-rate among their slaves , liberty for every female slave who reared five children to the age of seven , a bounty of £5 a head to every slaver whose cargo contained more young females than males.

It may be that these moderate men—Addington, at any rate, if not Jenkinson—really believed that regulation was a ' method ' of abolition But they were not to be allowed to salve their consciences without hearing some sharp home-truths. Fox was too old a parliamentary hand to let Dundas's specious promises go by unquestioned , and when Addington returned to his chair, he let fly at the policy of ' moderation ' with all his incomparable debating skill. Moderation in the slave trade, he said, reminded him of a passage in Middleton's *Life of Cicero*—' To break open a man's house and kill him, his wife, and his family in the night is certainly a most heinous crime and deserving of death , but even this may be done with moderation.'

Moderation in atrocity, in robbery and murder, in the pillage and destruction of a country ! The real question was not whether that execrable Trade required regulation, but whether it was fit to be continued at all And it seemed to him that in the scheme proposed something like a foundation had been laid for preserving it not only for years to come but for ever ' I note the terms in which the Trade has been reprehended by the two last speakers, but where is the proof that they will ever vote for the abolition of it ? ' And meantime, year after year, the Africans were being plundered and murdered and sold into slavery The rest of the speech was occupied with a further exposition of the horrors of the Trade, with a rebuttal of the suggestion that immediate Abolition would involve the British West Indies in the fate of St Domingo, and with a reminder of the constitutional importance of the petitions, which Dundas had carefully disparaged. ' I am certain of this ', he said. ' The table is never loaded with petitions but when the people of England feel an actual grievance and when the House ought to feel itself bound to give a remedy ' And for peroration he summed up his opinion of the Trade in terms that were certainly not ' moderate ' ' I believe it to be impolitic. I know it to be inhuman. I am certain it is unjust. I find it so inhuman and unjust that, if the colonies cannot be cultivated without it, they ought not to be cultivated at all   . As long as I have a voice to speak, this question shall never be at rest .   and if I and my friends should die before they have attained their glorious object I hope there will never be wanting men alive to do their duty, who will continue to labour till the evil shall be wholly done away '

Dundas was used to Fox's eloquence and knew how to deal with it When Fox sat down, he rose again, made a few dry, simple remarks in defence of his own position, and, to carry the question to an issue, coolly moved an amendment to insert the word *gradually* in Wilberforce's motion in favour of Abolition. Then came Jenkinson's speech ; and when he had done, the night was already over and dawn near breaking. But the debate could not conclude without a speech from the Prime Minister And exhausted as he confessed himself to be after listening for so many hours to such a host of words, Pitt spurred himself to an effort which even his critics admitted to be the finest he had ever made. His continued devotion to the cause of Abolition, unlike Fox's, had been widely doubted ' From London to Inverness ', Dickson had written to Wilberforce from Scotland, ' Mr. Pitt's sincerity is questioned , and unless he can convince the nation of his cordiality in our cause, his popularity must suffer greatly.' And Wilberforce himself had not forgotten that little disquieting outburst of impatience about St. Domingo. But when, after speaking for over an hour, Pitt sat down, all doubt had been dispelled

The first part of his speech was typically logical. He went straight to the main contention of the ' moderates ' that ' a gradual and in some degree a distant Abolition ' would better serve the interest of the West Indies than the more ' immediate and direct ' course. Immediate Abolition, he argued, would compel the planters to improve the conditions of their existing slaves and so increase their numbers and their labour. It would improve their finances by reducing their debts which—it was admitted—were due to speculation in slaves. And it would minimize the danger of insurrection which—again it was admitted—arose from the contact of newly imported negroes with the older and more resigned slaves. ' Surely, Sir, when gentlemen talk so vehemently of the safety of the islands and charge us with being so indifferent to it, when they speak of the calamities of St Domingo and of similar dangers impending on their own heads, it ill becomes them to cry out for further importation. . Let us vote that the Abolition of the Slave Trade shall be immediate. Will my right honourable friends answer for the safety of the islands during any imaginable intervening period ? '

From the argument from expediency Pitt then passed to the argument from legal prescription—an argument which, he pointed out, applied as much to gradual as to immediate Abolition and was in any case unfounded. Was it suggested

that ' the Slave Trade had received any such parliamentary
sanction as must place it more out of the jurisdiction of the
legislature for ever after than the other branches of our
national commerce ? ' Every new commercial regulation,
every new tax, every prohibitory duty affected some man's
property or some man's expectations : and if, on that
ground, Abolition was forbidden to Parliament, so were all
those measures. ' If for the sake of moral duty, of national
honour, or even of great political advantage, it is thought
right by authority of Parliament to alter any long-established system, Parliament is competent to do it.' And it
would be particularly offensive to suppose that Parliament
had ever bound itself to maintain such a scandal as the
Slave Trade. ' As well might an individual think himself
bound by a promise to commit an assassination ! ' And
what of the Act of George II which was cited as the binding
instrument ? It actually forbade any master of a ship to
carry off negroes from Africa ' by fraud, force, or violence,
or by any indirect practice whatsoever ', and inflicted a
punishment of £100 for each offence. In fact, nothing but
Abolition could prevent this law from being broken !

' And now, Sir,' said Pitt, ' I come to Africa ' ; and in the
second half of his speech he cut, as a statesman should, to
the very root of the question—the relations between the
two continents, one civilized and strong, the other weak and
savage. Why, first and last, he asked, ought the Slave
Trade to be abolished ? Because of its incurable injustice
to the Africans. So much the ' moderates ' admitted and,
so doing, give away their case for delay. ' If on the ground
of injustice it ought to be abolished at last, why ought it
not now ? Why is injustice suffered to remain for a single
hour ? ' What have we done for Africa—save robbing her
of fifty thousand people every year ?

' Long as that continent has been known to navigators,
the extreme line of its coasts is all with which Europe is
yet become acquainted, while other countries in the same
parallel of latitude, through a happier system of intercourse, have reaped the blessings of a mutually beneficial
commerce. . . . But Africa is known to you only in its skirts ,

yet even there you are able to inject a poison which pene--
trates to its very centre, corrupting every part to which
it reaches   What astonishing, I had almost said, what
irreparable, mischief have we brought upon that continent !
. . How shall we hope to obtain, if it be possible, forgiveness
from Heaven for the enormous evils we have committed, if
we refuse to make use of those means which the mercy of
Providence has still reserved for us for wiping away the
shame and guilt with which we are now covered ? . . Shall
we not count the days and hours that are suffered to intervene and to delay the accomplishment of such a work ? '
They must not wait for other nations to act with them Theirs
was the largest share in the Trade, theirs the deepest guilt ;
and other nations rightly looked to them to lead the way.
' It depends upon us whether other countries will persist in
this bloody trade or not ' Nor must they wait till ' a thousand favourable circumstances unite together. . . . Year
after year escapes, and the evils go unredressed. . . If you
go into the street, it is a chance but the first person who
crosses you is one, *vivendi recte qui prorogat horam.* We may
wait : we may delay to cross the stream before us till it has
run down ; but we shall wait for ever, for the river will
still flow on unexhausted.'

Pitt then briefly combated the argument that the Trade
relinquished by Britain would be at once absorbed by other
countries Would France take it, he asked, in the light of
events in St. Domingo ? Would Spain, Portugal, Holland ?
He doubted if they would have the will to go against our
lead , he was certain they would not have the money to
purchase the 30,000 or 40,000 slaves bought annually by us
at £40 or £50 a head. ' From what branch of their commerce will they draw together a fund to feed this monster ? '

And so he returned to Africa and to his final plea. It
was for Britain, he declared, to make amends for the past
by doing what she could to promote the civilization of
Africa. Let no one say that she ' labours under a natural
incapacity for civilization ', that such practices as human
sacrifice prove that ' Providence has irrevocably doomed her
to be only a nursery of slaves for us free and civilized
Europeans '. Human sacrifice had once been practised in
these islands, and Britons had been sold for slaves in Rome.
With equal justice some Roman senator might have pointed

to ' British barbarians ' and said, ' *There* is a people that will never rise to civilization—*there* is a people never destined to be free.'

' We were once as obscure among the nations of the earth, as savage in our manners, as debased in our morals, as degraded in our understandings, as these unhappy Africans are at present. But in the lapse of a long series of years, by a progression slow and for a time almost imperceptible, we have become rich in a variety of acquirements and favoured above measure in the gifts of Providence. . . From all these blessings we must for ever have been shut out, had other nations adopted in their conduct towards us the principles laid down as applicable to Africa . . Ages might have passed without our emergence from barbarism . and we, who are now enjoying the blessings of British civilization, British laws, and British liberty, might, at this hour, have been little superior in morals, in knowledge, or in refinement to the rude inhabitants of the coast of Guinea. If we shudder to think of the misery which would still have overwhelmed us, had Great Britain continued to the present times to be the mart for slaves for the more civilized nations of the world, through some cruel policy of theirs, God forbid that we should any longer subject Africa to the same dreadful scourge.'

It was now nearly seven o'clock in the morning , and while Pitt had been speaking, the climbing sun had begun to throw its rays through the windows of the House. It must have made singularly impressive, it may even have suddenly suggested, the prophecy of dawn in Africa with which Pitt closed his speech

' If we listen to the voice of reason and duty ', he said, ' and pursue this day the line of conduct which they prescribe, some of us may live to see the reverse of that picture from which we now turn our eyes with shame and regret We may live to behold the natives of Africa engaged in the calm occupations of industry, in the pursuit of a just and legitimate commerce We may behold the beams of science and philosophy breaking in upon their land, which, at some happy period, in still later times, may blaze with full lustre, and, joining their influence with that of pure religion, may illuminate and invigorate the most distant extremities of that immense continent Then may we hope that even Africa, though last of all the quarters of the globe, shall enjoy at length, in the evening of her days, those blessings which have descended so plentifully upon us—

Nosque ubi primus equis Oriens adflavit anhelis
Illic sera rubens accendit lumina Vesper . . .

It is in this view, Sir, it is as an atonement for our long and cruel injustice towards Africa, that the measure proposed by my honourable friend most forcibly recommends itself to my mind. I shall vote, Sir, against the amendment; and I shall also oppose to the utmost every proposition which in any way may tend either to prevent or even to postpone for an hour the total abolition of the Slave Trade '

' For the last twenty minutes ', said Wilberforce, who had himself suggested the theme of the civilization of Africa to Pitt the day before, ' he really seemed to be inspired.' And as Fox walked away from the debate with Grey and Windham, the three Whigs, none of them lovers of Pitt, agreed that the speech was ' one of the most extraordinary displays of eloquence they had ever heard '. And indeed throughout its closing passages the whole House had sat spellbound. Never had Pitt so nearly reached the level of his father's magic art But when it was over, when the young orator had at last sunk back into his seat, the spell was broken Back into members' minds thronged the memories of Paris and St Domingo, not easily effaceable by any eloquence or logic ; back, too, came their old love of compromise and the deep impression made by Dundas's exhibition of blunt common-sense. And so, hurriedly dividing, they carried his amendment by 193 to 125; then the motion as amended—' That the Slave Trade ought to be *gradually* abolished '—by 230 to 85 ; and then trooped out into the April sunshine in search of breakfast.*

* *Life*, 1 326, 345-6   *Hansard*, xxix (1791-2), 1055-1158   Pitt's *Speeches* (1806 ed), 50-82   Clarkson, ii 355-448

IV

The great debate of 1792 was the last of a series which formed the crowning experiences of this period of Wilberforce's life. They were to him like the battles at which the whole of a strategist's career is brought to an issue. Most of the steady, uneventful labour of the intervening days had been spent in preparing for them. On their result the success or failure of his lifework mainly turned. What, then, were his feelings at the close of this particular debate? Sanguine as ever and little knowing what lay ahead, he was not greatly disappointed. Something after all had been gained. A motion for Abolition, gradual alas! but still Abolition, had been carried for the first time and by a great majority 'against the united forces of Africans and West Indians'. He was not alone in his opinion. Many of his friends regarded the vote as a signal triumph, and letters of congratulation poured in on him. But one old friend saw farther ahead. 'I thought of you most unremittingly', wrote Milner, from his deanery at Carlisle, 'the whole day of April 2 and a good deal of the night which to me was a very restless one. . . . I think there can be no doubt that you have gained some ground . . . as far as respects public opinion; the opposers are plainly overawed and ashamed. The worst circumstance is this Dundas—nobody thinks well of him—duplicity and artifice are esteemed parts of his character—he is judged to do what he does unwillingly and with design, in the worst sense.'

The Dean was soon proved right on both points—in his belief that the direct opposition to Abolition had been weakened and in his recognition of the strength of the indirect opposition headed by Dundas. On April 23 and 27 the House discussed the resolutions proposed by Dundas in execution of his policy. The interval had enabled him to expand and polish up the 'method of regulation'; and the resolutions prohibited the carrying on of the Trade with foreign countries or in ships not hitherto employed in it, forbade the exportation of males over twenty years old and females over sixteen, and laid a lower customs-duty on females than on males. But the most vital resolution was that which, outbidding Denmark, fixed the date for Abolition at January 1, 1800. Wilberforce, Fox, and Pitt stood manfully by their guns , and the House was told by its Leader that it need not feel itself prevented by its previous decision from changing its mind and voting now for immediate Abolition. But their highest efforts had been made on April 2–3, and the most notable speeches of this debate came from another of the great young men of those days, as great in his way as Pitt and Wilberforce in theirs and a year younger than they. An amendment was moved by Lord Mornington, to be better known in time as Marquess Wellesley, substituting 1793 for 1800. ' We cannot modify injustice ', he declared ; ' the question is to what period we shall prolong it Some think we should be unjust for ten years . others think it is enough to be unjust for five years ; others . . that the present century should continue in disgrace and that justice should commence its operation with the opening of another ' These sarcasms went home. The House was undoubtedly uncomfortable , and it was soon evident that many of those who voted in the majority on the morning of April 3 really meant Abolition by gradual Abolition. Dundas's seven-year period was thrown out ; and after some haggling over the exact date, it was fixed at 1796 by 151 votes to 132.

' On the whole ', wrote Wilberforce, ' this is more than I expected two months ago, and I have much cause for thankfulness. We are to contend for the number of slaves to be imported , and then *for the House of Lords.*' He might well italicize the words. The obstructionists had still a trump-card in their hand The King had still his ' friends ' in the Upper House ; and the King, who used once to chaff Wilberforce about his ' black clients ', had become with the progress of the French Revolution an obstinate defender of the Trade. And Dundas, too, had his friends among the Lords—on both sides of the House ' Dropped in one day at Dundas's ', runs a naïve entry in the diary about this time, ' and much surprised to find Lord Loughborough

there '—Loughborough, *alias* Wedderburn, one of Dundas's
Tory colleagues not so long ago, but now among the Whigs
in the hope of finding there a less encumbered access to the
Woolsack, a cynical ' careerist ' not likely to be moved by
arguments of justice or humanity.   And in the Lords,
presiding over them, though near the end of his tether now,
was the perfidious Thurlow, bitter enemy of Pitt and of
every liberal idea.   On this ' unofficial ' subject of Abolition,
moreover, the attitude of the rank and file of the parties was
not the same in the Upper House as in the Lower.   Tory
peers could vote more freely against Pitt than Tory
Commoners, who, however un-Governmental the matter
might be, could not but be influenced by the lead, the
logic, the mere Olympic presence of the saviour of their
party and the mainstay of the Crown   And of the Whig
peers very few were ' Foxites ' ; for the most part they
were landed magnates of the Portland faction and dead
against Abolition.   Only one circumstance could conceivably
have undermined these bulwarks of vested interest.   If
Dundas's ' method ' had never been suggested, if the full
weight of the popular campaign—with electors' votes
behind those petitions—and the full force of the Abolitionist
speeches, especially Pitt's, had not been broken by that one
conscience-saving word, *gradually*, it is conceivable that
immediate Abolition might have been carried on April 3
And if this clean, uncompromising decision had come up
from the Commons, it is just imaginable, though not at all
likely, that the Lords would have accepted it.   As it was,
the result, despite Wilberforce's spirited battle-cry, was a
foregone conclusion.

The debate of May 3 was distinguished by the maiden
speech of William, Duke of Clarence, an honest young
Tory, who, like Rodney, had formed his own opinions of
the slave business during naval service in the West Indies.
So far from accepting gradual Abolition, he was against
Abolition altogether   ' He had been an attentive observer
of the state of the negroes, and had no doubt but that he
could bring forward proofs to convince their Lordships that
their state was far from being miserable : on the contrary,
that, when the various ranks of society were considered,

they were comparatively in a state of humble happiness.'
And he ventured on another argument, little dreaming of
the far-off day when he would give his royal promise to
create, if need be, sufficient Peers to carry the Reform Bill.
' An implicit obedience to the House of Commons ', he said,
' much as I respect that House, would make the House of
Peers useless, and thus the natural and constituent balance
in the constitution would be endangered.' But the Peers
did not require this princely lead With a great parade of
undertaking a burdensome duty, they repeated the solemn
farce which had been played with such effect a few years
earlier in ' another place '. Just as the Commons had
repudiated the evidence given before the Privy Council
Committee and insisted on hearing it anew for themselves,
so now the Lords repudiated the evidence given before the
Commons. Grenville vigorously protested, declaring that
the removal of a national disgrace brooked no delay, and
pleaded that, if evidence must be taken afresh, it at least
should be heard by a Select Committee, as in the Commons,
to save time But in the Lords the tactics of obstruction
were pressed to their limit. Lord Chancellor Thurlow had
the face to assure his fellow Peers that a Committee of the
whole House would not involve delay , and, amongst others,
the Archbishop of Canterbury had the folly to believe him
and to vote accordingly—on which account (for he was
a sincere Abolitionist) he had presently to write a remorseful
letter to Wilberforce So the comedy proceeded without a
hitch. Seven witnesses were heard at such intervals as the
whole House could spare , and then, on June 5, ten days
before the session closed, it was resolved to continue the
hearing of evidence in the following year

Sentence had been pronounced A hundred thousand
natives of West Africa had been condemned to death or
penal servitude Before another witness could attest their
sufferings in the House of Lords, war had broken out between
Great Britain and France. And year after year now, it was
less and less possible for English ears to hear the far, faint
cry of Africa beyond the guns in Europe.*

* *Life*, 1 314–53   *Hansard*, xxix (1792–3), 1204–93, 1349–55.
Clarkson, 11. 451–60   Holland Rose, *Pitt*, 1. 471–2

VI

INTERRUPTION

I

'HEARD of the militia being called out and Parliament summoned,' notes Wilberforce on December 3, 1792. 'Talked politics, and of the state of the country which seems very critical.' Modern opinion, wiser after the event, is sometimes tempted to make light of the anxieties of our forefathers in that troubled period. There was no cause for panic, it is true; but, none the less, strange things were happening. Working men were betraying an interest in politics which, save locally and transiently, they had never shown before. Radical clubs were springing up like mushrooms, proclaiming allegiance to Tom Paine, spreading cheap copies of his subversive pamphlets, and even demanding the suppression of a Parliament that had refused Reform by a National Convention on the French model 'After the example given by France,' wrote the London Corresponding Society to the French Convention, 'Revolutions will become easy.' As the rupture with France approached, the symptoms became slightly more feverish. French emissaries conducted a little futile propaganda among British artisans. 'No war with France' was chalked up here and there on the walls. Attempts were made to tamper with the army. At Sheffield a crowd, ten thousand strong, marched in procession with the tricolour at its head. In one or two towns there were riots Even more disquieting was the emergence of the Scottish people from half a century of political apathy. All the chief towns followed the English lead A Convention, representing forty-five societies, met at Edinburgh. A *liaison* was established with Wolfe Tone's United Irishmen. In Dundee, the hottest point, an effigy of Dundas, garbed with singular prodigality in satin waistcoat and breeches, was burnt by a cheering mob. And in both countries, while nothing very terrible was done, very terrible things were said. Hot-headed orators revelled in the sanguinary language of the Terror.

Now in all this there was little, if any, positive danger. There was no comparison between the social evils of France

and Britain. There was no real question of a British
Revolution, no more likelihood of the mass of Englishmen
becoming Jacobins in 1793 than of then becoming Bolsheviks
in 1919; and Burke's theatrical 'dagger-scene' in the
House of Commons was as much out of tune with the
realities of the situation as with the British temperament or
his own earlier sanity The Radical agitation of the war-
period was due to temporary and remediable causes—dear
corn, enclosures, low wages, unemployment, and the new
recognition of the impurities and inequalities of the existing
system of representative government. It was relatively
mild in operation, not a life was taken by the British
Jacobins, and it was confined to a very small circle. It
was, indeed, Pitt's greatest blunder that he did not leave
the forces of public opinion to do the work of repression,
unassisted by coercive laws and administrative persecution.
Nevertheless the anxiety of Wilberforce and his contemporaries is not unintelligible Never before had they seen
anything like this turbulence, heard anything like these
threats against English society, these greetings to England's
enemies. And, as they watched with horror the holocaust
in Paris, they remembered how quietly the fire had started
and how swiftly it had spread.

Wilberforce's attitude at the outset was a typical blend of
practical insight and a kind of spiritual fatalism. ' I will
frankly own ', he wrote at the end of 1792, ' that I entertain
rather gloomy apprehensions concerning the state of the
country. Not that I fear any speedy commotion—of this
I own I see no danger. Almost every man of property in
the kingdom is of course the friend of civil order, and if
a few mad-headed professors of liberty and equality were
to attempt to bring their theories into practice, they would
be crushed in an instant. But yet I do foresee a gathering
storm, and I cannot help fearing that a country which, like
this, has so long been blessed beyond all example with every
spiritual and temporal good, will incur those judgements
of an incensed God which in the prophets are often denounced
against those who forget the Author of all their mercies.'
' I think ', he writes again, ' of proposing to the Archbishop

N 2

of Canterbury to suggest the appointment of a day of fasting
and humiliation.' On its secular side, at any rate, it was
a pity that this attitude was not shared by Pitt. It would
have been well for his country and for his reputation if he
could have regarded those ' mad-headed professors ' with
Wilberforce's calm indifference instead of letting loose on
them the ferocity of a Judge Braxfield and his kind It would
have been well, too, if, following the same guide, he had not
left his old Reform plans on the shelf to await more tranquil
times, but at least had tried—though the prospects of support
in Parliament were far worse now than in 1785—to counter
anticonstitutional agitation with constitutional reform
' Unless some reforms be made,' said Wilberforce, ' though
we should get well through our present difficulties, they will
recur hereafter with aggravated force ' ; and for a man of
his day and of his somewhat conservative proclivities it
was a singularly wise saying. Who could have guessed in
1793 that the British people would be nearer Revolution
in 1832 than they were then ?

On the second great question of the moment Wilberforce's
standpoint was nearer Fox's than Pitt's. To most historians,
whether of Lecky's school or Green's, the outbreak of war
between Britain and Revolutionary France has seemed
almost as inevitable under the circumstances as it seemed
to the great majority of Englishmen at the time. It is not
to the point to argue that the terrible change which came
over the methods and objects of the French Revolution in
the autumn and winter of 1792 was largely due to the
menacing attitude of unregenerate absolutism in Central
Europe. The change was no less a fact. It is not to the
point to argue, either, that Pitt ought to have shown something warmer than his strict neutrality to the Revolution
at its onset, that he ought to have won over Parliament to
a policy of holding the ring and forbidding Austria and
Prussia to cross the French frontier, and that then the change
might never have occurred. For, Pitt and Parliament—
and, let it be added, the British people—being what they
were, to argue so is to argue *per impossibile*. Nor is it to
be wondered at that the beginnings of the Terror should

have seemed to throw Europe back into the atmosphere of St. Bartholomew's Eve and to have reproduced in English minds the passionate antipathy of the Elizabethans to an alien Antichrist It was hatred of the Jacobins, not panic, that made Englishmen all too ready to fight them. And when the easy triumph of Jemappes made Frenchmen all too ready to fight England, when a war for saving the Revolution from extinction in France became a war for imposing it on all the rest of Europe, something like a miracle was needed to prevent the open breach.

To Wilberforce, with his one supreme test for every thought and deed, the weeks before the rupture were weeks of ferment. He hated the excesses of the Revolution, hated especially its anti-religious bias ; but he also hated war. One reassuring fact he clung to through the autumn—Pitt's genuine desire for peace. He repeatedly assures his correspondents of ' the error of imputing to Mr. Pitt a war-system, as if it were his plan, his wish, his predilection to engage in war, and that he had set himself to consider how he could effect his purpose '. And, many years later, he reasserted his conviction and cited what was and is the best proof of its truth—Pitt's famous budget-speech of February 17, 1792, prophesying the continuance of peace for fifteen years. It was this trust in Pitt's pacifism that enabled him, after many searchings of his conscience, to support the Government in the debate on the Address when Parliament met in the middle of December He spoke last and briefly ' He frankly declared that, as at all times war ought to be deprecated as the greatest of human evils, so there never was a period when it appeared more likely to be injurious to this country than the present.   . If we should find ourselves compelled by the obligations of solemn treaties to engage in war, as men of conscience and integrity we must submit to the necessity ; but nothing less than this necessity would justify the measure.' A few days later the French Government disclosed its intention of violating the neutrality of Holland, Britain's ally, and French ships sailed up the Scheldt in defiance of the treaty, signed by Britain, which reserved its navigation to the Dutch. The necessity, it would seem, had arisen , yet Wilberforce still shrank from war. He clung desperately to the policy of holding the ring , but if that was impossible at an earlier stage, it was still more impossible now. The French were in Flandeis. Mere neutrality, mere diplomacy, on Pitt's part could not turn them out , and if they stayed, Pitt could not long be neutral. Yet Wilberforce believed that a public declaration of the fact that Britain was negotiating a pact of neutrality would have checked the intoxicated victors of Jemappes on the road to the Dutch frontier ' I never was so earnest with Mr. Pitt on any other occasion,' he afterwards declared And since Pitt could not be persuaded, he determined to urge his policy on the House of Commons. But he had not realized how strong the ties of friendship were , he had not yet steeled himself to reject a personal appeal from Pitt, to face an open breach with him. ' I was actually upon my legs to open my mind fully on the subject,' he writes of the debate of February 1, on the need for military preparations, ' when Pitt sent Bankes to me, earnestly desiring me not to do so on that day, assuring me that my speaking then might do irreparable mischief, and pledging himself that I should have anothei opportunity before war should be declared.' ' Sat very late,' the diary adds, ' and much disturbed afterwards.' It was not Pitt's fault that he never had his opportunity. For the next few days no business could be transacted for lack of sufficient members in the House ; and then the news came that on February 1, the very day on which Wilberforce had wanted to ' open his mind ', France had declared war on Great Britain and Holland.

Wilberforce was not one of those who interpret Christianity as vetoing the use of force in any circumstances. He believed that the war might have been prevented , but now it had come, he had no doubts as to his duty. ' I deemed it ', he says, ' the part of a good subject not to use language which might tend to prevent the unanimity which was so desirable at the outset of such a war.' And he sat silent when the House discussed the French declaration and Fox argued that the conduct of the British Government

had done much to provoke it—silent, but uneasy. He did
not love the Revolution, but neither did he love the *ancien
régime* or its champions in Vienna and Berlin. He realized
the dilemma we were in. It was one thing to stand by our
treaty and our ally against the Jacobins' assault on the
public law of Europe. It was another thing to set Englishmen shoulder to shoulder with Austrians and Prussians,
champions of the old absolutist order, and as greedy on
their part as the Jacobins for territorial aggrandizement.
If Wilberforce could have seen the long years of war
ahead, the rise of Napoleon, and Britain forced to pay those
continental legions to wage a war on land which she could
not wage successfully alone, he might not have been so
anxious to escape from the dilemma. As it was, he hoped
to wriggle out of it, to have Britain's cause somehow or
other dissociated at the outset from the cause of Austria
and Prussia. ' Vexed at Pitt and Dundas ', the diary says
of the debate, ' for not being explicit enough.' *

II

It was, of course, impossible for Britain to act quite
independently of her associates on the Continent, and
Wilberforce's distrust of them was quickly justified. The
First Coalition was a sorry failure. The chance of stamping
out the Revolution by a swift combined move on Paris was
missed , and while the lives of British troops were muddled
away in Flanders and eaten up in the poisonous swamps of
the French West Indies, Prussia was mainly preoccupied,
and Austria not much less, in butchering and dismembering
Poland And when, in 1795, Prussia drew off to masticate
her share and so brought the First Coalition to an end, the
only satisfactory event for Britain had been the demonstration on the Glorious First of June that, whatever might
happen on land, she was again supreme at sea
    War is a stern ordeal for any statesman. For Pitt, it

* *Life*, ii. 1–13 *Hansard*, xxx (1793–4), 79–80

was a tragedy. It had cut right across his career, shattering his dream of peace, bringing to a sudden end the steady work of reconstruction for which he was so admirably fitted and which, as he knew, he had so far done so well, and thrusting on him a new and tremendous task—a task he faced with all his father's patriotism and fortitude, but with none of his father's genius for war, and with a growing consciousness, as the years went by and peace still eluded him, that his proper life-work would never be accomplished. Hitherto so self-sufficient, so easily successful, he needed his friends now as he had never needed them ; and at the outset of his war-government his association with Wilberforce was almost as close and intimate as it had been at the outset of his peace-government nine years before. Nor was it only Wilberforce's earnest disinterested sympathy he valued, or his practical aid in counsel, though this he rated high. He recognized that Wilberforce was now a power in the country, that his opinion would have weight with all impartial Englishmen, and particularly with those religious-minded people who had been his most devoted followers in the Abolitionist crusade and amongst whom might be found the most dangerous, because the most impeccable, opponents of the war. Pitt strove, therefore, to win his old friend's mind as well as his heart. And since at first there was nothing in his conscience to forbid it, Wilberforce eagerly responded. A few months before the outbreak of war he had disclosed his golden opinion of Pitt to a friend who had sharply criticized his policy. ' Faults he has,' he had written, ' as who is free from them ? But I most solemnly assure you that I am convinced, if the flame of pure disinterested patriotism burns in any human bosom, it does in his. I am convinced, and that on long experience and close observation, that in order to benefit his country he would give up not situation merely and emolument, but what in his case is much more, personal credit and reputation, though he knew that no human being would ever become acquainted with the sacrifice he should have made. . . . Believe me, who am pretty well acquainted with our public men, that he has not his equal for integrity as well as ability in the *primores*

of either House of Parliament.' ' I am almost ashamed ',
he had added, ' of being drawn into this long panegyric,
but I will not burn it ; it is the language of the heart.'
It is easy to imagine, then, with what keen, serious pleasure
he resumed, at such a crisis in the country's history, his old
constant intercourse with its patriot leader, stood at his
side through the early disappointments of the war, shared
in his thoughts and discussed his plans—or those of them,
at least, which were not kept for Dundas's less sensitive
ears   The diary is full of it. ' To Holwood with Pitt in
his phaeton—early dinner and back to town '   ' Pitt's
birthday, 34 (May 28). .   . Dined Dundas' (with Pitt and
friends) and up too late.' ' To town to see Pitt—a great
map spread out before him.' ' Dined *tête-à-tête* with Pitt—
he disengaging himself to do so.' ' Slept at Pitt's—he very
kind.' ' Off to Holwood. Pitt and I *tête-à-tête*—he very
open and we discussed much.' ' Long political discussion
with Pitt on the King's speech '

The last-quoted entry is for January 18, 1794, and so
far their minds had moved as one. The Saint had become
as militant as the Statesman. ' House—Pitt uncommonly
fine on armed nation, etc ', says the diary for February 3.
But, as the year drew on, the harmony, daily scrutinized
and tested in the sanctuary of Wilberforce's conscience,
began sensibly to weaken. The cause of the Allies in
Europe went steadily from bad to worse. By the end of
the year they had evacuated Belgium ; and the French,
having occupied the whole of the left bank of the Rhine,
were overrunning Holland and forcing the States-General
to sue for peace. This unbroken record of failure made
a deep impression on Wilberforce   Clearly the war had
brought, seemed likely to bring, no tangible results. Was
it wise, then, for statesmen, was it right for Christians, to
persist in it ? For a time, however, the intimacy with Pitt
continued. In July Wilberforce is at Holwood and makes
the usual entry in the diary—' Dined *tête-à-tête* with Pitt,
and political discussion ' ; but in a letter to his old confidant,
Lord Muncaster, written before he left Pitt's house, he strikes
a new note. ' Pitt's speech ', he confesses, ' both from the

Treasury Bench and the Throne, was too pugnacious for me. It required our friend Hawkins Brown's nerves and warlike propensities to stand it. May God protect us ! ' By the autumn Wilberforce's peaceful propensities have hardened Writing again to Lord Muncaster in November, ' Little as one could hope ', he says, ' for a secure peace with such a set of fellows as the French Conventionalists . . I begin to think we can look for no good from the prosecution of the war ; and if so, it is time to stop for a while the ravages of that scourge of the human species.' Wilberforce was now well on to the diverging path ; and he was pushed a little farther down it, as it happened, by a Frenchman. Fugitives from France had been steadily trickling into England since the war began, and among them there arrived, that autumn, the Abbé de Lageard, who had shown such ' extraordinary humanity ' to the three young Englishmen in those far-off light-hearted days at Rheims Hunted for a year and a half through thirty Departments of France, he had slipped away at last from the guarded coast and, a pauper now and a pessimist, had found a refuge in London. His old acquaintances seized the opportunity of repaying his hospitality , they feasted him as he had feasted them ; they discussed the war with him and enlarged on the sea-power of Britain, on her reserves of strength, on the tenacity of her people But the weary exile shook his head ' Only the French ', he said, ' can conquer the French *Dieu vous garde, messieurs, d'une revolution.'*

There was another aspect of the war which confirmed the drift of Wilberforce's mind away from Pitt's. It was questioned at the time and it has been questioned ever since whether Pitt was right to lay so much stress on the acquisition of the French West Indies and to squander in those malarious islands British troops which might have been put to better use in Flanders. And, considering how many thousands of British lives were sacrificed and how little the loss of the islands affected the war-strength of France, the verdict has usually gone against him. But it is only fair to Pitt, and to Dundas, who was Pitt's chief prompter in the matter, to recognize how tempting the adventure must have seemed. Tropical 'sugar-islands' were regarded in those days as the richest plums of empire ; and if the French West Indies could be won and retained at the peace, it would deprive France of a great branch of her old commerce and reimburse Britain for the cost of the war And the winning of them, it seemed, would be an easy affair The position of the French colonists had gone from bad to worse since the first kindling of rebellion among the slaves of St Domingo. Undismayed by the results of its policy and affronted by the colonists' resolve to sever themselves from a motherland which persisted in such madness, the National Assembly had reasserted in 1792 the complete equality of all the freeborn inhabitants of the island, and had dispatched Commissioners to enforce its will. Two years later the logic of French radicalism was to go yet farther. In 1794 the Convention jumped the stage of abolishing the Slave Trade and abolished Slavery itself. At a stroke, throughout the French colonial empire, the slaves became free citizens. But if the new France could bestow the forms of Liberty and Equality on that unhappy mixed community which the old France had created, Fraternity, even in form, she could not give. The whites themselves, it has been seen, were divided from the outset ; and when the first Commissioners arrived in 1792, they did not scruple to use the blacks for the Jacobins against the Royalists. So St. Domingo remained an inferno of blood and fire. Already in 1791 and again in 1792 the Royalists had appealed to Pitt for the help which no one else could give them. But, though in the black days of the first slave rising the Governor of Jamaica had been allowed to provide them with arms and provisions, Pitt, rigidly bent as he was on peace and neutrality towards Revolutionary France, was bound to refuse any systematic or large-scale assistance, bound to ignore the desperate suggestion of annexation to the British Crown. But, when war had broken out, and when a firm offer was made on the colonists' behalf by so honest a man as Malouet, it was not easy to reject it, especially as the suppression of the insurgent blacks had now become highly desirable from the British point of view. For the rebels in St. Domingo were preaching Jacobinism throughout the Caribbean, slave-revolts were beginning to occur in British islands; and a general rising of the blacks against the whites seemed not unlikely unless British troops should intervene.

These arguments sufficed for Pitt and Dundas, but they did not suffice for Wilberforce Saracens are all alike to a Crusader, and a fanatical Abolitionist, his mind inflamed by grim anecdotes of slavery, might have ruthlessly argued that anything any planter suffered from any slave was in the nature of retribution. Now Wilberforce was no fanatic; he never forgot, indeed, to distinguish between good slave-masters and bad; and no one was more appalled than he at the horrors of the 'servile war' Yet it is natural to suppose that he was not altogether happy at the idea of using British troops against emancipated slaves And his antipathy to the West Indian 'side-show' went deeper than that. He did not want his country to acquire more sugar-islands, however valuable, for the simple reason that their acquisition and increased development by British settlers would create a new demand for slave-labour and heavily reinforce the case for an indefinite postponement of Abolition. It was a question, therefore, which touched the nerve-centres of his life As time went on, it deflected him from concentrating on the main issues of the war as much as, for opposite reasons, it deflected Pitt. The hatred of imperial expansion in that particular field became the nearest thing in his career to an *idée fixe*, till at last, in old age, he could seriously argue that British greed for sugar was the real cause of the war! 'I am myself persuaded', he wrote in 1828, 'that the war with France, which lasted so many years and occasioned such an enormous expense of blood and treasure, would never have taken place but for Mr Dundas's influence with Mr. Pitt and his persuasion that we should be able with ease and promptitude, at a small expense of money or men, to take the French West India Islands'

Once Wilberforce had come to a decision he felt bound to declare it publicly, though from the consequences of openly demanding peace from a Government still bent on war a smaller man might well have shrunk. War makes no allowances 'He who is not with us is against us' is its watchword. And the war-mind moves easily along the sequence of ideas from 'pacifist' to 'coward', 'defeatist', 'traitor'. It needed no little moral courage to pass from the warm friendship of 10 Downing Street out into the bleak frost of popular suspicion and abuse. 'Perhaps my differing from Pitt,' is Wilberforce's comment, 'by lessening my popularity and showing me my comparative insignificance, may not be bad for me in spiritual things.' But it was the personal breach that mattered most. To change from Pitt's intimate to something like his enemy! To work for his downfall? Even that might be his bitter duty. 'I would gladly get an end put to this war', he writes, 'without Pitt's being turned out of office, which will hardly be possible I fear, if it continue much longer.'

In the last six weeks of the year the decision was reached, 'cautiously and maturely'. 'Off at ten to Pitt's,' records the diary for November 19. 'Heard that Parliament would be prorogued until December 30, giving me time to make up my mind—strongly at present disposed to peace. . . . Threw out some hints of my state of mind, and accepted Pitt's invitation to dine.' On the 21st he met Pitt at dinner again, and on the 27th breakfasted with him to 'discuss politics'. That Pitt was clearly using all his powers of argument to win Wilberforce back is evident from an entry a few days later · 'At nine, Pitt's for political discussion till near one, and not bed till near two. Head and mind full, and could sleep but very distractedly.' But other influences were also brought to bear Christmas came with its special message ; and then, on the two following days, 'much political talk with Grant and Henry Thornton [two of his closest Evangelical allies], making up my mind.' On the 29th, at a dinner-party of friends—Duncombe, Muncaster, Henry Thornton, Bankes, and Montague—his course of action was agreed on On the 30th, after 'a disturbed night', in what he calls 'a very incoherent speech' he moved an amendment to the Address, declaring that it is 'advisable and expedient to endeavour to restore the blessings of peace upon just and reasonable terms ', but that, if such efforts should be ' rendered ineffectual by the violence and ambition of the enemy . . . the burdens and evils of a just and necessary war will be borne with cheerfulness by a loyal, affectionate and united people '.

The language of the Address, he argued, by its reference to ' that violent and unnatural system which is equally ruinous to France and incompatible with the tranquillity of other nations ', had suggested that we intended to prosecute the war until a counter-revolution had been effected. But was it feasible to impose a change of government by force on a high-spirited people ? A republic had now existed for some years in France , it had acquired a sort of stability ; there were no signs of disaffection to it in the army ; the royalist insurrections had been easily put down , and now that ' the furious and bloody tyranny of Robespierre ' was over, a ' somewhat milder ' system had been introduced If anything could bring about a counter-revolution, it was peace more likely than war Moreover, it was not so much to crush the Revolution that we had begun the war as to defend Britain from invasion by its evil principles ; and with the easy suppression of Jacobin agitation this danger had passed away The other object of the war had been the defence of our ally, Holland , but the Dutch were now on the point of making a separate peace. As to our other allies, ' it would be the extreme of dishonour to steal alone out of the general confederacy ', but Prussia, who was already giving us little active aid, and Austria, who could not go on fighting without our financial backing, were readier for peace than we were , and if the war continued, we should find ourselves alone. It was true, perhaps, that no secure or lasting peace could be attained. No trust could be put in the good faith of France. It would be necessary to maintain our forces in being on a costly scale. But war would be costlier still ; and cost was not war's only evil. Finally, it might be hoped that the French would also ' be glad of a little quiet ', and, however bitter their antagonism, would not be so hasty a second time to force a quarrel on their powerful neighbour.

It was harder for Pitt to answer Wilberforce's speech than to answer one of Fox's. It came from his own side of the House ; it was moderate in tone ; it was untainted by any suspicion of sympathy with the principles of the Revolution. But it had one weak point—its admission of the insecurity of any peace with the existing French Government. And on this Pitt fixed. He denied that the Address implied that we would never make peace with a French Republic , it simply meant that, till our resources were exhausted and all hope dead, we would never make peace without security. ' It had pleased inscrutable Providence that this power of France should triumph over everything that has been opposed to it. But let us not therefore fall without making any efforts to resist it ; let us not sink without measuring its strength ' What is to be gained by a temporary peace ? It would enable the Revolutionaries to strengthen a system of government, which, though Robespierre were dead, had not changed its principles nor abandoned its ambition of dominating Europe. It would give them a free hand to work their will on Holland. It would leave them in the possession of the Austrian Netherlands ; [1] and ' will my honourable friend say we ought to consent to that ? He will not say so.' Finally, it would dissolve for ever the Alliance of Europe. How could we hope to bring it back at our summons, when we had proclaimed our own weakness to the world ? When the war was resumed, we should be exposed alone to the fury of France The Alliance may have weakened, but what then ? If Holland falls, if Prussia withdraws, we must throw more British troops on to the Continent to fill the gap and hope for a diversion on the part of Italy and Spain. We can maintain, if not increase, our present efforts, but—and this is the main argument for fighting on—France cannot. Her incredible efforts have been financed by the confiscation of property and the issue of paper money. This system in turn has rested, could only rest, on fear. Now that the Terror is over, it must collapse. Let us carry on the war,

---

[1] Roughly equivalent to the modern Belgium, created in 1830

then, ' if not with the certainty of faith, yet at least with the confidence of expectation '

A resolute, but scarcely a cheering speech The majority voted down the amendment, as a matter of course, by 246 to 73, but they had received cold comfort ; and Wilberforce, voting uneasily with the Opposition, was unshaken. A month later, he repeated his case in the debate on Grey's motion in favour of opening peace-negotiations, and voted accordingly once more—in a minority of 86 to 269.*

III

It is said that only two public events in Pitt's life were so disturbing as to rob him of his sleep—the mutiny at the Nore in 1797 and Wilberforce's first open opposition. Strictly accurate or not, there is truth in the tradition Pitt's administration might be secure enough , but the defection of Wilberforce, notoriously disinterested and conscientious and in no man's eyes a fool, was a more serious blow to it than that of any other man in politics could have been. No one else could have given such a handle to his critics, so enhanced the daily strain of meeting the watchful, expert opposition of Fox and his Whig ' die-hards ' and the growing discontent in the country at a war which brought nothing but bad trade and unemployment and defeat. And the breach was more than political : it was personal. Only a Gallio, at such a moment, could have remained in intimate fellowship with the defaulter. So the lonely bachelor, who had found in Wilberforce some touch of spiritual kinship which he could rarely find in the obedient throng of hard-headed or second-rate men about him, became lonelier still And Wilberforce, on his part, was hit more hardly than by anything in his life before except the first pangs of his ' conversion ' or by anything after except family bereavement. He had foreseen that he would suffer, and suffer he

* *Life*, ii. 28-9, 45-7, 59-70, 391 *Hansard*, xxxi (1794)-5, 1016-27, 1230-8 *Pitt's War Speeches* (Oxford, 1915), 116-34 Fortescue, *British Statesmen of the Great War*, 94, 103-4 Rose, *Pitt*, ii, chap ix Stanhope and Gooch, *Life of Stanhope*, chap. viii.

did. Twenty-five years later the memory could still sting
him. ' No one ', he told a friend in 1820, ' who has not seen
a good deal of public life and felt how painful and difficult
it is to differ widely from those with whom you wish to
agree, can judge at what an expense of feeling such duties
are performed.' ' I felt queer, and all day out of spirits,'
confesses the diary for February 4 :- ' wrong, but hurt by
the idea of Pitt's alienation.' A week later comes this
poignant little entry : ' Party of *the old firm* at the Speaker's :
I not there '

He minded less the misconceptions and hostilities which
the very moderation of his policy aroused. Everybody
must be black or white in war-time, and he was grey. On
the main question of peace-negotiations he would vote
against the Government, but not on anything else if he
could help it. As long as the war continued, he would
support its measures for maintaining the British forces
abroad and keeping order at home. To most men such a
logical compromise seemed impracticable ; and at first the
Whigs were openly triumphant at the accession to their
resolute but small minority of so considerable a turncoat.
Fox was prompt to pay a friendly call ' You will soon
see ', he told Wilberforce, ' that you must join us altogether.'
But Fox was quite mistaken. Seven years later, in the
breathing-space of the Peace of Amiens, Wilberforce committed to paper, but not for publication, his opinions on
the ' hard and difficult case of a private member of Parliament in time of war and violent opposition ' with particular
reference to the circumstances ' in which our country was
placed during the last war '.

' There was an Opposition, able, vigilant, active, inveterate, powerful from their talents, formidable from their
principles, not very scrupulous in their means, and bitter
and uniform in their hostility, between whom and myself
there existed a difference not merely as to the mode of
prosecuting the war of which we all recognized the necessity,
but a fundamental difference as to the main principles not
only of political conduct but even of moral practice—in
whom I thought I saw (though neither in private nor in
public did I ever impute to them that they were not really

intending the good of the country, etc.), that prejudice and passion had so blinded them that they could see nothing to be apprehended in those principles and proceedings which appeared to me likely to sap the vitals of our country and to produce an explosion in which the whole fabric of our political and social edifice was likely to be buried in one common ruin. If by stating my doubts as to the wisdom of our counsels and the prudence of our measures, I should strengthen the cause of a party like that, how could I have made amends for the mischief I might have done, while, as before alleged, I could not have effected the purpose I had myself in view ? '

A few years later Wilberforce would have spoken in somewhat less alarmist terms of the radical proclivities of Fox and Sheridan and Grey ; but that was what he was thinking while he talked to Fox—very courteously and pleasantly, no doubt—on the occasion of that friendly call. And Fox soon had reason to abate his confidence. On January 5, 1795, less than a week after his ' pacifist ' amendment, at the end of the long and bitter debate on Sheridan's motion for the repeal of the recent Act suspending the right of *Habeas Corpus*, Wilberforce briefly stated his opinion that ' the hands of Government ought to be strengthened at such a time for the repression and punishment of faction ' ; his belief that ' Government had not abused the power committed to them ' ; and his intention to vote against the motion The significance of this little speech could not be missed Independent, Pittite-pacifist—whatever Wilberforce was—he was evidently not a Foxite

It seems curious, at first sight, that Wilberforce should have accepted so calmly the initial severities of Pitt's régime of repression Few gentlemen were democrats in those days, and he was assuredly not one of them. But the French Revolution had inspired no class-antagonism in him. He had none of Society's uneasy distaste for the ' lower orders ' He was constantly giving time and money privately to help the poor. There was no hidden streak of hardness in his nature. He was keenly sensitive to injustice. He could not be cruel. It has been seen, moreover, that though he hated Jacobinical doctrine and dreaded its influence on

English morals and religion—'God defend us from such poison', he exclaimed after reading Paine's *Age of Reason*—yet, until the black October of 1795, at any rate, he had no panic fears that the 'professors of liberty and equality' could sweep the country headlong into Revolution. Why then did he not protest against, why did he positively or tacitly accept the Government's harsh measures in 1793 and 1794? Did he approve the prosecution of the English Radicals? Did he tolerate Braxfield's grim mockery of justice in Scotland? From his public record, from what he said and left unsaid in Parliament, it would seem so. As to his private opinions, he speaks in the diary for December 19, 1794, of a 'conversation on the pending trials for high treason' at Pitt's and makes no comment—and that is all.

But the puzzle has its key. Something must be allowed for his confidence in Pitt, which, though the coming years were now and again to strain it, had by no means been destroyed by the difference of opinion on the war. Any action on his part, again, which might be publicly construed as sympathy with Jacobinism, could only be undertaken at the risk of far more serious damage to the cause he had most at heart than that already done by Clarkson's impulsive tongue. But probably the strongest motive for his acquiescence in Pitt's 'terrorism' lay in his understanding of the special responsibilities of public criticism under war-conditions. 'In war-time', he says in that private memorandum already quoted, 'often an honest man cannot [speak out], because he knows he will or may thereby do much public injury. Suppose him to see abuses. If by pointing them out he should, without procuring a reform of them, lessen, as far as his influence may extend, the estimation, attachment, and confidence which difficult times and times of war . . . render necessary to be had in Government, will he not be injuring the public interests?' And he enumerates particular abuses that might call for remedy—mismanagement and misconduct in the military and naval establishments, the need of parliamentary and municipal reform, 'corruption in our judicial system', and so forth. He is jotting down his thoughts on paper in this memorandum—

stating the difficulties, not solving them—laying down no
hard and fast rule ; but it is clear that he feels the difficulty
of opposition to be greater than the difficulty of acquiescence.
Thus, on the simpler problem of criticizing the actual conduct
of the war he has no hesitations at all. The honest man may
differ from Government as to the best measures and, if so,
he should state his alternative , but, that done, it only
remains for him, ' if he cannot procure the adoption of the
plan he would wish to see pursued, to endeavour to give
effect to that which is preferred to it—not to thwart, not
to impede, not to cripple '.

This line of conduct, while it made him useless to the
Opposition, did not palliate Wilberforce's defection on the
peace issue in the eyes of the war-party. It was, after all,
the supreme issue ; and the one lapse was enough to make
him abominably grey. The King gave the lead which Tory
society expected of him. He studiously cut Wilberforce at
the first *levée* he attended after moving his pacifist Amendment. Windham, as befitted a convert, let loose his bitter
tongue. ' Your friend, Mr Wilberforce,' he remarked to
Lady Spencer, ' will be very happy any morning to hand
your Ladyship to the guillotine.' Even Burke, so close
a brother-in-arms to Wilberforce in the cause of humanity
anywhere outside Europe but only living now on the
desperate longing to see the *ancien régime* triumphant over
a punished and humbled France, could not resist a sarcasm
' Mr. Wilberforce is a very respectable gentleman,' he said
to Pitt, ' but he is not the people of England.' Naturally
the country at large was no more tolerant than Burke, and
faithful Yorkshire was dismayed and angry   In the summer
of 1795, when the worst of the storm was over and Wilberforce toured the county in order to explain his conduct
and re-establish his popularity, he found the fires of resentment still smouldering   Women in politics are apt to be
more outspoken or less easygoing than men ; and there
were women in Yorkshire who were determined that the
refractory county-member should know what they thought
of him.   ' In one family of my most zealous partisans ', he
records, ' the ladies would scarcely speak to me.'   At

another house, while 'the coldness of the others seemed to give way by my being quite unaffected and undiscerning', the hostess refused to come downstairs

And if acquaintances were cold, friends were puzzled and disquieted. One of his most constant correspondents, Mr. Hey, wrote vigorous expostulations Dr Burgh, an old and tried adviser, told him frankly that 'above all evils he most deprecated a peace, in whatever form the present moment could obtain it'. 'Faction begins to claim you', he wrote; 'you are quoted and are growing into the subject of a panegyric. It is of infinite importance that you should not appear to the country as a leader of opposition. . . . Strange as it may sound, it is not so much the war that is in the mind of many of its supporters as the individual person of Mr. Pitt Though they like not his new connexions, yet still they attach themselves to him and do not love to see him opposed.' And no one was more anxious than Dean Milner As soon as he heard at Carlisle the news of Wilberforce's forthcoming Amendment he wrote an appealing letter, and another was soon posting at its heels. 'I do not perceive', he says in the first, 'the nature of the opposition to Pitt which you are likely to make Weigh it well, my dear friend. I hope you will not prove a dupe to the dishonest Opposition who will be glad to make use of you in hunting down Pitt and for no other purpose' The second letter is written when the report of the debate has told him all. 'I can truly say', he groans, 'I never was so much concerned about politics in my life, I was quite low, and so I continue . . I never conceived that you had intended to take so decided a part in this business as to lead the opposition against Pitt.' A few days later the loyal friend is at Cambridge, putting up an eloquent defence of Wilberforce in hostile combination-rooms.

It was a black, lonely time for Wilberforce. Solace indeed he could find and comradeship, in privacy, on his knees. But, little as he loved promiscuous society, he had none of the anchorite's self-sufficiency. The daily sitting in the House of Commons had lost half its fascination with Pitt there, so cold and far away. And, however congenial the company of his less political associates, the thought would come and come again that, in Downing Street or at Holwood, the ' old firm ' were gathered and he was not there.*

IV

Wilberforce's ordeal of isolation was happily short. In fact, the breach with Pitt had hardly opened before it began to close, for the simple reason that Pitt became gradually converted, as the year 1795 drew on, to the desirability of negotiating for peace. Presently, therefore, the broken threads could be tied up again, rather clumsily and comically, as befitted Englishmen   Pitt was shy and stiff, Wilberforce self-conscious and diffident. The diary for March 21 records their first meeting at a dinner-party—' 1 think both meaning to be kind to each other—both a little embarrassed ' Then, on April 15 ' Called at Pitt's the first time since the beginning of the session—he having the gout.' And on April 25 this quaintly typical entry · ' Called Eliot's, knowing that Pitt was there, and that Pitt knew I knew it, and thinking, therefore, that it would seem unkind not to do it.' But there was soon no need for these awkwardnesses and hesitations. Their relations responded like a barometer to the steady rise of Pitt's pacifism.   ' All Pitt's supporters ', says the diary for May 2, ' believe him disposed to make peace ' A few days later the mischievous Thurlow—still snarling at his expulsion three years earlier from the Woolsack and seeking to damage Pitt in the eyes of his more warlike followers by hinting that he has been in secret agreement with Wilberforce all along—lays a bet for five guineas with the Dukes of Leeds and Bedford that Pitt will vote with Wilberforce when the latter moves the next peace-resolution.   And certainly the Dukes might well have hesitated to take the bet if they could have overlooked the garden of Eliot's house at Battersea on the afternoon of May 12, and seen the two men, whose sharp estrangement was so recent and so

* *Life*, ii. 72–80, 102, 431–7 *Farington Diary* (London, 1923) i. 85

notorious, with Ehot and Ryder, ' walking, foining, laughing, and reading verses, as before '

There was indeed some substance in Thurlow's jibes. If Pitt was not prepared for some months yet to move publicly for peace himself, he was no longer unwilling, much less aggrieved, that Wilberforce should do so. Events seemed steadily to be proving him the better prophet of the two Prussia made her selfish peace. Holland, under her new masters, declared war on her old ally. The British troops evacuated Flanders. The French consolidated their hold on Belgium, and in the autumn annexed it finally to France. The ' First of June ' and the capture of Corsica, Martinique, St. Lucia, Ceylon, and the Cape of Good Hope were inadequate off-sets to the enemy's triumph on land. And Pitt's chief hope—the collapse of the French finances— seemed as far from fulfilment as ever Moreover, the reaction of the Moderates against the Terror was proving lasting and substantial. The Convention recovered its old authority. The leading Terrorists were executed or exiled. And, in the autumn, when young Bonaparte had whiffed away the feeble royalist rising in Paris, with his grape-shot, the new constitution of the *Directoire*, with its bicameral legislatine, was successfully established. It looked, indeed, as if Revolutionary France had at last put her house in order , and it became increasingly more difficult to plead that peace with security was unattainable. Finally, the serious dearth of corn and the growing destitution and discontent on this side of the Channel became daily stronger arguments for peace than they had been at the beginning of the year. But these developments were gradual, and Pitt was no hastier than Wilberforce in making up his mind. Its doors, however, were open to the idea of peace from the spring of 1795 onwards ; and it seemed not only harmless now, but positively advantageous, that Wilberforce should fly his kite. So, although Pitt declared in the House on May 27 that we must fight on a little longer ' and lamented and deplored ' Wilberforce's motion in favour of an honourable peace, he had actually discussed it with its author a day or two before the debate. ' I had shown my motion to Pitt on Saturday—he very kind now and good-natured ; he wrung from me to show it to others ; so I showed it to Grey and Fox '—a backstairs proceeding which Thurlow would doubtless have given his ears to ferret out. Pitt's colleagues, however, were not quite so ready as Pitt himself to make it up with the defaulter , and when he called at Downing Street to settle the time for his motion and found Grenville and Dundas there, he noted that while Pitt again was ' very kind ', Grenville was ' shy ' and Dundas ' sour '. And Windham was too passionately imbued with the anti-Jacobinism of his master, Burke, to follow Pitt's lead as to peace or the men who preached it. In his reply to Wilberforce's motion he derided his illusions and mocked bitterly at the ' Christian conscience ' of one who lauds his friend's ability to the skies and, in the same breath, is not too humble to oppose that friend's policy and to suggest that he could govern the country better himself. ' Too much hurt by Windham's personalities,' the diary confesses, not unnaturally perhaps. But there is balm now in Gilead Once more, like a refrain, come the salving words—' Pitt kind '.

The summer passed, and nothing happened to check the reviving harmony In the autumn Pitt showed how nearly he had reached a decision to try for peace by making advances to Wilberforce for the renewal of their interrupted habit of constant political discussion On October 24, twenty days after the monarchist fiasco of *Vendémiaire*, he wrote to urge him to come to London a few days before the opening of the session ' I cannot help being more anxious for this,' he says, ' as I think our talking over the present state of things may do a great deal of good, and I am sure at all events it can do no harm. It is hardly possible to form any precise opinion as to what is to be done, till we see the immediate issue of the crisis just now depending, but I cannot help thinking that it will shortly lead to a state of things in which I hope our opinions cannot materially differ. I need not say how much personal comfort it will give me if my expectation in this respect is realized Yours sincerely and affectionately, W. Pitt.'

Between the lines of this guarded letter Wilberforce read all he most longed for. He hurried to town, breakfasted with Pitt, and ' had a most satisfactory conversation with him '. Two days later he repeats ' another confidential and satisfactory conversation '. The fruits of this cabal were visible to all the world when Parliament met on October 29. The King's Speech declared that, if the termination of the constitutional crisis in France should be such as to afford ' a reasonable expectation of security and permanence in any treaty which might be concluded ', Britain would be prepared to reciprocate a disposition on the part of France towards a just peace. On December 8, the Directory being now firmly in the saddle, these overtures were renewed, and next day Pitt reaffirmed his willingness to treat with the Republican Government.

Meantime the renewed *entente* had been cemented by Wilberforce's stalwart support of Government at one of the two moments during the war when the tide of internal discontent rose nearest to actual danger-point. The crowds that clamoured for peace in the autumn of 1795 were no more Jacobin in spirit and motive than those that cheered the Radical demagogues in 1793 They wanted a more immediate necessity than Revolution ; they wanted bread. The bad harvest of the previous year had been followed by a peculiarly cold summer which blighted the corn and killed the shorn sheep , and heavy storms of rain in August increased the loss So, while unemployment was as rife as ever, the food-shortage became more serious In the middle of the summer a mob of hungry men at Birmingham was dispersed by the military, not without bloodshed. ' Are we to be starved to death ? ' they had shouted. ' War and Want or Peace and Plenty ' were the catchwords of a crowd in St George's Fields in July And all over the country the suffering poor grew more and more resentful at a war which brought such hardships and which, till Napoleon roused the instinct of self-defence, they never understood or cared about, and more and more exasperated with a Government which gave them neither victory nor peace. In July the windows of Pitt's house in Downing Street

were broken by an angry mob. But it was not till the autumn
that the unrest became seriously alarming. On October 27
a vast meeting was held at Islington under the auspices of
the London Corresponding Society   Nearly 150,000 people,
it was said, attended it ; and those of them at least who were
within earshot of the platform accepted a resolution declaring
that they were ready to take up arms, if need be, for peace
and constitutional reform. The circulation in London of
a leaflet on ' King-killing ' was less positively dangerous ;
but it gave a sinister colour to the unprecedented scene on
October 29 when George III drove to Westminster to open
Parliament through the hoots and hisses of the great crowd
that packed the Mall ' Peace ', ' Bread ', ' No Pitt ', ' No
Famine ', they yelled. The stage coach was struck by
a stone, and a pebble or some other small missile pierced the
window. On the way back to St. James's the curses and
threats were redoubled. The Guards could scarcely hold
the people back ; and when the King had entered the
palace, they wreaked their fury on his empty coach. It was
as well that the mob, in this mood, saw nothing of Pitt.
Certainly it was an ugly affair. The King had been shouted
at before, notably by a ' No Popery ' crowd on the occasion
of the passing of the famous Quebec Act in 1774 ; but never
had such bitter and violent animosity been displayed. And
coming in such close conjunction with the Islington meeting,
if it gave no solid reason for panic, it at least gave some
excuse. George III himself behaved throughout with
admirable *sang-froid* ; but Parliament and Society were
shocked and frightened, and two severe measures of repression, the Treasonable Practices Bill and the Seditious
Meetings Bill, were hurriedly framed and passed.

These Acts were unquestionably effective. There were
no more monster meetings, no more riots—a fact which
class-warriors like Lord Malmesbury regretted, now that
Government was so well armed for their repression   Reformers could only meet now in numbers that would fill
a small room   One or two leading spirits were arrested.
The Corresponding Society wilted away. Indeed the Acts
were too effective, since, continuing in force when any real

danger had passed over, they could be used, and were used, to keep the poor in sullen silence, to prevent the escape of much honest Reform steam, and to suppress the legitimate efforts of the workers to combine not against their country but against the taskmasters of the new and primitive industrial system   None the less, Pitt's violation of the British heritage of personal freedom may well have been justified at the time the Acts were passed.   It is for the hardened controversialist to say for certain they were not.

Wilberforce, at any rate, had no doubt whatever about the Acts   It was not now merely his enthusiasm for Pitt nor his shrinking from opposition in war-time that led him to support the Government   He had forgotten his cool reckoning of the invincible sobriety of ' every man of property in the kingdom '.   He was alarmed—as much alarmed as any member of the Government.   There is an anxious note in the diary on ' papers dispersed against property ' and ' prints of guillotining the King and others '   And when Pitt introduced the Bills in the House on November 10, Wilberforce showed once more the gulf that lay between his political temperament and Fox's.   Amid Tory cheers he declared that Parliament, not those newfangled clubs and assemblies, was the custodian of British freedom ; that in the right of petition—which, not forgetting the Abolitionist crusade of 1792, he insisted must be left inviolate— lay the only legitimate and effective safety-valve for popular grievances ; and that the Bills should, therefore, be regarded ' as a temporary sacrifice by which the blessings of liberty may be transmitted to our children unimpaired '   Next day he was closeted with Pitt at No   10 over the draft of the Seditious Meetings Bill—' altered it much for the better by enlarging '.   And the day after, he attended a further meeting ' at Pitt's about the Sedition Bill—after which supped with him and Mornington '   ' Never was a time ', he comments, ' when so loudly called on to prepare for the worst.'   And, a little later, comes a note of personal anxiety —a note which, be it remarked, would never have been sounded elsewhere than in the privacy of a deliberately introspective and candid diary   ' The people, I hear, are much exasperated against me. . . . I greatly fear some civil war or embroilment , and with my weak health and bodily infirmities, my heart shrinks from its difficulties and dangers ' Strange as it seems to us who know the quiet sequel, Pitt shared in these alarms. ' My head would be off in six weeks ', he said to Wilberforce at this time, ' were I to resign.'

It was in this almost Parisian atmosphere that a summons came to Wilberforce to face what seemed—groundlessly, perhaps, but none the less substantially at the time—a personal danger Yorkshire, it was reported, was up in arms against coercion. ' The Bills ', wrote Dr. Burgh, ' are obnoxious in this part of the world to an extreme degree.' The opposition party, determined to make its protest heard before the Bills became law, requested the High Sheriff, Mr. Mark Sykes, to call a county-meeting, and, on his refusing for fear that it would cause a riot, it hurriedly organized a private meeting of its own. ' Come forth in the spirit of your ancestors ', ran Wyvill's stirring appeal, ' and show you deserve to be free ! ' Wilberforce had already written to his friend, Hey, deploring the High Sheriff's timidity and asking for prompt news of further developments ' I shall ride at single anchor ', he said, ' ready to sail at a moment's warning.' The warning came as he was setting out to church one Sunday morning. It gave him little time, for it told him that the opposition meeting had been fixed for Tuesday. Sending his carriage to be prepared for the journey, he attended the service—he noticed that Sir George Shuckburgh ' talked ', and thought it a ' sad sermon '—then hurried off to Pitt, whom he found ' much disquieted ', and since Pitt's carriage was ready for instant use, he accepted his offer of it and, by half-past two, was off on the Great North Road, behind four horses, his secretary beside him. ' Almost the whole of Monday ', says the latter, ' was spent in dictating , and between his own manuscripts and the pamphlets which had followed him, we were almost up to our knees in papers.' If Wilberforce had not been so busy with his speech, his reflections might have been disquieting. ' If he ventured down ', he had been told by

Yorkshire friends, ' it would be at the hazard of his life.'
And one of the party at No 10 had cheered him on his way
by suggesting he would certainly be murdered ' if they find
out whose carriage you have got '. Meantime the mile-
stones were passing. He reached Doncaster on Monday
night and early next morning set out for York

A multitude of Yorkshiremen were converging on the
same point. All Monday the roads to York were thronged.
Over 3,000 horsemen were counted passing through Halton
turnpike alone. Many spent the night by the roadside ;
and next day they still came trooping in   The whole
county, it seemed, was going to be there ; and the High
Sheriff and all those responsible for the maintenance of
order grew hourly more anxious as the crowd within the
city gates increased and no one knew to which faction the
great mass belonged. But the friends of the Government
had not been idle , and when, on the Tuesday morning, the
two forces drew apart into separate camps, it was clear that
the ' Loyalists ' were more numerous than the ' Reformers '.
Some of the former gathered in the Castle Yard, the usual
place for a large-scale public meeting. Others forced their
way into the Guildhall where the meeting of protest was to
be held ; and a somewhat disorderly discussion was in
progress there, when suddenly, above the general tumult,
a great roar of cheering was heard outside the building
A chariot and four was slowly making its way along the
street   The crowd was yelling itself hoarse. The air was thick
with hats. Wilberforce, whom almost every one believed
to be in London, had arrived. ' What a row I made ',
he said to his son as they entered York by the same road
thirty-two years later, ' when I turned this corner in 1795. It
seemed as if the whole place must come down together '

Making his way through the throng in the Guildhall and
mounting the platform, Wilberforce entreated his old ally,
Wyvill, to bring his minority to the Castle Yard for a joint
discussion. ' He hoped ', he said, ' to have met his opponents that day face to face and convinced them of the
feebleness of their prejudices ' But Wyvill and his followers
refused to move ; and Wilberforce withdrew without them

to the Castle Yard. The crowd that packed itself round him as he stood on the old stone steps was over 4,000 strong, ' perhaps the largest assemblage ', said the local newspaper, ' of gentlemen and freeholders which ever met in Yorkshire '. His speech was brief ' I should have said much more ', he told Hey, ' if we had got into debate.' But it was enough to win once again the popular triumph which the ' shrimp ' had won on the same spot ten years before. ' A most incomparable speech indeed ', said one of his listeners. ' I never saw you but once ', wrote another, fifteen years afterwards, ' and that day you won my heart and every honest heart in the country. You made my blood tingle with delight ' To the malcontents who had stayed in the Guildhall the speaker might not have seemed so eloquent ; but there were still many doubters in his audience who doubted no more when he had done There was only one discordant incident and that in the vein of burlesque rather than of serious politics An officer stood up in full uniform—' that mad fellow, Colonel Thornton ',[1] said the chairman—informed the crowd that ' many of the soldiers were ready to join them whenever they should rise ', and then, ' after throwing off his regimentals to the rabble ', was borne away in a chair to the Guildhall. The supporters of the Government were thus left in possession of the field even more completely than before, and an address and a petition against seditious meetings and in favour of the King and Constitution were carried with scarcely a dissentient voice.

The lead thus given at York was promptly followed by the West Riding as a whole Bells were set ringing, exuberant meetings held, petitions signed in all the big towns And, according to Wyvill, it was Wilberforce's personal intervention which had turned the current of opinion. ' Many who, to my personal knowledge, came decidedly hostile to the Bills ', wrote Dr Coulthurst, ' were induced, on hearing your speech, to sign the address and petition. You have gained over almost every man in the

[1] Thomas Thornton, colonel of the West Riding Militia : see his life in *D N B*

five great commercial towns of the West Riding.' And one of the leading merchants in Leeds bore witness to the same effect Yorkshire's lead, moreover, was followed in turn by other counties, ' proving ', said Wilberforce, ' the justice of what Fox would often say—" Yorkshire and Middlesex between them make all England " '

There is, no doubt, a note of exaggeration in the mutual congratulations of the ' loyalists ', but there was enough at least in what had happened to dissipate Pitt's worst anxieties. Clearly the electorate had not been irrevocably estranged by his measures of repression. Clearly the country had not reached the brink of Revolution. November had been darkened by the shadow of the guillotine ; in December it was gone It was with real gratitude, therefore, that he welcomed the traveller back to London. That their fears had proved groundless detracted nothing from the instant courage with which Wilberforce had set out to face the unknown in the North. And whether or not its actual effects were as decisive as they seemed to some, he had dealt a great stroke for the Government. The personal reunion had been sealed and crowned.*

V

The effort and excitement of the Yorkshire adventure had proved somewhat exhausting. ' The last fortnight or three weeks ', writes Wilberforce on December 19, ' have been severe trials to a man weakly like me, and I have lost ground in health which I must recover ' But this Christmas was far more cheerful than the last. The clouds of popular disfavour had blown away. Society smiled once more on the intrepid champion of law and order. Majesty no longer turned its back. The King, indeed, so far unbent at the *levée* as to discuss with Wilberforce a current theological disputation between Gisborne and Paley. But the renewed note of happiness in the daily record of his life has little to

* *Life*, ii. 85–133 *Hansard*, xxxii (1795–7), 1–36, 292–5, 30 [.
Pitt's War Speeches, 137 Holland Rose, ii, chap xiii.

do with Society or the Court. The vital entries are those which tell of Pitt—how ‘very friendly’ he is now ; how ‘ very affectionately’ he accosts him when he calls , how they dine alone together and have ‘ long discussions about politics and people’ ; how he stays at Holwood and goes for country walks with his host ; above all, how ‘ very kind, open and fair ’ he is ‘ about peace, and I think wise too ’.

On this cardinal issue, indeed, they could not quarrel now. During the next two years, while the course of the war abroad and the distress and discontent at home went steadily from bad to worse, Pitt was anything but bellicose ; and in the spring of 1796 he made the first of a series of overtures for peace. Informal negotiations were set on foot at Basle ; but they soon broke down because the Directory demanded that France should retain all she had won in Europe while Britain surrendered all she had won elsewhere. By the autumn the situation was still less promising. Bonaparte’s astonishing career of victory had begun and the Austrians were fast being driven out of Italy. In October Spain, with her considerable fleet, entered the war on the side of France. So far from contemplating peace, the Directory were now proclaiming their intention of invading England. To many of Pitt’s supporters, to Windham and the ‘ Portland Whigs ’ who had joined forces with him in 1794, and of course to all the stubborn Royalists like Burke, this new provocation was a summons to fight on. But there was no such militant ardour among the people at large. Wilberforce’s correspondents in the country all told the same tale. ‘ My good Wilberforce ’, wrote Henry Duncombe, ‘ pray make Pitt conclude a peace , the country is quite tired of fine speeches ’ Moved by these appeals and by his own convictions, Wilberforce, who was spending August and September in industrious retirement at Buxton, determined to see Pitt , and, cutting short his ‘ holiday ’, he drove up to town and on to Holwood ‘ Full talk of all politics ’, he records · ‘ pleased with my interview on the whole.’

Pitt, indeed, needed no pressing towards peace. He had decided to make another effort, though the terms must now be hard for Britain if France were to be persuaded to accept them In October Lord Malmesbury made his slow journey over the neglected roads to Paris—' No wonder it was slow ', sneered Burke, ' for he went all the way on his knees '—with authority to offer the return of most of Britain's acquisitions overseas if France would only restore the conquests she had made from Austria in Europe. But he was soon back without a treaty in his pocket. The Directory had utterly refused to consider the severance of Belgium from France which Pitt, like every British states-man before him, regarded as essential to the balance and stability of the European system There was nothing for it, therefore, but to carry on the measures already begun for strengthening the forces in England for defence against invasion. And Wilberforce was fully as convinced as Pitt that, for the moment at any rate, peace was unattainable. In the debates on the Militia and Cavalry Bills and on the subsidy to Austria he vigorously supported the Govern-ment, and on one occasion, exasperated by what seemed to him the almost criminal factiousness of the Opposition, he let himself go ' I will not charge them ', he said, ' with desiring an invasion, but I cannot help thinking that they would rejoice to see just as much mischief befall their country as would bring themselves into office.' Sheridan at once replied with a bitter protest against Wilberforce's ' malice ', and ' insults ', and ' cant ', and a violent counter-attack on ministers ' begrimed and black with infamy '. But the chief object of Wilberforce's insults was a bigger man than Sheridan. Next day the diary admits a fear lest the speech ' had gone too far.   . But Fox very good-natured '.

With the New Year the gloom thickened Britain could hold her own at sea against the four next strongest naval powers in Europe. St. Lucia (for the second time) and Demerara had been captured in 1796, and now in February, 1797, came Jervis's defeat of the Spanish fleet off Cape St. Vincent with its first great example of the ' Nelson touch '. But, though the mistress of the seas might still defy invasion, it was clear that she would soon be left without a friend or foothold on the Continent ; for Austria was evidently weakening under Bonaparte's continued blows in Italy. Meantime a far graver domestic crisis was gathering to a head than the crisis of November 1795   Its prelude was a sudden and startling shock to the old prim self-confidence of the British business-world. ' This morning ', writes Wilberforce on February 26, ' Eliot came in and told me of the Bank going to stop payment to-morrow.' ' It disturbed my sleep at night ', he adds—and no wonder, for the suspension of cash-payments at the Bank of England by order of the Government seemed to herald a general financial crash. ' Anxious about great event ', notes Wilberforce next day   ' Went to General [Pitt's sobriquet among his closer followers]. . Letter from Lord Carrington stating that all going on well and stocks rising. They seemed cheerful and gay.' Ten days later Wilberforce was appointed on the Parliamentary Committee which took possession of the Bank and inquired into its solvency.

The financial danger soon passed off, but there was worse to come. On the morning of April 17 Wilberforce, who had gone down to Bath, was visited by Hannah More's sister, Patty, who brought with her a letter she had just received from Captain Bedford of the *Royal Sovereign* at Portsmouth. It contained the news of the mutiny in the fleet at Spithead. Since Burke was also at Bath, Wilberforce hurried off to his lodgings   It was, as it happened, their last meeting , for Burke's fatal illness was now within a few weeks of its end. ' The whole scene is now before me ', wrote Wilberforce some time after. ' Burke was lying on a sofa, much emaciated , and Windham, Lawrence, and some other friends were round him   The attention shown to Burke by all that party was just like the treatment of Ahitophel of old. It was as if one went to inquire of the oracle of the Lord   I repeated to them the account I had received, and, Burke being satisfied of its authority, we held a consultation on the proper course for Government to follow Windham set off to London the same night with the result of our deliberations '. Burke's advice, continues Wilberforce, was much the same as Sir Charles Middleton's when he was told on a previous occasion that a ship had mutinied. 'You know how ill I think these poor fellows have been used', he had said, 'but . . . you must order a 90-gun ship on each side of her and sink her on the spot if she does not at once submit.' In this case no such measures were practicable, for the whole fleet was soon flying the red flag. By reasonable concessions, however, to the sailors' reasonable grievances and by the personal intervention of the popular old admiral, Lord Howe, discipline was ultimately restored without bloodshed. But, meanwhile, a more dangerous mutiny—more dangerous because more seditious in its origin and better led—broke out in the fleet at the Nore. And that was not all. At the moment when England's 'wooden walls' had ceased to protect the country from invasion, there was trouble among the troops quartered in London On May 13 Wilberforce received an urgent message from Pitt and a personal call from Windham, Secretary at War. One of the fomenters of disorder, it appeared, was a certain Williams, an Anglican parson who, having drunk himself into destitution, had become one of the many recipients of Wilberforce's private charity. But 'wicked Williams', as he was popularly called, had proved irreclaimable ; and Wilberforce at last had written to tell him to expect no further aid. Whether from sheer malice or from incipient insanity he had taken this letter to various barracks, read out from it a warm expression of sympathy with the soldiers' discontents and a promise to bring their case before the House of Commons, and then showed Wilberforce's signature to confirm what he had read. On hearing this queer story, Wilberforce wrote to Pitt, recommending that Williams should be closely watched and that, since, it seemed, he had already confessed contrition to Windham, he might perhaps prove useful in Government service 'I dare say he is hungry', wrote the Saint. The absurd incident was soon closed, but not before the gossips had buzzed it about London that the Abolitionist fanatic had been trying to excite a mutiny. A day or two later the diary records yet another alarm : 'Pitt awaked by Woolwich artillery riot, and went out to Cabinet.' There were rumours abroad, too, that even the Guards were planning a revolt. But by midsummer this perilous fit of distemper in army and navy alike had run its course and Pitt was relieved of the worst strain he ever had to face.

To Pitt and Wilberforce, though not to Windham and the war-party, these grave internal troubles seemed to strengthen the case for peace. At the time of the Bank crisis Wilberforce had pressed for the reopening of negotiations. ' Called at Pitt's ', says the diary for March 31 ; ' a most earnest conversation about peace, and degree in which I may fairly differ from Ministry about it. Pitt exceedingly moved.' But after the mutinies Pitt needed no pressing. It was not indeed to be expected that the French Government would prove more accommodating now than in the previous autumn Camperdown had followed St. Vincent. Trinidad had been added to Britain's island captures. But there was heavier weight in the other scale. Bonaparte's magic soldiership in Italy had achieved its certain goal. Already in April peace-preliminaries between France and Austria had been discussed at Leoben ; and the cynical bargain of Campo Formio was about to be concluded, leaving Belgium firmly in the grip of France, and Britain alone without an ally. Nevertheless, since the French, it was rumoured, were growing tired of the war despite its triumphs, it was worth while to make one more attempt at peace. But the terms Malmesbury offered, when he crossed to France for the second time in July, were bound to be humiliating terms for Britain. If Austria were willing to leave her Netherlands in the grip of France, Britain would no longer insist on their release : and while France might retain her new frontiers, Britain would give up all her acquisitions except the Cape and Trinidad—Ceylon being set aside for exchange. And even as to this residue of British conquests Pitt was prepared in the last extremity to yield. It was a fine offer for France. Pitt had only wrung it from his Cabinet after two stormy meetings, with Grenville, Windham, Portland, and Spencer against him and the King behind them in the background. And yet it was rejected—though not by France. The majority of French-

men, both in the legislature and in the country, belonged to
the moderate or 'constitutional' party; and their representatives were on the point of coming to terms with
Malmesbury when the minority or Jacobin party, inspired
and directed by Bonaparte, 'purged' the Directorate by
the *coup d'état* of *Fructidor* and plunged France into a new
phase of terrorism at home and a new period of aggressive
and unceasing war abroad   Before long the whole situation
had been changed : the French Revolution had reached its
transforming climax in the virtual absolutism of Napoleon ;
and Britain was fighting not only for the general liberties
of Europe, but for her own existence as an independent
state *

VI

Meantime the question of the Slave Trade had inevitably
fallen far into the background   From the moment war broke
out, Englishmen had interests and troubles to think about
nearer home than the Guinea Coast and Mid-Atlantic.
Moreover, the actual rupture with Jacobin France at once
sharpened and concentrated the vague suspicions and
antagonisms that had begun to cloud the field of liberal and
humane ideals   Already, therefore, in 1793 public opinion
in the country as a whole had become as cool towards the
Abolitionist cause as Parliament had been in 1792. From
the reports that reached Wilberforce it might well have
been difficult to believe that the great petition movement of
the previous year had ever taken place   ' I do not imagine ',
wrote a Yorkshire correspondent, ' that we could meet with
twenty persons in Hull at present who would sign a petition,
that are not Republicans. People connect democratical
principles with the Abolition of the Slave Trade, and will
not hear it mentioned.' It was the same story in Norfolk.
In Suffolk it was said that ' a damp and odium ' had fallen
on the idea of ' collective applications '. So Parliament was
no longer out of harmony with popular opinion when it

* *Life*, ii 136-96, 211-20   *Hansard*, xxxii (1795-7), 1232-6.

continued the solemn business of killing Abolition by delay.

On February 26 Wilberforce proposed that the House should go into Committee on the Slave Trade in a few days' time   The attendance was thin ; and though a similar resolution had been carried in the previous year and though Fox and Pitt both warmly supported Wilberforce as before, the motion was lost by 61 to 53 and an amendment, postponing the question for six months, was carried.   Undaunted by this rebuff, Wilberforce determined that, if no progress could be effected with wholesale Abolition, at least some effort should be made to destroy that part of the Trade which had nothing to do with the British colonies.   On May 14, accordingly, he moved, and carried by seven votes, a motion for leave to introduce a Bill to suppress the British trade in slaves with foreign territories , and the Bill actually passed its first and second readings.   But it got no farther. The debate on the third reading was only attended by the few who, for different reasons, retained a lively interest in the question.   Hansard dismisses it in a sentence.   Pitt and Fox, it is elsewhere reported, were eloquent once more, and Warren Hastings's old enemy, Francis, made one of his able speeches.   Sixty members sat out the debate, and rejected the Bill by 31 to 29.

The House of Lords, it will be remembered, was supposed in the meantime to be examining witnesses with a view to considering the resolution passed by the House of Commons in 1792—that the Slave Trade should be abolished in 1796. They had made no further progress with this task in the session of 1793, when, on April 11, the anti-Abolitionists made a vigorous effort to strangle the question for good and all.   The Earl of Abingdon led off with a remarkable speech. He began with a fierce attack on the people of France, ' monsters in human shape ', ' wolves and monkeys ' as Voltaire had rightly called them, from whom proceeded, as from Pandora's box, ' all the evils and vices that human nature or the world can be inflicted with.'   ' Better were it for us that we were created toads to live on the fumes of a dunghill ' rather than endure the fruits of their philosophy.

' And what does the Abolition of the Slave Trade mean more or less in effect than Liberty and Equality ? What more or less than the Rights of Man ? And what is Liberty and Equality and what the Rights of Man but the foolish fundamental principles of this new philosophy ? ' The Abolitionist agitation proves in fact, that ' we too have in this country our Condorcets, our Brissots, our Abbé Grégoires, and our Robespierres '. And then, with a fierce jibe at Dr. Priestley's levelling (and Unitarian) teaching to his levelling (and dissenting) flock, the noble naturalist adds one more specimen to his Zoo. It means, he says, that ' all being equal, blacks and whites, French and English, wolves and lambs, shall, "merry companions every one", promiscuously pig together, engendering a new species of man as the product of this new philosophy, a nondescript in the order of human beings '. Finally, he swept aside the noxious bundle of petitions What was the ground of them ? Humanity ! ' But humanity is no ground for petitioning Humanity is a private feeling and not a public principle to act upon. It is a case of conscience, not of constitutional right And if petitions are to be admitted for conscience' sake, why not petition to alter the liturgy of the Church of England and to change the established religion of the country ? ' These petitions ' are consequently illegal, and being illegal, ought not to have been received, but, being received, ought wholly to be disregarded '. With this strenuous logic his lordship moved the postponement of the question for five months. He was seconded by the Duke of Clarence who breezily abused the Abolitionists, dead or alive. Mr. Ramsay, he declared, was ' one of the most tyrannical men who ever governed a plantation ', and as to the present promoters of Abolition, ' they are either fanatics or hypocrites, and in one of those classes I rank Mr. Wilberforce.' The Duke, and the Earl before him, had gone a little too far. It was more than the House could stomach. When Grenville, very grave in word and manner, protested against the attack on Wilberforce, there was general applause , and the Duke at once responded with a frank apology. ' He respected that gentleman's very high

character and certainly meant no personal or political
insult.' And Lord Abingdon, aware that the feeling was
against him, accepted Lord Mansfield's suggestion that he
should withdraw his motion. This did not mean, of course,
that the peers had changed their views on Abolition. It
was not till May 6 that they found time to continue the
evidence, and then only seven witnesses were examined
before the session closed.

To these repeated blows even the stalwarts of the Abolition
Committee began at last to yield In the winter of 1793
they sent Clarkson on yet another journey through the
country in order to bring their body of evidence against the
Trade up to date But they held few meetings in 1794 and
only two in each of the next three years After 1797 they
did not meet at all till the spring of 1804 Meantime they
had temporarily lost the services of their almost indispensable
agent. Clarkson's busy, impulsive, high-strung spirit was
harnessed to an inelastic constitution. In the last few years
he had done far more than any other man in the collection
of evidence and the informing of public opinion. His book
is full of calculations as to the thousands of miles he tra-
versed, the thousands of people he conversed with, the
hundreds of his correspondents. To search out and to register
minutely the sordid horrors of the Trade had been almost
the only, and not a healthy, occupation for his mind. He
began to brood about it. And he was specially harassed,
too, by a sense of responsibility for the misfortunes of many
of the witnesses whom he had personally persuaded to give
evidence. Pursued and persecuted by sundry champions
of the Trade, deprived sometimes of their livelihood, they
appealed for aid to Clarkson as ' the author of their miseries
and their ruin '. And, since Clarkson, over and above the
funds he drew for expenses from the Committee and from
Wilberforce's private purse, had spent money for the cause
with impulsive zeal out of his own very moderate means, he
was at his wit's end how to help them, until, to ease his
mind, Mr. Whitbread undertook to recompense all the
victims of this persecution for the future. The winter
journey of 1793-4 proved the last straw In the spring he

broke down completely. ' The nervous system ', he says
in his profuse, punctilious manner, ' was almost shattered to
pieces. Both my memory and my hearing failed me.
Sudden dizziness seized my head   A confused singing in
the ears followed me wherever I went. On going to bed the
very stairs seemed to dance up and down under me, so that,
misplacing my foot, I sometimes fell ' A long rest from his
obsessing duties was clearly called for, and a subscription
of £1,500 was quickly raised towards his support in retirement among the friends of the cause. Unfortunately
Clarkson's own activity in this matter jarred rather sharply
on Wilberforce's delicacy of feeling. Not long before, he
had received a petulant letter from his old collaborator
complaining that he had not sufficiently used his influence,
as requested, with Lord Chatham to procure the promotion
of his brother to a captaincy in the navy. ' I can have no
doubt ', Clarkson had said, ' but you have frequently
written to my Lord Chatham   . but you have not, I apprehend, waited on him often or insisted on his promise in strong
language. . . . I never will believe but that your own want of
firmness is the true reason why my brother has not succeeded
before.' Doubtless Wilberforce had made allowances for
Clarkson's strained health ; and he had replied, courteously
and at length, explaining that he was used to such remonstrances since, though he was ready to help his friends as
far as he could with propriety, he had always considered it
a matter of principle not ' to truck and barter away any
personal influence I may possess with some of the members
of Administration, which ought to be preserved entire for
opportunities of public service '. And now Clarkson bombarded him with letters, pressing him to canvass this man
or that. ' You do not know what ten days may produce,
particularly if we act together.' Wilberforce did as he was
bid His begging letters were full of Clarkson's praises and
of the debt the Abolition party owed him. The money was
duly raised. And Clarkson withdrew to ease his shattered
nerves and to contemplate the composition of the *History
of the Abolition of the Slave Trade*, published in 1808, in which
(it is only fair to state) he devoted less than 25 out of 1,160

pages to the eleven years of his personal inactivity. But the begging business, coming on the heels of that other matter of promotion, left the relations between Wilberforce and Clarkson a little strained ; and the seed was sown from which one day, when the first of them was dead, was to spring an unedifying controversy as to which had done more service to the Abolition cause—a controversy which was only closed in 1844 when Robert and Samuel Wilberforce honourably acknowledged to Clarkson, then in extreme old age, that they had not treated him justly in their biography of their father.

Clarkson disabled, the Committee dormant, the generality of his supporters despondent or preoccupied, it would not have been surprising if Wilberforce too had made a truce with the Trade, at least for the duration of the war. If he had done so, he would have been in many ways more comfortable. So long as he persisted in fighting for Abolition, he had to face an increasing measure of resentment or ridicule in political circles ; for in war-time the most good-humoured men are apt to be irritated by the persistent agitation of a controversial question not directly concerned with the winning of the war. And such little connexion as there was between the Slave Trade and the war told against Abolition. On the one hand, the war diminished the volume of the Trade ; only 7,157 slaves were carried from Africa to the West Indies in 1795 as against 26,971 in 1792. On the other hand, the war strengthened the argument for doing nothing to weaken the British mercantile marine. More tiresome, perhaps, for Wilberforce, and at times more alarming than the general atmosphere of opposition, was the hostility of individuals. Early in the campaign his life had been threatened by a Mr. Morris, a witness who had lost his temper under Wilberforce's effective cross-examination. A few months before the war a Captain Rolleston, of the Trade, had challenged him to a duel. He had evaded it on principles of which something will be heard later on ; and the incident was closed. About the same time he was assailed by another slave-captain, one Kimber, whom Sir James Stenhouse described as ' a very bad man . who would swear to any falsehood and who is linked with a set of rascals like himself'. He had been charged with barbarous cruelty by Wilberforce in the debate in Parliament in the previous April, and since then he had been tried for the murder of a negro girl and acquitted 'through the shameful remissness of the Crown Lawyers', according to Wilberforce's doubtless somewhat partial judgement, 'and the indecent behaviour of a high personage who from the bench identified himself with the prisoner's cause'. Thereupon Kimber wrote to Wilberforce demanding a public apology, £5,000 in cash, and 'such a place under Government as would make me comfortable'. Wilberforce consulted Pitt and on his advice dispatched a summary refusal. Kimber then lay in wait for his enemy in the street and accosted him, civilly enough at first, but, finding Wilberforce would give him nothing, he became loudly abusive 'Very savage looking,' reported Wilberforce's servant, Amos, when he came twice in one morning to the house. 'He went away muttering and shaking his head.' Wilberforce's friends took a serious view of Kimber's threats; and Lord Rokeby insisted on sharing his coach, with a pistol in his pocket, when he made a journey to Yorkshire. 'I can't say I apprehend much,' wrote Wilberforce himself to Lord Muncaster; 'and I really believe that, if he were to commit any act of violence, it would be beneficial rather than injurious to *the cause*' But the nuisance persisted. In the spring of 1794 the diary refers in what is now a rather anxious tone to 'this awkward business of Kimber's .. in which my life perhaps is at stake'. But the desperado was presently placated or intimidated into quiescence by the kindly offices of Lord Sheffield, one of the chief and most uncompromising defenders of the Trade. Less alarming, but somewhat irritating until he got quite used to it, was the ridiculous gossip about Wilberforce's private life inspired by the more unscrupulous members of the West Indian party. Once, when Clarkson was on his travels, and making the most of his opportunities of propaganda in a stage-coach, a fellow passenger took him up. 'Mr. Wilberforce', he said, 'is no doubt a great philanthropist in public ; but I happen to know a little of his private history, and can assure you that he is a cruel husband and beats his wife ' Scandal, indeed, insisted that the young bachelor was really married His wife was a negress, said one report , a lady's maid, said another. And one of his Yorkshire constituents, who himself had married his cook, wrote to congratulate him on defying ' the common prejudices of society ' and following ' his own path to happiness '.

Threats and libels, however, had no more effect on Wilberforce's determination than the discouraging indifference of the country at large ' It is said ', his friend, Dr Currie, had written at the outset of the war, ' that at length you faint in your course ; that tired of the obstacles which present themselves and fearful of embarrassing the Minister in his present difficulties, you are about to give up the cause of the poor African until a quieter season.' Wilberforce had at once denounced the ' calumny '. ' When the actual commission of guilt is in question ', he had written, ' a man who fears God is not at liberty ' There lay the key to his perseverance and its spring. The pursuit of Abolition might now seem to others an unprofitable, almost unpatriotic diversion, or, at the best, a noble waste of energy ; but Wilberforce could still hope on because, as Currie put it, his trust was not in man *

VII

In 1794 the prospects were, if anything, less promising than in 1793. The coalition of the Portland section of the Whigs with Pitt and the entry of its leaders into the Cabinet weighted the scale still further against Abolition. Windham was still for it, but the group as a whole, including Portland

* *Life*, i 356–7 , ii 17–23, 48–55 Clarkson, ii 462–71. *Hansard*, xxx (1793–4), 513–20, 652–60, 948–9. Harford, 141. For the Clarkson controversy, see Clarkson's *Strictures on a Life of William Wilberforce* (London, 1838) , Preface to the *Correspondence*, containing the biographers' reply to the *Strictures* ; and the editor's note in *Diary, Reminiscences, and Correspondence of Henry Crabb Robinson* (3rd ed), ii. 209–10.

himself, were strong supporters of the Trade. In 1792 Pitt had confessed to Loughborough that, in order to form a national administration, he would have to make concessions to the Whig magnates on Abolition ; and whether or not any definite assurances were given at the moment of coalition, it was now more obvious than ever that no sort or kind of Abolition could figure as a Government measure.

Wilberforce, however, was soon pressing once more for the cessation of the foreign Trade. Again he carried the Bill past its second reading in thin Houses. And there was now a new point in its favour. It was known that some of the West Indian party, realizing that the Bill could not directly injure their interests, were willing to accept it. ' It is a compromise ', wrote a planter to Wilberforce, ' which ought to attach every West Indian to you.' But very few of his *confrères* were so clear-headed , and the intransigeant majority had Dundas's heavy weight behind them. In vain Wilberforce privately appealed for his support. The cautious Scot had discovered a reason for opposing even this apparently innocuous instalment of Abolition ' I know with absolute certainty,' he replied, ' that the Bill will be considered by the colonies as an encroachment on their legislative rights and they will not submit to it unless compelled.' Not so many years ago, Dundas had ridiculed the claims of the thirteen American colonies to legislative independence ; but apparently he had taken the lesson of the Revolution deeply to heart. And if it was doubtful whether those little groups of planters would ever actually resist the sovereignty of the Imperial Parliament, it was true enough, as the future was to show, that they would bitterly resent its exercise over their domestic concerns. Anyhow, Dundas was very much in earnest. He told Wilberforce he had used all the influence he possessed with Pitt personally and his other colleagues, ' to prevent any question on the subject being agitated, at least during the war.' As it was, he could only make one concession to Wilberforce's plea. He would not publicly oppose the Bill ; he would keep ' perfectly quiet on the subject '—' and even to that I should feel it very difficult to reconcile myself if I did not believe that your Bill will not pass the House of Lords '.

Dundas's conscience was not in serious jeopardy This time, indeed, the Bill did pass its third reading in the Commons ; but it had no chance whatever in the Lords, and on May 2 it was swiftly done to death by 45 votes to 4. Only Lord Stanhope apparently supported it. Lord Abingdon told the bench of bishops that the Bill contained seeds of ' other abolitions ' which would one day grow up to their own downfall, and sustained his zoological reputation by quoting, *à propos* of those who drew profit from the foreign Slave Trade, the fable of the frogs and the boys who pelted them with stones—' this is sport to you, my boys, but remember it is death to us '. The result was a surprise to nobody. But there was one unexpected and very discouraging incident. Grenville, the soul of honour and solidity, who had championed Abolition as earnestly as Pitt since the day of that historic conversation beneath the Holwood oak, declined to press the Bill on the Lords as Pitt had pressed it on the Commons. It ought to wait, he said, till the conclusion of the general inquiry on which the House was then engaged. ' I am half vexed at Grenville,' wrote Wilberforce to Muncaster. Only half-vexed ? The friendly self-restraint sounds a little studied ; for did anybody still believe in the inquiry ? Two weeks earlier the Lords had rejected a renewed proposal, on Bishop Horsley's motion, that the hearing of evidence should be delegated to a Select Committee , and had done nothing since But Grenville's argument seems to have reminded them of their neglected duty. Four days later they summoned a witness to their bar. They listened to him and to one more. Then they shelved the tedious business for good and all.

At the beginning of 1795 the outlook was, if possible, still gloomier ; for it was the time of Wilberforce's break with the Government. His pacifism, as he knew well, was bound to strengthen the enemies' hands ; it was easy to imagine the gusto with which Lord Abingdon would say, ' I told you so—all Abolitionists are Jacobins.' And what would Pitt do ? At Christmas, just when Wilberforce was making up his mind for peace, Pitt had written him an encouraging letter He was intending, he had told him, to instruct Lord Effingham, who was shortly going to Jamaica, to clear up certain doubtful points in the Slave Trade case ' If any queries occur to you, pray send them to me ' But when, a few days later, the gulf had opened, when the friends were no longer on speaking terms, was it to be expected that Pitt would support the cause with the same warmth as before ? Might not his personal resentment move him to pay the defaulter back in his own coin ? Might he not, at any rate, sit stiff and silent at the next Abolition debate ? Such conduct would have been natural enough for the small mean Pitt of partisan lampoons ; but for the Pitt of history it was quite impossible. When Wilberforce moved on February 25 that the Slave Trade be considered, and pointed out that the date fixed for Abolition (1796) by resolution of the House was near at hand—and when Dundas, with almost disarming candour, declared himself still wedded to the doctrine of the ' middle way ', still admitted that Abolition was ' absolutely necessary ', and still insisted that it must be gradual—Pitt supported his recreant friend and combated his loyal colleague as firmly as he had ever done. He was at pains, further, to vindicate Wilberforce and his cause from the current imputation of Jacobinism ' I know not where to find ', he said, ' a more determined enemy of such delusions than my honourable friend, the proposer of this motion ' But Pitt's constancy availed as little as before. ' Beat,' notes Wilberforce. ' 78 to 61. Shameful ' And he confesses to Wyvill that this ' infamous vote ' has strengthened his belief in the need for parliamentary Reform

In the next session it seemed for a few short weeks as if at last the tide was beginning to turn The successful attempts of French agents to stir up slave rebellions in the British West Indies had stimulated the anti-Jacobin cry ; but, on the other hand, Wilberforce had completely dissipated all suspicion as to his own political orthodoxy by his vigorous support of the Government in the November crisis He was quick to make what capital he could from his renewed popularity. On December 15, fresh from his triumph at York, he gave notice of his intention of renewing his plea for Abolition after the recess. ' Now ', he declared, ' when we are checking the progress of licentiousness, now is the very time to show our true principles by stopping a practice which violates all the real rights of human nature ' And when on February 18 he moved for leave to introduce a Bill abolishing the Trade by a fixed date, the House, or at least the Government side of it, was readier to respond than it had ever been since war broke out, and Tarleton's motion for adjournment was negatived by 93 votes to 67. The diary is naturally jubilant. ' Surprise and joy in carrying my question. Speaker [Addington] asked me and Pitt to come to sup—thought it would be unkind to Pitt to refuse. He delighted with having carried it—very kind, and seemed vexed when I mentioned our little heat.'

It seemed, indeed, as if Wilberforce's perseverance was at last to be rewarded. He quickly drafted the Bill in close consultation with Pitt. On February 22 he heard it read a first time without opposition. On March 3 he thwarted an attempt to snatch a hostile division on the second reading by hurrying from his dinner-table to the House, and speaking against time till his supporters were in a majority of 32 When the Bill emerged from committee, where the date for Abolition was fixed at March 1, 1797, the majority rose to 45 ; and when it came up for third reading on March 15, its final passage seemed assured. But Fortune had still a trick to play on Wilberforce. Most of his new supporters, though prepared to attend and vote in ordinary circumstances, could scarcely be described as enthusiasts for Abolition ; and by a queer chance they were subjected that very night to a more powerful appeal than that of Wilberforce's eloquence or the far-off lamentations of the victims of the Trade. It happened that the evening of March 15 had been fixed for the first performance of a new comic opera, *I dui Gobi* or *The Two Hunchbacks*. Portugallo had composed the music. Vignoni, a favourite of playgoers in pre-war days, was to sing. ' There was a large and splendid audience,' reported the newspapers next day And somewhere among that audience, their whole minds happily absorbed in the jests and melodies of the opera, had been sitting some ten or twelve of Wilberforce's allies, while in the dull House of Commons the Bill was being rejected by 74 to 70. It was an infuriating disappointment for Wilberforce His austere views of the theatre must have made the frivolity of his truant supporters seem positively shocking. ' I am personally hurt,' he said. And the worst of it was that the loss of the Bill, so far from stinging the backsliders into repentance, confirmed their apathy. A few weeks later an attempt was made to palliate the unabolishable Trade by stiffening the regulations for the transport of slaves The Abolitionists, Pitt among them, of course supported it, and some of the foremost champions of the Trade, such as Sir William Young and Mr. Barham, were willing to accept it. But it soon perished of neglect. Three times it was brought up; three times the House was ' counted out '; and then Parliament was dissolved. It was indeed ' enough to try the patience of a saint '. ' This week ', notes Wilberforce on May 15, ' I have occasionally felt a sinful anger about the Slave-carrying Bill and the scandalous neglect of its friends.'

The following year was even more disheartening. Not only was the public mood more than ever averse in those black days from worrying about the negroes; but it now became apparent that the greatest of the Abolitionists—the one indispensable man without whose support, as time showed, the cause was literally hopeless—was beginning to relax his efforts. From the outset of the crusade, in every important debate, Pitt had been at his post and fought his hardest Every time he had pleaded unequivocally for immediate Abolition, in the teeth of more than half his Cabinet and in open conflict with his closest political comrade, Dundas. But early in 1797 a change began to come over him. The worst crisis, so far, of the war, at home and abroad, was at hand; and the unceasing burden of work and care, far heavier for him than for any other man, was beginning to weigh him down. Was it inexcusably faint-hearted or disloyal, then, was it not natural enough, that

he should want to ease the strain by compromising on the
Slave Trade ?   His own best efforts for Abolition had proved
quite fruitless.   Whether or not he continued them, it was
now most improbable that the Commons would accept it,
and it was quite certain, if they did, that the Lords would
reject it.   On the other hand, a settlement of the controversy,
if only a temporary makeshift, would remove an awkward
bone of contention between himself and his colleagues and so
far strengthen the Government for the prosecution of the war.

Such, no doubt, were the reflections which induced Pitt
to welcome the new proposal made in the spring of 1797 by
Mr C. R. Ellis, a member of an old West Indian family   He
declared himself a pupil of Dundas.   Like his master, he
desired gradual Abolition ; and he was convinced that the
West Indian colonists would not assent to Parliament legis-
lating over their heads in a matter which so closely affected
them.   He suggested, therefore, that the Colonial Governors
should be instructed from Whitehall to urge upon their
respective Councils and Assemblies the propriety of laying
down such ameliorative measures for the treatment of the
existing slaves as would promote their natural increase and
so in time destroy the Trade by making it unnecessary.   Here
was a compromise far more attractive to the planters and
the traders than the Foreign Slave Trade Bill.   It was
warmly supported by their representatives.   And no wonder.
The West Indian Councils and Assemblies—so at least it
was suspected—were not likely to respond very briskly to
recommendations from their Governors as to the treatment
of their slaves ; and in any case—it was notorious—they
were inexorably opposed to Abolition.   As Fox frankly put
it in the ensuing debate, the plan was just another ' indirect
attempt to perpetuate the Slave Trade '.   ' Abominable ',
Wilberforce called it.   And yet Pitt was anxious that
Wilberforce should accept it in some form or other.   ' Called
at the Speaker's ', says the diary for April 1, ' . . . Discussed
about Ellis's motion till very late—much hurt—Pitt wanted
me to close with it modified, but when I would not, stood
stiffly by me.'   In the debate on the 6th, Pitt maintained
this rigid loyalty.   The proposal meant, he declared, that
Parliament was formally to sanction the Trade for a quite

indefinite period, to go back on its resolve to end the Trade by a fixed date, and to accept an ineffective substitute for that total abolition which the honour of the country and the safety of the islands so badly called for. But he was only wasting argument once more. The motion was carried by 97 votes to 63. Ten days later, Pitt likewise supported Wilberforce's motion for leave to bring in a Bill for Abolition—now a regular annual incident—but he might as well have stayed in Downing Street. The motion, of course, was lost by 82 to 74.

So Pitt still loyally 'stood by' his friend; but, as Wilberforce was well aware, the loyalty was now a little forced, a little 'stiff'. It was against his own inclination. And every month now the strain which had pushed him the first steps along the path to compromise told more heavily. That significant discussion with Wilberforce had taken place in the middle of the financial crisis. It was followed by Leoben, the mutinies, Malmesbury's second mission, *Fructidor*, Campo Formio. Pitt met each blow as it came with unflinching courage; and nobody who marked his cool demeanour could have guessed that those months of anxiety were the beginning of a premature old age. After that turning-point Pitt seems never to have recovered his resilience; henceforward he was a tired man; and when, nine years later, the next crisis came, the patriot's heart-strings were as taut as ever, but this time they were to snap beneath the strain. In that same year, too, he suffered grievous personal blows. At its beginning he felt himself obliged, probably for financial reasons, to put an end to his one brief love-affair—if anything so shy and correct as his approaches to Lord Auckland's daughter can be so described —and in September, at the moment of Malmesbury's disappointing return from France, he lost his brother-in-law, Edward Eliot. 'Pitt has been almost overwhelmed with it', wrote Wilberforce of the latter blow to Hannah More, and one element in his own grief was the loss in Eliot, the 'robust Eliot' of the Rheims holiday, of 'a bond of connexion, which was sure never to fail, between me and Pitt'.

Through all these troubles Pitt's fortitude deceived his friends. Eliot's death, indeed, so shook him that he had to postpone his interview with Malmesbury, just returned from

France ; but next day, to all appearance, he was himself
again. And this illusion of unbreakable strength and spirit
explains what would otherwise seem to be inconsiderate
importunity on Wilberforce's part in pressing the claims of
his cause Thus, when Pitt refused to encumber the negotiations with France by introducing the extraneous question
of the Slave Trade, Wilberforce remonstrated with a petu-
lance that now seems oddly out of keeping with his quick,
perceptive, affectionate spirit ' I must honestly say ', he
wrote, ' I never was so much hurt since I knew you as at
your not receiving and encouraging this proposal. . . . Do,
my dear Pitt, I entreat you, reconsider the matter I am
persuaded of your zeal in this cause, when, amidst the
multitude of matters which force themselves on you more
pressingly, it can obtain a hearing ; but I regret that you
have been so drawn off from it. Indeed regret is a very poor
term to express what I feel on this subject. Excuse this,
from the fulness of my heart, which I have often kept down
with difficulty and grief '

James Stephen put it more bluntly, ' Mr. Pitt,' he wrote
to Wilberforce, ' unhappily for himself, his country, and
mankind, is not zealous enough in the cause of the negroes
to contend for them as decisively as he ought, in the Cabinet
any more than in Parliament.' But Stephen was not
strictly just. It is unnatural to suppose that Pitt no longer
desired Abolition ; that when he spoke of the need of stamping out the ghastly cruelties of the Trade and ridding British
honour of its stain, he no longer meant what he said. But
Stephen, and Wilberforce too, had seen half the truth Pitt
could desire Abolition. He could still declare his old convictions to the world. He could, and did, still ' stand by '
Wilberforce, time after time, in debate. But the spring,
the spontaneity, of his earlier efforts were gone. Never
again could his speeches be inspired by the passion and the
hope with which, five years ago, he had acclaimed the
coming dawn in Africa.*

---

* *Life*, ii 48–51, 82–5, 133–47, 195–6, 225, 234–8. Clarkson,
ii 472–5 *Hansard*, xxx (1793–4), 1439–49 , xxxi (1794–5), 467–70,
1321–45 , xxxii (1795–7), 737–63, 862–902 , xxxiii (1797–8), 251–94,
569–76. Holland Rose, i 472–9 , ii. 299–320

VII

THE SAINT

I

TWELVE years had now passed since the supreme event of Wilberforce's life   and the capacity it had given him to meet the ' blows of circumstance ' not merely with resignation but—in moments, at any rate, of solitude and contemplation—with serenity, had lost nothing of its power. We must understand this, indeed, if we would understand the man at all ; and it will help us, perhaps, though it seems a little intrusive, a little like eavesdropping, to watch him while the process is at work.   Observe him, then, for example, in the last week of August 1796.   It has been a bad year alike for his country and his own special cause. The last few months have brought the news of Bonaparte's first string of victories in Italy.   And the last session of Parliament has been distinguished above its predecessors by the eleventh-hour betrayal of the Foreign Slave Trade Bill to *I dui Gobi* and by the repeated, humiliating failure to obtain a quorum for the Slave-carrying Bill.   It is in a despondent mood, therefore, that Wilberforce writes to his old friend, Hey.   ' Public affairs look worse and worse,' he says ; ' . . . our national sins force themselves into my mind. . . I scarce dare hope for better tidings.'   And then, on the following Sunday, which is set apart, as usual, for reflection, he shuts himself up and carries his mind back to the transfiguring ordeal of 1785—to ' the singular accident, as it seems to me, of my asking Milner to go abroad with me ' and all that followed it.   And as he jots down his thronging thoughts pell-mell in his spiritual journal, the disappointments and anxieties of the times fade quickly into nothing   ' How much it depended on contingencies ! ' —that tour with Milner.   ' If he had been ill as he was afterwards or if I had known his character, we should not have gone together. . . . Doddridge's *Rise and Progress* having fallen in my way so providentially whilst abroad . . . My being raised to my present situation just before I became acquainted with the truth, and one year and a half before I in any degree experienced its power. . . What

a mercy to have been born an Englishman, in the eighteenth
century, of decently religious parents, with a fortune,
talents, etc.! Even Gibbon felt thankful for this; and
shalt not thou praise the Lord, O my soul? . . . My being
providentially engaged in the slave-business. I remember
well how it was. What an honourable service! . . . How
often protected from evil and danger! Kept from Morris'
hand and Kimber's. . . . Rolleston—and my coming away
from Bath so providentially—the challenge never cleared
up. . . . My illness in the spring, which might have been
fatal, well recovered from. My going into Yorkshire in the
winter. My election over with little trouble and expense. . . .'
And when he turns from these happier events and records
the troubles and discouragements and failures of his life,
these too seem now no less 'providential', no less for his
good because they help him to humility ' Do not I owe all
to the goodness of God? It is Thou, O Lord, that hast
given the very small increase there has been and must give
all if there be more.' And so he closes his confession and,
reassured and reinforced, goes out into the world again to
face the fortunes of the coming week

There lies the secret of Wilberforce's indomitable perseverance. These religious devotions would seem, indeed,
to have become an almost indispensable tonic for his
mercurial temperament. They steadied, refreshed, inspired
him , and he was always trying to secure more leisure for
them from the obsessions of his busy life in London There
are innumerable items in the diary like the following .
' Alas! what a hurrying life I lead, with little time for
serious reflection ! ' ' Some serious thought this morning,
and found the benefit of early rising, but it sadly wears my
frame.' Above all, he depended on his methodical observance
of the Sabbath. ' Often on my visits to Holwood,' he wrote
in old age, ' when I heard one or another speak of this man's
place or that man's peerage, I felt a rising inclination to
pursue the same objects, but a Sunday in solitude never
failed to restore me to myself.' Never, if he could help it,
would he let the day be used for work. Once or twice—
when, for instance, he was toiling against time in preparation

for the Abolition debate of 1791—he was obliged to break his rule. ' Gave up Sunday to slave business ', he confesses : ' I hope it was a grief to me the whole time to turn it from its true purpose ' He liked best to spend the day alone and hated going off for the week-end to less sabbatical homes, even to Holwood ' Though I never see *company* (so to be called) on a Sunday,' he prefaces an invitation to a new acquaintance, ' yet I sometimes ask a friend or two, who likes our way of going on, upon that day ' The way of going on was regularly prescribed. Family prayers, as usual, before breakfast , and after breakfast, ' morning church '. Then a stroll and a talk before three o'clock dinner. After dinner guests were left to themselves while their host withdrew for an hour and a half. ' I almost seem at this moment ', wrote Dr. Harford, many years after Wilberforce's death, ' to behold him on one of these occasions passing through the ante-room of his library, when about thus to retire, with a folio under his arm, and stopping me with a smile to tell me that his companion was a volume of Baxter's Works.' After this preparation, ' evening church ' ; then supper and talk or sometimes a reading of poetry by Wilberforce till bed-time

Twentieth-century England takes its week-ends differently, and so did the great majority of Wilberforce's contemporaries. Few signs of the times, indeed, dismayed or vexed him more ; for in his eyes it was one of the most unmistakable symptoms of a faint or forgotten faith. ' Looked into Swift's *Letters* ', he says once ; ' what a thoroughly irreligious mind—no trace of Sunday to be found in his journals or letters to his most intimate friends.' Public duties he regarded as no excuse for the profanation of the Sabbath, unless they could not conceivably be performed on any other day. In after days he drew this moral—and physicians might, perhaps, agree with him—from the suicides, in terrible succession, of Whitbread, Romilly, and Castlereagh. ' It is very curious ', he writes to Stephen after the last of the tragedies, ' to hear the newspapers speaking of incessant application to business, forgetting that by the weekly admission of a day of rest, which our Maker has graciously

enjoined, our faculties would be preserved from the effects
of this constant strain. I am strongly impressed by the
recollection of your endeavour to prevail on the lawyers
to give up Sunday consultations in which poor Romilly
would not concur. If he had suffered his mind to enjoy
such occasional remissions, it is highly probable the strings
would never have snapped as they did from over-tension.'
It was Wilberforce, again, who persuaded the devout
Perceval, when he was Prime Minister, to abandon the old
custom of fixing a Monday for the reassembling of Parliament on the ground that it involved members travelling on
Sunday. It was he, too, who persuaded Speaker Addington
to hold his *levées* on Saturday instead of Sunday evenings.
When Sunday drilling was made compulsory for the inhabitants of the Channel Islands in 1798 and the Jersey legislature, confronted with the passive resistance of certain
Wesleyan Methodists, passed a Bill to banish from the
island any one who refused the obligation, Wilberforce
promptly responded to the Methodists' appeal and succeeded
in persuading Dundas to get the Bill vetoed by the Crown.
Even when Napoleon was camped at Boulogne and every
one expected a landing on the Kentish coast, Wilberforce
was still vehemently opposed to the drilling of volunteers
on the only day when men of all occupations were at leisure.
' I am worried to pieces ', he wrote to Hannah More It
was simply ' shameful '. The recommendation of it was a
stain on the statute-book—for England at any rate : the
military men had confessed that ' Scotland would not have
it ' And presently he induced Parliament at least to cancel
its positive encouragement of the practice. He was shocked,
too, at the popularity of Sunday newspapers ; and in
1799, in conjunction with Lord Belgrave, he promoted
a Bill for their suppression, but without success. ' I got the
nineteen Sunday newspapers once for all the other day ',
the diary records in his later years, ' that I might the better
judge of their contents ; and assuredly such a collection of
ribaldry and profaneness never before disgraced my library '
  It was largely owing to these personal efforts on Wilberforce's part that a stricter observance of the Sabbath came

into general vogue by the end of the eighteenth century.
It became more and more the correct, almost the fashionable,
thing. And the new custom lasted. Wilberforce's Sunday
was the precursor of that orthodox Victorian Sunday which
seems nowadays as stiffly decorous as our grandmothers'
crinolines—almost an historical curiosity—a day of leaden,
listless hours, such as our elders have told us of, with not
overmuch regret at their passing—a day when girls might
do no needlework and boys read nothing but the Bible
A grey day in truth it was in many a stern household not
very long ago And a grey day it might have been in
Wilberforce's home but for Wilberforce, who could be
devout and yet no prude, earnest and yet no prig. ' There
was nothing of affected seriousness in his deportment or
manner on this day', writes a solemn admirer   ' All was
easy, natural and cheerful '.   Wilberforce would have
smiled at this description.   It was his smile, indeed, that
saved that careful Sabbath routine from pedantry and
cant and gloom. On Sunday, at any rate, he was incorrigibly
happy Indeed, whatever else the cynics might say of his
religion, they could not accuse it of making him miserable.
' You must allow that Mr. Wilberforce is cheerful ', a
sceptical friend was asked. ' Yes,' she replied, ' and no
wonder ! I should be always cheerful too if I could make
myself as sure as he does that I was going to heaven.'

None the less, his was an exacting creed. We have seen
him ' wearing his frame ', like any monk, with religious
exercises in the early hours. And just as in the first days of
his ' conversion ', so all through his life, he belabours
himself for his failure to live up to his ideal   ' What a
mystery of iniquity is the human heart ! ' he cries. And
why, particularly ? Because ' thoughts of worldly pursuits '
so often force themselves into his mind during ' devotional
exercises '. And, conversely, at other times (he complains
again and again), devotional thoughts are far too rarely
present The ' other-worldliness ' of the Evangelical revival
had given the desperately poor something to hold on to and
endure by through the miseries of the Industrial Revolution , but it was not so easy for fortunate, vivacious, busy

Wilberforce to bring himself to regard all the colour and movement of his happier world as transient shadows against a background of eternity. ' How little do we talk ', he says, ' like passengers who are hastening to a better country and here are in a strange one ! ' Yet few religious men could carry the logic of this conviction to such rigorous extremes. In 1797 he was once more very ill ' Feared I was about to be as bad as the former time ', he notes in the diary ; ' Suffered much—had death, as probable, in view, and felt, I hope, resigned, but no ardour or warmth.' After that, we need not be astonished at the following disclosure of the severity of his spiritual ordeal ' My eyes are very indifferent—tears always make them so, and this obliges me to check myself in my religious offices.' Such emotionalism is, perhaps, a little distasteful to our modern temperament. To the masculine-minded it savours of monkish morbidity ; and the up-to-date psychologist will promptly diagnose it as a neurotic complex. But let it be remembered that these ' religious offices ' were not the whole of Wilberforce's life. He was not a saint of the pillar or the gate. His agonies and ecstasies were the secrets of the inner chamber. And they did not enervate, they braced him, for the business of the active world outside Whatever we may call it, it was not morbidity which enabled this chronic invalid to fight down fatigue, to work as hard, day in, day out, as most stronger men ; to brush aside the worry of hostility and insult , to hold up, year after year, often almost single-handed, the drooping banner of his cause ; and finally to achieve as great a thing as any of his great contemporaries achieved for the good name of his country and the welfare of mankind.*

* *Life*, i 290, 316–17 , ii 23, 97, 165–6, 187, 315, 338, 424 , iii. 97, 151 , iv 340 , v. 66, 132, 135, 143 Harford, 4–7.

II

Wilberforce's religion was certainly not self-centred He had the missionary spirit. He was eager to bring others, through the same experience as his own, to lose and save themselves. And those gentle assaults upon his friends, which had been one of the earliest symptoms of his ' conversion ', became a regular and methodical business of his life. A curious document, dated January 12, 1794, has been preserved, bearing the title, ' Friends' paper ', and the instruction, ' To be looked at every Sunday '. It consists of a list of thirty of Wilberforce's friends with the appropriate notes ; for example :

> *S——and Mrs.* What books reading ? To give them good ones—Walker's Sermons. Call on Mrs S and talk a little Lend her Venn's last Sermon Education of their children, to inquire about. Prayer, etc. Their coming some Sunday to Battersea Rise to hear Venn. Call often, and be kind.
> *Lady A—— and Sir R.* Has he read Doddridge ? Be open to her, etc.
> *Mr. and Mrs. M——.* Encourage to family prayers, etc.
> *Lord and Lady J——.* See them. Get at them through G. Discover what books reading.
> *V——* Try what he believes and speak home truths.
> *The J——s.* Call and sound them on religion. Give them money to give away, etc. Little presents.
> *Lady E——.* Speak pretty openly, yet tenderly.

Little could these ladies and gentlemen have known what careful preparation their lively friend was making for their good. Little, too, could those who listened with delight to Wilberforce's fluent talk, with its mingled current of merriment and gravity, its unpretentious knowledge of the great world, its shrewd judgement of men and things, have guessed that he made a habit of keeping certain topics of conversation at the back of his mind which, if he could once introduce them, might be insensibly developed into a discussion of first principles He would often spend a quiet hour thinking out these ' launchers ' as he called them ; and he sometimes chastises himself in his diary for having attended some social

party without 'fitting himself for company' with a good
quiverful of them. There is an instinct in most civilized
human beings which makes them react to such well-meaning
friends like a hedgehog to a dog And Wilberforce, of course,
had many disappointments, frankly chronicled in the diary.
For example, 'Dined at Mrs. N 's to try to do her good, but
I fear it did not answer.' 'The ladies all good-natured',
he says, again, of a visit to a country-seat, 'but alas !
I make nothing of it. . . I think Lady Y. has a feeling of
religion   . . Though with Lord Y. I had some serious
conversation, I had no opportunity of any such intercourse
with the others, and I fear I seemed a gay, thoughtless
being.' And doubtless, then and often, he *did* seem 'gay'.
How otherwise, indeed, could his benevolent advances
which, however carefully prepared, must often have been
evident enough, have failed to offend the somewhat cynical
taste of eighteenth-century Society ? No doubt they
smiled at his pietism. There is a story Wilberforce used to
tell against himself of a visit to his ' old friend, Lord N——',
when he was ill : how he had sat some time chatting with
him, but without alluding to religious matters, when another
friend came in and asked the invalid how he was. 'As well
as I can be ', was the answer, ' with Wilberforce sitting here
and telling me I am going to hell.' But if they smiled at
' the saint ' they never derided him, nor ever voted him a
bore. When the little man came in late to a dinner-party,
bristling, maybe, with ' launchers ', every face, says a
contemporary, ' lighted up with pleasure at his entry '.

But Wilberforce's sense of mission could not be satisfied
with the spoken word He could not rest till he had told his
secret to a far wider circle than that of his friends and
acquaintances. So in the summer of 1793, after many
months of study and contemplation, he began to write.
On August 3, says the diary, ' I laid the first timbers of my
tract ' It was not an auspicious moment for a public man
to undertake an exacting literary task ; and the author
would have been starved into silence by the busy politician,
if the busy politician had not conceived the task as an
essential part of his business The ' advancement or

decline (of religion) in any country ', wrote Wilberforce in the preface, in answer to the possible charge that his work was outside the layman's field, ' is so intimately connected with the temporal interests of society as to render it the peculiar concern of a political man.' Thus, preoccupied as he was by the war and the Slave Trade, by his conscientious daily attendance at the House of Commons, by the local interests of his county, and by his charities and visitors and friends, he contrived now and again to get an evening undisturbed in his library and write another page or two, and occasionally, when Parliament was not sitting, he would break away into the country and devote a few untrammelled days entirely to the work. And so, in the course of three or four years, the tract grew gradually into a book of nearly 500 pages. By the beginning of 1797 the first draft was finished. Staying at Bath in February, he ' manages to be pretty diligent in the mornings ' in the work of revision · and when he returns to London, the manuscript is ready for the printers. ' April 12. My book out to-day.'

The book bears one of those long expository titles which were fashionable in the tractarian literature of the eighteenth century—*A Practical View of the Prevailing Religious System of Professed Christians in the Higher and Middle Classes in this Country contrasted with Real Christianity.* Its main object, says Wilberforce at the outset, is ' not to convince the sceptic or to answer the arguments of persons who avowedly oppose the fundamental doctrines of our religion , but to point out the scanty and erroneous system of the bulk of those who belong to the class of orthodox Christians and to contrast their defective scheme with a representation of what the author apprehends to be real Christianity '. The purpose, therefore, of the earlier chapters is to show how inadequate is the average Christian's conception of his faith—inadequate, first and foremost, in its failure to realize the supreme, the immeasurable importance of the subject, dwarfing to insignificance everything else in the world , in its strange indifference to the fact that ' this present scene, with all its cares and all its gaieties, will soon be rolled away, and " we must stand before the judgement-seat of Christ " ' , in its ' utter forgetfulness of its being the great business of life to secure our admission into heaven ' and to prepare our heart for its service and enjoyments '. Inadequate, next, because of its too easy confidence in salvation ; in its notion that a man can be a true Christian without taking pains ; in its refusal to face the reality and the awful consequences of ' original sin ' ; in its abuse of the idea of divine mercy to cover even unrepentant sinners, despite the ' clear and decisive ' warning of the Scriptures that ' the wicked shall be turned into hell '. Inadequate, too, because of its readiness to accept works without faith, because it regards ' amiable tempers and useful lives ' as if they constituted practical religion by themselves. All this, says Wilberforce, is ' only nominal Christianity ' The true Christian recognizes that the doctrine of grace is ' the cardinal point on which the whole of Christianity turns ' : that only by ' an absolute surrender of soul and body to the will and service of God ' can he hope for salvation ; that every purpose he has in his life must be tested by the pattern of the life of Christ

And so he comes to what he himself regarded as one of the most ' practical ' parts of the book, to the chapter headed ' A brief inquiry into the present state of Christianity in this country . . . and its importance to us as a political community ' True religion, he maintains, has been steadily declining in England. The growth of prosperity, the multiplication of great cities, the splendour and luxury of London, the prevalence, ' much as we are indebted to it ', of the commercial spirit—all this has led to ' the discontinuance of the religious habits of a purer age '. Christianity now ' seldom occupies the attention of the bulk of nominal Christians ' ; it is ' scarcely at all the object of their study '. And to be lukewarm is a stage towards unbelief. The tone of current literature is already sceptical. ' The time is fast approaching when Christianity will be almost as openly disavowed in the language, as in fact it is already supposed to have disappeared from the conduct of men ; when infidelity will be held to be the necessary appendage of a man of fashion, and to believe will be deemed the indication

of a feeble mind '. If any one doubts this, let him look at
France, where the same causes have produced their inevitable
result—' manners corrupted, morals depraved, dissipation
predominant, above all, religion discredited and infidelity,
grown into repute and fashion, terminating in the public
disavowal of every religious principle which had been used
to attract the veneration of mankind '. Against that picture
set the ideal of a community whose members all lead
Christian lives.

' If any country were indeed filled with men, each thus
diligently discharging the duties of his own station without
breaking in upon the rights of others, but on the contrary
endeavouring, so far as he might be able, to forward their
views and promote their happiness—all would be active and
harmonious in the goodly frame of human society. There
would be no jarrings, no discord The whole machine of
civil life would work without obstruction or disorder, and
the course of its movements would be like the harmony of
the spheres.'

For the supreme political value of Christianity is its direct
hostility to selfishness, ' the moral distemper of political
communities ', the cause wherever it appears—among
governors or governed, rich or poor—of political disorder
and decay.

' In whatever class or order of society Christianity prevails,
she sets herself to counteract the particular mode of selfishness to which that class is liable. Affluence she teaches to
be liberal and beneficent ; authority to bear its faculties
with meekness and to consider the various cares and obligations belonging to its elevated station as being conditions
on which that station is conferred. Thus, softening the
glare of wealth and moderating the insolence of power, she
renders the inequalities of the social state less galling to the
lower orders, whom also she instructs, in their turn, to be
diligent, humble, patient : reminding them that their
more lowly path has been allotted to them by the hand of
God ; that it is their part faithfully to discharge its duties
and contentedly to bear its inconveniences , that the
present state of things is very short . . . that the peace of
mind which religion offers indiscriminately to all ranks
affords more true satisfaction than all the expensive
pleasures which are beyond the poor man's reach . . and

finally that all human distinctions will soon be done away, and the true followers of Christ will all, as children of the same Father, be alike admitted to the possession of the same heavenly inheritance.'

It is on the thought of England as she thus might be and England as she is that the seventh and final chapter closes. It appeals to all 'true Christians', laymen and churchmen alike, to devote the whole of themselves to stemming the tide of unbelief by precept and example.

' Let them consider as devolved on them the important duty of serving, it may be of saving their country, not by busy interference in politics (in which it cannot but be confessed there is much uncertainty), but rather by that sure and radical benefit of restoring the influence of religion. . . . Let them be active, useful, generous towards others , manifestly moderate and self-denying in themselves. Let them be ashamed of idleness as they would be of the most acknowledged sin. . . . Let them cultivate a catholic spirit of universal goodwill and of amicable fellowship towards all those, of whatever sect or denomination, who, differing from them in non-essentials, agree with them in the grand fundamentals of religion. . . . Let them pray continually for their country in this season of national difficulty. We bear upon us but too plainly the marks of a declining empire. . . . It would be an instance in myself of that very false shame which I have condemned in others, if I were not boldly to avow my firm persuasion that *to the decline of Religion and Morality our national difficulties must, both directly and indirectly, be chiefly ascribed ; and that my only solid hopes for the well-being of my country depend, not so much on her fleets and armies, not so much on the wisdom of her rulers or the spirit of her people, as on the persuasion that she still contains many who love and obey the gospel of Christ ; that their intercessions may yet prevail ; that, for the sake of these, Heaven may still look upon us with an eye of favour.'* [1]

When Wilberforce submitted this book to Mr. Cadell the publisher, it was not very warmly received Mr Cadell was aware that the current demand for religious literature was meagre ; and though he accepted the book, he shook his head over its commercial prospects. ' He evidently regarded me ', reports the author, ' as an amiable enthu-

[1] Italics in the original text.

siast '. ' You mean to put your name to the work ? ' he
asked, ' Ah !   Then I *think* we may venture on 500
copies.' His daring was rewarded. The 500 were sold
out in a few days. By midsummer the book had become
almost a ' best-seller '. In August the fifth edition appeared,
making a total of 7,500 copies. And year after year the
demand continued   By 1837 only one more edition had
been produced , but fifteen impressions, some of them
running into thousands, had been struck off in England,
and in America no less than twenty-five   It had been
translated, moreover, into French, German, Italian, Spanish,
and Dutch.

The book's success surprised others besides Mr Cadell.
Many of Wilberforce's friends had feared that it would add
nothing, or less than nothing, to his reputation. Dean
Milner had earnestly tried to dissuade him from undertaking
the ' tract ' at all. ' A person who stands so high for talent ',
another friend had written, ' must risk much, in point of
fame at least, by publishing upon a subject on which there
have been the greatest exertions of the greatest genius '
But all such doubts had been instantly dispersed. Such
criticism as there was did but stimulate discussion and
increase the sale. A Socinian attack in the *Monthly Review*
made admirers of the book identify it with the very cause of
Christianity. Nonconformist dissatisfaction with its Angli-
canism endeared it all the more to the Church of England
' The bishops in general ', wrote Henry Thornton to Zachary
Macaulay, to whom he was sending a copy, ' much approve
of it, though some more warmly, some more coldly.' And
first among the warm ones was Bishop Porteus, Wilberforce's Abolitionist ally. ' I am truly thankful to Providence ', he told him, ' that a work of this nature has made
its appearance at this tremendous moment.' And, of
course, it was particularly welcome to divines of his own
Evangelical persuasion. ' I deem it ', wrote the venerable
Newton, ' the most valuable and important publication of
the present age, especially as it is yours ' ; and the old
pastor adds a touching compliment to his disciple of twelve
years ago. He had continued to write him letters of spiritual

advice from time to time ; ' but now ', he says, ' I shall be
glad to look to you (at least to your book) . . . to strengthen
my motives for running the uncertain remainder of my race
with alacrity '

And what of the folk to whom the book had more directly
been addressed ? What did Society, what did his own circle,
think of it ? At any rate they did not ignore it In Bath,
to quote a friend who was staying there with Wilberforce,
it produced quite a ' sensation ' and ' drew upon him much
observation ' ' Many of his gay and political friends
admire and approve of it ', wrote another, ' though some do
but dip in it.' A dip, we may suppose, was enough for the
Lord Chancellor ' I sincerely hope ', wrote Loughborough,
alias Wedderburn, ' that your book will be read by many,
with that just and proper temper which the awful circumstances in which we stand ought to produce.' Some of the
author's acquaintance found an intriguing personal interest
in the book : several, it is said, recognized in its pages the
likeness of themselves. But for many of its thousands of
readers the book satisfied a real spiritual need Arthur
Young was helped by it to something akin to the ' experience ' which Wilberforce himself had undergone and which
he had hoped through the book to impart to others. ' I read
it coldly at first ', he says in his autobiography, ' but
advanced with more attention. It brought me to a better
sense of my dangerous state ; but I was very much involved
in hesitation and doubt, and was very far from understanding
the doctrinal part of the book. This was well, for it induced
me to read it again and again, and it made so much impression upon me that I scarcely knew how to lay it aside.' An
anonymous reader told Wilberforce that he ' had purchased
a small freehold in Yorkshire that by his vote he might offer
him a slight tribute of respect '. Unhappily the opinion of
the man, whom, above all others, Wilberforce would have
liked to influence, is not on record. Of course he had sent
a copy at once to Pitt, recommending him ' to open on the
last section of the fourth chapter ' (entitled *Mistaken con-
ceptions entertained by nominal Christians of the terms of
acceptance with God*). ' You will see wherein the religion

which I espouse differs practically from the common system. Also the sixth chapter has almost a right to a perusal, being the basis of all politics, and particularly addressed to such as you.' It was the eve of the mutinies in the fleet : and whether the busy Minister did as he was told must remain a matter of surmise. At any rate his letter of acknowledgement—if there was one—was not warm enough to be quoted by Wilberforce's loyal bio- graphers There was another great man, however, of whose opinion there can be no doubt. Windham once told the House of Commons that Burke was comforted in his dying hours by reading Addison ; but we are also told by Mrs. Crewe, who was with him, that he spent a great part of the last two days of his life on the *Practical View*. ' If I live ', he said, ' I shall thank Wilberforce for having sent such a book into the world.' And one of the last messages he gave to Dr. Laurence was a word of gratitude for it to Wilberforce.

The publication of this book, then, must be reckoned as one of the outstanding achievements of Wilberforce's life. He could not himself be blind to its immediate and great success : but—it goes without saying—the buzz of interest, the chorus of congratulation, the admiring throng at Bath made no shade of difference to his demeanour. His chief satisfaction was to have declared his own opinions so frankly that in nobody's eyes in future need he fear to seem other than he was ' I cannot help saying ', he confessed to Newton, ' it is a great relief to my mind to have published what I may call my manifesto—to have plainly told my worldly acquaintance what I think of their system and conduct and where it must end.' *

* *Life*, ii 33, 104, 183, 190, 198–209, 405–6. Harford, 2, 9 *Auto-biography of Arthur Young* (London, 1898), 287–8 Bishop Wilson's *Introduction* to *Practical View* (6th edition, 1837).

III

The most malicious cynic could not accuse the author of
the *Practical View* of failing to practise what he preached
We have seen something of his unsparing devotions, his
untiring benevolence, his strict observance of the Sabbath ,
and he applied the same stern standards to all the details
of daily life. Wilberforce at thirty-eight had left very far
behind the care-free young man of the world who idled at
Cambridge and sported in London in the ' eighties '. Once
upon a time he had noted in his diary, ' My horse won at
the Harrowgate races.' ' Oh, what folly ! ' is his comment
now on the Newmarket meeting ' What forgetfulness of
God ! ' So strongly had he come to feel on the point that
he refused the formal office of steward at the York races
which custom had always bestowed on a member for the
county, and even diverted the member's usual subscription
to the funds of the county hospital. He was distrustful, too,
of less extravagant amusements. He shunned the theatre
He shied at cards. Quite late in his life, he can still comment, of a dinner-party at the Duke of Gloucester's, ' I felt
awkward about cards, though I declared I did not make a
point of conscience of not playing ' He was uneasy, too,
about dancing. At a big party at Bath, for instance, he was
once painfully surprised by a gentleman who had been
discussing with him the discipline of the Calvinist church
breaking off to join in a *cotillon*. And, indeed, to have told
his easygoing world in his book what he thought of it may
have soothed his conscience, but it had not made him any
more at home in it. Time and again he complains of his
discomfort. ' Taken in to dine at W. Smith's, with a vast
company. . . . I was not sufficiently guarded in talking about
religion after dinner.   . Came home, as if hunted, to
Thornton's quiet family party, and much struck with the
difference.' ' Dined at Dundas's . Lady —— and great
party. The conversation on natives of New South Wales,
duels, etc. I felt strongly how little I was fit for these
people or they for me. ("What doest thou here, Elijah ? ") '

Again, of that brilliant annual festival, the Royal Academy dinner, he notes. 'Sat near Lord Spencer, Windham, etc.— too worldly minded—catches and glees, they importunate for *Rule Britannia*—I doubt if I had much business at such a place. . . . Yet what a gay dream ! ' Of course, too, on more ordinary occasions the broad conversational taste of our forefathers must often have jarred on those Puritan ears, and the diary bears frequent witness to the 'improprieties' and 'profanities' of the fashionable company he moved in

When one is confronted with such comments as some of the above—quoted as they are so profusely by the filial biographers and clearly without the faintest qualms as to the effect on their readers—the old suspicion forces itself back on one's mind This calm, superior aloofness ! This self-conscious Elijah among the idolaters ! Surely the man was brimful of spiritual pride ? Surely he was a prig ? Well, the answer is the old answer—his contemporaries did not think so. There were others than the slave-traders— and there will be occasion presently to speak of them— who disliked Wilberforce, hated his politics, railed at his religion ; but none of them seems to have regarded him as arrogant or insincere That confident, full-blooded, supercilious *fin-de-siècle* Society, moreover, would have given short shrift to a prig : no prig could conceivably have won from it the genuine and kindly respect it showed to Wilberforce It is, indeed, remarkable that these fashionable folk, who regarded the enthusiasms and inhibitions of the new and very *bourgeois* Puritanism with mild amusement or positive distaste, should have treated Wilberforce's notorious fads with such singular deference ' Dined at the Duke of M's ', records the diary one day ' Many improper things said, which G. told me afterwards *they were themselves regretting on my account.*' One other instance out of many is yet more striking. In the year of Waterloo it chanced that Wilberforce was at Brighton during one of the Prince Regent's frequent visits to his favourite watering-place. He was invited to dine at the Pavilion ; and on his refusing on the ground of ill health, the Prince was told by one of

his companions that the Saint would never dine with him.
But the Prince persisted When Wilberforce came to pay
his respects a few days later, he treated him with marked
urbanity and reminded him of their first meeting at the
Duchess of Devonshire's ball in 1782, and of the particular
song that Wilberforce had sung on that occasion. It was
a rash opening. All unawares the Prince had provided
Wilberforce with a ' launcher ', and the result was delightful.
' We are both, I trust, much altered since, Sir '—was the
startling reply The Prince took a strong hold on himself.
' Yes ', he responded with somewhat laboured gravity .
' the time which has gone by must have made a great
alteration in us.' ' Something better than that, too,
I trust, Sir.' Even now the Prince was not deterred. He
repeated his invitation to dinner and assured Wilberforce,
with an engaging candour, that ' he should hear nothing in
his house to give him pain ' And so it was, both on that
occasion and at another dinner-party later on. There were
times when ' the first gentleman in Europe ' could live up to
his title.

A sincere and unpretentious virtue commonly commands
respect, but not so commonly affection. Those qualities in
Wilberforce, however, which had kept the young ' convert '
still lovable at the outset, persisted throughout his life
The confessions in the diary do not mean that he felt
himself personally, innately superior to his fellows His
moral standards were not, so to speak, of his own prescription. A revelation had come to him, without any conscious
volition on his part, and in the light of it he was bound to
try to live as he did. To any of those others, any day, he
believed, the same call might come and with the same
results. And his piety was no more tinged with the sourness
of conventional Puritanism than with its arrogance. It
would seem—there has been more than a hint of it in these
pages—that he had little real sense of humour but he had
something almost as good—a lightness and sweetness and
simplicity of manner which enabled him to obey his conscience in any society without offence. Fashionable hostesses were never afraid of his creating ' awkward moments '.

He could refuse to conform without seeming to condemn—a rare gift

Meantime, in the world outside the society in which he moved, Wilberforce's reputation for saintliness grew and grew. Englishmen in those days had good reason to doubt the disinterestedness of their politicians, but they never doubted Wilberforce's. His association with any enterprise was accepted by the public as a proof, not always of its wisdom, but always of its honesty. And when the world gave him and his little group of friends in Parliament the nickname of ' the Saints ', it was a genuine tribute : there may have been a touch of mockery in it, but none of sarcasm Wilberforce's name, in fact, became a by-word for scrupulous virtue—as witness Byron's famous anecdote. Sheridan, so he writes to Moore, was found by a watchman in the street one dark night, ' fuddled and bewildered and almost insensible. " Who are *you*, sir ? "—no answer. " What 's your name ? "—a hiccup. " What 's your name ? " —answer, in a slow, deliberate, and impassive tone . . " Wilberforce ".' *

IV

Wilberforce lived in two worlds One was the world of Pitt and the politicians and high Society, of Court *levées* and Royal Academy banquets and Ministerial dinner-parties. He was tied to it by his friendship for Pitt, by the necessities of his parliamentary career, and by his sense of social vocation. But he could always escape—and, with increasing frequency as time went on, he did escape—into quite another world. He had only to flit from his house at Westminster to his rooms at Clapham , and there, in what he could still describe as a ' rural fastness ', he found himself among a little *coterie* of more or less intimate friends, all thinking very much alike, all humanitarians, all Evan-

* *Life*, 1 276, 286, 315, 359 ; 11 28–9, 56, 86, 99, 137, 190 , 1v 277–8 ; v. 16, and *passim*. Byron's *Works* (1834 ed.), 111. 138 (Letter dated Oct 31, 1815)

gelicals   History knows them by a not inappropriate name—' the Clapham Sect '.

The patriarch of the community was Granville Sharp (1735–1813)—' the abiding guest and bosom friend ' of the younger brethren, says one who knew them well ; but intimate as he was with them, Sharp seems to have stood on a somewhat different footing from that of the others. He was some twenty years older than most of them : he was shy and diffident : he was relatively poor, too poor for a parliamentary career : he was rather the confidant and counsellor, therefore, than the comrade-in-arms.   The next in seniority—and also a little apart from the rest— was Charles Grant (1746–1823), who had entered the service of the East India Company in early life, and after twenty years' honest and lucrative employment had been appointed by Governor-General Cornwallis to the high post of fourth member of the Board of Trade at Calcutta.   On his retirement and return to England he joined the Company's Court of Directors, and in 1805 became its chairman.   From 1802 to 1818 he sat in Parliament, as member, most of the time, for Inverness-shire.   His eldest son was to go far in British politics, as far as the Cabinet and the House of Lords , and it is easy to understand the strength and the weakness of Lord Glenelg's notorious colonial policy when one remembers that it had its roots in Clapham soil.   The rest of the group— John Shore (1751–1834), William Smith (1756–1835), James Stephen (1758–1832), Edward Eliot (1759–97), John Venn (1759–1813), William Wilberforce (1759–1833), Henry Thornton (1760–1815), and Zachary Macaulay (1768–1838)—were more or less of an age.   Next to Wilberforce, Thornton was the dominant figure   His father, a successful banker, had been a devoted disciple of John Newton, helping to support him while he was at Olney and presenting him to the living of St. Mary Woolnoth ; and he had left his son a strong Evangelical and a wealthy man.   The great, lofty, oval-shaped library, designed by no less grandiose an architect than Chatham, in his house at Clapham was the regular haunt, the club-room, the meeting-house of the Sect. Between 1792 and 1797 Wilberforce lived in the house, as

Pitt had once lived with him at Wimbledon, and the garden of 'Broomfield', which he occupied for the next ten years bordered on Thornton's From 1782 till his death Thornton held the seat for Southwark. Like Wilberforce he was an independent-minded Tory, and if Wilberforce turned first to Stephen for counsel on the Abolition question, he relied most on Thornton's judgement in general politics. Stephen, who was in the House between 1808 and 1815, was also more or less a Tory, though he hated Pitt Smith, on the other hand, who sat for Sudbury, Camelford, and Norwich, was a Whig. All three, of course, supported Wilberforce to the end on Abolition, as the gentle Eliot, member for Liskeard, would have done if he had lived Macaulay was never in Parliament, but he was by no means the least active or useful member of the group He will presently appear in a leading rôle in the great adventure of Sierra Leone ; and his immense industry and admirable memory made him a kind of living encyclopaedia for the Abolitionists. If a date, a number, an incident were forgotten, if the authority for some point of evidence were doubtful. 'Look it up in Macaulay', they used to say. None of these men, not even Wilberforce as yet, was in any sense a great public figure ; and it was not till 1802, when John Shore, recently created Lord Teignmouth, came to live at Clapham, that the Sect obtained its most distinguished member. Shore, like Grant, had gone early to India to find there an even greater career than Grant's He had become not only a trusted official, but a friend, of Warren Hastings himself, and had accompanied him on his last voyage to England, but his reputation had not been overshadowed by the attack upon his chief. In 1787 he was appointed a member of Cornwallis's Council and became his chief collaborator in framing the historic Permanent Settlement of Bengal. In 1793 he succeeded Cornwallis as Governor-General : and, if his critics, while admitting the value of his five years' work in building up the new system of British administration in India, yet deplore his passivity in affairs beyond its frontiers, his adherence to the doctrine of non-intervention in native disputes, his dangerous acquiescence in the rise of the Mahrattas and the spread of French intrigue, he has his answer in the strict, explicit orders of Parliament and the Company. Rightly or wrongly, he obeyed them and he was rewarded on retirement with a peerage and a seat on Pitt's new Board of Control. Last but not least, John Venn, vicar of Clapham and shepherd of the flock, at whose parish church, as the tablet on its wall now witnesses, the brethren gathered every Sunday to worship and to listen to his sermons Add to these the intimates who did not live at Clapham but were constantly its guests—Milner, Gisborne, Babington, Clarkson, young Bowdler, and one or two more—and add the brethren's wives and the Grant and Stephen children as they grew up, and the roll of the Clapham Sect is complete.

It was a remarkable fraternity—remarkable above all else, perhaps, in its closeness, its affinity It not only lived for the most part in one little village ; it had one character, one mind, one way of life. They were mostly rich, living in large roomy houses ; but they all were generous givers to the poor. Thornton indeed gave away as much as six-sevenths of his income till he married, and after that at least a third of it They could mostly have been gentlemen of leisure , but they all devoted their lives to public service They were all what Wilberforce meant by ' true Christians ' And, as if to make them still more like a single family, they were interlinked by marriage. Thornton's mother was Wilberforce's aunt Stephen married Wilberforce's sister, Gisborne Babington's, Babington Macaulay's ; and Macaulay did not go far outside the circle when he married an old pupil of Hannah More's. It was doubtless this homogeneity, this unanimity that gave the group its power in public life. They might differ on party issues , but on any question of religion or philanthropy the voice of the ' Saints ', in Parliament or in the press, was as the voice of one man. It was, indeed, a unique phenomenon—this brotherhood of Christian politicians. There has never been anything like it since in British public life. ' Oh, where are the people ', asked the younger Stephen in 1845, when all the original members of the group were dead,

' who are at once really religious and really cultivated in
heart and understanding—the people with whom we could
associate as our fathers used to associate with each other?
No " Clapham Sect " nowadays ! '

Naturally Wilberforce was far more at home in this suburban fraternity than in London society, but he liked to take
a holiday, even from Clapham, and, then, obeying the
impulse which in most civilized men rebels from time to
time against the gregarious instinct, he would bury himself
in some remote part of England, sometimes alone, more
often with one chosen friend, most often of all with Gisborne
in his Staffordshire village. As has been seen, he regarded
occasional solitude as essential to his spiritual welfare
' I wish I could sentence some of my friends to a little
solitary imprisonment ', he once said ' They might then
see things in their true dimensions.' But, besides that, he
was a lover of the country and a hater of the town From
the first he felt stifled in London In his earliest days there,
before his ' conversion ', he tells his sister that none of the
pleasures and interests of London—not Mrs. Siddons, nor
the House of Commons—compensates for ' the loss of the
good air, pleasant walks, and what Milton calls " each
rural sight, each rural sound " '. ' I feel a load off my
mind ', he says, when he gets to Wimbledon In the next
period, similarly, he lives as much as possible at Clapham
and as little as possible at Palace Yard. And finally he
abandons Palace Yard, abandons even Clapham, in favour
of a house at Kensington Gore, so that, though Parliament
may force him to stay for months in London, at least it
shall not rob him of a garden. He took an intimate delight
in flowers. ' He would hover from bed to bed over his
favourites ', the *Life* records ; ' and when he came in, even
from his shortest walk, deposited a few that he had gathered
safely in his room before he joined the breakfast table.' So,
in all his homes, it was the garden that mattered most.
' I can never get there sufficiently early ', he writes, ' or
stay there in the morning long enough to witness the
progress of the spring ' His so-called ' study ' at Kensington

was a spreading walnut-tree beneath which he would read
and write whenever the weather permitted ; and when the
nightingales were singing, as, *incredible dictu*, they used to
sing in Kensington, he would linger out there late at night.
But a suburban garden is a makeshift at the best ; and
whenever Wilberforce got really out into the country, his
spirits automatically rose. It was the Lakes, then just
coming into vogue with English intellectuals, that called to
him most insistently. ' I long for the rocks and mountains
of Cumberland ', he tells Lord Muncaster whom he often
visited there , ' the very idea refreshes me ' The older he
grew, the more he longed for this refreshment. ' It is not
a mere imagination,' he writes to Lady Olivia Sparrow
from Barmouth in 1823, ' that in the case of a cold-blooded
creature like myself, a county of lakes and rocks and
mountains, like that which I am now inhabiting, appears to
call forth all the affections into augmented animation .   .
When I was a very young man (a *very* young man, understand), I was always in danger of falling in love when I was
an inhabitant of romantic countries · so even now the same
sublime scenery warms my heart with a double measure of
friendship.' One year he took a house for some months at
Lyme Regis and promptly fell in love with that romantic
sweep of coast past Golden Cap to Portland Two of his
best-remembered holidays were spent in visits to the wooded
valley of the Wye and to the strip of Devon coast where, in
rock-strewn steeps and combes, Exmoor falls to the sea.
He was perfectly content, however, with nature in her less
spectacular garb, never more content, indeed, than in
Needwood Forest which, then happily unenclosed, stretched
down to Yoxall Lodge Every day he would go rambling
there : and Gisborne would often hear him, far off among
the trees, singing away *fortissimo* for mere joy.

It was well that Wilberforce loved nature, for he took
little delight in art. Fortunately, he allowed his portrait to
be painted several times ; and in three cases at least the
result was admirable—for his earlier life, the Rising portrait,[1] now in private ownership ; and for his later years,

[1] Frontispiece

the Richmond, now in the Combination Room at St John's,[1] and the unfinished Lawrence, now in the National Portrait Gallery[2] But, though Gainsborough was still living when he came to London and though he used to meet Reynolds at any rate in those earlier, freer days, he never seems to have thought or talked about them afterwards. One is tempted to suspect that art and artists, though scarcely banned altogether like the theatre, lay dangerously near the moral pale And one wonders if his taste in architecture was any better than that of those kindred Methodists who had begun to sprinkle broadcast over England those edifices which, even if allowance be made for the rigours of economy, seem almost to assert a calculated and defiant contrast with the grandeur of the great cathedrals and the loveliness of the mediaeval parish-church. One sorry criticism, at any rate, escapes him ' The Pavilion in Chinese style,' he notes on the occasion of his encounter with the Prince Regent at Brighton , *beautiful and tasty* .
' though it looks,' he adds, as a happier second thought, ' very much as if St Paul's had come down to the sea and left behind a litter of cupolas.'[3]

In poetry, too, his taste, though strong, was limited, He used to combat Dr. Johnson's drastic opinion of devotional poetry ' Religion ', he would say, ' ought to be the very region of poetry.' And mainly, doubtless, on that account, his inevitable favourite among the poets was Cowper. During his lifetime, the stars of Keats and Shelley flashed and fell across the sky, but apparently he did not mark them. His one recorded allusion to Byron refers characteristically to his conduct rather than his poetry. When he was an old man, a neighbour read to him Moore's *Life* while he paced up and down the room ; and what particularly impressed the reader was ' his anxiety to find out anything in Lord Byron's favour ' ' There now,' he would stop and exclaim, ' surely there is good feeling there ! ' Scott's romantic ballads he devoured with a schoolboy's gusto. *Rokeby* ' interests him beyond measure '. He thinks

---

[1] At p 346 below.   [2] At p 396 below
[3] This *mot* has also been attributed to Sydney Smith.

Halidon Hill ' very beautiful ' But conscience is lurking in the background Though he reads *The Lady of the Lake* ' with delight and wonder ', and considers ' all that precedes and follows, *And, Saxon, I am Rhoderick Dhu*, quite inimitable ', he regrets ' there not being so much of a moral as in *Marmion* '. And these joys are dangerously intrusive Of *Rokeby* the diary confesses, ' Left off and locked it up during Sunday, and did not read it myself after the general reading, knowing that I could not finish it without sitting up late.' About the poet of his beloved Lake Country he can have had no such compunctions, but we only know his judgement of the man—and that in his post-revolutionary period—not of his work. ' Wordsworth, the poet,' notes the diary, a few weeks before Waterloo, ' breakfasted with us and walked garden—and, it being the first time, staid long —much pleased with him.' Shortly after he meets him again at a dinner-party, ' very manly, sensible, and full of knowledge, but independent almost to rudeness.' Three years later he is entertained by the poet's sister at Grasmere and sees ' the moon and a flood of light from Wordsworth's terrace '.

The same Puritan spirit broods over his enjoyment of what he calls ' light reading '. He is as frankly delighted with Scott's novels as with his ballads. A few years before his death he had a sequence of them read to him—*The Fortunes of Nigel, Heart of Midlothian, Old Mortality, Rob Roy*, and *Peveril of the Peak*. He listens eagerly to them all. Nigel haunts him ' strangely '. He is deeply moved by Jeannie Deans's ' truly Christian character and beautiful '. But he is glad when *Peveril* is finished. Because it bores him ? Not at all. ' This class of writing ' is ' too interesting '. It makes other books ' insipid '. He is uneasy, too, over Boswell's *Johnson*. It fascinates him. He leaves it ' with reluctance ' for more serious things. It detains him ' almost the whole evening ' And yet, he complains, it is ' mere chit-chat '. His conscience, in fact, always watching how the hurrying hours are spent, is only really at rest if the book is ' improving ' ; and his Puritanism, it seems, regards no book as ' improving ' unless it is either directly religious or

ethical in purport or adds something concrete and practical
to the reader's knowledge. There are of course exceptions.
He is never uneasy about Shakespeare. He often reads it
aloud in the evening with admirable voice and spirit. And
he shares the reverence of his age for the Classics. At one
time he is vowing to read at least a hundred lines of Virgil
every day ; at another he is closely annotating Horace's
Satires or committing an *Ode* to memory But the great
mass of his reading—and he was an insatiable reader all his
life—lay in those two 'improving' classes, and, of the
second class, particularly in history, ancient or modern,
from Ferguson and Gibbon to Voltaire. So engrossed were
he and Babington once in English history that they took the
book with them on their daily walks, ' one of them reading
aloud whilst his steps were guided by the other.'

It was the same with music. ' What ! ' he cried, when
invited, after his retirement from active life, to attend an
amateur concert at an early hour ; ' Music in the morning !
It would be as bad as dram-drinking.' And when, in the
evenings, he often joined, says an intimate, ' in singing or
chanting ', it was something very different, we suspect,
from the ballads and love-songs with which the young
songster from Yorkshire had once delighted fashionable
drawing-rooms Certainly in music, as in poetry, it was the
religious theme that moved him most. ' Quite overpowered
by the Hallelujah Chorus in the Messiah,' says the diary
in 1828 ; ' a flood of tears ensued, and the impression on my
mind remained through the day.' *

---

* *Life*, i 31-2, 279, 312, 327 , ii 143 ; iii 63, 70, 191, 237, 457,
461, 467 ; iv 92, 277, 390 , v 133, 199, 254, 268, 270, 285, 287, 291,
298, and *passim*. Harford, 8, 168. Sir J. Stephen, ' The Clapham
Sect ' in *Studies in Ecclesiastical Biography*, 521–82. *Letters of the
First Sir James Stephen* (privately printed, 1906), 87 J. C. Colquhoun,
William Wilberforce, his friends and his times (London, 1866).
D. N. B. sub nom.

V

With his busy life in London, with the brotherly society
at Clapham, with the unfailing companionship of books,
above all, perhaps, with his constant sense of communion
with another world to which this earth was but a stepping-
stone, Wilberforce had so far suffered little from loneliness
Quite early he seems to have discarded the idea of marriage,
partly, maybe, in view of his delicate health ; and when the
war came and continued year after year and the framework
of civilized society began to groan and crack beneath the
strain, he began to feel that not only the continual preoccupations and anxieties of his political career, but even—
strange as it seems now—its personal risks debarred him
from sharing his life with another. ' I doubt ', he wrote to
a friend in the autumn of 1796, ' if I shall ever change my
situation ; the state of public affairs concurs with other
causes in making me believe " I must finish my journey
alone ". I must differ from you in thinking that a man such
as I am has no reason to apprehend some violent death or
other I do assure you that in my own case I think it
highly probable. Then consider how extremely I am occupied. What should I have done had I been a family man
for the last three weeks, worried from morning to night ?
But I must not think of such matters now, it makes me feel
my solitary state too sensibly.' The last words are significant. There were moments now, at any rate, when he did
feel lonely. And, for all his protestations, the confession
was half-way to a surrender. By the following spring the
bachelor of thirty-seven had fallen deeply in love He had
made the acquaintance, at Bath, of Barbara Spooner, the
eldest daughter of Mr. Isaac Spooner of Elmdon Hall in
Warwickshire. On April 23 he proposed to her. ' *Jacta est
alea* ', cries the joyful diary that night. Not a word now of
the dangers and difficulties of the time, though it is only a
few days since the mutiny at Spithead. Ten days later,
however, the fears and doubts return. He has heard the
black news of Austria's separate peace ' Much affected by

it for *her* sake ', he comments. ' Wrote to her and told her that I would not hold her to engagement against her will.' Barbara Spooner's reply must have cleared away these hesitations for good and all. For, though nothing could be gloomier than his entry in the diary for May 28—' Daily reports of the soldiery rising . Pitt and the others now convinced that things *in extremis* I now feel exceedingly hunted and shattered '—yet, while he writes this, he is already on the road to Bath, and two days later he is married.

Mrs. Wilberforce would seem to have attained the Periclean standard of womanly virtue. She did not possess a ' dominating personality '. She was not one of those ' political hostesses ' who are almost as well known and as much talked of as their husbands. In all the Wilberforce tradition there is very little indeed about her. In the biography of their father the sons seem to have taken their mother for granted. But at any rate we know Wilberforce's own opinion. ' I believe her to be a real Christian ', he declared on the eve of his marriage ; and on his lips no lover's praise could be more fervent. We know, too, that at times of pain and illness and bereavement, she showed a wonderful fortitude, an heroic trust in her faith. We know finally—and it is all, perhaps, we need to know—that the family life, over which she presided so quietly for so many years, impressed every one who was admitted to it with its peace, unity, and concord.*

* *Life* II 214-15, 220.

VIII

PERSISTENCE

MRS WILBERFORCE was soon to discover that her husband's warnings as to the preoccupations and worries of his political life were not ungrounded. A week was all he could spare for the honeymoon, which was appropriately spent in a visit to Cowslip Green and Hannah More's schools ; and then he was back in his place in the House of Commons Not till the session closed in July could they leave London —first for a few weeks' stay with Wilberforce's mother at Hull, then a round of visits to Babington and other friends, and finally another course of waters at Bath. On November 1, 1797, they were back for the opening of Parliament. ' My dearest wife bears my hurrying way of life with great sweetness ', wrote Wilberforce to his sister in the following spring, ' but it would be a sort of gaol delivery to her no less than to myself to escape from this bustling town.'

If the worst strain had passed with the previous summer, the situation was still very critical during those winter months. All hope of peace had been destroyed by the triumph of the militant Jacobins in Paris who were now waiting for Bonaparte's return to launch him on the conquest of England And in facing this new danger England was thrice handicapped—by the insufficiency of her existing revenue, by the dire need and discontent of her poorer classes, and by the menace of rebellion in Ireland. With the first of these difficulties—the revenue— Pitt promptly grappled with characteristic courage He astonished Parliament and horrified Society by asking that the Assessed Taxes, which were levied on houses, windows, male servants, horses, carriages, and so forth, should be trebled, and in some cases quadrupled, for all taxpayers whose incomes exceeded £200, graduated abatements being allowed for lower incomes. The Opposition seized their chance with gusto ; for it seemed certain this time that Pitt was riding for a fall. ' A forced contribution of incomes by forced disclosure ', said Sheridan, was ' utterly irreconcileable to the spirit of a free and commercial country ' ; and Fox emerged from his dramatic retirement to denounce

Pitt as the author of his country's ruin   ' Storm louder
and louder ', reports the diary during these days : '   .
Anxious in the night about politics.   Much discussion
with Henry Thornton who sadly worried about assessed
taxes   Fox speaking well—much shaken ·   I think
Pitt must give them up '   Outside the clamour was no
less violent   Mayfair wondered ' how people were to live '
if the impositions were carried.   The City was up in arms ·
Pitt was told that he would be assaulted if he came there ;
and, a few weeks later, he was actually hooted on his
way to St. Paul's in a state procession   The bulk of
his supporters, however, responded to the necessity and
patriotism of his appeal, and none more effectively, despite
those transient doubts, than Wilberforce.   He did not like
the Assessed Taxes Bill   ' I dread ', he said, ' the venomous
ranklings it will produce.'   He complained, too, of its
pressing more hardly on the middle class than on the rich,
and he was ' much cut and angry ' at Pitt's rejection of
certain exemptions for which he asked.   But he confessed
that he was bound to accept the Bill for the simple reason
that there was no adequate alternative.   And this support
was, as usual, all the more valuable to Pitt because
of Wilberforce's reputation for political independence
Naturally the Whigs were no less irritated on that account.
To them, of course, the independence of a man who, ever
since that disappointing day when they had prematurely
welcomed the pacifist into their fold, had voted steadily
with Pitt, seemed an obvious and insufferable sham   And
on this occasion Fox himself was goaded into saying so.
Wilberforce had certainly tried his temper.   He had
wandered from the subject of taxation into a strong attack
on the famous ' Foxite secession ' which had lasted now for
a year and was to last for three years more—all critical war
years for the country.   It was a direct assault, he had
declared, on the principle of representative government : it
was a stimulus to the revolutionary spirit which sought for
some other guardians of the public interest than Parliament ;
and it had inspired the French Government with the belief
that the Whigs were allies at heart of France.   Fox at once

replied, first with a defence of his own conduct, and then
with a counter-attack on Wilberforce ' I do not know a
man in this House ', he said, ' who is so ready upon all
occasions to lend himself to Ministers, to profess to believe
what they profess to believe, to distrust what they distrust,
or to allege for them what he does not know to be true, or,
in short, to lend himself as a tool or instrument to Ministers
upon any occasion on which they may call for his assistance.
I say I know no man more ready to do all this than the
honourable gentleman himself, and this for the most con-
temptible party purposes ' ' I was sadly disturbed ', notes
Wilberforce, ' at Fox's imputations.   But I think I can
appeal to God that his charge was false.' He admits a fear,
however, that the attack may have weakened any influence
he might have had with the more moderate members of the
Opposition.

Meanwhile he was occupied in an appeal to the patriotism
of London ' Off to the city ', he records on December 18,
' to try to move the monied men to exertion.' His suggestion
was that a body of business-men should come forward and
invite the Government to propose a levy on property—' one
per cent. on the capital or so much on the income '—and in
a few days' time he actually succeeded in persuading a
well-attended City meeting to accept his plan and to submit
it to the Prime Minister. December 23 · ' Pitt's about the
plan. Found him rational and full of it. Talking with him
for half an hour.' In the end, however, the budget, as
originally conceived by Pitt, was retained ; and early in
January the Finance Bill was passed by large majorities
It marked an important phase in the education of public
opinion to the realities of the long war The contest with
Napoleon, it was evident now, was not a matter of active
fighting only, of strategy and fleets and armies . it was a
contest also in financial endurance in which the nation as
a whole must play its part.

The new spirit was revealed in the success of the Voluntary
Contribution. Early in the finance debate, Speaker Addington proposed that men of means and position should show
their recognition of the country's needs and so ease the

passage of the new taxation by making free gifts to the
State. Wilberforce warmly applauded 'I have been
writing to the Speaker and to Pitt', says the diary, ' con-
firming one and urging the other to a relinquishment of a
portion of their income during the war.' Incurably careless
of his private finances, Pitt was always hard up and almost
always heavily in debt ; but, as a matter of course, he rose
to the call. He and Dundas and other Ministers followed
the Speaker's lead with £2,000 apiece. Wilberforce contributed about an eighth of his income. The King subscribed £20,000 a year from the privy purse for the duration
of the war. The total was £2,300,000—a not unworthy gift
considering that the givers were also confronted with the
burdens of the new budget.

Wilberforce had had a special reason, and a good one,
for desiring Ministers to take a generous part in this process
of self-taxation. He recognized the justice of the Opposition
taunts A Government must be very sure its hands are
clean before it thrusts them deep into taxpayers' pockets.
And, if Pitt himself was incorruptible, was he keen enough
to scent corruption in others ? And had he seen to it that
the public revenue was economized to the utmost before he
asked for more ?

' It is in the highest degree important ', wrote Wilberforce
to Hey, ' that Administration should conciliate the goodwill, confirm the confidence, and animate the spirit of all
who are really attached to the constitution This can only
be done by reforming any manifest abuse, by retrenching
needless expenses, and by making personal sacrifices. . . .
I have been urging these considerations in private upon
Mr. Pitt, but unless my hands are strengthened, I doubt of
my success. He is really—I say it solemnly, appealing to
Heaven for the truth of my declaration—in my judgement
one of the most public-spirited and upright, and the most
desirous of spending the nation's money economically and
of making sacrifices for the general good, of all the men
I ever knew ; but I have met only with two or three (except
truly religious men) who have been able to do obnoxious
duties and above all to act in opposition to the feelings of
false honour by resisting the improvidence and restraining
the weakness of colleagues.'

It was an awkward subject even for Wilberforce to raise ;
and Pitt was nettled. ' Saw very little of Pitt this last
week—vexed him by plain dealing '—so the diary comments,
a little coldly, in November. But the chill was only
momentary. The following week, while the Assessed Taxes
debate is on, he sees Pitt almost daily and finds it not
impossible to return to the charge. ' Much serious talk
with Pitt, stating the necessity of economy and preventing
profusion and jobs.' *

II

Wilberforce was much less satisfied with the Government's attitude to the problem of destitution. ' Much
occupied about the scarcity ', he notes in February, 1800 ·
' urging Government, which sadly torpid and tardy ' And
again : ' I am much grieved at Pitt's languor about the
scarcity. They will do nothing effectual. Great sufferings
of the West Riding people.' His own proposals were not
ideal. He did not see that the most promising policy was
the enforcement of a living wage, adjusted to the price of
bread. Nor perhaps did he see that the supplementing of
wages out of parish poor-rates by the ' Speenhamland '
plan of 1795 was inevitably and disastrously pauperizing
the rural population of England. But he did see, at any
rate, that this method was inadequate either to cope with
the continual fall of wages or to convince the poor that the
England they were asked to starve for was not only an
England of the rich · and he pressed—both personally on
Ministers and in the House of Commons Committee, the
daily meeting of which he never missed—for direct assistance
from the State for all cases of extreme need and, at the
same time, for some curtailment of luxuries besides the mere
rationing of bread. But he could not persuade his colleagues
thus ' to gain the hearts of our people '. ' Though thinking
their measures too weak ', he complains, ' I am by far the

* *Life*, II 220–50. *Hansard*, xxxiii (1797–8), 1089, 1203–4,
1218–26 Holland Rose, II, chap xv.

most urgent in pressing forward those very weaker measures
to the execution of which they proceed languidly and luke-
warmly. It is really beyond expression vexatious to
experience such indifference ' And so it goes on, session
after session, while the English peasantry grow thin and
ragged and desperate. Wilberforce does what little he can
do by private charity In 1801 his gifts to the poor exceed
his income by £3,000. And he urges his acquaintances to
' abridge their luxuries and comforts and superfluities '.
One Yorkshire friend, he tells Muncaster, has resolved to
brew no ale and is striving to prevail on his neighbours to
form the same resolution. A year or two later, Dean
Milner reports Wilberforce as exhausting his strength on
this subject ' And how he does get misrepresented and
abused ! ' he writes. ' But you may kick him as long and
as much as you please . if he could but fill the bellies of the
poor, he would willingly submit to it all.'

The abuse came not only from those whose luxuries
Wilberforce was fussing to curtail. He was abused, too,
by those whose bellies he wanted to fill—and somewhat
more justly. For, genuinely anxious as he was that the
State should do something to relieve the poor, he would
not allow the poor to use the one weapon by which they
could relieve themselves. He regarded Trade Unions not
only as economically unsound, as tending to force up wages
to the detriment of trade in general, but—what was much
worse—as politically dangerous. Thus, with his Yorkshire
manufacturers at his back (but not the artisans !) he
supported the Combination Act of 1799 by which Pitt killed
Trade Unionism for a quarter of a century. Indeed, when
a smaller measure, dealing with combination in one industry
alone, had been introduced earlier in the session, Wilberforce
had been the first to ask for a wider Bill, covering every
trade. Such a Bill, he declared, ' might be of great service
to society.' He seems to have found no fault with the more
glaring defects of the Bill—such as the clause which allowed
a single magistrate to convict a man who might be in his
own employment—but neither did he oppose the amending
Bill of the following year which palliated some of them.

But why did he not detect the root injustice of it all?
Combination, it is true, among employers to reduce wages
was made illegal no less than combination among employees
to raise them. But did Wilberforce suppose, did any one
suppose, this side of the law would ever be enforced?
There is only one explanation, obvious enough. The
Combination Acts, passed as they were side by side with
an Act to keep the *Habeas Corpus* Act suspended, were
part and parcel of the anti-Jacobin reaction. In Wilberforce's mind and Pitt's, the idea of poor men repudiating
the salutary discipline of industrial life and coming together
in dark places to concoct a common 'strike' against
their masters was still crimsoned with memories of the
Terror   Industrial conspiracy!   Was it so long a step
from that to Revolution?   But there is a further question
If Wilberforce was so desperately eager to relieve the poor,
why did he not brave those political risks?   Partly, perhaps,
because he believed that Trade Unionism would defeat its
own ends by increasing the cost of production to the point
of falling trade and unemployment.   But mainly, surely,
because his sympathy for the poor had a curious limitation,
had, so to speak, its converse side.   Like Hannah More
and all his Evangelical friends, he felt that the material
hardships of this world were, after all, of secondary importance.   We have seen him in the *Practical View* almost
congratulating the poor on being saved by their poverty
from temptations that might endanger their salvation   It
may seem a hard doctrine—to some, perhaps, an odious
doctrine, when they think how little these good people knew
what poverty was—but at least it was sincere.   'I declare
my greatest cause of difference with the democrats', wrote
Wilberforce twenty years later, when distress and discontent
were rife again in England, ' is their laying, and causing the
people to lay, so great a stress on the concerns of this world
as to occupy their whole minds and hearts and to leave
a few scanty and lukewarm thoughts for the heavenly
treasure'   It was as much a cause of difference to the
democrats.   Nothing that Wilberforce might achieve for
suffering humanity in other lands could placate the Radicals'

hatred of his ' other-worldly ' attitude to the English poor
Most of them never forgave him for the Combination
Act.*

III

But the worst of England's difficulties in this crisis of the
war was not financial nor economic From the moment of
the collapse of Fitzwilliam's impulsive effort at conciliation
in 1795, Ireland had drifted first into lawlessness and
outrage, then into a bitter revival of the old religious blood-
feud, and finally, after a black period of repression and
reprisals in the North, into the Catholic Rebellion of 1798
On April 5 Wilberforce heard the news of the ' first blood
spilt in Ireland '. He had supported, it will be remembered,
Pitt's commercial proposals in 1785 , but since then, like
too many Englishmen of his own and later days, he had
given strangely little thought to the Irish problem · and
when on June 14 Sheridan opened the Whig attack on the
Government's Irish record, he felt unfit to join in the debate,
' not having pondered on the subject '. Five days later,
however, he plunged into a hot discussion as to whether the
militia should be allowed to go to Ireland. If suppression
were the policy, he argued, the stronger the force, the
shorter and more merciful the struggle. If concession, it
was still more needful to be ' unambiguously strong ', lest
generosity be interpreted as fear. As to the causes of the
rebellion he made no attempt to counter Sheridan's detailed
charges With that air of impartiality which so galled the
Opposition, he hazarded the opinion that the cause, if
carefully investigated, might be found to lie not in anything
the present Government had done but in ' old and long-
standing grievances as to which, according to the course of
Providence, we are now suffering the bitter consequences of
long-past misconduct and neglect '.

Happily, no great military effort was needed. ' Rebel

* *Life*, ii 358–60, 384–7 ; iii 4–6, v 36   J. L. and B Hammond,
The Town Labourer (London, 1919), 115–29.

camp at Wexford stormed ', records the diary for June 28 :
' all apparently suppressed.' But suppression was only the
first step. Some constructive settlement had to be attempted
if only to prevent this chronic wound in Britain's side from
breaking out afresh at some later crisis in the unending war.
And, little though he may have studied the Irish problem,
Wilberforce, like Pitt, possessed the first essential requisite
for its solution He had, as will be seen more clearly later,
a strong anti-Catholic bias ; but, belonging as he did to the
end of the eighteenth century and not to its beginning, he
wholeheartedly accepted the principle of religious toleration.
In England, at any rate, he held that the complete civil and
political disqualification of Catholics was an anachronism.
In 1797 he had carried a Bill through the Commons to enable
Catholics to serve in the militia, and had confessed himself
' too much incensed ', when the Bill was thrown out in the
Lords. And now he fully shared Pitt's irritation at the
opposition of the Ulster Presbyterians to any policy of
conciliation. He speaks of Pitt, in a confidential talk at
Holwood, ' resenting and spurning the bigoted fury of Irish
Protestants ' He was a witness, too, of Pitt's anger when
that hard coercionist, Lord Clare, attempted in the Upper
House to palliate and excuse the atrocities committed by
the Orangemen in their efforts to disarm the Catholic
peasantry on the eve of the Rebellion. ' " Well, suppose it
were so ", said Clare " but surely " I shall never
forget Pitt's look He turned round to me with that high
indignant stare which sometimes marked his countenance,
and stalked out of the House.'

But when it came to concrete proposals for a settlement,
Wilberforce was slow to follow Pitt's lead. It has been
a common experience of Englishmen who have tried to form
an unimpassioned judgement of the Irish question to be
buffeted by the naturally fiercer and more personal
opinions of their Irish friends , and in Dr Burgh Wilberforce
had a friend who was bitterly opposed to Pitt's plan of
Union. It was ' only to be done by force ', he said. It was
clear to Wilberforce from the first, moreover, that Pitt
regarded Union as ' opening the most promising way by

which the Roman Catholics may obtain political power'.
'Pitt sanguine', says the diary (January 25, 1799), 'that
after Union Roman Catholics would soon acquire political
rights resolved to give up plan rather than exclude them.'
And the admission of Catholics, including Irish Catholics
recently in rebellion, into the British Parliament seemed to
Wilberforce a far graver step than the admission of Catholics
in England into the militia 'Would you admit Papists
into the Parliament of the English ? ' he asks his old friend,
Hey, and bids him to be sure to answer. But, all the while,
he was subjected to Pitt's reasoning and Pitt's optimism.
'*Tête-à-tête* with Pitt' is again a constant entry in the
diary, and Ireland is the topic. The upshot was almost
inevitable 'Poor Burgh wild', he notes in January
'Bankes clear and strong against it. Auckland evidently
so secretly'; but he admits to Babington that his own
objections to the Union 'decrease if anything', though
'the preponderance of my judgement is against it on the
terms proposed'. A fortnight of reflection and much discussion with Bankes, and then 'My judgement at length
made up for Union'. 'Burgh is still on fire', he writes,
'and I dare scarcely tell him how decidedly I am favourable
to the measure.'

The passing of the Union Act and its sequel are a familiar
story. 'I have strange tidings to communicate,' wrote
Wilberforce to Muncaster on February 7, 1801, 'The King
and his Cabinet have quarrelled concerning the emancipation
(as it is called) of the Irish Roman Catholics—and Pitt,
Dundas, Lord Grenville, Windham, and probably Lord
Spencer also and Lord Camden are to go out of office
I think you will guess who is to succeed—the Speaker, with
Pitt's friendly concurrence. . . . It is strange, and certainly
argues great precipitancy and want of foresight, that this
was not settled one way or other last year when the Union
took place, or at least agreed on so far as to preclude all
difference at St. James's. . . . I fear the deed is done. The
King and Pitt part on affectionate terms—the King saying
that it is a struggle between duty and affection, in which
duty carries it.'

The Union had been crippled almost at its birth. Despite the inauspicious circumstances of its enactment, it is not inconceivable that the unitary form of government might gradually have guided Ireland into the same happy path as it had Scotland, if only it had brought with it—what was even more essential in the Irish case than in the Scottish— complete equality between the national religions. But it was not till Wilberforce's life was near its end that the English Tories reluctantly and imperfectly completed Pitt's design. And then it was too late. Nothing could then avail to lift the curse with which George III's sense of duty had blasted the Union in its cradle.*

IV

The crowding troubles of these war-years had not diverted Wilberforce from the main purpose of his life. Though almost all his comrades in the cause of Abolition had now resigned themselves to waiting till the war was over, Wilberforce still argued that the very fact that England was at war made it all the more imperative that she should instantly cleanse her shield of its blackest stain. ' Is not this a time ', he asked the House of Commons, ' in which all who believe in the superintending providence of God must feel desirous of averting His displeasure ? '

In 1798, therefore, and again in 1799 Wilberforce proposed his regular motion for leave to introduce an Abolition Bill. He was supported on the first occasion by Fox and on both occasions by Pitt. ' I always have been ', said the latter, ' and until my mind shall change its nature, I always shall be a friend to the immediate and unqualified abolition of the Slave Trade.' Nor can Pitt's speeches, though relatively short, be fairly described as perfunctory ; they were closely argued appeals alike to duty and to interest. Dundas, it will be remembered, had once fixed the year 1800 as the limit of his ' gradual ' Abolition, but only a simpleton would

* *Life*, ii 222–3, 278, 292, 297, 315–18, 324–5 ; iii 2–3 *Hansard*, xxxiii (1797–8), 1507–11.

have expected him on that account to support Wilberforce's motion in 1799. Once more he deplored his inability to agree with either side, once more he pursued a middle path; and this time his middle path was to leave it to the colonial Assemblies to bring the Trade to an end by means of regulations in accordance with the Address of 1797. Windham's attitude was more surprising. Hitherto a firm supporter of Abolition, he had suddenly changed sides He did not, of course—nobody did now—deny or whitewash the atrocities of the Trade. It was, he held, a choice of evils, since instant Abolition would endanger not only the safety and interests of the planters but also the happiness of the slaves. Loyal as ever to his master, he cited Burke as an early exponent of the method of regulation. But if Burke had lived, would he now have been content with regulation ? Would he have deserted Pitt and Wilberforce ? Would his hatred of the Revolution have clouded his mind so completely as to make him forsake the humanitarian field which he had made so specially his own, just because the Jacobins had run amok in it ? The defection of Windham was partly compensated by the adherence of a younger and more brilliant Tory. Canning came out decisively for Abolition in the debate of 1798, and in the following year he made a long speech on Wilberforce's side—one of those fluent, witty, incisive speeches which were quickly to set him in the front rank of British parliamentarians.

From the attendances and the voting it might seem as if Wilberforce was merely wasting time with these annual resolutions. In 1798 he was defeated by 87 votes to 83, in 1799 by 84 to 54. Yet the debates had not been altogether useless, if only for their revelation of the collapse of the case for the defence. It was an impressive fact that nobody now attempted to argue away the horrors of the Trade On the moral issue it stood condemned, and each year fresh revelations rubbed the verdict in Its advocates were driven back on such unconvincing pleas as the statement of Mungo Park (who had recently returned from his first exploration of the interior of Africa) that, in tribal wars up country, victorious chiefs would sometimes spare the lives of captives they would otherwise have slaughtered in order to sell them to the slave traders. More substantial arguments had been met and overthrown. Abolition, said the Trade, will endanger the islands and the Empire. The truth, replied Pitt, with unquestionable authority, is exactly the opposite. Abolition is the *sine qua non* of any improvement in the condition of the slaves, and this in turn is the only means of checking the spread of ' negro Jacobinism '. Well, then, said Dundas, let Abolition be brought about by the best method—colonial regulation. The answer to this was even more authoritative ; it came from the colonies themselves. In enacting regulations the Jamaican Assembly expressly declared that they were ' not with any view to the termination of the Slave Trade '. And it went farther. It disputed the right of the Imperial Parliament to carry Abolition against its will—a defiance which, despite his own argument a few years earlier, made Dundas (says Wilberforce) ' extremely angry with the Jamaica people '. And that was not all These Jamaica people finally showed up the *via media* as a blind alley by insisting that the waste lands of the island must be cultivated, and cultivated by slave-labour. On the basis of the distribution and supply of slaves in the past Pitt dryly calculated that this would involve the continuance of the Trade for 240 years.

Assuredly, then, these debates had some effect. The stalwarts of the Trade in the Commons now numbered only eighty or so. The rest of its old majority had already reached the stage of abstention. And since, though they kept away, they could not stop their ears to the echoes of Wilberforce's moral imperative and Pitt's logic and Canning's wit, the next stage—conversion to Abolition—was inevitably drawing nearer every year. And there was a further value in the debates They were accustoming public opinion to the idea that Slavery itself was only less abominable than the Slave Trade. The Abolitionists had very soon recognized that the assault on the Trade was only the first phase of a greater campaign. But they had hesitated to add fuel to the flames of vested interests and anti-Jacobin prejudices by raising the wider issue. As the case against the Trade developed,

however, the two questions could not be kept apart Again
and again the argument cropped up that the Trade should
cease, not only because of its inherent evils, but because it
provided new victims for the evils of Slavery. And the
inference was obvious

At the time, no doubt, it was difficult to realize the silent
cumulative effect of these annual debates ; and Wilberforce
confessed to the House in 1799 that the prospects of Abolition
seemed to him actually weaker now than they had been
when he first raised the question twelve years before. In
1800, moreover, he consented, for the first time, to a compromise Some of the leading members of the West Indian
party told Pitt that they were willing to support a suspension
of the Trade for five years , and to facilitate the introduction
of this measure Wilberforce agreed not to move his usual
resolution But he was reckoning without the ' die-hards '.
A public meeting was organized and the compromise so
vigorously attacked that it ' shook the resolution of our
timid converts and all except Sir William Young turned
round '. So Wilberforce's concession had done no good ;
yet, now that the annual sequence had once been broken
off, he decided to leave it so for a year or two, and it was
not till 1804 that the familiar resolution was again proposed.
In 1802, however, in moving for papers, he told the House
that he had not grown cold in the cause and that he would
shortly ask them to reconsider their verdict once more

Meantime, while he suspended his frontal movement for
wholesale Abolition, Wilberforce was busy with flank attacks
upon the Trade. In 1798 he drew Pitt's attention to an
Order-in-Council permitting ' notwithstanding the war, an
intercourse to subsist between our West Indian colonies and
those of Spain in which negro slaves are the chief articles
for us to supply ' and obtained his promise to rescind it.
In the same year he averted a more serious menace to the
Abolition cause. The conquest of Trinidad and the removal
of the Carib tribes from St Vincent to the mainland after
the insurrection of 1796 had provided new areas for cultivation of which the British planters were anxious to avail
themselves. Pitt had agreed with the Abolitionists that no

new slaves should be imported from Africa for the purpose ;
but he had almost consented to the planters' proposal that
slaves already in their possession might be transferred to the
new plantations, though it must surely have been obvious
that more slaves would then be bought to fill the gaps on
the old plantations, while, on the new plantations, since the
cultivation of virgin soil always involved a high death-rate,
the planters would soon be raising the old cry—and this
time with a better case—that they must import more slaves
or be ruined 'Lloyd's Coffee House',[1] was Stephen's
bitter comment, ' is in a roar of merriment at the dexterous
compromise Mr. Pitt has made between his religious friends
and his and Dundas's West India supporters.' Wilberforce,
however, had still a strong enough hold on Pitt to wreck
the scheme. He wrote to him, insisted on an interview, and
forced him to choose his side. ' At last,' he says, ' got the
(proposed) proclamation about slaves rescinded.'

He was not so successful in the matter of the Slave Trade
Limitation Bill, a measure brought forward in 1798 and again
in 1799 to protect part of the West African coast, especially
the neighbourhood of the new colony of Sierra Leone, from
the slavers' ravages. On its second reading in 1799 Wilberforce complains that ' Pitt coolly put off the debate when
I had manifested a design of answering P 's speech, and so
left misrepresentation without a word ' ; but he admits,
a little later, that Pitt is ' exerting himself ' for the Bill ;
he learns, indeed, that one of the anti-Abolition Ministers
has been given ' a severe dressing ' by his chief before the
whole Cabinet. So, in due course, the Bill made its way
through the indifferent Commons—the second reading was
carried in a tiny House of 60 by a majority of 16—and
finally reached the Lords where it was introduced by
Grenville, supported eloquently by Bishop Horsley, opposed
by Thurlow and the Duke of Clarence, and duly rejected.*

---

[1] The rendezvous of ship-brokers and marine insurance-brokers

* *Life*, ii 257–65, 277–8, 329–38. *Hansard*, xxxiii (1797–8),
1376–1415 , xxxiv (1798–1800), 518–66, 1092–1140. Clarkson, ii
475–88

V

During these barren years the Clapham Sect had been making, far away from apathetic Westminster, a bold experiment, which, it was hoped, might further the Abolitionist cause more effectively in the end than any amount of hammering at the conscience of Parliament. This experiment had originated in the curious social problem created by the first great act in the British rebellion against Slavery. *Fiat iustitia, ruat caelum*, Lord Mansfield had declared, when, in the course of the Somerset case, allusion was made to the awkward consequences of suddenly freeing the fourteen thousand slaves then estimated to be in England Justice had been done. The famous judgement had been given The slaves had been freed in their thousands. And while most of them had remained in the paid service of their masters or found other employment, some hundreds, unwilling or unable to get work, had drifted into idleness and destitution. The negro beggar had soon become a familiar sight in the streets of London ; and, some years later, the problem of the black unemployed had been aggravated by the demobilization of the negroes who had served with the British forces on land and sea in the American war and of whom some had been deposited in Nova Scotia, some in the Bahamas, and some in London. The private charity of the philanthropists had hitherto been the only means of relief ; Granville Sharp had himself supported from his slender means a considerable number of regular pensioners ; but now it had become evident that more concerted and radical action was required. In 1786, therefore, a ' committee for relieving the black poor ' was formed ; and the result of its discussions was the adoption of a proposal put forward by a certain Dr. Sweatman, an ' ingenious and honourable man '—to quote a contemporary—who had lived for three or four years at the foot of the mountains of Sierra Leone. He suggested that the indigent negroes should be transported *en bloc* from London and planted down as a colony in their native Africa. It was a novel

idea, but it commended itself to the Abolitionists as a means
of advancing civilization in Africa, and of proving their
repeated assertions that a profitable trade other than that
in slaves could be developed there. It also commended
itself to Government, who, anxious to rid themselves of the
growing nuisance, undertook to provide the cost of transport.
What the negroes thought of it is not reported.

In the spring of 1787, then, some few hundred negroes
and sixty whites were landed at Sierra Leone. A block of
fruitful coastland about twenty miles square, by St. George's
Bay, was purchased and in due course formally ceded by
King Naimbanna to the British Crown for the use of the
settlers, and work was begun on the building of a town
But the little community was soon beset by more than the
usual difficulties of an infant colony. Among the blacks
were many dissolute idlers who had done no work since they
had gained their freedom and, rather than do work now,
preferred to wander off into the bush. And among the
whites, by some amazing freak or blunder, were several
women of easy morals, whose presence was scarcely conducive
to the maintenance of health and discipline Near by,
moreover, were slave-dépôts, French and British, whose
agents did all they could to handicap and calumniate the
settlement. Finally it had been founded at just the wrong
season of the year. The fever-bringing rains set in before
the new-comers were acclimatized, and at the end of the
first year half of them were dead. The survivors struggled
on, their ranks continually thinned still further by desertion,
but now keeping disease at bay and cultivating the soil at
least enough to meet their immediate needs And then,
in 1789, fell the final blow. One of the inevitable petty
conflicts incidental to the Slave Trade had led to the
destruction of a neighbouring chief's village by British
sailors. In revenge he declared his intention of burning
the colonists' little town, and after three days' grace the
threat was carried out.

The promoters of the experiment refused to be dis-
heartened by this disastrous start. In 1790 the ' St George's
Bay Association ' was formed for ' opening and establishing

a trade in the natural productions of Africa ' and in the following year it was invested with a charter and incorporated by Act of Parliament as the Sierra Leone Company. Sharp was president, Thornton chairman, and Grant and Wilberforce among its first Directors. Its meetings at once begin to figure constantly in the diary. In canvassing subscribers Wilberforce is careful to emphasize ' the uncertainty of its turning out a profitable concern '. The civilization of Africa and the Abolition of the Slave Trade, not money-making, were its aims ' The design is noble,' he wrote to Wyvill, ' and I trust it will please God to bless the undertaking.' By such honest propaganda substantial capital was quickly raised. And, in the meantime, steps were being taken to save the settlement from extinction. A competent agent was sent out, some sixty of the scattered colonists collected, and a new town begun. In 1792 the negroes who had been demobilized in Nova Scotia requested the Directors to remove them to the more genial climate of Sierra Leone , and, Government having again undertaken to pay for the passage, over 1,000 of them were transported to the colony. Public interest in England was increased by this event , more subscriptions came in, till the Company's funds amounted to no less than £240,000 ; and the colony was well supplied with stores and equipment. A new town, Freetown, was built. A church, a hospital, warehouses were erected Schools were established and well attended. But, as Clarkson's naval brother, who acted as its Governor for ten months in 1792, soon discovered, the colony's difficulties were not over. Malaria was rife again, and among other visitations of nature, the colony was attacked by ' incredible swarms of ants '. At another time, a ship laden with African produce for England, worth £15,000, caught fire and was completely gutted Many of the recruits from Nova Scotia, moreover, proved far from satisfactory. They clung to the town and refused to cultivate the land They became insolent and refractory. They demanded a more democratic form of government, sent delegates to state their grievances in England, and when they returned unsatisfied, broke out in a feeble and short-lived insurrection. It needed a brave and patient man to govern this community ; but such a man the Company sent out in 1793, picked from the ranks of the Clapham Sect itself. Yet even Zachary Macaulay's strength was scarcely equal to the task. On him and one colleague the whole life of the place depended—administration, finance, justice, education, even the preaching of sermons and the celebration of marriages. And then there were detailed reports required by the Company and long personal letters demanded, in response to his own, by Wilberforce Still Macaulay held on, until, in 1794, came the crowning disaster. The colony was attacked by a French squadron, piloted by an American slave captain. No resistance was offered , but, despite the Governor's protests, the town was thoroughly pillaged by the Jacobin soldiers and sailors and some of the chief buildings burnt. No wonder that, soon after, Macaulay's health at last broke down ; but in 1795, after a short rest in England, he was back at his post. And now the tide began to turn. The French attack, it seems, had done some good. The disaffected Nova Scotians were now more willing to submit to discipline ; the damaged town was restored , agriculture and trade increased , in 1798 there were 300 houses and 1,200 inhabitants in Freetown, and a profitable business had been established with the surrounding native villages. When Macaulay left in 1799, he could claim that the colony was no longer an experiment but an established institution. In the following year, accordingly, the British Government committed itself yet further. The status of the Company was raised. It became the first of the Chartered Companies that were to play their historic part in nineteenth-century Africa—vested with supreme executive and legislative authority within the colony and endowed with grants from the British Treasury towards the cost of civil administration and defence. Seven years later the last stage was reached. The Company had done its pioneer work and the Government was ready to relieve it of further responsibility. On January 1, 1808, Sierra Leone became a Crown Colony.

Wilberforce had maintained from the outset the keenest

interest in this unique colonial enterprise He had discussed
its early troubles frequently with Pitt and Grenville. He
had kept up a steady correspondence with Macaulay. And,
despite its chequered fortunes, he could point in the end to
the colony as a proof of his old contention that intercourse
between Britain and Africa could rest on something better
than the Slave Trade. Nor was its example its only service
to the cause When at last the Slave Trade had been made
illegal, it was at Sierra Leone that British captains found
a home for the rescued victims of piratic slavers, by the
end of 1825 it was calculated that nearly 18,000 liberated
negroes had been located there. And it was at Sierra Leone
that in 1821 the head-quarters of British colonial government
along the West coast were established—a government which
was one day to prove the first and most powerful and most
persistent instrument for the suppression of the Slave Trade
throughout the dark interior of Africa.*

VI

Meanwhile the war dragged on into the nineteenth century;
and the prospect of a decision seemed no nearer. For a time,
indeed, the balance had swung sharply in Britain's favour.
In the year after the rupture of Malmesbury's negotiations,
Pitt's bold decision to re-enter the Mediterranean, where
for more than a year the flag of France had flown unquestioned, had been signally justified Nelson had missed
the French Fleet carrying Napoleon to Egypt, but he had
found it again in Aboukir Bay, and in the autumn of 1798
all England had been thrilled by his famous dispatch.
'Almighty God has blessed his Majesty's arms by a great
victory over the fleet of the enemy who I attacked at sunset
on the 1st of August off the mouth of the Nile.' ('Are not
you almost as delighted with Nelson's letter as with the

* *Life*, 1 305-7, 11. 157, 173, 233, 344   *Memoirs of Granville
Sharp*, 11 1-180 Lucas, *Historical Geography of the British Colonies*,
111 284-91 Sir G. O Trevelyan, *Life and Letters of Lord Macaulay*,
chap 1.

victory itself ? ' wrote Wilberforce to Hannah More.) The
Continental land-power, moreover, without which no decision
was attainable, had been once more added to the British
sea-power The Battle of the Nile, cooping up Napoleon
and his army in Egypt, had heartened the Emperors of
Austria and Russia to form the Second Coalition, and in
1799 Suwarow and the Austrians had reconquered North
Italy, while an Anglo-Russian force had landed in Holland
And then the scales had swung as quickly back again. In
the course of the autumn the Austrians had been heavily
defeated in Switzerland, the Anglo-Russian army had been
compelled to evacuate Holland, and Napoleon, slipping
away from Egypt, had returned to Paris and made himself
the virtual autocrat of France by the *coup d'état* of Brumaire.

Worse still was to come next year ; but before resuming
his career of conquest Napoleon made a skilful diplomatic
move. On the last Christmas Day of the old century the
uncrowned King of France addressed to George III and
Francis II a nobly phrased appeal for peace. Ardent
Bonapartists have held this act to prove that the greatest
war-maker in the history of Europe might have been, had
Fate allowed, its greatest peace-maker But Pitt and his
colleagues did not think so They believed that Napoleon
merely wanted peace in order to consolidate his new hold
on France, and, if peace itself were unattainable, hoped, at
the least, by these negotiations to break down the only
remnant of the Coalition—the Anglo-Austrian alliance
Most critics are agreed, however, that, whether their judgement of the offer was right or wrong, the manner in which
they answered it was mistaken. Grenville's reply, with its
slighting allusion to the First Consul's status and its suggestion that, if the French wanted peace, they had better restore
the legitimate monarchy, may have done some transient
good in Vienna ; but in Paris it did nothing but harm. It
merely made French nationalism more wholeheartedly and
more militantly attached to Napoleon and more bitterly
averse than ever from the Bourbons

Not unnaturally, the peace-party in England, who had
something yet to learn about Napoleon, were scandalized

at this hasty and offensive response to his proposals. The Whig attack on Pitt grew very bitter. And at last Wilberforce began to waver in his support of the Government's conduct of the war. ' I am grieved to the heart,' he wrote, on hearing of Grenville's dispatch : ' fearful that I must differ ', and he braced himself to resume the unpopular part he had played in 1795. But, now as then, he would not commit himself till he had heard Pitt state his case So yet another of those stern, protracted arguments took place. Once more Pitt recognized the stubbornness and the political influence of Wilberforce's conscience. Once more he tried his hardest to win him to his doctrine of ' no peace without security '. And this time he succeeded ' Wrote to Pitt, and he sent for me to town,' records the diary. ' I saw him Till then I was strongly disposed to condemn the [rejection] of Bonaparte's offer to treat ; greatly shocked at it. He shook me ' And then, three days later · ' Slowly came over to approve of the rejection of Bonaparte's offer, though not of Lord Grenville's letter '

Subsequent events, as in 1795, cemented this agreement. Napoleon's sword was a mightier argument than his pen. In May 1800, he crossed the Alps. In June he recovered Italy at Marengo. ' Pitt's language ', wrote Wilberforce to Bankes in July, ' is just what we could wish, firm but temperate. He is more sanguine than I am in his expectations, or rather in his opinions, that the Austrians *could* still drive Bonaparte out of the field, if they would exert themselves But there seems a proper sense of the probable necessity of making peace, with a disposition to assume a firm aspect in order to make it on tolerable terms.' But ' tolerable terms ' were not to be had for the asking , and Pitt's inveterate optimism was soon once more disappointed. In December the Archduke John was heavily defeated at Hohenlinden ; and in the following February the Treaty of Lunéville reimposed on Austria roughly the same humiliating conditions as those of the Treaty of Campo Formio four years before. Thus ended the Second Coalition, leaving Britain again with nothing but the mastery of the sea to confront the master of Western Europe.

The fact that this deadlock was as intolerable to Napoleon as to Pitt accounts for the strange interlude of peace which preceded the last, long, finally decisive struggle. The overthrow of British sea-power had become Napoleon's primary object. He sought it first by engineering a combination of the maritime states of the North against England ; but the League of the Armed Neutrality was abruptly dissolved by the assassination of its mad leader, the Czar Paul, and the destruction of the Danish fleet by Nelson off Copenhagen. Thus Napoleon was forced back on peace—a peace which would give him time to build an invincible French armada. Circumstances were favourable. In March, 1801, Pitt had resigned ; and for more reasons than one the new Ministers were readier than their predecessors to come to terms. ' If peace be made ', said Wilberforce, ' the Government may last.' So, on October 1, preliminaries were signed in London ; and five months later the Peace of Amiens was concluded.

Wilberforce was with Gisborne at Yoxall when letters from Pitt and Addington told him of the preliminaries. ' Fireworks at the Lodge for the Peace,' says the diary for October 6 · ' the children were delighted.' Next day he sets out for Bath and notes on his arrival . ' The people *intoxicated* with joy here and everywhere Grand illumination.' And he shared himself in the general relief and thanksgiving. ' God has, of His mercy to this sinful nation ', he declared, ' allowed a suspension of the work of death and desolation.' And he confesses that, if Government had refused the terms, he must have voted with the Opposition. He was rejoiced to find that Pitt approved them, though they were worse for Britain than any he had himself proposed. ' We shall have a scene of strange discordance,' he writes of the imminent debate : ' Lord Grenville is to oppose in the House of Lords and Lord Spencer also ; and Windham still more warmly in the House of Commons ; but Pitt will support with all his might ' Yet, if Pitt admitted that, since the dissolution of the Second Coalition, to make peace was to make the best of a bad job, he denied that he had changed his mind about Napoleon. ' I am inclined to hope everything that is good,' he said, ' but I am bound to act

as if I feared otherwise.' And Wilberforce, with all his
religious hatred of war, could not be more enthusiastic In
reply to Windham's denunciation of Ministers for signing
' the death-warrant of their country ', he could only urge
that, even if the peace should last no longer than three
months, it was right, none the less, to conclude it. It would
' give Europe a proof of our pacific disposition ' and enable
us to make ' friends who might be of service to us when we
should be compelled to enter into a new contest '. He
guessed, in fact, like most shrewd Englishmen, that the peace
was only a truce, only a ' suspension ', though no one's joy
would have been greater than his if indeed the nineteenth
century had brought with it the one thing needed to lighten
the dreary field of British politics, to ease the hardships of
the poor, and, among other accessories of a new age, to
ensure the swift triumph of Abolition.*

VII

Some of Wilberforce's friends had hoped that he might
be given a place in a Peace Government , and he confesses
himself that when the news of the change arrived, he
' was for a little intoxicated and had risings of ambition '.
But the following Sunday brought its usual antidote.
' Blessed be God ', he exclaims in his spiritual journal, ' for
the day of rest and religious occupation, wherein earthly
things assume their true size and comparative insignificance
Ambition is stunted. . . .' In any case, despite his ability,
his eloquence, his influence in the country, Wilberforce had
no chance of office. For Addington, though he had no great
love for the Slave Trade, was not prepared to face the
difficulties and discussions which lay in wait for a Prime
Minister who pledged his Government to Abolition. A
follower of Dundas's ' middle way ', he was by no means
so strong an Abolitionist as Pitt, and, if he had been, he was
not the man to dare what Pitt had never dared. Doubtless,

* *Life,* ii 312, 355–6, 373 , iii. 16–19. *Pitt's War Speeches,* 303.
Hansard, xxxvi (1801–3), 140–4

therefoic, he had little hesitation in deciding to leave Wilberforce's importunate conscience outside his Cabinet. But he could not altogether escape it. He had not been long at Downing Street before Wilberforce was there with a plan for including in the peace negotiations a proposal for a general Convention of the Powers to consider a joint suppression of the Trade ; and the New Year brought him a long, reasoned letter, begging him to take over the leadership of the great crusade and secure its triumph at the Conference of Amiens ' It is not (to a friend I may make the avowal) without emotion ', wrote Wilberforce, ' that I relinquish the idea of being myself the active and chief agent in terminating this greatest of all human evils , but *you* will readily believe me when I say that any unpleasant sensations on this head vanish at once before the prospect of effecting the desired object far more radically and completely than by any springs I could set in motion.' Nothing came of the proposal. It is doubtful whether anything could have come of it. Otto, the French minister in London, had indeed assured Wilberforce that ' if our Government would propose to negotiate for Abolition, then theirs would probably consent to it '. But their Government was Napoleon ; and Napoleon was already seizing the opportunity of the truce to pursue across the Atlantic the mirage of Empire that had failed him in the East. Undaunted by Pitt's experience he had recently dispatched some 25,000 French troops to fight against Toussaint and the yellow fever for the mastery of St Domingo ; and he was contemplating the transfer of Louisiana from Spain which, could he ever have enforced it against the veto of the United States, would have given France the whole of North America west of the Mississippi and south of the Canadian Lakes. The moment of launching such schemes of imperial expansion was clearly not the moment to abolish the Slave Trade, to antagonize commercial and colonial interests, to cut off the supply of labour for new settlements. Even, then, if Addington had surprisingly accepted Wilberforce's plan and still more surprisingly persuaded Parliament to accept it, the supreme surprise would have been Napoleon's concurrence.

Within a fortnight came another letter. The danger that the unoccupied lands in Trinidad and St. Vincent should be sold without safeguards against the importation of new slaves was again acute ' You perhaps may not know ', wrote Wilberforce, ' that for several years past Pitt has been assailed by sap and by storm in all directions and from all quarters . . but he never would give way ' And, on the heels of the letter, came Pitt himself, spurred on by Wilberforce. ' My dear Wilberforce,' he wrote next day, ' I have had a long conversation with Addington, and have great reason to hope from it that he has in no degree committed himself on any point that can lead to an increased importation of negroes . . . Ever affectionately yours, W. Pitt ' So far, so good ; but it was scarcely safe to leave it at that. ' Went after Canning,' says the diary a few days later. He found him ' staunch and warm for Abolition ' and persuaded him to raise the question of the unoccupied lands in the House The results of this move were more substantial. To a long and forcible speech from Canning Addington replied by pledging himself not to authorize the sale of any land in Trinidad without submitting the conditions to Parliament. He also professed a hope—but only a hope, as Wilberforce complained—that the policy of ' gradual Abolition ', which he had embraced so warmly in 1792 and so coldly neglected ever since, might be reconsidered next year.

But the events of the next year once more thrust the whole question far into the background. Wilberforce had refrained from moving his customary resolution in 1801 and again in 1802 in order that its almost certain defeat should not prejudice his new proposal for a European Convention. He was about to bring it forward, however, in the spring of 1803, when Parliament was informed by royal message of the recall of the British and French ambassadors and the imminence of war. ' You can conceive ', he writes to Babington, ' what would be said by Lord Hawkesbury & Co. if I were to propose the Abolition now.' The inevitable indeed had happened. Addington had spoken of the peace as ' a real reconciliation of the two foremost nations in the world '. Fox had been to Paris and come back a warm

admirer of Napoleon. But neither of them had heard
Napoleon confessing at the time that ' every treaty of peace
means to me no more than a brief armistice '. His deeds,
however, had soon proved more eloquent than words. He
had not even had the patience to wait till his great fleet
should emerge from the scaffolding that crowded every
dockyard in France. He had annexed Piedmont and Elba,
reinforced his hold on Switzerland, and maintained French
garrisons in Italy and Holland. And he had directly
provoked Britain by resuming his designs on the Levant—
discussing the partition of Turkey with the Czar, hinting at
a French occupation of the Peloponnese, and dispatching
a mission to Egypt which publicly reported that its reconquest would be an easy matter. Not unnaturally the British
Government had thereupon decided not to evacuate Malta,
the strategic safeguard of the Mediterranean, as the terms
of peace required. Protests and counter-protests had led
to the famous scene in Josephine's drawing-room when
Napoleon lost his temper with the British ambassador and
railed at him ' like a captain of dragoons '. ' He spoke
loud enough ', Wilberforce was told, ' to be heard by two
hundred people, and his countenance was perfectly distorted
with passion.' Though it was Britain that formally presented the ultimatum, that outburst of Napoleon's was
practically a declaration of war. In May hostilities were
resumed

Wilberforce was not exempt from the average Englishman's sentiments. ' The news ', he notes, of Lord Whit-
worth's recall from Paris, ' had the effect on the sudden of
making me feel a sort of intoxicating flush.' But, if he did
not think, as he had thought ten years before, that war
could be avoided, he held that British Ministers had needlessly impaired their moral case by insisting on the retention
of Malta as a condition of continued peace, instead of being
satisfied with its independence and neutrality. So strongly
did he feel on the point that, in the debate on the rupture,
as soon as Pitt had finished his defence of Addington's
Government and before Grey and Fox had opened the Whig
attack, he declared himself in opposition. ' Malta ', he said,

' is indeed a valuable possession, but the most valuable of all the possessions of this country is its good faith . This, then, is my grand objection to the conduct of Ministers, that by claiming the possession of Malta instead of its independence . . . they gave an inveterate enemy an opportunity of mis-stating our real views both to France and to Europe.' The House was ' very impatient ', ' they tried over and over again ', says Creevey, ' to cough him down ' ; and when it came to the vote, Wilberforce found himself in a minority of 67 to 398.

Fox knew Wilberforce too well by now to repeat his old mistake. There was no more question in 1803 than there had been in 1795 of his joining the Opposition camp. His conscience obeyed, his one vote of censure registered, Wilberforce was prepared to support Addington's Government no less loyally than Pitt's in its conduct of the war. And soon the rights and wrongs of pre-war diplomacy were driven from all men's minds by the instancy and gravity of the danger which the war itself brought. The domination of Europe, visions of Empire East or West, everything was now subordinated in Napoleon's purpose to the conquest of the island people whose stubborn independence seemed now the only barrier to the limitless extension of his power. The tents of the ' Army of England ' soon stretched along the coast from Ostend to Dieppe ; the ports were crowded with its ferry-boats ; while, divided between harbours as far apart as Brest and Cadiz and Toulon, the French and Spanish frigates waited for a chance to unite and hold the Channel for the few days needed to achieve the invasion. In face of such a danger all Britain was at last ' one breath ' for war as it had never been since Chatham's days. But, though party-spirit could be held in leash, though every one's desire might be to strengthen the Government's hands, the country and its representatives soon began to chafe at Ministers' seeming inefficiency. ' They seem everywhere in low estimation,' notes Wilberforce in the autumn of 1803. In the Pump-Room at Bath he meets visitors from all parts of England, and by them all (he says) ' they are accused of gross remissness and incapacity '. A little later he complains of the inexplicable delay in providing arms for his Yorkshire volunteers 'It is shocking work, yet, not being quite clear that there is much real blame, I do not like to speak of it in the House.' There were more militant critics who did not control their impatience. 'Windham & Co strong in opposition,' says the diary in December 'Fox manifestly drawing towards them. . . 'Tis said that Sheridan tried to frighten him by saying, " You will get Pitt in again, if you oppose ". He peevishly says, " I can't bear fools, anything but fools " ' It was indeed inevitable that Addington's capacity should be questioned, not so much, perhaps, on the intrinsic merits or demerits of his case as because he was standing in the shoes of an indisputably greater man. As even the Whigs were bound to admit, the country wanted the old ' pilot ' back on the bridge Pitt, however, refused to come out in opposition. He had pledged himself, when he left office, to support Addington, and though he thought his measures dangerously weak, he would not vote against them. But the tide of genuine, patriotic distrust and anxiety ran stronger and stronger ; and it was swelled by the lesser current of personal intrigue. Spirits so discordant as Fox and Grenville were thrown into strange alliance. And at last, in April 1804, convinced that the state of the country was now too critical to justify his holding any longer to his three-year-old promise, Pitt abandoned the aloofness that had dismayed and irritated his admirers, and followed Fox in an unequivocal attack on the Government.

Wilberforce had been deeply impressed by Pitt's earlier generosity to Addington, and he observed his gradual change of front uneasily. ' He is surrounded by men of party spirit without his integrity and of strong passions.' And though Pitt talked long with him and gave him his full confidence, his misgivings were not dissipated ' I fear he has been urged forward by people of less wisdom than himself.' What he personally desired and had personally pressed on each of them was a union of Pitt and Addington. He liked Addington despite his lukewarm attitude to Abolition He liked his peaceableness and his sobriety as much as he disliked

Windham's bellicosity or Fox's vehemence. ' I cannot help regretting ', he says, ' that Addington's temperance and conciliation should not be connected with more vigour.' And again, ' Poor Addington ! With all his faults I feel for him.'

Had he foreseen the upshot of the crisis, he would have been still more uneasy. It was Pitt's desire, as it was certainly the country's, that in this perilous hour the ablest men in all parties should combine , and he proposed to the King the formation of a Coalition Government including Fox, Grenville, and Windham. But George III was scandalized Make Fox a minister ! He was astonished, he told Pitt, that he should ' one moment harbour the thought of bringing such a man before his Royal notice '. And since, as it happened, the King was once more just recovered from a serious illness, Pitt could not fight him. For over three hours he argued with him as firmly as he dared With great difficulty he won his consent to the inclusion of the Grenvillites ; but, as he had previously confided to Wilberforce, he could not *force* Fox on him. And so it was once more the Minister, though this time the people were more certainly behind him, that submitted, and the wilful man, whom Lord Chancellor Eldon had recently described as ' my poor old master ', that had his way. It was Pitt's death sentence. Since the Grenville group rejected Fox's patriotic advice and refused to serve unless he were included, Pitt was compelled to form a Government of mainly second-rate men, half-Pittites, half-Addingtonians, with all a Coalition's drawbacks and none of its advantages. It meant that the enormous burden lay almost wholly on his own shoulders ; and presently it broke them.*

* *Life*, iii. 89, 97–101, 141–61. *Hansard*, xxxvi (1801–3), 1398–1408 *Creevey Papers* (1903 ed), i 15

IX
VICTORY

I

IN one sense Pitt's return to power was a personal loss to Wilberforce. His relations with the Prime Minister could not be so close and happy as his relations with the private citizen. At times, indeed, towards the close of Pitt's previous tenure of office, their old friendship had been sadly strained For Wilberforce, as the years went by, had begun to fear that Pitt was not doing all he might do for Abolition Surely, he kept on thinking, Pitt *could* carry it if only he *would*. Was he not indispensable now to King and country? Could he not compel his colleagues and his party to do almost anything he liked? And when Wilberforce found that even on subordinate Slave Trade questions, such as that of the unoccupied lands, it needed ceaseless watchfulness on his part to combat Pitt's apparent apathy or negligence, he was bitterly disappointed. He knew, too, that his importunity must often worry Pitt, however kindly he concealed it. ' Our friendship has starved for want of nutriment ', he confessed to a friend in 1798. ' I really love him for his public qualities and his private ones . . But how can I expect he should love me much, who have been so long rendering myself in various ways vexatious to him.'

On one occasion, about this time, Pitt certainly was vexed and did not hide it. The affair of Whit-Sunday, 1798, was a queer affair, one of the queerest in the personal annals of British politics. On that day, although it was in the course of a great war and his was the main responsibility for the conduct of it, the Prime Minister fought a duel with pistols against a member of the Opposition. It is true that Tierney's insistent and irresponsible abuse of Pitt and his policy had become wellnigh insupportable ; and it is true that, losing his patience at last, Pitt had insulted Tierney by charging him, not altogether falsely, with obstructing the defence of the country. Yet the challenge should neither have been made nor accepted , and it is not surprising that Wilberforce was shocked, ' more shocked than almost ever ', when he heard of it. It was not only that his

friend had risked his life, nor only that both men had set
their private feelings before their patriotism. Any duel,
under any circumstances, was in Wilberforce's eyes a defiance
of God ; he had himself on that account evaded Rolleston's
challenge ; and he was appalled that Pitt of all men should
have sanctioned such an impious barbarity by his own
example. He at once resolved to do what he could to
prevent such a thing happening again ; and he hurried up
to town to give notice of a motion against duelling. Pitt
was angry at this interference—all the angrier, perhaps, if,
now that the affair was over, his own conscience had begun
to prick him. He wrote Wilberforce a rather curt letter.
' Your motion ', he said, ' is one for my removal.' Other
friends joined their remonstrances to Pitt's ; and Wilberforce realizing, as he might well have done before, that
Pitt's part in the affair must preclude a straight vote on the
principle of duelling, withdrew his motion The incident
was closed in an epistolary *réunion.* ' I need not tell you ',
wrote Wilberforce, ' that the idea of my being compelled to
do anything painful or embarrassing to you has hurt me
not a little.' ' I am, and I trust I ever shall be ', he concluded, ' your affectionate and faithful friend, W. Wilberforce.' ' I cannot say to you ', replied Pitt, ' how much
I am relieved by your determination . . . Much less can
I tell you how sincerely I feel your cordial friendship and
kindness on all occasions, as well when we differ as when we
agree. Ever affectionately yours, W Pitt '

And always, in Wilberforce's heart, was the regretful,
almost resentful, feeling that he could never be as truly
intimate with Pitt as he could be with Thornton or Stephen
or almost any brother of the Sect. Some years earlier, in
1792, he had made an effort to renew that candid conversation of 1786, when he paid a visit to Walmer Castle
where Pitt had recently been installed as Warden of the
Cinque Ports ' Pitt received me very kindly ', says the
diary, ' and with great warmth of affection ' Next day he
had his chance. ' At night alone with Pitt, but talked
politics only—did not find myself equal to better talk.
I came here hoping that I might really find an opportunity

of talking seriously with Pitt. What am I to do so with
any one ? O Christ, help me.' Next morning he was at
it again. ' Had some serious talk with Pitt—interrupted
or should have had more ' It was his last opportunity ,
and while he confesses, at the close of his visit, his admiration of Pitt's ' integrity, public spirit, and magnanimity in
despising unpopularity ', he cannot give him the highest
praise of all : he cannot say he is religious. Indeed he even
wondered sometimes whether he ought to want so often
and so much to be with Pitt and ' the old firm ' ' This is
the day ', says the diary once, ' in which Pitt, Dundas,
P Arden, and Steele are at Hamels. I am disposed to wish
myself with them. I find that even here in religious society
I can have an earthly mind.' And when he is with them, he
is not altogether happy. The comments in the diary and
journal on a stay at Holwood in 1799 are eloquent enough.
' Pitt, Canning, and Pepper Arden came in late to dinner
I attacked Canning on indecency of Anti-Jacobin Evening
he and Pitt reading classics ' And next day ' My heart
has been moved by the society of my old friends at Pitt's
Alas ! alas ! how sad to see them thoughtless of their
immortal souls , so wise, so acute ! ' A few days later he
attends a party at Dundas's in Pitt's honour ' Pitt's
birthday — low-spirited — dined Dundas' great entertainment—Duke and Duchess of Gordon and others. I could
not assimilate, and all flat and cold '

So the old friendship creaked along till the change of
Government in 1801 at last freed Wilberforce from the
worry of Pitt's shortcomings over Abolition and freed Pitt
from the worry of Wilberforce's importunity. And, as it
happened, any such sense of disappointment or irritation
in that matter as lingered on in the back of Wilberforce's
mind was now lost at once in his unbounded admiration of
Pitt's conduct in supporting his untried successor The
diary overflows with eulogies. ' What wonderful magnanimity ! ' ' Unparalleled in a politician ' ' I do not wonder
if it is misunderstood. . . . Little minds cannot receive the
idea ; it is too grand for their comprehension But to any
one who fairly considers it in all its bearings .   it will

appear one of the noblest instances of magnanimity that was ever exhibited to the admiration and imitation of mankind.' And now the records of meetings and talks become more frequent again as if indeed something like the old intimacy was being at last recaptured ' Pitt and Rose dined with me quietly to-day. Pitt very pleasant, and we stayed chatting politics ' He meets Pitt at a country-house party, walks with him, and talks with him till after midnight, and has another ' long discussion ' with him after breakfast. On another occasion he and Pitt are talking *tête-à-tête* all day ' from breakfast to dinner ' There is real affection, too, in his anxiety at Pitt's taking command of 3,000 of the Cinque Port volunteers in the raising and equipment of which the Lord Warden was now spending all his time and much of his money ' I am uneasy at it ', he writes. ' He does not engage on equal or common terms, and his spirit will lead him to be foremost in the battle '— and so it might have been if, as every one expected, the French had landed on the Kentish coast. Yet his very anxiety forces the truth on Wilberforce. He knows it is not quite what he would have felt ten or fifteen years ago. He knows that the tie between them has gradually weakened, that in their inmost thoughts they have drifted apart. Indeed, as he reflects, he is almost surprised at his anxiety. ' For many years ', he tells Gisborne, ' there has been so little of the *eadem velle et nolle* that there cannot have existed much of what merits the name of friendship for that great man, yet I feel a good deal for him on account of the danger to which he is exposed.' That *yet* is significant There was a gap between them : it might be obscured, it might gradually be narrowed, during the interlude of Pitt's retirement : but it was bound to stand out nakedly again as soon as he returned to office. And unhappily there was time, before the end came, for each of them to widen it.*

---

* *Life*, i. 369 ; ii. 270, 280–1, 334–5 ; iii 19–21, 113, 131, 142.

II

It might be supposed that, since it was merely the King's prejudice that had prevented the formation of a Coalition, the new Government would have been conceded some measure of support or at least of tolerance from a united House of Commons inspired by the single purpose of saving the country from Napoleon. As a matter of fact, the opposition to Pitt, though it could no longer be urged that the safety of the nation required the removal of an incompetent Prime Minister, was no less vivacious than the opposition to Addington. Never, indeed, during his previous term of office had he been exposed to such a weight of attack. Fox and his followers were there as of old : they had returned from their tents before the Peace of Amiens ; and now they were reinforced by Grenville and Windham whose criticism of Pitt could scarcely have been more bitter if he had thrust them out of his Ministry with contumely instead of pleading earnestly with the King for their admission. It was a strong combination, and Pitt's colleagues were no match for it. Except for Dundas's experience and Canning's wit they were not a powerful parliamentary team and they worked ill together. Nor were any good recruits available outside. There was only Addington , and his appointment as President of the Council, with the title of Lord Sidmouth, at the end of 1804 betrayed the Government's weakness rather than added to its strength. To make bad worse, Pitt was dogged by a disheartening sense of insecurity. Five physicians were in attendance on the King, watching his aberrations; and every one thought that, if once he crossed the border-line and the Prince came into his own, Pitt would go out and Fox come in.

No lesser man than Pitt could have carried on the King's Government against these domestic odds in time of war— the greatest war in which Britain had ever been engaged and now, moreover, at its most critical stage—and Pitt at forty-five was a very different person from the young Prime Minister of 1783 The physical strain was now evident.

Men noted that he was thinner than ever and worried with a cough. But by drawing on his last reserves of strength he succeeded in holding his Government together and his enemies at bay. For nearly a year he maintained his majority in the House of Commons ; and then at last came a chance for the Opposition to inflict a blow which shook the credit of his Government, though it did not actually bring about its fall, and shook still more disastrously Pitt's fast-failing health.

In the winter of 1804 the political world was buzzing with rumours of a financial scandal at the Admiralty. The affair was some years old ; but since it dated back to Pitt's previous Government and since Dundas, who was now his First Lord of the Admiralty, was the villain of the piece, it was clearly the business of the Opposition not to let the scandal die. And, awkward as it was for him, Pitt, whose views on administrative corruption were notoriously strict, could not attempt to hush the matter up He had appointed a Commission to inquire into the allegations, and its report on those charges which implicated Melville was published in March 1805. It happened that Wilberforce was closeted with Pitt, discussing a Slave Trade question, when the first copy of it was delivered. ' I shall never forget ', he says, ' the way in which he seized it, and how eagerly he looked into the leaves without waiting even to cut them open.' There was good reason for his anxiety. The Report stated that Mr Trotter, Deputy Treasurer of the Navy, had used £10,000 of public money for private speculation and that Dundas, as Treasurer, could and should have prevented it Neither then, nor at any time, was it suggested that Dundas had profited himself by such transactions

The common belief that Pitt took this matter so deeply to heart because of his personal feeling for his old political comrade is exploded by Wilberforce's testimony He had closely marked Pitt's relations with Dundas Years ago, as we have seen, he had learned to regard that worldly Scot as Pitt's evil genius and he was inclined to ascribe to his influence most of Pitt's shortcomings as to Abolition and in other things. So it was probably with some satis-

faction that he had observed a rapid cooling of their friendship. A year before this crisis he had noted that ' Lord
Melville had not the power over Pitt's mind which he had
once possessed ' , and now he says, ' While it was generally
thought that Pitt defended Melville out of friendship, I knew
that they were scarcely upon speaking terms.' And, indeed,
a breach is not surprising. For the revelations of the
Commission had showed, if Wilberforce is to be believed,
that on this very question Dundas had lied to Pitt   ' Some
years before ', to quote Wilberforce's private memorandum
on the affair, ' Mr. Raikes [Governor of the Bank of England
in 1797] had hinted to him that the public money was
illegally employed. Dundas soon after coming in, Pitt said
to him at once, " Dundas, here has been Tom Raikes to me
with a long story of your way of employing the public
money , what does he mean ? " Dundas assured him that
it was their mistake, and that no money had been drawn
except for public service ' Under such circumstances Pitt
could scarcely have been blamed if he had left Dundas to
fight his own battle ; and for the credit of his present
Government, to adopt an aloof and impartial attitude might
well have been to make the best of a bad business. But he
determined on a more dangerous course. Was it because he
felt his own honour was involved ? Or did he shrink from
throwing so old a colleague to the wolves, although he had
betrayed his trust ? Or did he think that, his Government
being so weak, an attempt should be made to clear Dundas,
however great the risk ? That, at any rate, was the course
he took   When the Opposition opened its inevitable attack
on April 8 with Whitbread's resolutions, some of which
directly censured Melville, Pitt at once moved an amendment that the Commission's Report should be referred to a
Select Committee of the House for further investigation, on
the ground that the complicated Admiralty accounts and
especially Melville's share in them had not been adequately
examined. Could he secure his amendment, he might hope
in the end to carry the same majority with him either to
Melville's complete exoneration or at least to some milder
reflections on his conduct. But if he lost it, as well he might

on such uncertain ground, the defeat would be far more damaging to him and to his Government than if he had held his tongue. It might indeed involve his resignation.

Once before, it will be remembered, in the course of a debate on the conduct of a public servant, Pitt had been influenced by Wilberforce's conscience. This time he could not himself appeal to it. This time, on the contrary, he dreaded its effect on others. For it was just on a personal question of this sort, on a point of official morality, on the behaviour of Melville as on that of Warren Hastings, that Wilberforce's judgement was certain to carry weight ; and the very fact that Pitt had not consulted Wilberforce shows that he knew too well what that judgement was likely to be. It was a stormy night in the House Pitt's own speech had been interrupted by violent outcries from the Opposition, and as the debate dragged on into the early hours and the issue became more and more uncertain, the strain began to tell on him. When at last about 4 o'clock, Wilberforce rose from one of the front seats above the Treasury Bench, it was observed that Pitt lent forward and cast him an appealing glance. It reached its mark. ' It required no little effort ', confessed Wilberforce afterwards, ' to resist the fascination of that penetrating eye.' But the appeal was too late. Not without a painful struggle, Wilberforce had inexorably made up his mind on the basis of certain simple, undisputed facts contained in the Report. And now, in a short and quiet speech, he judged the case in the way posterity has judged it, in the only possible way. ' It seems to me ', he said, ' that, if I am willing to admit all which the advocates of Lord Melville argue for, yet I am equally bound to vote for the original motion If the House were to step out of its way to adjust all the shades of criminality which belong to this case, then indeed it might be necessary to take some proceeding or other similar to that which has been recommended to us by my right honourable friend, the Chancellor of the Exchequer. But here is a plain, broad fact which no subsequent elucidation can possibly explain away Here is Lord Melville publicly declaring on his oath that he has tolerated his dependent in a gross breach of an Act of Parliament for the purposes of private emolument. . If the House were once to suffer a Minister to say that he had connived at a breach of the law by a person who had been his confidential servant for a number of years, and that the superior was to pass uncensured because no personal corruption had been proved against him , if that were once to be admitted as a principle by which the House of Commons is to be directed, it would open a door to every species of corruption, and there would be no security left for the faithful discharge of any public trust ' After dealing, in a similar strain, with the plea that Mr. Trotter's transactions had not actually involved the country in any financial loss, he reminded the House that as the constitutional guardian of the people's purse it was on its trial no less than Lord Melville, and so sat down.

No wonder that, as soon as he had heard the first few sentences of this speech, Pitt sank back in his seat with a gesture of dismay. No wonder that, during the rest of it, his feelings, usually so stonily concealed, were evident to all who watched him. When, shortly after, the division was taken, it was clear that Wilberforce's speech had done its work. Some said he had turned as many as forty votes, but one would have been enough. The figures were 216 for the motion and 216 against. The Speaker's casting-vote was needed and all eyes were turned on the Chair. Abbot went ' as white as a sheet '. There was a painful silence. For ten minutes he sat still : and then, after a few words of explanation, ' I shall give my vote with the ayes ', he said ; ' and so the ayes have it '. Instantly the Opposition burst into a roar of triumph. ' Resign ', ' resign ', they shouted at Pitt. The hunt was up and one excited country-gentleman uttered a shrill ' view holloa ' and cried, ' We have killed the fox.' Other ungallant members crowded round the door to wait for the House to empty and ' see how Billy Pitt looked after it '. In earlier years there would have been nothing to see. He would have faced worse defeats and deeper humiliation without a change in that stiff, proud demeanour. But now, for the only time on record, he betrayed his emotions in public He sat still in his place with his little cocked hat pressed down over his forehead to hide his tears ; and presently, with a bodyguard of faithful friends to screen him from those vulgar spies, he was helped out of the House, dead beat and half unconscious of what was going on about him.

A year later, when Pitt was dead, a devoted Yorkshire Pittite told Wilberforce he could not vote for him at the election because of what he had done that night. ' I believe ', he wrote, ' that the delinquency of Lord Melville and the desertion of some of his oldest friends inflicted a wound upon his mind [from] which it never recovered, and [which] contributed to his premature death.' ' It did not injure Pitt's health ', is Wilberforce's ' docket ' on this letter. Maybe it did not, though the contrary seems probable ; but even if Pitt, like his father, had gone straight from Parliament to his death-bed, Wilberforce, though he must have been terribly distressed, could have felt no remorse. And surely, when it was all over, Pitt himself must have recognized that he had placed his friend in a dilemma, and that, knowing the man as he did, he ought to have foreseen which choice he was bound to make. In any case he showed no outward sign of resentment. For the little time that was left, his relations with Wilberforce were just as much short of intimacy as they had been before the Melville case—and no more He would have been scarcely human, however, if the affair had really made no difference to his feelings. He might blame himself in retrospect ; but the fact remained that the hand which had dealt him the deepest wound of his political life was Wilberforce's.

And what of Melville ? He at once resigned and retired to his Scottish home. But the Opposition continued its attack. It demanded and obtained his impeachment—and this with a bitter and exultant vehemence which soon overreached itself and swung back the tide of public opinion towards Melville as the victim of a factious persecution. From this spirit Wilberforce, of course, was wholly free He had done his duty, but he took no kind of pleasure in the result. Though he had detested Melville's worldly ways and deplored his influence over Pitt, though it was Melville more than any other politician who had prevented the success of the cause he had most at heart, he had always felt a liking for him. ' Must I join the triumph over a fallen friend ? ' he indignantly replied to one who urged him to join the deputation which carried up the resolutions to St. James's Inevitably, however, he was regarded by all Melville's partisans as the author of his ruin Indeed, it was the truth. For, although his impeachment before the Lords in the summer of 1806 resulted in his acquittal on all counts, that earlier vote in the House of Commons had made it impossible for him ever to serve again as a Minister of the Crown But Melville himself, assuredly no Puritan, possessed virtues which Puritans sometimes lack , and in his attitude to Wilberforce he proved himself bigger-hearted than his friends. A long time passed before the two men saw each other again , but about a year before Melville's death in 1811, they came suddenly face to face in the narrow passage between the Horse Guards and Downing Street. They recognized each other, as they were bound to do at such close quarters ; and for a moment Wilberforce thought Melville was going to pass him by without a word. But he was wrong. ' Ah, Wilberforce, how do you do ? ' cried the genial old Scot and shook him heartily by the hand ' I would have given a thousand pounds for that shake ', says Wilberforce, and adds ' I never saw him afterwards.' *

III

If Pitt's last Government had been stronger, the Melville affair need not have been so painfully important. Nor, if his Government had been stronger, need Pitt, in these last years, have exasperated Wilberforce more grievously than ever before by his conduct in the matter of the Slave Trade

It might have seemed, at first sight, as if the return of

* *Life*, III 218–30 *Hansard*, IV (1805), 255–322 *Lord Malmesbury's Diaries, etc* (London, 1844), IV. 338, 347. *Diary and Correspondence of Charles Abbot* (London, 1861), I 548 *Tenth Report of the Commissioners of Naval Enquiry* (in *Hansard*, III 1147-1212)

Pitt, who had always professed himself an Abolitionist, in place of Addington, who had always disliked and temporized with Abolition, was the only thing needed to bring about the long-awaited triumph of the cause. For now at last—there could be no mistake this time—the tide was coming in In a sense, indeed, the Abolitionists had decided the issue by their first crusade. From the moment the British people had been fully and authoritatively informed of the black truth about the Trade, Abolition sooner or later was certain. And it would have come sooner, despite the initial success of Dundas's obstructive strategy, if the first popular impulse had not been confused and checked by the counter-impulses excited by Jacobinism and the Revolutionary War. As it was, though the conviction of sin had been thrust into a corner of the nation's mind during the years of fighting, it had not been eradicated, and, all the while, it had been kept alive by the quiet propaganda of the Abolitionists The literature about the Trade had steadily increased The outspoken opinions of high-minded men all over the country had worked silently on their neighbours' thoughts. Almost every year men had read in the newspapers the report of Wilberforce's motion. Gradually, moreover, the anti-Jacobin fury had died down. For many years yet, it is true, any general advance of liberal ideas was still to be retarded ; vague suspicions of sedition among the working-classes could still inspire repression ; but Englishmen were not quite so ready as they had been in Robespierre's day to detect a red streak of Republicanism in every humane crusade Republicanism, moreover, was dead in France, slain, as Burke had long ago foretold, by a ' popular general's ' sword. It mattered less and less, then, that the cause of Abolition had once been tainted by its Republican supporters. And so, when the Peace of Amiens lifted for a time the obsession of war, and nullified for a time the anti-Abolition arguments based on the needs and dangers of war, all the conditions were favourable for the opening of another active campaign—all but one. That one, as has been seen, was Addington's dislike of Abolition

Yet, despite Addington and despite even the renewal of

the war, the hopes of the Abolitionists still rose. In addition
to the general re-awakening of the public conscience, the
cause now enjoyed two tactical advantages. First, the
Trade was divided. A majority of its supporters could still
indeed be persuaded by their extremist leaders to refuse a
single inch of compromise ; but a strong minority, alarmed
at the probable effect on their profits of the rapid cultivation
of sugar in the richer soil of Demerara, Berbice, Essequibo,
and Surinam, lately annexed from the Dutch, were ready to
accept a suspension of the supply of slave-labour for at
least a few years. Secondly, the Act of Union had
now brought to the House of Commons a hundred Irish
members, with no local interests in the Trade nor any social
or political connexion therewith, bound too by no previous
votes or pledges, and eager for the most part to assert their
national humanity by supporting Abolition.

Under these happier auspices, the Abolition Committee,
strengthened by the inclusion of Stephen, Macaulay, and
Brougham, resumed in the spring of 1804 the activities it
had suspended since 1797 , and it was decided that Wilberforce should once more propose in the Commons the familiar
motion he had dropped since 1799. No one, of course,
expected an immediate success. It was too much to hope
that the minority in favour of total Abolition, at once and
for all time, though it was certain to be greatly increased,
could be turned into a positive majority. But before the
day for the motion had been fixed Addington fell ; and the
Committee, hurriedly reconsidering its plans, decided that,
though Pitt would never give them all they wanted, he might
give them something—something that, at his bidding,
would certainly be carried. So, a few days after Pitt's
return to Downing Street, Wilberforce was there again,
entreating him now to take advantage of the division in the
ranks of the West Indian faction and, in concert with the
moderates, to propose himself, officially, a suspension of the
Trade for a period of years. Somewhat to Wilberforce's
surprise, Pitt at once consented ; and an interview with
Mr. Milligan, one of the moderates, was quickly arranged.
But nothing came of it. ' My conversation with Milligan ',

wrote Pitt to Wilberforce, the morning before the debate,
' amounted only to this, that he and other sensible West
Indians wished for the suppression , but the great majority
would oppose it, many from adherence to former opinion,
and more from the fear that, if once suspended, the Trade
would never be revived. In this state, and having had no
time to settle anything with any part of the Cabinet, I see
no use in moving the suspension, unless anything arises
in the debate to give a favourable opening for it.'

It was to be all or nothing then, when, on May 30, Wilberforce rose again to ask the Commons' leave to introduce
an Abolition Bill. Whatever their opinions might now be,
it was clear at the outset that at any rate members took a
deeper interest in the question. The House was by no
means full, but the attendance was twice as big as those
which had rejected the motion in several previous years.
In other respects the debate was like its predecessors.
Wilberforce once more outlined the whole case with
admirable clarity and studied moderation. Pitt, in a short
speech, welcomed the new converts to the cause and declared
that the best kind of Abolition was total Abolition, and the
best moment for it the earliest possible moment, but
promised—with an eye on his divided colleagues—to support
a partial or gradual measure if nothing better were attainable. Fox's speech was also short. His main point was that
the honour of the country was at stake. It was being
' whispered throughout Europe ', he said, ' that, however
we might like lessons of morality, we could not be prevailed
upon to give up a profitable branch of commerce very
readily '. Forty seconds, by Wilberforce's reckoning, was
enough for Addington's bald assertion that Abolition was
impracticable. Of other old supporters of the Trade,
Tarleton and Fuller and Manning stubbornly maintained
their opposition, but Barham announced his conversion.
The most striking incident was the intervention of the Irish
members. They had held that night, to quote the diary,
' a great Irish dinner, 33 or 34 dining together,' at which
Lord De Blaquière, their leader, had proposed the health of
Wilberforce for a toast. They had then trooped into the

House to vote for him ; and, rising last but one in the debate, De Blaquière declared that, though the question was new to Irishmen, they had no difficulty in coming to a unanimous decision on it A few minutes later, the division was taken. In a House of 173, no less than 124 voted for Wilberforce's motion and only 49 against it.

Success at last !—and far exceeding Wilberforce's hopes. Congratulations again poured in on him—amongst others from Jeremy Bentham whose friendship he had won some years before by his active, though unavailing, sympathy in the strange affair of the Great Panopticon And this time the congratulations were better justified. Twice before the House of Commons had voted for an Abolition motion, and nothing at all had come of it. But then the majorities had been slight and not to be depended on there had been no assurance that the House was ready to proceed beyond the stage of pious resolutions ; while now there seemed no reason why it should not see the matter through. And then for the last and grimmest obstacle ! ' I fear ', said Wilberforce, in replying to a cordial message from the aged Newton, ' I fear the House of Lords.'

No time was lost. On the very night of their triumph, the zealots gathered in Wilberforce's house. Thornton, Grant, Stephen, Macaulay, Brougham, and others were there ; and before going late to bed, Wilberforce discussed and settled the main lines of the Bill. Eight days later, on June 7, he moved its second reading. His previous exposition had made it unnecessary for his own part in the opening stage of the debate to be more than curt and formal ; but towards the end he rose again to clear Burke's memory from the imputation of unfriendliness to Abolition. Pitt's speech was longer and unequivocally for the Bill. And, though the defenders of the Trade made a desperate effort, brought up the heavy guns of Windham and Castlereagh, pleaded as of old for delay, for time to study the evidence, and stubbornly kept up the fight till 2 a.m., the division went against them almost as heavily as before—Ayes 100, Noes 42. On June 12 the Bill passed through Committee. In vain the West Indians strove to check its progress at the Report

stage when, says the diary, 'they slipped away, and,
leaving less than forty, counted us out.' In vain they
invoked all the old fears and prejudices and trotted out the
bogey of emancipation—thus, according to Fuller, the
slaves were saying, 'Massa King Wilbee wanted to free
them but the Parliament would not let him' The Bill
moved safely over their protests to its final stage. But just
before the last debate there was an anxious moment.
Abolition was not now so new a question to the Irish
members, and Wilberforce was dismayed to hear that
'they have been persuaded by West Indians that it is an
invasion of private property'. Barham's vote, too, seemed
for a time in danger 'Offended by my apparent inattention
to him', says the diary for June 23. 'I wrote him a letter
of apology, and all healed.' But far more disquieting than
anything else was the suspicion that Pitt's support was not
whole-hearted. In one of the debates a back-bench
Abolitionist, Mr Somers-Cocks, had asserted to Pitt's face
that, 'if he had employed the fair, honourable influence of
office,' the object he professed so cordially to desire would
long ago have been attained. More than once Wilberforce
had been tempted to think likewise he had become more
and more reluctant to recognize the difficulties of Pitt's
divided Cabinets; and now he was disappointed and
alarmed because Pitt did not give more time and more
energy to ensure the passage of the Bill. 'I never was so
dissatisfied with Pitt as this time', he complains in the
diary. But of time and energy Pitt had little to spare in
those days. His first duty, after all, was to fight Napoleon ;
and just at this moment his chief measure for the defence
of the country, the Additional Force Bill, was being bitterly
contested in the Commons. On June 8 his majority had
fallen to 40. 'The Opposition', notes Wilberforce himself,
'Foxites especially, in high spirits . . . The effect of these
bad divisions may cause the rats to run, and so pull him
down' Would it have been wise, at that moment, for Pitt
to irritate, perhaps to estrange, the anti-Abolitionists in
that weak majority of his by canvassing the cause of
Abolition more personally and provocatively than he did ?

As it was, his part was by no means neutral or nugatory. He attended the debates at every stage. He spoke frequently and always firmly for the Bill. And just before the end he personally defeated the last attempt at obstruction. Wilberforce himself had yielded to the Trade's demand that counsel must be heard ; but only one of them had spoken when the old plea for postponement was raised on the ground that members, especially the new Irish members, must have more time to consider the evidence. Pitt was on his feet at once. ' Warming in his speech ', says the diary, in a very different tone from that of its complaint of Pitt only two days before, ' [he] moved against hearing *counsel as well as* evidence, and carried it without a division ' It was obvious, indeed, that the question had been thrashed out long ago and that, as Pitt said, ' there was no reason to expect that counsel would throw any new light upon it.' It was manifest obstruction, in fact Yet could any one with less authority than Pitt's have swept it so peremptorily aside ?

The debate on the third reading took place on June 27. It was short and its result was never in doubt. Pitt's speech, indeed, was more concerned with the results of the measure than with its passage, but he may have won some votes by his tactful and timely handling of the question of compensation. He opposed the insertion of a special clause in the Bill, but he pledged himself to the principle that the State should meet all fair claims for personal losses caused by Abolition Later on, he interrupted Rose, a close friend and a member of his Government, in the middle of a vigorous speech against the Bill, on a point of order. Two or three old defenders of the Trade, led by its veteran champion, Sir William Young, gloomily paraded the weather-worn scarecrows of massacre and ruin The bigger men on both sides were silent. Neither Fox nor Windham, neither Canning nor Castlereagh spoke. Towards the end, Addington, speaking as ' a warm advocate for Abolition ', briefly denounced the Bill—because the negroes would be unable to distinguish between Abolition and Emancipation. Wilberforce followed him with ' some rather severe remarks on

him and his warm zeal for Abolition '—to quote the diary—
which he was glad, being always rather tenderly disposed
towards Addington, ' did not get into the newspapers.'
There were no further protestations of national humanity
from the Irish members , and their abstention explains the
drop in Wilberforce's majority. The figures were 69 for
the Bill and 33 against it

' The Supreme Disposer of all things can turn the hearts
of men, and before Him difficulties vanish '—so commented
Wilberforce on the conversion of the House of Commons
But only half the victory had been won ; and Wilberforce
might well pray for more than human agency to convert
the House of Lords. As he was ' carrying up ' his Bill, he
was met on the threshold of the House with disappointing
news from his old comrade-in-arms, Bishop Porteus. He
had discussed the prospects of the Bill with one of his
brethren, and they had come to the conclusion that its fate
ought not to be hazarded outright. The session was
advanced. Most of the bishops were away in their dioceses.
Several members of the Government in the Lords were
expected to oppose the Bill. Was it not wiser, then, not to
risk a positive rejection which would tell against success
another year ? A visit to Pitt was still more discouraging
The Cabinet, Pitt told him, had agreed that ' the subject be
hung up till next year '. Accustomed now to these swift
turns of fortune, Wilberforce at the moment took the
disappointment coolly, but the more he reflected, he confesses, the more bitterly he felt it. ' I own ', he writes to
Gisborne, ' it quite lowers my spirits to see all my hopes for
this year at once blasted, yet I can't help myself.' He says
nothing of Pitt , but he must have felt again that old
unreasoning resentment—unreasoning because Pitt's statement of the case, as clear and logical as ever, had convinced
him. The House of Lords, he had explained, ' from their
habits would not dispense with evidence ' , and for evidence
there was no time this session. He had argued, further,
' that it was best for the cause to be regarded as a new
question ', for Abolition to be urged *de novo*, mainly on the
ground of the increased and increasing danger to the West

Indies of permitting further imports of disaffected negroes. Nevertheless, Wilberforce was right to kick against conviction. For Pitt had not mentioned the real argument against immediate action in the Lords. The real argument was the old one—the division in his Cabinet and party. Had Pitt been strong enough to make Abolition a Government measure, to dragoon recalcitrant colleagues, and to press the Bill on the Lords with the united support of ministerial peers behind it, he would not have needed to make any other case for it than that which the Commons had accepted, and he could then have overridden those time-honoured habits in the matter of evidence—the near future was to prove it— as easily as he had crushed obstruction in the Commons.

As it was—it being understood among all parties that the Bill was not to be carried to a division—the debates in the Lords on June 28 and July 2 were a rather bloodless formality. But at least they revealed the weakness of Pitt's position. On both occasions it was a member of the Government, indeed a Secretary of State, Lord Hawkesbury, who opened the debate, not however as the Bill's official ' father ', but as its firm opponent. He was presently followed by the other Secretary of State, Lord Harrowby, who confessed to friendly feelings for the Bill, but did not presume to urge its merits on the House and supported his colleague's motion for adjournment. And, in between these Secretaries of State, the Lord Privy Seal, Lord Westmorland—' like himself, coarse and bullying ', notes Wilberforce, ' but without talent '—boasted his pride, ' as a peer of the realm ', that the admirable constitution provided one House at any rate in which the interests of the merchants and the colonists would be as carefully attended to as if they themselves were represented there. Finally, Lord Chancellor Eldon judicially admitted that he had never voted on the question, never indeed examined the voluminous evidence, but he advised the House, very gravely, to give ' the most mature deliberation ' to a measure which, if too suddenly adopted, would bring total ruin to so many individuals. Such was the Government contribution to the progress of the cause which the Prime Minister had so long and so openly supported. The Court, too, was to be reckoned with in the Lords: and four members of the royal family were in their places, prepared to vote with their spokesman, the Duke of Clarence, who, his old antagonism untempered by time, admitted that he chafed against the agreed adjournment and wished for an instant and decisive rejection of the Bill. The poor Bill, in fact, had only three defenders—for Lord Harrowby's speech was scarcely a defence—Horsley, Bishop of St. Asaph, who asked if a British House of Parliament really needed any great length of time to make up its mind on the notorious horrors of the Trade : Lord Stanhope, whose wild tirades and threats were worse than useless and who was only prevented by a timely remonstrance from the watchful Wilberforce from impulsively forcing a disastrous division . and Lord Grenville, who, like Pitt, had supported Abolition in his steady, serious way ever since that day at Holwood when, as Wilberforce now reminded him, Pitt and he had launched the young enthusiast on his long campaign. It was to Grenville, in fact, that Wilberforce had perforce appealed to champion the Bill as its ' natural guardian and protector ' in the Lords. And it is a final comment on Pitt's position that the man, who in days gone by—when he was a Secretary of State in Pitt's Government, when indeed he had been raised to the Upper House partly through Pitt's wish to have at least one firm friend of Abolition among so many of its enemies—would have ' fathered ' the Bill as a matter of course, should still, though he was now a leader of the Opposition, be the only man available to play the part

In due course the Lords adjourned the Bill by agreement till the next session. ' To be sure ', said Wilberforce, ' one session in such a case as this is not much ' , and he consoled himself with the prospect of a final triumph in 1805.*

* *Life*, iii 162–83. Clarkson, ii. 490–4 *Hansard*, ii (1804), 440–75, 543–58, 613, 649–62, 779, 848, 863–75, 926–33

IV

A final triumph in 1805 ? Of all Wilberforce's disappointments, that of 1805 was to prove the most exasperating.
Early in the year he was given a hint of impending danger,
but he does not seem to have appreciated it. ' You will,
I know, be glad,' Pitt wrote to him, ' independent of politics,
that Addington and I have met as friends ; but I hope
you will also not be sorry to hear that that event will lead
to political re-union.' Wilberforce was pleased at Pitt
communicating this news to him : ' it showed me ', he says,
' that he understood my real feelings ' He was still more
pleased with a talk he had with him as they walked round
the Park. ' I am sure ', said Pitt, ' that you are glad to
hear that Addington and I are at one again ' ' And then he
added with a sweetness of manner I shall never forget,
" I think they are a little hard upon us in finding fault with
our making it up again, when we have been friends from our
childhood and our fathers were so before us, while they say
nothing to Grenville for uniting with Fox, though they have
been fighting all their lives " '
It seems strange that Wilberforce should not have guessed
why it was that Pitt went out of his way to appeal to his
liking for Addington and to secure his express approbation
of the alliance. He knew its cause—the necessity for Pitt
somehow or other to strengthen his Government. But did
not he also know what one, at least, of its results must be ?
Had he forgotten that Addington's opposition to immediate
and wholesale Abolition had markedly stiffened in the last
few years ? Could he not foresee that the alliance would
make it harder than ever for Pitt to support it openly and
vigorously ? Anyhow, he soon learned the truth. Pitt
again sought his company ; but this time it was to lay his
dilemma candidly before him and to beg him to postpone
the reintroduction of the Abolition Bill But Wilberforce
had long ago determined never to ' make that holy cause
subservient to the interest of a party '. He was adamant.
Providence, it seemed, had at long last set the victory

within its grasp   It would be imbecile, it would be impious,
not to seize it, however much it might embarrass Pitt.   No,
he would not delay an instant   Within a week, indeed, of
his hearing about Addington he had given notice of his
motion.   Nine days later, on February 15, he moved for
leave to reintroduce the Bill and obtained it without
a division   On the 19th it was read a first time ; on the
28th it came up for the second reading.

When Wilberforce rose to open the debate, he had every
reason to expect that the result of the previous year would
be repeated   Opinion in the country at large was, if anything,
more interested, more favourable ; and nothing had happened at Westminster save the Pitt-Addington alliance,
and why should that alter individuals' votes ?   But as the
debate proceeded, he grew more and more uneasy.   With the
single exception of Barham, the first eight speakers were all
against the Bill.   Then at last Fox broke the silence of its
friends—combative, uncompromising, but not so confident
as usual   At the close of a short speech he expressed a
' strong hope ' that a favourable opinion in the Commons
would ' make a powerful impression on the public mind '.
He was followed by Mr Huddleston, warm for Abolition.
And then Pitt got up.   On every previous occasion, on the
debates on all of Wilberforce's annual motions, at every
stage of the Bill in the previous year, Pitt had declared,
quite clearly and firmly, that he personally desired immediate
Abolition.   To declare it again, he may have thought, was
a vain repetition ;   his opinion was notorious   Yet it is
surely strange, surely significant, that, on this occasion
only, he allowed it to be taken for granted.   His brief speech
was concerned mainly with the repudiation of an incidental
charge which a previous speaker had levelled against the
Government—a charge of making an official contract for
the purchase of slaves.   He said at once that he had not risen
' with any intention of entering into the debate ', and he sat
down without saying a word about the Bill   The chill
which seemed to have fallen on the Abolitionist rank and file
at the beginning of the evening now sank to freezing-point.
Those of them who had usually spoken on previous occasions

sat still in their places. It only remained for Wilberforce
to wind up the debate 'Though I thought we might be
hard run from the face of the House,' he said afterwards,
'I could not expect defeat.' A vigorous effort, however,
was obviously needed ; and his speech, though he felt,
he says, 'as if he could not go well', was easily the best of
the evening.   Boldly—perhaps overboldly—he met the
argument that the end of the Slave Trade would mean the
end of Slavery.   He would be mad, he said, to look for
Emancipation as the instant sequel to Abolition ; but he
hoped that one day the slaves of the West Indies would be
transformed into a free, moral, industrious, and happy
peasantry.   And he closed with the warning which more
than once, but not to-night, Pitt himself had uttered.   If
Parliament did nothing for the negroes, they would be
tempted sooner or later to do what they could for themselves.
A repetition by Lord Temple of the charge that Government
had purchased slaves—another curt denial from Pitt—and
then the division.   Seventy members voted for the second
reading, seventy-seven against it.

As they came away from the division, Mr. Hatsell, the
shrewd old ex-Clerk of the House, ventured to express his
sympathy. 'Mr Wilberforce,' he said, 'you ought not to
expect to *carry* a measure of this kind. . . . You and I have
seen enough of life to know that people are not induced to
act upon what affects their interests by any abstract arguments ' 'Mr Hatsell,' Wilberforce replied, 'I *do* expect
to carry it ; and what is more, I feel assured I shall carry
it speedily.'   And certainly there were excuses to be found
for the defeat 'All expressed astonishment,' says the diary.
'The Irish members absent, or even turned against us.[1] . . .
Some Scotch, I believe, who last year neutral, voted against
us.   Great canvassing of our enemies, and several of our
friends absent through forgetfulness or accident, or engagements preferred from lukewarmness.'   But explanations of
defeat are cold comfort ; and though Wilberforce was very
far from despair, though he could even make a show of

[1] Nine Irish members were present, and one at least voted for
the Bill

confidence to kindly pessimists like Hatsell, he was staggered
by the unexpected blow. 'I never felt so much on any
parliamentary occasion,' he confesses. 'Alas, my dear
Muncaster,' he wrote a few days later, 'from the fatal
moment of our defeat on Thursday evening, I have had
a damp struck into my heart. I could not sleep either on
Thursday or Friday night without dreaming of scenes of
depredation and cruelty on the injured shores of Africa. . . .
I really have had no spirits to write to you. . . . Still I will
do all I can. If we cannot stop the whole of this accursed
traffic, it is much to stop half of it , and I am resolved to
do what I can, I repeat it.' *

V

It was true that a good part of the Slave Trade could be
stopped without a wholesale Abolition Bill. It might be
possible to persuade Parliament to accept a partial measure
prohibiting the Trade with foreign countries only. And the
Government might take action, either on its own initiative
or under pressure from the House of Commons, to veto the
importation of new slaves into the old Dutch colonies,
recently annexed by Britain, of which the most important
was Guiana. Wilberforce had already taken up the latter
question in 1804, after the adjournment of his Bill in the
Lords. He had told Pitt that he was proposing to ask for
a resolution of the Commons ; but Pitt had assured him that
it was unnecessary. 'Called on Pitt (July 3), who positively
said he had no doubt of stopping the Trade by Royal
Proclamation. Very strong on this, and against any vote
of Parliament.' Wilberforce and his friends at once submitted. They dropped their plan of a resolution and waited
for the Government to act. But there was prolonged and
inexplicable delay. 'Let me beg you, my dear Pitt,' writes
Wilberforce, ten weeks later, 'to have the Proclamation

* *Life*, iii 210–16   Clarkson, ii 494–500. *Hansard*, iii (1805),
521–2, 641–74

issued. . . . It will not cost you half an hour to settle this.'
At last, in November, came encouraging news 'I am
hardly sure ', wrote Harrowby, ' that I am not a perjured
privy councillor in telling you that the order about Surinam
and all other conquered colonies was actually on the list
of council business on Thursday last ' But it was apparently
too low on the list. When the opening of the session of
1805 diverted the activities of the Abolitionists to the
greater business of the Bill, nothing more had been heard of
the Proclamation.

But the subsequent *débâcle* in Parliament threw Wilberforce back on to the Guiana question. ' I am resolved to
do what I can ' And, as the result of his bitter disappointment, there was now something stiffer, something almost
fiercer, in his resolution than ever before. He did not want
to quarrel with Pitt. An entry in the diary in the previous
summer shows how warmly he had still regarded him—
' Appointment with Pitt, who had answered my last letter
in a very friendly way—really affectionate, as I am sure
I felt and acted towards him.' But strange things had
happened since then. What was he to think of that extraordinary postponement of the Proclamation ? What was
he to think of Pitt's share in that disastrous debate ? He
notes in the diary that several half-hearted supporters of
Abolition excused themselves to him for not voting for the
Bill ' on the ground of Pitt's not meaning it to be carried '.
He makes no further comment ; but many of his fellow
Abolitionists were not so reticent. They now utterly
despaired of Pitt. They were convinced he had sold his
conscience to his Cabinet. And, though Wilberforce would
not go quite so far, though he still believed that his appeals
to Pitt's better mind might ultimately be successful, he was
determined now to be very firm with him. He would
certainly refuse again, as he had refused a month before, to
yield an inch to his personal or party difficulties. He would
use every weapon he had, even if it meant estrangement.
He would go, if need be, to the last extreme of open opposition. If there must be a quarrel, he could not help it.

In this mood he wrote Pitt a ' strong letter ' a few days

after the defeat of the Bill and followed it up in person That
interview must have been strained. Never before had he
actually threatened Pitt ; but now he told him that, unless
he promptly dealt with Guiana himself, he would force the
question on Parliament, and not merely as an independent
Abolitionist but in concerted alliance with Fox and Grenville. Whether or not so stern an ultimatum was really
needed, it quickly had effect Pitt was not merely as ready
to pledge himself as he had been in the previous year. He
put the matter at once before the Cabinet, and after its
next meeting he wrote to Wilberforce telling him that his
colleagues had unanimously agreed to stop the Trade with
Guiana and asking him to draft the requisite regulations.

Wilberforce was reassured. What he wanted to believe
of Pitt seemed to be coming true But other Abolitionists,
particularly the Whigs among them, were not so easily
satisfied. At the end of the month a meeting was called by
Lord Henry Petty at Lansdowne House, to consider what
steps should be taken to press the question to an issue
independently of Government. It was attended by some
twenty Abolitionists of all parties ; but the anti-Pittites,
Fox and Grey among them, were in the majority. Naturally,
therefore, Wilberforce's declaration of confidence in Pitt
fell rather flat. ' I saw certain significant winks and shrugs ',
he told Muncaster, ' as if I was taken in by Pitt and was too
credulous and soft ' However, the meeting, in deference to
Wilberforce, consented to adjourn for a few days, while he
and Bankes attempted, as its authorized agents, to obtain
a further pledge from Pitt The result was as unequivocal
as ever. Pitt told the envoys to report his answer to the
meeting—that the Government would, by Order-in-Council,
stop the Guiana Trade. It was a pleasant little triumph for
Wilberforce. The Prime Minister's explicit promise, given
not merely to a private friend but officially to the Lansdowne
House group, could scarcely be winked and shrugged aside.
So the meeting passed on from the Guiana question to that
of the Foreign Slave Trade and commissioned Lord Henry
Petty to give notice of a Bill for its abolition. It was afterwards decided, however, not to press for this second object

till the first was attained   They would wait for Pitt to
carry out his promise.

They waited for days . . . and weeks . . . and months

There can be only one explanation of this seemingly
astounding conduct   Notorious among all contemporary
politicians for his personal honesty, Pitt was incapable of
a mean deceit at the expense of Wilberforce and his collaborators.   The reopening of the Slave Trade issue in Parliament,
as his attitude in the last debate had shown, would certainly
have embarrassed him.   But this at least is incontestable—
he did not divert the Abolitionists from their purpose by
giving them a promise with the deliberate intention of
delaying his fulfilment of it as long as he possibly could
Nor, in this affair at any rate, was it a question of slowly
overcoming the susceptibilities of Sidmouth and his other
anti-Abolitionist colleagues   They had already given in ;
they had unanimously agreed to stop the Guiana Trade
The true, the only possible, cause of the delay was a complex
of two connected factors—the condition of Europe and the
condition of Pitt's health

If the one thought in Wilberforce's mind most of this
time was Abolition, the one thought in Pitt's mind all this
time was Napoleon.   The menace of invasion, though
custom and calculation of its difficulties had dulled its edge,
still hung overhead   And the old dominant problem of the
whole war—how to defeat Napoleon without Napoleonic
armies—remained unsolved.   In December 1804, Spain,
with her important fleet, joined France , but Britain still
stood alone.   Month after month Pitt laboured in vain to
create yet another Continental Coalition   The capricious
Romanov vacillated and bargained   The timid Hapsburg
preferred a dangerous peace to a still more dangerous war
The inept Hohenzollern waited with greedy eyes on the bait
of Hanover which Napoleon, but never Pitt, could offer
him.   None of them applied to his policy Pitt's single test—
' Will it save the liberty of Europe or not ? '   Meanwhile
Napoleon's power was rising to its zenith.   Directly or
indirectly he was ruler now of all the West of Europe.   In
May he crowned himself King of Italy at Milan   In June

he annexed the Genoese Republic. And thereby he succeeded where Pitt had failed. He had torn up the Treaty of Lunéville, he had destroyed the Balance of Power; and Alexander and Francis Joseph were at last goaded into war. The Third Coalition was formed   In the autumn the Austrian and Russian armies took the field, on the understanding, of course, that Britain as usual paid for them. With a selfishness fatal to herself as well as to the rest of Europe, Prussia held aloof

At length, then, with Napoleon's help, Pitt's long and anxious diplomatic campaign had proved, in part at least, successful; but its very success brought new burdens with it.   It intensified the violence of the Opposition; for Fox and the Whigs repudiated on principle a policy which had twice failed in practice and was, as a matter of fact, to fail again.   Further, it meant an increase of taxation to provide the subsidies, and that, in turn, meant fiercer enemies and cooler friends.   And in face of this new crisis Pitt's parliamentary position grew even weaker in 1805 than it had been before.   His initial defeat on the Melville affair in April was followed by endless and irritating debates on the question of his impeachment.   In the course of them the Addingtonians began to break away, and in July Sidmouth himself resigned.   A weaker man than Pitt might now have told his master that he had served him to the limit of his power, that he could no longer bear alone the intolerable load.   And Pitt, in his desperate need, went so far as to entreat George III once more to form a National Government by admitting members of the Fox-Grenville alliance to office, especially in view of the next budget   But the King was quite comfortably satisfied as to Pitt's capacity to carry on as before, and the idea of Foxites in the Government inflamed his unstable mind almost as much as that of Fox himself.   He talked wildly, it is said, about keeping Fox from his counsels at the cost of civil war   So there was no change

And, all this time, Pitt was obsessed with innumerable other cares than those of diplomacy and Parliament   He was taking a considerable part himself in the actual conduct of the war   He read and wrote countless dispatches.   He personally dealt with much of the departmental business both of the Foreign Office and of the War Office.   He was in constant consultation with the Lords of the Admiralty and with the Commander-in-Chief   The crucial decisions, for example, in the naval strategy which triumphed at Trafalgar were his as well as Barham's.   An endless string of callers at No. 10—generals, admirals, officials, politicians—was always waiting to fill the corners of his day with interviews— the most famous is his fine farewell to Nelson—and at night his sleep was often broken by the arrival of news that could not wait   The scale of his activities may seem small beside those demanded by our own Great War, but then as now there were only twenty-four hours in the day ; and Pitt, unlike more fortunate War Ministers, no longer possessed an even passably good physique.   Indeed, as his last year drew on, surely he must himself have suspected now and then that his strength was nearing its end.

Set in that perspective, Pitt's failure to redeem his promise in the matter of the Guiana Slave Trade no longer seems astounding.   Is it to be wondered at that he began to lose his old swift efficiency in every detail of government ?   Is it surprising that, when so many questions demanded instant settlement because they bore directly on the war, he allowed other questions to drift on unsettled from week to week ? But Wilberforce could not understand this strange, this ominous lethargy ; and his disappointment and vexation grew.   The pledge had been given in March.   By May Ministers had got so far as to consider the draft of the Order-in-Council ; but Wilberforce's discussions of it with Lord Camden, Pitt's War Secretary, and with Attorney-General Perceval are constantly interrupted and postponed.   He feels there is no driving force behind them, and, besides his almost daily calls at Whitehall, he is frequently importuning Pitt by letter or in person   At last the Order is framed, but ' so framed ', he thinks, ' as to be worse than none ', and he is off with it to Pitt to insist on emendations.   Otherwise, he declares, ' I really think we had better run the risk of losing all by trying to carry the measure in Parliament.'

Pitt asks him to draft his alterations. He drafts them. But,
ten days later—it is now June 4—the diary complains :
' Pitt has not yet settled it—too bad—though he authorized
Bankes and me to assure the meeting at Lord Lansdowne's
that he would do it. Sad work ! I write and call again
and again.' ' Procrastination ', he tells Muncaster, ' in one
whom you used to call " The General ", has increased to
such a degree as to have become absolutely predominant.'
And when, at last, on September 13, the Order-in-Council
is issued, Wilberforce cannot ascribe it to Pitt's awakened
conscience. It is chiefly due, he says, to the businesslike
methods of an anti-Abolitionist, Castlereagh, who had
succeeded Camden at the War Office.*

VI

Public men have often been permanently estranged by
more negligible grievances than those which Pitt and
Wilberforce inflicted on each other in 1805. Wilberforce's
speech had swayed the House of Commons to deal Pitt
the hardest blow of his career. Pitt's apathy and inaction
as to the Slave Trade must have seemed to Wilberforce
almost a betrayal of the cause he cared for most in life. But,
even so, the friendship was too old, too strongly founded
in mutual respect, to be more than temporarily clouded.
Throughout that difficult time they frequently met ; but,
if there was any unspoken resentment, any latent irritation,
on either side, there was never anything like a quarrel. And
in the autumn the cloud passed over. When at last the
Order-in-Council had been issued, there was no longer any
need for those persistent, importunate calls at No. 10 , and,
if Wilberforce was constantly dropping in, it was, as in
earlier days, just on the chance of finding Pitt free for
a tête-à-tête about less prickly things than Abolition Entries
like the following again recur in the diary : ' Drove into
town to see Pitt—had much talk with him upon political
topics, finding him very open and kind.'

* Life, iii 183–5, 216–17, 230–4. Rose, op cit , chap. xxiii.

In November came the double-edged tidings of Trafalgar. 'So overcome', notes Wilberforce, 'that I could not go on reading for tears.' When Pitt was awakened with the news in the early hours, he could not resume as usual his interrupted sleep ; and the dawn found him busy with the day's work. Had victory on sea been followed by victory on land, his life might have been saved. But Napoleon had discounted Trafalgar Denied sea-power, he could still show himself the master of the Continent. Already the 'Army of England' had been flung across Europe from the Channel to the Danube ; and on the day before Trafalgar 25,000 Austrians had surrendered at Ulm. A few weeks later, on December 2, the joint armies of Austria and Russia were crushed at Austerlitz. Napoleon had destroyed Pitt's Third Coalition almost as soon as it was made ; and he had destroyed Pitt too. The tremendous blow gave a fatal turn to what had seemed at first a transient attack of gout. On January 23 Pitt died.

Wilberforce was staying with Babington in the country and it was not till he returned to London on the 21st that he heard how ill Pitt was. Next morning, he was 'too unsettled and uneasy about Pitt' to stop at Clapham. He drove up to town and called on various friends All gave him a 'bad account'. Rose, who had come from the patient's house at Putney, told him that the doctors had given up hope. On the 23rd he heard from Bishop Tomline that the end had come about half-past four in the morning. When he set himself, that night, to record the final item in the diary wherein, for twenty-five years past, with the candour of the confessional, he had chronicled so much that was good and so little that was bad of his famous friend, his first thought was that his patriot *par excellence* had died as he had lived for his country, and his mind flew back to Trafalgar. 'Pitt killed by the enemy as much as Nelson,' he writes. But there is something solemn in Pitt's death that curbs the quick emotion he had felt at the news of Nelson's 'Deeply,' he says, 'rather than pathetically affected.' 'This late event', he writes to Muncaster two days later, 'saddens rather than softens my heart. There is

something weighing down the spirits.' And in the same
letter he reveals wherein the sadness lay. He had once
described Pitt as more genuinely patriotic and more pure-
minded than ' any man, *not under the influence of Christian
principles*, I ever knew '. He had never, of course, regarded
him as positively un-Christian, an infidel like Hume or
Gibbon He was to learn presently, indeed, that the dying
man had allowed Bishop Tomline to pray with him, mur-
mured the responses, asserted his faith, and declared that
he had tried, with many errors and failures, to serve God
and mankind. But Wilberforce, as we know, had wanted
more than that ; he had wanted Pitt to share in the fuller
revelation which had transfigured his own life ; and he had
dreamed of Pitt—years afterwards, as we shall see, he
confessed it—his great virtues thus supplemented and
illumined, his great powers reinforced, playing the part of
the ideal statesman of the *Practical View*, transfiguring the
life of England. He had never ceased to desire that, one
day, he might be permitted to be the instrument of such
a change in Pitt, to make him see the logic of his faith as
he saw it. Once, at least, during that visit to Walmer, he
had tried, and failed And now it was too late. ' I own ',
confesses Wilberforce, ' I have a thousand times (aye, times
without number) wished and hoped that a quiet interval
would be afforded him, perhaps in the evening of life, in
which he and I might confer freely on the most important
of all subjects. But the scene is closed—for ever.'

The last duties of his friendship were still to be fulfilled.
On January 27 a motion was proposed for a public funeral
and for the erection of a monument ' in the Collegiate
Church of St. Peter, Westminster, to the memory of that
excellent statesman '. To a later generation it seems, at
first thought, astonishing that the motion should have been
opposed ; but it is not easy in the middle of a war to take
a generous view of a statesman whose conduct of it has been
unsuccessful. And this was the morrow of Austerlitz
Neither Windham nor Fox, in fact, was merely factious in
his opposition. Neither denied Pitt's great abilities ; but

Windham maintained that the greatest national honours
should not be bestowed for merit, however high, unless it
were united with success, and Fox refused to subscribe to
the ' excellence ' of a statesman whose system of government had been, in his opinion, disastrous to the country.
It was one of those rare occasions when parliamentary
warfare is ennobled by the sincerity of the disputants and
the solemnity of their theme.   Pitt's friends and enemies
could speak of the dead man, as they never could of the
living, without a touch of personal bitterness, without
a thought of votes to be won or lost, but in simple loyalty
to their convictions.   Castlereagh's reply was temperate
and dignified , and Wilberforce, who followed him, warmly
acknowledged the honest motives of Pitt's critics.   But he
declared that it was neither just nor wise to make success
the criterion of honour ;   and then, venturing on more
contentious ground, he claimed that at least in one outstanding achievement Pitt had been successful—he had
saved England from ' the revolutionary spirit that had
convulsed France and alarmed the whole civilized world '.
' I feel this motion ', he said at the close of his brief speech,
' to be but a small tribute of deference to the memory of
a man who was ever the object of my esteem and admiration,
who was equally distinguished for great talents, for exalted
character, for enlarged views, for personal purity, and for
indefatigable patriotism. . . . To whatever regarded his own
interest he was perfectly indifferent.   He was always forgetting himself but always remembering his country.'

The motion was carried by a large majority, but, a few
days later, came another on which Wilberforce's views were
shared by few.   Always incorrigibly careless of his private
finances, Pitt had left some £40,000 of tradesmen's debts
behind him, and Wilberforce was one of those who did not
wish them to be paid by vote of Parliament, partly on the
principle that private debts should never be made a public
charge and partly for fear lest at a time of increased taxation
this extra burden, relatively slight as it was, should be
resented by the taxpayers and ' create a feeling very
injurious to Pitt's memory '   For three days, therefore,

he was busy canvassing his friends and the City for private
subscriptions ; but, with the exception of Perceval who was
' warm and generous as ever ' and, though not a man of
large means, promptly offered £1,000, he met with practically
no support   The diary bears witness to his disappointment ,
yet, strongly as he felt about it, he could not bring himself
to oppose the motion for public payment which was now
proposed in Parliament   Nor, of course, could he support
it, as Fox and Windham did.   He left the House, therefore,
before the debate on it began.

The funeral was held on February 22.   In the procession,
at Lord Chatham's request, Wilberforce was one of those
who carried the banner before the coffin, and his place in
the Abbey was in the forefront of the mourners.   Pitt's
grave had been prepared close to his father's ; and as he
stood beside it, it seemed to Wilberforce as if Chatham's
adjacent statue was ' looking down with consternation
into the grave which was opened for his favourite son '.

Fifteen years later, Wilberforce wrote down his mature
impressions of Pitt's character and career.   It is a document
of the first historical importance ; annotations and correc-
tions reveal the pains its author took with it ; and its
publication in 1897 was eagerly welcomed by students of
the period.   But, for present purposes, it is enough to draw
attention to one remarkable fact.   The document shows
that in 1821 Wilberforce's opinion of Pitt was, in all essentials
precisely the same as in 1806.   Fifteen years of experience
and reflection, fifteen years under other Governments with
other policies than Pitt's in war and peace, had only deepened
and clarified his earlier convictions.   His admiration is still
the same, still only clouded by the one regret that so great
a man should not have been greater still.   If only, at the
outset of his career, he had resolved ' to govern his country
by *principle* rather than by *influence* ' !

' All his faculties then possessed the bloom of youthful
beauty as well as the full vigour of maturer age , his mind
was ardent, his principles were pure, his patriotism warm,
his mind as yet altogether unsullied by habitually associating

with men of worldly ways of thinking and acting, in short,
with a class which may be not unfitly termed " trading
politicians ". . . . No one who had not been an eye-witness
could conceive the ascendancy which Mr. Pitt then possessed
over the House of Commons.' If only he had tried to
' govern by principle ', he would have succeeded And then
the whole English body politic would have been cleansed
and strengthened. Even so great a cataclysm as the French
Revolution would have left it unshaken. ' Such a spirit
of patriotism would have been kindled, such a generous
confidence in the King's Government would have been
diffused throughout all classes, that the very idea of the
danger of our being infected with the principles of French
licentiousness . . . would have been an apprehension not to
be admitted within the bosom of the most timid politician ;
while the various reforms which would have taken place,
and the manifest independence of Parliament would have
generated and ensured in the minds of all reasonable men
a continually increasing gratitude and affection for the
constitution and laws of our country. On the other hand,
the French, infatuated as they were . . . could never have
been so blind to their own manifest interest as to have
engaged their people in a war with Great Britain from any
idea of our confederating with the Crowned Heads of
Europe to crush the rising spirit of liberty in France. Hence
we should have escaped that long and bloody war. . . '

It is as old as politics, as old as the vision of the βασιλεὺς
φιλόσοφος — this idea of a favourite statesman rising
clean above the bounds of circumstance ; and there have
been others besides Wilberforce who believed that Pitt
could have done it, could have cut away all the oblique
supports of the old régime, dispensed with the votes he won
by the distribution of innumerable ' places ' and with the
votes the King won for him by the ' influence ' of the Crown,
and rested his authority on his ' principles ' alone. It is,
indeed, conceivable—though the speculation is idle enough—
that if Pitt had adopted and improved on his father's rôle,
if he had set himself, a second Great Commoner, at the
head of a real democratic movement in England, in temperate
alliance with the new ideas in France, he might have made
himself an almost omnipotent dictator But Wilberforce
is not thinking of anything like that. He does not even

presuppose some drastic measure of parliamentary Reform, something more than the suppression of bribery and corruption No : he would have us believe that, working within the structure, more or less unchanged, of the old eighteenth-century political system, Pitt, single-handed, could have moralized English politics. Almost a miracle ? Well, it was as something in the nature of a miracle that Wilberforce regarded it, as something, at any rate, beyond the unaided power of man For, when he speaks of ' government by principle ', he means much more than the government of a good man Before his eyes, all the time, is his vision of the ' true Christian ', and just as Pitt was in his mind, years before, when he wrote the passage on the ideal statesman in the *Practical View*, so now he is imagining Pitt as more than the bold reformer, as the ideal statesman himself And what a vista opens at the thought ! Consider, he says, the effect on Pitt himself and those about him, on his use of his brain and his faculties, on his choice of friends, on his official appointments in Church and State And consider how these men, in turn, in their appointments would have followed the same rules of choice, and so on throughout the descending sequence of the public service. ' Who can say what would have been the effect of those religious and moral secretions, if they may be so termed, which throughout the whole political body would have been gradually producing their blessed effects in augmenting its fulness, symmetry, and strength ! ' It was not the least of Wilberforce's tributes to Pitt's greatness to conceive him thus, if once his eyes had been opened to the truth, initiating and directing that one experiment in aristocracy which mankind has never cared or dared to try—a government of saints—and bringing down to English earth the incredible dream of a Christian State.

And there, as before, the deeper criticism ends. Wilberforce touches on a few minor foibles of Pitt's—his shyness amounting sometimes almost to *gaucherie*. (' He was one of the shyest men I ever knew,' is a pencil comment in the margin) ; a touch of pride, but none of arrogance , his occasional fretfulness in his later days , an oversanguine judgement of men and things. But these are trivialities beside his virtues—his honour, his truthfulness, his open mind, his incorruptibility, above all his selfless love of England. Long ago, in the first days of their friendship, the strength and purity of Pitt's patriotism had been impressed indelibly on Wilberforce's heart. Time might cool a little the warmth of his regard ; blemishes might be detected in other aspects of the man ; but that picture, at least, was safe from disillusion. It flashes instantly before him at the news of his death. And now, forty years after its first impress, it remains unchanged. ' No man ever loved his country with a warmer or more sincere affection.' *

VII

It is sometimes said that Pitt's death was a necessary preliminary to the Abolition of the Slave Trade ; and under all the circumstances it is probably true. But the censure implicit in the statement should fall on George III rather than on Pitt. Had Pitt been allowed to form a national administration, had he needed no longer to defer to inflexible colleagues and uncertain followers, had he been granted, in fact, a new lease of strength and freedom, there is no reason whatever to suppose that, as soon as it was clearly in his power, he would have hesitated to do what he had described, times out of number, as demanding instant doing. Nor does it detract in the least from the credit due to Fox to say that in this matter he was more fortunate than Pitt. When at last he was accepted perforce by George III as a Secretary of State in a Government composed of Foxites, Grenvillites, and Addingtonians, if he was obliged to assuage the royal fears of Catholic Emancipation, there was no need to compromise on Abolition. It could not, indeed, even now, be brought forward as a Government measure by a Cabinet which included Windham and Sidmouth ; but now, at any rate, for the first time, a decisive majority of Ministers,

---

* *Life*, iii. 238–54. *Correspondence*, ii. 71. Holland Rose, ii. 557. The ' Sketch of Pitt ' is printed in *Private Papers*.

headed by Grenville, their chief, were ready to support or at least to accept it. Meantime the reawakened public interest had not only been maintained, it had been strengthened. In the winter of 1805-6 Clarkson had emerged from his retirement, resumed after nine years' absence his seat on the Abolition Committee, and straightway, a giant refreshed, set off on another tour of propaganda. ' This journey ', he declares, ' I performed with extraordinary success.' What particularly heartened him was to find that the younger generation, who had grown up during the years of silence and inaction, embraced the cause with all the ardour of their elders in old days. So now, for the first time since 1792, there was something better than appearances to justify the hopes of the Abolitionists. Public opinion and political opportunity really coincided. The stars at last were in conjunction.

However deep his personal regrets, Wilberforce, too, must have realized at once that Pitt's death had opened a new prospect for his cause ; and he had lost no time in showing that, whatever might be the new alinements of political forces, the immediate advocacy of Abolition would be the supreme test of his allegiance. Once, during Pitt's lifetime, Fox had let fly a rather venomous shaft of wit at his professions of independence. ' If Wilberforce were compelled ', queried somebody at Sydney Smith's hilarious dinner-table, ' to desert either the cause of the slaves or the party of Mr. Pitt, to which would he adhere ? ' ' Oh,' said Fox, ' he would be for Barabbas.' But if Wilberforce, as was true enough, had always shrunk from opposing Pitt, it had been mainly on personal grounds. He had loved Pitt but not the Pittites. And, before Pitt was in his grave, he startled his friends by pledging his support to one of Pitt's warmest Whig opponents in the imminent by-election for the vacant seat at Cambridge University. ' My suddenly promising Lord Henry Petty,' records the diary for February 13, ' (which done too hastily from wishing to show Lord Henry how much both I and the cause felt indebted to him) has produced a sad degree of rufflement. Dear Dean [Milner] much hurt about it for my sake. I am accused of

changing sides.' Pitt's friends might have been still more
scandalized if they had known that Wilberforce was now
frequently closeted with Fox. And to Wilberforce himself
it seemed a strange turn of the wheel that had brought him,
on the same old quest, to Fox's door instead of Pitt's.
' Though intimate with Pitt ', he muses, ' for all my life
since earliest manhood, and he most warm for Abolition,
and really honest ; yet now my whole human dependence
is placed on Fox, to whom [all] his life [I have been] opposed,
and on Grenville, to whom [I was] always rather hostile
till of late years, when I heard he was more religious.' He
found Fox ' quite rampant and playful as he was twenty-two
years ago, when not under any awe of his opponents. . .
Talked as if we might certainly carry our question in the
House of Commons, but should certainly lose it in the House
of Lords ' This last confession took Wilberforce aback.
From Fox of all men this submissiveness, this scarcely
rampant attitude, towards an obstinate House of Lords was
not what he expected ; and he even wondered whether Fox
had been ' got at ' by the Court But the suspicion proved
unfounded. Fox had an entrée denied to Pitt ; and Wilberforce soon learned that ' the Prince had given his honour
to Fox not to stir adversely '. Meantime he was conferring
also with the new Prime Minister and even with Sidmouth ;
and it was presently decided that, before a wholesale
Abolition Bill was launched, soundings should be taken, so
to speak, by the introduction of a partial measure, taking up
and completing the work of Pitt's Order-in-Council On
March 31, accordingly, Attorney-General Pigott moved for
leave to introduce a Bill to prohibit the importation of
slaves in British ships into the colonies annexed by Britain
during the war or into the colonies of a Foreign state and
to prohibit also the outfitting of foreign slave ships in British
ports or the employment of British capital or labour therein.
' How wonderful are the ways of Providence ! ' exclaims
Wilberforce a little later : ' the Foreign Slave Bill is going
quietly on.' On April 18 it was read a second time—very
quietly indeed , the West Indians did not even divide the
House Very quiet, too, was the final stage on May 1 ; only

a handful of members troubled to attend, and the third
reading was carried by 35 votes to 13. In the House of
Lords the Bill was once more 'fathered' by Grenville;
but Grenville was now Prime Minister, the first to sit in
the Upper House since the beginning of the Abolition
movement; and, partly, no doubt, on that account, the
Bill had a far smoother passage than any of its predecessors,
far smoother than Fox might have supposed. The opposition obtained indeed a hearing for counsel on behalf of certain
London merchants and shipowners who had petitioned
against the Bill, the Duke of Clarence bluntly attacked it
on the second reading, and Westmorland and Hawkesbury
promised opposition at a later stage. But there was no
division. On the third reading the attack stiffened Eldon,
from the Woolsack, pronounced against the Bill. Lengthy
speeches were made against it by Hawkesbury, Westmorland, Sussex, and that old campaigner, Sheffield. On the
other hand there were favourable surprises. A rift appeared
in the hitherto united opposition of the Royal Family The
Duke of Clarence was answered by his cousin of Gloucester
in a maiden speech, condemning 'that shocking traffic in
human blood' and warmly supporting the Bill. And
Sidmouth, as the outcome possibly of Wilberforce's pleading,
declared that the Bill, as an instrument of 'gradual and
progressive Abolition' was entitled to his consistent vote.
At the end of a long debate the third reading was carried
by 43 votes to 13.

The result of these debates was even more auspicious
than might appear For though Sidmouth might choose
to ignore it, both Fox and Grenville had boldly shown the
whole of their hand. Fox had made it clear that this Bill
would soon be followed by another; that it was total
Abolition he meant to have, and quickly. 'The passing of
it,' he declared, speaking not only for himself but for several
of his colleagues, 'however unfortunate this Administration
might be in other respects . would bestow more true
glory upon it, and more honour upon our country, than any
other transaction on which we could be engaged' And
Grenville had denied that the Bill was, as its enemies had

said, ' Abolition in disguise '. It was Abolition, or a step
to Abolition ; but there was no disguise. ' I saw our
strength,' he told Wilberforce afterwards, ' and thought the
occasion was favourable for launching out a little beyond
what the measure itself actually required.' And it was
certainly remarkable that such candour had provoked no
desperate rally of the Trade, no stampede for safety and the
rights of property, among the rank and file in either House.
The omens, indeed, were so propitious that the three pro-
tagonists held ' anxious consultations ' as to the desirability
of attempting the final measure at once. ' It was almost
decided to try,' says Wilberforce. He was for it himself,
and so it seemed was Fox ; but Grenville's cool reason
prevailed. They would have no chance that session, he
argued, in the Lords, with the bishops leaving town and so
forth. One preparatory stroke, however, could be dealt before
the iron cooled. It was agreed that a resolution for total
Abolition should straightway be proposed in both Houses.

There was no delay. Procrastination, in this affair at
any rate, had disappeared with Pitt. At the beginning of
June the new proposal was discussed in the Cabinet. On
the 10th Fox moved a resolution in the Commons—its
language a deliberate echo of the resolution which Wilberforce had moved, year after year, in vain. And once more
Fox took occasion to lift the cause to a pedestal above all
others. ' So fully am I impressed ', he said at the outset,
' with the vast importance and necessity of attaining what
will be the object of my motion this day that, if, during
the almost forty years that I have now had the honour of
a seat in Parliament, I had been so fortunate as to accomplish that and that only, I should think I had done enough
and could retire from public life with comfort and the
conscious satisfaction that I had done my duty.' This time
there was a fuller House and the debate was more even and
protracted. The resolution was ably supported by Romilly,
the new Solicitor-General, Lord Henry Petty, Canning, and
Wilberforce. It was opposed by the Old Guard of the Trade
—Tarleton, Gascoyne, Young, Manning—and by Windham,
Castlereagh, and Rose. But the result was even more
decisive—114 to 15. A fortnight later the same resolution

was moved by Grenville in the Lords. Sidmouth, it seems,
had now taken alarm , and he opposed it on the curious
pretext of not wishing to have it put upon the Journals of
the House that any long-established custom of the country
was inhuman and unjust until some definite mode was
adopted for its abolition. Only Hawkesbury and Westmorland spoke with him   Erskine, the new Chancellor, the
Bishops of London and St. Asaph, and all the other speakers
were on Grenville's side.   The resolution was carried by
41 to 30.

Wilberforce, of course, was jubilant at this unbroken series
of successes. ' If it please God to spare the health of Fox ',
he says, ' and to keep him and Grenville together, I hope
we shall see next year the termination of all our labours.'
But there was still one more thing to be done this year,
one more point to be gained in that amazing session   He
feared, and Stephen agreed, that the passing of the resolution, foreshadowing as it did the triumph of total Abolition,
would spur the Trade to a hurried extension of the traffic in
the hope of securing such extra profit as it could before the
end.   The remedy was obvious—a preventive Act of Parliament—and in those strenuous days there could be no difficulty about a little thing like that !   Wilberforce hastened
to head-quarters. ' With Fox for one hour and a half. He
very rational and unaffected '   Seven weeks later the session
ended, but there had been time to rush through both Houses
a Bill to prohibit the employment in the Slave Trade of
any ships not hitherto employed therein.

It was, as has been seen, a concurrence of favourable
circumstances that had made it possible for so much to be
done towards Abolition in the session of 1806 ; but that it
actually was done and done so quickly was mainly due to
Fox's ardour for the cause.   His brief tenure of office, after
twenty-two years in opposition, was not marked by any great
achievements in the field of domestic or foreign affairs.   He
soon found that he could do no more than Pitt to stop the
war, to relieve the burdens of the poor, to appease and re-
invigorate Ireland.   But into the channel of Abolition the
pent-up stream of his passion for freedom and his hate of
cruelty could flow with an overwhelming rush   And no

one can help wishing that he had lived to see the end of it.
As it was, he was put out of action even before that one
session closed. At the end of June Wilberforce was dismayed
to hear that he was dangerously ill with dropsy, almost as
dismayed as he had been six months before by the similar
news of Pitt Yet it was only since then that he had really
seen Fox at close quarters Now and again, in earlier years,
he had been brought into casual contact with him on
Abolition business ; but, quite apart from the special
obstacle of Wilberforce's intimacy with Pitt, there had
never been any question of frequent or friendly intercourse
between them The respect which Wilberforce's genuine
philanthropy had won from Fox in the days before 1793
had been steadily overclouded by disgust at his servility—as
it seemed to him—to Pitt and Pitt's policy. And to Wilberforce after 1785, Fox's morals, his *amours*, his gambling,
his boisterous, indecorous, irreligious humour must have
seemed no less than horrible. Add to that his sympathy
with France in the days of the Terror, and who can wonder
if the Saint regarded him as almost an embodiment of the
vices and blasphemies of Jacobinism ? And though years
had passed, though Fox's violence had mellowed, though
he had become indeed in these latter days almost ' respectable ', a Pharisee would still have shrunk from him. But
it was not so with our Puritan. Now at last he really saw
the man and knew him ; and in a twinkling he had succumbed—as who did not ?—to the magic of his simple,
human personality. ' I quite love Fox ', he confesses, on
hearing the bad news, ' for his generous and warm fidelity
to the Slave Trade cause.' And then the familiar note
of regret—' Poor fellow, how melancholy his case ! He has
not one religious friend or one who knows anything about it.'
The end was not far off. He was already strictly confined
to his room, though he longed, he said, ' to go down to the
House once more to say something on the Slave Trade ',
and in three months' time he died—how differently from
Pitt—a happy man.*

* *Life*, iii. 255–74. Clarkson, ii 501–68 Rogers, *Table Talk*,
82. *Hansard*, vi (1806), 597–9, 805, 917–19, 1021–5 ; vii (1806),
31–4, 227–36, 580–603, 801–9, 1143–5.

VIII

It is eloquent of its altered fortunes that the Abolition cause was not set back by Fox's death. Whatever his earlier anxieties, there is no note of alarm in Wilberforce's comment on it. The old feeling that, year after year, his life is going by and the goal still unattainable no longer haunts his mind : and this time no regrets for a wasted session could cloud the joy with which, when Parliament rose, he fled from London and ' slipped into the snug and retired harbour of Lyme for the purpose of careening and refitting '. He was soon busily at work there, preparing for publication a final statement of the case for Abolition. ' A pamphlet ', he says, ' thrown in just in such circumstances, may be like a shot which hits between wind and water.' But in the middle of October his quiet labours were interrupted by a letter from the Prime Minister announcing the dissolution of Parliament. ' Sadly unsettled by the news,' he comments , for he knew that bad times and discontent, especially in the cloth industry, had strengthened the hands of his Whig opponents, and the last thing he desired at the moment was to divert his energies to an exhausting electoral contest. Very reluctantly, therefore, he posted off to Yorkshire, and was instantly engulfed in the dust and clamour of a hot election—speaking to ' scores of faces '—dragged wildly about in his carriage (' several run over, but not much hurt ')—escorted on his way from one town to another by ' sixty gentlemen on horseback '—chaired through the streets amid cheers and groans and missiles, one of which hit him on the forehead (' happily not hard, and I kept watching afterwards ')— until the last day came and set him once more at the head of the poll, though the opposition had succeeded in unseating his colleague, Lascelles. All this was precious time lost for the pamphlet ; and succinctness was not Wilberforce's literary *forte*. The pamphlet grew into a booklet of nearly 400 pages, and when at length it was published under the title of *A Letter on the Abolition of the Slave Trade addressed to the Freeholders and other inhabitants of Yorkshire*, the opening move had already been made in the last fight for Abolition.

It was evident, once again, at the very outset, under what different auspices the Abolitionists were now engaged : for Grenville, in consultation with Wilberforce, had decided to start the Bill in the House of Lords, and to make it, more-over, the first important business of the session. The new Parliament met on December 15, and the week before Christmas was devoted to the usual formalities. Then, on the second day of the New Year, on the Prime Minister's motion, ' A Bill for the Abolition of the Slave Trade ' was read a first time in the House of Lords. It was a simple, straightforward measure. After a reference in the preamble to the resolution of the preceding year, the first clause enacted that after May 1, 1807, the African Slave Trade and ' all manner of dealing and trading ' in the purchase of slaves in Africa or in their transport from Africa to the West Indies or ' any other island, country, territory or place whatever ' is hereby ' utterly abolished, prohibited, and declared to be unlawful ' ; and that any of His Majesty's subjects acting to the contrary shall pay £100 for every slave so purchased, sold, or transported. Clause II declared that any British ship thereafter employed in the Trade shall be forfeited to the Crown. Further clauses provided for the penalization of insurance contracts for safe-guarding the Trade ; for the payment of bounties for all slaves captured from British ships, or from enemy ships in war-time, to the officers and men engaged therein , and for the placing of such captured slaves at the disposal of the Crown either for service in the army or navy, or for a limited and regulated apprenticeship to private persons.

Before the Bill came up for second reading the little group of unrepentant champions of the Trade, headed by the Duke of Clarence and Lords Westmorland and Hawkesbury, made a last attempt to revive the obstructive tactics by which the Lords had killed Dundas's ' gradual ' Abolition Bill in 1792. Up to a point Grenville patiently gave way. The obstruction, he knew, could not last long since this time the general feeling of the House was not behind it. So the

papers asked for were duly laid on the table ; petitions
were accepted ; and counsel heard for the petitioners. But
that was enough. The further demand, the old demand,
that evidence should be called at the bar was resisted by
Grenville and successfully resisted without a division.
Thus a month, but no more, had been wasted when, on
February 5, the crucial stage was reached. The debate was
opened by Grenville in a speech which Wilberforce enthusiastically described as ' one of the most statesmanlike I ever
heard ' ; and certainly in its breadth, clarity, and logical
arrangement it reads like a speech of Pitt's. There is no
need to recapitulate its arguments : they rested mainly on
the two principles which Pitt had so often expounded—
justice to Africa and security for the West Indies   But the
peroration was unusual. It was not the familiar appeal to
the honour of the nation and the conscience of the House,
but a personal eulogy.

' This Bill will be supported in another place ', said Grenville, ' by a person to whom the country is deeply indebted
for having originally proposed the measure and for having
followed up that proposition by every exertion from which
a chance could be derived of success.   I cannot conceive
any consciousness being more truly gratifying than must
be enjoyed by that person on finding a measure to which
he has devoted the labour of his life carried into effect—
a measure so truly benevolent, so admirably conducive to
the virtuous prosperity of this country and the welfare of
mankind—a measure which will diffuse happiness amongst
millions now in existence and for which his memory will be
blessed by millions yet unborn.'

It may have been this tribute to Wilberforce which goaded
Westmorland into an equally personal peroration.   At the
close of a fighting speech on the losses to British property
and the gains to foreign traders involved in a surrender of
the traffic by Britain only, he declared that he would never
yield to popular declamation. ' Though I should see the
Presbyterian and the prelate, the Methodist and the field-
preacher, the Jacobin and the murderer unite in support of
it, in this House I will raise my voice against it.' ' Westmorland bespattered me ', reported Wilberforce to Mun-

caster ; ' but really it was a double pleasure to be praised
by Lord Grenville and abused by Lord Westmorland '
The noble earl was not holding the last ditch single-handed
Beside him stood a Prince of the Blood, an ex-Prime
Minister, an ex-Secretary of State, a great sailor, and a
great lawyer. The Duke of Clarence was as sturdily down-
right as ever, but ' worse (says Wilberforce) in point of
execution than usual '. ' Sidmouth ', to quote again that
eager listener, ' fretted and hurt me '—naturally enough ;
for Sidmouth, who had nearly slipped off the old, crumbling
via media in the previous year, had now recovered his
footing and, like an echo from Dundas's best days, insisted,
as an ardent and consistent seeker after Abolition, that it
must not be attained by an Abolition Bill but rather by the
imposition of a rising tax on slaves. The Jenkinson of
1792, similarly, showed himself still alive and little changed
in Hawkesbury, while St Vincent, with his heart in the
mercantile marine, was Rodney reincarnate—' the West
Indian islands ', he declared of his own knowledge, ' are
paradise itself to the negroes in comparison with their
native country ' Eldon, lastly, went back still farther,
dragging from a century's dust the memories of John Locke
and Somers to remind a feebler generation that the Trade
in their day had been sanctioned by the wise and good.
Lord Morton brought the speeches for the Trade to a total
of seven Ten, including Grenville's, were made against it
—by the Duke of Gloucester, the Bishop of Durham, and
Lords Selkirk, Rosslyn, King, Northesk, Moira, Holland,
and Suffolk Wilberforce was particularly pleased with
Holland and Moira, the latter of whom curtly referred his
fellow peers to the Old Testament and also, with better
judgement, to the New. When the division was finally
taken, the second reading was carried by 100 votes,
including 28 proxies, to 36, including 8 proxies—a majority
of 64 Next day the Bill passed through Committee, the
opposition only pleading that the words ' inconsistent with
the principles of justice and humanity ' should be cut out
from the resolution quoted in the preamble Of those who
had not spoken on the previous day, Lord Redesdale sup-

ported the amendment, and the Lord Chancellor, the Duke
of Montrose and Lords Carnarvon, Lauderdale, and Stanhope
opposed it. It was lost by 33 votes to 10 ; and this was the
last time the Upper House divided on the Bill. The final
stages brought out two more supporters, the Bishop of
London and the Duke of Norfolk. On February 10, after a
very brief discussion, the Bill was read a third time

Wilberforce had been a watchful visitor at all these
debates , and on more than one occasion members of the
House had sought him out at the close of the evening to
proffer their congratulations. ' Several peers ', the diary
quaintly notes, ' now speak with quite new civility.' ' How
striking to observe ', it goes on, ' Pitt and Fox both dead
before Abolition effected, and now Lord Grenville, without
any particular deference from Court, carries it so triumphantly But let us not be too sure.' And indeed when the
Abolition Committee met to consider the prospects in the
House of Commons and scrutinized the roll of members,
their minds were by no means easy Grenville himself
shook his head when he saw the ' terrific list of doubtfuls '.
But the time for calculating chances had gone by Battle
had been already joined. On February 10, the very day on
which the third reading was carried in the Lords, the first
reading was moved in the Commons It was not Wilberforce
who moved it, but, properly and significantly, the Minister
who had succeeded Fox as Foreign Secretary For Grey,
now Lord Howick and one day to be ' Earl Grey of the
Reform Bill ', was in most things, and not least in the matter
of the Slave Trade, the political heir of the man he had
followed through the wilderness for so many dreary years.
But in this initial skirmish, of course, there was little
fighting to be done , and Howick closed a brief debate by
conceding the enemy's request that the second reading should
be taken in a fortnight rather than a week. Brief as it was,
however, the debate had roughly shown how the forces were
divided ; and Wilberforce's spirits mounted at the evident
strength of the Abolitionists. ' Our prospects brighten ',
he records ; and throughout the fortnight of suspense his
hopes continued steadily to rise. On the morning of

February 23 he muffled his excitement in working hard to
perfect Howick's equipment—then dined with a few friends
—and so to the House.

It was clear at once that it was to be a ' great night '.
The House was unusually full and it betrayed, says Wilberforce, an ' astonishing eagerness '. The days of doubt and
discomfort and compromise were clean forgotten.   The
country gentlemen of Britain, free at last to lighten consciences which had never been quite easy since the grim tale
of crime and cruelty had first been told them, strove with
one another for the chance to strike a blow at the dying
Trade   A speech was hardly finished before six or eight of
them were on their feet to catch the Speaker's eye   If the
choice fell on an opponent of the Bill, they sat in frosty
silence.   Of the old stalwarts of the Trade, indeed, only
Gascoyne and Manning cared to face it · and not one of
its friends amongst the first-rank politicians said a word.
Windham silently carried his convictions into the lobby,
but Castlereagh and Rose did not even vote   Very different
was the swift response accorded to Abolition speakers—to
Howick when he challenged the appeal to seventeenth-
century wisdom and declared that ' the names of Pitt and
Fox are not inferior to any other ' ; to Roscoe, when he
said that, though Liverpool itself was his home, he had
never ceased to condemn the Trade for thirty years ; to
Fawkes, the new member for Yorkshire, when he expressed
his pleasure at being privileged to speak in unison with his
respected colleague for the county   All this time the
enthusiasm was steadily rising and it reached its climax at
the close of the Solicitor-General's speech.   Almost every
speaker for the Bill had followed Grenville's precedent and
ended with a compliment to Wilberforce.   But Romilly's
was the most eloquent, the most daring of them all

' When I look ', he said, ' to the man at the head of the
French monarchy, surrounded as he is with all the pomp of
power and all the pride of victory, distributing kingdoms to
his family and principalities to his followers, seeming when
he sits upon his throne to have reached the summit of
human ambition and the pinnacle of earthly happiness—
and when I follow that man into his closet or to his bed, and
consider the pangs with which his solitude must be tortured

and his repose banished, by the recollection of the blood he has spilled and the oppressions he has committed—and when I compare with those pangs of remorse the feelings which must accompany my honourable friend from this House to his home, after the vote of this night shall have confirmed the object of his humane and unceasing labours ; when he retires into the bosom of his happy and delighted family, when he lays himself down on his bed, reflecting on the innumerable voices that would be raised in every quarter of the world to bless him, how much more pure and perfect felicity must he enjoy, in the consciousness of having preserved so many millions of his fellow-creatures, than—'

the startling comparison in that tense atmosphere was like a spark on gunpowder. The House was on its feet, giving Wilberforce an ovation such as it had given to no other living man. Round after round, they cheered him, till the tumult echoed in the ancient roof that had looked down on every scene of Wilberforce's parliamentary career, but never on such a scene as this. It was the supreme moment of Wilberforce's life, but Wilberforce himself was scarcely conscious of it. In the middle of Romilly's noble tribute, when he spoke of his happy welcome home that night, his emotions overwhelmed him. He hardly knew when Romilly had finished or what that storm of cheering meant. Insensible, as he afterwards confessed, to all that was passing around him, he sat bent in his seat, his head in his hands, and the tears streaming down his face.

When presently he came to himself, a prolonged attack was being made upon the Bill by a Mr. Hibbert who had been connected with the Trade for many years but had only recently entered Parliament. At its close he rose to deliver his last Abolition speech. It was not in scope or form or substance one of his best. But indeed no great effort of argument or eloquence was needed ; and his main concern was to applaud the lofty and liberal feeling which the younger members of the House especially had shown that night, and to deprecate once more any bitter or exaggerated charges against their beaten enemies. The West Indian planters (he reminded the House) unlike their critics, had lived all their lives in the deadening atmosphere of slavery. . It was now late ; and after one or two more

short speeches, the question was loudly called for. So the
House divided : and when at last the figures were read out,
it was found that the second reading had been carried by
the tremendous majority of 283 to 16

The victory was final. It was useless for the Trade to
oppose the further stages of the Bill with such a majority
behind it. On February 27 it passed into committee without
a division The penal provisions were now inserted, and an
amendment to postpone the operation of the Bill for five
years was defeated by 175 votes to 17, Canning speaking
against it. On the other hand a concession was made to
the opposition on a point of sentiment. Howick suggested
to Wilberforce that the obnoxious phrase about ' justice and
humanity ' might be dropped from the preamble. ' The
whole merit of the great victory is yours ', he wrote, ' and
. . . I should be most unwilling to set up my judgement in
contradiction to yours.' But Wilberforce at once agreed.
It was politic and it cost nothing   ' The preamble ', he said,
' has not suffered in its substantial force.'   On March 16
Lord Henry Petty moved the third reading   Hibbert again
opposed it, at still greater length. And this time Windham,
who had voted among the sixteen opponents of the second
reading, broke silence with a speech of scornful scepticism.
' It is not true ', he said, ' that Parliament is about to
abolish the Slave Trade. We are only abolishing our share
in it. And it is even doubtful if, after all, this measure will
in any degree diminish the traffic in slaves on the coast of
Africa.' Castlereagh, too, was pessimistic. The only
results of the Bill, he thought, would be that the attachment
of the West Indian colonies to the mother-country would
be shaken, that they would smuggle in the slaves they were
forbidden to import, and that the mortality would therefore
increase. There was too much truth, it will soon be seen,
in these cold forecasts ; but to both of them Wilberforce
made a confident reply ; and since Windham had appealed,
as usual, to the great authority of Burke, he took occasion
once more to correct him. Burke, he told the House, had
often declared, both publicly and privately to himself and
his friends, that he fully shared their views on Abolition.

Francis, Sheridan, Henry Thornton, and Barham also spoke for the Bill. But there was no life in the debate. The opposition had recognized defeat and did not even press for a division. So the Bill was read a third time, without a dissentient vote , and on March 23 it returned to the Lords.

And then, at this eleventh hour, Wilberforce feared for a moment that the prize was after all to be dashed from his hands. For some weeks past the Government had been tottering, and now it was rumoured that it had actually fallen. What if the Bill should be lost in the chasm between two Administrations ? But Wilberforce was quickly re-assured. Perceval, who was marked out as the next leader of the Commons and was himself a loyal Abolitionist, told him that Eldon, Hawkesbury, and Castlereagh, the Bill's most powerful foes, had all accepted Parliament's decision and would themselves do anything that was needed to carry the Bill into effect without delay. Nor, indeed, was it true that Grenville had yet resigned. He had been given notice, so to speak ; the King had declared his intention of finding other servants ; but no other Government had been formed when, with one last protest from Westmorland, the Lords con-firmed the Commons' amendments. Two days later, on March 25, the King's assent was given and the Bill became law.

' Well, Henry ', said Wilberforce to Thornton, when the brethren of the Clapham Sect gathered at his house imme-diately after the second reading, ' Well, Henry, what shall we abolish next ? ' And never had the Saints been so triumphant, so light-hearted, as on that night. ' Let us make out the names of those sixteen miscreants ', cried William Smith. ' Never mind the miserable sixteen ', replied Wilberforce, looking up from a note he was writing as he knelt by the crowded table, ' let us think of our glorious 283 ! ' But, when the jubilant company had gone and Wilberforce was left alone, his thoughts turned wholly to humility and gratitude before ' the Giver of all good '. ' God will bless this country,' he said.*

* *Life*, iii 272–305. Clarkson, ii 569–80 *Hansard*, viii (1806–7), 257–9, 431–2, 468–9, 601, 613–18, 657–72, 677–83, 691–3, 701–3, 717–22, 829–38, 940–95, 1040–53 , ix (1807), 59–66, 114–40, 146. *Statutes*, 47 Geo. III, cap xxxvi.

X
SEQUEL

AT the passing of the Abolition Act, Wilberforce reached the zenith of his career He was now only 48 ; he was to live till he was nearly 74 ; but he was never to achieve another personal triumph equal to that of 1807. It would be quite false, however, to suppose that the rest of his life was a protracted anti-climax. His triumph over the Slave Trade had finally confirmed his unique position in the political and social life of England. High Tories might still shudder at his Evangelicalism and discover something of the old Jacobinical taint in his aberrations from the straight and narrow path on such questions as Parliamentary Reform and Catholic Emancipation. Radicals might come to hate the man who could cover the attempt to suppress the rising forces of democracy with a smoke-screen of pietism. But all the world between, the great mass of moderate men, the dominant opinion of the governing class—in Parliament, in Society, in the rank and file of the Evangelical body now growing to its fullest girth, and among his faithful Yorkshiremen—all this world accepted Wilberforce as the authentic keeper of the nation's conscience. Henceforth, till the end, for good or ill, his moral authority was almost pontifical.

It meant, of course, a still busier life for him. No organization of ' good works ' was complete without his patronage. At any philanthropic meeting his presence on the platform was almost a matter of course and always warmly recognized by the audience. On one occasion an emotional friend of his burst into tears ' at seeing him so applauded '. His house was more thickly thronged with visitors than ever. All sorts and conditions of men, from Cabinet Ministers to impoverished parsons, were always coming in. Absolute strangers, of either sex, called to ask his advice. Once, he records, ' a young female of twenty came into my library,

whose first words when we were alone were, "I have run
away, Mr Wilberforce!'" And a long piece of business have
I had with this young fugitive, whose companion, however,
I am assured, is of her own sex—her maid-servant' 'You
can scarcely conceive', he complains a few years later, 'the
prodigious amount of inconvenience which I sustain from
not thinking it right to allow my servants to say, when
I am within, that I am not at home.' The importunate
besiegers might be told that he was engaged or that he only
saw visitors by appointment. But it was not the least use.
'People will force their way in ... and you can little conceive
how difficult it often is for me to force my way out of my own
house.' So much fame and so much rectitude combined
indeed to drive him to a quaint expedient. He bought
a small house close by his home, and to this refuge, nick-
named 'The Nuisance', he would fly for privacy. 'Even
there', he says, 'I should be no more safe, if it were known
that I had such a lurking-hole, than a fox would be next
Mr. Meynell's kennel.' His correspondence, similarly, grew
to immense proportions. 'They are become an unspeakable
plague to me,' he says of his letters ; 'they form my chief
occupation', and his new colleague, Fawkes, exclaimed,
when he saw the day's tray-full, 'If this is to be member for
Yorkshire, the sooner I am rid of it the better!' Once,
indeed, the faithful, and always candid, Stephen told him
that he could not accept these minor preoccupations as
an excuse for neglect of the greater cause. He firmly bade
him '*make* time' for Abolition business. 'If you are to
be only a battering-ram to be pushed forward', he writes,
with an anxious profusion of metaphor, 'instead of a fore-
horse in the team to pull as well as guide the rest, the
Abolition is undone It will sink under the weight of your
daily epistles. Your post-privilege will be the bondage of
Africa, and your covers the funereal pyre of her new-born
hopes. Millions will sigh in hopeless wretchedness that
Wilberforce's correspondents may not think him uncivil
or unkind.'

But Wilberforce, being what he was, had to be civil and
kind. And it was not only the interviews and the letters

that stole his time   The calls of Society, too, now pressed
more hardly on him than before.   The most exclusive
hostesses were anxious to parade the hero of the day ;   and
it needed all his resolution to refuse and refuse again.
Yet refuse he had to ;   otherwise, as he said, it would ' lead
to an endless round of dinners '.   But there was one particular star of the fashionable world who would not endure
refusal.   It will be remembered that, when Wilberforce was
in Paris in 1785, it had been discreetly hinted to him that
a match between Mademoiselle Necker and Pitt might not
be inappropriate.   Whether the girl saw Wilberforce in those
days is not recorded;   but the famous Madame de Staël was
determined to see him now, and as a guest at her own table.
The assault was skilfully conceived.   She told Romilly that
she wished to make Wilberforce's acquaintance more than
that of any other man, and Romilly duly passed it on.   She
told the Duke of Gloucester that Wilberforce did not know
' how really religious she was ' and bade him ask the great
man and herself to dinner   The invitation of the Abolitionist
prince even Wilberforce could scarcely refuse.   He came,
and was overwhelmed with her compliments on Abolition.
' All Europe ', she told him, was thrilled.   She 'almost asked'
for copies of his books.   And before they parted, she insisted
on his dining with her in company with Harrowby and
Mackintosh, both Abolitionists of course.   ' I could not well
refuse ', is the diary's naïve complaint.   But in cold blood
he could not face it.   He wrote to excuse himself ;   and
though he said he might come in after dinner, when the time
came he shied even from that   But he was not to escape
so easily.   Madame de Staël was on her mettle.   Bets were
made among her friends as to the issue.   And Wilberforce,
when he heard about it, suffered ' much unpleasant doubting '.
But when he heard also—and this was her master-stroke—
that Madame de Staël was 'sure I should come *because I had
said I would* ', the game was up.   He went, and enjoyed it
vastly.   ' A cheerful pleasant dinner—she talking of the
final cause of creation—not utility but beauty—did not
like Paley—wrote about Rousseau at fifteen, and thought
differently at fifty.'   And, after dinner, a *salon*—' a brilliant

assembly of rank and talent '. ' The whole scene ', confessed
Wilberforce next morning, ' was intoxicating even to me.
The fever arising from it is not yet gone off.' ' I am sure ',
he adds, ' I durst not often venture into those scenes. The
seasoning is so high that it would render all quiet domestic
pleasures insipid.' Indeed the old Adam had been dangerously happy and in most vivacious form   ' Mr. Wilberforce ',
his hostess told Mackintosh afterwards, ' is the best converser
I have met with in this country   I have always heard that
he was the most religious, but I now find that he is the
wittiest man in England '   She was even tempted to read
his books   At any rate she praised them. *C'est l'aurore de
l'immortalité*, was her comment to a friend of Wilberforce's
on the *Practical View*.

A little later, Wilberforce made the acquaintance of another celebrated lady, who also knew something of France ;
and Madame D'Arblay was no less delighted with him,
though Fanny Burney's style is not quite so exuberant as
Madame de Stael's

' Let me steal a moment ', she writes to her father from
Sandgate, ' to relate a singular gratification, and, in truth,
a real and great honour I have had to rejoice in. You
know, my *Padre*, probably, that Marianne Francis was
commissioned by Mr. Wilberforce to bring about_ an
acquaintance with your F. d'A. . . . *Eh bien*, at church at
Sandgate, the day after my arrival, I saw this justly celebrated man, and was introduced to him in the churchyard
after the service by Charles. The ramparts and martellos
around us became naturally our theme, and Mr Wilberforce
proposed showing them to me   I readily accepted the
offer, and Charles and Sarah, and Mrs Wilberforce and
Mrs Barrett, went away in their several carriages, while
Mr Barrett alone remained, and Mr Wilberforce gave me
his arm, and, in short, we walked the round from one to
five o'clock. Four hours of the best conversation I have,
nearly, ever enjoyed ! He was anxious for a full and true
account of Paris, and particularly of religion and infidelity,
and of Bonaparte and the wars, and of all and everything
that had occurred during my ten years' seclusion in France ;
and I had so much to communicate, and his drawing out
and comments and episodes were all so judicious, so spirited,
so full of information, yet so unassuming, that my shyness

all flew away and I felt to be his confidential friend, opening
to him upon every occurrence and every sentiment, with
the frankness that is usually won by years of intercourse.
I was really and truly delighted and enlightened by him ;
I desired nothing more than to renew the acquaintance, and
cultivate it to intimacy But, alas ! he was going away
next morning. That his discourse should be edifying,
could not, certainly, surprise me , I expected from him all
that was elevated in instruction ; but there was a mixture
of simplicity and vivacity in his manner that I had not
expected, and found really captivating In contemplating
the opposite and alas, hostile shore which, to our fancy's
eye, at least, was visible, I could not forbear wafting over
to it a partial blessing, nor refuse myself beseeching one from
Mr. Wilberforce ; and the smiling benevolence with which
he complied has won my heart for ever *Addio, Padre mio*

F. d'A

But a deeper tribute than any that Fashion or Letters
could pay to Wilberforce was paid by the freeholders of
Yorkshire. Their allegiance had been tested, as has been
seen, in the autumn of 1806 ; six months later it was tested
again ; for in April 1807 the new Government decided on
a dissolution. And the result, this time, was a Yorkshire
election scarcely less famous in political annals than the
historic contests for Middlesex or Westminster. Both
parties had at once determined to fight, and, what was more,
to spend, to the last limit, in order to win those two cardinal
seats. Huge sums were promised on both sides ; one peer,
indeed, was ready to sacrifice the whole of his property
in the Barbados Even for the whole-hearted party candidate the prospect was alarming ; and Fawkes, brief as had
been his taste of the joys or toils of Parliament and large
as was his fortune, refused to face the cost. His place on
the Whig side was taken by Wilberforce's old opponent,
Lord Milton ; and Lascelles stood again for the Tories.
What chance, it might well be asked, had a man who had
always declared, and continued stoutly to declare, his
independence of both parties—unless indeed he were
a millionaire ? And Wilberforce, who was quite well-off
but not immensely rich, was advised by his friends to

withdraw from what must prove a hopeless struggle. He
was tempted to agree with them. He hated the violence,
he dreaded the physical fatigues, of an election. He was
no longer young enough to delight in battle with the
influence and wealth of the great Yorkshire families on
either side   'What greater enjoyment can there be in
life', asked the Duke of Norfolk, 'than to stand a contested
election for Yorkshire and to win it by one?'   Wilberforce
could have given him several answers. As he confessed to
Muncaster, he 'sickened at a contest'. And yet how could
he skulk away from his old supporters on the very morrow
of his triumph? How could he, with the cheers of the
Commons still ringing in his ears, confess by his withdrawal
that Yorkshire was bound to vote for money rather than for
merit? It was impossible. Immediately after the dissolution he posted off for York

He found that Lascelles and Milton had 'already engaged
canvassing agents, houses of entertainment, and every
species of conveyance in every considerable town'   It was
evident, indeed, in every way that the party organizations
were far more efficient and compact than anything an
independent candidate could improvise. But, if he could
not appeal to the spirit of party, he could appeal to the
spirit of independence ; and there were Yorkshiremen who
could put the second before the first. 'We cannot desert
Mr. Wilberforce,' said a member of his audience on nomina-
tion day, and promptly put down £500. Others caught fire
from his example , no less than £18,000 was immediately
subscribed ; and as the contest drew on, the flow of money
steadily increased. His opponents, however, had still the
longer purse as they had had the better start , and when,
on May 20, the polling began, it was evident at once that
Wilberforce must suffer heavily from lack of transport for
his supporters—so evident, in fact, that his legal adviser
from London declared, when the first day's poll had closed,
that he 'had obviously no chance, and the sooner he resigned,
the better'. But if Yorkshiremen wanted to vote for
Wilberforce, they were not going to be prevented by the
fact that nearly all 'the barouches, curricles, gigs, flying

waggons, and military cars ' (to quote the *York Herald*)
that crowded the roads round York for fifteen days belonged
to Milton or to Lascelles. ' No carriages are to be procured,'
reports a friend from Hull , ' but boats are proceeding up
the river heavily laden with voters , farmers lend their
waggons ; even donkeys have the honour of carrying voters
for Wilberforce ; and hundreds are proceeding on foot.'
One such party was met by a member of his committee on
the road from Wensleydale. ' For what parties, gentlemen,
do you come ? ' he asked. ' Wilberforce to a man ' was
the reply. One freeholder from near Rotherham had refused
to be deterred by lack of transport or the means to purchase
it He had come all the way, he boasted, behind Lord
Milton's carriage.

Ill organized though it was, this enthusiasm quickly told.
By the end of the fourth day, Wilberforce was 111 ahead
of Milton and 375 ahead of Lascelles. Every time-honoured
device was tried by his opponents Palpable lies were
whispered about or openly printed on handbills. What the
diary calls ' the mob-directing system ' was put in force.
' Twenty bruisers sent for, Firby the young ruffian, Gully
and others.' And when these were ' directed ' into the
storm that raged all day about the hustings, it was often
impossible for hours together for Wilberforce to gain
a hearing. But still, each night, he continued, though not
by much, to head the poll. On the twelfth day he fell ill
and could not leave his room. At once the word went round
that he was dead. But his victory was now secure ; and at
the final count the figures read—Wilberforce, 11,806 ;
Milton, 11,177 ; Lascelles, 10,989.

It is said that the combined expenditure of his two
opponents amounted to £200,000 The subscriptions which
poured in for Wilberforce, not only from Yorkshire but from
all over the country, reached in the end a total of £70,000.
But more than half of it was returned ; his actual expenses
were less than £30,000. These are significant figures Even
in those halcyon days of Old Corruption it was possible for
a great and scattered constituency to return the better,
though the poorer, man ; and even in an election which

was notorious for the strength of the party spirit it evoked, it was possible for such politically minded electors as the Yorkshiremen to set at the head of the poll a politician who had voted in his day for Fox as well as for Pitt, who had censured Melville no less than Hastings, and whose one great political achievement had been carried through from first to last outside the ring of party warfare *

II

After their brief tenure of office the Whigs returned to the wilderness for another twenty-three years ; so that, till almost the end of his life, and as long as he remained in politics, Wilberforce had to deal with a succession of Tory Governments, backed by fairly consistent majorities. His independence, therefore, was much the same kind of independence as that which Fox had jeered at in the old days. When Wilberforce declared he could bind himself to no party, it did not mean that he had no principles. ' Independents ' in the House of Commons have never been, can never be, absolute neutrals. And Wilberforce's principles were, in their general colour, Tory principles. Now as before, he sat on the Tory side of the House. His friends among its leading members were mostly Tories. He was never intimate with Grey. He could never really like Brougham. But his heart went out to Perceval, partly because he was, as he says, ' a most generous creature ' and ' sweet-tempered ', partly for the same reason which made him always friendly to Addington, because he was religious , he has been called, indeed, ' our first really devout Prime Minister '. Canning, too, for other reasons, he liked and admired , and his sentiments were so far reciprocated that Canning at one time made him his confidant in his queer, unhappy feud with Castlereagh and wrote him long letters, subscribed ' very sincerely and affectionately ', to justify his refusal

* *Life*, iii 315-35, 372, 458, 486-7, 526-7 , iv. 158-67, 265 , v 232 Harford, 47 *Diary and Letters of Mme. D'Arblay* (1905 ed), vi. 93-4.

ever to stand second to his rival. But this, of course, did
not prevent Wilberforce from being almost as shocked at
their duel as he had been at Pitt's and from wishing ' the
King would declare that neither of them should ever serve
him again in a public station '. Of Lord Wellesley, too, he
thought highly, and he came to regard even Hawkesbury,
soon to be Liverpool, as ' a really sensible man '. His
political *milieu* had been, in fact, decided for good and all
when he entered Parliament at Pitt's side in 1780 His
place was among the Pittites ; it could never be among the
disciples and heirs of Fox.

His attitude to the fall of Grenville's Government betrays
at once his Tory outlook. It had been practically dismissed
by George III on the old Irish question. Grenville himself
told Wilberforce that, when he refused an absolute promise
never to propose any extension of power to Roman Catholics,
' Then ', said the King, ' I must look about me.' And
Wilberforce was too satisfied with the result to think twice
about the means. ' It is in one grand particular ', he said,
' the same question as in 1784. My then principles, to which
I still adhere, would govern my vote, even if I did not think
so favourably of Perceval as I do.' What principles ? Was
it only because the Ministry of All the Talents, like the
Fox-North Government, was a coalition ? ' Coalitions ',
said Wilberforce, when one seemed likely to be formed
again in 1809, ' are odious things, and lead to the dissolution
of all principle and the loss of all credit in public men.'
But there was another significant point of similarity between
1807 and 1784. On both occasions George III had used his
prerogative to dismiss a Government he did not like and to
replace it with a pure Tory Government, willing to work
in unison with his personal policy And Wilberforce's
attitude to the prerogative was not the attitude of a
Whig.

So he resumed, naturally enough, the kind of independence
he had practised under Pitt. He publicly admitted his debt
of gratitude to those who had carried Abolition ; but he
denied that he had any right to repay it by parliamentary
support. And most of his Abolitionist intimates took the

same line. ' I am glad to find ', he writes, ' that Bankes, Babington, and I, and Grant, and Henry Thornton too, all settle down into trying the new Ministry and treating them as their measures deserve.' And on the most vital question of all it was easier for Wilberforce to treat their measures kindly than it had sometimes been in Pitt's day. The war had entered on its final phase. It was now, in a far more direct and generally accepted sense, a defensive war. There was no occasion now for Wilberforce to be torn between his allegiance to Government in war-time and his love of peace. Even he could not share in the renewal of pacifist agitation in 1807–8. For no man of any common sense could any longer believe in the possibility of peace till Napoleon abandoned his attempt to force Britain into sharing the subjection of the rest of Europe. But, if the primary issue between peace and war could not now be raised at Westminster, there was material enough for party strife, as bitter as of old, about the methods by which the war was prosecuted ; and in the course of the next few years Wilberforce was obliged to make up his mind on four outstanding controversial questions.

Far the most important of these was the question of the Peninsular Campaign. There was no party flavour in the universal enthusiasm with which the news of the Spanish Rising of 1808 was received in England. Since Austerlitz and the death of Pitt, Englishmen had ' rolled up the map of Europe ' ; they had abandoned, once for all, the heartbreaking policy of stimulating and subsidizing monarchical coalitions ; they had stood grimly aloof while Napoleon, having come to terms with the Czar at Tilsit, began to organize the whole Continent as a single subservient instrument for the economic destruction of England. And now, against all hope, a rift had suddenly appeared in that closedrawn net. Regardless of Spanish pride, the Corsican had coolly planted his brother Joseph on the throne of Spain ; and the Spaniards had risen, not at the bidding of an autocrat nor bribed by English pay, but aflame with the new spirit of nationality which was presently to kindle in other parts of Europe and to burn through the foundations

of the Napoleonic Empire. Naturally there was no doubt
in either English party as to the necessity of fastening on
this breach in the wall, of directing through it the pent-up
stream of British trade, of assisting the Spanish Juntas
with troops and arms and funds ' Every head and heart ',
writes Wilberforce to Muncaster, ' are full of schemes and
sympathies for the poor Spaniards '—Whig heads and hearts
as well as Tory. Sheridan, indeed, prepared a speech which
was meant, says the diary, to ' electrify the country ' But
' the opportunity being delayed, he, going upstairs, got so
drunk ' that, when he spoke, ' he was like a man catching
through a thick medium at the objects before him ' Wilberforce himself pressed for a Joint Address from both Houses,
committing the country to the Spanish cause But this
general enthusiasm and this concord of parties did not last
long. The new attempt at military intervention on the
Continent soon seemed as disappointing as the old. Wellesley's victory at Vimiero in August 1808 was robbed of its
fruits by the senior generals who took over his command
and signed the unfortunate Convention of Cintra. In the
winter Napoleon himself appeared in Spain with a quarter
of a million men to smash this impertinent Spanish revolt ;
and Moore's retreat to Corunna, though it brilliantly saved
his little army from the enemy's grasp, was none the less
a retreat. It was all certainly disheartening. The rising
seemed doomed. And, remembering the wretched series
of fiascos in Flanders, the Whigs for the most part turned
round and denounced the Spanish adventure They were
supported by a strong body of public opinion, but not by
Wilberforce The ' Independent ' voted, indeed, against
the Government in 1810 on the inquiry into the Walcheren
débâcle ; but when Ministers refused to jettison the Spanish
patriots, when in 1809, having taken Wellesley's measure,
they sent the unpopular general back to Portugal with
a British army, to win, before the year was out, the victories
of Douro and Talavera and the title of Lord Wellington,
and when thenceforward they made Wellington's policy in
the Peninsula their own, they could count on Wilberforce's
vote. He had instantly sympathized, like every one else,

with the Spanish revolt ; but he escaped the general sense of disillusionment because he had not 'looked for at least any great present triumphs '.

On the three other controversial questions arising in this final period of the war—the seizure of the Danish fleet in 1807, the quarrel with the United States in 1812, and the coercion of Norway in 1814—it was not so easy for Wilberforce to agree with the Government. The seizure of the Danish fleet could only in fact be defended by the casuistry of war. We know now—what Canning, then Foreign Secretary, half knew from his secret service and half guessed —that by the secret clauses of the Treaty of Tilsit Napoleon and Alexander had agreed to persuade or, if need be, to compel the Scandinavian Powers to join the Continental System and to place their fleets at the disposal of the anti-British alliance. Canning promptly countered this threat by dispatching a strong force of ships and troops to demand the surrender of the Danish fleet, though Denmark was still neutral. The Danes refused ; whereupon Copenhagen was bombarded, and the fleet carried off by force. Was Canning justified in thus anticipating Napoleon's plans and methods ? It was certainly a poser for Wilberforce's conscience. He discussed it at length with Sidmouth who condemned the *coup*, mainly because he believed the Danes were preparing to fight the French, and with Admiral Gambier who was ' quite satisfied of the rectitude and extreme utility ' of it, and spoke ' in high terms of the Divine goodness and of the protection of Providence '. ' After much (I trust impartial) reflection ', writes Wilberforce to Hey, ' I am convinced that, under all the circumstances of the case, the Danish expedition was just. . . . It was absolutely essential to deprive the Danes o fa fleet which, combined with that of Russia, would otherwise have soon conveyed a French army to Ireland or Scotland.' He confesses to Babington, however, that he could scarcely have dared to advise the expedition if he had been a member of the Cabinet ; and he insists that the captured fleet should not be used by Britain, but should be ' kept as a sacred deposit, to be restored on the termination of the war '. Such are the compromises to

which, as long as war continues, all but the most cantan-
kerous consciences must needs be driven.

The Norway case was similarly a product of war morals.
As the struggle with Napoleon neared its end, Prince
Bernadotte of Sweden was urged by the Czar Alexander
to join the Allies and create a diversion with a Swedish
force in Prussia. He agreed, but at a substantial price He
insisted, and the Czar promised, that in the event of the
final triumph of the Allies, Norway should be severed from
Denmark with which it had been united for nearly 400 years,
and annexed to Sweden. The fact that such a transaction
would be undoubtedly repugnant to the majority of the
Norwegian people was simply ignored. The compact was
signed in 1812 ; and in 1813 it was confirmed by Britain in
the separate Treaty of Stockholm with Sweden. In the
autumn of that year, the Swedish Prince and his army took
their part in the decisive battle of Leipzig. Napoleon's power
was broken, and Bernadotte claimed his reward. The
Danes submitted ; they surrendered Norway by the Treaty
of Kiel , their garrisons and officials evacuated the country.
But the Norwegians did not submit ; they refused to yield
to the hated Swedes. Force was therefore needed ; the
treaty of 1813 became operative ; and the British fleet was
ordered to reduce the Norwegians to obedience by a strict
blockade of their coast. The result was mercifully quick.
Confronted with famine and starvation, as well as Bernadotte's invading army, the Norwegians came to terms in
a fortnight. But, at the time the blockade was begun,
there was no saying how long they might have held out ;
and to many Englishmen the whole business was regarded
with deep aversion. In a debate in the House of Commons
in the spring of 1814—interesting, among other reasons, as
the occasion of the maiden speech of the young Whig who
was one day to be Earl of Durham—the Opposition violently
criticized the use of the British navy for so objectionable
a purpose. The Norwegians will say, declared Sir James
Mackintosh, ' Here are those boasted advocates of human
liberty, those deliverers of mankind, come to starve our
infants, because our countrymen will not submit to slavery '.

There could only be one answer, and Canning gave it. He
wished the treaty had never been made. He had himself
urged the House not to sanction it. He would pay any price
to be relieved of its obligations. But it had been sanctioned ;
it could not be evaded ; and honour required its fulfilment.
It was an inexorable argument, and Wilberforce perforce
accepted it   ' The idea of starving these poor people is
shocking,' he writes in his diary the night before the debate.
' Oh, how hideous are war's features when closely viewed ! '
But with a touch of practical shrewdness he adds . ' The
truth is Norway would not starve. She would submit, if
she knew she must.' That night, however, he ' slept but
ill, from uneasiness about the approaching Norway question '. And next day it was only with reluctance, and late
in the debate, that he spoke in support of Canning's case.
The whole treatment of Norway, he declared, was a piece
of flagrant injustice   ' I consider the partitioning of states
against their will a most despotic sacrifice of public rights.'
But the execution of the treaty was a matter of good faith ;
and he only hoped that the Government, who had not, it
appeared, originated the policy of the cession, would do all
it could, in carrying out its unpleasant duty, to minimize
the sufferings of the Norwegian people

If Wilberforce's ' independence ' had been flavoured with
Whig rather than Tory principles, he might perhaps have
taken sides with the Opposition over Norway. He would
almost certainly have done so over Denmark. And on the
third question—the quarrel with the United States—the
conflict between his natural instincts and his political
friendships was no less obvious. High Tory circles had
never forgotten, still less forgiven, the American Revolution.
The enthusiasm of Jefferson and his party for the Jacobins
and their unconcealed antagonism to Britain had confirmed
them in their opinion that Americans in the mass were
dangerous and rather disreputable Radicals, cloaking a spirit
of sheer licence with fine phrases about freedom. They forgot
the ties of common blood   They ignored the marked British
sympathies of New England. And they intensely disliked
having to treat this upstart nation as a fellow member with

Great Britain in the society of states. It is now admitted, on the other hand, by all impartial students that, when the quarrel came to a head, the attitude of the American Government was mistaken. They should have seen that Napoleon's Continental System was just as derogatory to the rights of neutrals as the Orders-in-Council with which Britain countered it ; and that British interference with their trade was only more palpable than French because Britain commanded the sea. They should have realized, too, galling as the British claim to search for deserters and to impress British subjects on American ships might be, that Napoleon's contempt for other people's rights and feelings was far more cynical and sweeping. But it is also admitted that though British Ministers did not in the least desire war with the United States—with a white population a third the size of Britain's and twelve times the size of Canada's—at the climax of the struggle with Napoleon, and though, indeed, their policy was by no means unconciliatory, yet in the exposition of it, in the able dispatches they penned for American perusal, they failed utterly in tact. It may be that President Madison and his followers would have had their fling at the Kingdom of George III in any case , but the cold, formal, superior tone of even the best-intentioned approaches from the Foreign Office was little calculated to placate their animosity It was no new thing, unhappily, in 1812. Ten years earlier, the American Minister in London, then Mr. King, had begged Wilberforce to use his influence with Addington and his Foreign Secretary to do what was most needed to promote an Anglo-American *entente*. ' I don't mean to insinuate ', he had written, ' that Ministers are deaf to justice and that they adopt measures of which we may justly complain No, it is the omission of minor offices, which, like an omitted visit, produces more coldness and finally dislike than a downright injury.' And Wilberforce had understood what he meant. He was one of the few Englishmen of the time who detected this half-unconscious failure in tact and appreciated its pernicious effects on American opinion. He was not handicapped by any political prejudice against the United States. He had

entered Parliament in 1780 as a declared opponent of the
American War, and his first and closest political comrade
had been Chatham's son. When the crusade for Abolition
absorbed his mind, he was drawn closer to America by the
knowledge that the first assault upon the Slave Trade had
been made by American Quakers ; and despite the special
difficulty of Slavery in the Southern States—or rather
because of it—he felt that the cause of Abolition should
appeal to America above all other countries. Shortly after
the triumph of 1807 he had written to Jefferson, urging an
Anglo-American compact for the final suppression of the
Trade. He took a liking, moreover, to the Americans he
met in London. They might not be—and who was ?—all
that he would have wished on the cardinal point ; ' I fear
there is little spirit of religion in America,' he once said ;
but he admired their directness, their simplicity of manners,
their common sense. 'Dined at Hampstead to meet Jay,
the American envoy, his son, etc ,' records the diary, ' quite
Americans—sensible—very pleasing, well-informed men.'

Wilberforce, therefore, was more dismayed than most
Englishmen when the quarrel began to drift towards an
open rupture in the winter of 1811–12. He speaks of ' the
grief and pain with which the very thought of a war with
America fills my heart ' And if it should come, ' I cannot
look forward ', he says, ' to the idea of victory in any war
between Great Britain and America.' When the question
was raised in the House of Commons on February 13 by
Whitbread's motion for the publication of the official
correspondence, he was only just convalescent from an
illness of some weeks' duration , but he insisted (' much
sooner, perhaps, than was prudent ', he confesses) on
attending and taking part in the debate He opposed the
motion, and thereby angered Whitbread who was ' very
rough and rude ' But in this case his attitude was not
governed by Ministerial sympathies He argued very
sensibly that the publication of the dispatches, just at this
moment, was far more likely to inflame opinion on both
sides of the Atlantic than to soothe it. And that led him
to the root of the trouble on the British side—the insular

aloofness and insensitiveness of the British official mind towards the outer world 'I confess', he said, 'that there is not at all times a sufficient attention in this country to the spirit of conciliation towards other countries and especially towards America. It would be well if persons in high situations of government had been more abundant in their civilities to that nation which, being a new one, is naturally more jealous of etiquette, possibly from feeling that it does not stand on as high ground as other and older states' This was precisely what needed saying and it was well said Three weeks later, on March 3, he supported Brougham's demand for an inquiry into the effects of the Government's main instrument of economic warfare with Napoleon, the Orders-in-Council They might or might not, he said, be a primary cause of the distresses of the mercantile middle-class, for which Brougham was the spokesman ; but they were certainly one of the causes of our quarrel with America 'I never was a warm friend to those measures,' he writes of the Orders-in-Council, 'or rather no friend at all but an enemy to parts of them. I am sick at heart from the sad prospect of a war with America.'

The Government was shaken by this general revolt. It conceded the inquiry ; it made up its mind to abandon the Orders ; it began the awkward business of climbing down An instant declaration might conceivably have forestalled the war, but unhappily, at this decisive moment, the whole machine of Government was temporarily put out of operation by the Prime Minister's sudden death On May 11 Perceval was assassinated by a lunatic. It was a great personal blow to Wilberforce 'Perceval had the sweetest of all possible tempers,' he sadly comments in his diary, 'and was one of the most conscientious men I ever knew.' His grief would have been deeper still if he had realized the public disaster which the private tragedy had involved. The formation of the Liverpool Ministry meant delay ; and it was not till June 16 that Castlereagh announced that the Orders-in-Council were immediately to be suspended. The sands had run out. Three days later, long before the news of the British concession could reach the other side of the

Atlantic, President Madison declared that the United States was at war with Great Britain. On July 19, little knowing that the tidings of the actual rupture were already far on their way across the ocean, Wilberforce declared, in the closing debate of the session, the sentiments which all Englishmen ought to have felt. ' I most earnestly trust ', he said, ' that we are not to be involved in the misfortune of a new war, aggravated by possessing almost the character of civil strife—a war between two nations who are children of the same family and brothers in the same inheritance of common liberty.' *

III

On the Government's war-policy, then, Wilberforce did not oppose his Tory friends. He was disquieted at their conduct towards Denmark and Norway, he criticized their American diplomacy, but he felt that in the main their case was justified · and on the supreme question of the Peninsular campaign he was wholly with them. In domestic policy, on the other hand, he could make a better claim to independence. On the two leading issues of Roman Catholic Emancipation and Parliamentary Reform he moved steadily away, during these years, from the orthodox Government faith. On neither of them could he ever be described as a Whig. But on both of them he was, or became, at least a Tory of the Left.

Most of the few Tories who had swallowed Pitt's moderate proposals for Reform in the 'eighties had long since succumbed to the anti-Jacobin reaction and joined with Pitt in driving the whole Reform movement underground. At the beginning of the nineteenth century it seemed as if Reform was dead ; and when presently it began to show signs of life and even to creep back timidly into parliamentary politics, the Tory rank and file had no doubts as to the

* *Life,* ii 57 , iii 307, 344–8, 426–8, 433, 458, 518 , iv 5–9, 17, 23–7, 37–40, 184–5 *Correspondence,* i 241–2 *Hansard,* xxi (1812), 788–91, 1150–1 , xxvii (1813 14), 834–64

propriety of killing it and this time really killing it. Not so Wilberforce He had indeed supported Pitt's system of repression : but he realized now that times had changed. True, he was as much afraid of Trade Unionism as ever. In 1806 he had been the leading member of a House of Commons Committee on the Woollen Manufacture and had drafted its able Report—chiefly memorable for the support it gave to the ' domestic system ' of production in the clothiers' village houses, which naturally appealed to Wilberforce's love of rustic life and faith in rustic morals and which he rightly believed could be carried on success-fully side by side with the ' factory system ' in the towns, and in the course of this Report he had repeated his case for the Combination Laws—not only the risk of wages being forced so high as to ruin ' the whole commercial greatness of our country ', but also the political dangers of any organized society of workmen. But this did not mean that Wilberforce, in these years at any rate, was an alarmist. Jacobinism was now a very old story Progressive opinion in the country, though far from contented with the operation of the constitutional machine, was not so high-strung as in those hysterical days. Now, surely, thought Wilberforce, was the moment for attempting Reform without the risk of its becoming Revolution. And so in 1809, when Curwen introduced his Bill for making the sale of seats in Parliament illegal, he supported it He stood, he said, where Pitt had stood at the outset of his career. If a moderate measure of Reform was desirable then, it was no less desirable now. ' Let us not be called upon to stand still, nor let us libel the constitution so far as to say that it is necessary to its preservation that we should cherish its radical defects.' At a later stage, he outspokenly attacked corruption in the bestowal of offices, titles, and contracts But he was not yet ready to tackle the basic question of representation, and he neither spoke nor voted for Burdett's drastic motion in the same session. Next year, however, a significant entry appears in the diary for May 5—' Wyvill breakfasted with me about Parliamentary Reform ' And on May 21 he votes for Brand's motion for a Committee to consider the means

of making the representative system ' more complete '.
A month later he presents a temperate Address from the
inhabitants of Sheffield ; and while dissociating himself
from ' wild measures ' and eulogizing the constitution, he
pleads again for the removal of the anomalies that
blemish it.

It was but a moderate line he took, but it was really
independent. His Government friends, though they could
not resist the attack on positive corruption and accepted
Curwen's Bill, set their faces against any tampering with
the ' rotten boroughs ', and they resented Wilberforce's
revivification of the younger and more liberal Pitt Even
Canning let fall one of his barbed sarcasms And some of
Wilberforce's Tory constituents in Yorkshire were up in
arms Letters of protest were addressed to their recalcitrant
member, reminding him of ' the general disinclination of
reflecting men to any change in the representation '. But
he maintained his independence. ' All seems quiet now ',
he notes ; ' but how little are men aware of the real dangers
of the country ! How little do they look forward to our
probable state fifteen or twenty years hence ! ' This was
written in 1810 By 1830 the continued refusal of Reform
had brought the country to the most acute political crisis
it had known since the days of the English Revolution

Similarly moderate, similarly independent was Wilberforce's attitude to Catholic Emancipation. He was not, it
has been seen, a bigot about Popery. Nor was he by any
means a Gallio. He was a zealous English Protestant : the
historic antipathy to Rome was in his bones. ' When
I recollect the history of past times ', he once said in the
House of Commons, ' I cannot but be jealous of the Roman
Catholic religion ' While, therefore, he accepted the
principle of toleration and utterly condemned the barbarism
and futility of trying, as the system of the Penal Laws had
tried, to stamp out Romanism in Ireland by blood and iron,
he was not prepared to move an inch beyond passive
tolerance He did not realize the tenacity with which the
national spirit of the Irish clung to its creed nor the responsi-

bilities which the Union had imposed on the Government of
the United Kingdom. To his mind one of the fruits—the
happiest, perhaps—of the Union should be the gradual
conversion of the Irish to Protestantism. ' So long as the
bulk of the Irish are Roman Catholics ', he once told
Grenville, ' the Protestants and the friends of Great Britain
will be in truth a garrison in an enemy's country ; and our
great endeavour ought to be to enlighten and thereby,
I trust, to convert the Roman Catholics. Much, I verily
believe, might be done in that way in twenty or thirty
years ' It is this strange idea that supplies the key to his
policy throughout. On that ground he repeatedly opposed
grants, whether by the Grenville Government or its successors, to the college of Maynooth for the education of a
Catholic priesthood—a ' most pernicious measure ', a ' very
dangerous ' development. And on that ground he defended
the maintenance of the Established Church in Ireland,
mainly supported though it was by compulsory Catholic
contributions. He admitted the anomaly ; but, like most
Englishmen of his day who thought about it at all, he saw
only one way to its removal—the way of ' enlightenment '.
More than half a century was to pass before Gladstone dared
to take the other way—the way of disestablishment. To
Wilberforce and most of his contemporaries such a surrender
was inconceivable. They would have regarded it as nothing
short of a betrayal of their faith, a cynical compact with
wrong, a dooming of the Irish people to the dark for ever.
As it was, Wilberforce was shocked at the sympathetic
references to Catholicism in Parliament ' It is grievous to
see ', he says to Stephen after a debate in 1808, ' that we
are only nominally a Protestant people.' ' I am not one of
those men ', he had himself declared in the previous year,
' who entertain the large and liberal views on religious
subjects, insisted on with so much energy by the honourable
gentlemen on the other side. I am not so much like a certain
ruler of whom it has been so happily said that he was an
honorary member of all religions '

The same motive—the avoidance of anything that would
strengthen the Catholic Church in Ireland—inspired his

attitude to the political issue. It has been seen how long
he hesitated over the Union, how he only succumbed at
last to Pitt's personal pressure, and how uneasy he felt at
Pitt's intention to complete his Irish settlement by the
political enfranchisement of the Catholics. And when Pitt
was dead, the fear of Catholics in Parliament took a stronger
hold on him. Was it not enough that Catholics now could
vote ? Should they also be allowed to sit ? It was on
this point chiefly that he differed from Grenville and the
Whigs at the very moment he was so closely tied to them by
the cause of Abolition. It was largely because they were
pressing for Catholic Emancipation that, once Abolition had
been carried, he was not altogether distressed at their fall.
' I feel deeply impressed ', says a letter of that time, ' with
the sense of the importance of not embarking on a Roman
Catholic bottom (if I may so term it) the interest and well-
being of our Protestant empire ' But he could not fold his
hands on that. The peculiar standing in politics which the
triumph of Abolition had given him forced him into closer
quarters with the problem. He had been lifted above all
personalities and parties as the friend of the oppressed ,
and there were some who thought that he must therefore be
a friend of the Irish Catholics Letters flowed in, entreating
him to add Emancipation to Abolition. ' I hope ', wrote
Sydney Smith, ' now you have done with Africa, you will
do something for Ireland. There is no man in England who
from activity, understanding, character, and neutrality
could do it so effectually as Mr. Wilberforce.' These
challenging compliments could not be run away from, and
Wilberforce applied himself to a new and fuller study of the
available literature on the question The result was scarcely
what Sydney Smith and his friends had hoped , but it was
something Guided always by that dominant religious
motive, Wilberforce gradually came to the conclusion that
it weakened the Protestant cause in Ireland to keep Catholics
out of Parliament when once they had been given the
parliamentary vote. ' The Catholic hierarchy ', as he put
it a few years later to his friend, Hey, ' can do just as well
through the medium of members of Parliament *called*

Protestants, but who, being elected by Roman Catholic voters and having little or no real religion themselves, are implicitly subservient to their constituents' purposes ' They can indeed do better, since such representatives ' do not call into action the Protestant spirit in the same degree '. The Catholic Church, meantime, increases its hold on its members by agitating the grievance of their exclusion from Parliament. Inclusion, on the other hand, will ' connect them to the Protestant system by the various ties which unite men who act together in Parliament and which would render it improbable that they would join a foreign enemy in separating Ireland from Great Britain '. ' Where can be the wisdom ', he sums up, ' of retaining the prison dress when you have set the men at liberty ? '

Wilberforce did not reach this position at one bound. As early as 1808, it is true, the diary admits, ' I strongly incline to their coming into Parliament, though not to their seeing with other men's [priests'] eyes ' But in a debate of that year he declares he must still resist the Catholic claim on the ground that public opinion in England is overwhelmingly against it. It can only raise vain hopes and make grievances more bitter ' Alas ! ' he complains, ' they are driving the Roman Catholics to rebellion. How mad to be thus stimulating them by telling them they are enslaved and oppressed ! ' But, year by year, he moves farther away from the intransigeant attitude of almost all his ministerial friends save Canning, farther away, too, from the prejudices of his own familiar circle Nor does his argument as to the anti-Popish instincts of the British public lose any of its force. When the question becomes a burning issue in 1813, the Protestants sweep the country, ' Meetings against Roman Catholics in all parts of England.' But it is characteristic of Wilberforce that the unpopularity of a cause stiffens him in his adherence to it. Slowly, somewhat anxiously, but steadily, he comes to conviction. ' I am very doubtful which way right ' ' Lord direct me ; all the religious people are on the other side ' ' It grieves me to separate from the Dean and all my religious friends , but conscience must be obeyed.' And so, in the course of the

William Wilberforce
From the unfinished portrait by Sir Thomas Lawrence P.R.A.
in the National Portrait Gallery

great debates of 1813, though public opinion is at least
as hostile as it was in 1808, he declares himself converted to
Emancipation. It is absurd, he argues again, to keep
Catholics from the House when you have already given
them the vote. And, forgetting his own alarms at the
dangerous effect of Whig speeches a few years back, he tells
the House that it cannot expect the Catholics to be satisfied
and tranquil 'Light and knowledge are spreading in
Ireland, and the more they extend, the more will the
Catholics of Ireland desire to enjoy all the privileges of
freemen. . We are now suffering from the follies and vices
of our forefathers. Ireland has been treated as a conquered
country ; and the remaining links of her ancient chains
press more severely on her because she has been admitted
to a part of the blessings of the British constitution.' He
begs the House, therefore, to see the wisdom of concession.
' This is a golden opportunity which may never return if
we now lose it '

The speech made a profound impression. As Canning
said, Wilberforce's opinion was peculiarly powerful because
it was known to be conscientious and had been so deliberately
formed. And it produced almost a sensation in the religious
world outside. The Evangelicals, fiery Protestants as they
were and largely responsible for keeping alive the hate of
Rome among the general public, were astounded. Even
Hannah More and her kinsfolk were within an ace of
quarrelling with Wilberforce about it. But there was no
call for these alarms. Emancipation had no chance in 1813.
The House of Commons might accept Grattan's resolutions,
as it did the one which Wilberforce supported ; but that
was all. The Government was not prepared to frame a Bill,
nor Parliament to pass it. Nor was Wilberforce prepared to
follow to the end the path to which Sydney Smith had
pointed. He could not do for Ireland what he had done for
Africa. Deeply conscious of the public influence he now
possessed, he would labour to form a true opinion on each
outstanding issue · he would fearlessly declare it and vote
for it ; but, if, as in this case of Catholic Emancipation,
popular prejudice was against him, he would not devote all

his time and strength to fighting it. He was not, it may be said again, an 'all-round' statesman : he could only go crusading in one cause.*

IV

Wilberforce, indeed, had begun to feel that the demands of general politics, which as member for so important a constituency as Yorkshire he felt bound to meet, were absorbing too much of his time. How conscientiously he performed his duties in the House of Commons has already been observed. 'There is scarcely any member of Parliament', he writes to one of his constituents in 1811, 'who has much, or I might almost say any, private business, who attends the discussions on public questions with anything like the same degree of regularity as myself or who takes part so much in them. . . . I have stayed till the very end of the session, I believe, every year of the last twenty-three or twenty-four.' Nor is there any other member, he adds, who is so consistently asked to serve on Committees of the House. And the infinite hours he spent at Westminster were not the only time he gave to his parliamentary duties. They pursued him home. Yorkshiremen, eager for a word with their member, increased the crowd that packed his waiting-room at Kensington ; and letters from constituents swelled the appalling bundle on his table. The strain of fulfilling conscientiously all these responsibilities weighed on him more and more. How long, he began to ask himself, could he endure it ? His first political obligation, after all, was to hold and extend the ground won by the Abolition Act ; and this, as will presently be seen, meant constant watchfulness and work. Was he not in danger of being cramped and crippled for that service by the business of general politics ? If he could not scamp his manifold duties, as Stephen wished, shut the door in strangers' faces, consign

* *Life*, iii 300, 307–11, 362, 408, 444–53 , iv. 94–9 *Hansard*, xi (1803), 602–4 , xiv (1804), 734–6, 979 , xvii (1810), 776–7 ; xxiv (1812–13), 1238–41 *Report of Committee on Woollen Manufacture*, July 4, 1806 J L and B Hammond, *The Skilled Labourer*, 184–7.

their letters to the waste-paper basket, ought he not to reduce his public obligations—even, perhaps, to resign the Yorkshire seat ?

And there were other considerations moving him in that direction. He was only fifty-two ; but his constitutional frailty had always forbidden him to count on a long life. Though he had never again been so near death as he was in 1788, he had once or twice been dangerously ill ; and he was frequently ailing and often confined to his room for a week or more at a time He was beginning, too, to detect, or to imagine he detected, the first advances of old age. His eyesight was not much worse than it had always been, but ' I am much impressed ', he notes, ' with finding my memory more decayed than I had conceived. . . . This is surely a strong argument for retiring. . . . I may forget engagements, declarations, and things which I have said.' But what weighed most of all with him was the fact that he now possessed a growing family and had far too little leisure to do a father's duty as he believed it should be done. Writing in 1810 from a country house at Hurstmonceux which a friend had lent him for a summer holiday, ' I have had an opportunity ', he says, ' of becoming acquainted with my own children who, it is no exaggeration to declare, seldom get a quiet minute with me during the sitting of Parliament.' There were six of them—four sons and two daughters—and at this date the eldest, William, was already twelve years old. He was never happier than in their company, nor they than in his. In his own unfading youthfulness of spirit he held the key to children's hearts. An historian of the Clapham Sect has recorded how its grave deliberations in Chatham's library were sometimes interrupted by a burst of merriment from the garden outside. It marked the approach of Wilberforce, striding across the lawn with a laughing boy clinging to each hand. He loved to read aloud to them on Sundays or to make them read aloud to him. And when he could snatch an hour or two from his London week-days he would carry them off to the British Museum or, better still, ' to see the great fish, and to toy-shops ' or ' to see some jugglers '. At home, too,

for all his years, the little man could be very strenuous—
' running races with them in the garden ' or ' playing blind-
man's buff for two hours ' on Twelfth Night. But this
casual intercourse, these jolly interludes, were not enough.
More and more, as they grew up, Wilberforce's mind was
troubled by the question of their education and his
parental part in it. It seemed to him a very grave
matter—perhaps too grave a matter. For he was always
wondering whether, when the time came, they would get
their supreme chance of felicity and take it, as he had been
led by divine accident to take it thirty years ago. ' I humbly
trust ', he wrote about this time, ' that I can say with truth
that the spiritual interests of my children are my first
object. I mean that I wish to see them become real Christians rather than great scholars or eminent in any other
way.' And we know how much he meant by ' real Christians '. He was wise enough, indeed, not to try to force on
them what, as he believed, could only come by Grace. He
was dismayed, for instance, and not unnaturally, when an
Evangelical friend of his told one of his boys, who had
just brought home a good report, that it was ' God's work
on the heart '. ' I fear above all ', he says, ' his being led
to affect more than he really feels.' But, none the less, few
fathers of those days can have seasoned their intercourse
with their children with so much of the moralities. Were
they reading a poem of Scott's, it was the moral of the tale,
not its romance, he fastened on. Were they studying
history together, it was the moral conduct of its characters
on which he tried to fix their minds. When the bell for
family prayers cut short their reading of Robertson's
History of America, he made its heavy tones chime with
the vices of the Spanish conquerors—a whimsical but very
effective aid to memory. ' To this hour ', confessed one of
his sons long afterwards, ' the sound of a bell insensibly
reminds me of his exclamation: " There it is again ! *Cruel*
Cortes ! *Perfidious* Pizarro ! " ' And often in the merriest
hours of a country holiday the children would be reminded,
in that simple, unaffected way their father had of mingling
grave and gay, of the author of all their pleasures. ' Mr. Wil-

berforce made us all very happy ', writes a friend at a family
picnic-party ' He read, and talked, and carved, and
reminded us of the benevolence of God.' And, of course,
there were also more direct methods of moral education.
The children were taken to church at an early age. They
listened to a multitude of sermons And their father, with
that rare capacity again for frank and easy talk on those
intimate matters about which parents usually find it very
hard to speak, would discuss and criticize their conduct
with them and especially their conduct towards one another.
When two of the boys were at school together, he provided
each of them with a paper of ' Hints ', ' to be often read
over ', bidding the elder to guard against his disposition to
dragoon the younger and bidding the younger not to resent
the elder's commanding ways ' Often reflect ', he tells
them both, ' that you are both children of the same father
and mother ; how you have knelt together in prayer ; have
played together as children, and have sat round the same
table on a Sunday in peace and love. Place the scene
before your mind's eye, and recollect how happy mamma
and I have been to see you all around us good and happy.'

To a father so devoted to his children, so anxiously
watchful of their little foibles, feeling so acutely his responsibility, it seemed increasingly regrettable, as they drew near
their 'teens and the difficult age, that in London, at any
rate, and while Parliament was sitting, he should be able to
see so little of them. It was this, indeed, more than any
other argument, that influenced him when in the session
of 1812 he came to the decision to resign his seat. It
was not lightly come to. The seat for Yorkshire was one
of peculiar prestige and authority in the unreformed House
of Commons ; the man who held it, though he might never
be a Minister, was always a parliamentary personage
Ties, too, that time has tightened and familiarized are hard
to break ; and how strongly the majority of his constituents
desired to maintain them had been very plainly shown by
their energy and enthusiasm in the great fight of 1807
Nor could Wilberforce obtain any unanimous counsel from
his friends. Grant and Henry Thornton were against his

leaving Yorkshire . and so, too, was the Speaker when he
called to ask his advice   Stephen and others were for his
migration from Yorkshire to some small seat which would
involve him in little, if any, local obligations and would
not necessitate his continual attendance at Westminster.
Babington advised a clean-cut retirement from Parliament
altogether.   Between these choices he wavered long ; but
at last he settled on the middle course.   It was hard enough
to abandon the great county, to step aside from the regular,
daily march of politics, to become, so to speak, an intermittent politician.   ' I feel very deeply ', the diary confesses, ' the loss of my high situation, and being out of the
dramatis personae whilst my friends are acting their parts.'
To go farther, to win entire freedom, to leave Parliament
altogether—that was impossible !   ' It is like closing my
account ', he wrote to Babington ; ' and I seem to have done
so little, and there seem some things which it would be so
desirable to try to do before I quit Parliament, that I shrink
from retirement as from extinction.'   It only remained, then,
to find a quiet seat , and there was little difficulty about
that in those days.   Lord Calthorpe had exactly the thing
in his pocket—the ancient borough of Bramber, now a tiny
out-of-the-world village near the Sussex coast.   And Lord
Calthorpe was Wilberforce's wife's cousin   No need, then,
for Wilberforce to fight an election for the seat, no need to
spend a fortune on it.   Lord Calthorpe would simply give
it him.   And so, in the autumn of 1812, on the eve of a
General Election, his ' resigning advertisement ' was published in the newspapers.   The Castle Yard at York, with
its crowd of cheering freeholders, knew him no more
Without any fuss or bustle whatever—by the mere transaction of a few formalities—he was duly ' elected ' for
Bramber   Lord Calthorpe begged him ' in the kindest
manner possible .   to consider it quite as my own '.

The migration was widely lamented in Yorkshire.   A meeting of the electors passed a unanimous resolution of gratitude
for ' his unremitting and impartial attention to the private
business of the county, and for his independent and honest
performance of his trust on every public occasion '.   From

his birthplace came a more diffuse and dithyrambic message
' As freeholders of Yorkshire resident in or near Hull ', runs
one of its paragraphs, ' we indulge in the grateful feelings
of an honest pride , we exult in the reflection that the
illustrious names of those incorruptible patriots, Marvell
and Wilberforce, adorn our records and shed a lustre on
this the place of their nativity.' And, of course, there came
innumerable private letters of regret from his constituents,
one of whom expressed the fear that Wilberforce's retirement would ' throw the county into the permanent possession of the two noble Earls who alone possess length of
purse sufficient to command it '. Other admirers, unaware
of his acceptance of Bramber, pressed him to stand for a
variety of seats—for Westminster, for Lewes, for Dover.
' Would you believe it ', he writes, ' R. really and gravely
asked me to stand for Warwickshire, in the Birmingham
interest, and to be the business member. I am not yet
quite insane ' But of all the tributes perhaps the pleasantest
came from an unexpected quarter. Soon after the Election,
Wilberforce was approaching the House of Commons one
day when Sheridan accosted him. When he heard of his
resignation of his Yorkshire seat (he told him), he had been
on the point of writing to him to urge him to reconsider his
decision, under the impression that it meant complete
retirement. ' Though you and I have not much agreed in
our votes in the House of Commons, yet I thought the
independent part you acted would render your retirement
from Parliament a public loss.' *

V

Wilberforce's retreat from Yorkshire is not to be wondered
at. It is astonishing, rather, that he should have held on so
long, considering the multitude and variety of his activities.
Besides the main preoccupation of the Slave Trade (which
must be dealt with presently), besides the unceasing routine
work for the local interests of Yorkshire, besides his careful

* *Life*, III. 469–78, 529–44 ; IV 53–70, 83, 91–2, 138–9, 205, 363.

studies and speeches on the main political issues of the day,
besides the innumerable visitors and letters and the elaborate
organization of his private charities—besides all this, he
was an unfailing attendant at almost every kind of meeting
for the promotion of religion and philanthropy. The diary
for four consecutive days in the ' May Meeting ' period of
1813 contains the following items   ' May 4th. Annual
sermon and meeting of Church Missionary Society for Africa
and the East. . . . Meeting afterwards, and spoke. Late
to Asiatic Society when took the chair   5th. British and
Foreign Bible Society anniversary—full meeting—I spoke
and well received . . . 6th. Prayer Book and Homily
Society—spoke, after a sermon. . . . 7th. Jewish Meeting
anniversary. . . . I spoke.'

Of these Societies—and there were others—two may be
singled out as the special objects of Wilberforce's busy
devotion.   The British and Foreign Bible Society was
largely his creation. No one felt more keenly the handicap
imposed on the cause of Christianity at home and abroad
by the difficulty of providing a sufficiency of Bibles. Now
and again he had himself given money for the purchase
of them to poor parsons in country districts ; and he had
warmly supported such spasmodic efforts as had hitherto
been made to secure a more widespread distribution. But
the need could not be fully met without some regular and
permanent organization   and early in 1803—in the days
of the truce and the invasion-scare—the diary records a
breakfast-party with three friends ' on Bible Society formation '. A few days later the discussion was resumed at the
counting-house of Mr. Hardcastle, a city friend, near Swan
Stairs on Thames-side ; and by the light of candles—so
dark was that April morning—the little group decided on
the inauguration of the Society, with Lord Teignmouth as
its first president   It was destined to do much more and
go much farther than its founders ever dreamed ; yet to
some religious minds it started on its career with a sinister
defect. It included Nonconformists as well as Anglicans.
Indeed, Wilberforce's filial, but by no means Evangelical,
biographers are at pains to defend their father's ' holy

daring '. To Wilberforce himself, however, this feature of the Society seemed one of its greatest merits   In earlier life, it is true, he had taken alarm at the growth of Nonconformity. In 1790 he had voted with the majority against the repeal of the Test Acts, but only after long hesitation and reflection, and the ' satisfaction ' the result gave him was, he confessed to Hey, ' by no means unalloyed '. By 1797 he had become definitely more liberal. So far from showing any bitterness or jealousy towards the ' Sects ', the *Practical View* appealed for the co-operation of all Christians who were agreed on ' the grand fundamentals '. In 1800 it was his personal intervention which prevented Pitt and his colleagues from tampering with the Toleration Act in order to suppress itinerant preachers. ' That they should think of attacking the Dissenters and Methodists ! ' he exclaimed. And he spent some hours with Pitt, ' at a *tête-à-tête* supper ', convincing him that that ' class of clergy ' were not positively immoral. With the Methodists, indeed, as was natural enough, he had become actively friendly ; and his admiration for ' that great and good man, Charles Wesley,' was so deep that for many years, together with two friends he asked to join him, he provided an annuity for his widow. In 1812 the Methodist body passed a public vote of thanks to him for his service to the principle of toleration. All this, of course, was looked askance at by Anglicans of the stricter school. Wilberforce was half a Methodist, they said : and it was actually one of the minor reasons he put to himself in favour of retirement from the House of Commons that the work he could do there might be better done ' by persons not labouring under the stigma of Methodism '. Nor was it unnatural, perhaps, in those days, that he should be suspect, devotedly loyal though he was and remained to the Established Church . for he stood quite frankly on its left wing, and there were plenty of Anglicans at that time who conceived collaboration with Nonconformists to be something akin to treason, and could never have regarded the Bible Society as a fine opportunity for the united labour of all Christians. So it seemed, however, to Wilberforce. It was a ' grand ' sight, he says of its sixth anniversary meeting—' five or six hundred people of all sects and parties, with one heart and face and tongue '.

Wilberforce was also one of the fathers of the Church Missionary Society, first discussed in his room at Battersea in the autumn of 1797, and founded in 1800, largely owing to his exertions. He was keenly interested, too, in the London Missionary Society, founded in 1794. Every one knows how great a work these and kindred bodies were to do, not only in their own religious field but also in maintaining a tradition of humane and honest conduct towards the native races with which Englishmen on the advancing fringes of the British Commonwealth were now to come increasingly in contact. It was inevitable that their missionaries should sometimes be ill suited to their difficult task that some of them should be feckless or fanatical, arrogant or even self-seeking. It was inevitable, too, that their supporters in London should sometimes show more zeal than knowledge and should be tempted—and use their influence to tempt the Government—to form hasty and unfair opinions. A time was to come when ' Exeter Hall ' was to be regarded with mild irritation or cynical amusement in some quarters at home as the shrine of impractical and goody-goody humanitarianism, and with something akin to hatred in some quarters in the colonies as the home of a lot of ignorant and prejudiced busybodies, avowedly hostile to the colonists and all their ways. And there were periods, it must be confessed, when missionary circles in London seemed obsessed with the belief that, if white men and black were in conflict, the white men were necessarily and entirely in the wrong, and the black necessarily and entirely in the right—a belief that, in so far as it affected policy, was as injurious in the long run to the interests of the weaker race as to those of the stronger

The most famous, and in the end the most mischievous, example of this one-sidedness belongs to South African history. The Great Trek is the national epic of the Boers—a romantic story of adventure on the open *veld*, of danger and death, of stubborn courage and achievement—but it was a great disaster to South Africa. It severed the political

unity which the nature and circumstances of the country
demanded ; it doomed it, over and above the troubles
between whites and blacks, to seventy years of friction and
strife between the two European peoples which had made it
their home. And in the complex of causes which brought
about the Trek, the strongest and most insistent thread is
the cleavage in principle between the Boers on the frontiers
of Cape Colony and the British Government in London as
to the manner in which the native races should be treated.
Disagreement, tension, there must have been in any event
for, while the new humanitarianism had so swiftly assailed
and captured public opinion in England, those remote, hard-
headed pioneers were still living in the atmosphere of the
Old Testament, still believing themselves authorized to deal
with the savage Kaffirs as the Chosen People dealt with
the Amalakites   In any event, therefore, the abolition of
Slavery throughout the British Commonwealth in 1834
must have produced a serious crisis in South Africa   But
it might not have resulted in the actual secession of the
recalcitrant Boers if it had not been followed by Lord
Glenelg's retrocession to the Kaffirs of the province of
Queen Adelaide in 1835. And Lord Glenelg, of course, was
none other than the son of Wilberforce's intimate of the
Clapham Sect, Charles Grant. But even the retrocession,
again, might not have proved decisive if it had not been
regarded by the Boers as the culmination of a deliberate
policy of friendship to the natives and enmity to themselves,
inspired for years past by the malignant slanders of the
missionaries. This was, of course, a prejudiced, an exaggerated view, but it was not entirely unfounded ; and for
such grounds as there were, Wilberforce and his friends were,
in part at least, responsible. They were biased—perhaps
inevitably biased   In dealing with the Slave Trade, they
had been at closer quarters with the abuses they attacked.
They saw the slave-ships ; they examined the slave-captains , the bulk of their evidence came from people engaged
in the Trade and very little of it from missionaries ; Newton
himself had been in it up to the eyes. The opposition,
moreover, the champions of the Trade, were on the spot ;

and the case against them had to be sustained under their
watchful criticism and powerful counter-attacks.   It was
possible, therefore, for Wilberforce to form fair and well-
balanced opinions on the Slave Trade without going himself
to the Guinea Coast or taking himself the Middle Passage.
But it was quite otherwise with regard to the sweeping
charges of inhumanity levelled against the Boers   Wilberforce never met a Boer   He knew nothing of the realities
of life on the Karoo or by the Kei.   Almost his only source
of first-hand information was the statements of the plaintiffs
in the case—the missionaries.   And for a man of Wilberforce's prepossessions this was fatal to fair judgement.
Secular evidence he would have weighed and winnowed :
but these were ardent, active Christians, sacrificing themselves to their faith, witnesses to the eternal truth   and he
was ready to believe almost anything these men of God
might say.

To what lengths this enthusiasm could carry him is illustrated by the famous Vanderkemp controversy.   Dr. Vanderkemp was a single-minded zealot in charge of the London
Society's Mission at Bethelsdorp.   He was particularly
obnoxious to the Boer farmers of the district, partly because
he maintained in happy security—or, as they held, in
demoralizing idleness—a number of Hottentots who might
otherwise have been obliged to work on their farms, still
more because his were the most vehement and vociferous
attacks on their humanity   And it intensified their chagrin
that he could reach the ears of Government.   ' If Mr. Wilberforce ', wrote Vanderkemp's colleague, Mr. Read, to London
in 1811, ' the friend of injured Africa, had a fair statement
of this business, he would surely exert himself.'   And so he
did.   He took the matter straight to the Prime Minister,
Perceval, and thence to Liverpool at the Colonial Office ;
and the upshot was a prompt request from the Secretary of
State to the Governor of the Cape to give the charges his
' most serious attention '.   A full inquiry was accordingly
instituted by four judges on what became known in South
African tradition as ' the Black Circuit '.   The results of it
were interesting.   Instead of the murders by the hundred

they had spoken of, the missionaries could only formulate
seventeen specific charges of the capital offence Of these
all failed. One of the accused was convicted of assault. Of
fifteen persons accused of violence, six were acquitted.
Vanderkemp's accusations were thus shown to have been
by no means all the outcome of fanatical imagination.
Undoubtedly there were Boers who were often cruel to their
slaves and native labourers ; and it was all to the good that
some of them had been detected, proved guilty, and
punished Wilberforce, so far, had been justified in his
exertions. But there was another side to it. The acquittals
had been more numerous than the convictions. And bitter
was the talk that ran from farm to farm up-country. Had
not the missionaries been shown to be reckless and undis-
criminating slanderers of innocent folk ? Had not their
high-placed friends in London unhesitatingly supported
them ? And was life tolerable under an alien and distant
Government, the strings of which such men as these could
pull ? In a long view, indeed, the harm done perhaps out-
weighed the good ; and Wilberforce, in his degree, must be
held accountable for both. When he was discussing the
matter with Liverpool and ' Lord N ', ' Vanderkemp ', said
the latter, ' is a worthy man, but an enthusiast.' ' Poor
Lord N ', is the diary's amazing comment ; ' Was not then
St. Paul an enthusiast ? '

It is easy to smile at such extravagances, easy to deride
the lop-sided dogmatism that sprang from too catholic a
trust in the divine inspiration of missionary evidence.
Certainly Wilberforce and his friends were sometimes over-
ready to believe evil ; but it should not be forgotten that
they had been face to face with the unquestioned horrors of
the Slave Trade. These were the things that white men had
done to black, and, so far as they could evade the Abolition
law, were still doing. And though the farmers of South
Africa were of a wholly different type from that of the West
Coast slavers, it was not quite unreasonable to suspect that
they might not maintain, at least without ' interference'
from Downing Street, a wholly different standard of conduct towards their uncivilized neighbours And this,

too, should be remembered. With all their limitations and mistakes those pioneers of the British philanthropic school were on the right side. It was they who planted in the public conscience of their countrymen not merely a sensitiveness to wrong, but a positive sense of obligation towards the backward peoples of the world. And in so far as the conduct of British Governments towards the native races in their charge was to be inspired throughout the coming century by the ideals of trusteeship, the honour of creating that tradition lay with them *

VI

The Church Missionary Society dealt with the East as well as Africa ; and the field in which Wilberforce was more keenly interested than in any other was India. At the outset of his political career he had been brought face to face with India and the problem of its government. He had listened in those early days to Burke's doctrine of trusteeship. He had wholeheartedly accepted it. He had played his part in securing the impeachment of Warren Hastings. But, as the effects of his ' conversion ' took a deeper and deeper hold on all his life and thought, he had begun to diverge from Burke's path. Burke's opinions about India were dominated by his respect for antiquity. The whole complex structure of Indian life, with all its immeasurable differences from our own, with all, too, that European critics must needs regard as defects or abuses, was too ancient, too venerable, to be rashly interfered with. He was not greatly concerned by the fact that its myriad inhabitants were not Christians. Religion, above all else, was a matter of old tradition ; above all else, an intimate, personal thing. It was not, he held, one of the duties of British statesmen to question or dictate the religious opinions of their fellow subjects in any part of the Commonwealth—not even in Ireland, nor yet in Canada. ' I would have us govern Canada ', he said, in his plea for

* *Life,* i 257–60 , ii 251, 360–5 ; iii 91–2, 407, 510–12, 536, 553 , iv 128–9   Sir G Cory, *The Rise of South Africa* (London, 1910), chap. 7, &c

the toleration of Roman Catholicism among the French
Canadians, ' in the same manner as the all-wise disposition
of Providence would govern it. We know that He suffers
the sun to shine upon the righteous and the unrighteous ;
and we ought to suffer all classes, without distinction, to
enjoy equally the right of worshipping God according to
the light He has been pleased to give them ' And in the
same spirit he conceived it to be no business of the British
Government to combat Hinduism or Islam in India. So
thought most Englishmen then and since, but not Wilberforce. For Wilberforce, while he could tolerate Nonconformity and, with an effort, Romanism, drew the line at
' heathen ' creeds. To him the notion of the British Government fulfilling a trust for the welfare of the Indian people
seemed almost farcical if it did nothing whatever to raise
them from ignorance and idolatry and to save them—so
indeed he saw it—from eternal damnation.

A member of Parliament in Wilberforce's time had an
excellent opportunity, at regular, if somewhat distant,
intervals, of airing his views on India. For, though by
Pitt's Act the British Government was now, so to speak, a
partner in the government of India, the active agent on
the spot was still the East India Company ; and every
twenty years the Company's Charter had to be renewed by
Act of Parliament. Twice, therefore, during Wilberforce's
tenure of a seat—in 1793 and in 1813—the whole Indian
question was fully discussed, not merely in one night's
debate, but at all the stages of the requisite Charter Bill.
And already in 1793 Wilberforce was convinced that it was
an essential, nay, *the* essential, function of the Government
not merely to permit but actively to foster Christian propaganda throughout the area of its Indian administration.
Accordingly, when the debate came on, he proposed a
series of resolutions, to be transmuted on acceptance into
clauses of the Bill, declaring the ' religious improvement '
of the Indians ' by all just and prudent means ' to be our
' peculiar and bounden duty ' and calling for the provision
of chaplains and schoolmasters throughout British India.
At the outset he was not without allies. He found Pitt,

indeed, indifferent, but he obtained Archbishop Moore's
blessing, and, still more useful, he won a promise of support
from the Minister in charge of the Bill, Dundas.   It was
mainly due to this last potent factor that the House accepted
the resolutions without demur.   Wilberforce was deeply
moved.   ' The hand of Providence ', he exclaims in his
religious journal, ' was never more visible than in this East
Indian affair.'   But his confidence was premature.   Like
a giant roused from sleep, India House began to stir.   The
Company had always set its face against missionary effort.
It had even refused, with one or two exceptions, to carry
missionaries to India on its ships.   It was a cardinal point
of its policy to abstain from any kind of tampering with
Indian beliefs and customs.   ' East Indian directors met ',
says the diary, ' and strongly reprobated my clauses.'   It
was the opening move of a swift and vigorous campaign.
Anglo-Indian opinion was solidly mobilized.   Influence was
brought to bear in Society and Parliament.   And when the
debate was resumed, Dundas, with his eye on the storm-
clouds, trimmed his sails.   Wilberforce was to suffer many
such sudden changes of fortune in the course of his career ;
but this was one of the first of them and it hit him hard.
In vain he strove to disarm the opposition.   ' It is not
meant ', he said, ' to break up by violence existing institutions and force our faith upon the natives of India ; but
gravely, silently, and systematically to prepare the way for
the gradual diffusion of religious truth.'   It was no use.
' The East India directors and proprietors have triumphed ',
he writes to Gisborne, ' all my clauses were last night struck
out on the third reading of the Bill (with Dundas's consent ! !
this is *honour*), and our territories in Hindustan, twenty
millions of people included, are left in the undisturbed and
peaceable possession, and committed to the providential
protection of—Brama '   ' How mysterious, how humbling ',
he meditates in the journal, ' are the dispensations of God's
providence ! . . . May not this have been because one so unworthy as I undertook this hallowed cause ? '

Twenty years later he returned to the charge with
undiminished zeal.   All that he heard, all that he read, in

the interval had intensified his horror at the abysmal depths
of Indian paganism. At times the thought of so many
million fellow men and fellow subjects blinded and doomed
seems almost to have got on his nerves : there is an almost
ranting note in some of his attacks on Hinduism and on the
lethargy of Government ' To me ', he writes to a clergyman in 1807, ' . . . our suffering our East India subjects . . .
to remain, without an effort to the contrary, under the
most depraved and cruel system of superstition which ever
enslaved a people, is . . . the greatest by far, now that the
Slave Trade has ceased, of all the national crimes by which
we are provoking the vengeance and suffering the chastise-
ment of Heaven.' And in the following year he is moved
to a queer outburst on hearing the rumour that Napoleon
was resuming on a grand scale his preparations for the
conquest of the East. He can scarcely have supposed that
Napoleon of all men would deliberately concern himself
with Christian propaganda in India ; but he could imagine
his cynical ambitions to be the instrument of a higher will.
' Should this country ', he writes to Hey, ' use the powers of
its government for the avowed purpose of shutting the
Scriptures out of our Indian empire, how could we hope that
God would not employ his French army in breaking down
the barriers we had vainly and wickedly been rearing and
thus open a passage by which Christian light might shine
upon that darkened land.' All the time, too, his work with
the Church Missionary Society, which largely owed its
existence to the failure to secure Government action in 1793,
was feeding his resentment at the discouragement and
frustration of missionary effort in the East One case made
a specially sharp impression. An unfortunate missionary,
refused a passage by the Company, had made his way out
to India, as other zealots had done, by a circuitous route.
On his arrival he was promptly ordered to depart—not
unnaturally, since he was without the requisite official
licence. ' On his stating that he had no money,' to quote
Wilberforce's account, ' he was told he might go before the
mast. The poor fellow—chiefly from grief—sickened
and died.'

It was with growing impatience, therefore, that Wilberforce awaited the expiry of the Charter ; and this time he
was determined not to fail from over-confidence or lack of
preparation Early in 1812 he began to plan his campaign
' It will be necessary ', he says, ' to call into action the whole
force of the religious world ' Sundry bishops were accordingly canvassed, and a meeting was held at Bartlett's
Buildings with the Archbishop of Canterbury (now Manners-
Sutton) in the chair. The fact that Perceval was still Prime
Minister was of good omen. He told Wilberforce that he
approved his object but ' saw great difficulties in the way '.
What, he asked him, were his positive proposals ? At the
least, replied Wilberforce, the insertion in the forthcoming
Charter Act of the same declarations of principle which had
been embodied in his resolutions in 1793 and also some provision for opening the doors of India to the missionaries.
That their entry should be regulated, that a licence-system
of some kind must be maintained, he was ready to admit ;
but he had formed no opinion yet as to who should control
it. Obviously not the Company Indeed he was fast moving
towards agreement with the Company's commercial rivals.
He was contemplating the abolition not only of the monopoly
but of the Company itself, ' rather than not insure the
passage for the entrance of light . . . into that benighted and
degraded region '.

But he found that the benighted and degraded condition
of Indians did not sting men's consciences so acutely as the
barbarities of English slave traders. ' I am sadly disappointed ', he confesses, ' in finding even religious people
so cold about the East Indian instruction.' And about this
time he received a warning which might well have revealed
to him the peculiar difficulties and dangers of the dubious
ground he was so confidently treading. He heard from
private sources a ' most alarming ' report that the Maha-
raja of Gwalior had written to the Secretary to Government
' resenting our measures for proselytising India '. ' Surely
this is the evil spirit's stirring up ', cries Wilberforce in
dismay. But Burke would have known better than that.
While Burke would not have palliated the survivals of

primitive barbarism which still figured among Hindu
religious customs, he would have understood, none the less,
the natural indignation of a prince of ancient Indian blood
at the charge that all his countrymen were living in a pit of
mire and shame   No wonder that Wilberforce's extremism
should have stiffened the opposition of those whose knowledge of India and its problems was wider than his   And
there were extremists on that side too, who held not only
that Government should itself have nothing to do with
mission work in India but that unofficial Christian propaganda of any kind—even the circulation of the Bible—
should be prohibited. By the time the Bill was ready for
discussion, the Anglo-Indian party as a whole had hardened
in the opinion that the licensing of missionaries should be
reserved in the new Charter as in the old for the Court of
Directors of the Company—in other words, that the question
should stand for twenty years to come as it had stood for
twenty years past.

The power of India House, however, was not all that it
had been in 1793. The financial position of the Company
was suffering from one of its periodic crises owing to the
cost of Lord Wellesley's ' forward ' policy ; and the clamour
of its rivals in the British business world for admission to
the Indian trade was the louder now that Napoleon had shut
them out from European ports. The Company itself, moreover, was not unaffected by the new ideas about the purposes of British rule in India. The old assumption that the
British were only in India in order to trade there had disappeared. Nor could those negative duties of maintaining
peace and justice, which had been almost automatically
created by the development of trade, long suffice for a Government inspired by a sense, however new and callow, of
trusteeship. Already the idea was in the air that something
should be done in India to protect and advance the general
well-being of the people, and not merely their material
well-being. It was in the Charter Act of 1813, accordingly,
that the first small step was taken in the gigantic task
of Indian education. It was provided that one lac of rupees
(about £10,000) should every year be ' set apart and

applied to the revival and improvement of literature and the encouragement of the learned natives of India, and for the introduction and promotion of a knowledge of the sciences among the inhabitants of the British territories in India '. But if once the door were opened to Western science, could it be shut to Western religion? The dilemma was vehemently pressed by Wilberforce. ' Is Christianity the only thing ', he asked, ' we refuse to offer to our Indian fellow-subjects ? ' And he was supported by at least one notable Anglo-Indian. His colleague of the Clapham Sect, Lord Teignmouth, spoke with the authority of an ex-Governor-General when he declared himself in favour of mission work in India provided that Government was only concerned to authorize and regulate it. Ministers, too, were sympathetic. Perceval was dead, but Castlereagh agreed with Wilberforce that it was no longer possible to reject the principles expressed in the resolutions of 1793 : and on the crucial question of missionaries' licences he proposed that, since it was impossible to exclude the Company from all authority in the matter, applications for licences should be made to the Court of Directors as before, but that, in the event of a refusal, the applicant could appeal to the Board of Control, *i. e.* the British Government. This was more than a compromise : it was giving all that Wilberforce could ask ; and it was hotly opposed by the Anglo-Indian body. But Castlereagh himself introduced it in the House of Commons ; and after warm debates it was duly incorporated in the Bill by safe majorities.

Wilberforce had not ventured, this time, to expect success. ' We carried it ', he says, ' beyond all hope. I heard afterwards that many good men had been praying for us all night.' But in truth he was fighting a winning battle ; and the two long speeches he delivered in the course of the debates and afterwards published, though they rank high among his parliamentary efforts, were not really needed to turn the scale Their value lies in their frank recognition of the inhabitants of British India as fellow subjects with Britons at home, no less entitled to enjoy, as far as might be, the benefits of British civilization. Sixty million Indians, he told the House, had been incorporated in one body politic with themselves ; but its cohesion could only be secured by the goodwill of both its parts. ' No government can be really secure which does not rest on the affections of the governed or at least on their persuasion that its main-tenance and preservation are in some degree connected with their own well-being.' And how was this frame of mind to be induced ? By extending to Indians the blessings of British laws and institutions, and above all by letting in ' the genial influence of Christian light and truth '. Opinions may differ as to the application of this doctrine of mutual goodwill ; but in principle it is incontestable ; and it was the doctrine by which British statesmanship in India was to be governed throughout the coming century But it is almost lost in the denunciations of Indian morals to which far the greater part of Wilberforce's speeches was devoted. His specific charges were not untrue. With his usual industry he had patiently built them up from the books or oral evidence of men who had been in India And it was well, perhaps, that Parliament should not overlook the dark side of the picture—the primitive and indecent character of many Hindu rites, the savage custom of infanticide or that which doomed the widow to immolation on her husband's pyre, and the prevalence of murder, rape, fraud, perjury, and all the crimes. But that was the only side that Wilberforce painted. He said not a word about the higher traditions of Indian life, about its philosophers and saints, about that ancient literature and learning which the very Bill before him was concerned to revive and foster. The incandescence of his faith had blinded him. He could see no good at all in paganism.*

---

* *Life*, ii. 24–8, iii. 350–3, 359, iv. 11–22, 101–26. Harford, 26–30 *Hansard*, xxvi (1813), 831–72, 1054–79 Ilbert, *The Govern-ment of India* (Oxford, 192 '), 73–9

VII

It was as well, perhaps, that Wilberforce could not give all his mind and time to vindicating the veracity of the apostolic Vanderkemp or to elaborating his indictment of Indian morals. These were but excursions from the field that he had made his own and trod with surer steps. Throughout these years the cause of Abolition was still his supreme interest and occupation For the passing of the Act had done much, but not all that needed to be done. It had done much because it was an Act of the British Parliament and Britain was mistress of the sea Without the British navy it might, indeed, have been almost a dead letter, but in 1807 the British navy began its long task of driving the Slave Trade off the water. It patrolled the Gulf of Guinea. It nosed round the West Indies Many a thick-skinned smuggler saw a British cruiser on his track and knew that the tables were turned—that the law had gripped him and his slaves were free. But, so long as the war lasted, there were far too few ships available for the complete suppression of illicit trade In 1811 the diary records a visit of Wilberforce's to the First Lord to urge him ' to clear the coast by a thorough sweep ', and another in 1812 for 'getting more naval force on the African coast ' ; and doubtless there were many more. Not yet, therefore, could the natives of the Guinea Coast feel quite secure from the raider and the kidnapper ; and even their protectors were still viewed with uneasy suspicion. One day, for example, a negro came out in a canoe, loaded with fruit for sale, to H.M S. *Assistance* which was lying near shore at anchor. Finding the Commodore on the quarter-deck, he asked him · 'What ship is this?' ' King George ship,' replied the Commodore (who tells the tale), ' man-of-war ship ' But the negro doubted. ' No,' he said, ' you Bristol ship.' Assurances to the contrary were useless. The man became more and more alarmed. ' Dom your heart, you Bristol ship,' he cried at last ; and leaping overboard and abandoning his canoe, struck out desperately for shore.

And illicit trading was not the only question. Windham's scornful prediction might have been a poor argument against the Abolition Bill ; but, on the face of it, it was true. Of course the Trade had not come to an end just because Britain had abolished it. Denmark had fulfilled her undertaking in 1803, and the American Congress had enacted Abolition three weeks before the British Parliament ; but all the other sea-powers were still engaged in the Trade. France, it was true, to whom the second largest share had once belonged, was temporarily shut out from it ; her ships could only venture on it, if at all, at the risk of falling prizes to their British enemies. But how could it be ensured that France would not return to it when once the war was over ? The same applied to Holland and Spain and Portugal, whose slave-ships were exposed to capture so long as they were in Napoleon's control. And the trade of neutral Powers, like Sweden, could only be abolished by the free choice of their own Governments. Thus, until, on the one hand, the existing Abolition Acts, especially the British and American, were rigidly enforced and smuggling completely suppressed and until, on the other hand, other Governments could be persuaded to follow the Abolitionist lead, the triumph of 1807 meant something much less than the total abolition of the Slave Trade.

To Wilberforce, moreover, the cessation of the Trade was but the first step in transforming the relations between white and black in Africa. He had always held—and Pitt had warmly agreed with him—that the Trade had inflicted a terrible injury on Africa, that it was not enough to stop inflicting it, that Britain must do what good she could to make amends for centuries of wrong. Pitt's greatest speech on Abolition had closed, it will be remembered, with a vision of a civilized and enlightened Africa. The same idea had inspired the bold experiment of Sierra Leone, which was now about to be transferred to Government. And it was with this object, as well as for the purpose of securing and extending the ground won for Abolition, that, a few weeks after the passing of the Act, the African Institution was founded, with the Duke of Gloucester as president, and

Wilberforce, the aged Granville Sharp, and other Clapham brethren among its first directors It was, so to speak, the heir of the old Abolition Committee and the Sierra Leone Company ; and it carried on and widened the work they had done to inform and stimulate public opinion. Grenville, Howick, and Perceval were original members ; and among those who attended its first anniversary meeting—'a magnificent day ', says the diary—were some fifty or sixty members of Parliament

But, as before, Wilberforce's main labours for the cause were personal and behind the scenes His letters on the subject formed the chief ingredient in that vast correspondence—letters to President Jefferson proposing that the British and American Governments should agree to allow the seizure by either navy of the slave-ships of either country ; letters to Consul Gambier at Rio, urging him to take measures ' to detect any British ships or men bringing slaves into Brazil ' ; letters to Perceval and Canning, pleading that special instructions should be sent to the revenue officials in Trinidad and Demerara to ' stimulate their exertions ' , letters to Lord Liverpool about the welfare of the West Indian slaves ; letters to Brougham and Lord Holland suggesting a tactful assault on the Spanish deputies visiting London , letters to Castlereagh on the Swedish treaty And there were innumerable interviews with people of all sorts and countries—strange, interesting people some of them, like Miranda (an unscrupulous Venezuelan adventurer who plotted with the British Government ' to insurge South America '), whose exotic figure flits across the pages of the diary, ' talking till half-past eleven and still untired ', bringing a Mexican friend to dine at Kensington Gore, appearing suddenly on the veranda in the middle of family prayers with two deputies from Carácas, triumphantly announcing the abolition of the Trade in Venezuela. Before long, too, the old parliamentary canvassing and wire-pulling were again required. For Wilberforce and his colleagues were forced to the conclusion that smuggling could never be effectively suppressed unless all the slaves in the British West Indies were officially registered, so that any illicit importation could be at once detected and the planter compelled ' to trust to the increase of his actual stock '. He began boldly with a direct assault on the Prime Minister ; and after some months he succeeded in persuading Perceval to make the experiment in Trinidad. There was some hesitation and delay in the Cabinet. The Law Officers shrank from overriding the colonial authorities. But finally in 1812 the order for registration was duly made. Meantime, in concert with Romilly and Brougham, Wilberforce had begun to move for an Act of Parliament, imposing a register on all the British West Indies. But this needed long and careful preparation ; and when they were ready to launch their Bill, they found the whole aspect of the world had changed. Napoleon at last was falling New vistas of peace and international concord were opening up. And the minor question of registration was temporarily shelved in order that the Abolitionists might be free to concentrate on working for a general international agreement for the suppression of the Trade.

Some progress had already been made since 1807 Some of the South American communities, severed from Spain by the war, had followed in the footsteps of the United States. Abolition had been carried in Venezuela in 1810, in Chili in 1811, in Buenos Ayres in 1812. Europe, too, was moving in the same direction At the time of the ill-famed Treaty of 1813, the Swedish Government, pressed by Castlereagh who in turn had been pressed by Wilberforce, disavowed the Trade and promised never to take part in it. But similar attempts to persuade the Spaniards and the Portuguese, when the Rising and the Peninsular War brought them into close contact with the British Government, had not been so successful. When their deputies first came to England in 1808, Wilberforce promptly set himself to get them ' well impregnated with Abolitionism '. The leaders of both political parties were pricked on to the assault, while he busied himself with the question of translating English propaganda into Spanish Later on, he collaborated privately with Castlereagh in bringing pressure on the Government of Portugal But Spain had refused to commit herself, and Portugal had tried to drive a bargain—' audacious and even atrocious ', Wilberforce called it—which would guarantee her in the uncontrolled extension of the Slave Trade south of Cape Palmas if she abstained from operating north of it.

Meantime the question of action by individual states was being merged into that of united action by all Europe. The end of the twenty years of fighting was in sight. Loyally supported by the Government, Wellington had stuck grimly to his task in the Peninsula. In 1812, by the captures of Ciudad Rodrigo and Badajos and the victory of Salamanca, he had opened his path to Madrid and permanently freed the south of Spain. Forced back for the moment into Portugal, he broke out again in the spring of 1813 and within six weeks he had driven King Joseph and the bulk of his forces over the Pyrenees. He was checked for a time on the frontier by the necessity of reducing San Sebastian and Pampeluna ; but in the autumn came his last magnificent struggle with Soult in the Pyrenees, and before Christmas the British army was encamped on the plains of France. In March 1814 they entered Bordeaux. Meanwhile Napoleon's fate had been determined at the other end of Europe. The phantom of world-dominion had lured him at last to disaster in the Russian snows. Yet even now, even after the Retreat from Moscow, he might still have saved himself if the 300,000 veterans, cooped up in Spain by Wellington, had been available. As it was, he raised incredible new forces with incredible speed. But, on the news of the Russian catastrophe, Central Europe was up in arms. In 1813 German nationalism, once betrayed to Napoleon by Prussia, was led by Prussia to deliverance. Russia once more moved West. Sweden came down from the North. Austria rose again in the South. On October 17 Napoleon, with 180,000 men, faced the circle of his enemies, 300,000 strong, at Leipzig. For three days he stood at bay, and then with half his army fled back across the Rhine. There were still anxious moments. Victory sets a strain on all alliances ; and the three great Continental Powers, each with a single eye to its own interests, wrangled and vacillated. The

Rhine frontier was feebly offered to Napoleon and insanely refused. But when at length the Allies, reunited under Castlereagh's firm lead, began to converge on Paris, the last inimitable efforts of Napoleon's soldiership could only postpone for a moment the inevitable end. ' How wonderful ', writes Wilberforce on April 9, ' are the events of the last few days ! After hearing that Bonaparte had dashed into the rear of the Allies, it seemed doubtful what would happen, when suddenly we heard on Tuesday that they were marching on to Paris. Then we hoped for the best, but how little expected that to-day, Saturday, we should hear of Bonaparte's accepting the Emperor of Russia's offer, renouncing the throne, and agreeing to retire to Elba ! ' ' My wife and children went out to see the illuminations ', records the diary, ' and stayed till late.'

Two thoughts came instantly into Wilberforce's mind when he heard the great news. ' How can I but wish ', he says in a letter he wrote that day to Hannah More, ' that my poor old friend Pitt were still alive to witness this catastrophe of the twenty-five years drama ? ' And his private paean of triumph closes with the cry . ' Oh, for the general abolition of the Slave Trade ! ' The age of war was over. A new age of peace had begun. And of all its promised fruits none seemed to Wilberforce so desirable as this or so certain of attainment. It was incredible that liberated Europe should reimpose on Africa the chains and torments of the Trade. ' It would be too shocking ', he writes to Gisborne, ' to restore to Europe the blessings of peace with professions of our principles of justice and humanity, and at the same moment to be creating—for so it would really be doing wherever the Slave Trade is extinct—this traffic in the persons of our fellow-creatures.' To this plank he clung steadily in the whirlpool of diplomacy in which the statesmen of Europe were now for many months involved. From the outset nothing else, except the blockade of Norway, in all that complex of interests and ideals really gripped his mind. Nor was he content merely to act, as hitherto, by personal pressure on British ministers. He took a hand in the game himself ' I am about to correspond with a real

live emperor,' he tells Gisborne, ' not merely such a sort of
Birmingham emperor as Bonaparte ' and within three
weeks of Napoleon's abdication he had dispatched to Alexander a voluminous epistle, detailing the history and the
horrors of the Trade and the measures so far taken for its
abolition and praying that the Czar might prove to be God's
' chief agent ' in delivering Africa as well as Europe. The
rôle appealed to Alexander ; but neither he nor any one
else could forcibly override the primary obstacle—the
opposition of France ' Their merchants ', reports the diary,
' are intent on gain anyhow. Grégoire and all the old *amis
des noirs* men are in exceedingly bad odour. No respectable
persons will have anything to do with them ' But Wilberforce refused to despair. He wrote a series of letters to
Talleyrand, one of which was printed as a pamphlet. He
wrote to the Archbishop of Rheims and to Lafayette. He
talked to Humboldt, who came to see him with Lafayette's
introduction. He then contemplated a personal assault on
Paris ; but he was persuaded that his presence might
embarrass the efforts which Castlereagh and his colleagues
were sincerely making to achieve what he desired , and the
less notorious Macaulay was sent instead But Macaulay
was no more successful than Clarkson had been in earlier
days. It is not surprising Frenchmen could scarcely be
expected to subscribe upon the instant to British doctrines
of philanthropy, which, after all, had taken many years
to win their way in Britain. Nor, perhaps, was a zealot
of the Clapham Sect the best-qualified of Englishmen to
expound them to Parisians. A little more sensibility, a
quicker tact, and the French Colonial Minister, Malouet, for
example, might not have been stung to the *brusquerie* with
which he met Macaulay's arguments. ' Do you English
mean ', he asked, ' to bind all the world ? ' Talleyrand was
too old an artist to be so blunt, but his replies to Wilberforce
were no less negative He rained compliments on him
and on his country ' Cette lettre, Monsieur,' he writes,
' a été pour moi l'occasion de renouveller toute mon admiration pour un pays dans lequel les plus grands hommes d'état
non seulement conçoivent les projets les plus utiles au

monde, mais en poursuivent l'exécution avec cette prudence, cette sagesse et cette persévérance qui en assurent le succès. . . Combien est heureuse l'Angleterre de posséder des hommes qui savent mettre vingt ans à établir une belle institution ! La méthode des mesures violentes et précipitées a failli perdre la France.   J'ai souvent tremblé pour la civilisation européenne. Je me rassurais en contemplant la sagesse, la raison, la prudence et les manières de vos hommes d'état.' How typically dexterous !—for all this, of course, is but a preface to a plea for delay. The writer himself—*ça va sans dire*—had long been a convinced Abolitionist ; but the majority of Frenchmen are still prejudiced   ' Vous connaissez la nature des préjugés : ce n'est point en les heurtant qu'on peut en triompher. Il faut des ménagements. Il faut surtout de la patience et du temps.' Talleyrand was saying, in fact, with his silken tongue what Malouet had said. France was not going to abolish the Slave Trade instantly at England's bidding ; and it was impossible either for Alexander or for Castlereagh to force her to. Wilberforce had urged that no West Indian island conquered from Napoleon should be returned to Louis XVIII without immediate Abolition ; and the British Government tried to bargain with islands and with money. But negotiations could not be broken off on that point only. Nor would such intransigeance really serve the cause ; for, as Liverpool explained to Wilberforce, to alienate France on that issue would stiffen the resistance of Spain and Portugal to Abolition. Could more indeed have been done than Castlereagh did ? Was it, under the circumstances, a grievous failure of diplomacy to obtain nothing but France's promise to abolish the Trade in five years' time, and in the interval to support Britain in urging the principle of Abolition on the rest of Europe ? Wilberforce, at any rate, thought so. Amid the storm of applause that greeted Castlereagh as he entered the House of Commons on his return from Paris, he alone sat silent ; and as soon as the Treaty had been laid on the table and the renewed cheers had died away, he was on his feet and in open opposition. ' 1 can assure my noble friend ', he said, ' that, if

I have not been able to concur in the salutations with which he has been welcomed on his return, it is not from any want of personal cordiality, but because, seeing him come up to the House bearing the French Treaty and calling to mind the arrangements made in it respecting the Slave Trade, I cannot but conceive that I beheld in his hand the death-warrant of a multitude of innocent victims—men, women, and children—whom I had fondly indulged the hope of having myself rescued from destruction.' *

VIII

But to lose the first piece was not to lose the game. The Paris negotiations were but a preliminary to the Congress at Vienna ; and Wilberforce's initial disappointment only intensified his eagerness to secure a general European Charter of Abolition. When, therefore, the Czar, who had come to London, expressed a desire to see him, he leaped at the chance. ' Got up by half-past six ', says the diary of June 12, ' that I might pray to God for a blessing on my interview.' So far as it went, the interview was a success. Alexander was very affable, very sympathetic. When Wilberforce spoke of his fears that the French might not keep their promise at the end of five years, ' We must make them ', he cried impetuously ; and then, correcting himself, ' We must keep them to it '. That the delay had been allowed at all was not his fault. ' What could be done ', he said, ' when your own ambassador gave way ? ' It was clear, indeed, that the Czar would prove but a broken reed unless Castlereagh were firmer at Vienna than he had been at Paris , and Wilberforce promptly threw himself into a lightning campaign to rouse the public opinion of the country. Once more the crusader's call was heard all over England ; and once more the response was prompt and over-

* *Life*, iii 360, 374, 382–5, 434, 459, 483, 505, 514, 546–7 , iv. 3, 19, 75, 132–7, 173–92 *Correspondence*, ii 284–6, 295 *Hansard*, xxvii (1813–14), 1078–82. *Memoirs of G. Sharp*, ii.

whelming. The triumph of 1807 had been no transient phenomenon ; the conscience of the British people had been permanently awakened ; the humanitarian tradition had begun. Within a few weeks 800 petitions, bearing nearly a million signatures, had reached the House of Commons, demanding that Parliament should, somehow or other, prevent the revival of the French Slave Trade. And this time Parliament itself needed no spur from outside. On July 27 Wilberforce moved an Address to the Prince Regent, regretting that so little had been done for Abolition at Paris and calling for more drastic action at Vienna ; and, since Castlereagh accepted it in principle, it was carried without a division. Two days later, an amendment to the Address upon the Peace, similar in content and also moved by Wilberforce, again found no opponents. These portents were not lost on Ministers. Whatever Jenkinson and Hawkesbury might have thought about it in the old days, there was now no warmer Abolitionist than Liverpool. ' If I were not anxious for the Abolition of the Slave Trade on principle ', he wrote to Wilberforce, ' I must be aware of the embarrassment to which any Government must be exposed from the present state of that question in this country.' No clearer mandate has ever been given by public opinion to a diplomat than that which Castlereagh took with him to Vienna. It was indeed so clear to all the world as to handicap the British plenipotentiaries. ' The display of popular impatience ' on this one subject in Britain—so Castlereagh grumbled to Liverpool—would be used by the foreign diplomats as an instrument for wringing concessions out of us in other fields. And, in any case, it can scarcely have seemed a grateful task—to urge idealism on Metternich and Talleyrand. What angry mutterings there would be in that jealous international congregation ! What resentment at the idea of Britain trying to dictate to Europe ! What sneers at the shopkeepers of the *Île Marchande*, for whom ' leur économie politique est leur raison d'État ', who had given up the Trade because they thought it did not pay and were now terrified lest their commercial rivals should prove, in keeping to it, that they had been mistaken !

Still, there was the mandate—an unequivocal, national mandate, only to be disregarded at the cost of losing office.

Castlereagh did not disregard it. He pressed obstinately for a convention But the crux of the matter was not at Vienna ; it was at Paris ; and Paris was apparently immovable. Not only had the Government set its face implacably against immediate Abolition ; it was contemplating the reconquest of St. Domingo from the negroes and its forcible return to the plantation system The appeal to humanity seemed wholly useless ; and Wilberforce fell back on the appeal to the pocket. Might not France give in, he asked, if England made further sacrifices, if she surrendered Mauritius, St. Lucia, or any other islands ? He was quickly undeceived 'Elle n'est point ici,' wrote Humboldt, ' comme elle l'étoit en Angleterre, une affaire d'argent ; elle est liée uniquement à des passions nationales.' The worst, in fact, had happened. The maintenance of the Trade had become a point of national honour. Nor was that all. The triumphant Royalists had not forgotten that the cause of Abolition had been linked with the beginnings of the Revolution. As in England twenty years before, so now in France it stank of Jacobinism 'French Royalists', wrote Lord Holland to Wilberforce, ' make no difference between you and me or between me and Tom Paine.' Even the institution of a new Abolitionist society in France was on that account impracticable. It would fatally recall the *Amis des Noirs*. ' Tout le monde ', said Humboldt, ' se gendarmera contre cette Société.' It was even impossible to persuade any publisher in Paris to face the financial risk of printing a translation of Wilberforce's public letter to Talleyrand. It was impossible, too, to get Abolitionist articles into the French newspapers The Trade, on the other hand, could command what space it pleased , and the French public, its national pride thoroughly on edge, read with gusto the affirmations of French independence and the innuendoes against Albion, and furiously clapped the allusions to the burning question which authors or actors inserted in the current drama.

But Wilberforce did not abandon hope. The cause, after

all, had been almost as desperate in England not so long ago. And there were Frenchmen, as he knew—some of them, indeed, were his personal friends—who stood above the current of popular passion, and who thought, as he did, that France had no excuse for the revival of an abuse which at the moment, as the result of the war, was quite extinct. He persisted, therefore, with his campaign. Leaflets and pamphlets in French and German were spread abroad by the African Institution. An essay by Sismondi and a reprint of that treatise on the impolicy of the Trade which Clarkson, who was now again in Paris, had once presented to Louis XVI, swelled the stream of propaganda But all his operations might have proved unavailing if Wilberforce had not found two powerful allies. The first of them was the King of France. Louis XVIII had been as keenly interested in the question as his ill-starred brother ; it was said, with pardonable exaggeration, that the only genuine Abolitionist in France was the King. ' That he is so,' wrote Lord Bathurst to Wilberforce in October, ' his letter to the Regent, a copy of which I enclose, will, I am sure, convince you.' The second ally was the Duke of Wellington, now British ambassador at Paris. To Wellington the suppression of the Slave Trade was a simple matter of clean humanity. Assured of the King's support, he was not inclined to make diplomatic allowances for national pride or Royalist prejudice ; and he fought as stubbornly at Paris as Castlereagh at Vienna, supplied, like Castlereagh, with copious ammunition from Wilberforce, Stephen, and Macaulay. When the French publishers refused, Wellington personally undertook to get the Letter to Talleyrand widely distributed ; and he persuaded Madame de Stael to provide a translation of Wilberforce's booklet of 1807, which, in an abridged form, he similarly circulated. Meanwhile he was using all his popularity at the Tuileries to stiffen the King's convictions and to bring pressure on his Ministers ; and presently, as the abandonment of the St. Domingo expedition showed, the mood of blank negation began to soften. At last, in November, came a surprising, if only partial, surrender An *ordonnance* was issued forbidding French subjects to engage in the Slave Trade north of Cape Formosa at the mouth of the Niger. Thus, the whole of the Upper Guinea Coast was officially secured from a revisitation by French slavers. The Duke promptly reported the good news to Wilberforce. ' C'est vous et Lord Wellington ', wrote Madame de Staël, ' qui aurez gagné cette grande bataille pour l'humanité. Soyez sûre que votre nom et votre persévérance ont tout fait. . . . Vous avez inspiré à votre héros Wellington autant d'ardeur pour faire du bien qu'il en avoit eu pour emporter les victoires. . . . Je me mets à vos pieds de tout mon cœur.'

There the matter rested for a few months longer; and then the decision was suddenly taken out of the hands of the kings and diplomatists at Paris and Vienna. In the last week of February 1815, the imperial exile broke from his prison in Elba. On March 1 he landed at Cannes. On March 20 he entered the Tuileries, vacated a few hours earlier by his Bourbon rival. But Napoleon knew well enough that Europe would not let him stay there without a struggle. He instantly began to prepare for it ; and while he extorted yet another army from exhausted France, he strove to disarm his opponents by fair words and to weaken them by intrigue. He informed the Allied Sovereigns, still gathered at Vienna, that ' his dearest wish was to make the Imperial Throne of France a bulwark for the peace of Europe '. He requested Marie-Louise to return with her child to Paris for the impending coronation. He strove to reawaken jealousy and discord between Russia and the Central Powers. He tried to re-establish contact with Talleyrand. And what of England ? He had not forgotten his most tenacious enemy. With instant understanding of the question which had troubled Anglo-French relations all the months of his exile, he struck boldly for the favour of the British Government and people by proclaiming the total and immediate Abolition of the Slave Trade. It was Napoleon's first move in the campaign which closed at Waterloo.

And when the Hundred Days were over, when Louis was back on the throne, when Wellington had become a still more commanding figure in the public opinion of Europe, it was impossible for the most stubborn Royalists to force the reversal of Napoleon's *coup* in direct antagonism to England. So Louis had his way, and the usurper's act was duly repeated. ' I have the gratification of acquainting you ', wrote Castlereagh to Wilberforce on the last day of July, ' that the long desired object is accomplished and that the present messenger carries to Lord Liverpool the unqualified and total Abolition of the Slave Trade throughout the dominions of France.'

Meanwhile Castlereagh had been faithful to his mandate at Vienna. From the outset of the Congress there was nothing for which he and his colleagues pressed so resolutely. Alexander, too, had kept his word and assumed the rôle which Wilberforce had urged on him. Talleyrand, likewise, kept the French promise to support the cause in principle ; and it was he who moved on December 10, 1814, for a committee of plenipotentiaries to prepare a general convention. On the part of Austria and Prussia there could be no difficulty , they were purely continental Powers, with no colonies or sea-borne trade. It was from Spain and Portugal that the opposition came They had to consider, they argued, the welfare of their colonies, though, as matter of fact, their colonies were already practically lost to them They could not at once suppress the Trade. They would need, they said, at least eight years' grace And in any case, in the light of the recent treaty with France, it was too much, perhaps, to expect an agreement for immediate Abolition. An agreement on the principle, however, could be and was obtained. On February 8, 1815, the representatives of the Eight Powers adopted a joint declaration condemning the Slave Trade and declaring their intention, without any precise commitment as to dates, to secure its universal abolition as quickly and effectively as possible. The text of this declaration was one of the documents annexed to the Final Act which was signed on June 9, and nine days later sealed at Waterloo.

In 1815, therefore, of all the European peoples who had ever had a hand in the Slave Trade, only the Spaniards and the Portuguese were still engaged in it ; for liberated Holland had renounced it early in 1814. And Spain and Portugal, it was manifest, could not long resist the explicit moral judgement of all Europe to which they had themselves subscribed. To have secured that explicit moral judgement did not mean, as will presently appear, that the Trade had been destroyed ; but at least it was a long step towards its destruction. And unquestionably the dominant factors in this achievement were the lead which the greatest slaving Power had given in 1807 and the remarkable exhibition of the strength and unanimity of British public opinion in 1814. Nor can it be questioned that for both these factors Wilberforce had been primarily responsible. A crowded Abolitionist meeting in London in 1814 had addressed him as ' the father of our great cause '. And now he had added to his fame among his countrymen a fame throughout all Europe. As the Slave Trade became a leading issue in the general politics of civilized society, so he took rank among the world's great men. In every capital his name was known : in every enlightened circle he had his readers and disciples. The Sovereigns and Princes of the great Alliance, gathered in London, each paid his tribute. His conversation with the Czar was the first of many ; for the vein of mysticism in Alexander had found something kindred and attractive in the pious Englishman's conviction of the providential ordering of the world. The Duchess of Oldenburg insisted on an interview. The King of Prussia presented him with a set of Dresden china—' the only thing ', he said, ' I ever got by spouting '. Prince Blücher dispatched his *aide-de-camp* from the field of Waterloo to tell the story of the battle to the Prince Regent—and to Wilberforce. But all these tokens of his fame left his simplicity quite unspoiled. It touched him far more deeply than did any of these gilded compliments when, during his holiday that autumn, he came to a secluded village in North Devon and, it being known that Wilberforce was there, the bells of the little church were set ringing.*

* *Life*, iv. 192–267. *Hansard*, xxviii (1814), 267–97, 438–42. C. K. Webster, *British Diplomacy. 1813–15* (London, 1921), Nos. cxx, cxxix, cliii.

XI

THE SHADOW

I

ALREADY before Waterloo was fought, there were signs that, as far as the internal condition of England was concerned, the end of the war was not to mean the beginning of an age of prosperity and contentment. The one boon above all others which the mass of the English people had expected peace to bring them was cheaper bread · and at first it seemed that peace had brought it. In 1814 the price of corn fell with a rush. But the effect on agriculture, abnormally diverted to corn-growing during the war, was naturally disastrous. Farmers by the score threw up their farms in despair. Many of them became absolute paupers. And the landlords, with derelict farms on their hands and rents falling, their new enclosures and developments no longer profitable, easy mortgages converted into crushing burdens, watched with dismay the rapid fading of their dreams of permanent war-prices and high rents Only one thing, it was thought, could save English agriculture—to shut out the corn which foreign producers, freed from the trammels of the war, were now ready to pour into England—and this thing a Parliament practically monopolized by the landlords was quite prepared to do. Nor was this class-interest the only interest. The war, as every war in which these islands are engaged must do, had planted in many men's minds the desire to make the country self-supporting in the necessaries of life. So, in the spring of 1815, the notorious Corn Law was passed, prohibiting the import of corn unless the price of wheat were more than eighty shillings a quarter. At a stroke the one supreme boon of peace for the masses was snatched away. The hungry poor were to go hungry still. No wonder that the patience, which had endured so much and so long because the war, it seemed, necessitated it, should now at last begin to break. ' Public discontent running high, Corn Bill *causa* ', notes Wilberforce early in March. ' Corn Bill in Committee—sad rioting at night. Both doors of the carriage which set down members opened, and member pulled out. None much injured.' ' Report of Corn

Bill. . . . Some mobbing, and people savage and inveterate—
alas ! alas ! Charles Grant and Mr Arthur Young, the
agriculturalist, slept with us for security.' ' Sir Joseph
Banks' house sadly treated ; all his papers burnt.'

If Wilberforce's house could still be regarded as a refuge
from the mob, it was only because he had not yet spoken
on the Bill, and before the debates were over, he felt
obliged to speak. ' At my prayers this morning ', says the
diary for March 10, ' I reflected seriously if it was not my
duty to declare my opinions in favour of the Corn Bill. . . .
I decided to do it   I see people wonder I do not speak one
way or the other. It will be said, he professes to trust in
God's protection, but he would not venture anything. . . .
Besides, it is only fair to the Government, when I really
think them right, to say so, as an independent man, not
liable to the imputation of party bias, corrupt agreement
with landed interest, etc ' Nor was the idea of ' log-rolling '
quite absent from his mind   He had already, indeed, when
pressed to speak, told Huskisson that he would do so if the
Government would support his Slave Registration Bill, and,
though he could not drive this particular bargain, he felt,
as he wrote to his eldest son, that to back the Government
now would render it more disposed to help him on missionary and religious questions. So, on the afternoon of
the 10th, he spoke.

' There was a general impression ', he said, ' that the opening
of our ports freely for the importation of foreign corn would
prevent agriculturalists from supplying our home-market
and would occasion a general decline and decrease of our
agriculture. If that were true, it was necessary for the
general weal of the Empire that the legislature should adopt
proper remedies before it was too late. . . . If the whole of
Europe were under one government—if it were one great
family—if all countries were as much disposed to dispense
happiness as they were often found inclined to injure one
another, he should then say, Let every country produce that
which the nature of its soil and other circumstances may
render beneficial, and let it supply other nations with its
superabundance. . . . But it was worthy of the most serious
consideration that those very countries from which we might
derive supplies were countries which, at no great length of

time, might be united against this nation. . . . No, there could not be any truth more certain than this—that a great country like England should be independent of foreign nations with regard to the supply of food.' Manufacturers were protected : why not agriculture too ? To save agriculture was to save the workers on the land. ' The House should consider the situation of the peasantry who could not attend to plead their cause. They should consider them as calling on Parliament with ten thousand tongues to protect them and their families. As to the cost of bread, he had not heard one single argument to show that, because the restricting price was fixed at 80 shillings, the price of corn must necessarily be raised to that extent.' At the same time he was personally in favour of the lower limit of 76 shillings.

This speech did not go unmarked. Early next morning, an old servant of Wilberforce's, who had set up as a greengrocer, went as usual to Covent Garden market to buy vegetables for his shop. ' So your old master has spoken for the Corn Bill ', he was told, ' but his house shall pay for it.' And, though the threat never materialized, it was thought prudent to station a sergeant, four soldiers, and a ' peace-officer ' in Wilberforce's house. ' Were you to enter the dining-room at family prayer time ', he wrote to his son, ' you would probably begin to think that we were expecting a visit from the ex-Emperor.' The following characteristic comment appears in the diary a few days later : ' The soldiers (Scotch) behave extremely well ; they come into prayers and pleased to do so.'

These incidents of 1815 are a significant introduction to the next seven years—the last years—of Wilberforce's active political life. What he did about the Corn Bill he felt it his duty to do about all the primary issues of that time. The welfare of his ' negro clients ' might still be the dominant interest of his life ; but the Member for Bramber could no more be silent about other leading questions than the Member for Yorkshire. In a sense all England was his constituency now. He was regarded by a large part of his countrymen as the nation's moral oracle. Writing in 1817, the poet Southey went so far as to say that ' the weight with which his opinion comes to the public' was 'far greater than of any other individual'. And that opinion he was bound to give, for silence would be as easily misunderstood as any old Delphic riddle. On behalf of his dominant interest, moreover, it was but common sense to acquire merit in the Government's eyes by honestly supporting its measures when he honestly agreed with them So he spoke —and his reputation suffered. For the 'Independent' was still, of course, a Tory: his speeches in this period were mainly Tory speeches, and it is doubtful whether the members of any party since Cromwell's have been so ferociously abused, in life and in their graves, as the Tories who ruled England for seven years after Waterloo.

Students of those days, whose hearts are not tutored by their heads, may find it difficult not to join in the chorus of vituperation, when they read of the bitter sufferings of the poor, of the ill-concerted and, under the circumstances, strangely temperate agitation of half-fed, desperate men, and of its blind and sometimes cruel suppression by a narrow oligarchy of the landed rich. But the historian who, at the risk of seeming smugly callous, tries to understand before condemning, who asks himself why those oligarchs, who after all were average Englishmen, acted as they did, will find two or three things to say in their defence. Some of those men, he will admit, who voted for the Corn Bill were prompted by sheer class-selfishness, but not all. There were some who genuinely agreed with Wilberforce that to save the landed interest was to save the country too And one of these was Huskisson, who, mistaken as he was on the Corn Laws, was soon to prove himself a not illiberal statesman and a sound economist. It is only fair, moreover, to remember that the most unselfish, the most philanthropic patriots could not have averted, and could not have done very much to ameliorate, the distresses of the poor. The forces of the Economic Revolution, industrial and agrarian together, were beyond the control of any Government or any party. Adjustment to so swift and drastic a change was only possible with time and with suffering. And meanwhile the most well-meaning Englishmen had nothing authoritative to guide them but the almost sacrosanct economic principle of *laissez-faire*. To improve the conditions or lessen the hours of labour, to protect the poor from their masters or from themselves—all such interferences with the natural operation of economic laws were likely, the professors told them, to do more harm than good. And, if one is tempted to think that men so hated in their day must have given good cause for hate, it is only fair again to remember—and it is easy for the present generation to understand—the effects of the disillusionment that came with peace. So long as the war lasted, the wretched poor, overwhelmed through no fault of their own by inexorable economic forces far beyond their comprehension, could find at least the cold comfort of something to explain it all and somebody to blame. They cursed the war and endured it : they cursed Napoleon and beat him. But when the war was over, when bread was dearer, trade slacker, everything worse instead of better, they looked, with the added bitterness of disappointment, for something and somebody else to blame. It scarcely needed the Corn Law to expose the criminals. They turned and cursed the Tories, all the more savagely because those tyrants were their countrymen ; and as their misery dragged on and deepened, they cursed the whole of the political and social order which the Tories typified and dominated.

The Tories were aware of this ; and it explains, if it does not excuse, their hard and barren policy. The significance of those Corn Bill incidents is not exhausted. Those soldiers at family-prayers in Wilberforce's house give a true touch of high colour, an authentic hint of melodrama, to the picture of the time. If the poor detected their enemies in the debates on the Bill, the rich detected theirs in the riot and arson that ensued. The English governing class, it has been seen, had never quite abandoned their belief in the possibility of revolution, and now it gripped them again as firmly as in the blackest period of Pitt's repression. The alarm this time could hardly be called a panic. Nerves had been hardened since the days of the Terror. An English mob was scarcely so terrifying as Napoleon at Boulogne.

But, if Sidmouth and his kind were neither neurasthenics nor cowards, they were certainly afraid. They saw, and saw rightly, that the mass of the people were more actively discontented with the existing order than they had ever been. They failed to see that Jacobinism had never taken root in England and was now quite withered up. They failed to appreciate the striking fact that, in so far as this discontent was vocal, it called for no Gallic cataclysm but only for a quiet and a not so very sweeping change in the English Constitution. They failed to realize that the one thing that could drive those slow Englishmen to revolution was an absolute, permanent refusal of any measure of reform—the rigid maintenance of a system which gave to a small minority of rich men, mostly landowners, an almost complete monopoly of political power. To be so afraid and to be so blind—those were the Tories' cardinal sins. Afraid and blind, they set themselves, tragic patriots, to saving their country by the one means most likely to destroy it. And if ever they wanted to strengthen their resolution by appealing to some indisputable authority, if ever they wanted a name to conjure with, they recalled the memory of Pitt. Dark over all those frosty years—the great years of the Pitt Clubs, where full-blooded young Tories of the Right exuberantly toasted the hero of repression—lies the shadow of Pitt : but it was the old Pitt of the war-period, not the young Pitt in his first decade of office.

It is against this background of anxiety and negation that the conduct of Pitt's old friend through the seven years of reaction must be viewed. No one nowadays can deny that Wilberforce was one of the best of his class—really disinterested, really trying to act on principle rather than on prejudice. But he, too, was afraid. It was unfortunate, perhaps, for his judgement that he should have been appointed a member of the Secret Committee of the House of Commons which, together with a similar Committee of the Lords, was appointed early in 1817 to examine the papers in the Government's hands ' respecting certain practices, meetings and combinations in the metropolis and different parts of the kingdom, *evidently calculated* to endanger the public tranquillity . . . and to bring into hatred and contempt the whole system of our laws and constitution'. There was thus set out before him a terrifying array of evidence, some of it true and quite innocuous, some of it honestly mistaken, and some of it actually manufactured by 'Oliver', the Government spy and *agent provocateur*. He read of the agitation and unrest which had grown with the growth of want and misery since the trouble began over the Corn Law—of great mobs harangued in violent language by demagogues like Hunt and Thistlewood, of intermittent rioting and arson, of the distribution in one or two cases of arms, of Luddist outbreaks for the destruction of machinery, of people waiting in provincial towns for the arrival of the mail-coach to bring them the expected news that London had risen and 'the Tower and the Bank were in the hands of the insurgents', of the Radical Cartwright and his Hampden Reform Clubs, of Spence's Societies for the nationalization of land. Some of it at least was alarming, and all of it was one-sided. Wilberforce and his colleagues had no personal contact with the poor, no direct knowledge of their real desires, and there were no 'go-betweens' to bridge the gulf of class and to tell them that the mass of the English people were not out for revolution. Almost inevitably, therefore, Wilberforce's alarm increased. Three days after the appointment of the Secret Committees he writes to his family at Hastings : 'We are here in the midst of accounts of plots, etc., but a gracious Providence, I trust, watches over us. Remember to pray in earnest against sedition, privy conspiracy, and rebellion.' Already it is as bad as that. 'We are not to divulge', he writes again from the Committee-room a little later ; 'but thus much I may say . . . that the seizing of the ringleaders on Monday last prevented bloodshed from the Spa Fields mob on Monday.' So already repression is the remedy. It is clear, too, already that Wilberforce has made the fatal blunder of regarding bitter denunciation of the unreformed constitution as tantamount to sedition. His attitude to Cobbett betrays it. 'Hunt', he writes, 'is a foolish, mischief-making fellow, but no conspirator, though the tool of worse and deeper villains. Cobbett is the most pernicious of all.' Now Cobbett's power in creating and mobilizing Radical opinion was unquestionably tremendous. The *Political Register*, especially when its price dropped to twopence in 1816, sold at the rate of 50,000 copies a week and was eagerly devoured by the discontented throughout the country. And Cobbett's language was immoderately bitter, often grossly unfair, sometimes quite inaccurate. But the most important fact about Cobbett was that he pleaded definitely for constitutional action and definitely discouraged violence. But against Cobbett Wilberforce's whole being revolted. He could not give him his due. He could not help conceiving him as a Paine, if not a Robespierre. And the cause of this almost instinctive repugnance was the cause of most of his prejudices. The man was irreligious. When the Prince Regent, of all men, in his talk with Wilberforce at Brighton in 1815, ' spoke strongly of the blasphemy ' of Cobbett's writings, the diary adds, ' and most justly ', with amazingly unconscious irony. So far as saints can hate, Wilberforce hated Cobbett : and Cobbett, without any qualification, returned his hatred.

The result of the Secret Committees was a foregone conclusion—the question indeed had been frankly begged in the terms of their reference. Their almost identical reports declared that a widespread conspiracy was afoot, organized by secret societies, for the subversion of the constitution and the spoliation of property. Armed with the weapon it had asked for, the Government promptly introduced a Bill for the suspension of the *Habeas Corpus* Act till the end of the session together with two other instruments from Pitt's armoury—a Seditious Meetings Bill, which prohibited all unlicensed assemblies and for such as aimed at changes in Church or State prescribed the death-penalty for a refusal to disperse, and a Bill to punish attempts to tamper with the allegiance of soldiers and sailors. All these measures were duly passed by big majorities. The Secret Committees, meantime, were too useful to be dispensed with. They continued to investigate

the stream of alarmist evidence and to report their belief
in the existence of a ' traitorous conspiracy '. And indeed,
once this belief had entered men's minds, there was enough
happening in England that spring and summer, not merely
in spies' note-books but in the light of day, to give it firm
root. Fires were still strangely frequent in rural areas.
Riots continued in towns, sometimes with loss of life. The
march of the Manchester Blanketeers on London termin-
ated, it is true, in a pitiful fiasco ; only twenty of them got
as far as Staffordshire ; but at the moment of its initiation
it had seemed a serious business. Ten thousand men had
gathered for the send-off ; and several hundreds had taken
the road. A little later there were outbreaks in Yorkshire
and the Midlands, which, feeble and futile as they were,
seemed ominous enough to those who did not know that
they had actually been provoked by ' Oliver '. At any rate
the Secret Committees were more than ever convinced of the
reality of the danger ; and in June the Government asked
for and obtained an Act to prolong the suspension of the
Habeas Corpus Act till March 1, 1818.

Ministerialists and Grenvillites alike stood solidly behind
the Government throughout the session : and Wilberforce
was with them. ' Seditious Meetings Bill. I spoke first
opportunity, strongly defending the Bill.' He took no part
in the debate on the first *Habeas Corpus* Suspension Bill,
but he supported the first reading of the second. The
disaffection, he argued, which unquestionably existed, was
mainly due to deliberate corruption of the ignorant. The
object of the Bill was to enable the Government ' to take
away those who infused the poison '. Would the power be
abused ? ' He could not easily believe that the noble lord
(Sidmouth) would so far forget the character he had always
sustained as to employ the authority entrusted to him for
wicked or oppressive purposes. Although Parliament might
not be sitting, no case of cruelty or hardship could remain
unknown in the present state of the Press, and every such
case would most certainly be canvassed whenever Parliament should be reassembled. . . . When Ministers pledged
themselves that this measure was necessary, he felt himself,

however reluctantly, compelled to yield to such necessity.
He certainly thought it an evil . at the same time he hoped
that the natural good sense of the people of England would
at length restore to them their ancient rights   Till then,
he must, for the sake of the patient poor, for the sake even
of the turbulent themselves, consent to the passing of the
Bill.' Romilly and Brougham protested in vain. The bulk
of the Tories, not so reluctant as Wilberforce to tamper with
the English tradition of personal liberty, nor so anxious as
Canning to prove justification, waited impatiently for the
division and carried it by more than two to one.

Wilberforce's attitude had quickly become notorious ;
and, as in Fox's day, it was all the more irritating to the
outvoted Opposition because of the additional weight which
his reputed independence gave it. In the debate on the
third reading, Sir Francis Burdett vented the bitter feelings
of most Radicals in a personal attack. ' I confess ', he said,
' I am astonished at the concurrence in this measure of an
honourable and religious gentleman who lays claim to a
superior piety. . . . Nothing could be more anti-Christian
than to shut up persons in solitary confinement. . . . The
honourable and religious gentleman recollects, no doubt,
the denunciation of Jesus against the wicked : " I was
hungry, and ye gave me no meat. . . . I was sick and in
prison, and ye visited me not." .   The honourable and
religious member was shocked the other day at the description of Africans chained and carried into slavery. How
happened it that the honourable and religious member was
not shocked at Englishmen being taken up under this Act
and treated like African slaves ? ' As the speaker harped
on his refrain, loud cries of ' Order ' were raised, and not
from the Tory side of the House alone. But Wilberforce
could look after himself. When Burdett had done, he rose
at once in response to ' the sort of call made upon him by the
honourable baronet '. In a short speech, none the worse for
being unprepared, he reiterated his conviction of the danger
of leaving at large ' those who had long been employed in
spreading a poison that had already attacked the vitals
of the constitution '. Then, turning towards Burdett,

' How ', he asked, ' can the honourable baronet talk as he
does of those religious principles on which the welfare of the
community depends ? I would fain believe that he desires
as sincerely as I do myself to perpetuate to this country the
blessings she enjoys. But if I could be base enough to seek
the destruction of those institutions which we both profess
to revere, I will tell him what instrument I should choose.
I would take a man of great wealth, of patrician family, of
personal popularity, aye, and of respectable talents I am
satisfied that such a one, while he scattered abroad the
firebrands of sedition under pretence that he went all
lengths for the people, would be the best agent for the
malevolent purpose of destroying their liberties and happiness ' ' Never in my parliamentary life ', said a member
afterwards, presumably no Radical, ' did I hear a speech
which carried its audience more completely with it or was
listened to with such breathless attention.'

Next session a similar but less offensive attack on Wilberforce was made by Tierney, now the Leader of the Opposition. The occasion was the second of the two fiery debates
in the spring of 1818, in which the odious machinations of
' Oliver the Spy ' were thrust into the light Ministers were
in an unenviable position. No one now believes that
Sidmouth deliberately employed ' Oliver ' as an *agent
provocateur*; but, unwilling to confess the lesser crime of
employing him at all in such life-and-death matters without
sufficient knowledge of his character, they decided to brazen
it out and trust to their majority. What, then, was Wilberforce to do ? One cannot help regretting that he did not
do what Romilly expected of him—that he did not forget
for once his personal respect for Sidmouth and insist at
least on an inquiry, But in the first debate—on a motion
for referring the question to the Secret Committee—while he
reprobated the use of spies at all as ' equally repugnant to
honour or morality or to the feelings of a gentleman and
almost as objectionable on the grounds of political expediency ', he gave his vote against the motion. And in the
second debate—on a motion for instituting an inquiry *de
novo*—he spoke and voted in the same way. But the House,

it seems, had not been sure of it. Charges of 'trying to catch the member for Bramber's vote' were bandied across the floor. And it was this that gave Tierney his cue.

' I do not wish ', he said, ' to speak disrespectfully of the honourable member for Bramber ; and certainly there is no individual more capable of giving effective support to Ministers and their measures when he chooses to turn out (*cheers and laughter*). What his vote will be on the present occasion it is not, perhaps, easy to prophesy. . . . Generally, his phraseology is happily adapted to suit either party ; and if, now and then, he loses the balance of his argument and bends a little to one side, he quickly recovers himself and deviates as much in an opposite direction as will make a fair division of his speech on both sides of the question ' (*continued cheers*).'

The taunt brought Wilberforce to his feet. The last speaker and himself, he said, were old soldiers in parliamentary warfare ; and he quite understood that the Leader of the Opposition had to say what was expected of him.

' But to what length must party-feeling have reached in this House, when it is asserted that, because a person is not systematically opposed to every motion of Government, he cannot form an honest opinion on any subject presented to him in Parliament. (*Cries of No, No, from the Opposition.*) Well, if gentlemen are anxious to disclaim such an injustice, I hope that I and an honourable friend of mine [William Smith] will in future be treated with somewhat more respect.'

' Wished not to speak ', he notes that night , ' . . . Tierney gave the last prick which forced me to rise ; though not at all ill-naturedly, I am glad to say. Nor was I ill-natured, I hope . thank God, I did not feel so.' *

---

* *Life*, iv. 244–9, 277, 308, 319–29, 373. *Hansard*, xxx (1815), 116–18, xxxvi (1817), 1109–43, 1246–9, xxxvii (1818), 363–6, 375. 850–61 J. L and B Hammond, *The Skilled Labourer* (London, 1920), 372–4.

II

In the latter part of 1817 and throughout the following year trade steadily improved. Unemployment decreased. The poorest classes climbed for a moment above starvation level And, immediate and significant result, the spasmodic turbulence ceased : the ' traitorous conspiracy ' faded into the background But the relief was transient. The reputation of the Tories—and of Wilberforce—was yet to receive its darkest stain To meet the new demand from the Continent the manufacturers overproduced, just as they had done at the close of the war. Continental purchasing-power was quickly exhausted : employers were left with big unmarketable stocks slump succeeded boom : and in 1819 unemployment and want were as bad as ever. Immediately and significantly the political agitation revived. But its character was still scarcely Jacobinical. The organization of nocturnal drilling was alarming, and doubtless intended to alarm. But that was the worst. Popular discontent no longer showed itself in violent outbreaks, in riots and burnings, but in relatively orderly mass-meetings for the single object of demanding Parliamentary Reform. It was one of those gatherings, however, that set the stage for tragedy. The crowd which assembled on August 16 in St. Peter's Field on the outskirts of Manchester to listen to Hunt and other orators was neither armed nor bent on violence ; but it was enormous—it numbered between 50,000 and 60,000 men, women, and children. And the Government can hardly be blamed for holding a small force of cavalry in readiness. The responsibility for what occurred lies almost wholly with the local magistrates. They allowed the meeting to begin and then, suddenly losing their heads, they ordered the Yeomanry, ill-trained for such a task and ill-suited for it by their political sympathies, to make their way through the throng and arrest Hunt ; and finally, when the Yeomanry were entangled and hustled in the crowd, they ordered the colonel in command of the Hussars to charge The result was the ' Massacre of Peterloo '. Eleven were killed or died of their hurts, and several hundred were injured by sword-cuts or horses' hoofs, or crushed in the panic rush for safety. It was not the tragedy itself, but its subsequent conduct that blackened the Government's record. Without pausing to investigate the facts, Ministers thanked the magistrates; declared, on very dubious ground, that the meeting had been illegal; and committed Hunt and some of his colleagues to trial for ' a conspiracy to alter the law by force and threats '. Lastly, as if to justify this hasty prejudgement of the case, they pleaded once more, when Parliament met in October, that measures of general repression were imperative. This time they did not move the suspension of the *Habeas Corpus* Act : it has never been suspended in Britain since 1818 ; but they moved and carried the ' Six Acts ', the kernel of which was the prohibition of unofficial public meetings and an attempt to tax the Radical Press out of existence. The agitation for Reform was to be silenced.

Wilberforce came up to this stormy session with the fear of revolution more firmly fixed than ever in his mind. ' Seldom has a boy returned on a black Monday ', he writes to a friend, ' with more reluctance than I to St. Stephen's. I dare not be too confident that we may not witness scenes of something nearer to civil war than this land has exhibited since 1646.' However groundless it may seem to cool students at the safe distance of a century, however reassuring the fact, admitted even in the Secret Committees' Reports, that the people at large showed little sympathy with rioters and incendiaries, this fear was now shared by almost all the members of Wilberforce's class, by Whigs as well as Tories, by business-men as well as landlords. When Wilberforce asked his correspondents in the country for first-hand information as to the conditions in their neighbourhood, their replies were uniformly sombre. A Yorkshire friend tells him, for example, in October, ' that the West Riding of our county is in an alarming fermentation—the lower orders generally corrupted and the merchants and higher manufacturers scarcely daring to resist the tide of blasphemy and sedition '. ' You may remember ', writes

Wilberforce, passing the news on to Stephen, ' the assassination of a merchant three or four years ago near Huddersfield, when it was said that, at the time the fatal shot was
fired, there was a general shout of triumph from the tops of
the houses, hay-stacks, and other elevated situations.' In
Leicester, again, so he heard, ' the lower orders are in the
habit of meeting by night in parties of twenty-five to practise
the pike-exercise '. But what most alarmed and repelled
him—what spurred him to repression more than all else—
was the agitators' open defiance of religion. ' Heretofore
they inveighed against the inequality of property,' runs a
private memorandum of this period, ' and used every artifice
to alienate the people from the constitution of their country.
But now they are sapping the foundations of the social
edifice more effectually by attacking Christianity '

And so, on Peterloo as on ' Oliver ', his voice and vote
were Sidmouth's It was not, of course, a blind, automatic
conformity : he could scarcely give Sidmouth what he had
never given Pitt. And on Peterloo he was certainly
influenced in some degree by an opinion given him by a
' very sensible and dispassionate man (no partisan of
Ministers) who halted at that place a short time after the
tumult ' The colour of this opinion is suggested by
Wilberforce's comment—' I think the magistrates have been
unjust to themselves in not publishing what may be called
their *case*.' And so, when Tierney moved a moderate
amendment to the Address, asking for a parliamentary
inquiry, Wilberforce opposed it, partly on the ground that
the law-courts were the proper place for ascertaining the
truth of criminal charges and not the House of Commons,
where evidence could not be tendered on oath, and partly
because an inquiry would cast a slur on the whole body of
magistrates on whose loyal service the local administration
of the country rested. But he committed himself no farther
than that When an angry opponent charged him with
' warmly defending ' the magistrates' conduct, ' I am not
prepared ', he replied, ' to defend any more than to attack
them.' Still less, it goes without saying, could he be
accused of any lack of sympathy with the victims of the
' massacre '. ' Can there be one man here ', he asked, ' who

does not from his soul lament these transactions ? If there
be, it must be one who has learned to look to slaughter and
civil war for the regeneration of his country ' No less firm
was his support of the ' Six Acts '. Opposition to them, he
believed and said, could only be inspired either by reckless
coquetry with revolution or by blindness to the reality of
the danger. ' It is one of the peculiar excellencies of the
British Constitution ', he declared when he urged that the
Seditious Meetings Bill should be passed, but should run for
three years only, ' to be able in times of popular commotion
to strengthen the hands of the executive government, and
afterwards, when the danger is past, to revert to our former
state of liberty and freedom '

Towards the end of that angry session the following entry
occurs in the diary : ' Dec. 16th.—Took my place, as for
some little time past, the last seat on the Opposition bench.
Finding that Opposition complained of it, I named it this
evening to Tierney who behaved very kindly about it.'
All things considered, the complaint was not unreasonable *

III

Certainly there were Radicals who hated Wilberforce.
Francis Place, the stubborn champion of Trade Unionism
and the backstairs architect of Reform, described him in his
analysis of the Peterloo debate as ' an ugly epitome of the
devil ' Cobbett's hatred dated back to his unregenerate
days, when, in strange contradiction to his later self, he was
the close ally and constant correspondent of so stiff an
oligarch as Windham There are one or two angry thrusts
at the uncongenial ' saint ' in his letters about the odious
Peace of Amiens. Fox, he declares, in his attacks on Windham's war-party, ' is most insidiously and malignantly aided
by Wilberforce ' , and alluding to a speech of Wilberforce's
in Yorkshire he begs Windham to obtain for him ' these
precious morsels of eloquence '. Wilberforce, too, it appears,

* *Life*, v 34–46 *Hansard*, xli (1819–20), 135–6, 319–22, 800–2.
H A Bruton, *Story of Peterloo* (John Rylands Library Bulletin,
October 1919, and separately printed)

is at the back of the mischievous attacks on the manlier
sports, especially bull-baiting, which Windham so queerly
loved and the popularity of which in Staffordshire and
Lancashire Cobbett associated with the peculiar bravery of
the troops enlisted in those counties. So it was with the
gusto of an old feud that Cobbett in later days assailed the
preposterous ' Independent '. Above all the other victims
of the *Political Register* he enjoyed putting Wilberforce in
the pillory ; and when he used his frequent and very effective
device of a Public Letter, he reiterated that too-widely
respected name with special zest—' Well, Wilberforce. . . .
Now you will observe, Wilberforce. . . . Mark it, Wilberforce ;
note it down. . . . ' Still more pointed is the climax of the
final crescendo in his often-quoted letter to Orator Hunt,
written after his flight to the United States on the suspension
of the *Habeas Corpus* Act in 1818.

' Think of it. A hundred brace of wood-cocks a day. Think
of *that* ! And never to see the hang-dog face of a tax-
gatherer. Think of *that* ! No Alien Acts here. No long-
sworded and whiskered Captains. No Judges escorted from
town to town and sitting under the guard of dragoons. No
packed juries of tenants. No Crosses. No Bolton Fletchers.
No hangings and rippings up. No Castleses and Olivers.
No Stewarts and Perries. No Cannings, Liverpools, Castle-
reaghs, Eldons, Ellenboroughs or Sidmouths. No Bankers.
No squeaking Wynnes. No Wilberforces. Think of *that* !
No Wilberforces ! '

The Radical dead-set against Wilberforce is nowhere
better illustrated than in Hazlitt's *Spirit of the Age*, published in 1825. Those lively ' studies in contemporary
biography' are admirable reading ; but drab history must
regard them primarily as a warning against a too easy
acceptance of contemporary judgements. Hazlitt pokes
fun, though not unkindly, at Jeremy Bentham ; he makes
him out an industrious, benevolent, amusingly childish
pedant ; and he denies that the man, whose influence was
to do more in the long run for the better government of
England than that of any other of his day, ' has given any
new or decided impulse to the human mind '. Coleridge,
' by dissipating his intellect and dallying with every subject

by turns ', has done little or nothing to justify the high
opinion of his friends Two pages of venom are devoted to
the Tory politics of Scott—his unworthy acts of adulation ;
his littleness, pique, resentment, bigotry, and intolerance ,
his forgetfulness of all that was due to the pride of intellect
and the sense of manhood, the moment his own interest or
the prejudices of others interfered, and so forth. Sir Francis
Burdett, on the other hand, whom a sober-minded historian
of by no means illiberal views has lately described as ' super-
ficial and self-advertising ', is pictured as ' a plain, unaffected,
unsophisticated English gentleman ' , ' one of the few
remaining examples of the old English understanding and
old English character ' ; ' never violent or in extremes
except when the people or the Parliament happen to be out
of their senses, and then he seems to regret the necessity
of plainly telling them he thinks so '. After that it is no
surprise to find Lord Eldon and Wilberforce classed and
limned together on the Plutarchian plan But it is a little
surprising to find Hazlitt painting Wilberforce blacker than
Lord Eldon. He depicts Eldon and the Tories of his type
as spoiled children, fractious and selfish, all urbanity and
good-humour until their interests are threatened. It is
a bitter enough picture, but not so malignant as that which
follows.

' Mr Wilberforce is a less perfect character in his way. He
acts from mixed motives. He would willingly serve two
masters, God and Mammon .   We can readily believe that
Mr. Wilberforce's first object and principle of action is to
do what he thinks right , his next (and that we fear is of
almost equal weight with the first) is to do what will be
thought so by other people. . . . His " conscience will not
budge ", unless the world goes with it. He does not seem
greatly to dread the denunciation in Scripture—" Woe
unto you, when all men shall speak well of you ". We
suspect that he is not quite easy in his mind, because West-
India planters and Guinea traders do not join in his praise.'
(This is hard hitting, but worse is to come) ' Mr. Wilberforce's humanity will go all lengths that it can with safety
and discretion , but it is not to be supposed that it should
lose him his seat for Yorkshire, the smile of Majesty, or the
countenance of the loyal and pious. He is anxious to do

all the good he can without hurting himself or his fair fame. His conscience and his character compound matters very amicably. He rather patronizes honesty than is a martyr to it. His patriotism and philanthropy are not so ill-bred as to quarrel with his loyalty or to banish him from the first circles . . He has had two strings to his bow—he by no means neglects his worldly interests while he expects a bright reversion in the skies. Mr. Wilberforce is far from being a hypocrite ; but he is, we think, as fine a specimen of *moral equivocation* as can well be conceived. . . . He carefully chooses his ground to fight the battles of loyalty, religion, and humanity , and it is such as is always safe and advantageous to himself . . . He has all the air of the most perfect independence, and gains a character for impartiality and candour when he is only striking a balance in his mind between the *éclat* of differing from a Minister on some vantage-ground and the risk or odium that may attend it.'

And so on, till, at the close of the essay which is certainly the most vindictive of the set (for Hazlitt mingles his abuse of Scott with some kindly praise of his novels), Wilberforce is robbed even of the credit which Fox and Grey and Romilly and Mackintosh, nay, all but the most spiteful opponents accorded him.

' Something of this fluctuating, time-serving principle ', runs the final paragraph, ' was visible even in the great question of the Abolition of the Slave Trade He was, at one time, half inclined to surrender it into Mr. Pitt's dilatory hands, and seemed to think the gloss of novelty was gone from it and the gaudy colouring of popularity sunk into the *sable* ground from which it rose It was, however, persisted in and carried to a triumphant conclusion. Mr Wilberforce said too little on that occasion of one compared with whom he was but the frontispiece to that great chapter in the history of the world—the mask, the varnishing, and painting The man that affected it by Herculean labours of body and equally gigantic labours of mind was Clarkson, the true Apostle of human Redemption on that occasion, and who, it is remarkable, resembles in his person and lineaments more than one of the Apostles in the *Cartoons* of Raphael. He deserves to be added to the Twelve ! '

These caustic pages have been quoted at some length because so many good opinions of Wilberforce have been recorded in this book. It is needless to check the string

of epigrams or to reopen the Clarkson controversy. Readers
of the foregoing chapters can form their own opinions. Nor
will they find it difficult to understand why anti-Tory rancour was thus concentrated on Wilberforce's head. When
party feeling runs high, the man who tells you he is neutral
and seems always to side with your opponents is more
provoking than a down-right inveterate enemy, especially
when his profession of neutrality is so far believed in by
a great part of the public as to give unusual weight to his
opinions. That this palpable Tory, this man of wealth and
property, as stiffly bound to the interests of his class as any
landlord, should pose as an impartial arbiter above the
heat and dust of party conflict—it was intolerable. Still
more galling, the pontiff was a pietist A frankly cynical
tyrant is more endurable than one who crushes his victims
in the name of God ; and to men like Hazlitt and Cobbett
the ' other-worldliness ' of the rich and comfortable Wilberforce's religion seemed positively nauseating. They gnashed
their teeth at his genteel tributes to the ' patient poor '.
And his Puritanical activities outside politics, his campaigns
for stricter morals and a sterner Sabbath—what were they
but one more symptom of class-tyranny, an attempt to
rob the poor of their harmless sports and to deaden their
meagre leisure-hours while the profligacy and idleness and
irreligion of the rich went unrebuked ? Wilberforce, in
fact, was the obvious target for the hostility with which
many Radicals then regarded the Churches—and not
without reason. For organized religion in England as a
whole was on the classes' side, not the masses' The sudden
revival of zeal for the Established Church in the days of the
French Revolution was largely due to the belief that
Jacobinism and Atheism were inseparable twins, that the
rights of property would be remembered as long as Christianity were not forgotten. The agitation for the building
of more churches needed no ulterior motive when the fast-
growing towns had only ' church-room ' for one in seven of
their population and when at Manchester, for example, the
vicar had to read the banns for at least 120 couples every
Sunday , and Arthur Young was right, when he took a lead

in this agitation in 1798, to insist that new churches were particularly needed for the poor. But the ulterior motive was always there. ' Where are they [the poor] ', asked Arthur Young, ' to learn the doctrines of that truly excellent religion which exhorts to content and to submission to the higher powers ? ' And when the agitation at last bore fruit, when, in 1818, Parliament voted no less than a million pounds for church-building, there was no concealing—there was little attempt, indeed, to conceal—the conviction that the Church was the natural ally of the State in the conflict with Reform. As Liverpool, the Prime Minister, told the House of Lords, the political aspect of the matter, the prevalence of dangerous influences in crowded centres of industry, was one of his reasons for regarding the New Churches Bill as actually ' the most important measure he had ever submitted to their lordships' consideration '.

Take account of such facts as these and of the ease with which party spirit exaggerates and generalizes, and it is easy to see why Wilberforce was anathema to the Radicals ; why the blood rushed to Cobbett's head when the Saint inveighed against the profanation of the Sabbath or bestowed the benediction of his faith on the existing political and social order ; why those vigorous haters would have hated him more, not less, if they had known that his decision to support the Corn Bill was made at his prayers.*

IV

Party feeling cannot be bothered with fine distinctions. It can only sustain itself by digging the dividing ditch as deep as possible and making the best of everything on one side of it and the worst of everything on the other. Since, therefore, Wilberforce's neutrality was merely nominal on

* *Hansard*, xxxviii (1818), 709–14. Hazlitt, *The Spirit of the Age* (London, 1825). Wallas, *Life of Francis Place* (1918), 147. Melville, *Life and Letters of Cobbett* (1913), i. 154–68; ii. 106–7. J. L. and B. Hammond, *The Town Labourer* (1919), 127–9, 221–46. Mathieson, *England in Transition* (1920), 153–5.

the main issue, since he supported Sidmouth's general system of repression as consistently as Pitt's, he was classified by the fiercer Radicals as an uncompromising reactionary with nothing to offer to the discontented but a policy of blank negation. And this was unjust For, while he spoke and voted for repressing agitation, he pleaded also for positive measures to remedy the ills on which agitation fed—the destitution and the ignorance of the masses. In one of his speeches on Peterloo he declared that it was everybody's duty ' to do all that was possible for relieving the distresses of the laborious poor '. He drew attention, very rightly, to the bad effect on character of the disastrous ' Speenhamland ' system of parish aid ; and suggested that the Government should find some means of providing paid employment. Later in the session he emphatically supported the proposal of Bennet, the Whig, for public relief work on roads and canals. ' Every possible plan ', he said, ' should be tried.' And when, in a debate on a petition on behalf of the Scottish poor, Castlereagh argued that Scottish landowners should tax themselves for poor-relief as heavily as their English *confrères* before England could be fairly asked to share Scotland's burden, Wilberforce insisted that, whatever the unfairness, it would be inhuman to allow these long-suffering Scots to suffer absolute want Of this debate the diary notes : ' I am told, and I fear justly . . . that I was extremely harsh against Castlereagh.' In the same session he pleaded for the education of the poor. ' Have you reflected ', he wrote to Dr. Chalmers, ' on the effects produced in this country by the newspapers ? They are almost incalculably great, and on the whole, I fear, very injurious. It is my persuasion that our safety will henceforth be to educate our people up to the newspapers, if l may so express myself. We must so much enlighten them that they may be armed against those delusions.' In the same strain he told the House of Commons that, until it made amends for its long neglect in this matter, he saw no prospect of tranquillity or prosperity in England. Education could not be left to evolve itself. If people were destined to be free, they must be made fit to enjoy their freedom. . . . Flat platitudes,

no doubt, to-day; but not platitudes in 1819. To many
Tories of the Right, in fact, such arguments must have
seemed mischievously false.

One could scarcely expect, however, that these mild
suggestions would tell in Wilberforce's favour with the
Radicals. He did not press them far—never so far as to
embarrass the Government. He started no great campaign
for relief works or for education. That was not his vocation.
And so the critics, if they marked these little signs of grace
at all, merely added them to their sum of the pasteboard
saint's hypocrisies. It is rather more surprising that Cobbett
and his friends gave Wilberforce no credit for his opposition
to the full Tory doctrine on minor issues. It was dishonest
of Hazlitt to mock at Wilberforce's humanity where white
men were concerned and to say not a word of his fight
against the increased severities of the Penal Code and
especially the Game Laws by which the more ruthless
section of the propertied class strove to deter the destitute
from stealing that they might not starve. Over seventy
offences were made capital during the reign of George III.
At the date of Peterloo death was the penalty for stealing
five shillings from a shop or two pounds from a dwelling-
house, for damaging an embankment or a hop-plantation
or cutting down a tree, for stealing a sheep or linen from
a bleaching-green or destroying a machine, for being found
disguised on a highroad or for impersonating a Greenwich
pensioner. Still more outrageous and still more senseless
were the Game Laws. For, as the results proved, no fear
of penalties, however barbarous, could keep the hardy
English peasant from trying to catch a rabbit on the squire's
land so long as he had no food or even so long as the London
poulterers were never punished for buying and selling the
game he poached. In 1816 the landlords passed an Act
enabling two magistrates to order the transportation for
seven years of a person found at night in an enclosure with
any instrument for killing or trapping game; and all
Romilly's protests could not persuade Parliament to go
farther than to limit the penalty in the following year to
persons found with any weapon of offence. Even to

threaten an assault with intent to prevent a poacher's arrest was a capital crime. As far as the death-penalty was concerned this savage code defeated its end For nineteen trivial capital offences out of twenty, ' injured persons would not prosecute , judges laboured to procure an acquittal ; juries perjured themselves rather than convict '. But the twentieth cases were numerous enough. And the convict who was not hanged was condemned to transportation to Botany Bay—which sometimes proved worse than a death-sentence—or to the foul and degrading conditions of English prisons

The severities of the Penal Code, like those of the Slave Trade, could not long survive the appeal to ordinary humanity and common sense. But in the one case as in the other, vigorous and pertinacious spokesmen were required to make it heard ; and as in the one case Wilberforce could rely on the support of Romilly and Mackintosh, so in the other Romilly and Mackintosh could rely on the support of Wilberforce. It will be remembered that, as early as 1786, inspired by Romilly's first protests, he had carried a small ameliorative measure through the Commons.[1]. ' The barbarous custom of hanging ', he had then declared to Wyvill, ' has been tried too long and with the success which might have been expected of it ' In a letter to Stephen in 1810 he deplores his being prevented by an attack of fever from hearing Romilly's speech in the House on capital punishment. And his heart was not hardened, as the heart of Eldon and others of his class, by the arguments of the era of repression Shortly after the Corn Bill riots—the soldiers had only left his house within the fortnight—he notes in his diary a typical instance of what he baldly calls ' our bloody laws ' : ' An affecting visit from Mrs. B., the wife of an attorney of respectable station and character, near thirty years in Leeds, convicted of forgery on stamps and deeds, and to be hanged this day week.' Again, he notes in 1818 : ' Mrs. Fry called early about a poor woman under sentence of death for forgery ' ; and once more he inveighs against ' our murderous laws '. In 1819 he pre-

[1] See p. 54 above.

sented to the House of Commons a petition on the subject
from the Society of Friends. In the course of his speech—
a speech which reminded the Whig chronicler, Greville, of
' the better days of the House of Commons '—he recalled
the devotion of the Quakers to all humane causes and not
least to that of Abolition ; and, amid general cheers, he
paid an eloquent tribute to Romilly whose tragic suicide
had occurred a few months before. That he should assume
himself the task of revising the ' hanging laws ' was, as he told
a friend who urged it on him, utterly impossible. ' I can
write but little,' he pleaded, ' I can scarcely read at all.'
And in his speech he called for ' some individual of competent
knowledge, industry, and ability ' to undertake the task.
It was clear enough to whom he was pointing as Romilly's
successor ; and when, a few weeks later, Mackintosh moved
for a Select Committee to consider the laws prescribing the
death penalty for felonies, Wilberforce vigorously supported
him. ' I have never heard ', he said, ' a more able address,
a more splendid display of profound knowledge of the
subject with such forcible reasoning of the facts.' ' He spoke
admirably,' notes the diary, ' I very middling.' But
Wilberforce's opinion, however he expressed it, carried votes.
The Committee was obtained by 147 to 128, and Wilberforce
was appointed on it. Its work procured in the following
year the repeal of several of the more flagrant laws ; and in
1821 Mackintosh, supported again by Wilberforce with
voice and vote, carried further measures, dealing with horse-
stealing and forgery, through the Commons. But the pace
had become too fast for the Lords, particularly for Lord
Eldon ; and further progress was barred till Peel succeeded
Sidmouth at the Home Office and himself took up the cause.

On the Game Laws Wilberforce was equally vocal and
persistent. In 1817 he supported Romilly's one successful
attack—on the sweeping application of the penalty imposed
in 1816. It was unjust, he said, to punish so severely ' an
act, which it was contrary to the natural feeling of mankind
to say was, in itself, a crime and which men could never
be brought to think a crime merely because there were
legislative provisions against it '. ' It was not right to make

up in severity for a defect of power.' And he went farther.
' I strongly object ', he said, ' to game being put on the same
footing as other property.' ' It is not considered any crime ',
he said later in the session, ' to purchase this sort of luxury
for a gentleman's table, while the poor wretch who purloined
it may suffer the loss of his liberty and perhaps be led to
the gallows.' In 1819 he declared the Game Laws to be
' so opposite to every principle of personal liberty, so contrary to all our notions of private right, so injurious and so
arbitrary in their operation that the sense of the greater
part of mankind is in determined hostility to them.' But
on this question Wilberforce had to vote with minorities.
Stealing five shillings or masquerading on the highway—such
felonies as these might be more leniently regarded by the
landlords' Parliament ; but poaching was the unforgivable
sin And Wilberforce had retired for some years from
politics before, in 1831, a Bill promoted by Althorp, himself
a landlord and a sportsman, and carried through both
Houses amid all the turmoil of the Reform Bill, swept the
whole bad business of the Game Laws into limbo.

Nor was Wilberforce silent on other abuses in the penal
system. He frequently referred in the House to the evils
of transportation ; and in 1819 he supported Bennet's
motion for a committee of inquiry in a long speech which
closed with an appeal to Castlereagh to reconsider his
opposition to it. With the scandal of the prisons he had
been brought into touch some twenty years earlier through
his friendship with Bentham. He had then tried to secure
more effective support from Pitt and Dundas for Bentham's
Utopian penitentiary, the ' Panopticon ' ; and had angrily
deplored the distress and loss of money in which the failure
of the scheme involved its creator. ' Bentham cruelly used '
is a recurrent note in the diary of those days And Bentham
deluged him with characteristic letters ' Kind sir,' runs
one of them, ' the next time you happen on Mr Attorney-
General (one day to be Lord Eldon) in the House or elsewhere, be pleased to take a spike, the longer and cheaper
the better, and apply it to him by way of a memento that
the Penitentiary Contract Bill has, for I know not what

length of time, been sticking in his hands.' A few years
later Wilberforce was again involved in the question of
prison reform, but not this time on the side of the reformers.
The shocking management of the Cold Bath Fields jail
might possibly have received impartial treatment in Parliament in 1798 if it had not been a party issue But it
happened that many of the suspected Jacobins, arrested
after the suspension of the *Habeas Corpus* Act, had been
imprisoned there , and it was Sheridan and the Whigs who
pressed the case for an inquiry Pitt refused it, and Wilberforce supported Pitt. Finally, in 1818, Wilberforce was
introduced to the heroic work of Mrs Fry among the female
prisoners in London. One day in February the diary
records a Quaker dinner-party in his house—' Mr and
Mrs. Buxton, Mr. S. Hoare jun., Mrs. Fry, Miss Priscilla
Gurney—very interesting talk indeed, and agreed to meet
to-morrow at Newgate '. So next day, ' Went with our
party to meet Mrs. Fry at Newgate. The order she has
produced is wonderful—a very interesting visit—much talk
with the governor and chaplain—Mrs. Fry prayed in
recitative—the place from its construction bad.' ' Much
impressed ', he notes a few weeks later, ' by Mr. Buxton's
book on our prisons and the account of Newgate reform.
What lessons are taught by Mrs Fry's success ! I am still
warmed by the account. Were I young, I should instantly
give notice of the business, if no one else did.' And in the
following year, when Alderman Wood presented a petition
from the City Corporation complaining of the crowded state
of Newgate, Wilberforce joined with Brougham in its support.

There was one more field of Wilberforce's interests in
which the champions of the poor might have found, if they
had wanted to find, something to mitigate their sweeping
condemnation. These years saw the first symptoms of the
reaction against industrial *laissez-faire*. Men were beginning
to feel that the heartless logic of the ' dismal science ' would
no longer justify the State in allowing the wholesale sacrifice
of children to the Moloch of British trade. More than a
decade had passed since Sir Robert Peel, the elder, had
proposed and carried in 1802 the first of the great series of

Factory Acts, forbidding apprentices in cotton or woollen mills to work before six in the morning or after nine at night or for more than twelve hours a day, excluding time for meals. Wilberforce had warmly backed this measure ; and his ardour had been heightened by a personal appeal he had received from ' an honest and hard-working couple whose child was barbarously torn from them and sent down to a distant cotton-mill '. ' I have since conversed with these people ', he wrote, ' and seldom have heard a more artless, affecting tale.' This was doubtless one of the influences which led him to press for the extension of the Bill to cover ' free-labour children ' as well as apprentices ; but Sir Robert opposed the proposal and it failed. This extension, however, was precisely what Sir Robert himself brought forward in 1815 and again in 1818. For the progress of the Industrial Revolution and the growing concentration of cotton-spinning in the towns had involved the increasing employment of children who were not apprentices and so unprotected by the Act of 1802. That Act, in fact, as its author admitted in the House, had quickly become ' almost a dead letter '. Ten times the number of children were now employed and most of them were worked for at least fourteen hours out of the twenty-four. He now proposed, therefore, that no child under nine should work in cotton mills or factories and none under sixteen should work more than $12\frac{1}{2}$ hours, including one hour and a half for meals. Together with Huskisson and the younger Peel, Wilberforce heartily commended the Bill : but he asked for a further limitation. ' It is cruel to imagine ', he declared, ' that children of nine years of age are able to sustain labour as long as those of fifteen or sixteen years ' ; and he suggested that children from nine to twelve should be allotted shorter hours than those of twelve to sixteen. It mattered little, in the upshot, that this suggestion was not adopted : for the Bill, having passed the Commons, was slaughtered in the Lords. Next year, however, the Lords themselves initiated, and the Commons duly accepted, a virtually identical measure except for the significant extension of the hours of work from $12\frac{1}{2}$ to $13\frac{1}{2}$.

Wilberforce's humanity was likewise engaged in the cause of the chimney-sweeps It is now almost forgotten that, a hundred years ago, the chimneys of the rich were swept by little boys—about five hundred of them in London, it is reckoned, and as many more in the provincial towns—who were forced to climb the flues, spurred up by their masters, if need be, with fire or pin-pricks or the whip ; scraping the skin from knees and elbows , incurring malformations and diseases in bodies often left unwashed year in, year out ; suffocated sometimes in a mass of soot at some far corner in a labyrinth of ancient flues or burned to death when ordered to extinguish a ' chimney on fire ' or when crawling by mistake into a lighted flue. But so it was , and it remains one of the grimmest puzzles of that age that, despite persistent ventilation of it, the scandal was permitted to go on One mild Act of Parliament alone was passed to deal with it, in 1788, and that was not enforced. Societies for superseding Climbing Boys, founded in London and in Yorkshire towns in 1803 and onwards, laboured in vain. At last in 1817 a concerted move was made in Parliament. Petitions were presented, a Committee was appointed, and it presented a sensational report. Thereupon Bennet brought in a Bill to prohibit boys from climbing chimneys in the future, with the exception of existing apprentices over fourteen years old : and as in his campaign against the Criminal Laws and the Game Laws, so in this Bennet found a sturdy ally in Wilberforce who assisted him to prepare the Bill and seconded his motion for leave to introduce it. On this occasion Wilberforce read a letter from a clergyman in a county town, reporting that within the last few months ' two children had stuck fast in chimnies and perished in that shocking state from suffocation ' The Bill passed safely through the Commons, but was held up in the Lords ; and next year the Lords threw out a second Bill. In 1819 Bennet proposed a third Bill ; and this time the Commons proved more restive But Wilberforce rose to the occasion with a fighting speech He met the argument that the masters could be trusted in their own interests to protect their boys with the conclusive example of the Slave Trade.

And he met the argument that a life-saving device, like the new sweeping machines, would quickly overcome custom and prejudice and come into general use without interference by the State with the equally telling example of vaccination. ' In a long course of years, machines may get the better of old habits ; but what numbers of wretched boys will suffer in the meantime ! ' The speech told. The Bill was carried. But the Lords once more destroyed it. Then Bennet made his final effort. He moved and carried a Bill, not to prohibit climbing—for that was clearly useless—but to limit the age of employment and otherwise to improve its conditions, just as Wilberforce, when the Abolition of the Slave Trade had seemed hopeless, had pressed at least for limitation. The result was no better. To the tune of Lauderdale's economic dogmas and Eldon's flippant sarcasms, even this mild measure of amelioration was rejected by the Lords.*

V

On all those issues Wilberforce was on the liberal side, and there was one other issue on which he showed a genuine independence—an issue which, in the course of 1820, set all other political issues in the background and which in the result did more than anything else, more than Peterloo and the Six Acts, to discredit the Old Tories. The affair of Queen Caroline was a very controversial and a very sordid business. It was precipitated, it will be remembered, by the death of George III at the beginning of the year. The new King's official wife, who for some years past had been living a life on the Continent, which, to say the least, was indecorous and indiscreet, was determined to assert her rights as Queen of England. George IV was equally deter-

* *Life*, i. 131 ; ii. 171–2 ; iii. 44–5, 440 ; iv. 256, 368–70, 376 ; v. 12–15, 48. *Hansard*, xxxv (1817), 346 ; xxxvi (1817), 925, 1157 ; xxxviii (1818), 171 ; xxxix (1819), 396, 452, 484, 828, 977, 1079 ; xl (1819), 379 ; v (N. S. 1821), 964. *Greville Memoirs* (London, 1896), i. 17. Mathieson, *England in Transition*, 117–19, 181–2, 213–14, 267–9. Hammond, *The Town Labourer*, chap. vii.

mined to refuse them, at the price, if need be, of instituting
proceedings for divorce on the charge of adultery, despite
the notorious looseness of his own domestic life. Ministers
were in an odious dilemma They must have recognized
the arbitrary egoism of the King's attitude. They must
have known that it would heighten his unpopularity with
the mass of the people. But they knew too that the King
was obstinate and was even capable of recklessly dismissing
the Government if it refused to carry out his will. They
therefore attempted a compromise. They agreed to his
demand that Caroline's name should be omitted from the
prayer in the Liturgy for the King and Queen, on the
understanding that any attempt to prosecute her should be
abandoned. But such a compromise was not at all accep-
table to Caroline. She set out from Italy for England.
At Montbard she was met by her staunchest champion,
Alderman Wood, and at St Omer by Brougham whom she
chose for her chief legal adviser. Nothing—or nothing at
least that George was prepared to offer—could now stop
her from finishing her journey On June 5 she landed at
Dover and proceeded to Canterbury. Next day she drove
through welcoming crowds to London

' She arrived about six in London—crowds greeting her ',
records the diary ' She approaches wisely, because boldly.
Fixes at Alderman Wood's Brougham in the house. How
deeply interested all are, indeed I feel it myself, about her !
One can't help admiring her spirit, though I fear she has
been very profligate.' But more was required of Wilberforce than an onlooker's interest. Public opinion had
turned instinctively to him, a few years before, on a question
in which party politics and royal morals had been similarly
interwoven—the question of the sale of official secrets by
the mistress of the Duke of York. And now, in this far
graver crisis, the call was clearer still. Justice and morality,
the prestige of the Crown and indeed of the whole system of
government it represented, were already drifting into the
whirlpool of party faction. Now, if ever, was the time for
the Independent to intervene, for the Keeper of the Nation's
Conscience to give the lead. But it was not a storm that

could be stilled by some fine moral gesture. King and
Queen were at open strife. Behind the obstinate man stood
the Government and the Tories of the Right. The obstinate
woman could count on Brougham's eloquence and Denman's
character, on the votes of other Whigs, if not their friendship
—the Whig ladies did not call on her till the crisis was over
—and on the almost passionate adherence of the English
people at large. With the principals in such a temper, their
forces aligned, and public feeling running high, all Wilberforce's adroitness, all his humanity and tact, might well
prove unavailing to prevent the horrid battle being fought
to a finish. He did not underestimate the difficulty himself.
Discarding all visionary ideas of reconciliation, he set
himself to postpone any official proceedings and gain time
for a compromise. What followed may be learned from his
own notes.

' I resolved, if possible, to prevent the inquiry , an object
which could only be attained by such an amicable adjustment as should give neither party cause for triumph. When
Lord Castlereagh had made a motion to refer the papers to
a Secret Committee, I endeavoured to interpose a pause
during which the two parties might have an opportunity of
contemplating coolly the prospect before them. Accordingly
I sounded the House (June 7) ; my proposition was immediately adopted and a pause was made with the declaration
that its purpose was to give opportunity for a final settlement. What followed is before the world—the correspondence, and subsequently the conferences which took place
between the King's servants and the Queen's law-
officers. The concessions made by the King's servants, as
Mr. Brougham afterwards declared in the House of Commons, were various and great. The name and rights of a
Queen were granted to Her Majesty without reserve, any
recognition of which had formerly been avoided. A royal
yacht, a frigate etc were offered. It was agreed that her
name and rank should be notified at the court either of
Rome or Milan—the capitals of the countries in which she
had expressed her intention to reside ; and that an Address
should be presented to the Queen, no less than another to
the King, to thank her Majesty for having acceded to the
wishes of the House of Commons.'

The one concession omitted from this list was the restora-

tion of Caroline's name to the Liturgy , and on this point
the King refused to retract the step he had compelled his
Ministers to take. Wilberforce himself wrote to him,
earnestly praying for this act of grace and frankly warning
him of the dangerous feeling in the country. But the King
made no move. Nor did the Queen. ' I fear ', laments the
diary on the following Sunday, ' lest it should please God
to scourge the nation through the medium of this rupture
between the King and Queen If the soldiery should take
up her cause, who knows what may happen—and is it very
improbable ? O Lord, deliver us ! ' Wilberforce's only hope
was that the Queen would yield on the Liturgy point, if
entreated so to do, not of course by the King, but by the
House of Commons Accordingly, on June 20, he gave
notice of a motion for an Address But there were soon
signs that this hope was scarcely justified. That very night
' just as I was going up to bed ', relates the diary, ' I heard
a knocking at the door announcing a letter from the Queen.
. . . Alderman Wood had given her a mistaken account of
my notice, and she wrote a warm, expostulatory letter—
her own ebullition ' Next day, ' Brougham brought me a
second letter from the Queen, more moderate '. On the
22nd, the day fixed for his motion, he received a communica-
tion from the Queen's chief agent which once more raised
his hopes, and not without reason. ' She will accede to
your Address ', wrote Brougham, ' *I pledge myself* ' [1] It
was in a confident mood, therefore, that he introduced his
motion in a crowded House Members were ' very noisy
and impatient ; would not hear Acland or even my own
reply quietly ' ; but the great majority were with him.
The motion was carried by 391 votes to 124 , and Wilberforce and three other members were appointed to present
the Address to the Queen. On the morning of the 24th they
donned their Court dress and proceeded to Wood's house in
Portman Street. ' There was a great mob about the door ',
wrote Wilberforce to his wife, ' which, if it had been night,
would have been very dangerous.' As it was, they were
hissed and booed ; but no stones were thrown. When they

[1] Italics not in the original.

reached the presence they soon found that their mission was a failure. The Queen had never really trusted Brougham. ' If my head is on Temple Bar ', she had said, ' it will be Brougham's doing.' And now she had listened to other counsellors who had made it their business to fan that distrust. Two days after she reached London, Cobbett had written to bid her ' beware of insidious and perfidious advice '. On the 10th he had told her that it is the universal hope that she will not suffer herself to be induced to accept *any compromise.* On the 12th he warned her that her enemies were now procrastinating in the hope of dealing with her when the public enthusiasm had died down. Finally, on the 23rd, the day before her audience with Wilberforce, he had told her, not indeed untruly, that the people would be with her if she rejected the Address. ' Mr. Wilberforce's motion is clearly seen through by the public ', he wrote, ' who have no doubt that it is intended to effect by supplication that which it is perceived cannot be effected by threats. . . The writer of this paper presumes humbly to express an opinion that the Answer to this Address should *explicitly reject the advice* contained in it. . . . An Answer of this description would, it is believed, put a stop to the efforts of Mr. Wilberforce ' So Wilberforce found the Queen steeled against compromise. ' Her manner ', he says, ' was extremely dignified, but very stern and haughty ' He read the Address. ' Alas ! the answer most decidedly rejected our mediation.'

Cobbett had certainly scored Wilberforce's efforts had been put a stop to He was angrily accused, indeed, of having misled and humiliated the House of Commons through his absurd illusion that the Queen would listen to its counsel : and the King's partisans denounced him as a feckless busybody who ought never to have interfered. He could easily have rebutted these charges. He had only to make public Brougham's explicit pledge. But this he refused to do—' a political forbearance ', confessed Brougham himself, ' which I never knew equalled '

Public battle was now inevitable. Since Caroline had refused a compromise, George was determined to get rid of her ; and his Ministers obediently prepared a Bill of Pains and Penalties as an instrument of divorce. But there were still some who believed that Wilberforce, if he had failed with the wife, might yet succeed with the husband. He was pressed to return to town in August, amongst others, by William Lamb (later Lord Melbourne) who thought there was ' great danger of serious popular tumult and insurrection '. ' If anything is to be done ', he wrote, ' your presence and influence will do it.' ' Mr. Wilberforce is looked up to ', wrote Madame d'Arblay to a friend, ' as the only man in the dominions to whom an arbitration should belong.' And Wilberforce himself had thoughts of urging the King ' to go to the House of Lords and declare he gives up his own wishes to the gratifying of his people '. But such hopes as he had were weakened by the open letter which Lord John Russell published in *The Times*. ' Although I generally differ from you in politics ', it ran, ' I warmly admire your generous efforts for the welfare of mankind, and I believe you capable of doing a great benefit to the country. You, sir, and some others whose support is the sole strength of Administration, are bound to interfere. . . . In your hands is, perhaps, the fate of this country.' ' How could he hope ', was Wilberforce's comment, ' that I should prevail on the King to accept my mediation as that of a neutral man, when publicly called upon to come forward by one of the strongest partisans of the Opposition.' Whether Lord John's letter made much difference or not, the King himself soon settled the matter. An impulsive go-between sent a messenger to fetch Wilberforce post-haste from Weymouth to Salt Hill to see the King who was informed that he was expected. George's reply showed that Wilberforce was right not to set out on such a hasty errand. He said that, if he conferred with Mr. Wilberforce, it must be on some political business, and that he never talked on political subjects with any but his Ministers.

So what has been justly called ' The Queen's Trial ' proceeded on its course. ' It will be long, painful, and disgusting ', Wilberforce had prophesied in the House, ' and what in my mind aggravates the evil, Parliament is not clear in

the matter. We marry our Kings and Queens contrary to
the laws of God and of nature, and from this source proceed
the evils which I am now anxious to avoid.' And he had
taken occasion to make clear his sense of the hardships
which the ill-used, if foolish, Caroline had endured. ' I am
strongly impressed ', he had said, ' with a feeling for the
Queen's situation in early life, and in what I lately proposed,
her advantage was especially intended.' No one can doubt
nowadays that Wilberforce's intervention *was* to her
advantage. Outwardly, it is true, she won the battle. The
Bill of Pains and Penalties passed the Lords by such slight
and falling majorities that Ministers ultimately abandoned it.
' This morning ', says the diary for November 11, ' the early
coaches from London came in, men and horses covered with
white favours—emblematic, I suppose, of her innocence—
for the rejection of the Bill against the Queen or rather for
Lord Liverpool's giving it up when carried only by nine.'
Caroline had won the battle, but at a heavy price. Day
after day she had sat in the crowded Chamber, respondent
in a divorce-case, while the Crown Lawyers paraded their
wretched Italian innkeepers and chambermaids to try to
prove her adultery. One black day, the strain had been too
much. When the notorious Majocchi was produced, she
rose in agitation, crying ' Teodoro ![1] No ! No !' and
hurried from the House. And when it was all over, ' I do
indeed feel thankful ', she wrote, ' *mais hélas*, it comes too
late. . . . No one in fact care for me ; and this business has
been more cared for as a political affair dan as de cause of
a poor forlorn woman. . . . I feel very unwell, fatigued, and
ébayé.' Some months later she had so far recovered her
strength as to renew the fight. The King refused to allow
her the share she claimed in his Coronation. The Privy
Council decided against her claim. The Primate told her
that he could only officiate by ' orders from the Sovereign '.
Undaunted, she drove to Westminster Abbey on the day of
the ceremony and asked to be admitted. She might have
got in, alone and unattended, but at the last moment she
turned back. The watching crowd, once so mad for her,

[1] Or ' Traditore '.

broke into laughter. ' Shame ! ' they cried, and ' Off ! '
So she drove away, and within a fortnight she died. Her
official husband continued to live his customary life for nine
more years.

It was pathetically true that most of her champions had
cared for her cause ' as a political affair '. Was Brougham
thinking only of the ' poor, forlorn woman ' ? Was
Cobbett ? She had better have trusted Wilberforce. For, if
he too had another motive than mere chivalry or justice, at
least it was not partisan : it was not to truckle to the King
nor yet to discredit him, not to serve the Government nor
yet the Opposition, but simply to terminate the scandal and
save the country from a disgraceful and demoralising
exhibition.*

VI

The Queen's Trial marks the turn of the political tide.
In 1820 the septennium of reaction was nearing its end
When Castlereagh committed suicide in 1822, Canning, who
had resigned in 1820 from loyalty to his friendship with
Queen Caroline in earlier days, became, in the teeth of the
King's enmity, Foreign Secretary and Leader of the House
of Commons ; and he soon secured a place in the Government for his comrade, Huskisson, with his Pittite tendencies
towards Free Trade. Peel, meantime, had succeeded Sidmouth at the Home Office and set himself to sweep away
the whole dirty system of *espionage* and intrigue, to resume
Mackintosh's campaign against the Penal Code, and to
establish law and order on the firm basis of an efficient
police force In two years' time, through the remarkable
alliance of Hume and Huskisson, the Combination Acts were
repealed. The positive repression of the poor had ceased

But nobody was yet prepared to take up the Radical cry
for Parliamentary Reform If the young Tories had been
converted to it, the Government and the party would have

* *Life*, v 54–88 *Correspondence*, ii 435 *Hansard*, i (1820),
1390–2. Melville, *Life and Letters of William Cobbett*, ii 148–57.
Diary and Letters of Mme. d'Arblay, vi 386–7 Spencer-Walpole,
History of England from 1815 (1914 ed), ii, chap. vi

instantly split in two. And on this fundamental question
the Whigs were still divided. Young Lambton had already
begun to lose his temper with his father-in-law, Lord Grey,
who told him in 1820 that he had no reasonable hope of
Reform being carried in either of their lifetimes, and with
other pundits of the party, like Lord Holland, who had
said, a year before, that, if it were carried, ' it would be as
bad as a revolution'. It was not strange, therefore, if
Wilberforce did not move in this decade beyond the point
he had reached in 1810. ' I continue friendly ', he tells a
Yorkshire friend in 1817, ' to the moderate, gradual, and
almost insensibly operating Parliamentary Reform which
was last brought forward by Mr. Pitt ' ; but, ' I am firmly
persuaded ', he adds, ' that at present a prodigious majority
of the more intelligent people of this country are adverse
to the measure' A year or two later, the fact that the
Radical demagogues were preaching Reform—a fact which
should really have been reassuring—frightened him off the
whole question, just as it frightened Grey who at this time
detested the Radicals and had no doubts of ' the wickedness
of their intentions '. So, in the course of a speech in 1819,
Wilberforce confessed that he had once favoured ' a moderate
reform of the system of representation in that House ', but
' now ', he declared, ' nothing like a moderate reform will
satisfy the discontented. No ! Nothing will now satisfy
them but the utter destruction of the Constitution.' With
the subsidence of agitation and the end of the Sidmouth
period, he became again a moderate Reformer, but with a
little more stress now on the ' moderate '. He was shier
than before of altering the representative system. He
intended to speak on Lord John Russell's motion for Reform
in 1822 and he voted for it , but next day he regrets in the
diary that he did not explain ' the principles of my vote ',
i.e ' that it was to put an end to the moral corruption of
elections in the smaller towns where drunkenness and
bribery gain the day '. Those are the evils, he writes a
little later, ' which call by far the loudest for reform.
I verily believe, and have long believed, the constituent body
to be more corrupt than the representative.' Very moderate
sentiments indeed ! Still he never barred his mind, like

many Tories and some Whigs, against the reality of Reform :
and in 1831, when the old man in his retirement heard the
news of Russell's introduction of the first Reform Bill,
while he confessed to his son that he ' almost trembled ' at
the thought of its consequences, nevertheless, in another
letter, he admitted that ' on the whole I think I should have
been favourable to it '.

There was nothing so hesitating and half-hearted in
Wilberforce's attitude to the Irish question. Time only
strengthened his adherence to the liberal view. In April,
1819, the diary betrays him closeted at Grattan's house
with Plunket, Tierney, Brougham, Mackintosh, and other
Whigs, and agreeing with them on the terms of a motion for
Roman Catholic relief. When Grattan died in the following
year, he joined with Grant in echoing Mackintosh's noble
tribute in the Commons. And in 1821 he made a fine speech
for the second reading of Plunket's Roman Catholic Dis-
ability Removal Bill. ' Persecution for religious opinions ',
he declared, ' is not only one of the wickedest, but one of
the most foolish things in the world ' ; and he confessed that
England's treatment of Ireland was ' enough to awaken
every generous sympathy in the human mind '. He recalled
the days when Ireland was called ' The Mother of the
Saints ' and ' possessed more pure religion than any other
country in Europe '. He reminded the House that the
Glorious Revolution had brought liberty to England but
not to Ireland ; that England had treated Ireland as a step-
mother her step-child. ' Can it be wondered at ', he asked,
' that she has struggled to shake off the yoke of her oppres-
sors ? ' Passing to the Union, he repeated his previous
assertions that, of his personal knowledge, Pitt had considered the emancipation of the Catholics as the essential
complement to Union. He was not alarmed by those
critics of the present Bill who thought no Catholic would
be satisfied with any concession short of a seat in Parliament. Was that so great an evil ? If Catholics are hostile
to this country, if they are subservient to their priests, all
the more reason for bringing them into the British Legislature where their prejudices can be softened by a closer
knowledge of this country and its Constitution. If the

Irish were supposed to be ill qualified for orderly politics, whose fault was it ? Has good treatment ever made a generous and high-minded people into rebels ? The difference between the English and the Irish was significant. The Englishman's peculiar characteristic was his willingness to submit his conduct to the law of the country. The Irishman's was directly the reverse—a natural impatience at the restraints of law. From what could that difference spring but from the Irish being denied the enjoyment of the British Constitution ? To give the Catholics the vote and go no farther was to let them out of prison and keep them in their convicts' dress. It was an effective speech— ' I was complimented ', says the diary—and it was followed by a more elaborate effort by Canning. But the day of Catholic Emancipation, though a little nearer than the day of Reform, had not yet come. The Bill passed the Commons by small majorities and was rejected in the Lords by 159 votes to 120.

In foreign policy, likewise, Wilberforce was on the liberal side. He entirely approved of Castlereagh's attempt to disentangle England from the coils of the Holy Alliance ; but he was prepared to go farther than Castlereagh, to proceed with Canning from a negative aloofness from Reaction in Europe to a positive alliance with Liberalism. Hazlitt's venom was never more reckless than when he wrote of Wilberforce : ' Not a word has he to say, not a whisper does he breathe, against the claim set up by the Despots of the Earth over their Continental subjects, but does everything in his power to confirm and sanction it.' Yet in 1821— four years before Hazlitt published his essay—in the debate on the imposition of a constitution on Naples by the Holy Alliance, Wilberforce had denounced the conduct of the three great military Powers as unjust, abominable, and hostile to every idea of liberty. Castlereagh's guarded language, he said, was not enough for him ; and in answer to his argument that the Powers would be deterred by their mutual jealousy from any territorial aggrandizement, he told the House to remember the fate of Poland and that ' each monarch has a way of taking a slice '. Again, in the following year, he came out in opposition to Castlereagh on

the Greek question. ' It is a disgrace to all the Powers of
Europe ', he said, ' that, long ere now, they have not made
a simultaneous effort and driven back a nation of barbarians, the inveterate enemies of Christianity and freedom,
into Asia . I know of no case in which the power of a
mighty country like England could be more nobly, more
generously, or more justifiably exerted than in rescuing the
Greeks from bondage and destruction.'

Manifestly, then, Wilberforce's place was on the left,
not on the right of the Tory party. His political friends
were not Castlereagh nor Sidmouth in those days, still less
Eldon, but Canning and Huskisson He was a welcome
guest in the latter's country home, and with Canning he
became so intimate that one night, as they walked away
together from a late sitting of the House, he spoke to him
of the serious things that lay nearest his heart. ' He had
neither father nor mother to train him up ', comments the
diary. ' I always wondered he was so pure.' Indeed, if
Wilberforce had continued in Parliament after 1823, he
would certainly have failed to maintain the last vestiges
of a claim to ' independence ' ; for he would have found
himself in close accord, on every dominant issue, with the
party which Canning and Huskisson led If Wilberforce
was Pitt's political brother, these were his political sons.
All three had felt the shadow of Pitt's war-period and
accepted a second era of repression in his name. But
Canning and Huskisson had not forgotten the sanguine,
liberal, unwarped Pitt of the days before the war ; and it
was this Pitt, and no other, that Wilberforce had really
loved. ' A vile picture ', he commented on seeing, about
this time, Hoppner's striking portrait of Pitt as he was in
his later days ; ' a vile picture—his face anxious, diseased,
reddened with wine, and soured and irritated by disappointments. Poor fellow, how unlike my youthful Pitt ! ' *

* *Life*, iv 315, 349 , v. 16, 73, 95–6   *Private Papers*, 264–6.
Hansard, xli (1819), 913 , 1(1820), 1062–3 ; iv (1821), 883–5, 1290–2 ,
v (1821), 356–8 ; vii (1822), 1651–2. Hazlitt, *Spirit of the Age* (1825),
359   Stuart Reid, *Life and Letters of Lord Durham* (1906), i. 129–31
G. M Trevelyan, *Lord Grey of the Reform Bill* (1920), 188

XII
SECOND CRUSADE

I

SINGLENESS of purpose is the crusader's characteristic virtue and the secret of his power , and throughout those clouded and restless years after the war, though Wilberforce was obliged, as has been seen, to play his part in current British politics, his mind was still mainly engaged in the fortunes of the negroes oversea The sovereigns and statesmen at Vienna had only willed, they had not carried out, the general Abolition of the Slave Trade, and, with one exception, the will of the British delegates alone was ardent and sincere. The exception was the Czar of Russia, and Russia was not a sea-power. So, if anything was to be done towards converting the resolutions of Vienna into realities, it was soon evident that the British Government would have to do it virtually single-handed. And since its mandate in the matter from Parliament and public opinion was as clear and vehement as ever, it did not shrink from the task. Pressure on Spain and Portugal, the only two Powers which had not yet agreed to Abolition, was vigorously resumed. In 1815 the Portuguese Government agreed, not without a grant from the British Treasury by way of compensation, to limit its share in the Trade to the west coast of Africa south of the Equator, and made fair promises of total Abolition in the near future. The Spanish Government was more backward   It pleaded that its colonies were not so well stocked with slaves as the British colonies had been in 1807. It complained of the economic loss involved and the difficulty of compensating its traders. It rubbed in the fact that Britain had already seized sundry Spanish slave-ships and refused to restore them. But it did not close the door to any settlement : it hinted at a bargain after the Portuguese model. ' With unfeigned joy I state to you ', wrote Wilberforce to Stephen in 1816, ' that I have just heard from Lord Castlereagh that the Council of the Indies, to which the whole question of the Abolition had been referred by the Spanish Government, has reported in favour of total and immediate Abolition. But a minority of seven, of whom

one has large property in Cuba, has protested against the
others and made a separate report. Even they, however,
have recommended abolishing north of the Line immediately and totally in five years. But all the Council seems
to wish to make it a condition that we should give them
money or at least give up their captured ships.' These
were the lines on which negotiations somewhat haltingly
developed. ' April 30, 1817. Almost immediately after
breakfast forced to town to Castlereagh on Spanish Abolition—with him for above an hour. He really takes much
pains for the cause. He says he has written more on this
head than any other. The Spaniards are pressing hard for
£600,000 and a loan.' The upshot was the signature of a
treaty in Madrid in September, 1817, under which Spain
undertook to abolish the Trade straightway north of the
Equator and totally in 1820, and Britain undertook to pay
£400,000 to compensate for the captured slave-ships and
' for the losses which are a necessary consequence of the
Abolition of the said traffic '. So the Spaniards secured their
bargain, because the cause of Abolition had taken so strong
a hold on Englishmen that they were willing to pay other
peoples to follow their example   In ordinary times £400,000
might not have seemed a very large sum. As Castlereagh
confessed, when he commended the Treaty to the Commons
in February, 1818, the Spanish merchants at Havana had
offered five times that amount for the privilege of continuing the Trade. But these were not ordinary times
Britain was in the trough of post-war financial depression.
' If the coffers of the country were full ', protested Sir Gilbert
Heathcote, ' I should be willing enough to give the noble
lord even a million of money if he wanted it ; but, now the
coffers are empty, we cannot afford unnecessary expenditure,
and I am averse to granting 400 pence to any potentate in
Europe.' This protest brought Wilberforce up. If the
country were really determined, he said, to bring about a
universal Abolition of the Slave Trade—and Heathcote
had admitted that—the method of bargain was cheaper
than the method of force. The removal, moreover, of this
obstacle to friendly relations with Spain might well lead to

an increase in our commerce with that country. And in any case it was right for England, treading this new and difficult diplomatic path, to be generous. ' Generosity is only justice. Considering the many blessings which the Almighty has showered on this country, it would be shameful to refuse such a sum for so great a purpose.' Mackintosh and Grant supported Wilberforce. There was practically no further opposition, even from those who felt most acutely the effect of bad times and heavy taxes on the condition of the poor. ' I believe ', said Bennet, ' that, if you went from house to house, you would have no difficulty in raising a contribution for the purpose of putting down this traffic.' In a small House of 60, only four votes were cast against the grant.

Thus, by 1818, all the leading countries of the Western world had made the Slave Trade illegal or pledged themselves to do so in a few years' time. But this did not mean, even when those few years were up, the cessation of the Trade. As a matter of fact it actually increased. And the reason was quite plain. Of all the states which had enacted an Abolition law, only Britain made any serious effort to enforce it. Under strict orders from a Government sincerely bent on executing the almost passionate determination of the British people, the British Navy made it virtually impossible for the Trade to be carried on in British ships. But foreign Governments were not so zealous. They had passed their noble resolution at Vienna ; and then, relieved of the tiresome philanthropy of Castlereagh and Alexander, they had done nothing at all. True to her undertaking France abolished the Trade by law in 1818 ; but the penalties for its infringement—fine and confiscation—were not enforced ; and for years afterwards slavers, French and other, continued to sail under the French flag. Spain and Portugal likewise fulfilled their promises and enacted total Abolition under relatively mild penalties—Spain in 1820, Portugal, after some procrastination, in 1830. Yet, as late as 1836, the British officials at Sierra Leone reported that ' there is nothing in the experience of the past year to show that the Slave Trade with Spain has in any degree diminished '. And, as late as 1838, Palmerston brusquely told the Portuguese Minister ' that the Portuguese flag is

lent, with the connivance of Portuguese authorities, to serve
as a protection for all the miscreants of every other nation
in the world who may choose to engage in such base pursuits '. The United States had abolished the Trade in the
same year as Britain ; and the Anglo-American Treaty of
Ghent in 1815, in tune with the Treaty of Vienna, had
denounced the Trade and pledged the two signatories to
use their best endeavours for its universal Abolition. In
1820 Congress proved the earnestness of its intentions by
making direct participation in the Trade an act of piracy,
punishable with death ; and in 1821 Wilberforce paid a
warm tribute to the zealous co-operation of American cruisers
with British off the African coast. Nevertheless, as time
went on, the Stars and Stripes were more and more misused,
till it became a literal truth that of all the flags of the Atlantic
nations the Union Jack alone was no protection to a slaver.

In the face of these disquieting facts there was only one
means by which the British purpose could be realized.
Somehow or other, the other maritime states must be persuaded either to co-operate with Britain in joint police-
work or to allow Britain to do their share of it by giving her
permission to inspect suspicious vessels flying their flags
and, if found to be slave-ships, to arrest them. It was on
this object, therefore, that Castlereagh concentrated his
diplomacy ; and he succeeded in including in the Treaty
with Spain clauses permitting a reciprocal right of search
and detention and instituting two mixed Anglo-Spanish
Commissions to decide the fate of ships so captured. Similar
arrangements were made in 1817 with Portugal and in 1818
with Holland. But, though British diplomacy continued
stubbornly to press the point, it was years before any
further success could be attained. There need have been
no lack of opportunity for a general discussion and an
international accord. The Powers at Vienna had agreed
to hold annual conferences for the furtherance of their
declared desire for universal Abolition But it was not till
1818 that the first of such congresses assembled at Aix-la-
Chapelle ; and then Castlereagh's proposal that a reciprocal
right of search should be conceded, to be carried out by

turned down   For the Powers—always, and intelligibly,
jealous of British sea-power—felt that the right of search,
however reciprocal and however guarded, would give the
British Navy something like a licence to interfere, at
pleasure, with all their sea-going trade.   An alternative
proposal by the Czar for the establishment of an international Board of Control on the African coast with an
international fleet under its direction was no less decisively
rejected.   In 1822 a second Conference was held for the
same purpose at Verona.   Castlereagh had recently committed suicide ; but the British case for Abolition was safe
in Wellington's hands, and Wilberforce again appealed to
Alexander's better self, both in a public and in a private
letter.   The latter, he confessed, ' though civil in terms, was
frank in matter : and it plainly intimated that we should
have no favourable opinion of his religious or moral
character if he did not honestly exert his powers on our
behalf '.   But neither Duke nor Czar could dictate to
Europe.   Verona was as fruitless as Aix.

No less stubborn and more lasting was the opposition of
the United States.   By 1841 all the other unpledged Powers
—France, Austria, Russia, Prussia, and Denmark—had
agreed to the reciprocal right ; but the American Government and Congress still resisted it, mainly because the
right of search was precisely the question on which American
opinion was most sensitive, especially where Britain was
concerned.   Again and again, therefore, the advances of
British diplomatists were courteously, but very firmly,
repelled.   And the case became still more intractable when
it was entangled in the domestic American controversy over
slavery itself.   The Governor of Liberia reported in 1839
that ' the chief obstacle to the success of the very active
measures pursued by the British Government for the suppression of the Slave Trade on the coast is the American
flag '.   There were Abolitionists, of course, in the United
States, no less ardent and sincere than those in England.
Protests were constantly made.   Leading American statesmen demanded action.   But the law remained unenforced,
and when in 1842 the Treaty of Washington provided for
joint operations by British and American cruisers off the

African coast, the American side of the bargain was never effectively nor consistently executed So, by the middle of the nineteenth century, the great bulk of the Slave Trade, now grown to proportions far greater than when Wilberforce first took up the cause of Abolition, was still safeguarded from suppression by the simple device of hoisting the Stars and Stripes. Not till the quarrel over slavery had come to an issue, not till Lincoln was in power and the Civil War had actually broken out, could the scandal be swept away In 1862 an Anglo-American Treaty was at last concluded, conceding a mutual limited right of search and establishing mixed courts on the African and American coasts.

Wilberforce, happily, could not see so far ahead. But already between 1815 and 1823 the obstacles to making Abolition a reality were distressingly plain. The lessons of Aix-la-Chapelle and Verona sank into his mind. He could not explain away the failure by any lack of sincerity or effort on the part of the British representatives. It is true that he had concurred with the other Abolitionists in sending Clarkson to Aix to watch their case. But, as he said at the time, he had ' no suspicion of Castlereagh ' ; and when the Foreign Secretary returned from the Congress and in a long interview told him ' all that had passed between him and the other Powers ', he did not question that everything possible had been done. At the Congress of Verona, similarly, he was more than satisfied with the Duke of Wellington's ' admirable zeal, perseverance, judgement and temper '. ' Dieu défend le droit ', he wrote to Macaulay ; ' I shall love all generals the better for it as long as I live.' No ; Britain was not to blame ; and what hope was there of overcoming the indifference and jealousy of foreign Powers ? Could the Slave Trade, Wilberforce began to ask himself, ever really be abolished as long as slaves existed ? Could that branch of evil ever be destroyed unless the whole tree from which it sprang were dug up by the roots ? *

* *Life*, iv 284–5, 320, 330 , v 1–10, 121, 136–7, 152–3 *Hansard*, xxxvii (1818), 67–80, 232–60 ; v (1821), 1331–2 T F. Buxton, *The African Slave Trade and its Remedy* (London, 1840), chap. ii. W E. B Du Bois, *The Suppression of the African Slave Trade in the United States of America* (Cambridge, U S A , 1896), chaps ix and xi

II

There was another train of events which was turning
Wilberforce's thoughts in the same direction and with
greater force. One of his chief arguments against the Trade
had been that the cessation of the importation of fresh
slaves into the islands would compel the West Indian
planters, in their own material interests, to treat the slaves
they already possessed with greater care for their health
and strength and to introduce any such improvements in
their social and moral conditions as would permit an increase
in the birth-rate. But, year after year, the Abolitionists
waited in vain for the realization of these hopes. New
slaves were still smuggled in, contrary to the law, under
foreign flags. There were just as many charges of ill treatment and moral degradation. And they were just as difficult to bring home to the culprits. ' I am quite, quite sick
of the West Indies as a field of labour in our cause ', Stephen
confessed to Wilberforce. ' To load the shelves of a Minister
with laboured memorials, to haunt him with conferences for
years, and at last to be turned round by the whisper that a
Governor stands well with great men and must not have his
toes trod upon, is beyond all patience. . . . I really think we
shall do nothing effectual to check colonial crimes till we
blazon them to the English public and arm ourselves with
popular indignation.' Wilberforce's patience, too, was
strained , but he clung to the idea that the planters would
still accept reform if only smuggling could be stopped, and
he believed it could be stopped by the passing of an Act
of Parliament requiring all slaves in the British islands to
be registered. He had begun to work for this measure (it
will be remembered) before 1814 and had only dropped it
in order to concentrate on his campaign for an international
repudiation of the Trade. But early in 1815 he took it up
again. ' Meeting on West India conduct at the Duke of
Gloucester's ', records the diary for February 15 . ' long
discussion—Lords Grenville and Lansdowne there, Babington, James Stephen, sen. and jun., and Harrison. Resolved

on pushing Registry Bill immediately.' ' March 1st. An
interview with Liverpool, Bathurst, and Vansittart, when
they told us they could not support the Registry Bill for
want of proof of actual smuggling of slaves ' When Napoleon
broke out of Elba, Wilberforce was inclined to postpone
'the Bill once more, but he was overruled at another Abolitionist meeting at the Duke of Gloucester's house, attended
by Grenville, Lansdowne, and Romilly amongst others.
' I against bringing on the measure this year. But Grenville
strongly for it, and all the rest gave way.' Accordingly,
five days before Waterloo was fought, Wilberforce introduced the Bill to the Commons in a speech of nearly two
hours. ' Got through pretty well ', he notes. Romilly
backed him, while Marryatt opposed for the planters Barham supported the Bill in principle but called for a preliminary inquiry into the condition of the slaves. Castlereagh admitted that the Government was bound by its
pledges to favour any measure that would facilitate Abolition ; but he asked Wilberforce not to press the Bill forward
with undue haste, if only to give the colonies time to understand it. The best thing, he suggested, would be for the
colonies to carry such a measure through their own legislatures In his reply, Wilberforce acknowledged that the
Bill could not be pressed to its conclusion in that session ;
and ' leave to introduce ' was granted without a division.
The result of the first reading debate, three weeks later,
was the same ; but Wilberforce took the opportunity of
nipping Castlereagh's suggestion in the bud. ' I have heard
enough of the West Indian legislatures ', he said, ' not to
have any very sanguine expectations from that quarter.
It is melancholy to reflect that, notwithstanding all the
admonitions which they have received on the subject of
mitigating the state of slavery, so little has been done by
them.' To compare them, he went on, with Parliament was
ridiculous. ' What sort of British constitution is it when
nine-tenths of the people are not even virtually represented
in the legislature ? '

No more could be done that session ; but the campaign
had been opened and the ' West Indians ' were hurriedly

taking down the weapons that had lain on the shelf since
their great defeat in 1807. ' I am assured ', Wilberforce
tells Macaulay, ' that they are mustering all their forces and
all their natural allies against us. . . . The British merchants
are joining the general body of our opponents ' And of all
the planters' weapons none was seized again more heartily
than the stabbing-knife that was stained with Ramsay's
blood ' If all that was published about me were true ',
said Wilberforce in 1816, in a debate on a petition from the
Bristol merchants against the Registry Bill, ' nothing but
a special Providence can have prevented my being hanged
thirty years ago.' A few weeks later, the slaves themselves
made a present to their masters of a stick to beat their
friends with. Like the troubles in St. Domingo in 1791
and in Jamaica in 1795, so now the slave revolt in Barbados
was ascribed to the criminal folly of the Abolitionists. The
slaves had broken out on the night of Easter Sunday, and
with drums beating and horns blowing had set to work to
fire their masters' sugar-canes and destroy the overseers'
houses and sugar-works. Some sixty estates were more or
less damaged. No European was killed. And the rebels,
wandering about with a vague purpose of destruction and
no military organization at all, were easily suppressed by
the troops. Several hundreds were shot in action, and many
of the prisoners were tried and executed. From the
uncouth banners they had carried—one of them representing
the King of England bestowing a crown upon a negro—
and from their own confessions, it was clear that they
believed themselves to have been freed from slavery by the
British Parliament and only retained in it by their masters.
They seem, indeed, to have been surprised at the intervention of British troops in a quarrel which did not concern
them. It was not such a very serious affair, then, but
enough for the planters, with a little exaggeration and a
little titillation of the baser race-instincts, to fashion
into a savage indictment of the Abolitionists. ' If anything
happens to our island ', Lady Malmesbury had said in 1791,
' I should certainly, if I was a planter, insist on Mr. Wilberforce being punished capitally ' And if English gentlewomen

were not quite so savage now, the rancour of the planters was fiercer than it had ever been. Wilberforce met their charges as he had met them before. In the debate of June 19 he reminded the House that from the very outset of the movement the West Indian party had accused the Abolitionists of aiming at wholesale and immediate emancipation. ' Nor have they confined their assertions to this House or to this country. They have actually printed and published in the West Indies that the design of the friends of Abolition was to make all slaves instantly free. . . . Though unable to read, the domestic slaves could obtain and promulgate the notion that their friends in Great Britain were labouring to give them liberty while their masters were the only persons that opposed it. I beg leave, therefore, to say distinctly that I and my friends are clear of the blood so unhappily shed.' And he went on to review some of the other ' grand arguments ' used against him in the course of his long campaign for the betterment of the negroes' lives. ' They charge me with fanaticism. If to be feelingly alive to the sufferings of my fellow-creatures is to be a fanatic, I am one of the most incurable fanatics ever permitted to be at large.' All these weapons had been used before, he said, and he had beaten them and would beat them again. And why was he so confident ? ' Because the people of England are religious and moral, loving justice and hating iniquity. . . . I rely upon the religion of the people of this country.'

A trust so complacent, so unctuous, and, as they knew in their hearts, so well-grounded could only intensify the planters' anger. They felt, as the frontier-farmers in South Africa felt, that this insufferably pious busybody was making infinitely more difficult the difficult task of keeping a black race in due subordination to the white. They felt, too—and the future was to prove them right—that the freer the negroes became, the less work their masters would get out of them. So they redoubled their efforts ; they even laid a voluntary tax on the export of their sugar to finance their propaganda ; and their invective became more virulent than ever. ' A more scandalous attack I have seldom seen ', wrote Wilberforce to Stephen of an article in a West Indian newspaper, ' but I am rather animated than discouraged by it. . . I get more and more to disrelish these brawlings and to be less and less touchy as to my character.' This unconcern for slander has come, he thinks, from advancing years and ' the decay of natural spirits ' and ' some little, I hope, from a growing indifference to human estimation '. But not all his collaborators were so hard-skinned ; and there was one who was almost as sensitive as the unhappy Ramsay. ' He is in so nervous a state ', Wilberforce tells his wife, ' that there is great cause for serious alarm about him. It is anxiety and, even still more, vexation at himself for being anxious that so harasses him. A cheerful temper is a great blessing.'

Certainly the cheerful Wilberforce was not to be hindered by calumny from pressing on the Registration Bill, nor yet by the caution or apathy of Ministers If the Government were against the Bill, he told Liverpool in 1816, he would fight it, painful as it might be . and he would win, because, in the long run, ' the religious and moral part of the community will never sit quiet and leave six or seven hundred thousand human beings in a state of studiously preserved darkness and degradation '. What did, however, give him pause was the increasing gravity of the situation in England. All through 1816 the clouds of popular discontent were banking up ; and Wilberforce began to wonder whether it was wise to urge the grievances of the West Indian negroes in competition, so to speak, with the grievances of the English poor. At the end of that dark year he entered the following quaintly characteristic note in a manuscript-book devoted to West Indian materials ' Against precipitancy— Moses 80, Aaron 83 years old, when God sent them to lead out the Israelites from Egypt Abraham 100 years old when Isaac born.' A little later his mind is made up for delay. ' I have for some time ', he tells Macaulay in January, 1817, ' been unwillingly yielding to a secret suggestion that it would be better perhaps to lie upon our oars in the Registry Bill and West Indian cause When Parliament meets, the whole nation, depend upon it, will be looking up for relief

from its own burthens ; and it would betray an ignorance
of all tact to talk to them in such circumstances of the
sufferings of the slaves in the West Indies. We should
specially guard against appearing to have a world of our
own and to have little sympathy with the sufferings of our
countrymen.' This letter would have been grist for
Cobbett's mill For, when Parliament met, it was not so
much the sufferings of the poor as their supposed sedition
that it fastened on. Before the end of a month Wilberforce
was engulfed in the Select Committee. And from that
moment, for five years to come, all legislative proposals on
the slaves' behalf were shelved as the Revolution and the
War had shelved them from 1793 to 1804.

It did not mean, of course, that the cause had lost its
sovereign place in Wilberforce's mind. He had decided not
to press it on a distracted Parliament and public ; but he
would not let it be forgotten. Just as in that earlier interlude of waiting he had moved his annual resolutions for
Abolition, so now from time to time he moved, with full-
length speeches, Addresses to the Regent deploring the
continuance of the Trade under foreign flags and reiterating
the obligation laid specially on Britain by her previous share
in it to leave nothing undone to protect and enlighten the
injured Africans. But there was now this difference. The
resolutions had been lost. The addresses were carried *nem.
con.* And during these years, again as in that previous
interlude, the cause of the slaves was being steadily
strengthened by the accumulation of evidence as to their
condition and by its regular submission to Parliament.
Thus, on April 22, 1818, two motions were made for papers
respecting the treatment of slaves in the West Indies—one
by Wilberforce, the other by Romilly ; and the latter's
speech was devoted to an *exposé* of things which, by official
admission, had happened in Dominica and St. Nevis. One
planter, for instance, had assaulted one of his female slaves,
bound her neck and limbs in an iron chain, and fractured
her arm. He had been duly charged for these offences by
the Attorney-General ; but the local grand jury had thrown
out the bill and had thought fit to remark on the dangerous

consequences of this and similar indictments. Another planter had ordered two slave boys, accused of receiving a stolen pair of stockings, a hundred lashes apiece, and a sister of one of them thirty lashes for shedding tears when she saw them beaten. Again the Attorney-General had been satisfied that the evidence justified a prosecution and again the grand jury had rejected it. Moving on another occasion for papers on St. Christopher, Romilly described the case of the Rev. Mr. Rawlins, manager of an estate in that island. A runaway slave had been caught and brought back to the plantation in an exhausted state. Next day he was severely flogged and, the day after, was set to work chained to another slave. He complained of pain and hunger and tried to lie down, but was beaten to his feet, Mr. Rawlins being present. In the course of the day he died, still chained to his comrade. This time the law could not be wholly evaded. The coroner's jury did their best for Rawlins : their verdict was ' Died by the visitation of God '. But at the trial Rawlins was found guilty of manslaughter and sent to prison for three months with a fine of £200. By colonial standards, as Marryatt indeed admitted to the House, this punishment was regarded as very severe, but not by British standards. The Colonial Secretary, Lord Bathurst, frankly told the Governor that ' Mr. Rawlins could not have been guilty of manslaughter : it must have been murder or an acquittal '.

These were not isolated cases. It was clear, in fact, that while Governors and Law Officers, vigorously supported no doubt by the Colonial Office, might try to enforce the laws against the maltreatment of slaves, they could do little or nothing without the co-operation of the planters. And the planters as a body, it was increasingly evident, had stopped their ears to all humanitarian appeals from England. It is not to be supposed that as a body they were cruel to their slaves ; but interference had hardened their hearts and closed their ranks. They would tolerate cruelty rather than allow the conviction of any member of their little community to be hailed as a triumph by those pietists in London. They would do their best to evade and nullify such laws and regulations as were thrust upon them from outside. And, if a sop must be thrown to the ' Saints ', they would themselves pass laws and regulations—and leave them unobserved ' As to those laws ', said Romilly in the House, ' which look so well on paper, which appear so well calculated to benefit the slave population, they not only are not executed, but were never intended to be executed.' And he quoted the following passage from a dispatch from Governor Prevost : ' The Act for encouraging the better government of slaves lately passed in Dominica appears to have been considered, from the day it was passed till this hour, as a political measure—to prevent the interference of the mother-country in the management of the slaves.'

In eliciting and publishing such facts as these Wilberforce and his allies were really doing more for the slaves than in pressing any legislative measures. They were convincing themselves—and taking the first steps to convince Parliament—that the slaves could not be protected from cruelty and degradation by a Registration Bill or any other measure which depended for its ultimate effects on a ' change of heart ' among the planters. In 1822, the year which marked the liberal renascence in the internal politics of Britain, a liberal movement began which was to determine the destiny of an infinitely vaster number of human beings than the inhabitants of Britain or of Europe. By 1822 the Abolitionists had decided to undertake a second and a greater crusade. And this time they leagued themselves not merely against this or that monstrous product of the slave-system. They were going out to transform the very basis of the relations between Englishman and African in the tropics. They were going out to abolish Slavery itself throughout the British Empire.*

* *Life*, iv 239–63, 283–8, 304–7 *Hansard*, xxxi (1815), 772–85, 1132–3 , xxxiv (1816), 722, 1151–68 ; xxxvi (1817), 1321–36 ; xxxviii (1818), 294–323, 1201–7 ; xl (1819), 1542–7 ; v (1821), 1325–34. *Life and Letters of Sir Gilbert Elliot* (London, 1874), 1 401 Bryan Edwards, *History of the British West Indies* (London, 1819), v. 102–7 ; see also v. 96–201 for an abstract of the laws respecting slaves passed by the West Indian legislatures from 1788 to 1817.

III

The anti-Slavery crusaders were accused, not always without justice, of painting the results of emancipation in too gorgeous colours. But Wilberforce's idealism was not altogether untempered by common sense. He certainly believed that the freed slaves would become an industrious, prosperous, and relatively civilized peasantry. Doubtless he underestimated the time this transition would take. But the present condition of a large part of the negro population of the British West Indies stands to witness that it was not altogether a fanatic's dream ; and recent developments in British West Africa have given a striking proof of the ability of negroes, unstunted by slavery and protected from European adventurers, to cultivate with energy and profit the produce of their own lands. But what of other human faculties ? To what point could their civilization rise ? How far, how deep could their education go ? Could they develop the business-like qualities on which the white race prides itself—orderliness, efficiency, organization ? Had they any capacity for politics ? . . . The world still awaits a final answer to these questions. In the life of mankind, so long and yet so short, the day when Africa emerged from the unknown and joined the common stream of human life is still as yesterday. In Wilberforce's time it was almost literally yesterday. Yet to all those questions he was already inclined to give an optimistic answer. It was mainly his religion, of course, that made him sanguine, his faith in the providential progress of the human family ; but there was one practical experience, one curious yet very characteristic episode in his life, that served to confirm his trust. This episode was his ' mentorship ' of the King of Hayti.

Christophe was a negro, born in slavery at St. Kitts. His capacity and honesty had already raised him above the dead level of manual labour when he became involved in the revolution in Hayti (or St. Domingo). It gave his natural gifts a chance to be proved ; he became one of Toussaint's chief lieutenants and under his rule he gained a rough-and-ready knowledge of administration. He took a leading part in the successful rising against Toussaint's sanguinary successor, Dessalines, in 1806 , and thereupon he assumed the government of the north part of the island, the south part falling to his fellow officer, Pétion, a mulatto. In 1807 he promulgated a Napoleonic constitution under which, as President and Commander-in-Chief for life, he virtually perpetuated his own military autocracy. A few years later he converted the Presidency into an hereditary Kingship. The coronation was held on the Champ de Mars at Cape François, in great state, with the whole army in attendance ; and still true to the Napoleonic model, King Henry the First of Hayti himself assumed the crown before he was crowned again by his archbishop. But it was not to Napoleon that his political sympathies turned. The French were his natural enemies. He and his people lived in constant fear of French attempts to reconquer the old French colony and to force the free citizens of the new kingdom back to their old slavery. Such a reconquest had indeed been attempted by Napoleon in 1802–3 and contemplated by the restored Royalists in 1814 ; and to avert this danger it was to England that Christophe looked. On the night of his coronation, at an official banquet to which the resident British and American merchants were invited, the King himself gave the toast—' My dear brother, George ! May his life be preserved by the Great Ruler of the Universe, and may he oppose an invincible obstacle to the unbridled ambition of Napoleon and remain always the constant friend of Hayti ! ' Christophe was far too shrewd, indeed, not to realize that in British support lay his best chance of maintaining an independent negro state. He had a remarkably well-disciplined army and a little fleet of one 44-gun frigate, nine sloops, eleven brigs, and sundry small craft ; but what was that against the power of France ? This, however, was not the only motive that led Christophe to invoke the sympathy and help of Wilberforce and his group. Security had to come first ; but when he had done all he could, by instituting a system of conscription, by enforcing laborious military training, and by building forts, to make himself secure, he turned with no less zeal to improve

the civil condition of his people The royal treasury was
full ; and he determined to spend lavishly on education.
Schools and colleges were to be established and staffed, so
far as might be, by qualified Englishmen. For the spirit
and method of the system were to be English. His people
must learn to speak good English instead of bad French ;
and they must be changed, if possible, from Roman Catholics
into Protestants. ' They wish to annihilate every trace of
a Frenchman ', a visitor reported.

In 1817, accordingly, Wilberforce received a personal
appeal from King Henry. It interested and attracted him
enormously ; and after satisfying himself in an interview
with Liverpool that the Government had no objection to his
corresponding with a foreign potentate, he warmly responded.
A voluminous and protracted correspondence ensued. ' He
has requested me ', wrote Wilberforce to Stephen, ' to get
for him seven schoolmasters, a tutor for his son, and seven
different professors for a Royal College he desires to found.
Amongst these are a classical professor, a medical, a surgical,
a mathematical, and a pharmaceutical chemist.' He was
given wide powers. Not only the choice of individuals, but
the amount of their salaries, within limits, was left to his
discretion ; and over £6,000 was transmitted to him for
making advances to the men he might appoint. It was no
light charge. It meant yet more fatiguing letters. It meant
a great many interviews with candidates and the most
careful consideration of each case. ' Much harassed ', the
diary confesses, ' by applications for recommendations to
Hayti by people of whom I know nothing.' And, of course,
as soon as the rumour of this benevolent and wealthy
monarch of the Caribbean got abroad, it was not only men
of missionary spirit or an enthusiasm for educational experiment that pricked up their ears. ' Rely on it ', wrote Stephen,
who had lived there himself, ' that in general there are only
two motives strong enough to keep any man or woman,
without necessity, six months in the West Indies—religious
zeal and *auri sacra fames.*' It was certainly a harassing
task and it put a heavy strain on Wilberforce's none too
abundant strength. ' Never have I worked harder ', he tells

Babington, ' than at my Haytian letters, and yet at last
the ship went away without much that she was to have
carried. But we shall have another opportunity, D.V., in
about a fortnight.' At one time he invites two rival candidates to his house ' that they might stay with me a few days
and enable me the better to take their dimensions '—an
austere ordeal for them ' I have succeeded in finding
a physician,' he writes to Hey, ' but I still want a surgeon,
and much more a divine. Oh, what would I give for a clergyman who should be just such as I could approve ! ' And his
friends and allies shared his enthusiasm ' Were I five and
twenty ', wrote Joseph Banks, ' as I was when I embarked
with Captain Cook, I am very sure I should not lose a day
in embarking for Hayti To see a set of human beings
emerging from slavery and making most rapid strides
towards the perfection of civilization, must I think be the
most delightful of all food for contemplation ' Wilberforce
felt just the same ' How I wish I was not too old, and you
not too busy, to go ! ' he exclaims in a letter to Macaulay.

Yet all this enthusiasm and all this hard work could not
achieve the impossible At first there were encouraging
reports One of the schoolmasters Wilberforce appointed
wrote that ' the youths applied to their work with almost
unexampled zeal and that their progress was really greater
than he had ever witnessed in the same time '. But not all
the Englishmen sent out to Hayti were so keen or so successful. It was not that the salaries offered were insufficient
to tempt good men. Christophe engaged a Court Painter
from England at 5,000 dollars a year ; and he declared his
intention of sending home two of his best schoolmasters,
when their time came to retire, possessed of independent
means. Nor was Wilberforce's judgement quite unpractical.
Writing to a friend to ask his assistance in finding a good
tutor for the King's son, ' I should prefer ', he says, ' a man
of sound sense and of some knowledge of the world, provided
he was really a practical Christian . . to any man of great
religious zeal who might be likely to push matters further
than the state of the King's mind or the circumstances and
disposition of the population in general would probably

bear '—sound enough missionary doctrine from Vanderkemp's admirer The difficulty was to find sufficient good
men to face so great an adventure, a climate to which the
lives of so many British soldiers had notoriously been sacrificed in the war, and conditions so uncertain, so seemingly
contingent on Christophe's single personality, that their
new careers might well be brought to an end before they
had well begun. So the men found were not all good men ;
and the strain of tropical life is quick to expose the weak
streaks in any white man's character. Some of the professors
quarrelled with each other or took to drink and vice , and
even the best of them, the men who could bear the strain,
began presently to write desponding letters home. No
wonder Wilberforce was anxious No wonder he had misgivings, for example, about some simple ploughmen whom
the unflinching Christophe requisitioned, ploughs and all,
to teach his people English methods of agriculture. ' My
heart quite fails me ', he told Macaulay, ' at the idea of
sending those four raw creatures into so distant and to them
so strange a clime, without preparing them more for what
they have to expect.' And, in truth, one wonders what
became of them !

But if the results of the experiment were disappointing, it
was not Christophe's fault—unless it was a fault to try at
all to civilize his people. He was held up to ridicule or
detestation by his enemies in Europe—and he had plenty
of them in France and in West Indian circles in England—as
a grotesque black military despot and a monster of depravity
and cruelty. ' You know, I doubt not enough of the case ',
wrote Wilberforce to Archdeacon Wrangham, ' to prevent
your being misled by the scandalous falsehoods which are
so shamefully propagated against King Henry's character.'
And there is at least one piece of substantial evidence to
show that Wilberforce was right in the main. In 1814
a British naval officer of repute was sent to Hayti by his
admiral to examine the conditions of trade. He reported
that the principal resident European merchants, some of
whom had been there ever since Christophe's accession,
were unanimous on the most vital point. ' We conceive

our persons and property under the protection of the King ',
they told him, ' to be as safe as in Kingston unless the French
land an expedition ' ' Nor could I hear ', adds the officer,
' of one act of injustice that could fairly be attributed to the
King. He is sharp in his dealings and in making them fulfil
their contracts But it is almost needless to mention how
far a merchant adventurer will go for gain and how necessary
it is to watch them.' In 1818 the same officer paid a second
visit to the island and wrote a long account of it which
carries on its face the stamp of impartiality. The following
are extracts ·

' The King is in his person what in England you would
call a fine portly looking man. . . . He is now growing stout ;
and on horseback, where he certainly looks his best, has much
the appearance of old George . . . He is quite black, with
a manner and countenance, when in good humour (and I
have never seen him in any other) very intelligent, pleasant,
and expressive. . . I am told by those who have seen him
in one of his gusts of passion that it can only be compared
to a hurricane for its fury ; but fortunately the fit now comes
very seldom and does not last long . . . None but the Queen
dare go near him in these paroxysms. . .
' His avowed intention is a religious, moral, and political
change. How far he is sincere and how far he possesses
talents capable of bringing about so great a change, time
will best show. . It is *his* mind and his alone that governs
all ; he has the ablest men of his kingdom employed about
his person, but they are mere executors of his will One
proof of his being neither a very changeable nor cruel man
is that almost all the great officers of the palace, who were
there four years ago, are there now , and they bear, generally
speaking, the characters of good and just men.'

The rest of the account is mainly concerned with the
details of Christophe's educational schemes, especially the
' four schools under Englishmen on the Lancasterian
system '. Two of the young Englishmen in charge—one had
been a monitor in a London school in the City Road, the
other was ' a young Aberdeen collegian '—had already made
good. But the two others had already failed. One was dead
' and an excellent riddance'; the other had been found by the
King ' drunk at 12 o'clock in the day amongst his scholars '

and was ' certain of dying this season by all accounts '.
There is a special tribute, further, to the hospitals. ' Dr.
Stuart,[1] the Professor of Anatomy, is come out with
Mrs Stuart—he appears a man of about twenty-eight and
very clever—he has taken charge of the hospitals, and no one,
not even the Governor, dare ask him a question—he orders
what he likes and it is immediately given him—in short,
he says that there is nowhere in Europe a more liberally
endowed hospital ' Finally, before he left, our witness
had an audience of the King.

' He was in high good humour and received me as an old
friend . . . We conversed a great deal upon the changes that
had taken place since my last visit. In answer to something
complimentary which I had said of his schools, he said,
" My wish is that my fellow-citizens may be made capable
by education of enjoying the constitution I intend for them ;
and if I live long enough, the world will see that this has
always been nearest my heart and occupied all my thoughts
But I must have time " . . . He has offered, through England,
twenty millions of dollars to France to make an independent
peace guaranteed by England, but without the guarantee
he would not give 20 dollars . He certainly is bringing that
great question to a fair trial—whether the negroes possess
sufficient reasoning powers to govern themselves or, in
short, whether they have the same capacities as white men.
And he is the only man, I think, in the world who could
have given it so bold a trial.'

That question needed a longer trial than Christophe or
any other man could give it in the normal span of a life.
And Christophe was denied even that. In 1820, only two
years after the above account was written, a group of officers,
resenting the continued maintenance of Christophe's rigid
discipline, mutinied ; they were backed, it seemed, by most
of the army ; and Christophe, deserted and desperate,
committed suicide. The news was a shock, but not altogether
a surprise, to Wilberforce. He had heard of Christophe's
stern military system and he had been uneasy. ' I know
not that a day has passed ', he said, ' that I have not prayed
for him ' But he recognized that this militarism was enforced
on Christophe by the insecurity of the international status

[1] The right spelling seems to be ' Stewart '.

of his kingdom and particularly by the danger of attack from France. Wilberforce, indeed, had hoped against hope to secure an acknowledgement of Haytian independence from the Congress of Aix-la-Chapelle, though he knew that Castlereagh, however firm on Abolition, was scarcely likely—being, as he remarked, ' a fish of the cold-blooded kind '—to venture on this thorny side-issue Nor, even if Castlereagh had been willing to press the claims of Christophe, would the Continental Powers have conceded them in the face of an indignant France. So Wilberforce was not far beside the mark in thinking that the character of Europe was at least as much to blame as the character of Christophe for the tragedy that destroyed him and his dreams.

For his dreams died with him. The educational system quickly collapsed. ' Every day something transpires ', wrote Dr. Stewart from Hayti six months later, ' to show the importance of King Henry to the Haytians. His greatest enemies now acknowledge that they never had a chief whose powers of mind and body were so fitted for command.' And perhaps the mere demonstration of his capacity, pointing a moral which Wilberforce and other philanthropists in Europe could not miss, had been Christophe's greatest service to his race For fourteen years he had kept in discipline and order an uncivilized people, degraded by slavery and barbarized by the horrors of a servile war. He had recognized their moral and mental backwardness, and had devised and begun to construct the machinery for their enlightenment. He had corresponded closely and lengthily with one of the most famous men in Europe And he had been born a slave.*

* *Life*, iv. 352–61 ; v. 1–5, 31, 42, 82–4 Bryan Edwards, *op. cit.* v 129–207.

IV

And so, one motive interlacing with another, the abolition
of British Slavery was determined on by the men who had
abolished the British Slave Trade. But as the years passed
in which they stiffened to their purpose, it became increasingly apparent that the leader of the first crusade would be
unable to lead the second. In 1821 Wilberforce was only
sixty-two, and many statesmen over sixty have fought and
won great battles ; but the infirmity which had dogged him
all his days was now beginning to get the upper hand. It
was not only the increasing failure of his eyesight—and
there were times when he could not read or write at all—
nor only his permanent gastric weakness. He had also
developed a tendency to lung trouble which made the close
atmosphere of the House of Commons on a damp or chilly
night peculiarly dangerous. In more than one winter he
was kept away from the House by repeated illnesses. ' I fear
that I shall do little more good ', he confesses in the diary,
when the complaint first takes hold of him. ' Alas that I
have not laboured more to make the best use of my faculties !
. . . It is a stroke which I own I feel.' But he faced the
inevitable with his usual temper. ' It is suitable ', he said,
' for an aged Christian to show himself willing to retire and
let others take the more leading stations.' Moses, he had
told himself, was an old man when he started on the march
from Egypt , but he had not led his people into Canaan.
' And the Lord said unto Moses, Behold, thy days approach
that thou must die : call Joshua.'

After consultation with Stephen and other intimates, his
choice of a successor fell on Thomas Fowell Buxton, whose
acquaintance he had made through his friendship with the
Norfolk community of Quakers. Buxton was born in 1786
and as a young man he had become keenly interested in the
question of the criminal law and the management of prisons.
In 1817 he had published a pamphlet on prison discipline
which was warmly praised by Wilberforce and Mackintosh,
and in 1818 he had entered Parliament as member for

Weymouth. Wilberforce had taken to him from the first.
He was a serious man. ' He never was a child,' said a friend
' he was a man when in petticoats.' And he was profoundly
religious. Wilberforce was impressed, too, by the solid
capacity he showed in the House—the capacity of one ' who
could hew a statue out of a rock ', he once remarked, ' but
not cut out faces upon cherry stones '. Moreover, he was,
like himself, an ' independent ' in politics ; and it was, in
Wilberforce's eyes, the ' old honourable distinction ' of the
cause in which Pitt and Fox, Grenville and Grey, had
worked together that it transcended parties. So, on May 24,
1821, having been particularly impressed with a speech of
Buxton's on the Criminal Laws on the previous night, he
made him a definite proposal.

He reminded him that, thirty-three years ago, when about
to begin his campaign against the Slave Trade, he had been
smitten by an almost desperate illness and had begged
Mr. Pitt to promise to undertake it in his place. ' I thank
God, I am now free from any indisposition ; but from my
time of life and much more from the state of my constitution
. . . I ought not to look confidently to my being able to carry
through any business of importance in the House of Commons. Now for many, many years I have been longing to
bring forward that great subject, the condition of the negro
slaves in our Trans-Atlantic colonies and the best means of
providing for their moral and social improvement and
ultimately for their advancement to the rank of a free
peasantry . . . I have for some time been viewing you in
this connection ; and after what passed last night, I can no
longer forbear resorting to you, as I formerly did to Pitt,
and earnestly conjuring you to take most seriously into
consideration the expediency of devoting yourself to this
blessed service. . . Your assurance to this effect would give
me the greatest pleasure—pleasure is a bad term—let me
rather say peace and consolation.'

This appeal from scarred and laurelled 62 to unblooded 35,
from one, too, who was regarded by all Buxton's circle as
the best, if not the greatest, man in public life, was not to
be resisted. Buxton had not hitherto paid close attention
to the details of the negro question ; but he had joined the
African Institution, his heart and his vote had been always

with Wilberforce, and he recalled how his Quaker mother had impressed the iniquity of slavery on his child's mind, how his sister's refusal to eat slave-grown sugar had made him think while he laughed at her, and how his first speech at Trinity College, Dublin, and his first public pronouncement at a meeting at Tower Hamlets had each been concerned with the Slave Trade. To devote himself henceforth to the overthrow of Slavery was no break with his past. Nothing indeed could better accord with the traditions of his social *milieu* and the promptings of his own serious ambition. He accepted the proposal. An alliance, which as Wilberforce put it, ' may truly be termed holy ', was struck up.

For a year or two it could still be an alliance. Wilberforce could not banish altogether the odious thought of retirement, but now that he had secured the succession, he was determined to hold it at bay as long as he could ; and, provided he could keep his health, his parliamentary powers were not yet by any means exhausted. It was the veteran, therefore, who opened the campaign against Slavery by attacking it in one particular field. Slavery had been customary among Europeans in South Africa since the old days of the Dutch occupation of the Cape ; but a new situation had been created in 1820-1 by the introduction into the eastern part of Cape Colony of some five thousand British settlers. This ' Albany Settlement ' had been organized and executed by the Government as a minor palliative for unemployment in Britain ; and it had been made a condition of the grant of lands that predial or farm slavery should not be practised. But to Wilberforce slavery in the house was as bad as, in some respects it was worse than, slavery in the field ; and on July 25, 1822, he moved an Address, urging that all slavery, domestic as well as predial, should be prohibited in the new settlement by a ' fundamental law ', as it had been from the first in the colony of Sierra Leone. Perhaps the most interesting passage in his speech was one in which he showed that he had grasped what statesmen have often failed to grasp—the essential singleness of Africa. ' Let me earnestly conjure the House ', he said, ' to estimate this motion at its just importance. The countries which we are now beginning to settle are of very vast extent , but, still more, by imperceptible boundaries they communicate with the almost interminable regions of the African continent. And my object is to secure, throughout that vast extent, the prevalence of true British liberty instead of that deadly and destructive evil which would poison the whole body of the soil and render that prodigious area one wide scene of injustice, cruelty, and misery.' But still more important for the future was the affirmation—or the pointed re-affirmation—of his general purpose. ' Not I only,' he said, ' but all the chief advocates of the Abolition of the Slave Trade—Mr. Pitt, Mr Fox, Lord Grenville, Lord Grey, and every other—scrupled not to declare from the very first that their object was, by ameliorating regulations and more especially by stopping that influx of uninstructed savages . . . to be surely though slowly advancing towards the period when these unhappy beings might exchange their degraded state of slavery for that of a free and industrious peasantry. There was a miserably thin House to listen to this declaration, but among the few members present, of course, was the new ' ally ' and he was well rewarded. ' This was the best speech ', said Buxton, in after years, ' that I ever heard him make '

But this Address was only a ' local operation '. Something more was needed to launch a general attack all along the line. That winter the Abolitionists met in what Wilberforce called ' a secret Cabinet Council ', and it was decided that a definite call to the new crusade should be issued to the country. And the voice, it was agreed, must still be Wilberforce's. So, early in the year, he shut himself up in his new country house at Marden Park and worked away at a public statement. Stephen had thought of helping him as Babington had helped him in preparing the case against the Slave Trade in earlier days. But on the whole, he writes, ' you would do better without me '. ' My province would be that of the driver only . . and then Mrs. Wilberforce will flog the driver every day if she thinks we do too much (she gave me fair warning of it on Sunday), and I shall flog myself

if we do too little.' So Wilberforce toiled on alone, and he
found the strain far heavier than he had in 1790. 'At work
on my Manifesto,' says the diary for January 26, 1823, 'but I
cannot please myself.' 'I am become heavy and lumbering,'
he confesses to his old collaborator, Babington, 'and not
able at once to start into a canter, as I could twenty years
ago. Happily it is a good road and in the right direction.'
'I get on slowly,' he complains a few days later. 'Music
in the evening To have friends in the house sadly consumes
time, though no one loves music better than I do ; yet the
time is short with me and I must husband it.' Meanwhile
he was encouraged by news from Macaulay of the activities
of the 'conspirators' in London. 'I have had two long talks
with Brougham ', he wrote, 'and have gradually opened
to him our feelings and views. I cannot help hoping that
we have gained him ' In the middle of February Wilberforce returned to town with ' a good deal of my piece ' ready
for press, but ' sadly out of heart about it '. Early in March
it was published. It is a pamphlet of fifty-odd pages,
entitled *An Appeal to the Religion, Justice, and Humanity
of the Inhabitants of the British Empire in behalf of the Negro
Slaves in the West Indies*. It gains by its relative brevity.
It is well packed with facts and well argued. The tone is
not in the least fanatical. Indeed Wilberforce is careful,
more than once, to insist that his charges must not be
construed too sweepingly, that not all slave-owners regard
or treat their slaves in the same way. And the presentation
is simple and effective—first, an analysis of the conditions
of slavery ; secondly, a rebuttal of the old argument that
the colonial legislatures should be left to improve those
conditions and prepare the way for emancipation by themselves ; lastly—and here, perhaps, confidence has to take
the place of proof—an assurance that the negroes will not
only be more moral and more Christian as freemen than as
slaves but will also work harder. On the whole, a very
serviceable piece of work, and Wilberforce need not have
been so diffident about it ; for it produced a quick effect
on public opinion—all the quicker because this second appeal
was not a novelty like the first. The campaign against the

Slave Trade had prepared the ground. It had revealed the horrors of Slavery itself as an essential part of its case. It had galvanized the public conscience and created a new and very sensitive humanitarian tradition. Opinion, therefore, responded at once. Again the letters of congratulation and approval poured in from all quarters, the most remarkable, perhaps, being one from a West Indian planter who declared that he hoped the Appeal would achieve its purpose—so moved was he by reading it—even at the cost of all his property. And again the Quakers were to the fore. They drew up a petition entreating Parliament to follow up the good work it had done, and was still doing, for the destruction of the Slave Trade by taking measures to redeem the hundreds of thousands of their fellow human beings now in bondage in the British colonies. And again the presentation of it in March, 1823, was entrusted to Wilberforce. He reminded the House that it was the Society of Friends who had first petitioned Parliament against the Slave Trade— quiet, retiring people, only obtruding themselves on the public at the imperative call of justice and humanity. ' It certainly is an extraordinary anomaly ', he went on, ' that the freest nation that ever existed on the face of the earth . . . should be chargeable with the guilt and inconsistency of allowing slavery in any place under its control. . . . Never, perhaps, since the world began has there been such a strange instance of the sufferance of an evil in consequence of its being removed out of sight.' He regretted now that he and his friends had not attacked Slavery itself from the first ; but they had felt that to press for the greater object might weaken their chance of achieving the less. They had always looked forward, however, to emancipation as their ultimate goal. Even Mr. Dundas had proposed that Slavery and the Trade should end together. ' I am fully aware ', he concluded, ' of the feelings entertained and the difficulties I had to encounter when I first brought the question of the African Slave Trade before Parliament between thirty and forty years ago. I well remember that those who were neutral as well as several who were friendly repeatedly told me that it was impossible I should ever succeed I determined, however, to persevere, for I felt quite sure that, in England, such a cause must be finally successful. I say the same now.' Directly Wilberforce had finished, Canning rose. ' Is it my honourable friend's intention ', he asked, ' to found any motion on the petition ? ' ' It is not,' replied Wilberforce, but referred to ' an honourable and esteemed friend of his ' ; whereupon Buxton gave notice of a motion, to be submitted a month hence, that the House should take into consideration the state of slavery in the British colonies.

Wilberforce had taken the lead for the last time, and he was thoroughly dissatisfied with his performance. ' Fatigue rather stupefied me,' he complains, ' and I forgot the most important points. But Canning's generalship admirable ' He had expected, it seems, a full debate ; and Canning's precipitate question had taken him aback. He had been ' thinking over the topics to be ready for reply ', he says, ' and was quite confounded. All of us *abattus.* Never almost in my life was I so vexed by a parliamentary proceeding. I felt as if God had forsaken me. . . . I could scarcely get to sleep and was ashamed to see my friends, though they tell me the effort was better than I had conceived.' So much distress at so slight a set-back—he had suffered many far worse reverses in the old days—suggests over-strain.

Happily Wilberforce was more contented with the part he took in the debate on Buxton's motion on May 15. Public opinion had had time in the interval to make itself further heard. ' The country takes up our cause surprisingly,' comments the diary ' the petitions, considering the little effort, very numerous ' It was therefore with a sense that the electorate was awake and watching and in something like the exciting atmosphere of 1791–2 that the House listened to Buxton's introductory speech. To Wilberforce it must soon have seemed that he had chosen his successor well. It was an admirable speech, full of substance, point, and interest. And it was a bold speech ; for it did not evade, it quickly and frankly faced, the oldest and, for timid minds, the most effective of all the opposition's arguments.

He admitted, at the outset, the danger of a negro insurrection.

'Wherever there is oppression there is danger . . . The question is how that danger can be avoided I assume that it is to be avoided by giving liberty for slavery, happiness for misery.' And he effectively quoted Pitt's assertion that ' it was impossible to increase the happiness or enlarge the freedom of the negro without adding in an equal degree to the security of the colonies '. ' But even supposing the danger of giving to be as great as the danger of withholding— there may be danger in moving and danger in standing still, danger in proceeding and danger in doing nothing—then I ask the House whether it be not better for us to incur peril for justice and humanity, for freedom and for the sake of giving happiness to millions hitherto oppressed than for slavery, cruelty, and injustice ' So much for the appeal to fear , next, the appeal to the sanctity of property. The Abolitionist proposal was to declare the freedom of all children born of slaves after a certain day. This plan of progressive abolition had already been applied successfully in the northern part of the United States , and under its operation slavery was already dying out quite peacefully in the British Empire itself General Brownrigg and Sir Alexander Johnston had introduced it in Ceylon, Sir Stamford Raffles at Bencoolen, and Sir Hudson Lowe at St. Helena. But the public had not marked these things, even in St. Helena about which a veritable library of books had recently been written. ' Generations yet unborn shall know that on such a day in July Sir Hudson Lowe pronounced that the weather was warm ; and, that, on such a day in the following December, Bonaparte uttered a conjecture that it would rain in the course of the week. Nothing has escaped the researches of the historian—nothing has been overlooked by the hungry curiosity of the public. Yes ! one thing has been ; that Sir Hudson Lowe gave the death-blow to slavery in St. Helena ' The plan then had been tried ; it was actually in operation on British soil , but none the less the West Indian planters would resist its application to themselves. ' I know the answer that will be given. " The father is mine ; the mother is mine ; and therefore the child is mine." But is that justice ? You have made it a crime to go to Africa and enslave a full-grown man there. How is it less a crime to make a new-born Creole a slave ? . . . It is a crime to murder a man ; is it no less a crime to murder a child ? It is a crime to enslave a man, is it no crime to enslave a child ? ' The claim, moreover, to a right of property in the man-slave was not unimpeachable The planter, say, had inherited him from his father who had bought him from a neighbour who had bought him at Kingston slave-market from a trader who had bought him from a man-merchant in Africa. ' So far you are quite safe. But how did the man-merchant acquire him ? He stole him he kidnapped him. . . . ' A daring attack this, on the citadel of property ; and Buxton very wisely followed it up with a hint at compensation. ' When I say that the planter has no claim against the slave, I do not say that he has no claim against the British nation If slavery be an injustice, it is an injustice which has been licensed by British law.' Finally he enumerated his definite proposals— the emancipation of all children born in slavery after a cer- tain date and the amelioration of the lot of existing slaves by attaching them to the soil, by giving them a higher status than that of chattels in the eyes of the law, by removing all obstructions to manumission, by providing religious instruc- tion, enforcing marriage and making Sunday a day of rest, and by restraining the master's authority to punish—and on this basis moved the general motion, ' That the state of Slavery is repugnant to the principles of the British Constitu- tion and of the Christian Religion , and that it ought to be gradually abolished throughout the British colonies, with as much expedition as may be found consistent with a due regard to the well-being of the parties concerned.'

This time a full debate could not be avoided. But the Government was not yet prepared to go all the way with the Abolitionists ; and when Canning followed Buxton, his denunciation of the evils of slavery was scarcely less vigorous, but he did not commit himself so definitely to its extinction. He moved a group of resolutions, as amendments to Buxton's motion, emphasizing first the need for ' effectual and decisive measures ' for improving the conditions of the existing slaves, and looking forward to ultimate emancipa- tion when, as the result of a ' determined and persevering, but at the same time judicious and temperate enforcement of such measures ', the time should be ripe for it. It had been arranged that Wilberforce should answer Canning , but again Canning's tactics had taken him aback. He had watered Buxton's wine and yet not robbed it altogether of its body. To make the right reply to this move, to accept the offer as it stood or insist on more, to make the choice on the instant—it was certainly, as the diary says, 'an awkward situation'. 'I could not learn what our friends thought and I never got up so utterly unprepared, but D. G. I believe I hit the point' He began by reinforcing Buxton's case that Slavery was inconsistent with British political and religious ideals This was familiar ground, and as he covered it with easy eloquence, he came to his decision not to break with Canning. ' I thanked God I judged rightly', he afterwards wrote to one of his sons, ' that it would not be wise to press for more on that night.' So he expressed agreement with Canning's desire that emancipation should come gradually with the growth of moral improvement in the slaves—and had not Buxton himself admitted that they were not ready for it yet ?— rather than by the sudden stroke of Parliament. ' But when we consider ', he said, ' the claims of these unhappy people and the time that has been already lost in accomplishing this great and high duty, we ought not to prolong their slavery an hour more than is absolutely necessary.' And, in any case, the task of improvement must not be left to the colonial legislatures ; it must be taken in hand by Parliament itself. ' After all that my right honourable friend [Canning] has conceded ', he concluded, ' we stand in a new situation. . . . We have now an acknowledgement on the part of Government that the grievances of which we complain do exist We have also the assurance that a remedy shall be applied. . . . I will no longer detain the House than by expressing my confidence that we shall this night lay the foundation of what will ultimately prove a great and glorious superstructure.'

It was certainly no more than a foundation. Slavery was to be prolonged for a good many hours more—for over ten years But it is easy to understand, and not so easy to condemn, Canning's desire to evade a rapid forcing of so big an issue Wilberforce's speech, at any rate, secured it for him. It muzzled the ' Saints ', and the other side, the planters' representatives, could not venture to quarrel with any policy that postponed their doom It will be remembered how scornfully they had met the first attack upon the Slave Trade—with what wholesale denials of its inhumanity and assertions of the falsehood of the Abolitionists' case, with what confident appeals to commercial and national interests as necessitating the indefinite continuance of the Trade But now it was clearer than ever that the first crusade had achieved more than its own deliberately limited purpose In eliciting the truth and educating the British people for the destruction of the Trade, it had cut away the supports of Slavery. So, when Charles Ellis rose to put the planters' case, he could not defend Slavery ; he could only describe it as an unfortunate system in which the unhappy planters, through no fault of their own, had been involved. He could not plead for its continuance ; he was bound to promise his support to Canning's resolutions. All he could do was to put his own interpretation on them, to suggest that their purpose could best be realized (in words that Abolitionists themselves, he pointed out, had once used) ' by a benign, though insensible, revolution in opinions and manners, by the encouragement of particular manumissions and the progressive amelioration of the condition of the slaves, till it should slide insensibly into general freedom . . . in short, an emancipation of which not the slaves but the masters should be willing instruments or authors '. There was no necessity for Canning to accept or to reject this interpretation of his policy ; and the long debate ran smoothly on Only Brougham, who came out definitely for Abolition with a full-dress speech, ventured to doubt the efficacy of the amending resolutions, though he did not question their sincerity But at the very end the Abolitionists tried to pin Canning down. At the close of Buxton's reply, Canning declared, by way of making his position perfectly clear, that he did not accept the principle that the children of slaves must always be slaves. ' Then one day ', said Buxton promptly, ' every child shall be free When will that day come ? ' ' I say ', replied Canning, ' I abjure the principle of perpetual slavery ; but I am not prepared now to state in what way I would set about its abolition ' With that Buxton had to profess himself content ; and Canning's amendment was carried without opposition.*

* *Life,* v 128–31, 154–80 Wilberforce's *An Appeal, &c* (London, 1823) *Memoirs of Sir T. F. Buxton* (London, 1849), 125–7 *Hansard,* vii (1822), 1783–95 , viii (1823), 624–30 , ix (1823), 257–360

V

The cause was now formally launched, and the Abolition Cabinet held constant meetings, some of them in the early morning at Wilberforce's house, reminding him ' of the old bustle of a Kensington Gore breakfast '. But for the moment, having tied their hands by accepting Canning's pledges, they could do nothing but await their execution. And for Wilberforce at any rate it was anxious waiting. ' I wish ', he tells Macaulay, ' I could be as easy about insurrections as you and Stephen ' His fears were quickly justified. The Government's first step, while it went to prove its sincerity, revealed the practical difficulty of the policy of gradual amelioration leading up to freedom. Canning's resolutions were sent out to the Governors of the West Indian colonies together with a letter from Bathurst, the Colonial Secretary, urging, as an immediate measure in compliance with the wishes of Parliament, the abolition of the flogging of females and of the use of the whip in the field. The news of this positive interference instead of mere pious declarations from Westminster and Downing Street produced a storm of indignation among the planters. An Address was moved in the Jamaica Assembly for the removal of Bathurst from the Government. Other speakers declared that Jamaica should sever herself from the British Crown. And the Assembly unanimously carried a protest against a ' decree ', ' whereby the inhabitants of this once valuable colony (hitherto esteemed the brightest jewel in the British Crown) are destined to be offered a propitiatory sacrifice at the altar of fanaticism.' Worse was to happen in other colonies. The planters of Barbados, suspecting that one of the local missionaries had sent home bad reports on the condition of their slaves, destroyed his meeting-house, and drove him from the island When the Governor offered £100 reward for the detection and conviction of the rioters, they issued a counter-proclamation that ' the good people of Barbados would take care fitly to punish such person or persons as should make any discovery '. There was a still

graver outburst in Demerara. Governor Murray, alarmed
at the 'feverish anxiety' displayed by the planters when he
communicated Bathurst's dispatch to them, decided to
conceal its contents from the negroes. But the planters did
not conceal their angry talk, and there were slaves who
overheard it. From plantation to plantation ran the rumour
that the King of England had set them free and that their
masters had suppressed the edict. In part of the colony
the slaves refused to work. That, it seems, was their only
active rebellion, but the troops were called out and the
'insurrection' was suppressed with heavy loss among the
slaves. No white man was killed. Dozens of 'insurgents',
however, were tried by court-martial and executed. Five
received the ghastly punishment of 1,000 lashes each.

The news from Demerara reached London in an inevitably
distorted form. The slaves had risen *en masse*, said rumour ;
and white men had been murdered. 'What ! ' cried Wilberforce on hearing of it. 'have they given such an order
without preparation, and without explaining their purpose
to the slaves—why it is positive madness ! ' 'The whip is
the grand badge of slavery', he said again ; 'they should
have begun with all those reforms which would have had a
wonderful influence without seeming directly and suddenly
to weaken the master's authority.' But such reasonable
protests were of little use. They could not save Wilberforce
and his friends from the old recriminations. Government
had blundered, and they were the obvious scapegoats.
Even Canning's private secretary, the gossip ran, had
declared that the insurrection 'had been *instigated* by
Wilberforce, Buxton, and Co.' Once more the hunt was
up. The West Indians redoubled their abuse of the old
arch-hypocrite who had dyed his hands with British blood ;
and British journalists, led by Theodore Hook, joined in the
hue and cry. But, if Wilberforce was more worried than he
had once been as his own failings, he was quite inured to
calumny. ' *John Bull*, for three or four weeks past ', he
writes, ' has been abusing me grossly. . . . One of his paragraphs was sent me the other day, with only these three
words, " Thou vile hypocrite ! " . . . My judgement is clearly

that it will be best to let him go on , to give him rope, according to the common saying '

Far more important—the cause had received a set-back. Canning was not the man to drop the fiery business altogether because he had burned his fingers. But his performance in 1824 was not up to his promise in 1823 On March 16 he laid before Parliament a full statement of the Government's policy in the form of a draft Order-in-Council for ameliorating the condition of the slaves in Trinidad, accompanied by a draft Proclamation to be issued in all the West Indian colonies, referring to the erroneous belief that emancipation had been carried and to the acts of insubordination it had caused and declaring that the slaves ' will be undeserving of our protection if they shall fail to render entire submission to the laws as well as dutiful obedience to their masters '. The Order-in-Council was a lengthy document. It established a new Government official, the ' Protector and Guardian of Slaves ', charged, in the first instance, with the duty of acting on a slave's behalf in all major legal proceedings in which he might be involved. It prohibited the use of the whip or any other instrument for enforcing labour. It limited the number of lashes that could be inflicted for any offence on any one occasion and forbade any whipping at all if the effects of a previous punishment were still uncured. It abolished the whipping of female slaves entirely. It prescribed that a record book should be kept on every plantation in which exact particulars of every punishment, exceeding three stripes, must be recorded, together with the nature and place of the offence , and that a literal transcript of the entries in this book should be presented by the owner or manager of the plantation every quarter to the commandant of the district and an oath taken that the entries were complete and the transcript exact ; and that all these returns should be forwarded by the commandant to the Protector and Guardian of Slaves It made provision for the issue of licences authorizing any clergyman or priest or public teacher of religion to solemnize the marriage of slaves ; and it forbade the separation of husband from wife or parent from child by sale. It endowed slaves with the

full right of acquiring, holding, and disposing of property.
It established saving-banks for slaves   It forbade the levy
of any tax on manumission beyond a registration fee of
twenty shillings.   It removed all obstacles to a slave's
purchase of his freedom at a price to be fixed, if necessary,
by a process of official arbitration.   It prescribed that any
slave should be admitted to give evidence on oath if he was
certified as fit to do so by any religious minister or teacher.
It required the submission of an annual report by the Protector and Guardian of Slaves to the Governor, on the
performance of his duties and the detailed operation of the
various clauses of the Order, and the transmission of his
report to the Secretary of State.   Finally, it laid heavy
penalties on infringements of the foregoing clauses and in
particular provided that any owner, manager, or overseer,
twice convicted of cruel or unlawful punishment, should, in
addition to the penalties, be disqualified from acting in such
capacity in future, and that, in the case of an owner so
convicted, his slaves should be confiscated to the Crown.

This thorough-going Order, Canning explained, was to be
applied to Trinidad and also to St. Lucia and Demerara,
the other colonies which possessed no legislatures of their
own and in which, as he said, the power of the Crown was
unshackled   He hoped the results of it would quickly lead
to the enactment of similar legislation by the Assemblies in
Jamaica and the rest of the West Indies   But when he sat
down, he can scarcely have believed that he had satisfied
the Abolitionists.   The Order-in-Council itself was patently
sincere , and it was a far more detailed and drastic interference in the handling of the slave-question than any
Government had yet attempted since the abolition of the
Trade   But that was all that could be said of it · and
Buxton was quick to point out how far it was from fulfilling
the pledge contained in Canning's own resolutions of the
previous year.   He had promised amelioration for all the
slaves in the West Indies.   The Order only dealt with the
35,000 slaves in Trinidad and a few more in the other subject
colonies, and left the welfare of the rest of the 700,000
slaves in the West Indies to the proved indifference of the

island legislatures   He had promised, further, that this
general amelioration should lead in the fullness of time to
general liberation.   The Order only dealt with individual
manumission.   It said not a word to suggest, that, even in
Trinidad alone, slavery was not to last for ever.   'Canning
opened in a very guarded speech', was Wilberforce's disappointed comment.   'Buxton strong, above concert pitch.
I was better voiced and better heard than usual.'   And
certainly this speech—his last full-dress speech on the theme
he had made his own—can stand beside the best of its
predecessors   With his old clear insight he seized on the
cardinal point   'The House must not conceal from itself',
he said, 'what the grand principle—the practical point at
issue—really is.   It is simply this—whether the slave-system
is to be put an end to by the imperial legislature or by the
colonial Assemblies.'   And as long as Parliament left it to
the planters, the slaves would despair of any real relief and
in their despair they might take their cause into their own
hands and endeavour to effect their own liberation.

'It is my daily and nightly prayer—it is the hope and desire
I feel from the very bottom of my soul—that so dreadful
an event may not occur   But it is a consequence which
I cannot but apprehend, and, as an honest man, it is my
duty to state that apprehension.   Only consider what a
terrible thing it is for men who have long lived in a state
of darkness, just when the bright beams of day have begun
to break in upon their gloom, to have the boon suddenly
withdrawn and to be consigned afresh to darkness, uncertainty, nay, to absolute despair!   Whatever Parliament
may think fit to do, I implore it to do it quickly and firmly.
Do not proceed with hesitating steps   Do not tamper with
the feelings you have yourselves excited.   For hope
deferred maketh the heart sick.'

But Canning was not to be shaken from his course.   He
declared in his reply that he stood between two extremes.
One side wanted him to promise that no more should ever
be done than was now proposed   The other side wanted
him to say what more he would do and when he would do it.

'I will not consent to be fettered by any engagements.
I will not be led by either side or in either sense to declara-

tions from which it may be impossible to advance and dangerous to retreat. . . . The question is not—it cannot be made—a question of right, of humanity, of morality merely. It is a question which contemplates a change, great and difficult beyond example, one almost beyond the power of man to accomplish—a change in the conditions and circumstances of an entire class of our fellow-creatures—the recasting, as it were, of a whole generation of mankind If this be not a question requiring deliberation, cautious and fearful deliberation, I know not what can be so '

It was hard to resist the force of this reasoning. Even Wilberforce must have recognized that the abolition of Slavery, which, as Canning had pointed out, had only been commended to Parliament for the first time nine months ago, was a far graver matter than the abolition of the Slave Trade which had lain before Parliament for nearly twenty years. And there was another point of difference The men who had obstructed and procrastinated in those earlier days and pleaded for ' gradual ' abolition, had, most of them, desired in their hearts to do nothing at all. But as Wilberforce knew, Canning was sincere He saw that Slavery in the end must follow the Trade. But Pitt's heir had inherited some of Pitt's encumbrances. Eldon, for instance, was back on the woolsack, obstructing and procrastinating. And Canning, for his own part, possibly because he had friends, and one intimate friend, George Ellis, among the West Indians, had not yet despaired of persuading the planters—despite what had happened in Jamaica, in Barbados, in Demerara, everywhere—to do what must be done themselves For the time, he had his way. The House was with him There was no division.

Wilberforce's effort that night had overtaxed his strength. He was able to attend the debate, a few days later, on ' Lord John Russell's motion about the French evacuating Spain '—' Canning invincibly comic,' he notes—but then he collapsed with a severe attack of pneumonia He weathered it, but it was more than two months before he could leave his room. On June 1, however, he was again in his place in the House. It was rash, no doubt ; but indignation forced him there The last entry he had made

in his diary before his illness had mastered him was this.
' Poor Smith, the missionary, died in prison at Demerara !
The day of reckoning will come '; and, as he lay in bed,
he had brooded long over this extraordinary affair. John
Smith was a Nonconformist missionary who had lived on an
estate in Demerara since 1816 The exposition of Christianity to a slave or subject people is, as contemporary
events in South Africa were showing, a delicate matter. It
calls for discretion on the missionary's part, and John Smith
may not have been discreet. His converts among the
slaves were many and devoted to him ; he sympathized with
their resentment at the suppression of the orders from
England ; and on the Sunday preceding the strike or
' insurrection ' of 1823 he chose an unfortunate text for his
sermon · ' If thou hadst known, even thou, at least in this
thy day, the things which belong unto thy peace ! But now.
they are hid from thine eyes ' On the same day he had
talked with a slave named Quamina. On Monday, on that
very estate, the strike began. On the two following days,
while the strike was at its worst, Quamina again visited
Smith and was taken to task by him for threatening to use
force. It would be un-Christian, he said, and also quite
futile Finally Quamina and his followers were persuaded
by Smith to promise that no blood should be shed. Meantime, Smith warned the manager of an adjacent estate that
the trouble might spread Those are the bare facts. They
were enough for the military authorities. Two days after
the declaration of martial law, Smith was arrested and
confined in the colonial jail. ' The upper chamber of the
building . . . was exposed to the scorching fury of a tropical
sun The lower chamber had a damp mud floor.' For
nearly two months Smith was confined there, his wife
voluntarily sharing his imprisonment. He had been arrested
on August 21 on October 13 he was tried by court-martial
—for martial law was still in force, although the ' insurrection ' had been completely suppressed in two or three days.
The Colonial Fiscal conducted the prosecution Smith had
to defend himself. Slave-evidence was then admissible in
Demerara, unlike most West Indian colonies, in accordance

with the old Dutch custom, and the main evidence against Smith was given by some slaves The chief of these witnesses afterwards confessed that his evidence, at a planter's instigation, had been falsified. Leading questions, moreover, were put to these witnesses and the prompted answer was usually given. And much of the most damaging evidence was not evidence of fact such as would be admitted in an orthodox British court. The witnesses were allowed to repeat conversations they had listened to—to say what they had heard somebody say to some one else about Quamina or the prisoner. The President of the Court Martial made no objection, nor did the President of the colonial Civil Court, who, having been hastily appointed a colonel of militia, was one of the judges and the only lawyer among them. Smith, in his ignorance, made no objection either. But as soon as he testified himself, in his defence, to things that he had heard, the Court decided that no more hearsay evidence could be accepted. Smith, moreover, was compelled to testify against himself. His private journal, in which he had opened his heart in passionate resentment against the treatment of the slaves, was produced as evidence against him. The result was certain. Smith was convicted of fomenting discontent among the slaves with intent to excite revolt and on other more detailed charges, such as neglecting to arrest Quamina. He was sentenced to death, with a recommendation to mercy, which was promptly granted by the Home Government. Some months afterwards Smith died in prison. But his enemies' hatred was unappeased They forbade his widow to attend the funeral. They tore up the railings which two negro members of his congregation set round his grave.

Such was the business which summoned Wilberforce from his sick-room to the House of Commons. He could not, of course, make the effort of speaking himself, but he had the satisfaction of hearing Brougham and Mackintosh say everything that needed saying. The Government had already gone so far as to reverse the proceedings of the court : but that was not enough for those who were determined to vindicate Smith's innocence beyond all question ;

and Brougham proposed a motion denouncing the whole
trial as ' a violation of law and justice '. The debate was
almost a re-trial. Brougham himself minutely reviewed the
constitution of the court, the character of the witnesses, and
the methods employed in their examination, with copious
quotation from the *verbatim* reports. Wilmot Horton did
his best, with counter-quotations, to state the other side,
but he could not go farther than to ask the House to suspend
its judgement. He was answered by Mackintosh who easily
demonstrated the *prima facie* incredibility of much of the
evidence against Smith, denounced the production of the
journal as ' precisely the iniquity perpetrated by Jeffries in
the case of Sidney ' and showed from the very statements
made in court that Smith had done all he could to persuade
the slaves to be patient. ' He appeals to their prudence :
the soldiers, says he, will overcome your vain revolt   He
appeals to their sense of religion : as Christians you ought
not to use violence. What argument remained, if both these
failed ? ' All these were lengthy speeches, but the House
was too keenly interested to allow the debate to close that
night. It was adjourned till June 11 ; and in the interval
Wilberforce rapidly gained strength. ' I very much wish ',
he told Stephen, ' if my voice should be strong enough, to
bear my testimony.' When the day came, he felt able to
make the effort   Before the debate opened, he went to
Stephen's house ' to be quiet for three or four hours, and
was so, and read papers and thought '. Nevertheless his
speech was not on the level of Brougham's or Mackintosh's,
nor indeed of many of his own. ' I quite forgot my topics ',
confesses the diary, ' and made sad work of it ' But those
facts in the case which stood unquestioned scarcely needed
eloquence to make them tell ; it had been clear from the
first that the House as a whole had been greatly shocked by
them , and Ministers had not ventured to propose a decisive
counter-motion. They simply moved the previous question ;
and even on this they were in some danger of defeat. But
Canning had not yet spoken ; and any one who questions
that Canning was a great parliamentarian should read his
speech   Once more he refused to be forced into one of two

extremes—to say either that the proceedings of the court were entirely correct or that Smith was entirely innocent of any charge. On the second point, while clearly betraying his belief that the charges actually brought had not been sustained and that the sentence therefore was excessive, he argued that Smith had at least been guilty of withholding from the Governor his knowledge of impending trouble, not indeed because he desired to foment it but because he dreaded playing an informer's part. It was a clever point, not very strong, perhaps, but strong enough to make many of his listeners hesitate to pass a wholesale condemnation on the officials of a British colony. And the cold, impartial tone of the speech was in effective contrast—in that unemotional House—with the passion of Brougham's reply. It was enough, not to ensure the Government's customary majority, but to carry ' the previous question ' by 193 votes to 146.

' I greatly doubt ', says the diary after this debate, ' if I had not better give up taking part in the House of Commons ' And certainly the doubt was justified by the increased feebleness of intellectual as well as physical power which his last illness had left behind it. But he had undertaken to present a petition for the abolition of Slavery from the town of Carlow and its neighbourhood ; and he felt it to be an opportunity, perhaps the last, ' of entering his solemn protest against the plan of Government as hopeless and dangerous ' ' It is nothing short of infatuation ', he remarks, ' to depend on the colonial assemblies for initiating a model to be set up in Trinidad ' Accordingly he nerved himself for a short speech on June 15, and this time he did not fail It was a clear and convincing assertion that the planters could not be expected, on any reasonable view whatever of their conduct and opinions, to extinguish Slavery or even to ameliorate it of their own motion.

' I am disposed to think ', he said, ' that my right honourable friend deceives himself as to the probable conduct of the West Indian Assemblies by insensibly admitting the persuasion that the West Indian proprietors in this country—many of whom are his own personal friends and men of the most humane and liberal minds—reflect the opinions and feelings of the colonists actually in the islands. Nothing, alas ! could be more different . . . The West Indians abhor alike the end we have in view and the means by which we hope to attain it. They frankly tell us that the emancipation of their slaves would be their inevitable destruction , and their prejudices make them disapprove of the various measures we recommend for the improvement of the negroes' condition. . . . When both means and end are alike obnoxious, it seems to me far too sanguine to look to their giving up their opposition and at length adopting the principles we recommend. . . . But only let the imperial legislature assume its proper tone and maintain its just authority, and all will go on quietly · you will soon witness with delight the accomplishment of your benevolent purpose. Hence it is that I have felt it my imperious duty to disavow the system of conduct which Government is now pursuing It is with reluctance and pain I have come forward , but I believe it my absolute duty to protest against that policy. *Liberavi animam meam.* May it please God to disappoint my expectations and to render the result more favourable than I anticipate.' *

VI

It was Wilberforce's last debate. Ten days later he was taken ill again on his way to pay a visit in the country , and on arriving at his destination, he was ' but just able to be helped upstairs to bed '. For a month he lay in a critical condition , and when, at last, he struggled back to health, it was clear that, for a long time to come, no work of any kind was to be thought of. He retired to a small house bordering on Uxbridge Common and lived there in complete seclusion, ' never visiting, scarcely receiving a single visitor '. But in the autumn he moved, on the doctor's advice, to Bath, which he found by no means so restful. ' There is walking between the glasses and after the glasses,' he writes to his daughter, ' and then in rolls the tide of visitors as

* *Life,* v 200–23 *Hansard,* x (1824), 1046–1198 , xi (1824), 961–1076, 1206–1313, 1406–27 The authorities confirm the accuracy of Spencer Walpole's account of John Smith's case, *History of England since 1815,* iii 398–402

regularly as that of the ocean, and like that, this human influx makes its way through and over every obstacle. . . . Continued knockings while I have been writing, and at last one intruder has actually made a lodgement.' It was a pleasure, none the less, for Wilberforce to meet some of his older friends and acquaintances again. ' Venerable Rowland Hill dined with me—aetat. 80 ', notes the diary, and again, ' I talked with Mr. Nevill in the Pump-room, whom I had met at Exton near fifty years ago he 82 aetat —an astonishing man.' And before he returned to Uxbridge to spend Christmas with his family, he paid a visit to the oldest and almost the closest of his spiritual comrades. ' Sat with Hannah More about an hour and a half, and she as animated as ever I knew her, quoting authors, naming people, etc.—off about one, after praying with her.'

With the coming of the new year the question of retirement could be postponed no longer. Doctors and friends were strongly for it : to continue in Parliament, they said, might mean a fatal seizure but Wilberforce struggled hard against it. He confesses to Macaulay that the idea is ' very painful '. ' It is to me almost like a change of nature to quit parliamentary life,' he told his son. And he had done so little ! ' I am filled with the deepest compunction ', he writes to a friend, ' from the consciousness of having made so poor a use of the talents committed to my stewardship. The heart knows its own bitterness ' To be forced ' to retire from public life *re infecta* '—that is the burden of all his complaints. Indeed, he could not bring himself at once to an instant and abrupt resignation. He would put it off just a very little. He would resign—quite certainly—as soon as the present Parliament were dissolved. Then his friends attempted, not very hopefully, an alternative plan The offer of a peerage was arranged. But Wilberforce courteously declined the initial suggestion. ' I have done nothing to make it naturally come to me,' he said. At last, however, he surrendered to the inevitable. As was his wont, he noted down the reasons for his decision—' I hope I may employ my pen to advantage if I retire into private life , and my life just now is peculiarly valuable to my family.—I am not

now much wanted in Parliament ; our cause has powerful
advocates who have now taken their stations —The example
of a man's retiring, when he feels his bodily and mental
powers beginning to fail him, might probably be useful.'
Accordingly he requested Buxton to apply on his behalf
for the Chiltern Hundreds—Buxton rather than Canning
or Grant or Brougham, as sundry friends suggested, because
he desired it to be a ' testamentary designation and to hold
him forth as the depositary of my principles on West Indian
matters ' ' It is the first place that I ever asked for myself ',
he wrote, ' and for near thirty years for any one else.'
Buxton finely quoted in his reply the inscription which the
Carthaginians set on Hannibal's tomb—' We vehemently
desired him in the day of battle '

It was a notable event in the life of the House of Commons
when Wilberforce passed through its doors for the last
time. He carried history away with him, this little, stooping,
frail old man Almost alone among living members of the
House, he had stood among the giants, their contemporary
and their equal, in the golden days of Pitt and Fox and
Burke. And now for nearly twenty years, when all those
others had gone, he had enjoyed the same kind of prestige ;
obtained from the House the same kind of respect, willing
or unwilling ; exercised over it, in many great matters, the
same kind of power, as that which had been given to those
others and to them alone. Like them, too, he had been a
great figure in the country. The overthrow of the Slave
Trade had given him something like the position in the
public eye which Waterloo had given Wellington. Liverpool
or Castlereagh, Grey or Brougham, Canning or Huskisson—
none of them was famous in his generation quite as
Wilberforce was famous ' When Mr. Wilberforce passes
through the crowd ', an Italian diplomat once remarked on
the day of the opening of Parliament, ' every one contemplates this little old man, worn with age and his head sunk
upon his shoulders, as a sacred relic—as the Washington of
humanity ' *

* *Life,* iv 373 , v 223-17

XIII
REST

I

'We have bought a house about ten miles north of London,' wrote Wilberforce to Gisborne shortly after his retirement. 'I shall be a little *zemindar* there : 140 acres of land, cottages of my own, etc.' Highwood Hill, as this estate was called, lay about a mile from Mill Hill 'Late when got home', comments the diary on the day he took possession, ' and had a too hasty prayer for first settlement in a new house—all in confusion.' The confusion soon subsided into a regular routine of life A systematic ordering of the day had been characteristic of Wilberforce ever since his ' conversion ' ; but now his abandonment of politics and his seclusion from society and its sudden calls and interruptions made it easier to keep strictly to the time-table. He rose soon after seven o'clock and spent an hour and a half at his devotions Three-quarters of an hour were then allowed for dressing and listening, as he dressed, to his reader At half-past nine came family prayers for half an hour, Wilberforce always reading and expounding a passage from the Bible Invariably after prayers, if the weather permitted, he spent a few minutes in the garden. Breakfast was late, usually about ten ; and if friends were of the party, they often sat talking round the table till midday. Then Wilberforce retired to deal with the day's letters , but by three o'clock, when the post had gone, he was out in the garden again, pacing up and down the sunny path, preferably with a friend—' now in animated or even playful conversation ', one of them records, ' and then drawing from his copious pockets some favourite volume or other, a Psalter, a Horace, a Shakespeare, or Cowper, and reading or reciting passages, and then catching at long-stored flower-leaves as the wind blew them from the pages, or standing before a favourite gum cistus to repair the loss '. He liked to stay out of doors till dinner-time which was never later than five. After dinner he went up to his room, rested for an hour and a half, sometimes sleeping and always coming down again as fresh and vigorous as if the day had

just begun. And then came the ' family reading '. It was
in these first years of his retirement that he indulged in so
many of Scott's novels with that typical regret that their
purpose was not more serious. ' They remind me of a
giant ', he says, ' spending his strength in cracking nuts.
I would rather go to render my account on the last day,
carrying up with me *The Shepherd of Salisbury Plain* than
bearing the load of all those volumes, full as they are of
genius.' Naturally, therefore, novels were not by any means
the only reading. History still holds its place—Clarendon,
Orford, Pepys, Hallam. ' Independent ' to the last, he
regularly subscribes to both the *Edinburgh* and the *Quarterly*.   •
And of the poets, Shakespeare, at any rate, and Cowper are
usually at his side or in his pocket ; but not, one may guess,
the most celebrated or notorious poet of his own day—
not Byron. One wonders, indeed, if Wilberforce was ever
aware of the doubtful compliment Byron paid him—if he
ever read the three tributes to his name and fame in the
pages of *Don Juan*. After reading, talk ; and then evening
prayers , and then more talk and more, usually till midnight
if there were old friends in the house, and often beyond it.
And so at last to a short and often broken night's rest.

For a casual visitor at Highwood Hill those evening talks
were an unforgettable experience. They saw the old man
at his best, pouring out the treasures of his long memory,
arguing, criticizing, orating on some favourite theme, and
all with an astonishing facility and freshness and vivacity.
' If he was lighted up ', says an acquaintance, ' and in a
small circle where he was entirely at his ease, his powers of
conversation were prodigious ; a natural eloquence was
poured out, strokes of gentle playfulness and satire fell on
all sides, and the company were soon absorbed in admiration.
It commonly took only one visit to gain over the most
prejudiced stranger.' The easy conquest of one such
stranger is recorded. Some cynical friend had given her a
thoroughly unpleasant idea of her host , but, after one
night in the house, she dashes off a long dithyrambic letter
to her sister, ' Oh, he is a dear, good, admirable old man ! '
she exclaims. How could any one, indeed, regard this

lively, indomitably youthful creature as a fanatic or a
hypocrite ? For he retained to the end his transcendent
gift of youth   That dangerous talent for mimicry, for
instance, had never been quite abandoned ; and he would
sometimes plunge the household into uproarious laughter
by his imitation of some public man till, conscience pricking,
he would ' check himself and throw in some kind remark '.
' The close union between the most rigid principles and the
most gay and playful disposition '—that was what still
struck Lord Milton, his old rival of the hustings, as the most
remarkable thing about him.   And when his two sons came
to write his biography, they were obliged to confess their
inability to do justice to this ' great and leading feature ' of
their father's character.   Perhaps the younger Stephen is
nearest it when, in a letter to Henry Taylor a few days after
Wilberforce's death, he quotes a line of Coleridge as
' expressing his nature to perfection as far as it goes '—
' Delight in little things, the buoyant youth surviving in
the man.'

Time had thinned the company that used to gather
for those great evening talks ; but many of the old friends
are still there—Stephen and Gisborne and Buxton and
John Joseph Gurney and Macaulay, and, now he is of
age, Macaulay's son.   ' Macaulay and Tom came to dinner,
and night ', says the diary in 1825.   ' Tom infinitely overflowing with matter on all subjects, and most good-
humoured ' : and next day, ' Macaulay off   Tom fertile
and fluent to the last, and with unaffected good-nature.'
That fertility and fluency were soon to be famous   ' I am
much pleased with a review of Tom Macaulay's in the
Edinburgh ', notes Wilberforce a few years later : ' it is
not merely the very superior talent which it indicates, but
(scarcely an ' independent ' judgement this !) its being on
the right side.'   He keeps in touch, too, with allies, new and
old, who are not of the inner circle.   Sir Stamford Raffles
and his wife are frequent guests.   One day he pays a visit
to the other survivor of the three who had talked of Abolition
under the Holwood oak.   ' To Dropmore, where received
very kindly , walked with Grenville for an hour before and

after dinner ; it grieved me to see him so feeble. Said he
had profited more from Aristotle's *Rhetoric* than any other
work.' Another day, ' Lord Harrowby rode over to see
me . . . very clever and entertaining as always.' But the
inner circle itself was never now so constantly in session as
it once had been ; the brethren of the Clapham Sect no
longer lived at each other's doors. And it had shrunk.
Death had taken toll of its members and their families.
John Venn the preacher had died in 1813, Henry Thornton
and his wife in 1815, Mrs. Stephen, Wilberforce's only surviving sister, in the following year, and Isaac Milner in 1820.
In 1821 Wilberforce had lost one of his own children, his
eldest daughter. But the family was growing ; his two
elder sons were married or on the point of marrying ; and
in his grandchildren Wilberforce was soon to discover one
more proof of God's amazing mercy to an unprofitable
servant. There were one or two friends, moreover, with
whom, late as he had come to know them, he had quickly
become intimate—foremost among them, Mackintosh.
Wilberforce had naturally been drawn to him by his eloquent
championship of humanitarian causes—' splendid ' and
' beautiful ' are the diary's epithets for his speeches—but it
was something more than that. There was something
kindred, it seems, between those two ; and certainly
Mackintosh was as great a talker as Wilberforce himself.
He had taken a house at Clapham ; and ' this extraordinary
man ', says Wilberforce, ' spends, they tell me, much of
his time in the circulating library-room at the end of the
Common, and chats with the utmost freedom to all the
passengers in the Clapham stage as he goes and comes from
London '. Two such talkers, indeed, could never have been
friends if they had yielded to the besetting sin of their class.
But both of them could also listen. Wilberforce spoke of
Mackintosh as ' full of information and sparkling like a
firefly '. ' I drew the highest prize in the lottery ', says the
diary, of a big dinner-party ; ' I sat by Sir J. Mackintosh.'
Again, ' Mackintosh came in and sat most kindly chatting
with me during my dinner—what a paragon of a companion he is ; quite unequalled ! ' ' If I were called upon

to describe Wilberforce in one word ', said Mackintosh on his side, ' I should say he was the most " amusable " man I ever met with in my life. Instead of having to think what subjects will interest him, it is perfectly impossible to hit one that does not. I never saw any one who touched life at so many points ; and this is the more remarkable in a man who is supposed to live absorbed in the contemplation of a future state   When he was in the House of Commons, he seemed to have the freshest mind of any man there. There was all the charm of youth about him. And he is quite as remarkable in this bright evening of his day as when I saw him in his glory many years ago.'

And so, in regular routine, in prayer and correspondence and infinite talk, the quiet months went by. There was rarely any break, except the intermittent visits to Bath for the ' potations ' which the doctors ordered. Frequent or lengthy journeys soon become too great a strain. But in 1827 the old man set out on one last great tour. He wanted ' to revisit the scenes of his childhood and early youth ' before it was too late ; and early in the summer he drove off for Yorkshire, stopping for a time on the way at his old haunt at Yoxall Lodge among the trees   ' Much as I had admired it before, I never saw its riches displayed in such overflowing profusion.' In Derbyshire he noticed how the country had been improved by the growth of woods on the bare hillsides of forty years ago. But it was in Yorkshire that the passing of time inevitably struck him most. At Huddersfield he met ' a warm-hearted shopkeeper, originally from Hull—knew me when himself a boy—remembered the ox roasted whole ' ; but at Hull and elsewhere the answers to his inquiries after the companions of his youth were all too often the same   ' Oh, he has been long gone ' or ' He died years ago '. His ' progress ' round his native county was slow and thorough. Of his many visits to friends' houses, the last—to Wentworth House—was in a way the most moving of all. ' The cordiality and kindness with which I have been received in this place ', he wrote to Stephen, ' has deeply affected me   Lord Fitzwilliam might well have been forgiven if he had conceived an unconquerable antipathy to me.' And he recalls his famous first election as the member for Yorkshire in the teeth of Fitzwilliam's opposition, when he was only twenty-four, ' a mere boy ', without a single friend among the county magnates, and identified with Pitt against whom Fitzwilliam had ' conceived a deadly hostility '.

So back at last to Highwood Hill (' What cause for thankfulness after six months' absence and thirty-six visits ') ; back to the peaceful routine, the garden-path, the household devotions, the daily letters, the family reading, and the talk.*

II

When Wilberforce left the House of Commons, he shut the door tight on politics. ' I am now no politician ', he declared, not without some secret satisfaction ; for the party conflict had always jarred on him, and his excursions into other fields than the negro question had always seemed a matter of duty and rather an unpleasant duty, forced on him by his knowledge that so many people expected him to say something and were so strangely influenced by what he said. So while England moved on into the sharpest political crisis in its history since the last ripple of the English Revolution had ebbed away in the alarms of ' forty-five ', the oracle was silent. That he was not indifferent, that he followed events in the newspapers and had his opinions on them, is clear from his private letters. ' In what a dreadful state the country now is ', he writes to his son at the time of the ' Swing Riots ' in 1830. ' Gisborne, I find, has stated his opinion that the present is the period of pouring out the 7th Vial, when there is to be general confusion, insubordination, and misery. . . . Your mother suggests that a threshing-machine used to be kept in one of your barns. If so I really think it should be removed. I should be very sorry to have it stated that a threshing-machine had been burnt on the premises of the Rev. Samuel Wilberforce ;

* *Life*, iv. 229, 272, 299 ; v. 27, 50, 109, 248–53, 272–98, 314–15. *Letters of the First Sir James Stephen* (privately printed, 1906), 33–4.

they take away one of the surest sources of occupation for
farmers in frost and snow times.' A week later, the old
Tory observes with no dismay the long-delayed advent of
the Whigs to power. ' Assuredly ', he writes, ' this Government is greatly to be preferred before the last.' But, as had
always been his way, it is the men rather than their measures
that he looks to, and their morals rather than their brains.
' Brougham better than Copley ', he says, ' and several
highly respectable besides, the Grants (Charley is in the
Cabinet), Lord Althorp, Sir James Graham, Lord Grey
himself, highly respectable as a family man ; Denman a
very honest fellow ', and so forth. He expressed, as has
been seen, a not unfavourable opinion on the first Reform
Bill ; and when both the first and the second Bills had been
rejected by the Lords, he was given a chance of understanding, better perhaps than he had ever done, how fiercely the
English people were bent upon Reform. Recluse as he was,
he was brought into personal contact with the wildest of
those outbreaks in the autumn of 1831, which showed how
near now the country really was to the revolution he had
dreaded in Pitt's day and in Sidmouth's. On the red Sunday of October 30 he was staying with his friend Harford
at Blaize Castle, four miles from Bristol. News of rioting
in the city reached him after church that morning ; and at
night he saw the sky lit up with the glare of its burning
buildings. A few days later, when all was quiet again, he
went with his host to inspect the damage. ' It was dangerous
to move forward ', writes Harford, ' for fear of the sudden
crash of tottering walls ; and it was appalling to stand still
and contemplate the surrounding scene ' ; but nothing
could daunt old Wilberforce's eager interest ; he insisted
that they must ' examine and localize every principal
feature of the recent outrages '.

Only one cause—his own—could now drag Wilberforce
before the public ; and even to combat Slavery he was very
loth to leave that quiet house and garden. ' It seems like
wishing to retain the reins when I can no longer hold them,'
he told Babington. And he positively declined to join in
those deputations to Ministers which he had so often led.
' I am a bee ', he said, ' which has lost its sting.' But he

yielded to repeated appeals that he should take the chair
at a great meeting of the recently founded Anti-Slavery
Society during the first winter of his retirement. ' Above
all, we feel the loss of you ', Macaulay had written : ' heart-
stirring occasions are in prospect, when I should have been
delighted to see you engaged *cominus ense.*' ' Got to the
meeting at twelve ', the diary reports ; ' took the chair.
Very kindly treated throughout, both by the very full
room and the speakers.' But the results of these new
efforts of the Abolitionists were not very ' heart-stirring '.
Canning's regulations had been duly applied in Trinidad,
Demerara, Berbice, and St. Lucia, and were about to be
applied, in a modified form, in Cape Colony ; and that
was all. In vain Bathurst urged the authorities in Jamaica
to take the example to heart and by their own legislation
to anticipate the interference of Parliament. True, they
passed an Act in 1826 ; but it was so meagre and on
essential points so deliberately indefinite that Huskisson,
who succeeded Bathurst, actually refused to sanction it.
In 1828 Huskisson's untimely death brought Murray to the
Colonial Office ; and he lost no time in telling the planters
that an amelioration of their slave-laws, which three
successive Secretaries of State had urged on them, was
' a matter of necessary policy '. But another year passed
and they had done nothing at all. Meanwhile the Abolitionists were chafing at the Government's inaction ; and
in the spring of 1830 they appealed once more to public
opinion with a monster meeting in Freemasons' Hall; and
once more Wilberforce, over seventy now and rather shrunk
and feeble, was prevailed on to attend. ' All the old friends
of the cause ' were there, says the diary ; and it was
Clarkson who moved that ' the great leader in our cause '
should take the chair, to which Wilberforce responded with
a tribute to his ' friend and fellow-labourer ' and a reference
to the days ' when we began our labours together, or rather
when we worked together, for he began before me '. So the
patriarch sat enthroned above the crowd, while Joshua
moved the resolution ' for effecting at the earliest period the
entire abolition of Slavery throughout the British dominions '.
It was Wilberforce's last public appearance in London. ' The

prohibition of my medical adviser is clear and strong', he wrote, when invited to a similar demonstration in the next year.

But the meeting of 1830 had given a greater impulse to the cause than the meeting of 1825, and the Abolitionists decided to join battle again in Parliament Though Buxton, as has been seen, was Wilberforce's official heir in the conduct of the Abolition question in the House of Commons, there was another and more famous Parliamentarian whom the 'Saints' seem to have regarded, at his time, as also, in some sense, their leader It is said that Wilberforce, on his retirement, had urged Canning to put himself at the head of the group, ' assuring him that their support would give him a strength which to an ambitious man like him was invaluable ' ; and that, Canning refusing, the reversion was accepted by the no less ambitious Brougham. It was Brougham, at any rate, who reopened the issue in Parliament with his motion for the consideration of the state of the slaves ' in order to the mitigation and final abolition of their slavery '. He made a powerful speech ; the subject was well suited to his lurid style , but the motion was lost by 56 votes to 27. Something, however, had been gained. Brougham was committed to the cause, and Brougham was certain of high place as soon as the Whigs came into office. Outside Parliament, meantime, the Abolitionist propaganda had been forcing the question to the front , and at the General Election which soon ensued, Slavery, though over-shadowed, of course by Reform, was for the first time an important electoral issue. Naturally it was nowhere more important than in Wilberforce's county. Brougham himself was a candidate for one of four seats which Yorkshire had now acquired—almost certain of success with Wilberforce's name and the organized support of the Abolitionists to back him ; and he and the other three members elected were all definitely pledged to Abolition. ' The election ', wrote Brougham to Wilberforce, ' turned very much on Slavery, your name was in every mouth, and your health the most enthusiastically received.' *

* *Life*, v 249, 262–3, 317–18   *Private Papers*, 258–9, 271–3. *Hansard*, xxv (1830), 1171–92   Harford, 230–2   *Greville Memoirs*, ii. 128   Colquhoun, *Wilberforce and his Friends*, 375.

III

Just at this time the evening calm of the life at Highwood Hill was rudely broken. Wilberforce suddenly lost the greater part of his wealth. All his life he had been a rich man ; but his gifts of many thousands in public and still more in private charity had prevented him from adding to his capital. ' I never intended to do more than not exceed my income,' he once told his eldest son. ' But believe me, there is a special blessing on being liberal to the poor and on the family of those who have been so ; and I doubt not my children will fare better, even in this world, for real happiness than if I had been saving £20,000 or £30,000 of what has been given away.' But since his retirement he had been involved in unusual expenses. The return on the capital spent on the purchase of Highwood Hill was much reduced by his dropping all the rents of his tenants between 30 and 40 per cent. At his first inspection of Highwood, moreover, he had been ' most struck by its distance from a church—three miles ', and he had not been there long before he resolved to build a chapel for the use of himself and his tenants and the neighbouring hamlet of Mill Hill. After a protracted and very irritating controversy with a local parson, he carried out his project at a heavy initial cost. He was ill prepared, therefore, for the disaster which overtook him in 1830. His eldest son, William, had not received, like his three brothers, a call to the Church. He had intended to practise at the bar ; but it had soon appeared that his health was not strong enough for it, and Wilberforce had set himself to find a career for him in agriculture. A promising opportunity was presently forthcoming. A business-man, in whom he had acquired a complete, but quite mistaken, trust, was prepared to launch a farming enterprise. It was to be on a large scale. William would take a remunerative part in it. Only capital was needed. And Wilberforce produced the capital—a very large sum—by selling out stock. Before long he had lost it nearly all.

It was a blow, and the kind of blow which hits an old man

hardest. But Wilberforce took it with perfect calm. ' A
solitary walk with the psalmist—evening quiet ' is the entry,
two days after the full extent of his loss was known. ' What
gives me repose in all things ', said the Saint and meant it,
' is the thought of their being His appointment.' But of
course the loss necessitated a great change in his way of life.
He was not left a pauper ; but it was now quite impossible
to keep up Highwood. He must find, at seventy-one,
another home—unless, indeed, the man who had given so
much in charity were ready to receive in charity. Six of
his countrymen, to their great credit, as soon as his change
of fortune was known, offered to make good the whole of
the damage. One of them was a ' West Indian '. Another
was Lord Fitzwilliam. But Wilberforce refused to accept
anything for himself. Only towards the completion of the
unfinished chapel—it cost altogether about £4,000—would
he allow his friends to help. So Highwood was abandoned ;
and he and his wife went to live, for alternate periods, with
their second and third sons. Samuel was already installed
in the vicarage of Brighstone (or Brixton) in the Isle of
Wight, six miles from Newport ; and Robert was shortly
presented by Brougham to the living of East Farleigh, not
far from Maidstone and almost within a mile of Barham
Court with its memories of the Middletons and Ramsay
and the first beginnings of the assault on the Slave Trade
more than forty years ago.

The death of his second daughter in 1832 made Wilberforce more dependent than ever on the affection of those
two sons and their families. They were intensely devoted
to him, and he was intensely fond and proud of them and
their vocation. ' You are able from experience to judge ',
he writes to Babington, ' how a parent must feel in witnessing
the pastoral labours of his own child.' It did not trouble
him that they had moved away from his own Evangelical
standpoint. He had always been broadminded in those
matters. But perhaps it was as well he could not know that,
when they came to write his biography, they would be
constrained to make excuses for his sympathy with Nonconformists ; that Samuel would one day be an Anglo-Catholic

prelate, suspected of Romanism, and that Robert—preceded by his youngest brother, Henry, and followed by his eldest brother, William—would one day even cross the frontier into Rome. No such clouds were visible about his sunset. The months at Brighstone or at Farleigh were as peaceful and as contented as the years at Highwood. ' I can scarce understand ', said the old man once, ' why my life is spared so long except it be to show that a man can be as happy without a fortune as with one.' So the days went on as before. He could do in his sons' homes exactly what he had done in his own. Those long evening talks were rarer ; he was too far away from Mackintosh and the rest of the London circle. But there was still a garden ; and at Farleigh, as of old, he would pace up and down the sunny gravel path, and at Brighstone he would venture out sometimes to the top of the downs or along by the sea below the cliff. In the spring of 1832 both sons were with their father for a time, Robert spending his holiday at Brighstone. ' Like a first summer day,' says the diary for April 4. ' The air singularly mild and balmy, and not a leaf stirring. S. engaged in a cottage reading. R. drove me out in the pony-chaise, which very pleasant.' And for April 5 : ' Day, if possible, even sweeter than yesterday ; as balmy and more air. Walked with my sons up the hill.' Happily, almost to the end, Wilberforce was strong enough to enjoy these pleasures of the country ; and his mind, if it began to move more slowly, was never clouded ' I thank God ', he tells a friend, ' my health is in about its ordinary state , though I am becoming yearly more and more stiff and crazy.'

Of course he had quite abandoned work of any kind. When he first retired from Parliament he had meant to write. ' I hope not to be idle in private life ', he had remarked, ' though less noisy.' And the diary reveals what he had meant to write about · ' Oh, that God would enable me to execute my long-formed purpose of writing another religious book I have also a wish to write something political ; my own life, and Pitt's too, coming into the discussion.' Presently he began to plan out a work on the Epistles. But nothing came of it, nor of his political auto-

biography. Sometimes, indeed, he would take out from its
drawer the sketch he had made of Pitt's character some
years before, and read it over, and make a little correction
here and there. For he had never forgotten the greatest of
his friends ; always he noted his birthday in his diary :
' Poor Pitt dead above twenty-one years,' it reads in 1827,
' to-day he would have been sixty-eight.' ' I never knew
so extraordinary a man,' he used to say in these latter days.
And so he would sit brooding, and sometimes talking to
his sons, about Pitt and the far-off days of his own youth
and prime. . . . The grammar school at Hull with the big
robustious usher Milner . . . Putney . . . Pocklington . . .
Cambridge . . . the plunge into London . . . Pitt in the
gallery and at Goosetree's . . . that wintry day in the Castle
Yard at York and the election for the county . . . Pitt at
Wimbledon, in Paris ; Pitt Prime Minister, fighting the
Coalition . . . and all that gay London life and those gay
London people . . . the Duchess of Gordon, Mrs. Siddons,
Mrs. Crewe—No ; he must not think of those days, except
to thank God for the ten-thousandth time for his deliverance.
. . . But after that, the wonderful gift of grace, the torments,
and old Newton, and the new tranquil life that followed . . .
and that long, strange talk with Pitt about it all . . . and so
back, with a change of heart, to politics and the Hastings
case . . . and presently the talk beneath the oak at Holwood
and the beginning—how nearly it had been no more than
a beginning !—of the long, long fight with the Slave Trade
. . . the quick success at first, the rousing of the country,
Pitt's great speech ; and then the Revolution . . . and those
dreary, disappointing years, under the shadow of that
endless war ! . . . The cause of Abolition hopelessly shelved ;
and Pitt, still the incomparable patriot, but changing,
ageing, drifting apart. . . . Years only brightened by his
marriage, and by the growth of those new intimacies at
Clapham, and by the success of the *Practical View* . . . and
then at last the sudden revival of the cause . . . Pitt's death
and Fox's zeal . . . and the great night when Romilly (poor,
noble Romilly) had praised him and the House had rung
with cheers. . . . And the busy time that followed ; the

crowd of visitors at Kensington Gore , the efforts to enforce
the British abolition of the Trade and to secure abolition
abroad, at Paris and at Vienna . And then the final phase
of his political career—the Corn Law and the soldiers in
the house, Peterloo and the Queen's Trial, Christophe and
John Smith, and the opening of the anti-slavery campaign .

A great life , but Wilberforce could not judge it as we
judge it. ' I am a sadly unprofitable servant ' was all he
could say. None the less—for humility can be sincere and
yet not blind—Wilberforce must at least have hoped that
his maintenance of Christian principles in public life had
not been quite without effect ; that if the tone of Parliament
and politics was higher now than it had been forty years
ago, it might perhaps be partly due to the influence of the
' Saints '. And, belittle it as he might, Wilberforce must
have known how large a part he had played in the abolition
of at least the British Slave Trade and how long a step that
had been towards the abolition of Slavery itself at least
within the British Empire. But, humility apart, Wilberforce
could never have guessed the full magnitude of his achievement. For it was not till the nineteenth century was growing
old that Britain's dealings with tropical Africa extended
appreciably beyond that fringe of trading-stations on the
Western coast. But when one vast area and then another
was brought, directly or indirectly, within the orbit of the
Empire till at last the British Parliament and people had
become responsible, in the last resort, for the peaceful and
orderly government of a great part of Central Africa, then
indeed it was evident how decisive and how timely the
achievement of Wilberforce and his allies had been. If the
conscience of Europe had not been roused in time, if Slavery
and the Slave Trade had still been tolerated by a lax or
fatalistic public opinion, the second phase in the relations
between Africa and Europe would have been even blacker
than the first. The plantation system of the West Indies
and the Southern States would—one must suppose—have
been reproduced on a gigantic scale wherever the teeming
soil could be cleared and cultivated from Cape Verde to
Mozambique ; and not beyond the Atlantic only but in

their native land, vast armies of negroes would have toiled
in slavery beneath the white man's whip. Nor was it from
that African nightmare only that Wilberforce, more than
any other man, saved the world He had done something
positive More than any other man, he had founded in
the conscience of the British people a tradition of humanity
and of responsibility towards the weak and backward black
peoples whose fate lay in their hands. And that tradition
has never died Never since have cynics or fatalists dared
to justify or palliate the old deliberate sacrifice of Africa
to Europe and America. Selfish and cruel things have been
done in Africa , now and again the morals of commercial
exploitation have been indistinguishable from the morals
of the slave system ; but, within the frontiers of the British
Commonwealth, at any rate, such things could only be done
in the dark and could not be done at all if British Ministers
in far-off London or their officials on the spot were quick
enough or strong enough to stop them For, as the world's
need for the produce of the tropics grew, there grew with it
the conviction that the economic development of Africa
need not, and must not, mean the subjection and degradation
of the Africans The dawn Pitt heralded may be broadening
very slowly into day ; but at least the civilization of Africa
is now something more than a theme for a peroration.
British rule in Africa is not pure altruism. Its standards
may not always or in every quarter be the same. But on
the whole—only ignorance or prejudice can question it—
British rule in Africa has been true to the principle of
trusteeship , it has striven to protect the moral and material
interests of the natives ; it has saved them from African
as well as European slave-masters ; it has given them
stricter justice and truer freedom than they could have got
for themselves, it has begun the long task of their education ,
it has tried to regard them as fellow members with Englishmen of a world-wide society, weak, ignorant, undisciplined
as yet, their faculties for the most part cramped and stunted,
but capable of a development to which only the centuries
ahead can tell the end.

To contrast the principles and practice of British tropical

administration in our own day with what was said in defence
of the Slave Trade by leaders of British opinion in the
eighteenth century and what was done in pursuit of the Trade
by British traders, is to measure the effects of what Wilberforce and his friends achieved. It was nothing less, indeed,
than a moral revolution ; and to those who see the world's
life as a whole, as an intricate, shifting complex not only of
states and nations but of continents and races, discordant,
yet interdependent, heterogeneous, yet all belonging to one
human family, will give a high place in history to the
Englishman who did so much to bring about that revolution,
so much to transform the moral basis of the relations
between Africa and Europe.*

IV

Meantime, the ' Second Crusade ' was once more on the
move ; and Wilberforce's friends began to wonder if indeed
the victory might be won before he died. The return of the
Whigs at the election of 1830, despite Brougham's committal,
had led to no immediate step towards Abolition. Grey and
his colleagues were naturally determined to subordinate all
other issues to the great struggle for Reform ; and when
Buxton again pressed his cause on Parliament, they were
still unwilling to grasp the nettle. But a novel suggestion
was put forward by Althorp. The planters, he pointed out,
had not yielded to persuasion, but they might yield to a
bribe. Why not lower the duties on the import of sugar
from those islands which definitely undertook to improve
the condition of their slaves ? The Government clutched
at this compromise, and Goderich issued a circular dispatch
from the Colonial Office promising measures of fiscal relief
to those colonies whose legislatures would adopt, in full
and unaltered, the Order-in-Council already in force in
Trinidad and the other colonies under Crown control.
Meanwhile the immediate manumission of all slaves belonging

* *Life*, v, chaps. xxxviii, xxxix.

to the Crown had been ordered. The result of these half-
measures was the miserable result which had followed
half-measures before. The slaves in Jamaica once more
believed that the King of England had given them their
freedom. Was not the manumission of the Crown slaves
a proof of it ? And in December they ' struck ', gathered
into gangs, and began to destroy the plantations. As before
they killed no white man. As before they were easily
suppressed. As before the punishment was rigorous. And
as before the Assembly ascribed the cause of the rebellion
to the ' unceasing and unconstitutional interference of his
Majesty's Ministers with our local Legislature '. But this
time, Ministers, less masterful than Canning, acted as if the
charge were true. They voted a considerable sum to make
good the damage done to the planters' property. They
agreed to a proposal for a committee of the Upper House
to consider the interests of the West Indian trade. And,
though the Reform issue was now out of their way and though
Brougham, their own Lord Chancellor, presented a petition
signed by 135,000 persons against any further delay in the
enforcement of Abolition, they did nothing more. When
Parliament met in 1833 no mention was made of Slavery in
the Speech from the Throne. But Buxton was as irrepressible as Wilberforce. He at once gave notice of a motion on
the question ; and resisted all the subsequent efforts of the
Government to induce him to postpone it. ' Well ', said
Althorp at last, ' if *you* will not yield *we must*,' and he
fixed a definite date, April 23, for a statement of the Government's views and a full debate. Ministerial changes gave
them a little more breathing space. Goderich's promotion
had brought Stanley to the Colonial Office, and Buxton
agreed to give the new Minister three weeks' further grace.

May 14, then, was to be the first day of the decisive battle ;
and the Abolitionists, uncertain of the Government's
intentions, set themselves to create an overwhelming
demonstration of public opinion. An effective pamphlet,
by a young clerk who had just returned from the West
Indies, describing the scenes of suffering he had witnessed
and showing from the official figures the terrible increase

in regular floggings in the Crown colonies that had resulted
from the disuse of the whip in the field, was hurriedly printed
and nearly two hundred thousand copies were distributed
Meetings and lectures were organized all over the country
Petitions poured in—the total of their signatures fell not
far short of a million and a half   Over three hundred
delegates, appointed by Abolitionists in every considerable
town in the British Isles collected in London and marched
in a body to 10 Downing Street to present an address to
Lord Grey.   The campaign of 1833, in short, was an even
more impressive demonstration of public enthusiasm than
the campaign of 1792.   And Kent, like other counties, was
caught up in it.   A meeting was arranged at Maidstone
for April 12 and a petition circulated for signatures in the
neighbourhood.   It came, of course, to Wilberforce, at
East Farleigh , and Wilberforce, into whose eager ears
Buxton and Stephen, on a short and a last visit to him, had
poured all the details of the movement, was not content
merely to sign it ;   against all his previous resolves and
promises he actually agreed to attend the meeting and to
propose its submission to Parliament himself.

His speech was not long, and there was only one controversial passage in it.   Like all such movements, the anti-
Slavery movement had its extremists, who regarded Buxton
as half-hearted, watched jealously for any unwarrantable
concessions to the enemy, and above all denounced the
proposal to compensate the planters for the loss of their
slaves.   A fanatic of this type Wilberforce had never been ;
he had always declared not only that compensation was just
in itself but that ' smart money ', as he called it, was owing
by the British nation for its old encouragement of the Slave
Trade   So he spoke out clearly for compensation.   ' I say,
and I say honestly and fearlessly, that the same Being who
commands us to love mercy, says also " Do justice " ;   and
therefore I have no objection to grant the colonists the relief
that may be due to them for any real injuries they may prove
themselves to have sustained '   The speech was obviously
an effort ;   his voice, feeble now and broken, could not fill
the Town Hall as it had filled the House of Commons ;   but,

at the very last, the audience caught an echo of what
Wilberforce had been. ' I trust ', he said, ' that we now
approach the end of our career ' And at that moment, by
a strange coincidence, just such another beam of sunlight
broke into the hall as had lit up the close of Pitt's greatest
speech against the Slave Trade more than forty years
before ; and Wilberforce wove it, as Pitt had woven it,
into his last words. ' The object is bright before us,' he
exclaimed, with a new gleam in his eyes and a stronger
ring in his voice ; ' the light of heaven beams on it and is an
earnest of success '

A week later he moved from East Farleigh to Brighstone,
and there he had an attack of influenza from which he seemed
to make a poor recovery. It was hoped, however, that the
waters of Bath would exert their usual influence on his
general state of health , and to Bath accordingly he went
on May 17, three days after Stanley had moved and carried
the resolutions on which his Bill to abolish Slavery was to
be based. But Bath could no longer work its annual charm.
A sort of langour settled on him and he suffered a good deal
of pain. On July 6, while at dinner, he was suddenly taken
very ill. ' I ran for a medical man ', records his youngest
son, Henry, ' and before I returned he was got to bed. He
was suffering much from giddiness and sickness. . . . When
his medical attendant came, " Thank God ", he said, " I am
not losing my faculties." " Yes, but you could not easily
go through a problem in arithmetic or geometry." " I
think I could go through the Asses' Bridge," he replied ;
and began, correcting himself if he omitted anything. . . . '
Nothing but death itself could quench his youthful spirit ;
and indeed he seems to have felt that death was coming
near. ' What cause have I for thankfulness,' he kept on
saying. Once he began talking of the joy his married life
had given him. ' Think what I should have done, had I been
left, as one hears of people quarrelling and separating
In sickness and in health was the burden, and well has it
been kept ' Just then Mrs Wilberforce entered the room
' I was just praising you,' he said. ' I am a poor creature
to-day,' he confessed a little later. ' I cannot help thinking

if some of the people who saw me swaggering away on the hustings at York could see me now, how much they would find me changed.' That evening some one mentioned Toussaint L'Ouverture and he inveighed against Napoleon's treachery. 'None knows what happened. What a story there will be there when this world shall give up its dead!' But, after all, the end was not yet; he was presently able to get up; and on July 17 he could be moved a stage on the road to London—the road the dying Pitt had travelled in 1806. On the 19th he arrived at William Smith's house in Cadogan Place. 'I am like a clock that is almost run down,' he told one of the many friends who hastened to his side.

Within a mile of his lodging the House of Commons sat debating Stanley's Abolition Bill The new Colonial Secretary had thrown himself at his task with the imperious vigour, the contempt of obstacles, and the dashing eloquence of 'the Rupert of Debate'. True to character, he had tried at first to frame his proposals without seeking the advice of the permanent officials of his department, at whose influence over transient Secretaries of State the newspapers had been grumbling for some time past. But he had been obliged, before long, to have recourse to the experts, and, chief among them, to James Stephen's son who was already winning a commanding position as an official at the Colonial Office. For more than ten years past the younger Stephen had given most of his time to the study of the Slave Question. 'This task devolved on me by inheritance,' he said; but there was more than that in it. His labours were inspired also by an almost reverent devotion to his father's famous friend He once told his wife to see that their eldest boy 'observed' Wilberforce. 'Try to fix in the dear child's mind some recollection of him. He may live to be as old as Mr. W himself without ever meeting any man whose image would be so worth retaining.' To Stephen, therefore, no duty could have been more welcome than the duty of 'coaching' the new Minister; and the final outcome of their collaboration was certainly at least as much Stephen's work as Stanley's

The scheme, expounded by Stanley on May 14 in a long and moving speech, was drastic and direct. Once for all he rejected the plea that the colonial legislatures could be trusted to do their duty. His review of their past record was as damning as even Buxton could have desired But his plan of emancipation was not quite the same as Buxton's He objected to the enfranchisement of all children born after a fixed date, on the ground that a young generation of freed negroes could not live beside an old generation of slaves. He proposed instead an emancipation of all existing slaves in a year's time, to be followed by twelve years of apprenticeship to their former masters Refusal to work was not to be dealt with by the masters but by specially appointed magistrates only. The planters were to be mollified by a loan of fifteen million pounds. From both sides this scheme was attacked ; but Stanley was ready to placate, if not altogether to satisfy, the Abolitionists, by reducing the period of apprenticeship to seven years, and to buy off the more dangerous opposition of the West Indian interest by transforming the loan into a free gift of twenty millions. These modifications ensured his triumph The resolutions, after six days' debate, were carried by 286 votes to 209. On July 22 the Bill itself—drafted by Stephen in two days at the cost of his Sabbatarian principles and his health besides— was read a second time On the 24th the gift of twenty millions was approved in Committee by the narrow majority of 158 to 151 On the 25th the reduction of the period of apprenticeship was agreed to without a division The final passage of the Bill was now secure.

As it carried the noblest measure in its history the House of Commons did not forget the man who had done most to educate his country up to it ' When Mr. Wilberforce hears of it ', said Stanley himself, in the course of these debates, ' he may well exclaim, " Lord now lettest Thou thy servant depart in peace ".' And, of course, the news of the successive stages of the Bill was quickly carried to Cadogan Place. ' Thank God ', he said, on the 25th, ' that I should have lived to witness a day in which England is willing to give twenty millions sterling for the Abolition of Slavery ! ' It was, in truth, his *Nunc Dimittis*. ' Mr. Wilberforce is very poorly,' reported the younger Stephen on the 26th. ' I do not think he can last long ' Next morning he seemed better. He read the family prayers with something like his usual fervency, and talked to the old servant, who wheeled him out in his invalid chair, with something like his usual animation. But he was taken ill again that night , and next day, Sunday, he had an alarming succession of fainting fits. In the evening, in an interval of consciousness, ' I am in a very distressed state ', he said to his son ' Yes,' replied Henry, ' but you have your feet on the Rock.' ' I do not venture to speak so positively, but I hope I have.' He did not speak again There was one deep sigh, and, about three o'clock on the Monday morning, he died.

On the news of his death a letter was addressed to his son, requesting that he might be buried in Westminster Abbey. ' I am authorized to add ', wrote Brougham, ' that nearly all the members of both Houses of Parliament would have joined [in signing it] had the time allowed ' The funeral was on August 5. The long train of mourners' carriages was accompanied from Cadogan Place to the Abbey ' by immense crowds of people who flanked it, in moving columns, on either side '. The body was laid near those of Pitt and Fox and Canning

A year later, at midnight on July 31, 1834, eight hundred thousand slaves became free. It was more than a great event in African or in British history. It was one of the greatest events in the history of the world.*

---

* *Life*, v. 352–78. *Hansard*, xvii (1833), 1193–1262 , xviii (1833), 112–66, 204–36, 308–60, 458–509, 515–53, 573–98 , xix (1833), 1056–69, 1184–1220, 1234–42, 1252–70. Harford, 241, 248 *Buxton Memoirs*, 329–43 *Autobiography of Henry Taylor* (London, 1885), 1. 130–7. *Letters of the First Sir J. Stephen*, 16–17, 28, 31. *Annual Register*, 1833, Chronicle, 114–15 Walpole, *History of England since 1815*, iii. 410–13

INDEX

Printed in England at the Oxford University Press